CHILD AND ADOLESCENT THERAPY

A Multicultural-Relational Approach

Also by Edward Teyber

Helping Children Cope with Divorce

Interpersonal Process in Psychotherapy

CHILD AND ADOLESCENT THERAPY

A Multicultural-Relational Approach

Edited by

Faith H. McClure, Ph.D.

Edward Teyber, Ph.D.

Harcourt Brace College Publishers

Fort Worth   Philadelphia   San Diego   New York   Orlando   Austin   San Antonio
Toronto   Montreal   London   Sydney   Tokyo

Publisher	Ted Buchholz
Editor in Chief	Christopher P. Klein
Project Editor	Publications Development Company
Senior Production Manager	Kathy Ferguson
Art Director (cover)	Melinda Welch

Cover Image: © Walter Hodges / Tony Stone Images

ISBN: 0-15-501453-6

Library of Congress Catalog Card Number: 95-79404

Copyright © 1996 by Harcourt Brace & Company

Address for Editorial Correspondence: Harcourt Brace College Publishers, 301 Commerce Street, Suite 3700, Fort Worth, TX 76102.

Address for Orders: Harcourt Brace & Company, 6277 Sea Harbor Drive, Orlando, FL 32887-6777. 1-800-782-4479, or 1-800-433-0001 (in Florida).

Printed in the United States of America
5 6 7 8 9 0 1 2 3 039 9 8 7 6 5 4 3 2 1

To Our Families

PREFACE

PURPOSE AND AIMS

Children comprise a substantial proportion of referrals to mental health settings. Nonetheless, individual adult psychotherapy has been the primary training and treatment model across mental health disciplines. In recent years, however, there has been a growing recognition that child and adolescent treatment must become a primary thrust for clinical training. In parallel, greater sensitivity to issues of race, culture, and diversity must be emphasized in all clinical training, and especially in child and adolescent treatment. Thus, the purpose of this book is to provide a graduate-level psychotherapy text that addresses child and adolescent treatment from a multicultural perspective.

Three fundamental needs in counselor training are addressed. First, the text elucidates how ethnographic factors (e.g., culture-specific beliefs, values, and behaviors), demographic factors (e.g., gender), affiliation (e.g., religious), and status (e.g., economic) impact child and adolescent treatment. There are two primary schools of thought within the multicultural field. Some scholars' emphasis is largely ethnographic. Although they acknowledge that there are individual differences within groups, their training centers on the cultural characteristics of various groups. In contrast, other scholars view multiculturalism more broadly: they include socioenvironmental factors such as family structure, religious affiliation, and economic status. These scholars, while acknowledging the salience of ethnographic factors (e.g., culture-specific beliefs, values, and behaviors) also view the individual differences of members of these groups as being significant. This text views multiculturalism in the latter, broader perspective and addresses multicultural factors as they impact each counseling relationship. For counselors to be effective, they must give ongoing attention to the clients' subjective worldview as shaped by cultural, familial, and individual experiences. Thus, this text illustrates how multicultural factors impact the treatment process when dealing with the most salient clinical disorders and problems that children and adolescents present.

Second, for novice therapists, working with culturally diverse clients amplifies the complexity and challenge of treating children and adolescents. Effective clinicians must be practical people who can draw flexibly from multiple theoretical perspectives. Clinicians can find much of use, but also significant limitations, within every theoretical approach. Typically, therapists selectively apply aspects of different theoretical approaches and techniques to clients. Counselors-in-training often find this eclectic approach maddeningly vague; they need more specific guidelines for where they are going in counseling relationships and how they will get there.

This text articulates a more practical and integrative relational framework for conceptualizing treatment plans and guiding intervention strategies. Increasing attention to attachment theory, object relations theory, and the social dimensions of cognitive behaviorism have highlighted the relational aspects of psychotherapy—the interaction or process that transpires between the therapist and the client. Thus, the second aim of this text is to provide a conceptual model that uses the therapeutic relationship as an integrating focus for organizing different theoretical perspectives into specific treatment plans and intervention guidelines.

More specifically, clients do not merely talk with therapists about their problems; in their real-life relationship with their therapists, they actually reexperience or reenact critical aspects of those problems. The case studies in this text illustrate that when the interaction or process that transpires between the therapist and the client enacts a resolution of the clients' conflicts, rather than a repetition of them, all intervention techniques become far more effective. With its focus on the specific interpersonal responses that a particular client needs from a particular therapist, this idiographic approach to treatment is highly syntonic with the Multicultural-Relational approach to be described.

The third aim of this text is to address clinical training needs and help trainees work more sensitively and effectively with young clients. Practicum instructors and clinical supervisors often articulate the same problem: How can we teach trainees to conceptualize their clients' problems or dynamics and translate those formulations into specific treatment plans and intervention guidelines?

Books devoted to theory provide interesting but broad assistance in conceptualizing clients' problems. Similarly, books on "technique" and skill development suggest "what to do." In contrast, clinical instructors often have difficulty finding readings that demonstrate how theory leads to practice. Trainees need specific guidelines to help them formulate a conceptualization of their clients' problems and then to use this conceptualization to guide treatment plans and intervention strategies.

Following an overview of the Multicultural-Relational approach in chapter 1, each successive chapter (2–13) uses a standardized organizational format to illustrate how a Multicultural-Relational treatment approach can be effective in treating a range of child and adolescent disorders and problems. Each case study explicates how sociocultural issues were conceptualized using a Multicultural-Relational approach and how they influenced treatment planning and the therapeutic process. The case studies selected are representative of the most salient child and adolescent clinical disorders and problems. Extensive case dialogue and therapist reflections are provided

throughout each treatment chapter, allowing the reader emotional participation in the treatment process. By providing a case study in each chapter
that illustrates this case conceptualization process in a programmatic way,
this text attempts to meet this fundamental training need. In addition, it
does so by utilizing ethnically diverse therapists and clients who are working together on the most important disorders and problems in the field
today.

CONTENT AND CONTRIBUTORS

After Chapter 1, each successive chapter follows the same organizational
structure. This parallel format allows ethnically diverse therapists to present cases of ethnically diverse clients, and ensures that the same essential issues are addressed in the same manner across all the topics discussed. In
each case names and other identifying information have been changed to
preserve confidentiality.

Each treatment chapter addresses one of the specific problems or disorders that clinical trainees are likely to encounter among child or adolescent
clients: Eating Disorders, Comorbid Depression and Anxiety, Sexual Abuse,
Parental Divorce, Borderline Personality Disorder, Attention-Deficit/Hyper-
activity Disorder, Gender Orientation, Separation Anxiety, Rape Trauma Syndrome, Severely Emotionally Disturbed Children, Conduct Disorder, and
Spiritual Values Clarification. The chapter authors are from ethnically diverse
backgrounds and are experts in relational approaches to child and adolescent
treatment. Because they are clinical instructors as well as skilled practitioners, they are close to the students' experience of becoming counselors.

STYLE AND APPROACH

Clinical training is personally challenging and we have aimed to provide a
text that is student-oriented and empathic to the complexities of becoming a
therapist. Clinical material, often affect-laden and poignant, can be uncomfortable or personally disruptive to beginning therapists. To make this anxiety-arousing material less threatening, we have tried to keep the text simple,
direct, and straightforward—straying deliberately from the traditional academic style. We have found that instructors and trainees alike welcome
warmth and personal accessibility in dealing with these sensitive concerns.

In sum, this text is written for graduate students who are learning how to
become counselors. Through its extensive case studies, we have structured a
text that is practical, compelling, and clinically authentic, while still being
highly applicable. We have wanted our readers to "see" how the therapists'
own thinking and internal processing evolves during work with clients. From
these examples, readers will come to know how compassion and respect for a

client can develop from sharing in the clients' struggles; what counselors can say and do to nurture, affirm, and empower their clients; and, what "mistakes" therapists may have made and how they have used them as opportunities for change. We hope that readers will be able to recognize the personal satisfaction that working with these diverse children and adolescents has given the authors. We also hope that readers will, in turn, be encouraged to begin working with children and adolescents themselves.

CONTENTS

Chapter 1

THE MULTICULTURAL-RELATIONAL APPROACH   1

Faith H. McClure, Ph.D. and Edward Teyber, Ph.D.

Chapter 2

EATING DISORDERS   33

CASE ILLUSTRATION OF ALLIE: AN 18-YEAR-OLD BIRACIAL FEMALE

M. Dawn Terrell, Ph.D.

Chapter 3

PARENT–CHILD THERAPY WITH A DEPRESSED AND ANXIOUS CHILD   68

CASE ILLUSTRATION OF ORIN: AN 11-YEAR-OLD CAUCASIAN BOY

Dorli Burge, Ph.D.

Chapter 4

SEXUAL ABUSE   91

CASE ILLUSTRATION OF SHEILA: A 15-YEAR-OLD AFRICAN AMERICAN

Faith H. McClure, Ph.D.

Chapter 5

CHILDREN OF DIVORCE   124

CASE ILLUSTRATION OF MARY: A 12-YEAR-OLD NATIVE AMERICAN GIRL

Edward Teyber, Ph.D.

Chapter 6
BORDERLINE PERSONALITY DISORDER   160
CASE ILLUSTRATION OF JONATHAN: A 17-YEAR-OLD AFRICAN AMERICAN
Barbara N. Graf, Ph.D.

Chapter 7
ATTENTION-DEFICIT/HYPERACTIVITY DISORDER   185
CASE ILLUSTRATION OF TIMMY: AN 8-YEAR-OLD BIRACIAL CHILD
Faith H. McClure, Ph.D. and Edward Teyber, Ph.D.

Chapter 8
GENDER ORIENTATION   219
CASE ILLUSTRATION OF TONI: A 19-YEAR-OLD BIRACIAL MAN
Jan Aura, Ph.D.

Chapter 9
SEPARATION ANXIETY DISORDER   251
CASE ILLUSTRATION OF HENRY: A 10-YEAR-OLD LATINO CHILD
Anthony Zamudio, Ph.D. and Nancy L. Wolfe, M.S.

Chapter 10
RAPE TRAUMA SYNDROME   287
CASE ILLUSTRATION OF ELIZABETH: AN 18-YEAR-OLD ASIAN AMERICAN
Sandy Tseuneyoshi, Ph.D.

Chapter 11
GROUP THERAPY WITH SERIOUSLY EMOTIONALLY DISTURBED CHILDREN   321
CASE ILLUSTRATION OF SAM: A 9-YEAR-OLD AFRICAN AMERICAN CHILD
Cassandra N. Nichols, M.S.

Chapter 12
CONDUCT DISORDER   357
CASE ILLUSTRATION OF BRIAN: A 10-YEAR-OLD AFRICAN AMERICAN CHILD
David Chavez, Ph.D. and Nancy L. Wolfe, M.S.

Chapter 13
SPIRITUAL VALUES CLARIFICATION   393
CASE ILLUSTRATION OF LINDA: A 16-YEAR-OLD DEPRESSED DAUGHTER OF MISSIONARY PARENTS

John Powell, Ph.D.

About the Editors   *437*

About the Contributors   *439*

CHILD AND ADOLESCENT THERAPY

A Multicultural-Relational Approach

Chapter 1

THE MULTICULTURAL-RELATIONAL APPROACH

Faith H. McClure, Ph.D.
Edward Teyber, Ph.D.

The purpose of this text is to help counselors-in-training become effective child and adolescent therapists. Children comprise a substantial proportion of referrals to mental health settings, yet individual adult psychotherapy has been the primary training and treatment model across mental health disciplines. In recent years, however, there has been a growing recognition that child and adolescent training must be given equal emphasis for clinical training.

There has also been an increasing awareness that clinical training must facilitate greater sensitivity to issues of race, culture, and diversity in the treatment process (Vargas & Willis, 1994). The goals of this text are: (1) to show how multicultural issues can be incorporated into child and adolescent treatment, and (2) to provide a conceptual model that utilizes the therapeutic relationship and the process dimension to guide treatment plans and intervention strategies. We will begin with a brief review of the theoretical/historical contexts for multicultural counseling and interpersonal process. Following this conceptual overview, we will introduce the Multicultural-Relational approach.

MULTICULTURAL COUNSELING

When understood and appropriately applied, sensitivity to multicultural issues greatly facilitates the counseling process. Over the past two decades, the counseling field has begun to recognize multiculturalism as a powerful and significant force in the treatment process. In a Special Issue of the

Journal of Counseling and Development (1991, 70 (1)), it gained the label of the "Fourth Force in Psychology."

Historically, the emic and etic approaches have been representative of two primary schools of thought within the multicultural field. We will highlight the strengths and limitations of these two historical approaches and will then introduce a different, integrative multicultural approach that will be used throughout this text.

In the past two decades, cross-cultural counselors have emphasized culture-specific variables and the need for culture-specific counseling techniques (an emic approach). These scholars, who originally brought cultural awareness to the counseling field, have concentrated on the cultural characteristics of various groups. For example, the text by Gibbs and Huang (1989) takes this ethnographic approach to counseling children and highlights the characteristics of various ethnic groups that impact the counseling process. Although the differences among members within groups is acknowledged, the emphasis is largely ethnographic.

The emic approach developed in response to a lack of sensitivity to "worldviews" other than those espoused by middle- to upper-class European and European American individuals from whom the theories of the major therapeutic schools came. Sue and Sue (1990) note, for example, that culture-bound life experiences, class-bound values, and language variables shape individual identity and worldview. The values and variables are not similar across all ethnic, cultural, and racial groups, and, historically, these differences were not incorporated into traditional clinical training and practice. The primary limitation of the emic approach, however, is that beginning counselors may use this information in a stereotypic, workbook fashion, which fails to capture each particular client's subjective and unique experience.

In contrast, others have argued for the salience of commonalities or universal characteristics of people, thereby minimizing the need for alternative counseling protocols (an etic approach). This approach, which emphasizes the sameness rather than the differences between groups and individuals, is concerned that the emic, or culture-specific, approach may risk losing sight of the common threads that join people and make them all part of the family of humanity. Etic scholars, who write compellingly in an existential or humanistic vein, contend that only by attending to the humanness that connects all individuals can we foster effective counseling relationships (e.g., Draguns, 1989; Fukuyama, 1990; Vontress, 1979, 1985). Differences can be acknowledged and transcended when human experience is understood within the framework of a universal existential philosophy that says, to some extent, "all humans are cut from the same cloth" (Draguns, 1989, p. 13). However, this approach minimizes the salience of specific cultural experiences in contributing to children's presenting problems. This can have negative repercussions. For example, if interventions are not consonant with each child's particular cultural and familial background, premature terminations are likely because the treatment milieu is incongruent with family/cultural values.

More recently, there has been a call for a balanced and integrative approach to diversity, a combining of thoughtfulness and sensitivity to specific cultural background factors (an emic approach), attention to universal principles (an etic approach), and acknowledgment of the importance of individual differences. That is, the *multicultural* scholars (e.g., Pedersen, 1991; Speight, Myers, Cox, & Highlen, 1991) acknowledge the salience of ethnographic factors—including culture-specific beliefs, values, and behaviors—and recognize human universalities, but they also view as significant the differences among individuals within various groups. These clinicians' view of diversity is broadened to include, in addition to ethnographic factors, demographic factors (e.g., gender), affiliation (e.g., religious, political), and status (e.g., economic).

Within this broader multicultural approach, *therapists' sensitivity to clients' worldview and their responsiveness to each individual client's varying needs become the more salient features.* That is, the counselor attends to the young client's individual experiences and subjective worldview, which has been impacted by the child's familial experiences, all of which occur within a broader cultural context. In this approach, the therapist: (1) creates a secure, nurturing environment, (2) validates and affirms the *client's own worldview,* and (3) facilitates the client's connectedness to and expression of his or her own true "voice" and authentic relationships. These goals are syntonic with the views expressed by Gilligan and researchers at the Stone Center (Gilligan, 1982; Jordan, Kaplan, Miller, Stiver, & Surrey, 1991), who have suggested that socialization processes in this country (1) often encourage separation and individuation at the expense of relatedness and secure attachments and (2) include problematic cultural proscriptions about how boys and girls *should* think, feel, and act. This problematic socialization causes children to mute/disown/discredit (disconnect from) their own feelings and views (i.e., their true inner "voices"). It affects their capacity for empathy and intimacy in important relationships and interferes with their ability to remain in or establish authentic connections with others. These writers have suggested that the differential risk for psychopathology in children, which is higher for boys during the childhood years and for girls beginning at adolescence, may be due to occurrence of this self-alienating process at an early age for boys and at adolescence for girls. As we will see from the chapters that follow, the therapist can provide a "corrective" experience for clients by entering their subjective worldview, validating their subjective experience, and providing them with a safe, caring, and secure therapeutic relationship. Only from the safety of this interpersonal relatedness and the security of this relationship can the child's or adolescent's true feelings or authentic self emerge and be affirmed. A child's experience of connectedness to the inner self, while being simultaneously connected to the therapist, is a source of healing. Thus, the child's or adolescent's feelings and behaviors are best understood *within the context* of his or her complex culturally learned experiences and expectations. We believe that this treatment process, which emphasizes the counselor's responsiveness to the client's worldview, is central to the process of change, as will be illustrated throughout this text.

Therapist credibility is a key concept in this broader multicultural perspective. Sue and Zane (1987) have suggested the concept of credibility as an organizing construct for providing meaningful and culturally sensitive interventions. According to their description, there are two primary kinds of credibility: ascribed and achieved. Let's review both ways of attaining credibility with clients.

Ascribed credibility is assigned to the therapist on the basis of characteristics such as title, educational qualifications, age, race, gender, and so forth. For example, being an African American clinical psychologist is an ascribed role: it is based on external, identifiable criteria. Ascribed credibility seems to be particularly important to clients in the initial phase of therapy. That is, clients may be more willing to come to therapy initially because the therapist possesses specific characteristics that are important to them (e.g., the therapist is Latino and male, as is the client). Thus, at this initial phase, cultural match or fit (e.g., similarity in race, gender, age, sexual orientation, religious affiliation) may be highly valued. This occurs, for example, when a male Latino teenager refuses to talk to an Asian male therapist, believing that the therapist is unable to understand his worldview.

Achieved credibility results more directly from the skillfulness and effectiveness of the therapist's interventions. It becomes more salient beyond the initial phase and impacts whether the client stays in treatment and benefits from therapy (Sue & Zane, 1987). Thus, achieved credibility is an outcome of the therapist's sensitivity and skill and is specifically related to: (1) how the therapist conceptualizes the problem(s) (for example, is the conceptualization congruent with the client's belief system? Does it take into account this child's socioenvironmental history and living situation?); (2) how the treatment goals are set (for example, are the therapist's and client's goals congruent? What are the treatment priorities for the therapist, the client, the parent(s), and the school? Are these priorities realistic, given this child's family and cultural system?); and (3) how the process or interaction transpires between therapist and client (Are the means and processes culturally acceptable and compatible? How are the issues of language, role, level of interpersonal expressiveness, degree of formality, and so forth, operating?).

Using this construct of achieved credibility, the focus is not on culture or culturally specific techniques per se but on the therapist's credibility and effective use of interventions for this particular client. This concept endorses the importance of cultural factors (i.e., culture-specific characteristics) but links these specifically to their impact on the counseling process and the therapist's credibility. That is, counselors must attend to cultural factors (e.g., culture-bound beliefs, values, lifestyle) because these will substantially impact client presentation, process, and outcome. Awareness of culturally relevant behaviors and experiences will alert the therapist to potential credibility problems, which can then be addressed or responded to.

To illustrate, a "paranoid" African American male teenager is one who is probably very much in touch with reality, given the life experiences he may have had. A therapist who diagnoses this client as paranoid (which frequently occurs) and focuses on helping him see "reality" soon loses credibility. Similarly, a therapist's expectation that a child from a traditional Asian family will vent anger or other pent-up negative emotions may only engender increased anxiety in the child. If the child and the child's parents see the therapist's view as incongruent with acceptable behavior within their family and culture, the therapist's credibility as an effective helper is greatly impaired.

Knowing how ethnicity, gender, sexual orientation, age, developmental level, socioeconomic status, religion, and so forth, impact values, beliefs, behavioral styles, expectations, and philosophy of life is essential and *provides another layer of understanding.* Clinicians must, however, be careful in how they use this information in therapy: there are within-group differences. For example, knowing that *some* Asian Americans may speak softly and avoid eye contact when communicating with high-status individuals will decrease the likelihood of the therapist's assuming that an Asian American client who uses this communication style is unassertive, depressed, or shy. However, assuming that this behavioral style is an accurate descriptor for *all* Asian Americans would be in error and could result in misdiagnosis and negative therapeutic outcomes. A listing of how each of the variables identified above impacts the counseling relationship is beyond the scope of this or any book. However, useful references addressing these ethnographic characteristics include Atkinson, Morton, and Sue (1989), Gibbs and Huang (1989), Ito (1992), Sue and Sue (1990), Vargas and Koss-Chioino (1992), and Vargas and Willis (1994).

Faced with ambiguous guidelines for how to become more culturally sensitive counselors, trainees often try to learn lists of culture-specific characteristics and interventions. However, given the complexity of culture, and the differences within subcultures, this model often fails to capture the reality of each individual child's experience. Thus, we are proposing a multicultural approach that emphasizes instead *the therapist's ability to articulate and enter into the child's subjective worldview.* And, given the complexity of this multicultural approach, which acknowledges the role of individual uniqueness, cultural variables, and universal human principles, a relational or process-oriented framework is useful for becoming an effective multicultural counselor. In the following section, we introduce and illustrate the "process" dimension in counseling relationships, and then examine more fully this cardinal concept of what it means to understand or enter into the client's subjective worldview.

RELATIONAL ASPECTS OF PSYCHOTHERAPY

General Relational Variables

Attachment theory, object relations theory, and the social dimensions of cognitive behaviorism have brought increased interest in the interaction between the therapist and the client (e.g., Bowlby, 1988; Kahn, 1991; Kiesler & Van Denburg, 1993; Klerman, Rounsaville, Chevron, & Weissman, 1984; Teyber, 1996). In an excellent summary of therapy outcome research, Strupp (1989) concludes that the primary factors associated with positive outcomes are aspects of the therapeutic relationship. For example, relational variables, such as accurate empathy, active listening, compassion and warmth, focused attentiveness, and emotional availability, are essential features of effective therapy. Although such relational variables are essential, they do not provide counselors-in-training with the specific guidelines they need to formulate effective case conceptualizations and treatment plans. Below, we will examine how some interpersonally oriented clinicians have tried to utilize the therapeutic relationship in more systematic or programmatic ways to guide treatment. More specifically, we will review how they try to *identify the problematic relational patterns* that children are repetitively enacting in their play, living out with family members and others, and reexperiencing in their relationship with their therapist in order to:

1. Assess what is wrong for this child personally;
2. Clarify what needs to change in the child's current interaction or relationships with others;
3. Guide specific interventions within the therapeutic relationship.

Specific Relational Experiences

The central theme in the interpersonal or relational approach is provision of an experience of change: enacting a solution to the child's conflicts in the here-and-now, real-life relationship between the therapist and client. Variations of this central tenet have been found in diverse theoretical approaches and have received various labels, such as providing clients with a "corrective emotional experience" (Alexander, 1963), structuring opportunities for "enactive mastery" (Bandura, 1977), disconfirming "grim unconscious pathogenic beliefs" (Weiss & Sampson, 1986), "challenge to change" (Kiesler, 1988), or "interpersonal challenge" (Andrews, 1991).

In all of these interpersonally oriented approaches, the therapist's overriding diagnostic task is to identify the problematic relational patterns or "maladaptive transaction cycles" that repeatedly occur with parents and significant others and, especially, with the therapist. Among the therapist's primary intervention tasks are to: (1) utilize his or her own experience of the client to identify how aspects of this problematic interpersonal style that are occurring when the client interacts with others are also occurring in the client–therapist relationship or interaction; (2) engage the client in identifying, exploring, and understanding this relational pattern; and (3) work with the client to alter this problematic pattern, first in their relationship and then in interactions with others. The therapist must search for a supportive way to provide interpersonal feedback that clarifies, questions, provides alternatives, or fails to reinforce the old relational pattern both within and outside of the therapy relationship. In this way, the therapist does not permit the same problematic but familiar interpersonal consequences (e.g., to have to take care of or meet the needs of the adult/therapist, to not be taken seriously, to have to take sides in parental conflict, to experience unclear boundaries or a lack of limits), which the child expects when dealing with others, to be reenacted in the therapeutic relationship. Instead, the therapist tries to provide a "corrective emotional experience" and to offer a safer and more affirming solution to the child's relational problems in their current interactions and then helps the child to generalize this experiential relearning to other relationships outside the therapy setting. The case studies described in subsequent chapters give many concrete illustrations of this orienting construct.

Long ago, Frieda Fromm-Reichman (1950) captured this relational focus succinctly when she stated that clients need an *experience,* not an *explanation.* In other words, clients do not change when given explanations about how their problems developed, interpretations about what their behavior means, or advice about what they should do. Instead, *change is facilitated when clients have a real-life experience of change in their current interaction with the therapist.* Let's examine closely what this central concept means, and make an effort to help beginning therapists translate these relational concepts into tangible guidelines for "what to do" with child and adolescent clients.

Within every theoretical framework, some clinicians have highlighted the interpersonal dimension and observed that clients do not merely talk with therapists about their problems in the abstract. Instead, they reexperience their conflicts with others or bring critical aspects of these conflicts into their real-life relationship with the therapist. Early in treatment, it becomes very clear that children do not just talk about the issues that brought them to treatment; they behaviorally enact these issues in how they interact with the therapist (the process) and, symbolically, in the content of their play. If the child is to change, the therapist must enact a relationship with the child that is different from the prototypic and problematic relational scenarios that have been reoccurring with others. The following example introduces how therapists can begin using their current interaction with a client to guide their intervention strategy, begin formulating a case conceptualization, and ultimately provide a relationship that "resolves" rather than "reenacts" the client's conflicts.

Suppose you are treating Johnny, a 6-year-old boy whose parents are recently divorced. During your first session, your client begins to kick you. You intervene and tell him firmly that his behavior is unacceptable. Johnny begins to cry and runs out of the playroom. How can you begin assessing your best response at this particular moment?

By attending to children's worldview and the interpersonal processes that may transpire, different responses will be appropriate for different children. To begin structuring your thinking in this instance, however, *it is useful to hypothesize that Johnny is probably beginning to reenact with you a problematic and repetitive relational scenario with which he has also been struggling where others are involved.* For example, if you surmise from observations you have already made about Johnny and his family that Johnny has an intrusive parent who does not give him space, he may need a cooling-off period. In this case, you may need to let Johnny know that you recognize his need for some space (e.g., Therapist: "Looks like you need some time alone. When you're ready, come back to the playroom"). You would then sit several yards away and maintain sufficient physical distance from Johnny so he does not feel you are intruding.

In contrast, however, if your initial observations have led you to hypothesize that Johnny has a rejecting or uninvolved parent, he may need to know that you would like to continue to be actively involved with him. That is, Johnny may need help understanding that rejection of his behavior is not the same as rejecting him. This message would be especially significant if Johnny belongs to a racial or religious group that experiences frequent rejection from the larger social environment. In this case, evidence of your continued engagement with him may be important. You would then stay close to where Johnny is during his cooling-off period. While following Johnny out of the playroom and staying next to him, you might say, "You may be wondering if I'm angry and won't want to be with you. I don't like being kicked, but I do want to be with you. Let me know when you are ready to go back to the playroom."

Thus, whether the therapist is assessing merely how to respond to this particular interaction, or the broader questions of case conceptualization which we will discuss later, the process-oriented therapist tries to:

1. Identify the problematic relational scenarios that may be reoccurring with others in the child's life;
2. Anticipate how these relational patterns could be reevoked or reexperienced in the therapeutic process;
3. Provide new and more satisfying responses in the therapeutic relationship that help to resolve, rather than repeat, this familiar but problematic relational scenario.

To emphasize, Johnny's problem is dynamically or metaphorically reenacted in the therapeutic relationship if he elicits from the therapist the same pursuit/intrusion or distance/rejection that is problematic at home. In contrast, by providing the "intruded" Johnny with a cooling-off period alone, or the "rejected" Johnny with pursuit and contact, the therapist is responding at this moment in a new and different way that gives Johnny an experiential resolution of his conflict in the therapeutic relationship—at least for the moment. One trial learning will not be sufficient to alter a well-established behavioral pattern, but if the therapist can continue to respond, in the therapeutic relationship, in many other big and small ways that enact a solution to his conflict, Johnny is having the experience that relationships can be another way.

If the therapist continues to respond effectively and to use the process dimension in this specific and planned way to provide a corrective relationship, will it be sufficient to resolve Johnny's problems? Usually not, but, as we will see in the case studies that follow, it is relatively easy to generalize this real-life experience of change with the therapist to other real-life relationships beyond the therapy setting.

Furthermore, accompanying intervention techniques from educational, behavioral, cognitive, and other theoretical approaches all become more effective—they "take"—when they are utilized within the context of the therapist and client living out *together* a solution to the client's problems. In parallel, intervention techniques from every theoretical perspective will falter when the therapist unwittingly responds in a way that metaphorically or dynamically reenacts the client's problems. In this way, focusing on the current interaction between the therapist and the client provides a "meta-perspective" for understanding what is occurring and where to go in therapeutic relationships and, as we will see, can readily be integrated with other therapeutic modalities. The accuracy of this meta-perspective is further sharpened by an understanding of how cultural experiences have shaped clients' worldviews. These may have had impact indirectly, via family roles and values, or directly, via the client's personal experiences with poverty, discrimination, and other problematic conditions. For now, however, the following example may further illustrate the process dimension and how the therapist can either "resolve" or "reenact" the client's conflicts in the therapeutic relationship.

Suppose an inhibited, worried, and depressed 8-year-old child has learned from repeated parent–child interactions, "If I grow up, become stronger, and act more independently, I'm hurting my mother." In treatment, the child will repeatedly "test" the therapist to verify or disconfirm this pathogenic belief. For example, the child will test the belief by *acting* independently with the therapist (e.g., being insightful, disagreeing with the therapist's observations, asserting the direction of play, and so forth). Immediately after acting stronger or more independent in one of these ways, the child will carefully evaluate how the therapist responds to this new, anxiety-arousing behavior. If the therapist needs to be "right" or authoritative and takes issue with the child's observations, disagreement, or new initiative, the therapeutic relationship behaviorally confirms the child's belief

and reinforces the conflict. That is, the therapist in this instance is responding as though uncomfortable with the child's assertiveness or independence, thereby mirroring the child's mother. Even if the therapist has been
accurate in talking with the client about the content of the problem (e.g.,
"Your mother seems to need you to need her . . ."), this child cannot progress in therapy as long as the process is awry and is recapitulating the child's
conflict. *This reenactment of the child's conflict with the therapist along
the process dimension is a predictable and regular occurrence in counseling relationships.*

In contrast, by being wed more to the process (i.e., the way they are interacting) than to the content (i.e., what they are talking about), the therapist may disconfirm the child's pathogenic belief by welcoming the child's
independent expressions. That is, the therapist disconfirms the child's problematic belief by being interested in the child's insight even when it differs
from the therapist's. The therapist also allows the child to progress in treatment by being receptive to the child's disagreement or open to a criticism of
the therapist, and by being responsive to the child's initiative or new direction. As the therapist repeatedly responds in these effective ways, resolving
rather than reenacting the child's conflicts, the child is having a real-life experience of change in the therapeutic relationship. And here, as in all relationships, what has been done by the therapist counts, not what has been
said.

Further, if the child is a member of a group that has been consistently
discriminated against or treated as inferior, the therapist's acceptance and
validation of the child's point of view may begin to diminish the impact of
the damaging sociopolitical messages the child has had to contend with.
Over time, the child may be empowered to become increasingly self-
affirming, self-directing/independent, and self-regulating. These qualities
will develop within the context of the child's cultural values. That is, the
multiculturally sensitive therapist can help the child become more independent while still continuing to maintain family and cultural values, such as
respect for elders, loyalty to family, and so forth.

In play therapy with younger children, these relational principles are
even more applicable because the "doing"—the play activity—is the therapy.
Thus, for example, if a play therapist unwittingly tells a child that this is his
play time and can choose what to play, then restricts certain play activities,
the reversal may dynamically replay the child's conflict, such as an experience with a noncustodial parent whose promises are seldom fulfilled. This
child may interpret this experience as a "confirmation" of the untrustworthi-
ness of people and what they say. Or, if the play therapist is seeing a child
with obsessive-compulsive symptoms and the therapist habitually picks up a
toy or crayon immediately after the child drops it, or asks the child to clean
up after activities right away, these responses may convey that the therapist
values order and needs to be in control in a way that reinforces the child's
symptoms and problematic expectations.

Finally, it is important to emphasize that from the neutral vantage point of reading, observing a colleague's therapy session on videotape, or supervising a case, it often seems easy or obvious to enact a solution to the client's conflict along the process dimension. However, beginning therapists should be aware that *it is much harder to do this in affect-laden relationships than it is to say.* Why? As emphasized above, children and adolescents are going to recreate or play out with the therapist the same conflicts they are having with others, especially along the process dimension or the way in which they interact with the therapist. In particular, the object relations theorists have emphasized the subtle but powerful pull for children to reenact the same relational dramas they are having with others. Going beyond the traditional psychodynamic concepts of transference and countertransference, or the Sullivanian concepts of "eliciting maneuvers," they discuss "projective identification" and other ways that clients tend to systematically evoke specific feelings in their therapists (e.g., boredom, irritation, inadequacy), engendering the same conflicts with the therapist that the client has been having with others. In this regard, helping supervisees understand their own emotional reactions to the client becomes one of the most important functions of supervision for process-oriented therapists.

THE MULTICULTURAL-RELATIONAL APPROACH

As we have just seen, the relational emphasis is on understanding what is occurring between the therapist and the client and systematically utilizing this understanding to provide a new and different kind of relationship that resolves rather than repeats these problems. This is a highly idiographic approach to treatment in that it focuses on the specific interpersonal responses that this particular client needs from the therapist at this time. Historically, the relational approach focused on individual and familial factors that contributed to the client's problems and coping style. Adding a multicultural perspective sensitizes the therapist to other, broader contextual variables that have contributed to who this client is (e.g., socioeconomic status, religious or other affiliations, sociopolitical history). Thus, the idiographic process-oriented approach is highly syntonic with the multicultural approach, which provides a richer, more accurate understanding of clients and their needs.

Clearly, multicultural and relational approaches have several perspectives in common. Both acknowledge the paramount role of the treatment process to treatment outcome. If case conceptualization, treatment process, and treatment goals are culturally discrepant or reenact the client's generic conflicts, treatment will not be effective. Some clients will not continue in treatment or, if they do, progress will not occur until either the therapist or the client is able to reestablish a new and more effective therapeutic process.

These approaches also emphasize the need for personal awareness, particularly of the factors that contribute to client and therapist *worldviews.* Awareness of these worldviews includes assumptions, biases, thoughts, and feelings, as well as the factors that have contributed to identity development, such as race, ethnicity, gender, familial experience, and sociopolitical experience. Both approaches view these factors as having significant impact on the therapy process and outcome. Further, they emphasize the influence of sociocultural and interpersonal factors on development, and they see these as significant sources of emotional health and pathology. Finally, sensitivity to the uniqueness of individual histories, acceptance of the client and what the client brings to the therapy setting, and ongoing attempts to meet the client where he or she is are generic to these perspectives. Together, a Multicultural-Relational approach to therapy yields rich, integrative counseling that provides a focus for organizing different theoretical perspectives and individual and cultural factors into specific treatment plans and intervention guidelines.

Elaborating further the central concepts of worldview and personal awareness, effective Multicultural-Relational therapists have in common an active, lifelong orientation toward expanding their own self-awareness. More precisely, they are aware that they have evolved their own worldview and are cognizant of the *subjectivity* of their own perceptions. In other words, they are aware that the basic beliefs and organizing perceptions that comprise their worldview are not universal reality or "the truth." Their worldview is merely the personal construction they have evolved to make sense of their own life experience, which in turn has been shaped by familial, cultural, and other personal characteristics. *This awareness of the subjective nature of their own worldview seems to make effective counselors willing to suspend their worldview more readily and to enter more fully into the subjective experience of others.* In this way, they are more responsive to the varying individual needs, developmental histories, and multicultural experiences of every client.

When counselors possess this cognitive, affective, and interpersonal flexibility, they can meet the child or adolescent *on his or her own terms.* That is, when therapists feel secure enough to relinquish attempts to control or direct the client, they can suspend their own worldview, de-center, and enter fully into the client's subjective experience. Only with this capacity can therapists recognize and appreciate the highly personal meaning that a particular symptom or problem holds for a client. This empathy, in turn, is the avenue that leads counselors to become more accepting, compassionate, and respectful of the client. This cognitive and affective flexibility allows the therapist to understand better *why* this child has formerly responded in seemingly self-defeating ways, and to *appreciate the adaptive way in which this child's symptomatic behavior "makes sense" and has been a reasonable or functional attempt to solve his or her dilemma.* In these ways, the multicultural and relational approaches hold a shared emphasis on expanding counselor awareness of one's own and the client's subjective worldview.

As previously mentioned, it is beyond the scope of this text to list all the factors that may potentially impact worldviews. However, familiarizing oneself with culture-specific information (see Tharp, 1991, for a review of therapy with diverse children and adolescents) and then assessing directly with the client and the client's family how this information applies to them can be very useful. The result is a richer contextual frame than is typically used in counseling practices where individual and family history are traditionally assessed, but the impact of broader contextual cultural factors (e.g., socioeconomic status, religious background, sociopolitical experiences due to race, and ethnically based beliefs and values) is not taken into account. Our premise is that these need to be included in clinical assessments. They will allow counselors to enter more fully into the client's subjective experience or worldview, which enables counselors to respond in more sensitive and effective ways. To elaborate further, a Multicultural-Relational approach provides an especially rich and often different understanding of the person and the presenting problems of each client. What may seem like "pathology" or "illness" may, instead, be revealed as this client's best possible adaptation at a time when he or she was forced to cope with adverse circumstances. Multicultural-Relational therapists, in taking this perspective of trying to understand the healthy attempt at mastery embedded within symptoms, are better able to provide the client with a *secure base* or safe *holding* environment where the painful emotions that accompany stressful life circumstances can be understood and cared about. In this safe place, all the client's experiences—and especially the accompanying pain—can be expressed and responded to by the therapist. We find that this affirmation of clients' original attempts to cope with their dilemmas (which they have often had to manage with limited resources), coupled with having their pain "held" or "contained" by an emotionally responsive therapist, empowers clients to begin seeking new solutions to their problems.

In sum, we believe that an effective Multicultural-Relational therapist recognizes the relevance of cultural diversity, appreciates the dilemmas it can create for clients, and strives to gain further knowledge and deeper understanding of sociocultural issues of race, ethnicity, gender, religion, sexual orientation, and economic status. As noted earlier, we are thus defining multiculturalism broadly to include sensitivity to a wide range of social-system variables. Lee (1991), Locke (1990), and others criticize this inclusive definition of multiculturalism, believing that it stretches the meaning of multiculturalism to any group that considers itself "different." In response, we return to the concept of worldview and agree with Speight, Myers, Cox, and Highlen (1991) that multiculturalism is *generic* to all counseling. Thus, in our approach, we are challenging therapists to cognitively de-center and empathically enter into the subjective experiences of each individual client.

Appreciating the cultural context that *every* client brings into treatment gives the therapist one more layer of understanding. Thus, following closely from the work of Ibrahim (1985, 1991), Pedersen (1991), Wrenn (1985), and others, we further define effective Multicultural-Relational counselors as follows:

1. They recognize that a plurality of cultural factors and experiences contributes to each individual's subjective worldview; that is, they accept unequivocally that reality is not defined according to one set of cultural assumptions or stereotypes.
2. Having examined/considered the cultural factors that have contributed to their own worldviews, they respect the client's differing realities.
3. They are sensitive to variations among individuals and understand their own worldview sufficiently to have the security or capacity to relinquish it and enter the client's worldview.
4. They focus on the therapy process, which frees them to draw flexibly from a range of techniques, rather than being wedded to one theoretical point of view.
5. They are able to validate their clients' experiences, even when these experiences differ vastly from their own. In doing so, they support the clients' own initiative and sense of efficacy, which we believe is at the heart of effective child therapy.

In the 12 chapters that follow, a Multicultural-Relational perspective provides a broad context for understanding child and adolescent symptoms. This pluralistic conceptual approach narrows the treatment focus to a highly idiographic or individualized response to each child. Let's look more closely at how the Multicultural-Relational approach can be utilized to understand the therapeutic relationship and guide intervention strategies.

THE THERAPEUTIC RELATIONSHIP AS AN ORGANIZING FOCUS FOR TREATMENT

In the Multicultural-Relational approach, the therapeutic relationship takes center stage and is the principal arena for therapeutic action. The interaction that transpires between the therapist and client is the therapist's most important source of information about the child and it is the primary means of effecting change. Restating the essential concepts presented above, therapists effect change by trying to enact a solution to the client's problems *in the therapeutic relationship.* That is, they provide clients with a real-life experience of change in their current interaction and then help clients generalize this experience to other relationships.

This is easy to say but not so easy to do. Therapists must be able to identify the hurtful interpersonal scenarios that have been repeated many times between the child and significant others (e.g., the parentified child has had to take care of the parent's needs at the expense of the child's; the child has experienced being devalued by teachers or classmates because of poverty or belonging to a minority race). In treatment, aspects of this repetitive interpersonal conflict will come into play or be activated between the therapist and the client *along the process dimension.* That is, the child will be subtly attuned to taking care of the therapist or meeting the therapist's need, rather than risk relinquishing some control and allowing the therapist to respond to the client's emotional needs. Or the client may expect to be devalued by the therapist and may take an offensive stance of trying to assert personal worth in an aggressive way; or may be withdrawn and uninvolved, feeling that he or she has nothing of value to convey. This recapitulation repeatedly occurs, and when it does, the therapist must respond in a way that resolves rather than thematically reenacts this conflict. The following example illustrates these principles and suggests how sensitivity to cultural issues facilitates the treatment process.

Suppose a therapist is seeing a depressed 10-year-old Hispanic girl from an alcoholic family. During one session, the therapist has a cold, looks sick, and doesn't feel well. The client says, "You have a bad cold. I'll do some coloring while you take a rest." Let's consider several possible responses.

On the one hand, suppose the therapist says, "Thanks, but this is your time," yet proceeds to be minimally engaged with the child throughout the rest of the session. This parentified child will readily and subtly adjust her behavior to accommodate the therapist's needs and minimize demands on the therapist. Thus, in this seemingly benign offer to color, the family dynamic and the child's central conflict of accommodating and suppressing her own needs in order to meet others' needs is being introduced into the therapeutic relationship. In this example, the therapist's disengaged response confirms or reenacts the child's conflict in the therapeutic relationship, and little progress will be made until the process changes.

On the other hand, suppose the therapist says something like, "No thanks, this is your time and I would like to respond to you," and remains more actively engaged. By not repeating the familial dynamic, this response may work well for some children, but it poses a dilemma for this particular child. She is relieved of the burden of having to take care of another's needs, but an essential component of her cultural expectations to be helpful and caring is not being validated in this therapeutic context. Thus, relief from others' needs may be gained, but the price she has to pay in terms of cultural role and identity is dear.

In contrast, a Multicultural-Relational response that is sensitive to both cultural and process issues might be, "Thanks, I really appreciate your concern for me. I do have a cold today, but I would still very much like us to spend this time doing something together. What would you like to do today?" If the therapist then proceeds to be actively engaged and responsive to the client's needs, she will experience a corrective relationship in which her needs can take priority at times or, at least, can coexist in the presence of the needs of others. The therapist has not recapitulated the parentified child's caretaking role in treatment or rejected her culturally prescribed expression of caretaking. Thus, this third response has tried to underscore both the legitimacy and importance of her needs and has begun to convey to the client that her caretaking style, which may be necessary for survival and validation at home, is not always necessary in this or other settings.

In sum, the therapist needs to do more than just establish good rapport with clients, clarify the dynamics of problematic behavior, or change reinforcement contingencies in the environment. Although these are usually helpful interventions, therapists must also provide a real-life, behavioral experience of change in their current interactions with clients. When process enacts a solution, all types of intervention become more effective. To fully understand this, however, we need to clarify further the *process dimension* and to examine the concept of *client response specificity*.

How the Process Dimension Differs From the Content

The content of what the therapist and client discuss (e.g., failing grades, depressed or otherwise preoccupied parents, intimidating classmates) is different from the process or way in which the therapist and client interact together. Although therapists do not usually literally reenact with clients the same hurtful responses they have received from others, we have already seen how the way in which they interact tends to thematically evoke conflicts along the process dimension. Let's examine further this distinction between the process and the content.

The following illustration highlights how therapists can enact a very different process with a client while discussing the same content. As before, the significant point is that the different types of process they enact can provide either a partial reenactment or a resolution of the client's conflict. For example, suppose a novice child therapist and her 9-year-old client are talking together for the first time about the girl's sexual contact with her stepfather. The content of what they are talking about is sexual molestation. Depending on the process they enact, however, the effectiveness of this discussion may vary greatly.

On the one hand, suppose the therapist is initiating this discussion and is pressing the child for full disclosure about what occurred. The therapist is a graduate student who is genuinely concerned about the child's safety, but her "need" to know is intensified by her concerns about her legal responsibilities as a mandated reporter and her awareness that her supervisor will want her to know all of the details about this potential molestation.

In response to the counselor's continuing pressure for disclosure, the child complies with the therapist's authority and reluctantly speaks. Although useful information may be gained under these circumstances, the opportunity for greater therapeutic gain will be lost because aspects of the child's conflict are being reenacted thematically in the interaction with the therapist. That is, the girl is again being pressured to obey an adult, comply with authority, and do something she doesn't want to do. Being pressured to talk about something she doesn't want to disclose in no way traumatizes the child as the original abuse did. However, the process of demand/comply is awry, and it is likely to reevoke in the child the same core affective concerns of helplessness and compliance that the abuse initially engendered. Because the process is reevoking the original conflict, her disclosure will likely serve to hinder her progress in therapy and slow the process of reempowerment.

The situation may be further complicated if the child belongs to a cultural group where family loyalty is highly prized. The child in this situation is thus being asked to violate rules that are sanctioned by the cultural group to which her family belongs. Although other family members and friends may not approve of the stepfather's behavior, they may deny this child the support she needs because she took this information to someone outside the family. For example, although disclosure violates family rules and loyalties for most victims, this may take on additional significance and add much more stress for a Native American child.

What should the therapist in this example do instead? Wait nondirectively for the child to volunteer this information—while she may continue to suffer ongoing abuse at home? Of course not. But by attending to the process dimension, the therapist may be able to begin providing the client with a corrective therapeutic experience while gathering the same information. That is, instead of pressing for disclosure, what if the therapist *honored* the child's "resistance" or cultural prescriptions? For example, the therapist could make a process comment and/or inquire supportively about the girl's reluctance to speak:

THERAPIST: You do not want to talk with me about this right now. Something doesn't feel safe. I'm wondering what might happen at home if you talk with me about this.

Can we talk instead about what your mother might think or what your stepfather might do? Is there a family member you would feel safer talking to?

If the therapist can help the girl identify and resolve her concerns about disclosing (e.g., her mother won't believe her; her stepfather will be sent away; she will be told it is all her fault; she will be chastised for not keeping it in the family and trying to resolve it there), the child may find it relieving to disclose to the therapist what happened and participate more actively in this discussion.

Although this process difference may seem subtle, its effect is powerful and far-reaching indeed. In the second scenario, the child is already beginning the healing process by the way in which she shares her trauma. She is not just hearing supportive words from the therapist, which have limited therapeutic impact anyway. Instead, she is having a real-life experience of change in her current interaction with the therapist. That is, through the therapist's attempts to understand and to work with her reluctance to speak, she is empowered to speak for herself rather than merely to comply again. As the therapist and client continue to interact in this and other ways that enact solutions to her conflict, she will feel empowered in her relationship with the therapist and on her way toward resolving her abuse.

In sum, therapists must be able to think and intervene on multiple levels. Sensitivity to cultural factors also will give therapists one more layer of understanding to respond more effectively to their clients. And, whenever they use the process dimension to resolve clients' conflicts, clients have a real-life experience of change that is far more compelling than words alone can ever provide.

Client Response Specificity

Client response specificity is also a central concept in the Multicultural-Relational approach. As illustrated previously, sensitivity to individual and cultural influences demands that therapists tailor their responses to fit the specific needs of each individual child. There are no cookbook formulas or generic techniques for responding to the complex problems, diverse developmental experiences, and multiple cultural backgrounds that children and adolescents present. In this regard, *the same therapeutic response that helps one child or adolescent progress may only serve to hinder another.* In play therapy, for example, children are often encouraged to hit a punching bag as an appropriate expression of their anger. This activity may reduce an inhibited child's anxiety over expressing anger, especially if the child's parents are cold and strict. Alternatively, it may evoke intense anxiety for a child for whom it is culturally unacceptable to resolve conflict via this overt form of aggression. Or, the same technique may have still another outcome for a child who is living in a disorganized and unpredictable home, who may not sleep in the same bed every night, and who receives little adult supervision. For this child, hitting the punching bag is likely to foster further, unwanted acting-out and aggression.

Let's use a different example to look more closely at client response specificity. Suppose a male counselor has just self-disclosed to an early adolescent boy how the counselor felt when his own parents divorced many years ago. If this client's parents are too preoccupied with their own marital distress to be able to communicate with their son, the counselor's disclosure may be helpful and may foster further sharing and investment in the relationship.

In contrast, the same disclosure from the counselor may have very different effects on another client. For example, if the second client has a parent who is depressed and leans on the son for emotional support, the therapist's well-intended self-disclosure is likely to be unwanted and burdensome to the client. Or, if the divorcing parents communicate with each other through the client and embroil the son in their ongoing battles, the therapist's self-disclosure may be counterproductive and may arouse a high degree of anxiety. That is, the client may feel he has to "take sides" or is being exposed to privileged information that potentially changes the boundaries, as occurred in his family.

In still another circumstance, this therapist's credibility could possibly be jeopardized by the nature of the disclosure and how the conflict was resolved. For example, self-disclosure of an issue the therapist had great difficulty resolving could be viewed as unprofessional by some Asian clients and might raise doubt about the therapist's ability to be helpful to them. However, the same disclosure to certain African American clients may be welcome and could convey to the client that the therapist is human and less likely to be judgmental. In this way, the Multicultural-Relational approach emphasizes client response specificity, as therapists try to assess and provide the specific interpersonal responses that a particular client needs in order to change.

UTILIZING THE MULTICULTURAL-RELATIONAL FRAMEWORK WITH OTHER THEORETICAL FRAMEWORKS

It is difficult to treat children and adolescents, and novice therapists find it even more challenging to begin working with culturally diverse clients. One aspect of this difficulty is that effective clinicians must be practical people who can draw flexibly from multiple theoretical perspectives and function within a multicultural context. Clinicians can find much of use within each of the major theoretical approaches, although each also possesses significant limitations. They similarly learn much from the literature on cross-cultural psychology, but this information is distal to intervention strategies and could result in an ineffective, cookbook approach to treatment. The common solution to the problem of these strengths and limitations has been to selectively apply, in treatment of clients, aspects of different theoretical approaches and techniques. Counselors-in-training often find this eclectic approach maddeningly vague, however, and need more specific guidelines for where they are going in counseling relationships and how they can get there.

In contrast to the lack of specificity in the eclectic approach and the limitations of adopting any single point of view, the Multicultural-Relational approach can serve an integrating focus for treatment. In this regard, beginning counselors can best think of this Multicultural-Relational perspective as a "meta-approach" that can be used by therapists working within different theoretical orientations and with different cultural groups.

The Multicultural-Relational approach is a central aspect of effective counseling and provides the context within which therapists operate. Therapists can then use concepts and techniques from other theoretical approaches (e.g., family systems, psychodynamic, cognitive, and behavioral) while attending to the process and the extent to which it impacts the therapist's credibility as an effective helper.

In the chapters that follow, for example, clinicians present case studies that illustrate the Multicultural-Relational approach. These therapists are often thinking about the client in family systems and dynamic terms, enriched by an appreciation of the additional understanding that multicultural sensitivity can provide. Observers note, however, that the therapists are often responding to clients using educational and behavioral interventions, which are also enriched by a sensitivity to the process being enacted.

In sum, all of these concepts and techniques are helpful, but each will be more effective when the interaction or process that transpires between the therapist and client is enacting a solution to the client's problems. Conversely, therapists of every theoretical orientation will be less effective when the client's conflicts are metaphorically reenacted along the process dimension. Further, if the process violates or asks clients to violate strongly held cultural values, the therapist will lose credibility and the client may not stay in therapy. In this regard, effectiveness in therapy is not necessarily predicated on the degree of religious or ethnic similarity between therapist and client, gender and age matching, or even personality characteristics or theoretical orientation of the therapist. Client matching will certainly facilitate some clients entering therapy, and it will be essential for others. Over the course of treatment, however, the therapist's achieved credibility (i.e., the effectiveness of the process that transpires between therapist and client) will largely determine the outcome of therapy.

For example, the dropout rate after the first session is extremely high for African American clients. This may occur because the therapist does not establish credibility as an effective helper; that is, the therapist fails to listen actively to the client, fails to convey understanding and respect, or too quickly suggests solutions that do not take into account the client's socio-familial history and current living situation. To illustrate, if a therapist is seeing an African American teenager who has had many conflicts with authority figures, being perceived as aloof, detached, and directive will truncate the therapy process. Instead, establishing a partnership or collaborative alliance by being warm and respectful, and acknowledging/validating the adaptiveness of the client's original stance toward authority figures, will facilitate the client's continuing participation in treatment. Similarly, if a therapist is quick to interpret a client's lateness to therapy as "resistance" when in fact the client does not have personal transportation and depends on others for rides to the sessions, the therapist will be perceived as judgmental and the client will not stay. A more effective stance would be one that is collaborative, validates how difficult it might be to find rides, and then helps the client explore various solutions to the problem. The therapist may then also query, in a gentle and supportive way, how the client feels about coming to therapy, so that if other, more dynamic resistance issues are operating, they can also be addressed.

Thus, clinicians working within any theoretical framework can employ a Multicultural-Relational perspective. Regardless of theoretical orientation or techniques selected, clients improve when the therapeutic process resolves rather than reenacts their conflicts. Further, the therapist's sensitivity to and respect for these cultural differences will greatly enhance the therapist's credibility and subsequent ability to provide clients with the relational experiences they need in order to change.

BECOMING A MULTICULTURAL-RELATIONAL THERAPIST

As noted earlier, Multicultural-Relational concepts are often easier to read about and understand than they are to put into actual practice. Before looking at how different therapists have put these concepts into practice with clients, let's examine several reasons why this approach can arouse anxiety among novice counselors. Following this, specific guidelines for conceptualizing clients and tracking the treatment process within a Multicultural-Relational perspective will be provided.

Personal Aspects

As supervisors, we find that beginning counselors try very hard to help their new clients and are deeply moved by their clients' pain. Strong anxiety is generated in clinical trainees as their sincere efforts to help their clients and their strong needs to feel adequate in their new careers press against ambiguous guidelines for how to proceed. To contain these inevitable performance anxieties, many counselors "foreclose" on the developmental process of evolving a professional identity and seek the security of adopting a structured formula for how to proceed with clients.

To work within a Multicultural-Relational framework, however, beginning therapists must be able to tolerate ambiguity. This means that the counselors must be able to encourage clients' initiative and support their interests even when cultural and personal differences make the clients' perspective very different from the experience or worldview of the therapists. Further, therapists must be able to respond to what clients present and must forgo the safety of structuring the material that clients bring up. In this regard, the therapists must have the interpersonal skill and flexibility to be able to respond to the interaction that is occurring *in the moment.* This also means that *counselors must be oriented more toward understanding their own internal responses to the client, and their own reactions to what is transpiring between them, than toward exerting control over the client's feelings and behavior.*

Counselors do need specific guidelines for where they are going with clients and how they will get there (see Process Notes and Case Conceptualization, this chapter), and the detailed case studies that illustrate this will be provided in the chapters that follow. As we will see, however, these specific treatment plans and intervention guidelines are generated more by counselors' highly individualized conceptualizations of particular clients and their interactions or processes, than by generic treatment programs, diagnostic categories, or group characteristics of religious/cultural/social class membership.

Said differently, an effective Multicultural-Relational therapist must have the flexibility to deal with the complexity of each individual client. The therapist's ability to respond to the unique and varying needs of each client is essential to treatment outcome. In this regard, Kluckhorn and Murray (1956) stated long ago that every person is like all persons, like some persons, and like no other person. That is, therapists must have the flexibility to work with the human similarities, the cultural variations, and the individual differences that exist in every client. When counselors can blend human universals, cultural characteristics, and individual differences, they have the best possibility of understanding the full complexity of their clients' experiences.

Other issues also make it difficult to begin working within a Multicultural-Relational perspective. For most of us, talking directly with clients about what is going on between us breaks the social rules we have grown up with. For example, most beginning therapists are uncomfortable using process comments like those listed here, or talking with clients about what is occurring between them:

- "How does this control battle you are describing with your mother go on between us? Where do you see the control in our relationship?"
- "How do you think I am going to respond if you decide to do that?"
- "What do you think I want you to do in that situation?"
- "It sounds to me like we're starting to have an argument about this, just like you and your dad do at home. What do you see going on between us?"
- "You're throwing the ball very hard at me right now. Perhaps there is something you want to say to me?"

If therapists do not find sensitive and tactful ways to address or inquire about the process dimension, they will not see how the client's conflicts are reoccurring in their relationship. When therapists are willing to take the risk of making the process dimension overt, however, that step usually reveals how some important aspects of the client's presenting conflicts are occurring with the counselor as well. Once this parallel is made overt, counselors and clients have the opportunity to resolve rather than reenact this problematic relational scenario. That is, the counselor and client can agree to work together and find ways for each of them to change the current interaction with each other and resolve this problem between them. Once clients experience that relationships can be "another way," therapists can readily help clients generalize this real-life experience of change with the therapist to parents, teachers, siblings, and others beyond the treatment setting (Teyber, 1996).

However, it is threatening for most beginning therapists to take this interpersonal risk, discuss their current interaction with the client in direct ways, and explore how the client's conflicts may be occurring in their relationship. In particular, making process comments and "talking about you and me" will feel highly taboo for counselors who grew up in authoritarian families where there were strong, unspoken rules against such forthright communication. Discussions about "you and me" can discomfort therapists from almost every familial/cultural background, but they may be regarded as especially impolite among counselors from certain cultures. However, counselors can learn to provide clients with a context for process comments (e.g., "I know people usually don't talk together this way, but can you and I talk very directly with each other about something?"). When counselors provide a helpful context such as this and judiciously use process comments with sensitivity, tact, and respect for the client, several important results follow.

Routinely, process comments like these will reveal how a client's conflicts are being enacted between the therapist and client along the process dimension. They will also evoke the client's feelings more fully and intensify the personal meaning that the relationship holds for both the therapist and the client. Such direct communication makes for a closer, more authentic person-to-person relationship, which is essential because meaningful change does not occur in a one-up/one-down or hierarchical relationship. The Multicultural-Relational therapist is not a safely distant technician or a professional who is merely enacting a "role." Instead, it is *the immediacy of the relationship and the genuine meaning it holds for both the therapist and the client that gives this new experience of change its impact.* In this way, it is challenging but highly rewarding when therapists can use themselves and the real-life relationship they enact with clients to help clients change.

Conceptual Aspects

Counselors in training need help to begin utilizing these concepts with their clients. In addition to mentors' supervision and their own reading of case studies that illustrate this approach, therapists need specific guidelines to help them organize their thinking about their clients in Multicultural-Relational terms. To accomplish this task, we recommend two exercises. We encourage counselors (1) to take a few minutes after every session to complete *process notes* that specifically address relevant Multicultural-Relational issues (a standardized format for process notes is provided); and

(2) to write a *case conceptualization* for their clients. The time and effort required are usually rewarded by a more focused and "even" course of treatment as well as more effective outcomes. A structured format for writing process notes and case conceptualizations within a Multicultural-Relational framework is presented in the next section.

PROCESS NOTES

Date: _____

Client: _____

1. Client behavior: What is the client doing in this session?

What were the principal concerns expressed (in discussion or play themes and behavior)? Was the focus on previously raised issues or on new issues? What were the primary emotions experienced and what characteristic relational themes or interactions were evidenced? How do these relate to the presenting problems and treatment goals set? How do I and others typically react to these coping strategies or interpersonal style?

_____

_____

_____

_____

_____

2. Therapeutic relationship: What can I learn from our current interaction?

How did I feel about myself during this session and what were my personal reactions toward the child/adolescent? Do my emotions typify the reactions of others toward this child/adolescent (e.g., angry, bored, frustrated, protective) or do they suggest my own countertransference? How may the current interaction or process be both different from (resolving) and similar to (reenacting) what transpires with significant others.

_____

_____

_____

_____

_____

3. Treatment plans: What are my treatment goals?

Where am I going with this client? What issues do I need to explore further in order to understand this client better? To what extent (and how) do I interact with parents and/or school officials in this case? What specific relational experiences must I provide now and over the course of treatment in order to help this child/adolescent change? Have there been any significant changes in the child/adolescent's life situation or therapy to alter any treatment plans? Have I missed any factors (including cultural ones) that impact my treatment plan?

_____

_____

_____

_____

_____

4. Intervention strategies: Which interventions were effective in this session and which were ineffective?

What interpersonal processes and intervention techniques did I use to try and reach my goals (e.g., clarify relational pattern, interpret play themes, elucidate predominant affect, validate predominant affect and/or experiences, role play, provide affective containment, provide interpersonal feedback, reframe, educate)? How did the child/adolescent respond to these interventions? Were the techniques and interventions used congruent with the corrective interpersonal process I was trying to enact with this client? With this understanding, what can I do next time to differentiate myself and our process from the problems that have characterized other important relationships, and to create greater interpersonal safety for this client? How consonant are my strategies with the client's familial and cultural background?

_____

_____

_____

_____

_____

CLIENT CONCEPTUALIZATION

Gathering information and history is important and useful, but therapists must not lose sight of the process they are enacting. That is, data gathering should, to the extent possible, follow from the specific issues the client/family is presenting. This section suggests appropriate activities for the therapist and indicates the self-questioning the therapist will find beneficial.

Formulating the Problem(s)

Summarize the client's presenting problem(s) and provide a diagnosis with your rationale. Specify your source of information (e.g., parents, teachers, testing, self-report, and/or observation of behavior). How does the client feel about self (e.g., unlovable, worthless, vulnerable) and how is this manifested (in statements made or in play or other behavior)?

Reveal why treatment is being sought at this particular time, especially if the problems have been long standing. What concerns may exist about having a problem or needing to ask for help (personal, familial, cultural)?

What are the client's experiences with significant others (per client's and/or significant others' report) and what expectations does client have of significant others (e.g., are they experienced as critical, withholding, intrusive)? How have cultural factors (e.g., race, gender, sexual orientation, religion) impacted client and his or her experiences with significant others? What are the conflicted feeling states that result (e.g., is client anxious, depressed, ashamed) and how are these states manifested (in mood, statements, play, or other behavior)?

Take special note of attention span, motor activity, language, cognitive abilities, response to the therapist, and interaction with parent(s) or other caretaker(s).

The Developmental Context

How did these problems originally come about? Note the developmental history, including whether developmental milestones (e.g., walking, talking) occurred within normal limits. Reveal parenting practices (e.g., how do they typically discipline and nurture; what important family rules govern family interaction); configuration of the family (including all individuals living in the home, regardless of biological relationship), familial roles (e.g., rescuer, peacemaker, scapegoat), family systems, interaction and communication patterns (especially nature of marital relationship, alliances and coalitions, and clarity of intergenerational boundaries), attachment history, and trauma or other developmental experiences that may have shaped current problems.

Assess family history of psychiatric disorders.

Evaluate the client's cultural context (e.g., ethnic values, religious beliefs, socioeconomic status, sociopolitical experiences), how it has contributed to the client's worldview, and how it may contribute to current presentation.

Identify coping strategies, family strengths, and client and family supports (if any).

Investigate the quality of the family's social life (e.g., family activities) and client's relationships with peers. Relate child's hobbies and other play activities and academic and school adjustment. When you do not have sufficient information, formulate working hypotheses about potential developmental experiences that may have transpired. Suggest how these developmental experiences (individual, familial, and cultural) could interact with current stressors, crises, and social supports to shape the client's worldview and conflicts. In particular, identify the most central dysfunctional or pathogenic beliefs the client holds about self and expectations of others.

Goals and Interventions

Where do you want to go with this client and how do you plan to get there? Consider the client's, the parents', and possibly the school's interest in the outcome and their involvement during the therapy process. Focusing on shared goals that are realistic to you and experienced by the child/adolescent as his or her own, utilize your interpersonal and developmental formulations of this child/adolescent's problems to clarify what you are trying to accomplish right now (short-term goals), your intermediate goals, and your long-term goals.

Delineate your intervention strategies for reaching your goals, and the kinds of activities you may use. How do you plan to use yourself and the relationship you provide this client to reach these goals? Articulate as specifically as you can the interpersonal responses or experiences this particular client will need from you in order to receive a corrective emotional experience and change (e.g., for clients with detached parents, actively helping them generate possible solutions; in contrast, minimizing suggestions, homework, and directions for clients with intrusive/controlling parents, while validating all expressions of the client's own initiative). Evaluate the appropriateness of the goals set and interventions to be used, given this child's personal, familial, and cultural history and context.

What is the sequence of issues to be addressed and specific interventions or techniques to be employed (e.g., interpersonal feedback, cognitive reframing, educational inputs, process comments, affective containment, highlighting of repetitive relational patterns, validation, role playing)? If certain behavioral and cognitive techniques are to be used (e.g., modeling, training in self-instruction, role playing, reframing, cognitive restructuring), consider how you hope to accomplish this with very young children and how the play activities will serve as a metaphor. Assess the appropriateness of referrals to group therapy and/or parent training.

Treatment

TREATMENT FOCUS

Elucidate the maladaptive patterns or relational themes that recur for the client in his or her presenting problems, current and past significant relationships, and with you. For example, regarding the client's internal working models or relational templates: (a) What does the client want, or wish for, from others (e.g., to be cared for)? (b) What does the client expect from others (e.g., to be criticized or rejected)? (c) What is the client's experience of self in relationship to others (e.g., inadequate, burdensome, isolated, and disconnected)? and (d) What are the conflicting affective states that typically result (e.g., contempt and shame; affection and security)? In terms of these relational patterns and the client's expectations of others, what are the client's interpersonal strategies for coping with these relational problems (e.g., complying with others, withdrawing, acting out)? What do these interpersonal coping strategies tend to elicit from the therapist and others? Provide a focus for treatment and integrate your formulations of this client's problems into two or three themes that capture what you think is wrong for this client, or needs to change.

THERAPEUTIC PROCESS

What has counseling focused on to date, and how have the therapist and client interacted together? How does the therapist tend to feel toward the client, and is this similar or different from how others tend to feel toward the client? How does the client bring his or her conflicts into the therapeutic relationship? More specifically, consider several ways in which the therapeutic process you are enacting with the client is both different from and similar to core relational patterns that the client has been struggling with in other relationships? For very young children, play behavior and themes in this behavior may serve as metaphors.

IMPEDIMENTS TO CHANGE

If the client terminates prematurely or treatment is not successful, what factors could contribute? What role do parents and significant others play in this? Did parents need to be warned that temporary increases in acting out or other distress-signaling behaviors are not uncommon?

Identify specific situations, relational scenarios, or affects that are likely to trigger the client's anxiety. How will the client express and/or defend against this anxiety in his or her relationship with you (e.g., distancing, acting out, or complying when therapist disagrees)? How was/is this being expressed, in play and/or other behavior? Why have this child/adolescent's anxieties and modes of defense made sense or been adaptive in terms of his or her worldview or previous experience?

Consider how the child/adolescent's relational patterns could be reenacted in the therapeutic relationship and how the client's conflicts or interpersonal style might interact with the therapist's own countertransference propensities.

A Note on Equipment and Practice

If you are working with young children, what play "equipment" will you make available to the child? Among the more common playroom items are a sand tray with an assortment of miniature people, trains, cars, trucks, animals, dinosaurs, trees, houses, furniture, and so forth. In addition, clay or Play-Doh, puppets, paper, crayons, watercolors, markers, finger paints, stickers, and construction materials such as glue, scissors, and string are standard. Dolls and a dollhouse, play telephones, blocks, Tinkertoy sets, erector sets, balls, masks, and dress-up clothes are often useful. Many therapists begin with these items and add to their collection over time, often bringing in items that they feel might be especially relevant for the child they are working with.

Students who are not yet seeing clients of their own are encouraged to take videos of therapy with children or adults (e.g., Gloria series with Rogers et al., Richard series with Strupp et al.) and evaluate these using this framework. Students might (a) write a "case conceptualization" and "process notes" for the session observed, and (b) identify what further information was needed to achieve a fuller understanding of the multicultural-relational aspects of the case.

Looking Ahead

As clinical instructors, we have found that practicum students struggle to conceptualize their clients' problems and translate these formulations into specific treatment plans and intervention guidelines. Thus, the third aim of this text is to meet this fundamental clinical training need by providing, in each chapter, an extensive case study that illustrates this case conceptualization process in a standardized format.

In each of the remaining chapters of the book, a different clinician uses a case study format to address one specific topic or disorder in child or adolescent treatment. We have selected the most relevant disorders and presenting problems that counselors-in-training are likely to encounter: Eating Disorders, Comorbid Depression and Anxiety, Sexual Abuse, Parental Divorce, Borderline Personality Disorder, Attention-Deficit/Hyperactivity Disorder, Gender Orientation, Separation Anxiety, Rape Trauma Syndrome, Severely Emotionally Disturbed Children, Conduct Disorder, and Spiritual Values Clarification.

To elucidate how these therapists integrate a Multicultural-Relational approach into their case conceptualizations and treatment plans, each chapter follows the same organizational format. A general description of the disorder or topic—including DSM-IV* characteristics if relevant, incidence data if available, and any developmental variations—is given at the start of the

---

*Throughout this text, DSM-IV is to be understood to represent American Psychiatric Association. (1994). *Diagnostic and statistical manual of mental disorders* (4th ed.). Washington, DC: Author.

chapter. The introduction also describes generic social and cultural issues relevant to diagnosing and treating this population and indicates how symptom presentation and clinical interventions are potentially modified by cultural background. Next, an extensive case illustration of this disorder or problem addresses the following factors in a uniform sequence:

Presenting problem;

Initial session;

Case conceptualization;

Orienting constructs;

Treatment plans and intervention strategy;

Therapeutic process;

Termination and therapist's summary thoughts.

Readers will find some minor variations in these headings in a few chapters where group treatment of children or extensive familial participation is involved. Following the case study, each author will provide suggestions for further reading in this area. This parallel structure ensures that the same essential treatment issues are addressed in the same manner across each chapter. Contributors present these multicultural cases within the same integrative conceptual framework.

Finally, we are well aware how challenging it is to become a therapist. Beginning counselors need material that links theory to practice and that is accessible, practical, and clinically authentic. Thus, the contributors chosen for this volume are both clinical instructors and skilled practitioners with special expertise in each topic area. They are aware of the personal experience of becoming a therapist and they have been sensitive to the questions, concerns, and aspirations of counselors-in-training as they have prepared their respective chapters.

REFERENCES

Alexander, F. (1963). The dynamics of psychotherapy in light of learning theory. *American Journal of Psychiatry, 120,* 440–448.

Andrews, J. (1991). *The active self in psychotherapy: An integration of therapeutic styles.* Boston: Allyn & Bacon.

Atkinson, D. R., Morton, G., & Sue, D. W. (Eds.). (1989). *Counseling American minorities: A cross-cultural perspective* (3rd ed.). Dubuque, IA: Brown.

Bandura, A. (1977). Self-efficacy: Toward a unifying theory of behavioral change. *Psychological Review, 84*(2), 191–215.

Bowlby, J. (1988). *A secure base.* New York: Basic Books.

Draguns, J. (1989). Dilemmas and choices in cross-cultural counseling: The universal versus the culturally distinctive. In P. Pedersen, J. Draguns, W. Lonner, & J. Trimble (Eds.), *Counseling across cultures* (pp. 3–22). Honolulu: University of Hawaii Press.

Fromm-Reichmann, F. (1950). *Principles of intensive psychotherapy.* Chicago: University of Chicago Press.

Fukuyama, M. (1990). Taking a universal approach to multicultural counseling. *Counselor Education and Supervision, 30,* 6-17.

Gibbs, J., & Huang, L. (Eds.). (1989). *Children of color: Psychological interventions with minority youth.* San Francisco: Jossey-Bass.

Gilligan, C. (1982). *In a different voice: Psychological theory and women's development.* Cambridge, MA: Harvard University Press.

Ibrahim, F. (1985). Effective cross-cultural counseling and psychotherapy: A framework. *The Counseling Psychologist, 13,* 625-683.

Ibrahim, F. (1991). Contribution of cultural worldview to generic counseling and development. *Journal of Counseling and Development, 70*(1), 13-19.

Ito, M. H. (1992). *Minority children and adolescents in therapy.* Newbury Park, CA: Sage.

Jordan, J., Kaplan, A., Miller, J. B., Stiver, I., & Surrey, J. (1991). *Women's growth in connection: Writings from the Stone Center.* New York: Guilford Press.

Kahn, M. (1991). *Between therapist and client.* New York: Freeman.

Kiesler, D. (1988). *Therapeutic metacommunication: Therapist impact disclosure as feedback in psychotherapy.* Palo Alto, CA: Consulting Psychologist Press.

Kiesler, D., & Van Denburg, T. (1993). Therapeutic impact disclosure: The last taboo in psychoanalytic theory and practice. *Clinical Psychology and Psychotherapy, 1*(1), 3-13.

Klerman, G., Rounsaville, B., Chevron, E., & Weissman, M. (1984). *Interpersonal psychotherapy of depression.* New York: Basic Books.

Kluckhohn, C., & Murray, H. (Eds.). (1956). *Personality in nature, society and culture.* New York: Knopf.

Lee, C. (1991). Promise and pitfalls of multicultural counseling. In C. Lee & B. Richardson (Eds.), *Multicultural issues in counseling: New approaches to diversity* (pp. 1-13). Alexandria, VA: American Association for Counseling and Development.

Locke, D. (1990). A not so provincial view of multicultural counseling. *Counselor Education and Supervision, 30,* 18-25.

Pedersen, P. (1991). Multiculturalism as a generic approach to counseling. *Journal of Counseling and Development, 70*(1), 6-11.

Speight, S., Myers, L., Cox, C., & Highlen, P. (1991). A redefinition of multicultural counseling. *Journal of Counseling and Development, 70*(1), 29-36.

Strupp, H. (1989). Can the practitioner learn from the researcher? *American Psychologist, 44,* 717-724.

Sue, D. W., & Sue, D. (1990). *Counseling the culturally different: Barriers to effective cross-cultural counseling* (2nd ed.). New York: Wiley.

Sue, S., & Zane, N. (1987). The role of culture and cultural techniques in psychotherapy: A critique and reformulation. *American Psychologist, 42,* 37-45.

Teyber, E. (1996). *Interpersonal process in psychotherapy* (3rd ed.) Pacific Grove, CA: Brooks-Cole.

Tharp, R. (1991). Cultural diversity and treatment of children. *Journal of Consulting and Clinical Psychology, 59*(6), 799-812.

Vargas, L., & Koss-Chioino, J. (Eds.). (1992). *Working with culture: Psychotherapeutic interventions with ethnic minority children and adolescents.* San Francisco: Jossey-Bass.

Vargas, L., & Willis, D. (1994). Introduction to the special section: New directions in the treatment and assessment of ethnic minority children and adolescents. *Journal of Clinical Child Psychology, 23*(1), 2-4.

Vontress, C. E. (1979). Cross-cultural counseling: An existential approach. *The Personnel and Guidance Journal, 58,* 117-122.

Vontress, C. E. (1985). Existentialism as a cross-cultural counseling modality. In P. Pedersen (Ed.), *Handbook of cross-cultural counseling and therapy* (pp. 207-212). Westport, CT: Greenwood Press.

Weiss, J., & Sampson, H. (1986). *The psychoanalytic process: Theory, clinical observation and empirical research.* New York: Guilford Press.

Wrenn, C. (1985). Afterword: The culturally encapsulated counselor revisited. In P. Pedersen (Ed.), *Handbook of cross-cultural counseling and therapy* (pp. 323-329). Westport, CT: Greenwood Press.

Chapter 2

Eating Disorders

Case Illustration of Allie: An 18-Year-Old Biracial Female

M. Dawn Terrell, Ph.D.

The Disorder

It seems like I spend every waking hour consumed with thoughts about food, wanting it but feeling I shouldn't have it, or not wanting it but knowing I'll have it anyway. I even dream about food! I feel like I'm fighting this battle to control food and my weight and everything related to it, but really it all controls me. The thing that's really scary, though, is that when I manage not to think about food or my weight for just a little while, sometimes I feel even crazier. I feel more scared . . . or even worse, totally empty. So I end up going back to obsessing about food . . .

The quote above came from Allie, a multiracial woman who at 18 sought help at her university counseling center because of a long-standing pattern of eating problems. Her words portray the sense of struggle experienced by individuals with eating disorders. Food is no longer seen simply as nourishment, to be taken in when internal physiological cues signal hunger. Eating disordered individuals often no longer know how to respond to such cues. Instead, they view food as an object to be controlled and used to ward off feelings of all sorts, from physiological hunger to anxiety to desire for closeness. For some individuals with eating disorders, food becomes a symbol for all that is feared. For others, food comes to represent what is longed for.

Whether feared or longed for, or both, food becomes the stand-in or substitute for something absent in the individual's life. Preoccupation with food often covers over an inner emptiness, as Allie's words suggest. Many clinicians believe that what is absent in the lives of individuals with eating disorders is the experience of having been appropriately nurtured and cared for, an experience that is necessary for the development of a secure identity and the capacity for intimacy. The love/hate struggle with food that seems to define the life of an individual with an eating disorder is thus at its core a struggle with unmet needs for nurturance and with associated identity and intimacy problems (Zraly & Swift, 1990).

This chapter describes the work Allie did in therapy to understand and overcome her struggle with food and to resolve the underlying issues that gave rise to that struggle. The emergence of Allie's eating disorder and her work to overcome it were tied to her experience as a person of mixed ethnocultural heritage. A review of the large literature on eating disorders, with special reference to the role of ethnocultural factors, will set the stage for Allie's case illustration. Information about the clinical features of eating disorders will be presented, along with a discussion of the prevalence and etiology.

Clinical Features

For individuals who are diagnosed with *bulimia nervosa,* food may be both feared and longed for. This ambivalence is expressed in alternately taking in large quantities of food, that is, binging, and then purging through such means as vomiting, taking laxatives or diuretics, or using other methods, such as excessive exercise to compensate for the binge. To be considered bulimic, an individual must report an average of at least two binge-purge cycles each week for three months according to the *Diagnostic and Statistical Manual of Mental Disorders,* Fourth Edition (DSM-IV; American Psychiatric Association, 1994; hereafter, DSM-IV). Many bulimics will binge and/or purge several times in a single day, especially during times of stress. Like Allie, bulimics also report feeling a lack of control over their eating behavior, and their self-evaluations are unduly influenced by a persistent overconcern with weight and body shape (DSM-IV). Two types of bulimia nervosa are recognized in DSM-IV: *purging type,* which involves reliance on vomiting or use of laxatives or diuretics as a compensatory activity following a binge episode, and *non-purging type,* in which other compensatory activities are carried out following binge episodes.

In individuals diagnosed with *anorexia nervosa,* fear of food and of becoming fat predominate. The fear of becoming fat is so great that the individual refuses to maintain a normal body weight and restricts food intake drastically or uses other means (including purging) to prevent weight gain. Anorexics are diagnosed as being either *restricting type,* or *binge-eating/ purging type,* depending on their primary method of maintaining low body weight. Low body weight, and some of the means used to achieve it (e.g., excessive exercise), will result in amenorrhea in women, defined for diagnostic purposes as the absence of at least three consecutive menstrual cycles otherwise expected to occur (DSM-IV). Anorexics (and many other women with eating problems) have a seriously distorted view of their body size and weight and may report feeling fat even when emaciated and/or may deny the seriousness of their disorder (Zraly & Swift, 1990). Body image distortion, however, varies according to ethnicity. Kuba and Harris (1992) suggest that cultural differences in preferred body type may account for the findings that anorexia in ethnically diverse clients may not always be accompanied by severe body image distortion or even abnormal fear of weight gain. According to DSM-IV, an individual must have a body weight that is 85% or less of his or her normal weight or expected normal weight according to growth charts to be diagnosed with anorexia nervosa. It should be noted that some clinicians who work with eating disordered individuals feel that this weight criterion is too restrictive, particularly when assessing individuals from ethnic groups where typical body build is either larger or smaller than the average.

Earlier concerns about the general restrictiveness of the diagnostic criteria for eating disorders resulted in an increase in the weight criterion from 75% of expected body weight, listed in DSM-III (American Psychiatric Association, 1980), to the current 85% and also led to the creation of a third diagnostic category. *Eating disorder not otherwise specified* is the diagnosis that would be given to individuals who show symptoms of either anorexia nervosa or bulimia nervosa but do not meet all the diagnostic criteria for those syndromes (DSM-IV).

Although compulsive overeating is not currently considered a distinct eating disorder in DSM-IV, those with a history of chronic overeating share common clinical features with bulimics and anorexics. They too will typically experience overconcern with weight and body size and will try to compensate for periods of binging with attempts at restricting food intake through dieting (Zraly & Swift, 1990).

Eating disorders most commonly arise during adolescence, with anorexia nervosa having an earlier onset. The immediate precipitant is often a period of weight gain followed by dieting, usually in conjunction with a major disruption in the adolescent's life (e.g., move to new school, shift in relationships). However, it may simply be the normative changes of adolescence that trigger disordered eating behavior. I frequently have had clients report that they[1] started dieting when they reached puberty, equating the development of a more womanly shape to "getting fat."

As discussed earlier, eating disorders reflect underlying struggles with identity and intimacy, which helps to explain the emergence of eating problems during adolescence. Adolescence is a period in which the chief developmental task is forging a positive sense of identity, partly through the development of close relations with peers (Erickson, 1959). For some

---

[1] By far, most of the clients I have seen with eating disorders have been female.

individuals, this new developmental challenge is frightening; they report feeling "overwhelmed" at the prospect of growing up and are unable to cope with the demands of adolescence. They may resort to disordered eating to ward off their feelings of inadequacy. The feelings of inadequacy are in turn compounded by feelings of shame and guilt associated with the disordered eating behavior. Thus begins an often painfully spiraling cycle of resorting to attempts to control food as a means of coping with difficult feelings. As Bruch (1984) noted, binging and purging, or the anorexic's restricted eating, becomes a habitual means of coping, "a psuedosolution for . . . problems of living" (p. 10).

Disordered eating is frequently associated with depression and low self-esteem (DSM-IV). Biochemical changes brought on by the disordered eating may account in part for the mood disturbances, though the latter may have been present at the onset of eating symptoms. Suicidal ideation and impulses are also common clinical features in individuals with eating disorders and need to be carefully assessed and worked with in therapy (Zraly & Swift, 1990). Therapists can address suicidal concerns by asking about them directly and by establishing a contract in which the client agrees to seek specific help (e.g., contact the therapist or a crisis line) should suicidal feelings mount.

Prevalence and Etiology of Eating Disorders

Although reports of the clinical syndrome of anorexia nervosa date back to the prior century, and the practice of purging following consumption of large quantities of food has been around for many centuries, it is only in the last two decades that a great deal of attention has been focused on understanding the prevalence and etiology of eating disorders. This shift coincides with a marked increase in the incidence of eating disorders, especially among young women. Females account for 90% of all cases of anorexia and bulimia (DSM-IV). Recent prevalence estimates suggest anorexia nervosa occurs in less than 1% of adolescent females; bulimia nervosa is more prevalent, with recent estimates suggesting that 1% to 3% of the female population are bulimic compared to .01% of the male population (DSM-IV). Other estimates suggest that as much as 8% to 20% of the female population experience episodic binging and purging (Zraly & Swift, 1990).

Sociocultural Factors and Eating Disorders

The far greater prevalence of eating disorders among females has been explained by sociocultural factors. Some theorists (e.g., Orbach, 1978) argue that eating disorders have increased largely as a result of cultural trends in society that set thinness as a standard of beauty, power, and status for women. Certainly, social pressures to be thin have led to widespread dissatisfaction with body size among women, resulting in what has been termed "a normative discontent" with weight (Rodin, Silberstein, & Striegel-Moore, 1984). Research consistently shows that men are less concerned about, and more satisfied with, their weight and body size and hence may be less at risk for developing eating disorders.

Indeed, until recently anorexia and bulimia were thought of as disorders experienced only by young, affluent White females (Bruch, 1984). As Root (1990) notes, the stereotype that eating disorders occur only in this population has meant that relatively few studies of the prevalence of eating disorders have included people of color in their samples. Those studies which have been more inclusive indicate that eating disorders not only occur in people of color but also suggest that ethnocultural factors may play an important role in the development of an eating disorder (Kuba & Harris, 1992; Root, 1990).

For example, many ethnocultural groups hold values concerning body size that diverge distinctly from those of mainstream culture. This divergence can present a source of acculturation stress for some young people of color struggling to achieve a sense of identity, particularly where mainstream values stereotype people from other cultures as unattractive and therefore unworthy. As Allie's case will illustrate, acculturation conflicts concerning body size and distress associated with negative racial/ethnic stereotypes may place ethnoculturally diverse individuals at greater risk of developing an eating disorder. Root (1990) writes that "the development of an eating disorder may, in fact, become a vehicle for attempting a resolution for biculturality" (p. 531), i.e. for coping with acculturation stress. She says too that the "double oppression" experienced by young women of color may create such distress that they resort to disordered eating to cope with or ward off difficult feelings.

Psychodynamic and Family Systems Views of Eating Disorders

While sociocultural stereotypes and acculturation conflicts play an important role in the development of an eating disorder, prevailing theories concerning the etiology of eating disorders place greatest emphasis on the early psychological experience of the eating disordered individual. Psychodynamic theorists focus on the mother-child relationship and particularly the child's difficulties in successfully separating from the mother. Family systems theorists look more broadly at the nature of family alliances and norms in accounting for eating disorders.

Hilde Bruch (1973, 1984) developed the most widely cited psychodynamic formulation of the etiology of eating disorders. She argued that mothers of individuals who develop eating disorders fail to respond appropriately to their very young child's needs during the separation-individuation process. For example, an infant's hunger cries might or might not elicit a feeding. A young toddler's wishes to play may go unheeded by the mother who is not attuned to the signals her child is giving. The child therefore has little opportunity to develop a sense of his or her own needs, or of the internal cues that signal those needs. Bruch argued that as a consequence of repeated empathic failures in the separation-individuation process, the child is unable to form a stable and positive sense of self and will instead experience overwhelming feelings of inadequacy and ineffectiveness in confronting normative developmental tasks. This sense of inadequacy reaches a crisis point as the child approaches adolescence. The emergence of disordered eating at this time represents an attempt to defend against the feelings of inadequacy by attempting to exert control over one's body.

The exact nature of the mother-child relationship and of the empathic failures in separation-individuation leading to disordered eating appear to differ for anorexics and bulimics. Johnson (1991) suggests that the anorexic's primary caretaker is overprotective and controlling. The child is subtly or overtly punished for any attempts to master self-regulation. Indeed, all initiative and attempts to move toward separation and autonomy are likely to be discouraged during the child's early life. The child is instead expected to be compliant with parental expectations and often strives to be the "model" child. This adaptation suffices during childhood and latency but becomes untenable as the child reaches puberty and confronts developmental pressures to separate. The refusal to eat so characteristic of the early adolescent anorexic may represent a stab at separation from the overinvolved parent.

The bulimic's parent, conversely, is often underinvolved (Johnson, 1991). Instead of rigidly controlling the child's movement toward autonomy, the child is expected to take on the role of meeting his or her own needs early on and perhaps those of the parent as well. Expression of needs for nurturance and mirroring are thus discouraged. Although the child may appear to be more independent and comfortable with separation as a result, this is at the expense of feeling safe or taken care of. The bulimic, pushed too soon to be independent, will also likely feel overwhelmed when confronted with developmental challenges. The experience of having to care for self, however, may account for the later onset of symptoms in bulimics compared to anorexics. It may be that they are better able to cope with some early developmental tasks, though the push for intimacy during late adolescence will be especially difficult because of their experience of unmet dependency needs.

It should be noted that discussions of the role of separation-individuation vicissitudes in the development of eating disorders assume that achievement of separation and autonomy is the cornerstone of psychological health. Such an assumption is of course based on a Eurocentric and androcentric (i.e., male dominated) model of mental health. Steiner-Adair (1991) notes that this model may not be adequate in discussing the development of young girls, which is also shaped significantly by the core value of relatedness. Steiner-Adair argues that young girls are caught in a terrible bind precisely because they are expected to conform to both the androcentric values of separation and autonomy and the value of relatedness. She argues further that the confusion and internal distress evoked by this bind is a significant contributor to the development of eating disorders.

Young women from ethnoculturally diverse backgrounds face a still more complicated picture in their development. For many young girls of color, the values of interdependence, belongingness, and family loyalty clash with the mainstream value of separation and autonomy (Kuba & Harris, 1992). Coping with the clashes among the cultural values of one's own ethnic group, those of one's gender, and those of mainstream culture creates a heightened vulnerability in young women of color as they confront the task of achieving a positive identity. The complicated process of identity formation in young women of color may thus place them at risk for developing eating problems (Root, 1990).

Discussions by family theorists (e.g., Minuchin, Rosman, & Baker, 1978; Schwartz, Barrett, & Saba, 1984) can help shed light on how socialization experiences within the family and larger cultural milieu may impact the development of eating disorders. Drawing from structural family systems theory, which talks about the inherent separation difficulties of children growing up in "enmeshed" (i.e., overinvolved) families, family theorists see eating disorders as a symptom of family dysfunction. Enmeshed families typically have strong family rules, whether overt or covert, that prohibit expression of conflict or any intense, negative emotion such as anger, sadness, or fear. Compliance with family norms is enforced through withdrawal of affection or other means. The child in such a family grows up unable to express strong emotions and without a firm sense of personal identity. Hence we would again expect difficulties for the child when confronting the developmental tasks of adolescence. The family system is poorly equipped to launch the young adolescent, who may become "sick" as a way of coping with the conflicts that arise as he or she moves toward separation (Minuchin et al., 1978). Though not all families of eating disordered individuals are enmeshed, they all fail in some way to provide an appropriate environment for supporting the child's development of an independent identity and capacity for authentic relating.

It has also been observed that families of eating disordered individuals tend to be particularly preoccupied with food and appearance (Bruch, 1984; Schwartz et al., 1984). Parents may make intrusive comments about the developing child's size and weight or otherwise evoke anxiety in the growing child about his or her appearance and food intake.

All families have their own values and rituals concerning food and weight, and these may become important in the child's susceptibility to an eating disorder. For example, some families may use food as a reward for children or as a symbol of nurturance. Others may see eating together as a sign of family closeness, while still other families will promote a feeling of deprivation and secrecy around food and eating. Some families value thinness as an ideal body type, while other families see plumpness as pleasing.

Family values and rituals concerning food and body size will be strongly shaped by the cultural milieu of the family, and ethnocultural differences in values and rituals concerning food are often important in the development of eating disorders in people of color (Kuba & Harris, 1992; Root, 1990). For example, it has been observed that the children of immigrants may develop eating problems because they experience great distress at being caught in the middle of two competing family messages: to "fit in" with the dominant culture and thus strive to be thin while, at the same time, maintaining allegiance to the culture of origin, which may value a non-thin body type (Kuba & Harris, 1992).

The preceding discussion of sociocultural, psychodynamic, and family systems views of the etiology of eating disorders suggest that the nature of the child's cultural and interpersonal world are central factors in the development of eating disorders. The Multicultural-Relational approach to therapy, with its focus on the recognition of cultural and interpersonal issues in the unfolding relationship between client and therapist, is thus a powerful and highly appropriate mode of treatment for individuals with eating disorders. Recovering from an eating disorder will require the development of new modes of coping with feelings and relating to others. Therapy is thus aimed at helping the client to discover a new way of being, and the chief vehicle for this is the therapeutic relationship. Allie's case illustration will highlight how recovering from an eating disorder involves resolving interpersonal difficulties in the context of the therapeutic relationship.

CASE ILLUSTRATION

Presenting Problem

Allie sought treatment because of an upsurge of episodic binging and purging following the breakup of her first serious romantic relationship. She reported binging and then vomiting as many as five times a day in the 2 months since the breakup, a significant increase over the two to three episodes she had averaged each week since the age of 15. Current triggers for binging were her acute feelings of rejection and sadness related to the breakup, and her anxiety about being able to continue to live up to her high standards for academic performance. She was having difficulty carrying out daily activities such as studying and attending classes and had also begun to avoid socializing with friends. Fear that her increased binging would lead to weight gain was the primary reason she sought treatment, though she also hoped that being able to talk about her feelings about the breakup might help her to reduce the episodes of binging.

CLIENT DESCRIPTION

Allie was a short, attractive 18 year old. Though I readily recognized that she was of mixed racial/ethnic heritage (my own biracial background perhaps heightening my awareness of telltale signs), Allie seemed to obscure any signs that she was not White. She straightened her long, dark, and naturally curly hair to heighten her resemblance to a well known musical celebrity (who ironically also identifies as White though of mixed heritage). Allie's careful makeup was not effective in covering up the dark circles under her eyes, a feature that frequently occurs in bulimics. Although thin, she also had the puffiness along the jaw line that is characteristic of active bulimics (due to swelling of the parotid glands). She was dressed in a baggy sweat-shirt and fashionable jeans.

Allie seemed to experience a great deal of shame initially in talking about herself, making only sporadic eye contact and sinking into her chair as if to hide. While her discomfort in talking may reflect cultural constrictions on drawing attention to self and seeking help for psychological problems, Allie was at that time highly identified with mainstream cultural values. Her reticence seemed to reflect instead her feelings of self-disgust about her eating patterns. She also remarked that she had little experience talking about her feelings to anyone, particularly feelings of sadness or anxiety, her primary affects at the beginning of therapy.

Allie met all of the diagnostic criteria for bulimia nervosa. While her inability to carry out normal daily activities, low energy, sadness, and low self-esteem might well be accounted for by the bulimia, it was only as the sadness and low energy abated with the reduction of bulimic episodes that I was able to rule out an underlying depression.

SOCIAL CONTEXT

Allie's parents, Gloria and E.J. (Earl Jr.), were teenagers when they married just a few months before Allie was born. Their families strongly disapproved of the marriage and of the pregnancy that prompted it. Gloria's parents, Rafael and Alicia,[2] were immigrants from Mexico who had worked hard to secure a middle class lifestyle for their only child, and they were bitterly disappointed that Gloria postponed going to college to care for Allie. They also disapproved of the marriage because E.J. was of a different ethnicity and religion. E.J. was biracial, himself the product of a brief teenage romance between his African American father, Earl Sr., and a young Dutch woman studying in the U.S. Raised by his paternal grandparents, Earlene and James, E.J. was well aware that his birth had disrupted his father's educational and athletic aspirations and he was determined that marriage would not derail

---

[2] Allie's given name is Alicia, in honor of her grandmother.

his own ambitions to become a professional athlete. Because they were well-off, Earlene and James were able to assist the young couple financially, and E.J. finished college while married to Gloria.

During the 4 years of their marriage, the couple lived for some time with Earlene and James, and Allie developed an especially close bond to her great-grandparents. Gloria, however, did not get along with her in-laws and frequently clashed with them about child rearing practices. Earlene and James, consistent with African American cultural norms, encouraged Allie to play actively with other children even as a young toddler. Gloria tended to be more restrictive with Allie and felt her play should be limited to "lady-like" activities like doll play. Mounting tensions between Gloria and her in-laws, and resentment that E.J. was able to pursue his goals while she was not, contributed to the demise of the marriage.

Following the divorce, Gloria moved back in with her parents for 5 years, and Alicia and Rafael were primary caretakers for Allie from ages 4 to 9. Allie remembers them being warm and affectionate with her, as her father's family had been, in sharp contrast to her mother, who tended to be a strict disciplinarian with high expectations. Gloria's parenting style was at odds both with her parents' and her culture's values. Gloria's goal as a parent was not only to help her child achieve upward mobility as her own parents had but also to help Allie assimilate into mainstream culture as well, something Gloria's parents had never sought to do, remaining tied to the close-knit Mexican and Mexican American community in the city they lived in. Gloria herself felt a strong need to assimilate to "get ahead." She worked a series of jobs during this time, while attending and completing college part-time.

At age 9, Allie abruptly moved with Gloria across town from Alicia and Rafael, and Gloria cut off all communication with them. Allie later learned that this was because the two disapproved of a romantic relationship Gloria had started with a then married White politician, Greg. Gloria remained estranged from her parents but allowed Allie to visit for holidays and special occasions. Allie found these visits increasingly painful because her grandparents were quite critical of Gloria, especially after Gloria's marriage to Greg when Allie was 11.

Following her mother's remarriage, Allie once more made a major move, this time to a very exclusive, predominantly White suburb about an hour from the more working class, ethnically diverse city in which she grew up. The move was difficult for Allie, who missed family and friends. She found it difficult to make new friends at first, and felt out of place. Nevertheless, she worked very hard to get good grades and to fit in so that her family would think of her as a model student and daughter.

Because of Allie's very light complexion, most of her new classmates and neighbors assumed that she too was White, and Allie never corrected their impression or said anything when they would repeat racist jokes or stereotypes. Racist comments were not uncommon given the climate of racial polarization in a neighboring metropolitan city. From the age of 11, all of Allie's classmates and friends were White.

When Allie was 13, her mother and Greg had a daughter, Jennifer, and it was decided that Greg should adopt Allie so that she would have the same last name as her mother and half-sister. It was at this point that Allie officially changed her first name, though she'd had the nickname of Allie for many years. Her grandmother does not know that she changed her name from Alicia.

Allie started high school at 14 with a new name and a new family. She got along well with her stepfather, who left all parenting decisions concerning Allie to Gloria. Allie was at first thrilled with the birth of Jennifer but found frequent requests that she look after the baby burdensome once she became more active at school. Allie began to have frequent arguments with her mother, with Gloria complaining that Allie had become selfish since the move. Allie felt that her mother was too demanding and resented the long established expectation that she be "mother's little helper." The arguments reached a peak when Allie became a cheerleader in her sophomore year of high school. Allie also started dating and was spending more and more time away from home.

The arguments with Gloria dropped off dramatically after the sudden heart attack death of Earlene the spring of Allie's sophomore year. Though never close to her former mother-in-law, Gloria was nevertheless deeply affected by Earlene's death and began telling Allie that it was important to live as if death could come at any moment. She still, however, voiced high expectations for Allie in terms of appearance and school achievement and was critical if Allie did not look and act like the model daughter. Allie was devastated by her great-grandmother's death and felt guilty about not having visited Earlene as much since she'd become more popular at school. Allie cherished the relationship to Earlene in part because it was her primary link to her father, who had become a quite well-known professional athlete. Gloria's continuing animosity toward her ex-husband, and his own preoccupation with his career, meant that Allie had had virtually no contact with her father since the divorce. Earlene had tried to console Allie about her father's lack of contact. Allie responded to Earlene's death by redoubling her efforts to be a model child.

At the start of her junior year of high school, Allie began dating John, a 17-year-old, White senior. Allie was attracted to John because he was "smart, ambitious, and gorgeous." The two began to date seriously midyear, after John learned he had been accepted by a prestigious college back East, and they became sexually intimate shortly thereafter. Gloria and Greg approved of Allie's relationship with John, though Gloria constantly hinted that Allie should be taking precautions to avoid pregnancy. Allie's maternal grandparents, Rafael and Alicia, whom she saw only sporadically, were less impressed with John, though they assured Allie that they just wanted her to be happy.

Wanting to "look good for John," Allie began to purge after large meals about the time the couple started dating seriously. She had first heard of the tactic from a fellow cheerleader and did not initially see it as a problem, though she was very secretive about purging from the beginning. It was not until she also found herself seeking opportunities to eat secretly that Allie became concerned about her behavior, for she would force herself to throw up after these binges. She was terrified that John would find out and was actually relieved when their relationship switched to being long distance once John went away to college. Concern about her eating problems was a factor in her decision to attend the large, public university near the city she had grown up in rather than attempting to go to a more prestigious college nearer to John's school. Noting a relationship between her binging and purging and experiences of stress, she felt that she could not handle the stress of another big move or of a rigorous academic program.

Allie's immediate and extended family were pleased that she chose to stay close to home for college, though the decision caused tensions in her relationship with John, who felt Allie had limited her options. Other differences began to emerge between John and Allie, particularly John's discomfort with Allie's relationship with her father's family. After several arguments about his reluctance to spend any time with them, John admitted that he had some prejudices against African Americans and that he probably would not have begun dating Allie had he known she was part African American. Allie stopped asking him to spend time with her father's family and again drastically cut down the time she spent with them as she had before Earlene's death. John and Allie continued to date through her freshmen year of college, but John decided he wanted to date other people, just before the beginning of Allie's sophomore year. At this time, Allie was living in a sorority with eight other young women, one of whom was a close friend from high school.

Initial Session

Individuals with eating disorders, like substance abusers, often enter treatment denying the extent of their problems. They may be terrified of giving up their symptoms, thus losing their primary means of coping with difficult issues. They frequently come to therapy at the behest of a friend or family member and may be reluctant to commit themselves to the therapy process, hoping instead for a quick and preferably spontaneous recovery. Although they may be engaged in an apparently strong interpersonal network, I have found that clients with eating and substance abuse disorders rarely have had experiences of deep and sustaining relationships in which their needs and feelings can be fully expressed. The intensity of the therapeutic relationship is therefore often particularly anxiety provoking for them since they are uncomfortable with the intimacy it entails. At the same time, these clients often present in acute distress associated with their disordered eating or abuse of substances, and they are looking for ways to control the distress. The challenge in seeking to engage an individual with an eating disorder in therapy is to offer help in handling distress while also confronting denial and wishes for an easy or quick way out. The challenge is complicated by the necessity of avoiding a replication of the individual's early experience of not having his or her needs responded to appropriately. The therapist must be able to listen attentively for the unmet dependency needs while avoiding gratification of wishes for easy solutions. I was cognizant of these challenges in beginning to work with Allie, and sought to address them in our first meeting.

FIRST CONTACT

I knew before meeting Allie that she had concerns about food and eating, as she had requested an intake appointment after seeing my name on a flyer for an eating disorders therapy group. (At the time of her request, she made it clear that she was seeking individual and not group therapy.) In addition to gathering the usual information in an intake, I therefore sought to obtain a thorough history of her experiences with dieting, weight fluctuations, binging and purging episodes and also explored family history and attitudes concerning food and eating. This fact-finding approach may seem to overemphasize food and weight, yet I have found it helpful in conveying from the very beginning of therapy that *anything* related to eating concerns can be discussed openly and honestly, without recriminations or the cloak of secrecy most individuals with eating disorders are used to. This approach also tends to counteract denial, since it becomes quite clear to both client and therapist that the disordered behavior is not a very effective means of weight control, let alone a successful coping strategy, because of its great emotional and physical toll. Below is a sample of our discussion of Allie's eating history. It illustrates how a fact finding approach may help uncover relationships between disordered eating and problematic feelings and also the meanings the client attaches to food and weight.

THERAPIST: It sounds like the episodes of eating and then throwing up become more frequent when you're under a lot of stress or when, like now, you're dealing with a difficult and painful experience.

CLIENT: Yeah. It's always been like that, since I started, though in the beginning I just wanted to keep my weight down.

THERAPIST: How often were you having these episodes.

CLIENT: At first once or twice a week, then two or three times, sometimes more.

THERAPIST: So you found yourself binging and then purging more and more over time, just to keep your weight down?

CLIENT: (pauses, then in a softer voice) I guess so.

THERAPIST: Is this something you've thought about before?

CLIENT: Well, yeah, I guess I knew I was doing it more and more, even before the breakup, but it just was a way to not get fat.

THERAPIST: Tell me more about your concerns about not getting fat.

CLIENT: Well, you know, guys are so into their girlfriends looking just right, and I have some family members who are kind of heavy, and I'm short and I can't afford to gain any weight . . . and my mother really gets on me about my weight . . . so I've just really always had to watch it to not get fat.

THERAPIST: What would it mean to you to be fat?

CLIENT: I'd be a failure, and no one would love me.

Allie's association of fat and failure came to the surface readily with the fact-finding approach. This approach also brings to the surface the client's fear that the therapist will try to control the client's eating behavior or force her to gain weight, a fear having its roots in an often overcontrolling mother-child relationship. The fear needs to be addressed explicitly in the initial contact, as it was with Allie:

CLIENT: My ideal weight is 100, anything over that and I feel fat.

THERAPIST: Why 100?

CLIENT: That's what I weighed when I looked my best and was happiest, when I started dating John.

THERAPIST: Sometimes there are fluctuations in a person's base weight—by this I mean the weight a person can naturally maintain without needing to diet or to use excessive methods to control weight. If you think about the period of time since puberty when you've been able to maintain a certain weight without resorting to dieting or purging, what would that weight be?

CLIENT: Well, maybe 110 or even 115.

THERAPIST: So 110 or 115 might be a weight it would be more possible for you to maintain than 100.

CLIENT: I don't want to weigh 115, and I don't want to be fat. If I have to get fat to get better, then I'm not sure it's worth it.

THERAPIST: I can hear that you have real concerns about getting fat. I'm sure there are lots of reasons why this issue is so important to you, and I hope we can talk about those reasons. I want to assure you that my goal is *not* to make you get fat. Instead, if we were to work together, I would want to help you find healthier ways to achieve your goals, including not getting fat. It seems like it would be important to help you find a way to really like yourself as you are and not feel like you have to throw up to be a certain weight.

CLIENT: Yeah, well, that would be good, if it could happen.

Another major issue in joining with Allie, as with any client with an eating disorder, was to make it clear that the therapeutic relationship would be collaborative and that her experiences would be important to me. I wanted to convey to Allie my belief that she could get better. Instilling a sense of hope is a key curative factor at the outset of any therapeutic relationship, but it is particularly important for individuals who are feeling helpless in overcoming their problems.

CLIENT: I've tried everything to stop, and I just can't.

THERAPIST: Well, it's not easy and it may take some time, but my sense from all you've told me is that you really do want to get a handle on this. I'd like to be able to help. Everybody's experience is unique, and we'd have to really get to the bottom of understanding how eating got to be such a problem, but I do think that it's possible to get to the place where eating is not the problem it is for you now.

CLIENT: I guess you know a lot about these kinds of problems.

THERAPIST: Some, yes, but like I said, everybody's unique. If we were to work together I would want to get to know *you*. We'd have to find solutions that work for you. What do you think?

CLIENT: (silently starts to weep) Yeah . . . yeah. (seems unable to speak for a moment or two) If we could, you know, find a way for me to get a handle on this. If I could get better . . . I mean, I really want to. I'd really like to do this. I'm willing to try.

THERAPIST: OK. That's a good place for us to start.

This was an intense interaction for Allie. I was later to learn that she responded as she did largely because I had emphasized that while I would help her, she would be the one to "get a handle" on her eating problems and the handle would be one that met her needs, that is, one that would really help her to cope. My work with Allie thus taught me once again the importance of providing support in a way that also allows the client to feel empowered.

ESTABLISHING A WORKING ALLIANCE

One of the issues relatively neglected in the voluminous literature on eating disorders concerns the often strong initial reactions of both client and therapist to each other as they begin to work together. The therapist, particularly if a woman, must confront personal feelings about appearance and body size and about the methods eating disordered individuals use to avoid weight gain. The client will often be acutely aware of the therapist's comfort or lack of comfort with issues of appearance and with disordered eating. The client, preoccupied as he or she is with food and appearance, may in fact be especially curious about the therapist's use of food and more than usually sensitive to the therapist's appearance. For both client and therapist, a major question is whether they will be able to identify with each other sufficiently to form the basis of a working alliance. As will be seen, cultural differences and similarities will also be important in the early formation of the therapeutic relationship.

When I met Allie, I had been working with women with eating disorders for only a few years, yet I had had an almost lifelong history of weight problems. A key issue for me, therefore, was to separate out my own experience from Allie's while at the same time using my experience where appropriate to gain insight into what Allie might be feeling.

In our initial sessions I found it more difficult to maintain my objectivity with Allie than with other clients with eating disorders I had worked with for reasons I at first could not pinpoint. I was more than usually aware of how I looked to Allie and wondered what she thought of me. The source of the extra self-consciousness did not become clear until we began to discuss Allie's perceptions of me. This discussion brought to the surface how important the issue of cultural identity was for Allie and helped clarify why I was feeling so scrutinized by her. The following dialogue shows how Allie had immediately recognized the fact that I was racially mixed, just as I had recognized her mixed heritage. She was unusually curious about me because she wanted to know how I saw myself.

CLIENT: You know, you're really not what I expected.

THERAPIST: (I thought she was probably referring to the fact that I was overweight.) How am I not what you expected?

CLIENT: Well . . . I don't know, you're just not.

THERAPIST: Maybe we can look at this a little closer . . . it's important for us to know how I meet your expectations or don't . . . and how you feel about that. I imagine too that you may wonder how I see you, and we may want to talk about that as well.

CLIENT: Umm . . . (a noncommittal shrug follows).

THERAPIST: You don't seem too sure about whether it's a good idea (at this point I wasn't too sure either, wondering if I had jumped the gun in suggesting we look at our perceptions of each other).

CLIENT: Well, I don't want to offend you or anything.

THERAPIST: We've talked about how you can say anything you want to here. We can always talk about my reactions if you feel worried about what I might think.

CLIENT: Well, it's just that most people think only White girls get eating disorders, so I was kind of surprised you aren't White.

THERAPIST: (Because I'd been thinking about my weight, I'd missed the possibility that her first statement referred to our ethnic differences and was thrown off guard when she brought them up directly.) How is it to work with someone who's not White?

CLIENT: Well, I'm not prejudiced, if that's what you mean. But it makes me curious . . .

THERAPIST: Curious about . . . ?

CLIENT: Well, I was wondering what your background is . . . I mean, how you got started working with people with eating disorders.

I was pretty sure at this point that Allie was asking about my cultural background as well as expressing curiosity about my interest in eating disorders. I felt it was important to explore why these questions were important to her before answering them directly.

THERAPIST: Seems like there are two questions here—what my background is, and how I came to do work in this area. I'll be glad to answer both questions, but I'm curious too. I'm wondering why you might want to know about me and my experience and what my answers might mean to you.

CLIENT: I was just wondering if you were mixed, you know, um, racially mixed. Cause I am. I mean some of my family are not White.

THERAPIST: Yes . . .

CLIENT: So I thought maybe if you were mixed too maybe, you know, you might understand about that.

THERAPIST: About what it means to be of mixed heritage?

CLIENT: Yeah.

THERAPIST: Well, it's something we could certainly talk about. Especially if you have some feelings about it, or questions.

CLIENT: So are you?

THERAPIST: Yes. My mother is White and my father was Black.

CLIENT: So what does that make you?

THERAPIST: I see myself as Black.

CLIENT: Oh. (pauses, looks directly at me for one of the first times in our work together) My grandparents—actually they're my great-grandparents—on my father's side are Black.

I have thought a good deal about whether I handled this interaction appropriately, and I would undoubtedly handle it differently if I had it to do over. I was aware that we had left her other question unanswered and that we had not fully explored why she wanted to know about my background or experience. I also felt that by declaring a monocultural identity, I might have made it difficult for Allie to explore her own experience of being ethnically mixed. My response was prompted by my own solution to the question of identity, which had little relevance for Allie's current ethnocultural identity. However, this is one instance where a therapeutic mistake provided an opening for productive work. When we talked later about how my answer affected her, Allie said that I had given her the idea that I felt good about myself and my ethnicity. She thought that perhaps then I might really be able to help her learn to feel good about herself after all. She also said that she thought of how proud her great-grandmother, Earlene, had always been of being Black. Unknowingly, I had tapped into an early experience Allie had had of being cared for by Earlene, and this was to become significant in the transference Allie developed. I thus gained a certain amount of credibility with Allie for addressing the issue of cultural identity directly, and this proved important in establishing a working alliance. Allie became more open in our work together, and she also gradually became more comfortable exploring how she felt about our relationship as it unfolded.

Case Conceptualization

The emergence of Allie's disordered eating was associated with her first serious romantic relationship. The upsurge in binging and purging that led her to seek treatment was triggered by the breakup of that relationship. It thus appeared clear that intimacy issues were important in understanding Allie's bulimia. I speculated that Allie's many early disruptions in relationships were central in explaining her apparent difficulty with intimacy. It seemed likely that the disruptions, particularly the divorce and the abrupt parting from first one set of grandparents and then another, had seriously impacted Allie's sense of self and her ability to trust that she would be cared for. She had experienced little continuity in care giving. Though her early experiences with her extended family were warm and affirming, she soon learned that responding to her grandparents' warmth meant possibly incurring the wrath of her mother, the only figure consistently present in her life. I imagined that, like many young children, Allie had blamed herself for any conflicts her mother had with others and for her parents' divorce and that she had come to feel she was therefore unworthy of love and affection. Neither parent provided Allie with the opportunity to disconfirm her beliefs about her unworthiness, and her father's absence and Gloria's criticism in fact may have exacerbated her feelings. Her attempts to be the model child may well have been a response to the self-blame and sense of unworthiness. The attempts served to defend against the self-blame but in no way resolved it.

I hypothesized that the self-blame was an underlying theme helping to explain Allie's very self-destructive bulimic behavior. My experience in working with individuals with eating disorders led me to believe that Allie, like other clients I had seen, did not believe she deserved to be loved and cared for appropriately. The bulimic episodes were at least partly an expression of this inner sense of unworthiness. As long as she binged and threw up, Allie felt that she was defective. Allie was thus acting out an inner conviction, but in doing so she was perpetuating the faulty assumption. A major focus of the therapy was to help her understand the underlying feelings of unworthiness that were being acted out in bulimic episodes. More specifically, I knew that Allie would need to be able to recognize that the feelings of unworthiness were tied to her past. They were based on a child's valiant but flawed attempts to understand the attitudes and behavior of the significant adults in her life.

I also hypothesized that the bulimic episodes expressed a good deal of ambivalence on Allie's part—a wish to take in something on the one hand and a fear of that same something on the other. As noted, the bulimia seemed tied to intimacy conflicts, and like Zraly and Swift (1990) I believe that individuals with bulimia are profoundly ambivalent about intimacy. They experience the universal need to be close to others, yet have learned early in life that being close carries psychic costs. For Allie, those costs included having to suppress her own needs to gain her mother's approval. I thought that aspects of the relationship with John replicated Allie's early experience, making the relationship difficult to sustain.

Certainly, one way in which the relationship was similar was that Allie once more had to deny her own unique individuality to please John. At least, she felt that she had to. Rather than believing she could be loved as she was, she felt she had to look a certain way to earn John's approval and affection. An all too common experience for young women, yet one doubly distressing for Allie since "looking good" to John also meant denying her mixed ethnocultural heritage. Because John was uncomfortable with her father's African American ancestry, Allie cut herself off once again from her father's family. She was in a sense trying to live a lie, at the cost of having to deny the connections to some of the people in her life who had been most affirming of her. Being close to John required that Allie deny her real self, and that she cut herself off from family members who had affirmed that real self.

It is perhaps not surprising that Allie's symptoms emerged in the relationship with John, since the symptoms themselves have to do with living a lie. In binging and purging, the bulimic typically tries to hide her concerns about weight from the world. It is a way of maintaining a fiction that one is normal—at least of normal weight. The symptoms also serve to hide any other concerns the individual has from the world and, most importantly, from herself. Allie's preoccupation with maintaining a certain weight to please John meant she did not have to look more closely at the relationship to determine whether it could really meet her needs. She managed feelings of unworthiness in the relationship with John by focusing on her appearance and avoiding any examination of the roots of these feelings or of how the relationship exacerbated the feelings. Allie's bulimia thus served certain defensive functions. While the bulimic symptoms caused her emotional and physical distress, they nevertheless helped her to keep out of awareness the ways in which her basic needs for appropriate care and affection were not being met. In warding off this awareness, Allie remained out of touch with the feelings associated with the unmet needs: self-blame and unworthiness. I assumed that the bulimic symptoms more generally served to ward off awareness of difficult feelings and that the symptoms had increased because Allie was confronting an upsurge in such feelings following the breakup with John.

I speculated that the feelings of sadness and rejection Allie was experiencing when she began therapy had not only to do with her current loss of the relationship with John but also might reflect unresolved issues associated with earlier losses. Allie had never had the opportunity to discuss, let alone fully work through, her feelings about her parents' divorce and the loss of her relationship with her father. As discussed in the chapter on counseling children of divorce, very young children often respond to divorce and the disengagement of a parent following divorce with acute feelings of abandonment. Children need to be helped through these feelings. Allie was not helped because of bitterness about the marriage and divorce on both sides of her extended family. I hypothesized that Allie's feelings following the divorce were so painful that she had to cover them over, only to have them stirred up again by the breakup with John.

While Allie's bulimia indicated to me that she had serious psychological problems, I was also aware that Allie had many strengths. She was a very bright young woman who had maintained an excellent academic record while engaged in a variety of extracurricular activities in high school and college. She had warm feelings for her immediate and extended family and was well liked by her peers, though she tended to keep her friendships fairly superficial. I believed that Allie possessed a solid set of coping skills to manage many aspects of her life and to develop relationships. Her coping skills seemed deficient primarily when it came to handling intimacy and strong emotions, such as sadness. I hoped that her more general coping ability would be an asset in our work together, and it did prove critical to the success of her work to gain control of her bulimic symptoms.

Orienting Constructs

In formulating a conceptualization of Allie's case, I drew heavily from the literature on the etiology of eating disorders discussed earlier. It was clear from Allie's early history that her mother had failed in many ways to respond appropriately to Allie's needs and to support her development of a firm sense of self. Gloria's high expectations of Allie, reliance on her as a helper, and insistence that she assimilate to mainstream cultural values even to the point of denying her mixed ethnocultural heritage all served to foster in Allie a sense that she must deny her real self and her own needs to be loved and cared for. Allie's lack of comfort with intimacy, feelings of unworthiness, and unresolved sadness were readily understandable in light of her early experience. I could see how Allie might have turned to disordered eating as a way of coping with intimacy conflicts and difficult feelings, as other facets of her development may have predisposed her to develop this particular "pseudosolution" to her problems in living.

Allie had been caught in the bind that Steiner-Adair (1991) suggests is an important factor in the development of eating disorders. Allie was expected to both be independent and excel academically and to be able to form romantic relationships with males. Unfortunately for many adolescent females, these expectations may often be experienced as contradictory. Young women often believe that to be attractive to men they must deny their own academic and independence strivings so they are not viewed as threatening to the males they are involved with. Allie experienced a great deal of anxiety in trying to reconcile the two expectations once she became intimate with John, and she recognized that the anxiety was a source of stress that prompted her to binge and then purge. Her bulimia also afforded her a way out of the bind: she decided not to go to a prestigious school because she feared her bulimic episodes would become worse.

Allie's situation was further complicated by pressures to deny her ethnic heritage and to adopt cultural values that denigrated her family background. Indeed, as therapy progressed it became clear how much mainstream cultural messages about appearance and attractiveness confused and distressed Allie. The following discussion illustrates this confusion, and indicates its role in her disordered eating:

CLIENT: It was really hard, at school, to be with people when they would make these totally racist comments, talking about how ugly Black people were, or how lazy Mexicans were.

THERAPIST: What would you be feeling when you were with people making these comments?

CLIENT: These people were my friends, and I'd be thinking to myself that must be what they really think of me, or it's what they would think of me if they knew that members of my family were Black and Mexican. So, of course, I didn't want them to know.

THERAPIST: So you were feeling like you couldn't let your friends know who you really were.

CLIENT: I knew that the things they were saying weren't true, at least not about the people in my family that I loved, but it was hard to fight back. I felt that if I told them I'm part Black and part Mexican and I'm not ugly or lazy, they would just totally reject me instead of changing their views. And in a way, maybe I was agreeing with them by trying so hard to be White. Because I never wanted anyone to think of me as ugly, and I guess I did believe you had to be White to be pretty.

THERAPIST: You talked a lot about needing to be seen as pretty and how that tied in to your starting to purge. How do you think your need to be seen as attractive ties in with the racist comments your friends would make?

CLIENT: Well, I guess I really believed the things they said at some level, cause you know I would hear it so often and see it too in the way people get portrayed, and I guess I *felt* unattractive. So I would obsess about it and then try to make myself more attractive. That meant being thin, and it also meant being White. I was terrified they would find out I wasn't all White, so maybe I focused on trying to be thin.

Kuba and Harris (1992) discuss the concept of *internalized oppression* to describe the experience of young women of color who adopt mainstream values concerning appearance and feel themselves to be unattractive as a consequence. These authors believe that internalized oppression is a central factor in the development of eating disorders among women of color. Though conflicts in her ethnocultural identity were apparent from the beginning of our work together, it was not until therapy was well under way that Allie was able to see how they contributed to her pattern of disordered eating and how they related to her deeper feelings of being unworthy.

There is an emerging body of literature (e.g., Helms, 1993; Sue & Sue, 1990) which suggests that ethnocultural identity develops in sequential stages. In early stages, individuals view themselves in terms of the values and stereotypes of the dominant culture; later they will begin to question these values and stereotypes, often as a result of exposure to racism or to competing cultural views. For the young child of color, the earliest stage of ethnocultural identity is thus often characterized by self-rejection if their cultural milieu is not able to offset the values and stereotypes of the dominant culture. Developing a more positive ethnocultural identity will typically involve immersing oneself in one's own culture for a time, and rejecting mainstream culture, and then questioning *any* view that automatically denigrates members of other cultures. The final stage of ethnocultural identity development involves the integration of a positive sense of self as an ethnic being and an openness and acceptance of others who may be different. Children are helped to develop positive ethnocultural identities by affirming experiences with others and by the opportunities to interact with role models who themselves have positive identities.

Allie's extended family provided her with experiences that helped to offset some of society's stereotypes about African Americans and Mexican Americans, but she had only sporadic content with them from age 11. Since her parent's families did not get along with each other, they were not able to help Allie develop an identity that integrated their separate cultural traditions. Perhaps more significantly, Allie's mother had herself not been able to forge a positive ethnocultural identity. Gloria remained strongly identified with mainstream cultural values and had in fact cut herself off entirely from her parents and from her cultural heritage. Allie's primary role model thus could not help her to move beyond the earliest stage of identity development, and her environment from age 11 on also served to keep Allie stuck in this earliest stage. I began to suspect that Allie's inability to move through the stages of ethnocultural identity contributed to her disordered eating. Had she been able to see herself more positively as a person of mixed ethnocultural heritage, she might not have felt the need to make herself over into the thin, mainstream cultural ideal.

Treatment Plans and Intervention Strategy

INITIAL TREATMENT PLAN

My initial view of the treatment with Allie was that it would likely unfold in three stages. My goals for the first stage were to: (a) establish a therapeutic relationship of trust and cooperation, (b) help Allie gain mastery over her bulimic symptoms, and (c) help Allie begin to make connections between her symptoms and underlying feelings and conflicts. I hoped that achieving these short-term goals would make it possible for us to do more in-depth work in the second stage. My goal for this second stage was to trace Allie's problems with intimacy to her early experiences of disruptions, and to help her understand where her feelings of unworthiness and sadness came from. I assumed that this second stage would involve exploring the nature of our relationship, as typically relationship themes are reenacted in the therapeutic relationship before they are fully understood by clients (Teyber, 1996). My goals for the final stage of our work together were initially quite simple: I hoped that Allie would be able to forge a positive sense of self so that she would no longer feel the need to resort to binging and purging to make herself into a lovable person. I knew this new sense of self could be stimulated by corrective emotional experiences in the therapeutic relationship, and I presumed that this would mean Allie would have the experience of being truly understood and accepted as she was rather than for how she looked or how hard she worked.

Many clinicians (e.g., Bruch, 1984; Johnson, 1991; Zraly & Swift, 1990) have talked about how essential, and sometimes difficult, it is to gain the trust of eating disordered clients in the initial stages of treatment. Because they often have little experience in truly intimate relationships, eating disordered clients may initially find it hard to trust that the therapist is really available to help them. Instead, as mentioned earlier, they may expect to be controlled. I have already highlighted my attempts to help Allie see that our relationship would be collaborative rather than the more hierarchical relationship she expected and feared. I did, however, indicate that I could help her only if she was willing to take active steps to understand and eliminate her symptoms. As Bruch (1984) suggests, I found it helpful to outline briefly my understanding of what eating disorders represent and how treatment might proceed:

THERAPIST: One thing I want to share with you is that, in my past work with people with eating disorders, I've found that we can almost always trace the binging and purging to other problems in a person's life. So a lot of our work is about understanding those problems and finding better ways of coping with them than binging and purging.

CLIENT: What kinds of problems do you mean?

THERAPIST: Well, we've already talked about how you've been purging more since the breakup with John. Most people have a really hard time with breakups, but maybe we might look at this relationship and find that there are some reasons—below the surface, things you're not necessarily aware of—that make the breakup particularly painful. So we would try to understand the feelings, but also try to find ways of coping besides purging.

This first stage of therapy with eating disordered individuals, like work with substance abusers, is typically focused on helping the individual to stop the disordered or addictive behavior. Many clinicians believe that the insight-oriented work of relational therapy can not proceed until an individual is well into recovery, that is, has given up reliance on disordered eating or substances. This belief is based on the fact that disordered eating and substance abuse are used defensively to avoid experiencing painful affects, and hence these affects are not available to explore in therapy as long as the client continues the symptoms. My own experience bears out the importance of focusing on strategies for reducing and eliminating symptomatic eating at the beginning of therapy. I do believe, however, that clients are able to gain insight into the role of the disordered eating from the beginning of therapy and that care and attention must be given to helping the individual maintain recovery *throughout* the therapy. Exploration of particularly painful material during the course of therapy may prompt relapses, and these must be addressed immediately to ensure continued progress in recovery and in the therapy. I further believe that the therapeutic relationship forged in the initial stage of treatment is what makes possible the later work in therapy.

A good deal of the work Allie and I undertook during the initial stage of treatment, which lasted about four months, was aimed explicitly at eliminating Allie's reliance on binging and purging as a means of coping with stress and conflicts. This involved some informational work, as Allie needed to learn facts about the consequences of bulimia, the need for proper nutrition, and healthy strategies for weight management and stress reduction. I was able to refer Allie to a time-limited support group run by the university health center as a supplement to our work, where the psychoeducational format provided Allie not only with the information she needed but also with a forum to answer her questions about diet, and so forth. Where clients are unable to attend such psychoeducational support groups, I have found that making suggestions about reading materials and a referral to a nutritionist are important.

It is also important during this stage to have the client carefully monitor the emotions and events that trigger episodes of disordered eating. For many clients, being able to identify the triggers of their disordered eating is an empowering step. They are surprised to learn that the episodes that once seemed completely out of their control actually follow a certain pattern. Identifying the pattern is a first step in gaining control over the disordered eating. The next step is to develop a repertoire of new coping strategies for handling the emotions and events that trigger the episodes. Although clients may ask the therapist for suggestions about new strategies, their fear of being controlled means any suggestions from the therapist are likely to be resisted. I have found that clients—when it's pointed out that they are the ones who have to use the strategies—can readily list ways of coping that have worked for them in the past or that seem to work for people they admire. The feasibility of strategies has to be explored, and the client should be encouraged to actually put new ways of coping to the test. Below is an example of the kind of work Allie and I did to explore one possible trigger for a binge and to help Allie discover other ways of handling the situation:

CLIENT: I was noticing that whenever I get angry with Margi [her room-mate], I want to eat lots of candy.

THERAPIST: Do you have the urge to binge whenever you're angry, or just when you're angry with Margi?

CLIENT: I haven't really noticed it with anyone else, but now that you mention it, I don't get angry much. When I was angry with John, I wouldn't say anything, but I would try to sneak away and eat. It was a way of getting back at him, behind his back.

THERAPIST: Seems like anger is hard for you. What else could you do when you find yourself feeling angry, say with Margi?

CLIENT: I could avoid her.

THERAPIST: Hmmn. Isn't that what you're doing by binging?

CLIENT: I could ask her for some space.

THERAPIST: How would that be for you?

CLIENT: Hard.

THERAPIST: Any thoughts about why it might be hard? Why anger is hard for you to express?

CLIENT: I hate it when people get angry—you know, when they yell and scream.

THERAPIST: Do you yell and scream when you get angry?

CLIENT: No. I just eat. (laughs) I guess I'm afraid people will yell and scream at me if I tell them I'm angry at them, like my mom does if I let on I'm not 100 percent happy with her.

THERAPIST: Is Margi like your mother?

CLIENT: No.

THERAPIST: Will she yell and scream if you ask for some space?

CLIENT: No.

THERAPIST: Or tell her you're not 100 percent happy with her?

CLIENT: (laughs at my using her terminology) No, I guess not.

THERAPIST: And if she did?

CLIENT: I guess *then* I could leave.

THERAPIST: Would you binge then?

CLIENT: Probably. What else could I do?

THERAPIST: You tell me. We've talked about some of the things you find helpful when you're stressed—like running, going for a drive, seeing a movie, reading a magazine. Would any of those things satisfy rather than a binge?

CLIENT: Maybe going for a drive, though I might run over someone!

THERAPIST: Yeah, seems like you've got to find a way to get some of the anger out without attacking a candy bar or a poor pedestrian.

CLIENT: I could always go downstairs and play video games.

THERAPIST: I think it will be important for us to look at why anger is hard for you, but in the meantime playing video games sounds better than binging and then wanting to purge. Maybe you could try this the next time you're feeling angry with Margi.

In this interaction, Allie found a short-term solution to handling an interpersonal trigger to binging. Gradually, Allie was able to build a repertoire of these short-term solutions. The longer term goal of also understanding the inhibitions in expressing anger is alluded to, though exploring the roots of Allie's conflicts with anger in more depth was a second stage goal. Although Allie had developed some ease in the therapeutic relationship, as indicated by her use of humor and her willingness to take some risks to acknowledge conflictual feelings, I did not feel yet that we had established a solid enough alliance to explore her anger fully or to work on ways of communicating her anger more directly.

Although it is generally a very positive experience for clients to begin to respond differently to events that formerly triggered disordered eating, clients may also experience a sense of loss as they give up their symptoms. They may also begin to experience for the first time the stronger emotions they have been warding off with the disordered eating. Finally, they will almost invariably experience some relapses in their attempts to eliminate disordered eating. The therapist must attend to the shifting moods accompanying the early stage of recovery and help the client to hold onto gains while working through temporary setbacks and/or the exploration of more intense material. As noted earlier, even as the client begins to make significant gains in recovery, it is important to continue to explore the use of disordered eating as a coping mechanism and to help the client avoid relapses.

As Allie began to gain some mastery over her binging and purging, reducing her bulimic episodes to two times a week and eventually being able to go without purging even after a binge, I felt we were able to move to exploring more charged material. During this second stage, which lasted from about the fourth to the twelfth month, I was alert to nuances in our relationship that might give clues to Allie's core conflicts. Anger at my being away for vacation, disappointment following a misinterpretation, and feelings of warmth following an empathic connection were all explored as they arose in our relationship. This exploration of Allie's feelings toward me often led us to the roots of the feelings in earlier experiences. In this way, relational reenactments between Allie and me became a vehicle for us to understand how Allie originally had come to feel her own needs did not matter.

There was no discrete turning point between the second and third stages of therapy with Allie. Instead, as Allie began to examine her early relationships as a result of exploration of relational reenactments, she found that her attitudes toward her family and herself began to change significantly. This was most immediately discernible in her shifting ethnocultural identity. After a period of testing in our relationship, Allie began to talk about feeling she could trust me and this reminded her of her close bond to her great-grandmother, Earlene. In reexamining this relationship, Allie was particularly struck by how Earlene had tried to reach out both to Gloria and to her father's Dutch mother. Allie felt that Earlene, though strongly identified as African American, had been able to embrace women of different ethnicities. Allie herself had felt totally embraced by Earlene, and remembering

this allowed Allie to begin herself to embrace the different ethnicities represented in her parentage. It is perhaps noteworthy that our own therapeutic
relationship replicated this bridging of ethnicities.

Less immediately, but no less significantly, Allie came to understand
how her feelings of being unlovable were linked to her parents' divorce. Giving voice at last to the feelings of loss, anger, and bewilderment freed Allie
from the pervasive sense that she had been to blame and helped her to see
that her parents, like herself, were imperfect people who had not been able
to cope with a difficult situation. Her need to be the model child/adult also
abated, though the skills she had developed in pursuing perfection in
schoolwork still stood her in good stead.

BALANCING GOALS

The chief task in the early stage of therapy was to balance the goal of helping Allie gain mastery of her eating behavior while beginning the exploration of the core conflicts that were being masked by the disordered eating.
As with many eating disordered clients, Allie would readily talk about a specific binge episode, but she had more difficulty relating it to her feelings
and to past experiences. As Allie gained information about bulimia through
the psychoeducational group, and also developed strategies for coping with
situations that triggered bulimic episodes, her narrow focus on specific
binge episodes shifted to a focus on understanding the underlying causes of
disordered eating.

REVISED TREATMENT GOALS

The treatment goals did not significantly shift during the 18 months of therapy, though my understanding of the specific targets of treatment did. One
dynamic underlying Allie's eating behavior that I had missed in my conceptualization was her difficulty with anger, and as we explored the roots of
this difficulty, it became clear that Allie had a great deal of unresolved anger
towards her mother, because Gloria had taken her away from the two family
situations in which Allie had felt most loved and affirmed. I thus began to
pay special attention to how Allie defended against her anger in the therapeutic relationship and found that exploration of anger was a key part of the
relational reenactments that characterized the second and third stage of
treatment.

Therapeutic Process

RELATIONAL REENACTMENTS

Relational reenactments proved to be pivotal points in the therapy. The
reenactments were often stimulated by separations or breaks in our work
together. One especially critical reenactment came four months into the

therapy, and it was the stimulus that led us to deeper exploration of Allie's difficulties with anger. In the session following a three week holiday break, Allie for the first time was able to express anger directly:

CLIENT: It was the trip from hell from the beginning, and when I got back up here no one was around to talk to about it. My first night back I went straight to Taco Bell and just totally pigged out. It's been really hard since. All those things we talked about doing, well, I haven't done any of them. There doesn't seem to be any point.

THERAPIST: I'm sorry it's been such a hard time for you Allie. Do you want to talk about what made the trip hard? Was it the things we talked about before you went home?

CLIENT: I don't remember what we talked about, I only know it was bad, and I've been eating like a pig ever since.

THERAPIST: I imagine my being away didn't help any.

CLIENT: You have to take your vacation, right?

THERAPIST: Right, but it seems like it was a hard time for you, and maybe you're feeling upset about my being away.

CLIENT: What makes you think that?

THERAPIST: I notice today you're not looking at me much, and you sound like you're not happy with me, to use your phrase. And also, I know *I* would probably be angry if I needed to talk to someone and my therapist was away.

CLIENT: That's crazy, therapists have the right to take vacations.

THERAPIST: They have the right, but that wouldn't stop me from feeling mad or at least disappointed. How do *you* feel about my being away?

CLIENT: I don't know. Maybe I am disappointed a little, I don't know, like you make it seem like things are going to get better, and then you disappear just when they get worse . . . So maybe I am a little pissed. Mostly, I just wonder if this is really going to do any good.

THERAPIST: Well, I'm really glad you could tell me you're pissed at me. Seems like now that I've let you down, you're wondering if it's safe to trust me again, trust that the therapy can be helpful.

CLIENT: It's not that *you* let me down.

THERAPIST: Well, you needed me and I wasn't here.

CLIENT: I know it's not your fault. I mean, I should know how to handle things by now without having to eat like a pig.

THERAPIST: Allie, do you see how you went from being able to acknowledge that you were mad at me to blaming yourself for feeling bad that I was away? Why do you think that happened?

In this interaction, Allie directly expressed her anger and also reenacted her tendency to immediately try to placate the object of her anger. I had to explicitly invite Allie to express the anger. Typically I will refrain from naming affects with clients to avoid imposing my assumptions of what a client is feeling. However, I have found that some clients need help being able to recognize and give voice to their feelings. This has been particularly the case with my eating-disordered clients. I felt that Allie would be able to express her anger directly only with some prompting. My invitation to Allie to express her disappointment with me was a very new experience for Allie, and she clearly expected me to invalidate her anger. After all, therapists need vacations. Rather than invalidate it, I tried in this interaction to show Allie not only that her feelings were understandable but also that I cared about what she felt. I went on to tell her that I was sorry that I had not been there for her. My apology came later rather than earlier because I did not want Allie's anger cut off prematurely. Instead, we talked about how she herself tried to cut it off. We went on to explore the many interactions with others, especially John and her mother, that had taught her that it was not okay to be angry. We had already discussed how her unexpressed anger was a trigger for binging, and this first direct expression of anger toward me signaled a significant drop in Allie's disordered eating. Following this corrective experience, Allie not only began to express her anger and disappointment more directly with me and with others but she became more comfortable expressing other feelings as well, including sadness and pleasure.

It may seem strange that Allie would have had difficulty expressing pleasure, but another major reenactment in our work together indicated that Allie experienced pleasure as threatening. In particular, she feared that she would lose the source of her pleasure because of retaliation from a jealous other. The reenactment occurred in the 14th month of therapy, as Allie was preparing for a summer study course abroad. By this time in therapy, Allie had made substantial progress in recovering from her bulimic episodes, and she was much more insightful about the underlying roots of her problematic eating. She was, in fact, beginning to talk about terminating therapy. The reenactment was prompted by my countertransference to Allie's impending trip and to the termination.

In one session, as Allie talked about a side trip to Paris, I began to question her about whether she thought it was really a good idea to go off on her own away from her travel companions. After she herself began to mention reasons why the side trip might not be such a good idea, I noted that Allie was not looking at me, and she had become less engaged in the discussion. In short, she reminded me of the shy, reticent young woman I had begun working with. I immediately realized that there was a part of me that missed the old Allie—the one who needed my help. Here she was going off to Paris (a city I'd always wanted to visit myself), and I realized how much I would miss her when she left. I was proud of the work she had done, yes, but apparently I was not yet ready to let her go. I believe I was reenacting with Allie an important dynamic in her relationship to her mother. Like Gloria, I was having a hard time recognizing Allie as a person in her own right, capable of existing without me. We were able to talk about this when I acknowledged my countertransference:

THERAPIST: You know, Allie, it's just hit me that I've kind of poured cold water on your idea about Paris when I should be celebrating with you the opportunity to go.

CLIENT: What do you mean?

THERAPIST: Just that the very fact that you're looking forward to doing something on your own, for yourself, is something to celebrate, and instead I seem to be trying to discourage you.

CLIENT: I did think you were being kind of negative, but then I thought maybe you know something about Paris that I don't know.

THERAPIST: No, I'm sure you know more about Paris than I do. Maybe that's the problem. You're going somewhere I've never been. But I'm happy for you. This is a big step for you.

CLIENT: I don't know. Maybe it's too big a step.

Here Allie was ready to talk herself out of the pleasure of independent travel in her efforts to keep her overprotective therapist from feeling bad. When I pointed out this dynamic to Allie, she immediately related it to a relationship pattern with her mother. Allie had learned not to relish her steps toward independence because Gloria would respond by finding fault with those steps. When this pattern repeated in our relationship, I responded in a different way than Gloria. I acknowledged the feelings behind my response and also supported Allie's right to experience pleasure in her impending independence:

THERAPIST: When I think of your trip to Paris, I realize that I'm a little envious, and even more, that I'm going to miss you. But I'll enjoy thinking of you in Paris. I *am* really glad for you, Allie. It seems like you're on your way in more ways than one.

CLIENT: Yeah, it does, and I guess deep down I'm really happy about it too.

Recognizing and sharing my countertransference with Allie was an important part of the therapeutic work, particularly as we drew closer to termination. I was able to do this because we had developed a very strong working alliance during the course of therapy. For the most part, our relationship was characterized by warmth and positive feelings on both sides. As already mentioned, Allie quickly transferred to me the warm feelings she had had to her African American great-grandmother. She saw Earlene as wise and was willing to entertain the expectation that I too would be wise with her. Although we explored the roots of these transferential feelings, it is worth noting that I did in fact try hard with Allie to be the wise woman role model she needed at that stage in her development. First, because the wise woman is part of my own cultural heritage and is an image I consciously aspire to. Also, I shared with Allie the experience of being of mixed ethnocultural heritage, and I wanted to help her achieve a more positive sense of her ethnocultural identity.

IMPEDIMENTS TO TREATMENT

The chief impediment to treatment was Allie's initial discomfort with the idea of giving up her bulimic behavior. Purging was a strategy Allie consciously used to ward off unwanted weight gain. As she developed new, healthier strategies to manage her weight (e.g., healthy eating, exercise, stress management techniques to counteract urges to binge), Allie was left with only the unconscious motive for purging—to ward off difficult feelings. At first she resisted exploring these feelings by finding new ways to avoid the experience of painful feelings. Instead of binging and then purging, she would come to session late or miss a session, or come and talk only about superficial things. We discussed how scary it was for her to not resort to the disordered eating to protect herself from feeling painful affects and also about how important it was for her to find a way to feel safe in the therapy before exploring the feelings directly. Allie and I often went in circles as she would move closer to core conflicts and then feel the need to defend against her awakening awareness by resorting to distancing strategies. Allie herself became astute in recognizing how she defended against painful affects. Examining our relational struggles helped Allie to understand how she avoided being close to others because she feared they would find her unlovable.

Anger and sadness were particularly difficult affects for Allie to experience deeply, and as already noted these would often first be addressed in terms of our relationship. The continuous relational focus provided Allie with corrective emotional experiences of being understood and accepted by someone even as she was feeling threatening feelings of sadness or anger. In turn, she learned to understand and accept her own feelings.

Allie's resistance to experiencing anger and sadness in therapy made sense in light of her history. She had not really had the opportunity to express these feelings fully in most of her relationships and had as a consequence learned to cover them over to such a point that she often failed to recognize them in herself. The disordered eating helped her to cover these and other feelings over, and it was only as this defense was removed that Allie began to explore the roots of the feelings of sadness and unworthiness in her early experiences with disruptions.

In giving up the strategy of purging, Allie had had to learn to tolerate the physical sensation of having a full stomach. Once the strategy had been given up, she faced the more difficult task of learning to tolerate the experience of deep and intense feelings of loss. For example, Allie experienced really for the first time the pain and bewilderment evoked by the essential demise of her relationship with her father following her parents' divorce. How could her father have abandoned her so completely? How could her mother have allowed the abandonment to happen? Allie had to finally ask these and other questions out loud and to experience the resulting anger and desolation, to realize that she had unconsciously believed that she was to blame for her parents' failure to appropriately nurture her. Engel and Ferguson (1990) have used the term *imaginary crime* to describe how an individual unconsciously assumes guilt for parental inadequacies, and they discuss the many ways in which the self-blame for imaginary crimes gives rise to self-punishing psychological problems. As Allie began to mourn her early losses and to experience the confusion they evoked, she realized that her feelings of unworthiness were rooted in situations she had had little control over. Instead of protecting herself from the feelings through purging or protecting her parents from her anger through her self-blame, Allie was able to finally gain some sense of mastery over the feelings by experiencing them fully in the relative safety of the therapeutic relationship.

Termination and Therapist's Summary Thoughts

Therapy ended almost 15 months after it began when Allie left to go abroad. Although the timing for termination was prompted by an external event, both Allie and I felt that she had made sufficient progress to end treatment. As noted, I had some countertransference reactions of wanting to hold on to Allie. She, for her part, was delighted to have come so far but was a little apprehensive about ending therapy altogether. She had some realistic concerns about how she would carry with her the insights she had gained in therapy but had over the prior year gained real mastery over the bulimia and did not feel in danger of relapse. She also was no longer plagued by the sadness that marked her entry into therapy but was instead able to feel a wide range of affects, none of which was disabling.

One of the reasons I believed that Allie was ready to terminate was that she had moved through experiencing and expressing some of her anger toward her mother and had come to have a fuller appreciation of who Gloria was—her deficiencies as a mother but also her strengths. Allie was able to see that Gloria had struggled against enormous odds to raise a child without the help of a partner and that Gloria had been overprotective on the one hand and unresponsive on the other because of the issues she was struggling with, rather than because Allie was in any way a defective child. These realizations helped Allie forge a more open relationship with Gloria, though it was still marked by high expectations from Gloria. Allie no longer responded to the expectations with efforts to be the model child but with clearer assertion of her own goals and wishes. Perhaps most importantly, she was able to maintain this sense of identity even under pressure from Gloria to be once again the model child.

Allie ended therapy having come to understand her issues in relationships and the reasons for those issues. While her sense of self had also undergone marked changes, she still had not fully integrated a sense of identity as a worthy, deserving young woman. She was still, for example, consolidating an ethnocultural identity that integrated her mixed ethnic background.

She also still experienced anxiety when beginning relationships with men, fearing that they would not care for her once they really knew her. I fully expected that Allie would be able to take these further steps toward a positive sense of self as she entered new relationships and continued the self-examination started in therapy.

We ended therapy acknowledging how much each of us had valued the experience of working together:

CLIENT: I remember you said it could get better, and I'm really glad I believed you way back when, cause it has.

THERAPIST: I'm glad you believed me too. You've really worked hard, Allie. You should be proud of yourself. I'm glad I got a chance to get to know you and to see how far you've come.

CLIENT: Yeah. It's been good.

THERAPIST: Not always easy, right?

CLIENT: No, but I did feel like you were there to help. I'm really going to miss coming to see you.

THERAPIST: I've enjoyed working with you, Allie, and I'll miss you too.

One of the things we discussed in our last session was Allie's fear that she would not be able to find another therapist she could work well with should she seek help again. Although I was able to hear her expression of appreciation for our work together, I talked with Allie about the importance of realizing that she had been the one to make use of whatever help I provided. She could grow with another therapist if she needed to and would continue to grow on her own. I said goodbye to Allie with the sense we had accomplished much. The struggle with disordered eating had been resolved.

REFERENCES

American Psychiatric Association. (1980). *Diagnostic and statistical manual of mental disorders* (3rd ed.). Washington, DC: Author.

American Psychiatric Association. (1994). *Diagnostic and statistical manual of mental disorders* (4th ed.). Washington, DC: Author.

Bruch, H. (1973). *Eating disorders; Obesity, anorexia nervosa, and the person within.* New York: Basic.

Bruch, H. (1984). Four decades of eating disorders. In D. M. Garner & P. E. Garfinkel (Eds.), *Handbook of psychotherapy for anorexia nervosa and bulimia* (pp. 7–18). New York: Guilford.

Engel, L., & Ferguson, T. (1990). *Imaginary crimes. Why we punish ourselves and how to stop it.* Boston: Houghton Mifflin.

Erickson, E. (1959). Identity and the life cycle. *Psychological Issues,* Monograph 1. New York: International Universities.

Helms, J. E. (1993). *Black and White racial identity. Theory, research and practice.* Westport, CT: Praeger.

Johnson, C. L. (1991). Treatment of eating-disordered patients with borderline and false-self/narcissistic disorders. In C. L. Johnson (Ed.), *Psychodynamic treatment of anorexia nervosa and bulimia* (pp. 165–193). New York: Guilford.

Kuba, S. A., & Harris, D. J. (May, 1992). *Eating disorders in women of color: The ethnocultural context in the identification and treatment of eating disorders.* Paper presented at the Annual Meeting of the American Orthopsychiatry Association, New York.

Minuchin, S., Rosman, B., & Baker, L. (1978). *Psychosomatic families: Anorexia nervosa in context.* Cambridge, MA: Harvard.

Orbach, S. (1978). *Fat is a feminist issue.* New York: Paddington.

Rodin, J., Silberstein, L., & Striegel-Moore, R. (1984). Women and weight: A normative discontent. *Nebraska Symposium on Motivation, 267*–307.

Root, M. P. P. (1990). Disordered eating in women of color. *Sex Roles, 22,* 525–536.

Schwartz, R. C., Barrett, M. J., & Saba, G. (1984). Family therapy for bulimia. In D. M. Garner & P. E. Garfinkel (Eds.), *Handbook of psychotherapy for anorexia nervosa and bulimia* (pp. 280–307). New York: Guilford.

Steiner-Adair, C. (1991). New maps of development, new models of therapy: The psychology of women and the treatment of eating disorders. In C. L. Johnson (Ed.), *Psychodynamic treatment of anorexia nervosa and bulimia* (pp. 225–244). New York: Guilford.

Sue, D. W., & Sue, D. (1990). *Counseling the culturally different. Theory and practice* (2nd ed.). New York: Wiley.

Teyber, E. (1996). *Interpersonal process in psychotherapy. A guide for clinical training* (3rd ed.). Monterey, CA: Brooks-Cole.

Zraly, K., & Swift, D. (1990). *Anorexia, bulimia, and compulsive overeating. A practical guide for counselors and families.* New York: Continuum.

SUGGESTIONS FOR FURTHER READING

Garner, D. M., & Garfinkel, P. E. (Eds.). (1984). *Handbook of psychotherapy for anorexia nervosa and bulimia.* New York: Guilford. This compilation includes excellent chapters outlining psychodynamic, feminist, and family systems perspectives on eating disorders as well as discussions of cognitive-behavioral treatment approaches. Different modalities of treatment are described in separate chapters, including group therapy and pyschoeducational principles. Although now somewhat dated, this book includes the work of some of the most prominent clinicians specializing in the treatment of eating disorders.

Root, M. P. P. (1990). Disordered eating in women of color. *Sex Roles, 22,* 525–536. Root provides an illuminating discussion of the cultural and familial dynamics that underlie the emergence of eating disorders in women of color. A therapist with extensive experience working with women with eating disorders, Root integrates discussion of sociocultural factors with a family systems perspective on eating disorders. She has also written elsewhere about the experience of racially mixed individuals.

Teyber, E. (1996). *Interpersonal process in psychotherapy. A guide for clinical training* (3rd ed.). Monterey, CA: Brooks-Cole. Teyber provides a detailed introduction to the relational approach to psychotherapy, helping the beginning therapist develop a sound understanding of the theoretical rationale for such an approach. The text includes extensive case vignettes and discusses major issues in the unfolding process of psychotherapy.

Zraly, K., & Swift, D. (1990). *Anorexia, bulimia, and compulsive overeating. A practical guide for counselors and families.* New York: Continuum. This short book provides an easy to follow overview of the features, dynamics, and treatment of eating disorders. The authors draw on their years of experience working with individuals with eating disorders to argue that common early experiences underlie the different expressions of eating problems.

Chapter 3

PARENT-CHILD THERAPY WITH A DEPRESSED AND ANXIOUS CHILD

CASE ILLUSTRATION OF ORIN: AN 11-YEAR-OLD CAUCASIAN BOY

Dorli Burge, Ph.D.

THE DISORDER

Recently, diagnostic criteria for depression in children have become more uniform and more sensitive to developmental changes. Contrary to a long held psychoanalytic belief that children's psychic structures were not mature enough to permit the experience of depression, childhood depression has been found to be relatively common and is often the precursor of a long-standing depressive disorder (Carlson & Kashani, 1988; Cytryn, McKnew, & Bunney, 1980; Harrington, Fudge, Rutter, Pickles, & Hill, 1990). Symptoms may include: (1) depressed or irritable mood, (2) anhedonia in all or most activities, (3) appetite and weight changes, (4) sleep difficulties, (5) psychomotor agitation or retardation, (6) loss of energy, (7) feelings of worthlessness or excessive guilt, (8) problems with concentration, and (9) suicidal thoughts according to the *Diagnostic and Statistical Manual of Mental Disorders,* Fourth Edition (DSM-IV; American Psychiatric Association, 1994; hereafter, DSM-IV). Somatic complaints, irritability, and social withdrawal are commonly observed in depressed children. Clinically significant distress or significant impairment of functioning, such as poor school performance, is necessary for the diagnosis of a Major Depressive Episode. Somatic complaints, irritability, and social withdrawal are commonly observed in depressed children.

Developmental psychopathologists see depression as a disorder that interferes with the attainment of important developmental milestones. The failure to master crucial developmental tasks (such as separation-individuation in toddlerhood or the formation of peer relationships) sets the stage for subsequent difficulties in coping with the environment and for low self-esteem, which leads to further vulnerability to recurrence of depression (Cummings & Cicchetti, 1990). In fact, it has been shown that the rate of relapse of depression in children is as high as it is for adults (Asarnow et al., 1988; Kovacs et al., 1984; Ryan et al., 1987). In addition, there are suggestions that childhood depression is associated with recurrence of depression in adulthood (Harrington et al., 1990). Thus, the identification and treatment of childhood depression may prevent impairment over a lifetime.

Childhood depression often occurs in the context of long-standing family history of depression (Hammen, 1991). Depression runs in families partly, no doubt, because of biological vulnerability but also because of the psychosocial difficulties that are associated with depression. A depressed parent does not have the energy, emotional resourcefulness, resilience, assertiveness, and flexibility that successful parenting demands. Many studies have shown that the parenting of depressed mothers is different from that of normal control mothers and that the children of depressed mothers have a variety of difficulties, including depression (Burge & Hammen, 1991; Downey & Coyne, 1990; Gelfand & Teti, 1990; Gotlib & Hammen, 1992). Developmental psychopathologists suggest that the emotional unavailability and inconsistent parenting of depressed parents results in insecure attachment of the children who may carry forward working models of relationships that result in greatly increased vulnerability to depression (Cummings & Cicchetti, 1990). A child who experiences maternal inconsistency and rejection may develop a working model including the belief that he or she is not worthy and cannot expect another's enduring care and involvement and that relationships are always unsatisfying, frustrating, and anxiety provoking. While longing for stable, trusting relationships with others, the child anticipates and is highly sensitized to rejection and inconsistency in the social environment. Minor conflicts may be interpreted as evidence of personal unworthiness, eroding self-esteem, and increasing vulnerability to depression. Children's internal working models have been found to mirror the mothers' working models. The parents themselves are likely to have had dysfunctional relationships with their parents, which become reenacted in their interactions with their children (Main, Kaplan, & Cassidy, 1985). Thus research and recent theoretical formulations point to the importance of including the parents of any depressed child in the treatment. Depression does not simply reside in the child but is a result of transactions with the social and familial environment.

Recently, there has been increasing awareness of the fact that depression is often comorbid with anxiety disorders and conduct disorders (Cole & Carpentieri, 1990; Kovacs et al., 1989; Puig-Antich, 1982; Ryan et al., 1987).

Thus, a child who presents with depression may not only have parents with depression but also present with other disorders, complicating treatment process and planning considerably.

Orienting Constructs

Doing therapy with anyone, whatever color and cultural background, the therapist needs to explore the individual's expectations, hopes, and experiences of interactions rather than relying on preconceived assumptions. The therapist has to be sensitive to subtle differences in people's contexts and inquire about them. Basic humility and a strong sense of curiosity are particularly helpful in working with parents.

The present author's approach to treatment is eclectic with a basically psychodynamic, object-relations focus that incorporates aspects of family systems theory. This framework emphasizes the importance of early relationships for understanding the child's and the parents' psychological makeup, defense mechanisms and symptoms. Within a family, a negative working model of relationships may prevail that is destructive but familiar. Each individual in the family carries an image of others as basically critical, hostile, and unavailable. Caught in a vicious cycle, each family member behaves in such a way as to reconfirm the expectations of the world, self, and the other family members as critical, hostile, and unavailable. The therapist's task becomes to explicate the nature and destructiveness of these negative working models and to help alter behavior that has maintained negative expectations.

While these are the basic guiding principles in my thinking about a child and his parents, other techniques, such as parent education, behavioral management, and cognitive-behavioral techniques, might be incorporated into the treatment as needed. As different modalities are used, it is of paramount importance to stay aware of the impact of each intervention on the individuals in the family, on their relationship with each other, and on their relationship with the therapist. To be successful in the treatment of childhood disorders in the context of the family, a therapist needs many different skills and comfort with a range of treatment modalities.

Treatment of any child with any diagnosis requires sensitivity to both the child's and the parent's issues. Child treatment without including the parent is not likely to be effective, unless there are special circumstances, such as the parent suffering from serious mental illness or parents that are so focused on their own problems that their cooperation is minimal. However, in such circumstances the person who cares for the child should be included, and parents need to be involved on whatever level is possible. The social environment of the child, and particularly the relationship between parent and child, exerts a tremendous influence on the child. The therapist may offer a safe and benign environment for one or two hours a

week, but if the child is buffeted by emotional storms or emotionally neglected the rest of the time, treatment will have relatively little effect and
certainly not be effective in the long term. Because adolescents' developmental tasks include developing a sense of identity separate from the family, treatment issues shift. While work with adolescents often is facilitated
by inclusion of the family, an adolescent may benefit significantly by individual treatment.

The therapist has the task of providing both the child and the parent*
with a healing experience in the here and now. As the parent experiences
being listened to, empathized with, and taken seriously, the parent's needs
are met in a way that may help her provide these healing experiences for
the child. As the therapist works with the parent-child dyad, awareness
has to be maintained not only on the content but on the process of the interaction. The parent's working models of relationships are operative in the
relationship with therapist as well as in her relationship with her child. Dynamics that occur in everyday life are recreated in the treatment room. For
example, a parent who had a rejecting, critical mother expects any person
in authority to be similarly rejecting and critical and carries an image of
herself as unworthy and incompetent. The parent is likely to be hypersensitive to any attempt on the therapist's part to suggest alternative parenting
techniques and to interpret them as put-downs and criticisms. In her interactions with her child, she may interpret any oppositional behavior of the
child as a rejection of her as a person as well as proof that she is an inadequate mother and may find it very difficult to deal with such behavior
in constructive ways. Each failure in the interactions confirms her feelings
of helplessness and unworthiness. Such feelings may contribute to more
depression, which saps her energy for dealing with the child actively and
effectively. Repeated transactions like these result in an overall sense of
hopelessness and mutual negative feelings. Similarly, the child is likely to
create his world in a microcosm in the treatment. A child with an unassertive, helpless parent who finds it difficult setting limits is likely to
experience the world as unsafe and uncontaining. In the therapy room,
such a child may test limits repeatedly, both recreating the experience at
home and testing whether the therapy environment is more containing.
Such a child may evoke feelings of helplessness, parallel to the mother's, in
the therapist.

Being alert to one's own reactions is as necessary as constantly monitoring what the clients' experience of interactions might be. Continually staying
aware of the process is often particularly challenging and difficult when
children and their parents present a multitude of symptomatology and

---

*I will be referring to the parent with female pronouns since the primary caretakers of chil-
dren in contemporary society tend to be the mothers.

crises. The therapist often has to rely on the support and help of supervisor or colleagues to see beyond the seeming chaos and stay aware of the metacommunications of child and parent, as well as the reactions they elicit in the therapist. For example, a family might move from crisis to crisis, engaging the therapist in repeated efforts to "put out the fire." The therapist may feel powerful and indispensable, on the one hand, but carry the frustrating sense of running around in circles, on the other hand. The metacommunication of the family to the therapist may be to make him understand the chaos and hopelessness in their lives as well as to express the yearning to have the therapist be in charge and take care of the distress in the family. Only by staying aware of this metacommunication can the therapist start addressing the basic sense of helplessness in the family and help each member to become mobilized on his or her own behalf.

Parent-child therapy conceives of the treatment proceeding in a parallel fashion. Difficulties between parent and child and failure of adaptation in the child often arise at developmental thresholds that evoke emotional echoes in the parent and bring the parents' unresolved emotional conflicts to the surface. The therapist's task is to help the parent identify the emotional crisis from his or her own past that has been elicited by the child and help work through it. The process of working through such a crisis proceeds on two levels: (1) on an intellectual level, the parent gradually learns to understand how unresolved issues from his or her own background affect the process of parenting; (2) on an emotional level, the parent has the experience of being listened to empathically, of someone attempting to tune in emotionally. Most importantly, the parent is allowed to have the experience of revealing emotional secrets without being judged. This experience is incompatible with a working model of others as untrustworthy and uncaring and, ideally, will result in a revision of basic assumptions and expectations about relationships.

As parents feel emotionally understood, they feel less threatened by the therapist and their child. The therapist's comments and the child's behavior are not necessarily interpreted as rejection and criticism any more but can be weighed and evaluated for what they are. The parents become more flexible in their coping and behavior. At this point, they may become able to incorporate new techniques and skills the therapist might suggest into their interactions with their children. Selma Fraiberg has eloquently described this mode of treatment with mothers of infants (1980).

A basic challenge in working with children and their parents is how to engage the parent in the treatment initially. The therapist can approach the parent as a fellow problem solver. The parent has much to contribute to treatment planning because of her intimate knowledge of the child over the years. Such an approach will elicit commitment to treatment from the parent more than an approach that implicitly communicates that the therapist is the expert and will tell the parent about the child and what the solution to the problem is. The metacommunication of the former is that the parent has strengths and resources while that of the latter is that the parent is incompetent and helpless.

Many therapists working with children find themselves identifying with the children and experiencing strong negative, often competitive, feelings toward the parents. The beginning therapist, in particular, often has fantasies of rescuing the child from the negative influence of the parents. This sometimes stems from the therapist's unresolved issues with his or her own parents and an overidentification with the child. It often seems simpler to blame the parent rather than stay aware of the complexities involved in the parent-child interaction with attendant ambiguities and uncertainties of how the interaction came to be what it is. In addition, the beginning therapist may still have feelings of omnipotence that have not been tempered by a range of positive and negative experiences. But wherever a hostile attitude toward parents comes from, it is likely to be counterproductive. If the parents sense hostility in the therapist, they are more likely to withdraw from the treatment. The therapist has to be curious about the transactional cycles between parent and child, about the historical underpinnings of these transactions, both in terms of the parent's background and in terms of the history of the present dyad. The parent enters the relationship with the child with a complex emotional history and expectations about relationships and parenting learned from her or his own parents. The child is born with temperamental predispositions. From the very start, the parent and child engage in interactions that form and influence the other. It is often easier to identify parenting gone awry than to notice the subtle influence that the child has on the parent. But inevitably, the child's response or lack of response to the parent will influence the parent's future expectations of the child, the parent's sense of efficacy as a parent and person, and ultimately, the quality of the next interaction. And the therapist has to be humble in assuming that he or she knows what a given behavior of the parent or child means, why the parent behaves in a given way, or what the parent understands about his or her impact on the child. This humility is particularly important when the therapist deals with parents and children from different ethnic groups.

Work with children and their families demands much flexibility in treatment modality. The child may be at a stage during which he will express himself best through play therapy or in a therapeutic peer group setting. The parent may need exploration of how his or her own family background relates to parenting in individual psychotherapy sessions, as well as education about child development and parenting skills (Chethik, 1989). Often referral to social service agencies is necessary as well to ensure that basic needs of the family are taken care of. No parent is likely to be able to muster the energy necessary for therapy if there are pressing concerns about housing or feeding the family.

Parenting is a highly complex task that is continually changing as the child develops and matures. Parenting demands emotional openness, flexibility, resourcefulness, energy, and commitment. How an adult approaches this difficult task is, at least, to some extent determined by the parenting the parent has experienced, as recent research on the continuity of attachment has shown (Bretherton, 1985; Main, Kaplan, & Cassidy, 1985) and as sensitive clinicians have long been aware of (Bowlby, 1988; Fraiberg, 1980; Scharff & Scharff, 1991).

The parent-child dyad has a complex history of many transactions, which affects how they experience each other and react to each other in the present. This history affects the expression of symptomatology in the child. By closely observing the interactions in the present, learning to understand the factors that shaped the interaction and staying sensitively attuned to the needs of both parent and child and the sociocultural context in which they operate, the therapist can potentially become a powerful agent of change for both child and parent.

Case Illustration

Presenting Problem

Orin, an 11-year-old boy, originally was brought for treatment into an urban clinic because he was unable to sleep alone in his room. He also was hesitant about letting his parents, Lisa and David, go out and felt anxious as long as they were away. He was unwilling to sleep over at friends' houses. His mother usually slept in his room with him but neither parent appeared particularly concerned about this. A friend recommended they seek treatment because the sleeping arrangement did not seem normal. I was assigned the case in my capacity as a psychology intern at the clinic.

CLIENT DESCRIPTION

Orin presented as a very bright, verbally precocious hip-looking youngster who chronically underachieved in school and was virtually socially isolated except for occasional contacts with some of his cousins. His verbal fluency and "coolness" contrasted with his very childlike facial features. He professed not being interested in peers because none of them were very interesting. Teachers at school repeatedly complained about Orin's lack of effort. During individual sessions, Orin's verbal wit and superiority gave way to a sense of great sadness and severe lack of self-esteem, feelings of being dumb and useless, hopelessness about the future, and self-blame for his father's depression. During these initial sessions, Orin brought action figures I was unfamiliar with, talked at length about how much they had cost, and ridiculed my lack of familiarity with them: "You just don't know anything, do you?"

Possessing these toys appeared to make him feel special and superior to others, at least temporarily. But even as I engaged with him around the toys and encouraged him to tell me more about them, he would suddenly lose interest and state that it was dumb to play with toys, that he was not interested in talking to me about anything, and that it would be too boring anyway. The artificial sense of superiority that the toys provided collapsed into feelings of worthlessness. The experience of being with Orin helped me comprehend why he had difficulties forming relationships with peers. Orin complained of periods of sleeplessness, poor appetite, and agitation. He also insisted that his sadness was totally normal and not worth talking about. The picture was one of a dysthymic youngster with occasional major depressive episodes, during which his symptoms worsened and sleeplessness and poor appetite became particularly pronounced. In addition, he showed the symptoms of Separation Anxiety Disorder, a diagnosis frequently comorbid with depression (DSM-IV). His parents were relatively unaware of his depressions.

SOCIAL CONTEXT

Initial assessment revealed that Orin's father, David, a slight, pallid-looking man who worked sporadically in the movie industry, had a long-standing history of depression and was disabled by his depression for long periods of time. A psychiatrist prescribed antidepressants for him. When his depression lifted, he was charming and witty. He was highly educated but felt like a failure in life. David seemed like a shadow when compared to his dramatic wife. Orin's mother, Lisa, an ex-dancer, was very dramatic-looking and exhibited a somewhat histrionic style. She had a history of drug and alcohol abuse but had been sober for two or three years and attended AA meetings frequently. Lisa reported that she used drugs regularly while Orin was small and felt much guilt about the impact this may have had on him.

In their daily lives, the couple exhibited a pattern of lack of planning for the future. The father's occasional work in the movie business brought in relatively large sums of money, but the family tended to spend lavishly and found themselves, repeatedly and despairingly, in financial straits. The parents showed a preoccupation with image, style, and possessions similar to that which Orin exhibited in his sessions.

The sociocultural context of the movie industry reinforced and mirrored the family's functioning in many ways. The entertainment industry's obsession with image was reflected in the mother's dramatic appearance and Orin's attempts to appear "cool," whereas the father's failure to live up to the image of a powerful "mover" in the industry reinforced his depression. Living within a subculture that tends to equate possessions and wealth with self-esteem encouraged Orin to attempt to gain peer acceptance by flaunting his new possessions but left him with a feeling of emptiness because he encountered envy instead. His parents' tenuous self-esteem was eroded in the long periods with a lack of income and led them to spend money recklessly when Orin's father did succeed in finding lucrative work. Trying to bolster their self-esteem by showing off possessions resulted in out-of-control spending that quickly led to yet another period of financial straits and the attendant feelings of hopelessness and helplessness and lack of self-esteem. The fickleness of the industry's esteem of its members, depending on whether luck and money is on their side, further eroded the parents' trust in themselves and others. The context of a subculture that values high drama more than psychological resolution and seeks instant gratification reinforced the family's style of functioning. When difficulties arose, they quickly escalated to seeming catastrophes that called for immediate dramatic interventions. Before treatment was initiated, the mother, as many members of the subculture do, coped by resorting to the "quick-fix" of alcohol and drugs.

The parents appeared intensely needy. However, they also were devoted to their son and committed to his welfare, a major strength that allowed the treatment process to proceed through subsequent crises. Treatment was facilitated by their intelligence and quick grasp of psychological concepts.

Case Conceptualization

Orin appeared never to have mastered the separation from his parents that usually occurs during the preschool years. His mother's alcohol and drug abuse and the inconsistency in behavior associated with it had made him highly insecure in his relationship with her. The recurrent withdrawal of his father into depressions was experienced by Orin as repeated losses of his loving father. When his parents were emotionally stressed, they tended to be as sarcastically critical of him as they were of themselves. The lack of consistency in his parents' attention to him engendered a sense that he was not worth loving, that there was something essentially defective about him, leading to seriously impaired self-esteem. The lack of financial stability in the family confirmed his sense that the world was not to be trusted. The family's involvement in the movie industry, where success often depends on luck and projects fail frequently for reasons out of control of given individuals, may have contributed to Orin's and the family's defeatism. Orin's aloofness and preoccupation with his parents interfered with the forging of relationships with peers. He appeared to feel that he had to protect his parents and to ensure that they did not quarrel. The parents, in turn, did not feel effective as adults and related to Orin more as siblings than as parents. Orin's depression matched the family atmosphere. Everyone felt a failure. The fact that Orin exhibited problems confirmed for the parents that they failed at everything. The parents were disengaged from each other. The mother joked she would not know how to relate to her husband if they slept in the same bed again. Thus, in Minuchin's sense there were role confusions (i. e., Orin watched over his parents as if he were their caretaker), boundary violations (i.e., the mother slept with the son; the son participated in marital quarrels), as well as triangulation (i. e., the couple communicated with each other primarily around issues concerning Orin) (Minuchin, 1981).

Treatment Plans and Intervention Strategy

Initial short-term goals were (a) to forge a working relationship with both parents and Orin, and (b) to help the parents realize that Orin's difficulties with separation and depression might interfere with his further development as a preadolescent.

Intermediate goals were (a) to help the parents develop a plan that would facilitate Orin's sleeping by himself, (b) to work at alleviating Orin's depression using cognitive-behavioral techniques, (c) to help the parents feel more effective as parents by reminding them of their strengths and exploring with them what they understood the role of a parent to be.

Long-term goals were (a) to strengthen the couple's relationship by providing therapy sessions that focussed on the parents' relationship, rather than Orin; (b) to help Orin feel more secure within his family and with his own feelings so that he could start separating and develop appropriately as a preadolescent.

INITIAL PHASE OF TREATMENT

Neither Orin nor his parents had a sense that any of their circumstances were amenable to change— that is, Orin would always be sad, underachieving, isolated, lonely, and would never learn to sleep by himself. The parents did not feel that they could help Orin in any way. The father wryly joked that if he had not managed to help himself, he was not going to be able to help his son. The whole family subscribed to a depressive point of view. The family's sense of hopelessness resulted in pervasive lack of motivation to engage in therapy. During several sessions, I outlined a behavioral program that might facilitate Orin's sleeping by himself, but the whole family responded by explaining the impossibility of changing the way things were. In individual sessions, Orin essentially did not want to talk to me insisting that talking about things would just make things worse. For example, I invited him to tell me about his experience when he attempted to go to sleep by himself. Orin was dismissive: "What's the point of talking about it? All it does is make me feel bad, and it is not going to change anything. I am just not going to talk about it." And he changed the subject to talk about a recent movie. Attempts at interpreting his avoidance were met by accusations that I was trying to read his mind. I experienced this as highly frustrating and needed to spend time in supervision dealing with the feeling of hostility and impulse to blame the parents, as well as a sense of creeping hopelessness that mirrored the family's hopelessness. Dealing with my own responses helped me understand better how Orin and his parents experienced their world.

CRISIS PHASE

However, soon a crisis occurred. Orin's school was about to have its annual camp-out. During a therapy session, Orin expressed his interest in participating in this outing and persisted even though his mother quickly told him he would not be able to sleep away from home. Orin's impulse to join his peers appeared highly threatening to Lisa. I encouraged Orin in his wish to participate in this age-appropriate peer activity and discussed with him ways that would make it easier for him to feel comfortable. By taking Orin's side and supporting his wish to join his peers I severely unbalanced the family system. With the parents' help, arrangements were made with the school for one of the teachers to take him under his wing. Orin, with some anxiety, continued to make plans and prepare for the outing while his mother became increasingly uncertain about whether she wanted Orin to go. In his sessions with me, Orin discussed in detail what activities were planned at the outing, which of the other children he might spend time with. He did not express anxiety overtly, but rather dealt with the impending experience in a highly intellectualized manner. Orin left on the outing without becoming hysterical as his mother had expected. However, within an hour of his leaving, Lisa became intensely upset and put in a crisis call to me. She reported feeling torn apart, consumed by grief and guilt that she let Orin go even though she knew he would be distraught, and imagined his panic at being by himself. She expected her son to be rageful at her for not having protected him better. Clearly, this incident triggered many issues for the mother: fears of abandonment, a sense that the world was inherently dangerous, and fear of retribution if she was not always perfectly available to her child, a threat to her sense of self-worth bound up with being the all-protective mother. The intensity of her emotion was both unexpected and overwhelming for me. I struggled to be supportive to her and yet provide a sense of reality: "Orin has just gone on a camping trip. He is with adults he knows and trusts. If he is upset when he comes back, it can be dealt with." Lisa's husband, meanwhile, lapsed into one of his depressive episodes, mirroring his style of withdrawal during conflict. Orin, in fact, spent the weekend with his peers, experienced some sadness but appeared to respond to the comforting of the staff and the children. He quickly realized, however, how upsetting his trip had been to his mother. The state of his parents upon his return must have confirmed to him his sense that they needed him for their well-being. The next week, he refused to go to school. Using a behavioral approach, I encouraged the parents to get Orin to school every morning and do whatever they could to help him rejoin his class. The first few mornings Orin was able to stay one hour but this time became progressively shorter. During this time the parents' sense of powerlessness was reconfirmed. With encouragement from my supervisor, I became directly involved in getting Orin to school by meeting the parents in the morning and staying with Orin in the classroom. For a brief time, it appeared that he would reintegrate into the school. However, when his teacher became more rigid and refused to accommodate Orin's special needs in any way, Orin became adamant that he would not return to school.

Lisa's intense anxiety elicited similar feelings of panic in me. I felt that I might have done something terrible by encouraging Orin to go on his overnight outing. Getting caught in the family cycle, I started sharing the belief that neither the parents nor the child could handle this. I responded to and encouraged numerous crisis calls during subsequent events until I became aware of the process and realized that the family needed "emotional containment." I was able to draw on my considerable developmental knowledge to reassure myself that an 11-year-old's going on an overnight outing was an appropriate activity. Consultation with the supervisor was very helpful in anchoring my reactions in reality.

"Emotional containment" is a demanding process for the therapist. He or she fully empathizes with emotions expressed and is able to communicate this empathy to the client. However, in the midst of the intensity of emotion observed in and experienced with the client, the therapist maintains an observing self that is able to convey to the client that emotions will not overwhelm him or her, that the intensity of the pain will decrease, and that the upsetting event is not catastrophic.

Regular brief sessions with the mother were arranged twice a week for a two-month period. These sessions focused on containing her anxiety and helping her see that the problem was being worked on. She was helped to see that her fear of Orin's rage at her stemmed from experiences with her mother who would lash out at her if Lisa was not attuned to her needs. Lisa's experience of being contained subsequently helped her tolerate and contain Orin's affect rather than enter an escalating cycle of mutual anxiety and fear with him. For example, in the past, when Orin became anxious about being on his own, she would assume that his emotions were overwhelming and destructive and, rather than talk with him about his fears, immediately made arrangements so he would not have to be on his own. After some therapeutic work, however, she was able to encourage him to talk about his feelings and empathize with how scary they seemed but then work with him on making a brief separation tolerable.

In therapy sessions, Orin insisted that no one at school cared about him and that appearances to the contrary were false. His depression worsened. Soon, he refused to talk about himself or school and declared that talking just made him feel worse. Instead, he started bringing transformers and Mutant Ninja Turtles to the therapy. His fantasy play was extremely violent. By the end of the session all the figures would be killed. If one figure attempted to protect another it was subject to particularly vicious attacks. Orin, at this point, reacted very negatively to any kind of interpretation of his play. However, it was evident that he experienced the world as a threatening, dangerous, uncontained environment. He appeared to be afraid that any feelings would overwhelm him and therefore preferred not to acknowledge them at all. Taking his cue, I essentially became an observant commentator of his play. For example, I would simply say, "Michelangelo seems to want to help his friend, but the other guy is killing him"; or, "Everybody is getting hurt; no one seems safe." However, his behavior elicited feelings of helplessness and hopelessness in me, mirroring what had happened between Orin and his parents. In addition, the unrelenting violence of his play left me feeling concerned and sometimes overwhelmed, no doubt reflecting Orin's own fears of becoming overwhelmed. With supervision, I reaffirmed my sense that I was able to offer Orin something. The therapeutic goal became to help him experience the safety of the contained therapy room and the presence of a supportive adult who was not afraid of his feelings—or his violent play.

Despite attempts at intervention, the principal of Orin's school eventually stated that they were not willing to work with the family any more. The parents decided to search for another school that would be better able to meet his needs. As his career at the school was reviewed, his mother brought in writing samples that appeared to be those of a learning disabled child. Testing with another staff member was instituted and revealed that he was a gifted child with a significant learning disability. This helped explain Orin's sense that he was stupid and lazy. He was able to evaluate his work as not up to standard but had always been told by parents and teachers that he simply did not work hard enough. I had to deal with a sense of guilt that I had interpreted Orin's conviction that the school did not care about his needs as cognitive distortions when, in fact, the school had not been attuned to some major deficits and his special needs.

BALANCING GOALS

The crisis around Orin's school refusal acted as a catalyst. The parents now became invested in the therapy process and were able to acknowledge that problems in the family had been long-standing. They revealed that they had had to spend most of Orin's kindergarten year at the school, that since Orin's birth they had spent virtually no time as a couple because he demanded all their attention and because they were afraid to leave him. Both parents carried abandonment issues from their own families of origin.

Lisa's mother had relied on her daughter to take care of her emotionally from a very young age. When Lisa failed to discern what her mother wanted, the mother would become rageful and verbally abusive and ignore Lisa for days. Therefore, Lisa had the experience of being intensely connected with her as long as she devoted all her emotional attention to her but of being emotionally abandoned when she focused on other, usually age-appropriate matters.

David came from a wealthy, highly educated family. But both of his parents suffered from recurrent depression and had little patience and emotional energy for their son. They spent time with him when it was convenient for them and expected him to be on his best behavior when they were available. He was sent to a boarding school at a very early age and remembered becoming depressed then. As a teenager he refused to attend boarding school any more and stayed home but was terribly lonely. He rarely saw his parents who were either busy with a social schedule or depressed.

The emotional scars from the parents' respective backgrounds were addressed insofar as they had an impact on their interaction with their son. Raising their son had become their primary source of self-esteem. Orin appeared to sense this burden and felt overwhelmed and helpless. A regular schedule of therapy sessions was established, with some sessions for the couple and some sessions for each parent individually. The supervisor on the case worked with the mother while I worked with the father, the couple, and the child. As stated earlier, multiple diverse needs often have to be met when working with parents and children. The clinic setting enabled me to offer more comprehensive treatment than might have been feasible in a private practice setting. Goals were similar to the ones outlined above except that Orin's learning disability also needed to be dealt with. Addressing separation anxiety issues and their developmental antecedents became a more central goal in Orin's treatment. His difficulties with peers were addressed by including him in a latency-age boys' group.

The parents' helplessness was evident when they essentially wanted the staff to find a suitable school. Although providing resources, the staff encouraged the couple to visit and evaluate schools themselves to help them feel empowered and capable and become aware that they had personal resources as well as intuitions and knowledge about what their child needed. I repeatedly reminded them about their intimate knowledge of their child, the observations they had made over the years, and their intuitive sense about what kind of setting would be a good match for Orin. They became increasingly active in this search and eventually acted as highly effective advocates for their child in obtaining funding from the public school system to send their child to a private school for learning disabled children. As the staff worked with them on some of the steps in the process, the parents' sense of self-efficacy increased dramatically. They started feeling powerful and able to fill the shoes of parents.

This new sense of power in dealing with authorities and bureaucracy in their advocacy for their child was built upon as issues of parenting were discussed. The couple needed to be reminded repeatedly that they were the adults in the family who had power and could make a difference. When Orin's fears of being by himself were discussed, it became evident that both parents shared his fantasy that something devastating would happen to him if he had to sleep on his own. Upon reflection, David and Lisa realized that his distress evoked painful memories of being abandoned by their own parents. At times of emotional crisis for Orin, they became unable to fulfill their parenting functioning, caught in the same pain he was in. Orin's mother was able to identify that she had dulled this pain by substance abuse. Lisa's chronically depressed mother had been essentially emotionally unavailable to her. Lisa had spent much of her childhood trying to cheer up her mother. From these childhood experiences she carried a sense of crushing failure, as well as guilt for even aspiring to anything that felt her own. When Orin became angry at her, she experienced his anger as if it were her mother's and felt desperate that she would lose his love. For the father, Orin's distress would trigger memories of the awful loneliness and depression he had experienced in boarding school.

I also encouraged Orin's parents to reflect on their own process with me and reminded them of the time of initial crisis when I had become caught in an escalating cycle of anxiety with them. They realized that they had felt better only once I had extracted myself from this cycle and offered containment. Rather than continuing to encourage crisis calls, I suggested regular brief therapy sessions and pointed out to them that the crisis was manageable for them and Orin and that it would need to be resolved in steps. They had experienced my stance as soothing. This concrete example of a vicious escalating cycle and its resolution was very helpful to them and helped them gain perspective whenever there was temptation to "cycle" with Orin either in terms of his anxiety or his depression.

Subsequent to this session, with the help of behavioral techniques that the parents were able to utilize this time, Orin made significant progress in sleeping by himself. In consultation with the parents, a series of graduated steps of moving the parents out of Orin's room were developed. Both parents agreed that this was a reasonable and manageable plan and would not be too much for either them or Orin. Their active involvement in developing the plan was crucial for their subsequent cooperation. Thinking through the steps with me functioned as systematic desensitization of the parents to Orin's predictable distress at the changes. First, instead of sitting next to his bed, his mother would place the chair a few feet away. Then, she moved her chair next to the door. Then, she moved the chair outside the bedroom door, where Orin could still see. Next, she moved out of his sight. When he became panicky about being in his room by himself, both parents became more able to soothe and calm him and were less fearful that he would suffer harm.

In couple's sessions, Orin's parents were encouraged to focus more on their own relationship. They became aware that they had not had a "date" in years and, with much encouragement, started planning time for themselves. Initially, they needed help in even thinking about what they might do together. I had to encourage them to remember what they used to like to do together. They found many reasons why it would be impossible to do any of them. The sense of helplessness and hopelessness that had emerged in work around issues with Orin was present in the couple's work. It appeared that neither one of them felt that they deserved anything from the partner. The task of spending time together had to be broken down into small steps: (a) go for a brief walk together while Orin was in therapy, (b) go to lunch while Orin was in therapy, (c) go for a brief walk while Orin stayed at home with a trusted friend, (d) go out for short dinner, and so forth. As the tone of the sessions became less hopeless, the couple started talking to each other more and showed dysfunctional ways of relating to each other. Neither one could let the other one talk without interrupting. Expressions of negative emotional reactions to the behavior of the other were perceived as blaming and quickly escalated into angry outbursts on Lisa's part and total withdrawal on David's part. I intervened actively in pointing out this pattern repeatedly. I encouraged both partners to observe how I listened to and reflected their feelings and to use my behavior as a model. Lisa and David responded to the use of humor in this process and started referring to me as Mrs. Traffic Cop. Over time, their communication skills improved considerably, and they felt more and more that they could turn to each other for support and that each could be an emotional resource to the other.

Orin's father used his individual sessions to explore what he could and could not provide for his son. Initially, he attempted to use his verbal fluency and wit to deflect the focus of the sessions. He wittily talked about his previous experience in psychoanalysis and demonstrated how facile he was at interpreting dreams. As he told me stories about what he had learned about himself in analysis, I repeatedly asked him to reflect about how he felt about what he was telling me and how his experience might have affected his parenting of Orin. Gradually the emotional tone of the sessions deepened. He remembered how distant his own father had been from him and how he was forced into premature self-sufficiency when he was sent to boarding school at an early age. He carried deep sadness from his childhood. He felt ashamed and hopeless about his long-standing depression and repeatedly stated that there was nothing he could offer his son. I empathized with his pain and gradually helped him realize that he had much life experience to communicate to his son. In several sessions David reflected on choices he had made in the past that had been detrimental to him. For him, looking carefully and critically at the past and his own actions was a true act of courage because until then he had glibly asserted that no one had control over anything and that circumstances were to blame for all bad outcomes. I initially felt uneasy about encouraging him to engage in this process of evaluation, being concerned about appearing judgmental. However, it was only when David faced his own disappointment in himself and the sense of shame about giving up on life that he started feeling he could help guide Orin, help him learn from his own mistakes, and that his involvement and sensitivity would facilitate Orin's growth. Gradually, he and his son spent more time together going fishing and attending baseball games. Getting out more helped him feel less depressed.

Since Orin's mother's sense of identity appeared completely absorbed in being his mother, her therapist, my supervisor, encouraged her gently to try to get some work outside the home. With this permission, she started voicing her need for her own life and before long started an active job search. This led to one of the most significant events in Orin's therapy.

One of the mother's job interviews was scheduled concurrent with Orin's therapy session at the clinic. Generally, Orin's mother had either waited in the waiting room or gone on brief errands during Orin's therapy hour. But as the mother said good-bye to Orin this time, he became increasingly anxious, started holding on to his mother, and screaming inconsolably. I was faced with two people with conflicting needs: (a) Lisa needed confirmation that her attempt to have a focus other than Orin was acceptable, not "bad" and "selfish," and ultimately best for Orin. I, therefore, encouraged Lisa to leave, despite Orin's upset, and conveyed to the mother that I would be able to handle and tolerate his strong emotions. Implicitly, the therapist gave Lisa permission to take care of herself and to value her own goals, something that her mother had never been able to do for her. (b) Orin was panicked at the idea of his mother's leaving and did not think he could tolerate his fear. To him, I had to convey empathy for his distress and confidence in his ability to tolerate his intense feelings. Orin cried and screamed for about 30 minutes, attempted to run out of the building, and needed to be physically held. Through his screaming and crying, I told him repeatedly that I knew he was scared but that I was going to keep him safe. In the course of containing so much emotion, I had to work on containing my own anxiety. My experience as a mother and extensive experience in working with infants and toddlers helped me tolerate his distress.

Eventually, Orin calmed down and was able to continue with his usual play with his fantasy figures. He wreaked havoc with his action figures, throwing them, enacting repeated killings but, remarkably, this time some of them were resurrected and engaged in boisterous bragging about how strong they were. He became angry and berated me for not letting him run after his mother. My calm acceptance of his anger seemed to relieve him. Repeatedly, I said to him, "I know you are angry because I would not let you leave when you wanted to. But my job is to watch out for your safety, even if you are angry about it."

From then on his relationship to me changed. It was as if the incident had been a test to see whether I could tolerate his emotions. He became more trusting, talked more about himself, and initiated a new game he would continue for weeks: he wanted to play hide-and-seek like a very small child. Over and over, he would hide behind pieces of furniture for me to find him. Given that he was a large 11-year-old, he was never exactly hidden but he was clearly playing this game as a toddler might. I had to pretend I could not find him until I finally spotted him with glee. Orin appeared to need to experience over and over the sense of being separate from another person and then reconnecting after a delicious period of tension. I initially felt uncertain about whether I was doing my job, but Orin's urgency in playing the game quickly made me realize that he was attempting to master a crucial emotional task: separation in a context of total safety.

Following these events, the family stabilized. Orin was placed in a special school for learning disabled students. During the first two weeks, the parents stayed with him at school but with the help of the school staff gradually withdrew. Orin was able to tolerate the separation from them as long as he had a pager that allowed him to get in touch with them, an option he chose less and less frequently. For the first time in his life, he excelled academically. His depression lifted, and he became increasingly able to form peer relationships. Orin's mother obtained a part-time job and quickly became very successful at what she was doing. As her self-esteem improved, the couple's relationship became stormier because she asked more for what she needed and David often did not feel adequate to meet her needs. But at the same time, they were much more engaged with each other. Rather than avoiding each other, they talked their conflicts through. They were united in their efforts to parent Orin, set limits more appropriately, and became less indulgent.

The Therapeutic Process

RELATIONAL REENACTMENTS

As described above, Orin and his parents had a powerful impact on me. Repeatedly, the family members' behavior and reactions induced me to participate in the cycle of helplessness, hopelessness, and panic that Orin and his parents experienced and that immobilized them. Their helplessness and panic was so palpable that it was tempting to simply take over from the parents and tell them what to do as a way to ward off these uncomfortable feelings. However, stepping in and taking over would have been implicitly understood by them as criticism and confirmation of their essential incompetence and sense of worthlessness (incompetence that they had experienced in their interactions with their parents). It took much energy and determination on my (and my supervisor's) part to stay aware of the process and counteract it in order to provide truly therapeutic interventions.

Orin's state of panic when his mother had to leave for an interview exerted a strong pull to simply reenact interactional cycles of the past. His distress was so dramatic that I had fleeting fantasies that he would disintegrate and could not cope with the situation. I felt tempted to tell the mother that she would have to stay. Of course, these are exactly the reactions Orin's parents had had repeatedly when they had tried to deal with his separation anxiety. In response, they circumvented any situations that might have helped Orin to learn how to cope and find out that he could go through the experience of feeling frightened and master it. If I had encouraged the mother to stay, I would have reinforced Orin's sense that he could not deal with such situations and reinforced his fears of his emotions being unmanageable. In supporting him through his panic and subsequent anger I powerfully communicated to him my trust in his ability to cope. He seemed to feel reassured about my ability to contain him. Only after this event did he start dealing with his separation anxiety through repeated hide-and-seek games in the therapy sessions, revealing more childlike, and probably more frightening, needs and deficits.

Relational enactments in therapy helped me understand the emotional experience of Orin and his parents. Awareness of these enactments is only possible with meticulous attention to the process of therapy and willingness to monitor one's own often difficult and conflictual emotions in response to the clients.

IMPEDIMENTS TO TREATMENT

The family's initial stance that nothing could be changed about how things were was a powerful barrier to treatment. This stance engendered frustration and hostility in me that could have easily led to acting out in therapy sessions. I had to struggle to stay aware of and express, in supervision, feelings that were counter to my image of myself as a helping, caring, and patient individual. As the family went into crisis, dynamics of the family became clearer and it became easier to understand that the initial resistance had been an expression of the parents' and Orin's essential hopelessness and lack of personal power and efficacy.

During the crisis phase and in some interactions with Orin, I experienced feelings of helplessness that interfered with my sense of efficacy as a therapist. Again, this helplessness mirrored the parents' and Orin's. Once I acknowledged these feelings in myself, I could see them as mirroring the helplessness in the parents and Orin and as a communication from them. This allowed me to empathize with the helplessness, explore the antecedents, and then to gradually guide them toward recognizing their own strengths and abilities.

Orin's silent stance in play therapy was experienced as an impediment to treatment by me. I had the impulse to make him talk, to interact with him actively so I could show him what I had to offer and show myself that I was a "competent" therapist. But any such pushing was counterproductive, since Orin was afraid to talk about his feelings because he believed they would overwhelm him. Over time I understood that my empathic presence, and my quiet nonjudgmental observation of his play were reassuring to him. He was communicating his need of "being left alone" to deal with his emotions instead of having the adult intrude and take over, as his anxious mother often had done.

Impediments to treatment, negative reactions that clients evoke in the therapist, are often clues to important dynamics and should be regarded as powerful, if indirect, communications by clients. It behooves the therapist to attempt to decipher these communications.

Termination and Therapist's Summary Thoughts

A termination date had to be set because of the end of my internship. I had worked with the family for about 10 months. Lisa and David talked openly about their fears about whether they would be able to manage on their own.

They expressed their sadness about the loss of the relationship with me, a person whom they had grown to trust. They talked about their sense of my having stood by them through a violent storm. I experienced feelings of sadness and guilt at abandoning the family. However, the family's trust in the institution was helpful to them and a transfer to a new therapist was arranged. Orin became increasingly angry in the sessions prior to termination but refused to address the termination directly. As the transfer to another therapist was discussed, Orin stated that he would not talk to any other therapist because there was no point. At least indirectly, he communicated his sense of loss. But he insisted that talking about sadness, or saying good-bye, would make him feel worse. However, he listened intently when I spoke about my own sadness of having to say good-bye to him. In the termination session I gave the parents a certificate commending their courage in working at becoming real parents. Both of them beamed. Orin's certificate commented on his courage in playing about really important things. Orin seemed as pleased with his certificate as his parents were with theirs.

Although the family still had many problems to deal with, they appeared to have changed in crucial ways. The parents owned their own emotional pain about their childhood rather than living it through Orin. The couple was now able to turn to each other for emotional support, freeing Orin to focus on his own preadolescent developmental tasks. Both parents, but particularly Lisa, had a sense that they could make an impact on the world. Orin also felt that he could accomplish things in the world and that emotions were not inherently dangerous.

Several problems remained. David still had recurrent major depressive episodes and could not work regularly. However, the family now acknowledged David's depression and talked about it as a problem that David had to get help for, and that affected everyone in the family. Orin's depression had lifted, but he was hypersensitive to any rejection in his interaction with peers. Minor conflicts made him withdraw and feel depressed temporarily. In other words, he was still prone to depressive reactions but did not show the full-blown picture of clinical depression and dysthymia. Clearly, given the family history, he remained at risk for further depressive episodes. Although he spent more time with peers, he still had not formed any really close friendships. His learning problems remained a challenge, although he had a much clearer sense that he could succeed in school. In an ideal world, Orin and his family would have benefited from ongoing therapy with me. However, they were able to transfer to another therapist in the clinic and continued their work successfully. Possibly, the most crucial change that occurred for Orin and his parents was that they all had a sense of hope and confidence that the future could bring growth and positive experiences. A year later I heard that the family was basically stable and that they all weathered a change to a new school successfully, after Orin's school was closed down because of financial problems. Orin was now an A student and had several friends in the new school. I do not know any more information about

Orin's and his family's welfare since then. I still find myself thinking about them often.

The case study illustrates parent-child therapy as discussed in the introduction. It also demonstrates how depression does run in families. Orin presented with both depression and separation anxiety. Treatment that involved the parents as much as the child revealed to what extent the child's symptoms mirrored emotional scars the parents carried. Without the focus on both parents and child these might not have been uncovered and dealt with. Engaging the parents in the treatment process not only increased their cooperation but allowed them to feel powerful and effective possibly for the first time in their lives, giving them, and their son, hope for the future. Treatment moved back and forth between a number of modalities, depending on needs of the present. Sometimes psychodynamic exploration predominated while, at other times, active behavioral intervention was used. Family therapy and couple's therapy were part of the treatment as well.

For me, the process was a powerful learning experience. Initially, I experienced the whole family as extremely difficult and unmotivated and felt hopeless about being able to help them and hostile about their lack of motivation. As crises unfolded, the family's anxiety exerted a contagious pull and I needed containment from the supervisor as much as the family needed containment from me. The hopelessness, anxiety, and feelings of utter responsibility the family engendered in me paralleled what David and Lisa elicited in Orin and what their parents had elicited in them. My awareness of my own process helped me stay attuned to the process of the family. As I became clearer about how I might effectively work with the family, my confidence in my role effected the process between me and the family. In my work with the parents, I became a surrogate parent for them, helping them be aware of their own strengths and tolerating and listening to their pain. Instead of criticism and abandonment, which both parents had learned to expect in relationships, I offered empathy and a steady presence. I modeled for the parents how they might communicate with their son emotionally. As the parents had some of their emotional needs met and learned to meet each other's needs, they were able to cope with their son's developmental needs and emotions better. Their delight in the certificate at the end of treatment symbolizes their need for approval from me as well as their realization that they could be effective parents to their son. The work with Orin was alternately frustrating and exhilarating, as work with children often is. Orin vacillated between an adolescent defiant stance and the neediness of a much smaller child. The experience with family and Orin helped me grow as a person and as a therapist. I felt saddened at the necessary leave taking and wished that I could continue to follow their development.

Parent-child therapy demands flexibility, tolerance of ambiguity and complexity, as well as emotional openness of the therapist. It can be extremely time intensive and may be most feasible in settings where a variety of resources are available. But even when it is less comprehensive than in the case presented, it is a powerful intervention that can improve the quality of life for child and parent.

REFERENCES

American Psychiatric Association. (1994). *Diagnostic and statistical manual of mental disorders,* (4th ed.). Washington, DC: Author.

Asarnow, J. R., Goldstein, M. J., Carlson, G. A., Perdue, S., Bates, S., & Keller, J. (1988). Childhood-onset depressive disorders: A follow-up study of rates of re-hospitalization and out-of-home placement among child psychiatric inpatients. *Journal of Affective Disorders, 15,* 245–253.

Bowlby, J. (1988). *A secure base. Parent-child attachment and healthy human development.* New York: Basic Books.

Burge, D., & Hammen, C. (1991). Maternal communication: Predictors of outcome at follow-up in a sample of children at high and low risk for depression. *Journal of Abnormal Psychology, 59,* 341–345.

Carlson, G. A., & Kashani, J. H. (1988). Phenomenology of major depression from childhood through adulthood: Analysis of three studies. *American Journal of Psychiatry, 145,* 1222–1225.

Chethik, M. (1989). *Techniques of child therapy. Psychodynamic strategies.* New York: Guilford.

Cole, D. A., & Carpentieri, S. (1990). Social status and the comorbidity of child depression and conduct disorder. *Journal of Consulting and Clinical Psychology, 58,* 748–757.

Cummings, E. M., & Cicchetti, D. (1990). Attachment, depression, and the transmission of depression. In M. T. Greenberg, D. Cicchetti, & E. M. Cummings (Eds.), *Attachment during the preschool years.* Chicago: University of Chicago Press.

Downey, G., & Coyne, J. C. (1990). Children of depressed parents: An integrative review. *Psychological Bulletin, 108,* 50–76.

Fraiberg, S. (1980). *Every child's birthright: Clinical studies in infant mental health: The first year of life.* New York: Basic Books.

Gelfand, D. M., & Teti, D. M. (1990). The effects of maternal depression on children. *Clinical Psychology Review, 10,* 320–354.

Gotlib, I. H., & Hammen, C. L. (1992). *Psychological aspects of depression. Toward a cognitive interpersonal integration.* New York: Wiley.

Hammen, C. (1991). *Depression runs in families: The social context of risk and resilience in children of depressed mothers.* New York: Springer Verlag.

Harrington, R., Fudge, H., Rutter, M., Pickles, A., & Hill, J. (1990). Adult outcomes of childhood and adolescent depression: Psychiatric status. *Archives of General Psychiatry, 47,* 465–473.

Kovacs, M., Feinberg, T. L., Crouse-Novak, M., Paulauskas, S. L., Pollock, M., & Finkelstein, R. (1984). Depressive disorders in childhood: I. A longitudinal prospective study of characteristics and recovery. *Archives of General Psychiatry, 41,* 229–237.

Kovacs, M., Gatsonis, C., Paulauskas, S. L., & Richards, C. (1989). Depressive disorders in childhood: IV. A longitudinal study of comorbidity with and risk for anxiety disorders. *Archives of General Psychiatry, 46,* 776–782.

Main, M., Kaplan, N., & Cassidy, J. C. (1985). Security in infancy, childhood and adulthood: A move to the level of representation. In I. Bretherton & E. Waters (Eds.), Growing points of attachment theory and research. *Monographs of the Society for Research in Child Development, 5,* (1&2), 66–104.

Minuchin, S. (1974). *Families and family therapy.* Cambridge: Harvard University Press.

Puig-Antich, J. (1982). Major depression and conduct disorder in prepuberty. *Journal of the American Academy of Child Psychiatry, 21,* 118–128.

Ryan, N. D., Puig-Antich, J., Ambrosini, P., Rabinovich, H., Robinson, D., Nelson, B., Iyengar, S., & Twomey, J. (1987). The clinical picture of major depression in children and adolescents. *Archives of General Psychiatry, 44,* 854–861.

Scharff, D. E., & Scharff, J. S. (1991). *Object relations family therapy.* Northvale, NJ: Jason Aronson.

SUGGESTIONS FOR FURTHER READING

Bowlby, J. (1988). *A secure base. Parent-child attachment and healthy human development.* New York: Basic Books. Discusses therapeutic implications of attachment theory. Readable and wise.

Fraiberg, S. (1980). *Every child's birthright: Clinical studies in infant mental health: The first year of life.* New York: Basic Books. Compelling case studies of parent-infant interventions.

Kottman, T., & Schaefer, C. (Eds.). (1993). *Play therapy in action: A casebook for practitioners.* Northvale, NJ: Jason Aronson. A useful book with many clinical examples demonstrating various approaches to therapy with children.

Wachtel, P. L. (1993). *Therapeutic communication. Principles and effective practice.* New York: Guilford. Integrates psychodynamic and cognitive-behavioral approach to therapy, quite sophisticated conceptually, yet practically oriented with many clinical examples. Focuses on how to word interpretations and other interventions so they are most likely to be listened to. As useful for beginners as for experienced therapists.

Chapter 4

SEXUAL ABUSE

CASE ILLUSTRATION OF SHEILA: A 15-YEAR-OLD AFRICAN AMERICAN

Faith H. McClure, Ph.D.

THE DISORDER

Reports of the sexual abuse of children have avalanched. According to a 1988 U. S. Department of Health and Human Services Report, the incidence of child sexual abuse in 1986 was 2.2 children per 1,000. In a national phone survey of lifetime prevalence, Finkelhor, Hotaling, Lewis, and Smith (1990) found that 27% of the women and 16% of the men reported sexual victimization. However, reports of lifetime prevalence vary considerably in the literature, with reports ranging from 6 to 62% for women (see Damon & Card, 1992; Peters, Wyatt, & Finkelhor, 1986) and 3 to 31% for men (Finkelhor 1990; Peters et al., 1986). The substantial differences in reported prevalence rates are due to (a) discrepancies in definitions (for example, criteria may include varying age differences between perpetrator and survivor, may include only contact, that is, experiences where physical touching is involved, or may include both contact and noncontact experiences, such as exhibitionism and solicitation to engage in sexual activity without physical contact) and (b) methodological differences (for example, the data may have been collected by phone or in writing, or by face-to-face interviews and may vary in the specificity of the questions from the general "have you ever been sexually abused?" to more specific ones asking about distinct types of acts, and so forth). The significance of specifically assessing history of molestation was demonstrated by Briere & Zaidi (1989), who reviewed 100 charts of female patients seen in a psychiatric emergency room and found that the reported rate of sexual molestation was 70% among those who were directly asked about abuse, while the noted rate was 6% among those not specifically asked. Despite the definitional and methodological issues discussed, it seems clear that sexual abuse is a far reaching problem. It is therefore imperative that therapists who work with children and adolescents be knowledgeable about sexual abuse, its impact, and how to best intervene.

In the first section of this chapter, general information about sexual abuse and its impact will be presented. This will be followed by a case illustrating treatment of an African American adolescent incest survivor named Sheila (pseudonym).

Although there has been considerable discussion in the literature regarding how to define childhood sexual abuse, most clinicians agree that sexual contact between a child or adolescent and someone who is older (some suggest a five year difference) and/or someone who has more power and control (such as a teacher, youth group leader, or older sibling), is abusive. For most children, such incidents are experienced as violations and result in significant negative outcomes. The outcomes are moderated by a variety of factors, such as the child's age or developmental stage (see Downs, 1993); the child's emotional/psychological history; the type of assault, such as the use of violence or threats or bodily penetration; the number of incidents and number of offenders; and the relationship between the victim and the perpetrator, for example, a known and trusted neighbor or parent, versus a stranger. The most important moderator of outcome, however, is the way in which significant others, especially maternal figures, react to discovery of the abuse. (See Kendall-Tackett, Williams, & Finkelhor, 1993, for a review.)

As will be noted in the case illustration that follows, Sheila experienced severe emotional trauma because she had been molested by her stepfather (someone known and trusted), beginning at a very early age (age 7), and this had occurred frequently over a long period of time (until she was 15). In Sheila's case, there was bodily penetration and an emotional threat (loss of family support) if she rejected her stepfather's advances. Her symptoms were further exacerbated by her history, which included her mother who was probably depressed and frequently emotionally unavailable and who did not provide Sheila with unqualified support when the molest was reported.

There are a myriad of psychological sequelae observed in survivors of sexual abuse, including emotional impairment (e.g., anxiety, fear, anger, depression), cognitive impairment (e.g., poor concentration and memory, low self-esteem), impairment in interpersonal relationships (especially intimacy and trust), sleep disturbances (including nightmares), sexual difficulties, self-destructive behavior, and substance abuse (Finkelhor, 1990; Kendall-Tackett et al., 1993). Although some researchers try to distinguish between short and long term effects (see Beitchman et al., 1991; Browne & Finkelhor, 1986; Green, 1993; Finkelhor, 1990), the wide variation in symptomatology observed in sexual abuse survivors makes this distinction less meaningful. In fact, researchers have had great difficulty identifying a specific and definitive set of symptoms for sexual abuse survivors perhaps because of the varying circumstances in abuse experiences and individual differences in responses among the survivors. Each of the emotional effects noted above have been reported as both short-term and long-term effects. The research suggests that although many (26% to 55%) improve over time (including some who did not receive formal therapy), some (14% to 28%) get worse (see Finkelhor, 1990). As will be noted in the case illustration that follows, most of the effects identified above were evident.

The literature suggests that in general boys and girls show similar emotional responses to sexually abusive experiences and that when differences are noted they are usually due to the nature of the experience (e.g., abused by trusted friend or family member versus by a stranger). (See Browne & Finkelhor, 1986; Finkelhor, 1990.) It is important for clinicians to be aware that developmental factors are likely to impact the symptoms actually exhibited (Downs, 1993; Kendall-Tackett et al., 1993). Knowing, for example, that symptoms such as anxiety, nightmares, and sexually inappropriate behaviors are common among sexually abused preschoolers; that sexually abused school-age children tend to exhibit fear, aggression, and school problems; and that sexually abused adolescents frequently exhibit self-injurious behavior, running away, and substance abuse should sensitize counselors working with these groups to carefully assess the possibility of sexual abuse when these symptoms are present. At the same time counselors must be careful not to *assume* that sexual abuse is the only cause of behaviors of this sort but must evaluate this possibility. Therapists treating children who exhibit these symptoms can evaluate for the possibility of abuse by asking children if they have ever been touched in ways they are uncomfortable with. They can then, depending on the response, ask more specific questions regarding where they have been touched and by whom. Therapists are less likely to be accused of "planting" ideas of sexual abuse if they begin with more general questions and become more specific as the children's responses warrant (e.g., Have you ever been touched in ways that make you feel uncomfortable or yucky? Can you tell me what happened? Can you tell me who it was? Was anyone else there? Where did this happen? When did this happen? Did you tell anyone? Did he or she ask you not to tell? What did they say would happen if you told?). Useful suggestions for assessing children are provided by Damon and Card (1992), Heiman (1992), and McFarlane and Krebs (1986).

While most studies report negative outcomes in sexually abused children, clinicians should be aware that a few studies have found some sexual abuse survivors to be asymptomatic (see reviews by Finkelhor, 1990; Green, 1993). The reasons are not entirely clear and several hypotheses have been proposed (e.g., that there is minimization of symptoms by the children and their families, that there are limitations inherent in the types of assessments used so that they do not capture these childrens' distress, that these may be children whose symptoms will be exhibited later). The most parsimonious explanation is that these are probably children who have been responded to in effective and affirming ways by significant others (Finkelhor, 1990; Kendall-Tackett et al., 1993).

There is a vital need for research that elucidates protective factors, since knowledge of these factors can have profound implications for interventions with sexually abused or "at risk" children and adolescents. The available research suggests that childrens' ability to cope with trauma is moderated by factors such as social support, having a mentor, and having experiences that foster a sense of efficacy. However, our understanding of these factors and how they exert their impact is still in its infancy.

Diagnostically, none of the current categories in the *Diagnostic and Statistical Manual of Mental Disorders,* Fourth Edition (DSM-IV; American Psychiatric Association, 1994; hereafter, DSM-IV) adequately accommodates or captures the quality of sexual abuse trauma, due perhaps in part to the many (widely varied) symptoms displayed by survivors. Among the more common diagnoses given to sexual abuse survivors are one of the anxiety disorders (such as Post-traumatic Stress Disorder), Major Depression or Dysthymia, an adjustment disorder, or a "V-code" (Sexual Abuse of Child). Finkelhor and Browne (1985) suggest that a more useful conceptualization of the effects of sexual abuse is to focus on how the abuse impacts the children's views of themselves, others, and the world and their overall emotional adjustment. They suggest that the "traumagenic" (trauma-creating) effects of sexual abuse result in four primary processes, which are *traumatic sexualization, betrayal, powerlessness,* and *stigmatization.*

Let's examine each of these important consequences of sexual abuse for children and adolescents. According to Finkelhor & Browne, *traumatic sexualization* is the process in which childrens' sexual attitudes and feelings are "shaped in a developmentally inappropriate and interpersonally dysfunctional fashion as a result of the sexual abuse" (Finkelhor & Browne, 1985, p. 531). These children thus may exhibit inappropriate sexual behavior (e.g., masturbate in public, be sexually promiscuous), may have difficulty accepting and/or understanding their own sexuality, and may develop atypical emotional connections to sexual activities (such as confusing sexual activity and affection).

Betrayal results from the recognition that a significant other has manipulated them, caused them injury, and shown little regard for their well-being. This may include the perpetrator, of course, but also other significant people in their lives who failed to protect or believe them. Indeed it is not uncommon for incest survivors to experience an enhanced sense of betrayal by the non-offending (sometimes called nonprotective) parent. For many children, the sense of betrayal is magnified by the failure of significant adults in their lives to believe their reports of abuse and is made worse by requests to deny the reality of their distress (e.g., "It's over, so just forget it happened"; "Your father would never do anything like that"; or "Don't you ever say anything like that to anybody ever again . . . Do you understand me?").

Powerlessness results from being assaulted, coerced, manipulated, misunderstood, and trapped, robbing the child of his or her sense of efficacy and control. It can bring about a sense of helplessness, a sense of hopelessness about the future, and is a significant contributor to depression.

Finally, *stigmatization,* which includes childrens' feelings of being marred, shameful, guilty, lacking honor, and so forth, becomes part of the child's self-concept as a result of messages given to the child by the abuser and others who blame, shame, and in other ways characterize the child negatively. Sheila's case very aptly demonstrates all four of these effects.

In Sheila's case, the issues of powerlessness, stigmatization, and betrayal were more poignant because of her status as an African American female, a member of a group who by virtue of race and gender experience less power, are stigmatized as inferior, and often feel betrayed by the sociopolitical system. For Sheila, feelings of betrayal were intensified by her mother's lack of support.

Theories regarding the causes of child maltreatment in general focus on the relative contribution of cultural, community, familial, and individual variables. With regard to sexual abuse in particular, factors implicated include cultural and community attitudes toward children, such as viewing children as property. (Some writers have suggested that the preponderance of male compared to female perpetrators may be due in part to our patriarchal society in which men are accorded most of the power, control, and property rights.) In addition, child rearing practices and experiences, such as the prolonged absence of one or both parents, maternal employment outside the home, unhappy family life, parental discord, having a stepfather, and intergenerational patterns of incest have been suggested. It is important to note that although most who are abused *do not* reenact and molest others, individuals who do molest often report their own experiences of having been molested. Finally, alcohol abuse, poor impulse control, emotional immaturity and neediness, and inadequate coping skills, especially when combined with social and geographic isolation of a family, have also been implicated as risk factors for sexual abuse (see Finkelhor & Associates, 1986; Finkelhor et al., 1990).

Sociocultural Considerations in the Prevalence of Sexual Abuse

Research on the mediating impact of sociocultural factors on the prevalence of child sexual abuse is rather sparse, since most of the literature combines the various categories of abuse: physical abuse, emotional maltreatment, neglect, and sexual abuse. According to the 1988 U. S. Department of Health and Human Services Report, maltreatment, particularly physical abuse and neglect, were higher among those with low family incomes and larger family sizes (four or more children) but did not differ significantly by race or ethnicity.

With regard to sexual abuse prevalence rates, Wyatt and Peters (1986) evaluated studies on adults abused as children and noted that there is no evidence to support the notion of differences in these rates based on ethnicity, region, and survivor's current educational level and economic status. They suggest that sexual abuse is evident across all racial, social, and cultural boundaries. However, there are a few individual studies that do report differing rates based on race and/or ethnicity (e.g., Kercher & McShane, 1984; Russell, 1986). For example, Kercher & McShane (1984) reported higher rates among Latinos in Texas and Russell (1986) reported lower rates among Asian females.

The data regarding variations in the specifics/characteristics of sexual abuse by race or ethnicity is conflicting. For example, some studies report that sexual abuse begins early for African American women compared to White or Latina women (DeJong, Hervada, & Emmett, 1983), while others report the opposite (Wyatt, 1985). Some studies also suggest that African American children are less likely to be abused by a biological father than are White children (see Russell, 1986; Tzeng & Schwarzin, 1990).

In one study comparing child abuse reports to population distribution, Lindholm & Willey (1986) reviewed 4,132 cases of child abuse that were reported to the Los Angeles County Sheriff's Department. They found that in proportion to their population representation, rates of overall abuse were higher for Blacks than for Whites and Hispanics. However, the majority of the reported cases were for physical abuse, with sexual abuse constituting 24.5% of the reported cases. Within the sexual abuse category, Black children had lower rates of abuse (16.6%) than White children (26.7%) and Hispanic children (28.2%). The other findings, which are consistent with other reports in the literature, indicated that the majority of the perpetrators were male (95%) and that significantly more females than males were sexually abused. In this Los Angeles sample, intercourse occurred more often in Hispanic and Black groups, fondling more often in Hispanic and White, and oral copulation more often in the White group. Sodomy was rare but occurred more often to boys in the Hispanic group. Although the literature reports a preponderance of male sexual perpetration, anecdotal information suggests that female sexual perpetration may be higher than previously noted.

There has been relatively little research on abuse-related symptom presentation based on race or ethnicity. Most studies do not report their sample's racial breakdown. The few that have, have yielded inconsistent findings on the effects of race on outcome. For example, in one study, higher levels of psychiatric symptoms were noted in the minority compared to White women (Morrow & Sorell, 1989). In contrast, Wyatt (1990) found few differences in symptoms based on race in her sexually abused African American and White American sample. A more recent study suggests that there may be no *general* effects of race or ethnicity on symptoms but that the effects of race or ethnicity may be mediated by the specific attributes of the abusive event, for example, oral copulation, sodomy, or intercourse (Mennen, 1995). This researcher noted, for example, that penetration was especially traumatizing for Latina women.

Finally, the precise role of childrearing practices on the prevalence of sexual abuse is not well understood, although family composition (e.g., having a stepfather), family size (e.g., having a large family of more than four children), and the quality and quantity of parental supervision all seem to play a role (Finkelhor & Associates, 1986; Finkelhor et al., 1990; U.S. Department of Health and Human Services, 1988). Although most sexual abuse survivors do not molest others, the fact that most perpetrators report histories of their own sexual abuse is significant for purposes of intervention (see Araji & Finkelhor, 1986). Furthermore, it is important to note that while the majority of victims are female, the majority of perpetrators are male although reports of female perpetration are increasing. These findings suggest that socialization practices and gender roles may mediate how sexual abuse trauma is coped with behaviorally, even though survivors may exhibit similar emotional responses at the time of the abuse.

CASE ILLUSTRATION

Presenting Problem

Sheila, a 15-year-old African American female was brought to therapy by her foster mother following her release from a psychiatric hospital. Sheila had attempted suicide (by ingesting pills) and her hospital discharge diagnosis was Major Depression with Psychotic Features (Mood Congruent). She recently had been removed from her own home after she told a friend that she was being sexually abused by her stepfather, which began when she was 7 and now included intercourse. Her friend convinced her to report the abuse to the authorities. Sheila's stepfather was then removed from the home. Although her mother denied knowing about the abuse as it was occurring, and did not directly say she disbelieved her when it was reported, at no time did she overtly say, "I believe you and support you." In addition, her mother did not protect her from family acquaintances who asked her to withdraw the abuse charges against her stepfather. A few weeks after reporting, Sheila found her mother's lack of support intolerable and ran away from home. Upon arriving in the adjoining city, her sense of hopelessness became overwhelming and she contemplated suicide. Fortunately, she called her friend and told this to her friend. This friend then contacted the social worker assigned to the case. At this point Sheila was hospitalized. On release from the hospital, she was placed in a foster home. It was at this time that I saw her in therapy.

Therapy was initiated to deal with her depression and the sexual abuse. Most of the initial history was obtained from a Child Protective Services report and from the social worker who had been assigned to the case.

CLIENT DESCRIPTION

Sheila was a tall, overweight, taciturn 15-year-old at intake. She had short hair and her hazel eyes were very sad and often filled with tears. During the initial session she shuffled into my office, slouched on the couch, made occasional eye contact and barely said a word. Her energy level seemed to be extremely low—she was clearly severely depressed. After clarifying that Sheila knew why she was here (i.e., for counseling, rather than evaluation, so we would therefore not focus on obtaining a detailed history of the abuse), we discussed issues of confidentiality. My initial attempts to engage her were almost painful. There were long silences as I attempted to convey to her my availability, interest, and support, without "forcing" her to engage, as this would only dynamically replay the "demand-compliance" routine that she had endured at home. This meant tracking her behavior closely and responding to even slight nonverbal responses.

THERAPIST: Sheila, I know from the CPS report and from the hospital's report that you have had to deal with a very difficult situation at home and that it has been hard for you to talk about it . . .

CLIENT: (barely nods but turns her eyes toward me)

THERAPIST: I would like to know more about you. I would like to be as helpful as I can be. We don't have to talk about what happened with your stepfather right now unless you want to . . .

CLIENT: (tears in her eyes, shakes her head to indicate that she does not want to)

THERAPIST: Perhaps later when we get to know each other better we can talk about that. Would it be okay with you if I asked a few questions about your school, friends, and things you like to do?

CLIENT: (slight affirmative nod)

The session continued in this manner with Sheila responding with brief statements, nods, and shrugs. At the end of this session, I asked Sheila if she would be willing to return to which she nodded affirmatively. It is extremely important when working with adolescents to have them make the decision to return to therapy, even if it is just for a "trial" phase. The issue of choice is even more salient for sexually abused adolescents, since they have been forced to comply with others' demands. For Sheila, her status as an African American female, in a society where the power is often with those who are White and male, magnified the salience of giving her the opportunity to determine and control her options.

Although Sheila acknowledged suicidal ideation, she had no plan. I nevertheless asked her to enter a short-term "no suicide" pact with me, based on the severity of her depression, her ideation, and her history of attempts. Sheila met the criteria for both Major Depression and Post-Traumatic Stress Disorder. She had clearly been severely traumatized by the incest. She was hypervigilant and experienced frequent nightmares. She reported often being afraid of going to sleep, of waking up with choking sensations, and of sometimes having difficulty breathing. She reported hearing "voices" that told her she was bad and used terms such as "sinner." It was unclear if these "voices" were truly consistent with psychosis or whether these were simply intrusive self-condemnations with a dissociative quality to them. Although most of the statements made by these voices seemed to represent things that had been said to her, some appeared to be anticipated condemnations, all with a critical tone. At school, Sheila found it difficult to concentrate. She was sure all the kids at school knew that she was "marred." She saw no hope for the future and often thought about killing herself, although at the time of intake she denied having a suicide plan. In addition to seeing me, Sheila was taking antidepressants prescribed the agency's psychiatrist.

SOCIAL CONTEXT

Information about Sheila's family background and early life experiences was sparse. She had never known her biological father and was raised by a single mother until age 7, when her mother met and married Mr. B. Sheila had two younger half-siblings, a brother age 7 and a sister age 5. She had occasional contact with her maternal grandfather but never knew her maternal grandmother who had died prior to Sheila's birth. Sheila reported that as a young child she was very close to her mother. She was very proud of how her mother had coped as a young, single parent with little external support. She was determined to be an obedient daughter and had made every effort to be close to her mother. The consistency of her mother's emotional availability is unclear as Sheila describes always trying to please her mother, who often seemed sad. Sheila also described occasions during which she would hear her mother crying in her room. She states that she was therefore very happy when her mother met Mr. B. at their church since he seemed to make her mother happy. In addition, Sheila stated that she had always wanted a father and Mr. B. was very attentive and kind to her. So, initially, Mr. B. was very much welcomed into their lives.

Shortly after Mr. and Mrs. B. were married, Mrs. B. became pregnant and had a very difficult pregnancy. During this time Mr. B. became actively involved in several caretaking tasks such as putting Sheila to bed at night and helping her make breakfast in the morning. However, he was short-tempered and yelled a lot, although he never was actually physically abusive. Sheila learned early to obey to keep the peace and to try and win her stepfather's approval.

In the ensuing years Sheila continued her efforts to be an ideal daughter especially because she felt that it was her responsibility to make her mother happy. As she grew older she took on many household chores and played the role of peacemaker whenever her parents argued. Sheila's description of her mother suggests that Mrs. B. was severely depressed after the birth of both Sheila's siblings and had quite likely been clinically depressed for a substantial portion of Sheila's life. Sadly, the role reversal dynamic in which Sheila took on more adult responsibility appears to occur with some frequency in incestuous families. In Sheila's case, as in the case of many incest survivors, it short-circuited her childhood and resulted in a pseudomature facade.

Sheila's family went to church regularly and her stepfather was an elder at the church. This meant that he was respected and various members of the congregation often talked about what a "fine" Christian father he was. As we will see more fully later, although Sheila felt anxious whenever her stepfather's praises were sung, she never contradicted these statements and was sure that no one would believe her reports of abuse anyway. Furthermore, the cultural value of family loyalty and obeying one's elders, which was often extolled in her church and in her family, also played a role in Sheila keeping the incest a secret for so long.

The importance of understanding the contribution of culture in the assessment and treatment of sexual abuse has been receiving more attention in recent years (Heras, Gomez, & Thomas, 1992). Clearly, family values impact if and when sexual abuse is revealed. They also impact the treatment process. Children, like Sheila, who come from families where the viability of the family as a group is more important than the child's individual molestation experience may be censured for revealing their abuse experiences. These children may then be especially hesitant to discuss their full range of feelings toward the perpetrator and/or nonprotective family members. The therapist's ability to supportively acknowledge the role family values and loyalty issues play, without forcing the child to respond in any particular way, will be very healing. That is, the therapist must acknowledge the significance of the child's cultural context and help the child find a way to cope given that context.

The neighborhood in which Sheila grew up was a small, rural community, made up primarily of working class Mexican Americans and African Americans. The local school, however, was racially mixed, where many children were European American offspring of local farmers. Racial tension in the local school was often high, although the various racial groups tended to maintain separate activities. Sheila was a good student and she felt that this was something her mother valued. Although she had received positive responses from her teachers over the years because of her good school performance, she had always been self-conscious because of her race, gender, and weight. Consequently, she was not very assertive at school and participated in no extracurricular activities.

Initial Session

Adolescence, with its multiple social, psychological, and physiological demands, can be a difficult phase for many individuals. It is even more difficult for teens who have experienced betrayal and violation within their families. For African American females, feelings of powerlessness and pessimism are fueled by the sociopolitical climate. Sheila had to contend with all these factors as well as with attempts by her family and their friends to discount the impact of the abuse. Her stepfather had abused her for most of the 8 years he had been married to her mother (beginning with inappropriate touching and fondling at bedtime, later progressing to intercourse). However, when she finally risked disclosing her secret, many within her family circle suggested she recant her accusations and "just stay away" from her stepfather. Under these circumstances, Sheila's sense of being devalued, feeling powerless, and having a sense of futility about life and the future made absolute sense.

My initial therapy goals were to establish a relationship with Sheila where she would feel safe, valued, and could begin to develop hope that her future was not as bleak as she currently felt. Although there were frequent silences in the first few sessions, I attempted to convey to Sheila warmth, respect, and presence by my body language (e.g., leaning forward slightly), by listening attentively and "tracking" her closely (i.e., accepting and responding to her shrugs and brief statements as they occurred), and by approaching issues tentatively so she could easily let me know if she was not ready to deal with particular topics. Although I felt tense and questioned my competence repeatedly during these first few sessions, it seemed that in reality Sheila was quite anxious to have a nonjudgmental supporter and within a relatively short period of time began to initiate verbal discourse in therapy. Although Sheila's willingness to engage with me was probably expedited in part by my being an African American female, I am sure that my attentiveness to her body language (and mine) and my respectful, nonjudgmental stance were also significant in facilitating the development of our relationship. This stance, which represented my attempt to achieve credibility with Sheila, is supported by the research which suggests that African American clients often approach therapy tentatively until they can size up the counselor and his or her interpersonal competence.

Case Conceptualization

Sheila had been sexually molested by her stepfather for almost eight years and had not, until now, directly told anyone about the molestation. There were, of course, many symptoms and behaviors related to the abuse, such as depression, overeating, expressions of anxiety about staying home alone with her stepfather, and several suicide gestures (which included taking over-the-counter pills and leaving the empty bottles on her parents' bathroom counter). However, it was not until boys at school began showing interest in her and making sexual comments (such as remarks about how well she was "developing"), combined with the establishment of her first really close friendship, that Sheila directly told someone about the abuse. In an

ironic way, it was Sheila's desire to have a relationship in which she was valued and loved that made her vulnerable to her stepfather's abuse. Her stepfather then abused her trust and made her feel shameful and worthless.
Sheila's response was to search for ways to be found worthy of her family,
hence her compliant and caretaking stance.

Sheila believed that her mother knew about the abuse and, because she
had not intervened to stop it, felt that she was expected to continue to sub-
mit. Her suicide gestures (with the pills) usually followed nights when her
stepfather had intercourse with her. Neither her mother, nor her stepfather,
ever commented on the empty pill bottles. Sheila's mother later stated that
she had never seen these empty bottles. Sheila was acutely aware, however,
that her stepfather was much more aloof with her following these incidents.
This increased the tension in the family and Sheila would once again try to
find ways to please her parents so she could reconnect with them.

Although sexual abuse is abhorred in Sheila's cultural and religious community, some of the values held within this community, such as family loyalty
and obedience, may also have unintentionally contributed to her continued
submission to her stepfather and to keeping the abuse secret. Saying no to her
stepfather would have been disobedient and telling someone outside the family disloyal. At least this is what Sheila believed.

In addition to Sheila's sexual abuse, her early life experiences played an
important role in her development. Sheila was raised by a single, African
American woman with little personal, social, or financial support. She was,
however, able to provide a home and some stability for Sheila. At the same
time this mother was depressed and had difficulty sustaining emotional
availability. During her "good periods," she and Sheila engaged in fun activities and she was able to convey to Sheila that she was proud of her. Sadly,
her depressed periods were more frequent, and during these times Sheila
tried to do whatever she thought would ease her mother's load and make her
feel happier. For example, Sheila excelled in kindergarten, was seldom oppositional at home, and was very attuned (and responsive to) her mother's
likes and dislikes. This inconsistency in her mother was damaging and increased Sheila's vulnerability. Out of these early experiences, Sheila developed an obedient, people-pleasing attitude, and a pseudomature facade. This
became her template for relating to others, including her abusive stepfather.
In therapy, Sheila conveyed the feeling that her approval from her mother
and stepfather were highly contingent on her being "good," i.e., being compliant and responsive to their needs.

Religion also played an important role in her early experiences. Sheila's
understanding of religious principles was that she be humble and obedient.
She interpreted being angry, disobedient, or questioning as inconsistent
with Christianity. In fact, Sheila's "hallucinations" during her hospitalization and during the initial phase of therapy were moral and religious in nature, with the "voices" telling her she was not a good Christian. Indeed
Sheila was caught in a tremendous bind. Based on her interpretation of

Christianity, she was a sinner for having premarital intercourse but also a sinner for being disobedient and disloyal in reporting her stepfather.

Orienting Constructs

I believe that children's earliest relationships with significant others have tremendous impact on their developing self-concepts, serving as "templates" for future relationships. In Sheila's case, she internalized from her early relationships a sense of self as being good only when she was taking care of others and their needs. She was responded to positively only when she was compliant and pleasing others. This was, for example, evident in her relationship with her mother where she was often the caretaker, helping around the house, inquiring about her mother's needs, comforting her mother when she was sad, and rarely "burdening" her mother with her own needs. In her relationship with her stepfather, Sheila wanted to be cared for and special; she also wanted to avoid his anger at all costs. Her experience with him alternated between his being kind and helpful and his molesting her. When she resisted his advances, he became angry and withdrew from her. She felt that her only solution was to comply. In her desire to avoid his anger and maintain some level of relationship with him, she submerged her needs. Over time, Sheila's ability to access and even express her own needs or feelings was severely muted.

The ongoing violation, betrayal, and lack of nurturance and support for her own needs contributed further to her sense of unworthiness, powerlessness, and hopelessness about the future. It made sense that out of these experiences Sheila developed cognitive schemas (ways of viewing the world, herself, others, and the future) that were highly pessimistic. Beck and others write compellingly about the impact of people's attitudes or assumptions (referred to as schemas) that develop out of previous experiences, on the way they think, feel, and behave (see Beck, Rush, Shaw, & Emery, 1979). Beck et al. (1979) present the concept of a *cognitive triad,* which involves individuals' views of *themselves* as negative (worthless, defective, inadequate); *the world* (including others and experiences in the environment) as difficult, demanding, unmanageable, and uncontrollable; and *the future* as bleak, with goals unattainable and failure likely. Each of the components of this triad were evident in Sheila and their genesis vis-à-vis her life experiences made absolute sense.

Finally, for Sheila, her negative life experiences occurred in a sociopolitical context that devalued her status as an African American woman, fueling further her sense of being worthless, of the world as unmanageable, and the future as bleak.

Sheila's stance in therapy vacillated between trying to please me, being what she thought a "good client" should be, and being suspicious of my motives and the consistency of my presence and support if she acted out (which she tested in a variety of ways). Our roles (especially as they related to caretaking) and the boundaries of our relationship also were important in the therapy process, as Sheila tried to discover who she truly wanted to be and how she wanted to construct her relationships with others. I will elaborate on this later in the chapter.

A significant construct in my clinical work is to attend to the client's specific history, evaluate the client's templates and cognitive schemas, and then try to provide a corrective experience. What this means is that I am alert to replays of the client's interactions with significant others, which he or she has told me have evoked much pain. I then try to provide for the client a different experience from the one they have had. I ask myself repeatedly, What is the impact of the process we are now enacting? What sorts of responses does this client need and how might I communicate these? Beyond the words spoken, I question the message of the process we are engaging in. What, for example, is the message to the client if there is advice giving? The impact is likely to be very different for a client who comes from an intrusive family (i.e., they may resent it and/or interpret it as further evidence of their inability to manage) compared to a client who has had little parenting and nurturance (i.e., they may view it as a sign of concern and caring). Sociocultural background may further complicate the picture since taking on a teacher or advice-giving role may be acceptable and solicited by some but viewed as patronizing by others. I believe further that the therapeutic environment must be stable, consistent, and safe, so clients can express their full range of feelings, knowing they will be accepted, contained, and responded to. As the case unfolds, the process of responding to Sheila based on her individual, familial, and cultural experiences will be seen.

Treatment Plans and Intervention Strategy

INITIAL TREATMENT PLAN

As noted earlier, the initial therapy goals were to establish a relationship with Sheila where she would feel safe, valued, and could begin to develop hope that her future was not as bleak as she felt. Other important initial goals were to reduce her depression, suicidal ideation, and "auditory hallucinations," which I believed were really dissociated self-condemnations.

Middle phase goals were to explore her childhood experiences especially regarding her relationship with her mother and stepfather. Based on this, we would together try to understand the genesis of her symptoms and coping patterns. I wanted to help her work through the emotions associated with these difficult and disempowering developmental experiences so she could begin the process of more actively choosing and redefining how she wanted to relate to others.

The goals of the later phase were to further develop her self-esteem by finding ways to further empower her. I also wanted to try to help her establish new supports and gratifying relationships that were modeled on the affirming relational experiences I was trying to provide for her, rather than following along the exploited-powerless templates that had been structuring the relationships she had been forming.

The goals were thus:

Phase 1

1. Establish a relationship characterized by safety and trust.
2. Work to reduce her depression including her suicidal ideation, sense of hopelessness, and self-condemnations.

Phase 2

1. Help her explore her childhood history and sort through her range of emotions and needs.
2. Do the necessary guilt, shame, and grief work.
3. Help her tolerate, accept, and integrate various thoughts and emotions.

Phase 3

1. Focus further on self-concept and increase self-esteem.
2. Establish new supports and develop meaningful, gratifying relationships.

Phase 1.   Much of the initial phase of therapy was spent establishing the relationship and working to reduce Sheila's depression including her suicidal ideation, sense of hopelessness, and self-condemnations. The process of engaging Sheila in therapy was described in the initial contact section. The emphasis here was on closely tracking and together clarifying her words, gestures, tones, and underlying messages and beliefs. I was very careful not to violate Sheila's protective net, which meant that I broached potentially sensitive topics tentatively and always respected her right to choose to not deal with the issue at that time. I tried to convey, in words and behavior, that she was in control of the pace of therapy. One way of joining with Sheila was to explore and together clarify the linkage between her life experiences and her feelings. Her feelings of powerlessness, hopelessness, and futility about her future made absolute sense in light of her life experiences. Repeatedly throughout the course of treatment, I was trying to be validating of this, rather than minimizing the impact as many in her family had done, and this went a long way in solidifying our relationship. My purpose in part was to enact a process different from the ones she had previously experienced and to help her feel understood and cared about.

It became clear early on that one of the ways Sheila tried to make sense of things—given how hard she had tried and the betrayal she had experienced—was to conclude that she must somehow be flawed. It seemed as if the sexual trauma had become incorporated into her sense of self and she had begun to see herself as full of shame and unworthy of good things. It was thus important to talk about the fact that bad things had *happened* to her but that *she was not bad.* In doing this, I had to be with her (i.e., attentive and respectful) as she worked through her interpretations and understanding of moral and religious messages she had heard. In this I felt my task was to listen and ask her to evaluate and clarify these messages. I asked a fair number of questions in an effort to make overt her cognitive schemas. For example, I would often ask questions, such as "Is that what you think (or believe or expect)?" "What makes you think that way?" "Are there other ways of thinking about it (or Are there any other possible explanations)?" "Whose rule (or "should") is that?" "Is that what you choose (or want) to believe?" The process of making overt her views of God, self, others, and the extent to which she felt buffeted by events helped Sheila clarify her pathogenic beliefs, but it was also intended to convey to her that I valued *her* thoughts, feelings, and beliefs and that I saw her as having worth. This was significant given Sheila's history of submerging her feelings and being made to feel shameful and worthless. My unconditional stance of support also began the process of providing her with a sense that this was a safe place where all her feelings and experiences could be discussed.

It was clear that Sheila approached most situations with great pessimism and had no positive future expectations. The process of magnifying her schemas by having her take a closer look at each of the assumptions she held (i.e., "There's something wrong with me," "I can never do anything right," "Nothing I do is ever good enough, and I guess it will always be that way so there's no use trying"), their genesis (i.e., her lack of affirming childhood experiences, the violation, betrayal, powerlessness, and stigmatization that resulted from the molestation and the lack of support from her mother), their current functions (a way to make sense of events and try to instill order and some form of consistency where none existed), and evaluate their "reality" base (e.g., Where did these messages come from?; Did she really want to accept them as her own?; Were there other possible explanations?) was quite significant. She was able to begin grounding her feelings in reality and began to identify areas where she could make choices and have control. She was able, for example, to identify areas where she had been able to effect change (for example, she was no longer being molested by her stepfather) but also recognize that the molest was not her fault as a young child being coerced by a powerful significant other.

Over time Sheila's assumptions were less *automatic.* In the process of challenging her false beliefs, affirming her worth and dignity, and supporting her right to say no and be self-directing, Sheila took on the questioning model I had provided. She began to recognize her tendency to take on the negative characterizations made by others (e.g., "You are a very *selfish* child, what would it hurt to drop the charges against your stepfather and just stay away from him? How is he going to support the other children if he is in jail?" These were the types of statements she heard from people associated with her family). Furthermore, she began to "talk through" who the statement belonged to, whose view it represented. Although statements such as these continued to have impact, they no longer were automatically accepted as truth.

With regard to dropping the charges against her stepfather, Sheila agonized about the impact on her younger siblings of her father being jailed. In the end, she stated that she did not want to recant the abuse charge because doing so would "be a lie." Although she had difficulty articulating this, she conveyed the sense that recanting would epitomize her worthlessness. In maintaining her stance and being supported in this by me and some other people in her life, she experienced empowerment and acknowledged her self-worth. This was an especially delicate process, given Sheila's family's value of maintaining the family as a group at all costs. It was critical that Sheila, and not I as therapist, make the decision to keep the charge against her father. My job here was to help her give a *voice* to all her feelings, including the family loyalty issues, the censure likely to result if she refused to drop the charges, and what dropping or following through with the charge would mean to her and her sense of worth.

Sheila's history of compliance with significant others made it imperative that I be highly cognizant of the extent to which I was directive, yet her level of depression during the initial phase dictated that I be active. I tried to balance this by being active (which included providing information, asking questions such as "Is this what you want?" "Is this how you feel?" "What do you think about . . . ?" and trying to "normalize" her experience and validate her feelings: "When you describe how hard you tried, it makes sense that you would feel helpless . . .") but always maintaining awareness of the extent to which my activity might be construed as directive (i.e., experienced as demanding or controlling in terms of her internalized schemas). On many occasions I asked her directly if she felt that I had a particular agenda or wanted her to respond in a particular way and we were then able to work on this together. I also communicated my view that her needs, feelings, and choices were important by acknowledging them whenever she ventured to express them. In this way, I was trying to rework the role reversal and let her know that in this relationship, she would be responded to rather than have to take care of me. I always kept in mind her templates, which were to please others, take care of them, and submerge her needs below theirs. This process led naturally to the second phase of treatment to be discussed in the next section.

As previously mentioned, Sheila was also taking antidepressant medications prescribed by the agency's psychiatrist and these were especially helpful in assisting her with sleep. Her suicidal ideation was dealt with directly by establishing a "no suicide" agreement. As Sheila's depression lessened, so did her suicidal ideation. Further, her self-condemnations, which were impacted greatly by her religious beliefs, diminished as she began to explore her views of God and as she began to think of him as more benevolent and less judgmental. Her involvement in a new church was very important to this process. Fortunately she became involved with a church group that was affirming of her.

I also referred Sheila to a group for adolescent incest survivors. She was at first very reticent about this but agreed to attend at least one session. The group experience became a very significant adjunct to our individual work because the group provided information and further normalized and validated her experiences and her feelings. She was especially relieved to discover that she was not the only African American to have been molested by a family member.

Phase 2.   One of the major goals of this phase was to help Sheila explore her past relationships and try to understand how they contributed to who she was and how she coped. The process of exploring her childhood history was at times distressing, and Sheila would then consider engaging in behavior that was potentially self-damaging. For example, during one therapy session Sheila had talked about her closeness to her mother as a young child. She expressed her sense of loss when her mother did not stop the abuse, which was exacerbated by her mother "allowing" (from Sheila's point of view) other family members to ask her to recant her charge against her stepfather for molesting her. The following day, Sheila was caught stealing food at the school's cafeteria. She stated that she did not need or really want the food and anticipated being caught but did not care.

This episode represented self-destructive behavior and a sense of futility about the future, following a rather painful therapy session. I certainly questioned my interventions: Had we moved too fast in therapy? Were there other things I ought to have said or done during that therapy session? Were there things Sheila was trying to communicate to me that I was not hearing? I realized that the stealing occurred right after we had talked about her mother and her immense need to have been taken care of by her mother. It seemed as though stealing food was symbolic of her desire to be nurtured. Further, the blatant nature of the event suggested that she wanted me to be aware of her distress (much like the empty pill bottles she had left for her parents during her suicide gestures), and it became important that I respond clearly and protectively and not minimize the event. This incident, which could have had very negative consequences, provided me with an opportunity to respond differently to Sheila's cry for help than had her parents. We scheduled an emergency session that day, during which time I conveyed to Sheila directly that I heard her cry for help. For the first time in our time together, Sheila was able to allow herself to sob freely, which she did for a substantial portion of the session. I let Sheila know that I *wanted* to hear her—including her feelings, thoughts, and needs—and asked if she would communicate these to me directly in words to the extent that she could. She was able to let me know that she had not communicated directly in her family of origin because she feared that her feelings and needs would be minimized or ignored. We addressed how these issues might play out in our relationship. I explicitly asked Sheila to point out to me verbally whenever she felt as though I was minimizing or ignoring something of significance to her. I also asked Sheila for permission to directly confront her when I perceived her to be *acting out* rather than *talking out* her feelings. Our relationship as a *team* really solidified during this session. We were also able to talk about the potential that she might be self-injurious following painful disclosures and that we needed to identify together, in advance, alternative coping strategies.

During this phase Sheila and I spent a great deal of time talking about her stepfather's abuse of her. She recalled him coming home during times when he knew she was alone or coming to her room at night when the others were asleep. As we focused on this, Sheila experienced an increase in intrusive thoughts and was inundated with feelings of shame and of rage. I explained to her that this increase in pain was really a sign that she was working on healing and I used the medical analogies of chemotherapy and surgery to explain how the treatment, which is part of the recovery process, sometimes brings about a temporary increase in distress and discomfort before healing occurs.

I encouraged Sheila to bring her thoughts, feelings, and recollections to therapy. Talking about these in a supportive, nonjudgmental setting diminished the degree of secrecy in which they had been shrouded. It also reduced the shame she felt. Often, when I work with sexual abuse survivors, I encourage them to journal as an additional way of processing. Sheila was quite hesitant about this and concerned (in an appropriate way) about whether she could trust that what she wrote might be safe and remain private. Given the boundary violations she had experienced in her own home, it made sense that she questioned whether anything could be truly private and inviolable. We simply agreed that this was a tool she might choose to use at some later point in her life. However, in the session following, Sheila was rather withdrawn and quiet. The change in behavior was quite distinct from previous sessions, so I commented on it. I had learned in my time with her that I needed to let her know when it seemed as though there was something important that she wanted to communicate, even though I might not know what the issue might be. Changes in mood, verbal production, and body language were among the cues I attended to. I asked her if there was something we needed to talk about. She began to cry and stated that she "knew" I would be mad at her.

THERAPIST: Mad?

CLIENT: Well, I didn't start a journal.

THERAPIST: Yes?

CLIENT: I was supposed to.

THERAPIST: Only if you wanted to.

CLIENT: But you wouldn't have brought it up if it hadn't been something you wanted me to do. I'm sure you wanted me to do it (client has tears in her eyes).

THERAPIST: Sheila, I notice your tears. Would you talk to me about how you are feeling?

CLIENT: I've been afraid all week that you might be mad at me. I tried to do it once but just couldn't.

THERAPIST: I'm not angry with you Sheila, and I appreciate you bringing it up and talking about it. (Even though I might have explored further her expectation that I would be angry and the genesis of this, I felt that a direct answer with support for taking the risk to express her concern was the more important focus). I think it might be helpful if we talk about your expectation that I might be angry.

CLIENT: So I can still come and see you even if I don't do the journal?

THERAPIST: Absolutely. (Again I felt it important to let her know right away that we were still connected.) Can we talk about your concern that I might not want to see you?

CLIENT: I worry that if I don't do what you want, you might not want to see me any more. At home if I didn't do what they wanted, they stopped talking to me, and I hated the silences, so I always did it in the end.

THERAPIST: And you are concerned that I might act in the same way?

CLIENT: Yes.

THERAPIST: Sheila, I'm really glad that you brought this up with me. You don't have to please me for me to be here for you. I think it is terrific that you decided for yourself what you wanted to do. I appreciate it when you let me know that you don't agree with me. I also appreciate it when you let me know about your feelings and your concerns. (Even though I had not given her a *directive* about journaling, that reality was not important; what seemed most important here was her fear of abandonment if she was not compliant.) From what you have said about your family it makes sense that you would feel this way. (We then went on to talk about her compliant script, its probable genesis, how it might continue to be replayed in the present especially in our relationship, and what its consequences were and might be over the long term.)

This incident underscored the power of early templates and how relationship issues get repeated in therapy.

Sheila's religious faith also served a positive role. She reported talking to God as a way of processing and making sense of her life experiences. As mentioned before, Sheila had also joined a new church where she made new friends who were affirming of her and who did not see God as punitive and judgmental.

Sheila expressed much rage at her stepfather for violating her and making her feel so worthless. During one particularly poignant session, Sheila began pounding a pillow as she questioned why he had molested her. I quickly set up a role play, with several pillows representing her stepfather, and encouraged her to express her feelings. As she talked to him, her ambivalent feelings toward him emerged. In addition to her rage and feelings of violation, she also acknowledged how desperately she had wanted to be loved by him. At the end of the role play, Sheila was able to talk about some of his characteristics that she had valued; for example, helping her make breakfast or praising her for some accomplishment had made her think of him as a father. She struggled to understand how he could be so kind at times and then be so profane at times. Sheila's ability to acknowledge both the positive and negative aspects of her stepfather were crucial in helping her develop empathy for herself. An important part of this was realizing that life contained many gray areas and that people had good and bad parts to them. Further, that people, including Sheila, could be loved despite their flaws. Grasping this helped Sheila to not remain stuck in her rage toward her stepfather.

Sheila's case highlights the importance for clinicians who work with incest survivors to be very careful of expressing their own countertransferential feelings toward the perpetrator. Many incest survivors have ambivalent feelings toward their perpetrators. If therapists express their own negative feelings, they curtail the survivor's ability to deal with his or her full range of emotions toward that individual, which may include genuinely positive feelings.

The next day when I returned from running an errand during the lunch hour, Sheila was in my office, on the couch, curled in a fetal position.

THERAPIST: Sheila, are you OK?
CLIENT: (Opens her eyes but barely moves and responds in a scarcely audible voice) Yes, I just needed to come to a safe place.
THERAPIST: Sounds like you have felt threatened and unsafe. Can we talk?
CLIENT: I couldn't sleep last night, I could smell him (stepfather), I could see his shoulder, it was just hard . . .
THERAPIST: You have been having more memories of your stepfather and his abuse of you?
CLIENT: Yes, and I couldn't sleep. I went to school this morning but couldn't think so at lunch I told the nurse I was sick and came here. I slept a little here.
THERAPIST: I'm glad you found a safe place. How can I help?
CLIENT: Can I stay for a little while longer?
THERAPIST: Yes. I will wake you up in 15 minutes so we can decide where we go from here. (At this point it seemed to me that her need to feel cared for and responded to over-rode any potential boundary issues). (fifteen minutes later)
THERAPIST: Sheila, we have about 15 minutes to talk before my next client. I know we have been talking more about your stepfather, and from what you said earlier, it sounds like you have been very affected by that, perhaps having bad dreams and frightening memories.
CLIENT: (crying) I've been remembering some things and can't go to sleep and the medicine hasn't helped.

THERAPIST: Sheila, we have several options. I want you to feel safe, but I also realize that we need to talk about what happened with your stepfather more, so it won't have such a powerful effect on you.

CLIENT: (interrupts) All I know is I don't want to go back to the hospital. I think I could manage if I saw you more.

THERAPIST: That would be fine but first I need an agreement with you that you won't hurt yourself. (Knowing Sheila's history of suicide attempts, her increase in symptoms made me concerned for her safety).

CLIENT: I promise to talk to you first when things feel really bad, as long as I don't have to go back in the hospital.

THERAPIST: How many times a week do you think you would like to come in right now?

CLIENT: How many times can I come?

THERAPIST: We could meet daily if you thought you needed that. We could also meet less and perhaps arrange a specific time when you could call if you wanted to. What do you think? Lets start there.

CLIENT: I'd like to come everyday, but I know you have other people to see. Can I come twice and call you on the other days?

We then arranged for brief daily check-in times for the next two weeks and for the additional appointment. We agreed to review the need for the calls and additional session biweekly. It seemed that during this especially difficult period, Sheila needed to be able to touch "home base" even if briefly to feel safe. We also made an appointment later in the day for a psychiatric review of her medications, and the decision was made to increase these slightly at bedtime. This episode represented a balancing dilemma for me. I did not want Sheila to feel that I saw her as fragile and unable to cope but I *was* concerned for her safety—suicide attempts had been made before. I responded affirmatively to Sheila's request for more sessions and phone contact because I was aware that we were delving into very painful material and that she had felt unheard and unresponded to by her mother during her molest. It was therefore imperative that I provide for her a different experience: that I acknowledge how painful and destructive the abuse was and convey to her that I would respond and provide a safe place for her. Having more contact with her was part of that message. During the sessions I also conveyed my feeling that she had strength and that asking for support during a difficult phase demonstrated her strengths in knowing to ask for what she needed. I also emphasized that she had choice: we could increase or decrease the number of sessions and phone contacts depending on what she felt she needed. I understood that Sheila needed to feel safe and develop trust before she could truly venture out and become an autonomous adult—and that I represented her secure base at this point. I felt confident that as we explored and diffused this highly charged material (of her molest and the lack of protection she had experienced) she would be able to move on and would not need or want to call and/or come in as frequently, especially as she got involved in other social activities. And that is exactly what occurred. I would not necessarily respond to all clients in the way just described. Sheila's personal history, of her cries for help and security not being heard, suggested this particular response. Responses have to be specific to client needs and have to take into account the client's history.

At first Sheila presented with what seemed like intense rage at her mother for not protecting her. This rage was fueled by her conviction that she would have done anything in the world for her mother. As she moved beyond the rage, her profound sadness emerged. She had always fantasized that if she was a "good enough" daughter, her mother would love her and be there for her emotionally and physically. The issue of "good enough" is especially intense for minority children who are bombarded with negative stereotypes and ranked as second class citizens. As we will see later, it was important for Sheila to know that my caring about her was not contingent on her behavior, that is, that I would always view her as "good enough" to care about, even when she acted out.

At this point Sheila focused intensely on her mother's lack of active support and her emotional aloofness following the abuse disclosure. Further, since her mother did not intervene when some friends and family members asked Sheila to withdraw the charges against her stepfather, Sheila felt certain that this was additional indication of her lack of worth. Group therapy was extremely useful in untangling the issues here. Sheila's ability to have empathy for other incest survivors and the lack of protection they had experienced made it possible for her to consider explanations other than her unworthiness for what had happened to her.

I was aware of my own countertransference at this point, including anger at Sheila's mother for not protecting her, sadness for all she had suffered, and wanting to somehow make up for it. Yet I knew that Sheila was extremely resilient, and what she needed most was empowerment. I felt that this would come about as she began to heal and experience greater control over her life's course. I was also careful in how I conveyed my feelings because I did not want to limit the expression of her full range of feelings, including positive ones, toward her mother.

During this phase Sheila grieved the loss of her fantasized mother. She did this by talking about their relationship, her wishes, and her disappointments. She also, at this time, engaged in behavior that seemed to test the boundaries of our relationship. She seemed to be exploring if I would be willing to substitute as her fantasized mother. Given my feelings of sadness for the lack of protection and lack of consistent affirmation she had experienced, I had to work hard to keep my feelings in check and always asked myself if my responses were in her best interest.

CLIENT: Would you give me a ride home today?

THERAPIST: Sheila, I'm not completely sure what brought this request up today. Do you have any thoughts about this?

CLIENT: I just want you to give me a ride home, that's all.

THERAPIST: I would like to check something out with you. I could be wrong and if I am, just tell me so. One thought I have is that we have been talking about your mother and how much you wanted her to be there for you and take care of you. Does your request for me to drive you home have anything to do with wishing to be taken care of, perhaps by me?

CLIENT: (Silent, begins to tear up).

THERAPIST: (after several minutes): Could we talk about how you are feeling?

Sheila then stated that she was hurt and disappointed that I had not granted her request. I expressed my understanding of her feelings and appreciation at her willingness to share these with me. This gave her permission to express her anger at me, anger that I was available to her only on "my terms," that is, in the therapeutic relationship. She wanted more of my time and attention. Given her childhood deprivation, this was very understandable and I applauded her direct expression of feelings. Yet, her childhood had also contained boundary violations, so maintaining strict boundaries was absolutely essential. This was a very sensitive juncture and I tried to communicate to her that I valued her and our relationship and that I would not violate the boundaries of that relationship. I said this very concretely ("Your thoughts, feelings, and needs are important to me"), described the process of our relationship thus far, and indicated how this process reflected my attempt to convey that I valued her ("I listen closely and asks lots of questions because I want you to realize that I value you and your point of view") and would not violate the boundaries of the relationship ("I also want you to know that the rules of our relationship won't change and that I won't ask you to do things for me or act in ways that are not proper. You have told me how hurt and confused you were when your stepfather was kind and acted like a father at times but then forced you to have sex at other times. I want you to know that our relationship won't change. Driving you home would begin to change our relationship").

This became a very rich phase of therapy, with many of her issues being addressed in the context of our relationship. For example, she would occasionally ask me to do things for her which were outside the boundaries of our relationship like calling her teacher to excuse her from a particular class period. In Sheila's case, these requests were almost always connected to wanting to be taken care of. Over time she was able to make many of these connections herself and would with much humor say that soon she could be her own psychologist.

I considered it healthy that Sheila was, in our relationship, trying out the child role by asking to be taken care of rather than being the caretaker. We talked about this—the extent to which it was positive and the ways she could appropriately ask for caretaking in her everyday life. This in fact reduced Sheila's self-isolation in her foster home and she became much more integrated in the family and their activities. We did, however, also talk about the risks in asking to be cared for, especially if the person she was asking for caretaking might take advantage of her vulnerability as her step-father had done.

Sheila's earlier relationships had been characterized by support only when she was compliant and pleasing others. As discussed in the Orienting Constructs section, I was alert to these templates and carefully considered my responses so that I would provide for her a more corrective response. In the early part of therapy Sheila had continued this compliant and submissive stance. She always solicited my thoughts about various issues, rarely disagreed with me, and so forth. I responded to this by encouraging her to express *her* views and supported her expressions of her feelings and needs. On occasion, her caretaking script emerged. I had injured my knee and came to work in a knee brace. She immediately offered to reschedule the session so I could go home and rest. Knowing that she had often sought opportunities to meet her mother's needs, and that there had often been role-reversals in that relationship, I felt it important to convey to her that in this relationship she did not have to take care of me. My response had to be couched in as respectful and helpful a way as possible, since I did not want to suggest that taking care of others was a bad thing. So I acknowledged the kindness in the gesture but also the fact that it would be inappropriate for me to be taken care of by her. We connected this to other relationships (e.g., with mother and stepfather) and explored the appropriateness of the roles she had had to take in those relationships.

As time progressed Sheila tested the relationship further in several ways. For example, she began to call and ask to change appointment times. On one occasion she missed a session without canceling. I believed that each of these instances involved her testing our relationship. On each occasion, she expressed the expectation that I would be angry, and we were able to address her expectations and what she anticipated would result from my anger. These experiences provided me the opportunity to respond differently to her and convey repeatedly that although certain things were important to me, such as calling to cancel an appointment, violating my rules or expectations was not going to fracture our relationship.

In this process, Sheila was learning that she did not have to be a "good" client to have my attention and support. Knowing that we would remain connected even when she acted out helped solidify further the concept that she was worthy and that I cared about her, her "flaws" notwithstanding.

A stumbling block, which had to be dealt with repeatedly, was the issue of dissociation. While dissociating had at times been a functional coping strategy, it now had the potential of limiting her recovery and her ability to accept all parts of herself. I had to find a nonjudgmental way of addressing this, which I did simply by framing this as a coping strategy that was no longer useful. I then asked her permission to address this whenever it seemed that she was dissociating ("Sheila, you have suddenly become quiet, are you still with me?"). I encouraged her to self-monitor so she could recognize the early signs of detaching and ground herself in her physical environment by touching her chair, noticing that she was wearing shoes of a particular color, and so forth. Sheila became quite adept at this, which was very important in helping her be present with her thoughts and feelings. I believed that these steps were necessary for greater self-acceptance and integration of thoughts, feelings, and experiences.

Throughout the early phases of therapy, identity issues were touched upon and addressed within the context of early life experiences and how these had contributed to who she was. The task, as we moved into the next phase, was to work with Sheila on magnifying her strengths and support her acceptance of these. Further, we needed to address factors that may impede establishment of meaningful and gratifying relationships. Finally, as Sheila became more present and future oriented, we would deal with her hopes, dreams, and goals for the future.

Phase 3. Sheila had begun the process of self-redefinition when she decided not to recant her charges against her stepfather. In that process, she had begun to acknowledge her worth. In addition, by not recanting, she had made a choice that went against the wishes of the people who had been important in her life, a major departure from her old method of operating. This had, off course, produced tremendous anxiety in her, but she received a great deal of support from her incest survivors group, from a family who had befriended her at her new church, and from me. This process seemed to free Sheila to begin to acknowledge other, previously hidden, interests, such as her interest in music. She joined the choirs at church and at school, where she experienced an increased sense of competence and established new relationships. Sheila had always been very gifted academically but had not functioned to her potential. As her depression lifted and her ability to concentrate improved, her school performance also improved. These factors were significant in her current self-concept, and her old views of herself as worthless, helpless, and hopeless were now visibly challenged.

Several interpersonal challenges existed. Although she began to establish new relationships with people at her church and at her school, her old interpersonal script sometimes emerged and interfered. For example, she sometimes engaged in activities or responded in ways that she thought would please her friends, and she would later feel resentful. We worked on Sheila's identification of her wishes and on ways to express these, often role playing interpersonal scenarios. We also worked on identifying the costs and the benefits of various relationships and she was encouraged to actively and deliberately choose whom she wanted as close friends. Her new initiative in this paid off when she developed a best friend whose family also welcomed Sheila into their lives. The first real disagreement in this relationship was seen by me as a sign of progress: Sheila's willingness to disagree and express her own viewpoint with someone she valued was a sign of growth and normal adolescent behavior.

Sheila did in fact begin to look toward the future with increased positive anticipation. An interesting note about her future goals was that she thought she might like to become a nurse—certainly a functional and appropriate arena in which to be a caretaker!

REVISED TREATMENT PLAN

Although the overall goals did not change, the relative importance of the various issues shifted. For example, as my relationship with Sheila solidified, her profound sadness at the loss of her relationship with her mother emerged, and a substantial proportion of therapy was spent reminiscing about that relationship and addressing the loss she experienced. Although she initially focused on what she could have done differently or better to have maintained her mother's support, realizing that the past was not changeable and expressing her anger and sadness allowed her to move on and use some of her energy toward development of other support systems. Sheila also invited her mother to several therapy sessions. Although Mrs. B. was at first quite hesitant about this, she did later attend and this process was extremely useful in helping both mother and daughter develop empathy for each other and slowly begin the process of reestablishing a relationship. These sessions occurred in the later part of Sheila's therapy, when she was further along in her individual work. This was important because Sheila was now somewhat more realistic in her expectations of her mother and we continued to talk about these, so she would not expect too much and be disappointed. Having more contact with her mother also allowed Sheila increased access to her siblings, which was very meaningful for her. Unfortunately, I left the agency soon after this. At this point, Sheila and I had been meeting for almost 15 months. I had been seeing her once a week, except for a five month period during which I saw her twice a week. The therapist who took over the case had agreed to meet with both Sheila and her mother on an occasional basis. I was also aware that the whole family (Sheila, mom, and siblings) would probably need to meet together in therapy at some future time.

BALANCING GOALS

The issue of being an active but not a directive therapist had to be balanced. It was important that Sheila be encouraged to make choices for herself given her history of having to comply with the demands of others in her own home. Furthermore, in a society where she was faced with restricted options by virtue of her gender and race, empowerment was a critical therapeutic goal. Sheila's developing self-esteem, her increased involvement in rewarding activities, establishment of affirming relationships, and recognition of those aspects of her life in which she could make choices were all significant in this respect. I believe that in Sheila's case my status as an African American woman was important in providing a sense that while success might be more difficult for women of color, it was attainable.

Meyer (1993) writes compellingly about the need for survivors of abuse to have a holding environment with a therapist who can allow and tolerate "phase appropriate dependence" while also looking for opportunities to encourage growth and maturation. This is a critical balance, especially with children and adolescents, who have typically had inadequate nurturance and care but also clearly need empowerment and self-determination. I often found myself questioning my responses and looking for the most appropriate balance whenever Sheila requested more contact, advice, and so forth. I did not want to foster dependence yet wanted to convey caring and consistent support as she dealt with the very painful issues in her life.

Another balancing issue involved confronting memories of the abuse. While doing this yielded discomfort and intensified her symptoms, it needed to be done. The task became one of exploring while providing support. I had to be careful not to panic or overreact to an increase in symptoms, since she needed to know that I could tolerate and remain present with her in her pain and know that I believed she had the strength and resilience to cope with it. At the same time, I had to acknowledge the significance and intensity of her pain so she would know she was being heard. This was especially important in light of the fact that she felt her parents had not heard her when she had been suicidal earlier. So I acknowledged the enormity of her hurt and also affirmed her strengths and ways in which she had taken control of her life.

The issue of providing clients a secure, contained environment, where they can remember and feel without fear of being abandoned no matter what the intensity of their pain, while at the same time affirming their strengths and assisting them find even more adaptive ways of coping, is one I face repeatedly with clients and guides my work.

Therapeutic Process

RELATIONAL REENACTMENTS

As mentioned in the Orienting Constructs section, I believe that children develop frames or styles of relating to others based on early life experiences, especially experiences within their families. These then impact therapy, and the therapist-client relationship becomes an arena for reworking these templates. My goal as a therapist is to try to provide for the client a different experience from the one they have had, hopefully one that will be healing for them.

Many of the relational reenactments were described in the therapy process outlined. For example, in Sheila's family, the way to gain approval was to please others, regardless of the emotional cost. This issue was illustrated when Sheila tried to be what she thought a good client should be and wanted to please me by doing the journal even though it was something she did not want to do. In this instance, it was vital that I convey to her that our relationship was not contingent on her compliance or pleasing me. Furthermore, this process communicated acceptance of her feelings as legitimate and encouraged her expression of these.

Given Sheila's experiences with betrayal, her suspiciousness of the consistency and stability of our relationship if she acted out was really quite valid. If she directly violated a rule (as she had in reporting her stepfather), would I still support her? She tested this by canceling and rescheduling appointments (often on short notice) and once missed an appointment without canceling. We were able to address this, and still remain connected, which she had not experienced in her relationship with her mother after she reported her stepfather's abuse.

In Sheila's family, role confusion abounded. In addition to the sexual partner role she was forced into with her stepfather, she had been her mother's caretaker. It became important in our relationship that there be absolute clarity in our roles. Thus, for example, when Sheila offered to reschedule after I came to work with a knee brace, I communicated to her that she did not have to take responsibility for my welfare and indicated that I had chosen to come to the office that day. We were able to relate this to the roles she had had at home and talk in a supportive way of appropriate roles in relationships and of adults needing to take responsibility for themselves and their choices.

The boundaries of our relationship also were important in the therapy process and Sheila tested these. An example of this was her asking for a ride home. It was essential, given her experiences with boundary violations, that our boundaries be strictly maintained. Sheila needed to know that the rules of our relationship were firmly established and were not going to change as they had in her relationship with her stepfather.

In addition to the reenactments just described, I also had to be aware of my own countertransference. In many ways Sheila had not had good parenting and I frequently found myself wanting to be her parent and take care of her. I had to frequently remind myself that beyond providing support and assistance with decision making, Sheila was a teenager who needed to be provided with the tools that would empower her and affirm her growing confidence and autonomy.

IMPEDIMENTS TO TREATMENT

Probably the most extreme potential impediment to treatment in the early phases was Sheila's history of extreme compliance with significant others coupled with her severe depression, which made it imperative that I be active yet not directive. I had to be very careful that the changes she made in her life were not for the purpose of pleasing me but were meaningful choices she was making. I was very aware of the fact that she had not had much parenting, so looking to me for guidance made sense. Yet, given her history and the sociopolitical context in which it was embedded, she needed empowerment. Thus, encouraging her self-determination while remaining connected and supportive was important.

Other impediments included Sheila's history of submerging her needs, her decreased ability to access her feelings, and her tendency to dissociate. In providing Sheila with a holding environment for her pain and validating her responses as appropriate given her history, she began to remember and feel. My ability to be with her in her sadness, shame, and rage allowed her to master and integrate these profound emotions, emotions that adolescents cannot contain on their own.

Termination and Therapist's Summary Thoughts

This relationship had been a significant one for both of us. My own issues with caretaking emerged as I contemplated a job offer elsewhere. Sheila and I had together made great progress. However, it was reasonable to expect her to repeatedly rework many of the issues that we had addressed for greater mastery and integration. Other issues, which had not been addressed in our work together, would also need to be focused on. For example, although many adolescents with histories of sexual abuse act out sexually, Sheila was very uncomfortable and awkward in dealing with young men who showed sexual interest in her. Although she had begun to develop some platonic male friendships, one of her crises toward the end of therapy followed an occasion during which one of her male friends told her he was sexually attracted to her. She reported being attracted to men (in the abstract), but felt very awkward and uncertain about developing an intimate sexual relationship. This was clearly an area that needed greater attention, especially as she approached young adulthood. I realized, however, that Sheila was an incredibly resilient young woman who had survived tremendous loss and betrayal. She was doing well in school, was involved in extracurricular activities, and had developed new support systems. She had an affirming incest survivors group and would be able to continue therapy with a new counselor.

Sheila's response to my announcement that I was leaving the agency included alarm, a sense of being abandoned, and anger. She began by acknowledging how important our relationship had become to her and how afraid she was of getting as depressed as she had been. I, in turn, conveyed that this had been an important relationship for me and that it had been a privilege for me to work with her. I also invited her to share the range of feelings she might be experiencing:

THERAPIST: I appreciate you telling me how important this relationship has been for you. I wonder if my leaving raises any other feelings for you?
CLIENT: What do you mean?
THERAPIST: Over the past year we have found it helpful to talk about both the good and the bad feelings that come up in different situations, as

well as the good and bad feelings we have about people. I want to check and see if you feel you could talk with me about all the different feelings that my leaving raises for you.

CLIENT: (tears in her eyes) I'm frightened, and sad, and mad.

THERAPIST: Yes. There are lots of different feelings . . .

CLIENT: I'm afraid I might get depressed again and I won't have you to come to. And part of me is mad because I have come to trust you and told you lots of things and now you are leaving me.

THERAPIST: Part of you is angry with me because it feels as though I am abandoning you and it makes you wonder if it was a good thing to trust and share yourself with me?

CLIENT: I know you've helped me a lot and talking about my anger makes it seem as though I don't appreciate it.

THERAPIST: I know you appreciate me. However, your anger at me also makes a lot of sense. I appreciate it when you can share both the good and bad feelings you might have about me. It makes me feel that we can be honest and genuine with each other, that our relationship is not phony.

We spent much of the remaining eight weeks talking about her relationships with others and with me, underscoring her strengths and the gains she had made, and discussing the potential "mine fields" (i.e., her interpersonal tendencies that sometimes got in the way of developing fulfilling relationships). We also began to look forward, and Sheila spoke hopefully of going on to college. What a contrast from the despondent, hopeless young woman I had first seen at intake! I could see that Sheila was now responding to herself with the same caring attitude that I held toward her, and I felt that she was taking a part of me with her that might prove helpful as she encountered new challenges. I felt certain that her intelligence and her increased awareness of her strengths and weaknesses and of her patterns of relating to others would serve her well in the future.

REFERENCES

American Psychiatric Association. (1994). *Diagnostic and statistical manual of mental disorders* (4th ed.). Washington, DC: Author.

Araji, S., & Finkelhor, D. (1986). Abusers: A review of the research. In D. Finkelhor and Associates, *A sourcebook of child sexual abuse,* pp. 89-118. Beverly Hills: Sage.

Beck, A. T., Rush, A. J., Shaw, B. F., & Emery, G. (1979). *Cognitive therapy of depression.* New York: Guilford.

Beitchman, J. H., Zucker, K. J., Hood, J. E., DaCosta, G. A., & Akman, D. (1991). A review of the short-term effects of child sexual abuse. *Child Abuse and Neglect,* 537-556.

Briere, J., & Zaidi, L. (1989). Sexual abuse histories and sequelae in female psychiatric emergency room patients. *American Journal of Psychiatry, 46*(12), 1602-1606.

Browne, A., & Finkelhor, D. (1986). Impact of child sexual abuse: A review of the research. *Psychological Bulletin, 99,* 66-77.

Damon, L., & Card, J. (1992). Incest in young children. In R. Ammerman & M. Hersen, *Assessment of family violence.* New York: Wiley.

DeJong, A., Hervada, A., & Emmett, G. (1983). Epidemiological variations in childhood sexual abuse. *Child Abuse and Neglect, 7,* 155-162.

Downs, W. (1993). Developmental considerations for the effects of childhood sexual abuse. Special issue: Research on treatment of adults abused in childhood. *Journal of Interpersonal Violence, 8*(3), 331-345.

Finkelhor, D. (1990). Early and long-term effects of child sexual abuse: An update. *Professional Psychology: Research and Practice, 21*(5), 325-330.

Finkelhor, D. and Associates. (1986). *A Sourcebook on child sexual abuse* (pp. 15-59). Beverly Hills: Sage.

Finkelhor, D., & Browne, A. (1985). The traumatic impact of child sexual abuse: A conceptualization. *Journal of Orthopsychiatry, 55*(4), 530-541.

Finkelhor, D., Hotaling, G., Lewis, I., & Smith, C. (1990). Sexual abuse in a national survey of adult men and women: Prevalence, characteristics, and risk factors. *Child Abuse and Neglect, 14,* 19-28.

Green, A. (1993). Child sexual abuse: Immediate and long-term effects and intervention. *Journal of the American Academy of Child and Adolescent Psychiatry, 32*(5), 890-902.

Heiman, M. (1992). Annotation: Putting together the puzzle: Validating allegations of child sexual abuse. *Journal of child psychology and psychiatry, 33*(2), 311-329.

Heras, P., Gomez, M., & Thomas, J. (1992). Cultural considerations in the assessment and treatment of child sexual abuse. *Journal of Child Sexual Abuse,* 119-124.

Kendall-Tackett, K., Williams, L., & Finkelhor, D. (1993). Impact of sexual abuse on children: A review and synthesis of recent empirical studies. *Psychological Bulletin, 113,* 164-180.

Kercher, G., & McShane, M. (1984). The prevalence of child sexual abuse victimization in an adult sample of Texas residents. *Child Abuse and Neglect, 8,* 495-501.

Lindholm, J., & Willey, R. (1986). Ethnic differences in child abuse and sexual abuse. *Hispanic Journal of Behavioral Sciences, 8*(2), 111-125.

McFarlane, K., & Krebs, S. (1986). Techniques for interviewing and evidence gathering. In K. McFarlane & J. Waterman (Eds.), *Sexual Abuse of Young Children: Evaluation and Treatment,* New York: Guilford.

Mennen, F. (1995). The relationship of race/ethnicity to symptoms in childhood sexual abuse. *Child Abuse and Neglect, 1,* 115-124.

Meyer, W. (1993). In defense of long-term treatment: On the vanishing holding environment. *Social Work, 38*(5), 571-578.

Morrow, K., & Sorell, G. (1989). Factors affecting self-esteem, depression, and negative behaviors in sexually abused female adolescents. *Journal of Marriage and the Family, 51,* 677-686.

Peters, S., Wyatt, G., & Finkelhor, D. (1986). Prevalence. In D. Finkelhor and Associates, *A sourcebook on child sexual abuse* (pp. 15-59), Beverly Hills: Sage.

Russell, D. (1986). *The secret trauma: Incest in the lives of girls and women.* New York: Basic Books.

Tzeng, O. & Schwarzin, H. (1990). Gender and race differences in child sexual abuse correlates. *International Journal of Intercultural Relations, 14,* 135-161.

U. S. Department of Health and Human Services (1988). *Study of National Incidence and Prevalence of Child Abuse and Neglect: 1988.* Washington, DC: Author.

Wyatt, G. (1985). The sexual abuse of Afro American and White American women in childhood. *Child Abuse and Neglect, 9,* 507-519.

Wyatt, G. (1990). The aftermath of child sexual abuse of African American and White American women: The victim's experience. *Journal of Family Violence, 5,* 61-81.

Wyatt, G. and Peters, S. (1986). Issues in the definition of child sexual abuse in prevalence research. *Child Abuse and Neglect, 10,* 231-240.

SUGGESTIONS FOR FURTHER READING

Treatment of Sexual Abuse in Children and Adolescents

Everstine, D., & Everstine, L. (1989). *Sexual trauma in children and adolescents.* New York: Brunner/Mazel. Provides useful guidelines for assessment and treatment of children and adolescents.

McFarlane, K., Waterman, J., and Associates. (1986). *Sexual Abuse of Young Children: Evaluation and Treatment,* New York: Guilford. Very practical, especially for those working with young children.

Multicultural Issues in Counseling

Gibbs, J., Huang, L., and Associates. (1989). *Children of color: Psychological interventions with minority youth.* San Francisco: Jossey-Bass Publishers. Provides useful guidelines for assessing and treating minority children.

The following are journal references that address the issue of multicultural competence in counseling.

Multiculturalism as a fourth force in counceling [Special issue]. (1991). *Journal of Counciling and Development, 70*(1).

Sue, S., & Zane, N. (1987). The role of culture and cultural techniques in psychotherapy: A critique and reformulation. *American Psychologist, 42,* 37-45.

Chapter 5

CHILDREN OF DIVORCE

CASE ILLUSTRATION OF MARY:
A 12-YEAR-OLD NATIVE AMERICAN GIRL

Edward Teyber, Ph.D.

THE ISSUES

I am interested in how children maintain secure attachments under stress—and in understanding the life experiences that threaten children's all-important ties to their caregivers. As a child psychologist practicing in California since the 1970s, parental divorce and postdivorce family relations has been the most common family stressor and presenting child problem I have seen. Helping these children and their parents cope with marital disruption has given me a window to better understand how parents and children can lose or preserve the security of their emotional ties to each other. In pursuing these clinical interests that highlight for me what is most human about us, I have enjoyed finding that there is a wealth of empirical research on children and divorce that I could readily apply to help children adjust more successfully. In this first section, I will summarize these extensive research findings that differentiate the factors determining whether children will be able to attain a healthy or problematic adjustment to divorce. In the second section on treatment, I will use the case example of 12-year-old Mary and her family to illustrate basic guidelines for treating children of divorce.

Social Context and Prevalence of Divorce

Why are there so many divorces nowadays? Why do so many children have to cope with this profound disruption that evokes such painful feelings? Perhaps, as one sometimes hears, "People just don't care anymore." Such a simple assignment of blame is often heard, but it is not very accurate. Complex and far-reaching social changes have occurred throughout this century that have led to profound changes in family roles and relationships. Urbanization and industrialization throughout this century, women entering the work force during and after World War II, and control over fertility through birth control in the 1960s have all contributed to a shift in traditional roles, responsibilities, and decision-making power in the family. As a result of these sweeping social changes, and public policy changes, such as the adoption of no-fault divorce, the divorce rate doubled between 1960 and 1975. The divorce rate peaked in 1979–80, but it is still high. In fact, the U.S. Census Bureau predicts that about one half of all new marriages in the 1990s will end in divorce within ten years. As a result, over 1.1 million children will be going through divorce every year (U.S. Department of Health and Human Services, 1990).

Because of the escalating divorce rate, researchers began studying the effects of divorce on children intensively in the 1970s. As we will see, they have learned a great deal about children's reactions to divorce, as well as the family process variables that predict children's successful versus problematic long-term adjustment. Because familiarity with these normative reactions to divorce can help child therapists respond more effectively, these findings are summarized below. Readers interested in examining these research findings more carefully may examine several excellent reviews of the empirical literature (Hetherington, 1991; Emery, 1988; Grych & Fincham, 1992; Hetherington, Cox, & Cox, 1985; Rutter, 1987; Santrock & Warshak, 1986; Wallerstein & Kelly, 1980). The findings I will discuss are drawn from these research reviews.

Children's Reactions to Divorce

Marital disruption is profoundly painful to most children. Almost all children will be very upset by the initial breakup and show more anger, fear, depression, and guilt during the first year. Therapists should expect that most children do not understand what is happening, will be shocked and surprised by the separation even though it did not happen suddenly, and will not welcome the breakup in any way unless they have been witnessing physical violence. These troubled reactions that many children initially experience in response to the marital breakup and one parent moving out of the home usually lessen during the second year. In contrast to children's shorter term reactions, children's long-term reactions to divorce vary greatly. Thus, child adjustment does not depend on divorce per se, but on family process variables that determine how parents and significant others respond to the child during and after the separation. In particular, therapists should note that the most important factors that shape children's successful versus problematic long-term adjustment to divorce are: (1) the degree of parental conflict children are exposed to; and (2) the quality of parenting (especially discipline) they receive after the breakup. That is, children who are not exposed to ongoing parental conflict (Wallerstein, Corbin, & Lewis, 1988);

receive effective parenting and discipline practices (Maccoby & Martin, 1983; Hetherington, 1991); and experience warm and accepting relationships with both parents (Camara & Resnick, 1988; Guidubaldi, Perry, & Nastasi, 1987) usually adjust to divorce very well.

Children's responses to marital disruption are also influenced by socioenvironmental stressors children may be experiencing, such as poverty or living in a neighborhood with high crime and violence. As we will see below, most of the research reported here was done with Caucasian, middle-class families. While many of these responses are evident in poor and economically disadvantaged families, they are often magnified by the *multiple stressors* of economic deprivation and less time with the remaining parent who may have to work longer hours to make ends meet. Further, the stressful impact of divorce is likely greater in Asian, Hispanic, Catholic, and other ethnic/religious families where marital disruption is atypical and more or less unsanctioned. With these considerations in mind, let's see how children's reactions to divorce vary between boys and girls and how it can affect children differently at different ages.

Age Differences

PRESCHOOLERS

In response to the initial shock of marital disruption, preschool children will feel sad, cry more often, and become more demanding. Children will also regress and may resume thumb sucking, hitting siblings, or needing help to feed themselves. Boys tend to become noisier, angrier, and more restless, often disrupting group activities at nursery school and losing the ability to play cooperatively with other children. Some girls tend to become "perfect" and become overly concerned with being neat and good. Preschool children will also be anxious and have more nightmares, bedwetting, masturbating, and fear of leaving the parent.

SIX TO EIGHT YEARS OF AGE

Conflicting findings have been reported, but most researchers suggest that divorce seems to be especially difficult for 6- to 8-year-old children. Boys at this age are especially upset by the breakup and will usually be more distressed than girls. The primary reaction of children at this age is sadness. They are most likely to cry openly about the marital disruption and will often be sad and weepy. They tend to long for the out-of-home parent, and boys in particular may miss their father intensely. Sadly, children at this egocentric age are especially likely to believe that they have been rejected by the departing parent. As a result, they come to feel that they are basically "unlovable." This results in lowered self-esteem and loss of initiative and depression, evidenced by a sharp decline in school performance, as they have trouble concentrating in school. In particular, it is common for both the parents and the therapist to underestimate how *worried* these children are about their parents' well-being during and after the breakup, and how invested they may be in trying to prevent the divorce and restore their original intact family.

NINE TO TWELVE YEARS OF AGE

Whereas the primary feeling for 6- to 8-year-olds is sadness, it often changes to anger for 9- to 12-year-olds. These children may be intensely angry at both parents for the breakup or especially angry at the parent who initiated the separation (or at least the one who is blamed for the breakup). Unfortunately, *children at this stage are highly prone to taking sides with one parent against the other and to assigning blame.* As a result, these children are especially vulnerable to becoming embroiled in destructive parental battles in which one parent seeks to blame, harass, or get revenge on the other. In addition to aligning with one parent against the other, these children also express anger in other ways. In particular, many single-parent mothers report that it is "impossible" to discipline their 9 to 12-year-old sons. Simultaneously, these children may angrily reject their out-of-home father's attempts to spend time with them. Taking this one step further, boys who are temperamentally difficult and already challenging to parents may be especially vulnerable to the disruption of divorce.

As we will see in the following case study with Mary, anger is not the only reaction experienced by these children. They are also sad about the breakup, worried about their parents' well-being, afraid about what is going to happen to them, and lonely. In particular, children at this age feel *powerless.* They do not want the divorce, miss their intact families, long for the out-of-home parent, and feel helpless to alter the enormous changes occurring in their lives. These experiences are especially pernicious for children belonging to minority groups or from low SES families where lack of control and feelings of powerlessness are prevalent. Fueled by angry defiance and profound feelings of helplessness, school performance drops markedly for about one half of the children in this age group. Other symptoms, such as troubled peer relationships and somatic complaints (e.g., headaches, stomachaches) may emerge during this age period as well. Kinship ties often can serve as a helpful buffer or resiliency factor for these children.

Strong gender differences also have been found in school-aged children's reactions to divorce. In the two years following divorce, boys from divorced homes are far more likely to be in conflict with their custodial mothers and disobey them than boys from intact homes. In contrast, school-aged girls from divorced families are likely to function as well as girls in intact two-parent homes and get along well with their custodial mothers—at least until adolescence when the level of mother-daughter conflict often increases substantially.

ADOLESCENCE

Fewer adolescents experience parental divorce, as most divorces occur when children are younger. When divorce does occur, however, the responses of adolescents tend to vary greatly. On the one hand, adolescents adjust to the family disruption better than younger children. This occurs because they are becoming more independent and removed from family relations and do not need as much nurturance and guidance as younger children. Adolescents usually cope with the divorce by distancing themselves from the parental relationship and becoming more involved in their own plans and future. Refreshingly, some adolescents show a positive developmental spurt in response to the marital disruption. These young people are often very helpful to their parents and younger siblings during this family crisis. Their own maturity and compassion can be seen as they participate constructively in family decisions, help with household responsibilities, and provide stable, nurturing relationships to younger siblings.

On the other hand, many adolescents feel betrayed by the divorce. Some adolescents will angrily disengage from the family and may begin acting out sexually, especially if they see their own parents readily become involved in other sexual relationships. Other adolescents may become depressed, withdraw from peers and family involvement, or lose their plans and ambitions for their own futures. Like older school-aged children, adolescents are also going to have far more significant adjustment problems when they are pulled into "loyalty conflicts." Loyalty conflicts are common after divorce and occur when children feel they must take sides in parental arguments or choose one parent over the other, rather than being given permission to love and be close to both parents at the same time. For most adolescents, however, the main concern is about their own future. In particular, they often worry about how the marital failure will influence their own future ability to have a good marriage or their ability to go to college. Their concerns seem valid, unfortunately, as one of the primary long-term effects of divorce for some late-adolescents is a decreased ability to succeed academically in college and to achieve occupationally during their early adult years.

Gender Differences

In addition to these age differences, researchers find marked gender differences for children in the years following divorce. Although there has been increasing attention to joint custody and father-headed families, about 90% of all children of divorce in the 1990s still reside with a custodial mother.

There are disparate research findings here, but better controlled studies find that the problems caused by marital conflict, divorce, and life in the care of a single mother are more pervasive for young boys than they are for young girls. Boys in single-mother families, in contrast to girls in single-mother families and to children in intact homes, have more long-term adjustment problems. Younger boys tend to be more dependent and help-seeking, whereas older boys are more aggressive and disobedient. Compared to girls, boys in single-mother-headed homes also exhibit more behavior problems at school and at home, have more trouble getting along with friends at school, and have poorer school achievement. Two years after the divorce, preadolescent girls in mother-headed families tend to be as well adjusted as girls in intact two-parent homes. In contrast, there tends to be an increasingly widening gap over time between the problematic behavior of boys in mother-headed homes and the better adjustment of boys in two-parent homes. The evidence of greater difficulty in raising boys after divorce is especially noted in sibling relationships. Researchers find more anger and conflict between sons, and between sons and daughters, than between sisters. This greater difficulty in handling sons after divorce may be one reason why the 1990 U.S. Census finds that parents with sons are 9% less likely to divorce than parents with daughters.

These significant gender differences between boys and girls change as children grow into adolescence, however. Better controlled studies continue to suggest that divorce is harder for young boys than girls. This occurs because boys tend to lose their primary identification-figure and source of discipline when father moves out and to receive more anger and criticism from custodial mothers than girls. However, when girls reach adolescence, conflict often escalates between single mothers and daughters to match the level of conflict between young sons and mothers. In addition to increasing mother-daughter conflict, adolescent girls are likely to develop problems in dating and heterosexual relations—especially if their father has not been actively involved in their lives. Poignantly, they tend to have sex at an earlier age and with more partners and are likely to marry at a younger age and eventually become divorced themselves. These problems in heterosexual relations and in academic and occupational underachievement tend to continue on into early adulthood. These gender differences become even more complex as families traverse from single-parent divorced families to stepfamilies. For example, researchers also have found that boys tend to adjust positively to the introduction of a responsible stepfather, whereas girls are more likely to struggle with this new addition.

Therapists can often help divorcing parents respond more effectively to their children by educating them about these normative reactions and concerns. Some important qualifications must be emphasized, however. First, these findings on the effects of divorce on children are based on samples of middle-class, Caucasian children. To date, there have been only a few descriptive studies of cultural differences in adults' response to divorce (e.g., African Americans: Isaacs & Leon, 1988, and Fine, McKenry, & Chung, 1992; Mexican Americans: Neff, Gilbert, & Hoppe, 1991, and Wagner, 1988; and Italian Catholics: Dicosta & Nelson, 1988). With the important exception of an educational, school-based group intervention program for mixed race urban children (Alpert-Gillis, Pedro-Carrol, & Cowen, 1989) there is virtually no research on cultural differences in children's reactions to divorce. However, ethnic status and socioeconomic standing will modify how symptoms are manifested, coping styles, help-seeking patterns and willingness to utilize treatment (Tharpe, 1991). With much father absence postdivorce, for example, grandmother-mother-daughter relationships often predominate. In response, sons without a male role model may adopt or act out hypermasculine "protest" behavior. Or, when there are multiple stressors, such as poverty, and no kinship ties to support a single-headed household, family disorganization may result in increased risk for joining gangs.

Economic factors are an essential aspect of divorce that have not been fully understood. Most parents have more economic stress and can provide fewer resources and opportunities for their children following divorce, although the actual extent of economic decline for children after divorce is a very controversial issue in the divorce literature. Duncan and Hoffman (1985) report that only 20% of Black children and 50% of White children lived in families receiving spouse or child support 2 years after the divorce. These researchers also suggest that 40% of women have their incomes cut in half one year after the divorce, leading many children to live in poverty. Further, there is no question that poverty does increase the likelihood of divorce. The 1990 U.S. Census Bureau reports that poor families are twice as likely to dissolve as more affluent families. Such economic stressors lead to increased family mobility and a resulting decrease in kinship networks and family support systems. This becomes especially problematic when it deprives families of grandparents and other surrogate parents who can provide the essential "buffers" that single parents need to cope effectively in the aftermath of divorce. Children become more at risk for a wide range of personal, social and academic problems, as the multiple stressors of poverty, family disruption, and decreased familial supports tax the family's coping abilities.

Finally, it is important to emphasize that the research findings summarized above refer only to the effects of marital disruption on children. These findings do not generalize to other family changes, such as parental death, or to other family forms, such as never-married single parent families. Let's turn now from this general overview of children's reactions to divorce and move closer to the feelings and experiences that divorce can engender. The following case study of Mary will help us see what therapists can do to help children cope with divorce.

CASE ILLUSTRATION

Presenting Problem

Mary entered treatment as an anxious, overweight, and depressed 12-year-old girl. In the months following the stormy breakup of her parents' marriage, Mary changed from a polite, obedient, and overly responsible child, becoming sullen and withdrawn in her new home with her mother. She began quarrelling and arguing with friends and, for the first time, was becoming unresponsive and disobedient toward her teacher. Her school performance, predominated by As and Bs, had fallen off to Cs and Ds since the breakup. Upon the advice of her teacher, her mother reluctantly telephoned for counseling for Mary because she seemed so unhappy.

CLIENT DESCRIPTION

Mary's mother and father (Mrs. and Mr. A.) were both racially mixed: Caucasian and Native American Indian. "Mary" had an Anglo first name and a traditional Indian surname. Her facial features reflected her mixed heritage and she had straight black hair, reddish brown skin, and dark brown eyes. Consonant with cultural norms, Mary was a quiet and reserved child, but she could be engaging to both peers and adults. She was physically inactive and about 20 lbs overweight. Like many children of divorce, Mary was both sad and mad. Although at school and with friends she seemed angry in response to the breakup, her predominant affect was sadness. Diagnostically, Mary initially seemed to present with an Adjustment Disorder with Mixed Anxious and Depressed reactions to the divorce, but her low self esteem and long-standing dysphoric mood more accurately reflected a Dysthymic Disorder.

SOCIAL CONTEXT

Community.   Mary's family lived in a small rural Southwestern community. Mary felt safe and known by classmates and neighbors in their ethnically mixed neighborhood and school. This was a stable but economically-pressed neighborhood of working-poor and blue-collar families, with many working single-parent mothers. In the broader community, a conservative country western ethos was prevalent that emphasized traditional sex roles. Men were expected to fulfill macho roles, such as wearing boots and cowboy hats and carrying rifles in their pick-up trucks, while women were expected to remain in nonachieving work roles and nonassertive caretaking roles.

Although conformity to these traditional sex roles became a primary source of marital conflict for Mrs. A., both parents were highly acculturated and shared middle class values of upward economic mobility and achievement through education. Both parents actively sought advancement at work, attended night classes toward a college degree, and actively supported educational achievement for Mary. In this regard, both parents were uneven in integrating a biracial identity and achieving role flexibility. On the one hand, both parents had the interpersonal range and cultural flexibility to succeed in Anglo business settings (computer sales and office management). Both parents also chose to retain Native American surnames; they valued their Indian heritage, and their social networks included Anglos, Mexicans, and Indians from a range of blue-collar and middle-class families. Although they were successful in achieving this identity integration outside the home in the work and educational sphere, the parents were not able to establish shared values and mutually accepted roles within their marriage.

Family Structure.   The contradictions and uneven aspects of Mary's functioning reflected, in part, her parents' skewed marriage and their unstable family structure. On the one hand, Mary lived in a rigidly hierarchical family. Her father was highly authoritarian and not only demanded strict obedience to every demand but immediate compliance in tone and expression as well. Further, reasons for directives were not given, and compromises and verbal give-and-take were not permitted. Corporal punishment was condoned but not necessary, as Mary simultaneously feared her father and sought his approval. She would not even consider disobeying him—even after the breakup when so many children no longer obey noncustodial fathers. Thus, Mary was intimidated by her stern father but also looked up to him; she looked forward to shared activities, such as horseback riding, target shooting, and watching sports together on television. Mary was subservient to her authoritarian father and grew up watching her mother similarly comply with her domineering husband. There was no effective parental coalition—Mr. A. ruled the family. In Minuchin's (1974) structural terms, the family was organized as $\frac{F}{M\text{-}D}$.

In recent years, however, Mrs. A had became successful at work and earned the respect of her co-workers and superiors. As she received this validation and support at work, she felt more confident and tried to become more equal within the marriage. Her attempts to redefine the marriage in terms of more shared power ultimately failed and precipitated the divorce, but only after several years of escalating marital conflict, when Mary was exposed to her parents mutual yelling, insults, and threats.

Whereas Mary was subservient to her authoritarian father, she acted like a sister to her mother during the marriage and like a parent to her after the breakup. Thus, the rigid boundaries with her father were contrasted with a confusing role structure and lack of clear intergenerational boundaries with her mother. At times, Mary was a close confidante and "best friend" to her mother; at other times, Mary acted like a concerned parent who was worried about Mrs. A's unhappiness and loneliness. Sometimes, they behaved like bickering sisters or competitive peers. Fortunately for Mary, however, Mrs. A. was able to occasionally assume an effective parenting role. That is, despite these confusing role transfers, her mother could discipline Mary effectively and be a source of nurturance and understanding for her at times. These shifting family roles, alliances, and relationships contributed to Mary's complex blend of healthy and symptomatic features.

Initial Session

In treating children of divorce, as in other child therapy, critical events occur in the initial telephone contact and request for treatment that can significantly influence the course and outcome of treatment. In the initial telephone contact, for example, one parent may subtly but successfully enlist the therapist's allegiance in the parental battle. That is, the referring parent may successfully define the other parent as "bad" to the therapist, reconstituting in therapy the same splitting defenses or loyalty conflicts that may be central to the child's symptoms and distress. Or, as occurred in this case, the mother's initial "resistance" to treatment was immediately evident. Without my acknowledging and responding to her initial reluctance on the telephone, Mrs. A. may not have brought Mary to the first session. First, we will explore some important issues in the initial telephone contact with Mrs. A, and then look at how I tried to establish a working relationship with Mary in our initial session.

INITIAL TELEPHONE CONTACT

Although cultural and gender differences were operative between different family members and me throughout treatment, they were far more significant during these initial contacts than at any other time in treatment. For example, Mrs. A. was flat and distant with me in the initial telephone contact—emotionally unconnected. She sounded skeptical and resigned as we discussed Mary's situation—as though she had to comply by calling but did not really want to speak with me, although she knew that Mary was struggling and needed help. I assumed that, based on her life experience, there were very good reasons why she felt this way, although I didn't know what the specific reasons for this were yet. So, I tried to formulate some tentative possibilities or *working hypotheses* about her worldview that might help me respond to her more effectively until I could learn more about her. In particular, I was concerned that she might not follow through with bringing Mary to the initial session if I could not help with this initial resistance, change our interaction or process, and join with her in some way during this initial telephone contact. Rather than ignore her reluctance, wait until therapy sessions began, or simply regard Mary individually as my client, I groped to find ways to join with Mrs. A. In addition to inviting any questions, concerns, or reservations she might have about me or treatment, I tried to reach her by making an empathic connection: "Divorce is harder than most parents expect it to be. And after you work all day and come home to more demands and problems, it can seem too much some days. It really is hard to be a single parent . . ."

She brushed off this empathic attempt, so I looked for other ways to try and engage with her: "Well, it does sound like things have not been going well for Mary, and I can see how hard you've been trying to help her . . ."

Mrs. A. would not allow me to respond to her in this affirming way either, but when I suggested a limited commitment ("Let's just agree to meet for one session . . . I would like to meet with you for about 20 minutes, Mary alone for about 20 minutes, and you and Mary together for about 20 minutes . . . After that, you and Mary will be able to decide for yourselves whether I can be of help or not and, if so, we can decide together how to proceed from there"), she became more responsive and accepted this bid, scheduled an appointment, and brought Mary to the initial session.

Why did this response allow treatment to proceed? It seemed to empower Mrs. A. by giving her more control over the decision to enter treatment, as well as the ability to help shape the direction of treatment. Based on what I had already heard on the phone about both the marital relationship and her cultural expectations, I hypothesized that this response might be helpful because it held out the promise of getting the help she needed without having to comply with me as she may have had to do in other relationships. This initial working hypothesis about compliance and working with her reticence right from the beginning turned out to be important. As I later learned, many relationships with authority figures, and males in particular, had indeed confirmed her expectations of submission and compliance. In therapy, Mrs. A. told me that asking for help from anybody was "unacceptable" for her and that it was "stupid" to even think of asking a male for help. The simple act of having to ask for help for her daughter evoked multiple layers of interlocking conflict and pain for her, including (a) never having had her emotional needs met in her own childhood, (b) humiliating compliance from 12 years of marriage with her domineering husband, and (c) distrust of Anglo authority based on cultural expectations. In this initial telephone contact, Mrs. A. was behaviorally teaching me both what was wrong and how I needed to respond to her and her daughter in order to help them.

INITIAL CHILD CONTACT

Following the initial conjoint session, I began seeing Mary individually to talk about her parents' divorce. It was not a priority for me to obtain any specific history or to make any behavioral changes during the initial conjoint session with her mother or in our first individual session together. Similarly, I did not want her to feel any pressure for self-disclosure or to answer personal questions (Everett, Proctor, & Cartmell, 1983). It was clear from her serious and wary manner in our initial conjoint session that Mary was uncertain about seeing me and unsure of what this therapy business was all about. Simply being in the room with me was pressing against cultural sanctions on drawing attention to herself and seeking help for problems from outsiders. Thus, my initial goals were simply to help her feel okay about talking to me and to be willing to come back and meet with me again. The internal questions that guided my thinking and responses were, How could I establish some sense of safety for her in our relationship, find a way to "join" with her, and begin a more collaborative relationship?

Mary was controlled and somber when she sat down in my office. She folded her hands in her lap and looked at the floor. This was an intimidated and inhibited child, and I was a male, Caucasian, authority figure—with whom she had not felt much safety in the past. Per "client response specificity," it was essential to try and differentiate our relationship from problematic past experiences right from the beginning. My initial working hypotheses from talking to her mother and observing Mary led me to believe that it was essential that I was not perceived as dominating or directive like her father—but as friendlier and more egalitarian. Rather than go right to work on divorce-related issues, I tried to help her be with me in a different way:

THERAPIST: Have you ever seen a psychologist before?
CLIENT: (nonverbally shrugs no)
THERAPIST: What have you been told about why you're here and what we're going to do?
CLIENT: (shrugs shoulders again, suggesting "I don't know")

I made a big to-do about pulling a pocket watch and long chain out of my pocket and pretended to begin hypnotizing her. Mary liked my joke, smiled, and looked into my eyes for the first time. It was a friendly moment and allowed me to explain what therapy was and what we would be doing together. After that, it was much easier to take the next step and begin approaching her divorce-related concerns:

THERAPIST: I've heard your mom and dad are getting a divorce. What's happening?

Mary accepted my open-ended invitation and began telling me about the big events that had shaken her life. Keeping the compliance issues in mind, I followed her lead whenever possible and introduced a series of exploratory topics only as they followed naturally from the material she was presenting (these topic areas will be detailed). Like most children of divorce, she had observed much, had many worries and concerns, and ultimately had much to say:

CLIENT: My dad doesn't live with us anymore. My mom and I live in a new apartment by ourselves.

THERAPIST: That's such a big change. How is it going for you?

CLIENT: I don't know.

THERAPIST: What's the best thing about living in your new apartment with your mother?

CLIENT: Well, my mom and dad don't argue as much.

THERAPIST: That must be a big relief. It's scary to see your mom and dad fight.

CLIENT: Yeah, it's better now . . .

Later in the same session:

THERAPIST: Why did your mom and dad break up? What have you been told about all of this?

CLIENT: I don't know, they just don't get along I guess.

THERAPIST: Have your mom or dad ever talked to you about the divorce or why they broke up?

CLIENT: My Dad and I don't talk together much, and my Mom just starts crying.

THERAPIST: So you have had to figure out all of this on your own and handle everything yourself.

CLIENT: Yeah.

THERAPIST: Well I'm glad you're here with me now so you can have somebody to talk to about all of this. Are there any questions I can answer for you right now?

In this way, I explored a series of divorce-related issues in order to assess what was troubling Mary the most. In addition to assessment, I used this discussion to begin intervening and correcting some important misconceptions she had about the divorce. For example,

THERAPIST: Sometimes children tell me that they think they caused their parents to divorce. Have you ever felt like you were to blame?

CLIENT: Maybe.

THERAPIST: What did you do that might have caused your parents to break up?

CLIENT: Well, they argued about me a lot, you know.

THERAPIST: How so?

CLIENT: My dad would get mad at my mom for being too easy on me. And I think my mom disagreed with my dad because he was too strict with me. I would listen to them arguing about me like that a lot.

THERAPIST: So you think you caused your parents to divorce because they argued over how to discipline you?

CLIENT: Mm hmm.

THERAPIST: Well, yes, Mary, they were arguing with each other over how to raise you, but that doesn't mean that you *caused* them to break up. Lots of kids tell me they feel this way, but children are never responsible for their parents' divorce. You know how some things are child business and other things are adult business? Well, deciding to get married, having a baby, or getting a divorce are all adult decisions that children really have no control over . . .

Thus, by being friendly, interested, and giving her open-ended bids, this intimidated girl could talk to me in important ways about her parents' divorce. By understanding the difficult feelings that the divorce aroused for her and articulating more fully the dilemmas she was coping with, I began to establish credibility with her: ("It's really hard when you feel like you have to take sides between them because you want to be close to both of your parents at the same time"). Mary became increasingly animated and forthcoming with me over the course of our first few individual sessions. She was clearly a responsive and highly workable young client. That she could be so stiff or frozen, initially, and later respond so well, again told me that there were caring and safe aspects of her family life that coexisted along with real threats and problems. I anticipated that treatment would be successful if we could continue the collaborative interpersonal process that we had begun.

Case Conceptualization

I thought about Mary's treatment in three distinct phases. As we have seen, Mary initially presented as anxious, compliant, and overweight. Her parents had recently separated, she had moved to a new apartment with her mother within the past month, and I knew that she had been exposed to much parental wrangling during the breakup. I hypothesized that her compliance and obesity reflected longer-term developmental conflicts, but I did not yet know much about the potential causes and meaning of these symptoms. However, because of her parents' stormy breakup, I knew it was likely that she was highly anxious as a result of being exposed to ongoing parental conflict. To address her anxiety, and because this was the initial mandate I had been given for treatment, I began to assess and help her resolve a series of generic divorce-related issues. This first phase of treatment (6 sessions) was an active, educational and problem-solving approach. Phase 2 (parent education or "coaching" sessions with each parent) and Phase 3 (conjoint parent-child sessions) will be discussed later.

As I mentioned earlier, there has been a great deal of empirical research on the effects of divorce on children and the family process variables that predict how children will adjust. Guided in part by these research findings, I wanted to explore with Mary five topic areas that I find often are linked to how children adjust (Teyber, 1992). Thus the first six sessions comprising Phase One of treatment were spent talking about her parents' breakup in general, and exploring the following five content areas in particular.

   1. *Parental conflict.* Therapists must be sensitized to the fact that divorce will be most problematic for children when they are exposed to ongoing parental conflict. That is, although most children will be initially anxious in response to marital disruption, *children are almost certain to suffer intense anxiety and long-term adjustment problems when they are exposed to chronic or ongoing parental wrangling,* such as arguing, verbal or physical fighting, yelling, threatening, and so forth. In contrast, parents of children who make a secure and successful adjustment may not like or trust each other, but they have the good sense to *shield* children from parental conflicts. Further, they don't *undermine* the other parent to the child (e.g., "Your mother's an idiot, you don't have to listen to her" or "Your father's a liar, why do you want to see him?"). And, they don't *embroil* children in adult conflicts (e.g., "Tell your father the next time he's late with the support check . . .").

I asked Mary directly about this aspect of the breakup.

THERAPIST: How did your parents get along these past few months? Did they argue or fight a lot?
CLIENT: (nods . . . tears)
THERAPIST: They fought a lot, and you were really scared.
CLIENT: (looks down) Yeah.
THERAPIST: What was the scariest thing about their fights?
CLIENT: I was afraid that maybe my dad was going to hurt my mom.
THERAPIST: Yes, you were scared that it wasn't safe for her and she might get hurt. Tell me what happened?
CLIENT: Well, my dad would get real mad and start yelling at her and my mom would start crying and stuff.
THERAPIST: What kind of stuff would happen next?

   2. *Continuity of parent-child relationships.* By two years after the divorce, about one half of all divorced fathers have no regularly scheduled contact with their children. When one parent disengages and fails to fulfill an active part-time parenting role, children internalize responsibility for the parent's uninvolvement. These children usually feel that they are not loveworthy and become depressed, suffer a loss of initiative and decline in school performance, and cannot make realistic long-term plans for their future. Better adjusted children of divorce, in contrast, usually maintain physical and emotional access to both parents following the breakup and do not suffer the loss of a parent through the divorce. This issue quickly emerged in my explorations with Mary.

THERAPIST: What's the worst thing about living in your new apartment with your mother?
CLIENT: I miss my dad.
THERAPIST: How often do you get to see him?
CLIENT: On weekends.
THERAPIST: You wish you could see him more.
CLIENT: Yeah.

THERAPIST: Of course you do. You don't get to see him everyday like you used to. What could we do to help with that feeling?

CLIENT: I don't know.

THERAPIST: Does your dad know you miss him? Do you tell him?

CLIENT: Uh uh.

THERAPIST: What might happen if you told him how you feel?

CLIENT: I don't know. We never really talk together like that.

THERAPIST: What do you think he would do if you told him that you missed him, or if you asked him if you could talk together on the phone every Wednesday night at 8 o'clock?

3. *Loyalty conflicts.* Virtually all children who have long-term problems adjusting to divorce feel they have to take sides and choose between their parents. These children do not have permission to love and be close to both parents at the same time. Instead, these parents give children the message (often nonverbally or in subtle and covert ways) that they have to choose to be close to one parent at the expense of closeness to the other. For example, the mother may look sad or hurt when the son expresses how eager he is to visit Dad, or the father may feel mad when the daughter expresses how much she misses her mother. Therapists must keep in mind that almost every child wants to be close to both parents—no matter how limited or superficial that relationship may be described by the other parent or seem to the therapist. Children feel torn apart inside (i.e., stomachaches, headaches, peptic ulcers) when they are pressured by parents or grandparents to take sides between their parents. These already difficult circumstances are exacerbated for biracial children such as Mary. Mary not only had to cope with the challenging developmental task of establishing a biracial identity, but she had to do this in the bifurcated context of not being able to experience a relationship with both parents simultaneously. Feeling how immobilizing these loyalty issues were for her, I tried to help by asking directly about them.

THERAPIST: Your parents argue a lot and haven't been getting along very well. Do you ever feel like you have to take sides between them?

CLIENT: What do you mean?

THERAPIST: Do you ever feel like you get pulled into their fights or have to be on your mom's side or your dad's side?

CLIENT: Oh yeah, my dad gets mad sometimes and says, "You always take her side."

THERAPIST: That wouldn't feel very good to hear. Does your mom feel okay if you miss your dad or want to be with him?

CLIENT: Uh uh. I think it makes her kind of sad.

THERAPIST: This must be very hard for you because you love them both. It's unfair when kids feel they have to take sides and choose between their parents. Children should be allowed to be close to both of their parents at the same time.

CLIENT: Yeah, it is unfair.

4. *Parenting competence.* Divorce can seem commonplace because it occurs so frequently, but therapists must not become habituated to it because it is still an earth-shaking crisis for every family member when it occurs. Most separating parents deny how stressful the divorce will be both for themselves and their children and underestimate how much time and effort it will take to recover emotionally. Researchers find that it often takes parents two to three years to fully regain their equilibrium and that parents often reach a psychological low-point one year after the separation. As a result of their severe and prolonged personal distress, *most adults' parenting competence declines markedly following the breakup.* That is, most parents are not able to nurture, discipline or provide a predictable household organization as effectively as they did before the divorce. This is an especially unfortunate interaction, as children are distressed by the breakup and have heightened emotional needs of their parents at this time. For example, children find much-needed security when parents discipline effectively by providing clear limits and regularly enforced rules. Children also are reassured by predictable daily routines when so many other things in their lives are changing. Thus, a negative interaction often occurs as parents' diminished childrearing capabilities coincide with children's escalating needs. This negative interaction is one of the most important causes of children's symptomatic adjustment to divorce.

I was trying to assess this issue with Mary throughout the initial phase of treatment and wanted to determine if her parents were still parenting her effectively. More specifically, I wanted to know three things: (a) if and how she got her emotional needs met; (b) how discipline was handled in both households; and (c) how much structure, organization and predictability she experienced in her daily life. To answer these, I asked questions such as these:

1. "What do you do when you're sad? Who do you talk to when you're lonely? What would your mom/dad do if you asked him/her to hold you or just sit with you for a minute?"
2. "Are the rules the same or different at your mom's and your dad's house? What happens if you break the rules at your mom's/dad's house? Now that your parents are separated, is it easier for you to get out of doing the chores you used to have to do?"
3. "Tell me about dinnertime. Who decides what you're going to eat? Who prepares dinner? Who sits together? Do you sit at the table or eat in front of the TV? Who cleans up afterwards?" and, "What do you do every morning to get ready for school? Tell me everything that happens. When do you wake up?

Like most children, Mary had clear perceptions about these issues and could describe in detail how her mother and father handled each of these issues. Exploring these three areas confirmed my initial hypothesis that Mary was struggling with long-standing problems beyond the immediate divorce crisis and clarified further problems that needed to be addressed in treatment. In particular, these explorations revealed how Mary was (a) lacking in emotional support from her father and (b) serving as a parentified caretaker for her mother. These two issues became the basis for both the second and the third phases of treatment and will be discussed later.

5. *Explanation for the divorce.* Almost all parents feel painfully guilty about the divorce. Most parents want to do the best they can for their children and worry that their marital failure will hurt their children in some unknown but irreparable way. One of the many problems with excessive parental guilt is that it serves to keep parents from talking to their children about the divorce, in general, as well as from giving children a basic explanation for the divorce and what is going to happen. In the absence of effective parental explanations, children fill the void with their own egocentric and problematic explanations that inevitably blame themselves for the divorce.

For very young children under 5 years of age, and to some extent up to 7- and 8-year-olds, the principal concern that divorce arouses is separation anxieties and abandonment fears. Indeed, in children's eyes, their worst fear often comes true. For example, if dad can suddenly pack up and move out on Saturday morning without any forewarning and without telling children specifically when and where they will see dad next, it is understandable that children worry, won't mom go away too? Children need to be prepared in advance for departures and reassured repeatedly of the continuity of parent-child relationships. For example, parents can say:

> "Mom and dad have decided we are not going to be married anymore. We are going to get a divorce. We are going to live in different houses from now on, but we will still always be your mom and dad. That is never going to change. Dad is going to move to a new apartment on Saturday, and you will be with him at his house on. . . . Even though we are not going to be married anymore, you will always live with one of us. We will both always love you and work together to take care of you until you are grown up. We are going to need to talk together a lot about this, but are there any questions we can answer for you right now?"

Young children are egocentric in their thinking and place themselves at the causal fulcrum of family changes. If you ask preschool and school-aged children if they ever feel responsible or to blame for their parent's divorce, the majority of them will say yes. These children carry an unnecessary burden of blame and guilt for the divorce and occasionally hold fears of reprisals. As we saw earlier, Mary did indeed feel responsible for her parents' divorce because they frequently argued over how to discipline her.

Finally, children also need an explanation for the divorce that does not assign blame. Parents often give ineffective explanations for the divorce that demand children see only one parent's reality as "truth," embroil children in parental conflicts, or draw children into adult conflicts and concerns that are beyond their understanding. This occurs, for example, when one parent explains the divorce by saying, "Your father is leaving *us* for another woman!" or, "Your mother is destroying our family because she wants to meet her own selfish needs."

Such explanations undermine the parenting authority of the other parent to the child and take away that parent as a role model or identification figure. Such explanations cause the child to, in effect, lose a parent through the divorce. Similar to the explanation suggested above, Mary's mother had provided an effective explanation for the divorce that eschewed blame and had been reassurring to Mary. It was important for Mary to receive this effective explanation from her mother because her father insisted that the divorce was her mother's fault and wouldn't have occurred if her mother weren't so "stupid and selfish."

In sum, phase one of treatment lasted six sessions and was successful in reaching limited but important goals: (a) Differentiate myself from other males, authority figures, and Anglos by finding a balance between establishing a friendly working relationship in which Mary received permission to initiate and lead while maintaining the role of therapist and authority that was consonant with her cultural expectations; (b) Assess her current functioning and identify other nondivorce related issues that had been problematic throughout her development and contributed to her longer-term depression; and (c) Help her come to terms with the central worries and concerns precipitated by the divorce.

This short-term, educational and structured intervention reduced her presenting anxiety and improved her mood. Mary had important questions about the divorce answered, certain misconceptions clarified, and her emotional reactions to the breakup affirmed. Through discussions and role play techniques, she also gained some new strategies for coping more effectively with ongoing problems. For example, we worked on having her leave the room when her parents began arguing and telling her parents that she didn't want to carry messages back and forth to the other parent when they asked her to do that.

A brief, educationally oriented intervention such as this is sufficient to help many children of divorce. When parents are willing to participate in treatment and cooperate with guidelines from the therapist (e.g., stop fighting in front of children, ease loyalty conflicts and give children permission to be close to both parents, provide effective explanations for the divorce, and so forth), an effective divorce prevention service can be provided in a short-term modality. In some cases, however, developmental conflicts beyond the immediate divorce crisis will be identified—as occurred with Mary. Thus, rather than terminate after the initial phase, Mary, Mrs. A., and I all mutually agreed to continue meeting. Before examining this second phase of treatment, we will first highlight several orienting constructs that guided these interventions during Phase One.

Orienting Constructs

Guidelines for conceptualizing the first phase of treatment were provided, in part, by the extensive research literature on the effects of divorce on children. Coupling these research findings with my own clinical work with children of divorce, I have found these five topic areas to be closely linked to child adjustment:

1. The extent of interparental conflict;
2. Whether mother and father both assume an active parenting role after the divorce;
3. Loyalty conflicts;
4. The quality of parenting postdivorce; and
5. Parental explanations for the divorce.

I was interested in other issues, of course, but Mary's principal concerns were identified by exploring these five topic areas. As we have seen, Mary did have significant questions and concerns within each of these five areas. Working within this structured/educational modality would not have succeeded, however, without sensitivity to how cultural and gender differences between us were played out along the process dimension. Let's highlight these issues.

It was evident in our initial contact that Mary was anxious and distrustful with me—but also compliant. Her experience with males, authorities, and Caucasians had sometimes been dominating, demanding, and intimidating. Mary could not have taken in and utilized the divorce-related information, problem-solving strategies, and emotional support I offered if I had not: (a) differentiated myself from her past relational experiences and provided a corrective relational experience; and (b) balanced permission to stop complying and begin responding to her own needs with the realities of her cultural context. Let's examine each of these separately.

Mary needed a specific relational experience with me in order to improve in therapy—even in this short-term, educationally oriented modality. If I relinquished a professional role, began to self-disclose and tried to be more of a "friend," or was reluctant to inform, structure, or lead, Mary and I would have recapitulated the ambiguous, embroiled, and sibling-like relationship that she was mired in with her mother. She would have been left again without the security of having an adult effectively in charge. On the other hand, if I was too formal, demanding, or distant, I risked being experienced as her authoritarian father and activating the expectations that she may have to capitulate and comply with me as well. Thus, the central therapeutic task for me was to provide a new "authoritative" relationship where the adult was effective and in charge but still responsive, available, and encouraging. Let's examine this new middle ground more closely.

I tried to provide this corrective relational experience in many ways: being friendly and warm; respecting or honoring her limits and boundaries; being accepting and responsive to her disagreements; asking about and being responsive to any concerns she may have about me or about being in treatment; following her lead whenever possible and supporting her initiatives; and being interested in and responsive to whatever held meaning for her. Knowing that our relationship could have mirrored her problematic experience with her father if I asked questions, gave advice and directives, and she in turn answered and followed my suggestions, I utilized the concept of "giving permission." I encouraged her to talk about whatever was most important to her, took a genuine interest in her chosen topic, and brought in my areas of concern only as they followed naturally from the material she initiated. This collaborative alliance was enlivening for her, as she could lead rather than comply and follow for a change. In this regard, the passivity she evidenced in the beginning decreased in each successive session and was hardly a feature in our interaction by the fourth session.

In parallel, the initial phase of treatment was productive for Mary because her central conflict with her mother was not thematically reenacted in our interaction. As we will see, it soon became evident that Mary was enmeshed with her mother, and saw her mother as needy, vulnerable, and not effectively in control of her own adult life. By being interested and accessible, but still a professional who was capable and in charge, I did not "need" her and experientially differentiated myself from her mother. Clear therapeutic limits and boundaries were especially reassuring to Mary and served to provide a safe and corrective interpersonal environment for her. This was a corrective relational experience for Mary, in part, because it allowed her to feel close to me and let me help her without worrying about being responsible for me or taking care of me, as she had to do with her mother. These same familial patterns were operative on the cultural level as well.

Maintaining my credibility as an effective helper in the process ways described above also was consonant with her cultural expectations. It was important that I balanced giving permission to initiate, lead, and be more assertive with me with the reality of complying, being quiet, and going along, appropriate to her familial and cultural context. That is, I needed to help Mary distinguish situations/relationships where it was safer to be compliant and when this was not necessary. Within her cultural context, I also needed to affirm that following or being quiet and deferential were also valuable and appropriate ways to behave at times toward some others in her life. We will see how I had to balance Mary's cultural prescription to respect and honor her parents with permission to stop taking care of her mother and begin attending to her own needs as well. Without working with the cultural meanings that these changes held for her and helping her to make these important discriminations and find a new balance, I would have lost my "credibility" and been ineffective in helping her resolve her problems within the parameters of her life situation. Thus, assessing and providing the specific relational experiences that each client needs is a central, orienting construct for me, but I cannot do this effectively without appreciating the cultural context that shapes the client's subjective worldview.

Treatment Plans and Intervention Strategy

INITIAL TREATMENT PLAN

I formulated initial treatment goals for phase one, intermediate goals for phase two, and longer-term treatment goals for phase three, and corresponding intervention strategies for reaching each of these. In phase one, I simply wanted to engage this reluctant mother and daughter in treatment and establish a working alliance. Beyond this general aim, my goals in phase one were to (1) identify Mary's principal divorce-related concerns via exploring the five topic areas presented earlier and (2) begin assuaging these concerns wherever possible. More specifically, I tried to help with her divorce-related concerns by providing (a) explanations and normative information where needed, (b) validation for her emotional reactions to the breakup, and (c) specific problem-solving strategies to address certain problems with her parents that we had jointly identified (e.g., carrying messages back and forth between her wrangling parents).

During the second phase of treatment, my intermediate goals were to enlist both parents in a brief educational or "coaching" intervention to help them change certain parental interactions that were creating conflicts for Mary. Specifically, I wanted to (3) reduce her exposure to interparental warfare and (4) alleviate her loyalty conflicts and give her greater freedom to be to be close and involved with both of her parents.

During the third phase of treatment, my longer term goals were to engage both parents in treatment with Mary and try to ameliorate two long-standing developmental conflicts for Mary that were being generated by ongoing patterns of family interaction. Specifically, I wanted to (5) help Mary's father respond to her in a less authoritarian and intimidating manner, so she wouldn't be so anxious, compliant, and inhibited; and (6) facilitate clearer intergenerational boundaries and better parent-child role differentiation between Mrs. A. and Mary in order to relieve Mary's burden of parentification.

My initial goals and strategies for establishing an effective working alliance were detailed in the Initial Session section, and my goals for the initial phase of treatment were discussed earlier in the section on Client Conceptualization. Intermediate goals 3 and 4 for the second phase of treatment, which entailed parental involvement, have not been elucidated and comprise an essential aspect of treatment. This new aspect of familial intervention is examined below in phase two. As we will see, goals 5 and 6 evolved from this parental intervention and will be elaborated later.

The primary goal in the second phase of treatment was to reduce inter-parental conflict and/or shield Mary from her parents' ongoing battles. Mary and I had already made some progress on this third goal in our initial phase of treatment. We had worked on this by:

1. Affirming how scary it was to see her parents fight;
2. Clarifying that she was not responsible either for causing or stopping their battles;
3. Acknowledging that it is unfair when children are pulled into parental battles or pressured to take sides; and
4. Rehearsing and role playing what she could say and do to remove herself from her parent's wrangling.

Although each of these interventions offered some help, I believed that Mary would remain anxious and unable to attain a secure postdivorce adjustment as long as the parental battle continued. To attain this goal of greater security, I began the second phase of treatment by telephoning each parent and asking them to meet with me individually for one session.

As often occurs, mother was ready to participate but assured me that father would not be willing to meet. In general, therapists will find that many fathers will not participate in treatment if they are asked by the mother. However, most fathers will participate in treatment when the therapist (a) speaks directly to him rather than triangulating through the mother, (b) explicitly validates the continuing importance of his role in the child's life, and (c) asks him to share his understanding of what can be done to make things better for his child.

Mary's father accepted my invitation to meet for one session and attended this appointment. He began the session by announcing that he didn't believe in therapy and didn't like therapists. I accepted his point of view without challenge and clarified our common goal of helping Mary. During the course of this session, I was able to help him make the contingent connection between Mary's anxiety (nail biting, overeating, nightmares, losing homework) and parental arguments. He could see that parental arguments were upsetting for Mary and ultimately he agreed both to "conduct business" with his ex-wife only when Mary was not present. He was also willing to use me as a mediator with Mrs. A. in the future to resolve parenting disputes that they couldn't resolve and would otherwise embroil Mary. This complex issue was not resolved in one meeting, of course, but Mary was exposed to significantly less interparental conflict after this frank discussion. This reduction in exposure to interparental conflict was probably the single most important change that could have occurred for Mary.

Success in this cardinal arena was not matched by such significant improvement in other areas, however. Regarding the 4th goal of loyalty conflicts, for example, Mr. A. was rigid in his belief that his ex-wife was selfish and to blame for breaking up the family and that "Mary should know the truth" about her mother. Although he could acknowledge that this may put

Mary in a strained position between her parents, it was not possible for him to relinquish his externalizing view. Similarly, regarding the 5th goal, Mr. A. was unwilling to discuss or consider relaxing his harsh, authoritarian parenting style and offer Mary more approval, affection, or self-expression.

In many cases, however, therapists will be able to work individually with parents on childrearing issues, such as these, or conduct further conjoint sessions to help parents and children communicate more effectively with each other. In this case, however, Mary's father declined further involvement on these issues of parenting style and loyalty conflicts. Several factors contributed to this reluctance. He was angry about the breakup, but broken-hearted too. He had grown up in a brutally authoritarian family and the marital rupture evoked long-standing separation anxieties and the shame of being left and having unmet needs exposed. Like most of the men he knew and worked with, Mr. A. coped with these unacceptable feelings in rigid and externalizing ways—often through anger and alcohol abuse. I was afraid that if I pressed for more, which a part of me wanted to do, I would rupture the fragile alliance I had with him and threaten the limited but important gains we had made. Our ethnic differences and his cultural proscriptions against a man seeing a therapist also may have made it harder for him to become further involved in treatment. Therefore, I supported the changes we had agreed upon, validated his important contributions to Mary's development, and invited further contact at any time he wished to help with any future concerns that might arise.

Mrs. A. was also wary in our session together, but she could see that therapy was helping Mary. As a result, she also joined me in the 3rd and principal goal of shielding Mary from further parental conflicts. Although I spoke in terms of helping Mary, Mrs. A. was visibly relieved to have my support in finding ways to reduce the personal distress of her ongoing parental battles.

Mrs. A. was able to enter into these discussions more freely than Mr. A. and we evolved a joint plan of action. First, whenever parental conflicts were escalating in Mary's presence, Mrs. A. would terminate the conversation with a specific sentence ("I do not want to talk about this anymore right now. We will continue this adult conversation later when we are alone."). If that did not stop the escalating tension, she would announce that she would not continue this conversation further at this time and would physically depart without further comment. Ultimately, Mr. and Mrs. A. agreed to discuss issues only in a public restaurant where neither one would be likely to lose their temper or escalate conflict.

As with Mr. A., significant improvement occurred with the primary goal of shielding Mary from exposure to parental conflict, but few gains were made with the 4th goal of reducing loyalty conflicts. Mrs. A. believed that a girl belongs with her mother—which supported Mr. A.'s view that she had always undermined his relationship with Mary. As with Mr. A., I felt that I had more to lose than gain by pressing my agenda and deferred this goal.

Whereas Mr. A. was unwilling to work on the 5th goal of more effective, authoritative parenting, however, Mrs. A. was willing to participate further and examine other conflict areas. This introduced the third phase of treatment, which focused on the 6th goal of easing the mother's parentification of Mary.

REVISED TREATMENT PLAN

The third phase of treatment began as I started working with both Mary and Mrs. A. on the 6th goal of parentification. Mary had become inappropriately concerned about her mother's well-being and felt responsible for shoring up her mother's emotional equilibrium. Mary's parentified concern for her mother stemmed from three realistic concerns. First, Mr. A. was physically intimidating and often yelled and made threats toward her mother. Although these arguments had not erupted into physical violence, Mary accurately sensed that their emotions were out of control and the potential for harm was readily imagined. Mary's worry and concern about her mother's well-being also made sense in terms of their new living status. Following the breakup, Mrs. A. was tired and distressed. She worked full time and came home to the "second shift" of shopping, cooking, cleaning, and responding to Mary. Mrs. A. was guilty about the breakup and "hurting" Mary, sad about missing the good things in the marriage, and overwhelmed by the very real demands of a career, running a household, and caring for a child. Mary could see the sadness in her mother's face and the fatigue in her slumped posture. Sadly for both, she often saw or heard her mother crying.

Finally, Mary's preoccupation with her mother's well being was not based solely on the situational circumstances described above. Despite being a hard-working and successful office manager, Mrs. A. had probably been dysthymically depressed all of her life, with periodic bouts of Major Depression. Mrs. A.'s own childhood had been grim. Her own single-parent mother had been a chronic alcoholic and a schizophrenic and repeatedly had to send Mrs. A. away to live with relatives while her mother was incapacitated or binging. (Understanding the multigenerational family history is the best way for me to become more accepting of parents who are responding in hurtful ways to their children.) Mary was highly sensitized to her Mother's pain and hopelessness, and her basic sense of self was organized around the role of shoring up her mother. For example, Mary was vigilantly responsive to her mother's unspoken emotional needs and served as her mother's confidante and "best friend." Mary was much too grown up, helpful, and concerned about her mother's emotional well-being to be able to have her own childhood.

In order to resolve this role reversal, I met once weekly for the next 10 months in varying combinations with mother alone, daughter alone, or mother and daughter together. Many of the sessions in this final phase of treatment were with Mrs. A. individually in order to focus on her parentification of

Mary. As Mrs. A. made gains in our individual sessions in understanding how and why she was parentifying Mary, we would schedule conjoint sessions with Mary to address these issues in their relationship. At these conjoint sessions we would all talk together about this role reversal and, utilizing the personal gains she had made, Mrs. A. would own or make overt to Mary the specific ways she had been placing Mary in this adult role. Mrs. A. also would communicate how she felt stronger now, and, although it was loving of Mary to try and offer this support, she did not need Mary to assume this caretaking role anymore.

At other times, when they began to interact in this parentified mode during the session, I would describe their interaction to them and make overt how they seemed to be squabbling like siblings just then, how they seemed to be interacting more as confidantes and friends than mother and daughter at this moment, or how Mary was worrying about her mother and trying to take care of her as a parent in this interaction. Mary and her mother both became able to recognize and change their own participation in these familiar but problematic patterns. It was clear, however, that Mary could only relinquish her parentified status as she received directly spoken permission from her mother to do so. In this way, individual adult therapy or marital counseling can often be an integral part of child treatment. To examine this further, let's look briefly at the three issues Mrs. A. and I focused on in our individual sessions that allowed her to reclaim her appropriate parental role.

First, Mrs. A. felt guilty about initiating the divorce and selfish for breaking up the family just because she was unhappy in the marriage. This guilt, in part, kept her from effectively disciplining Mary and enforcing the rules she set. For example, rather than taking charge and simply telling Mary to wash the dishes, Mrs. A. ineffectively complained and tried to cajole her. Mrs. A. increasingly recognized how her guilt led them to squabble like sisters, with no parent effectively in charge of the family.

Second, Mrs. A. also needed to develop a better support network for herself. After the breakup she now had to do many things herself that her husband used to handle, and being a single parent was far more demanding than she had imagined. However, Mrs. A. also felt guilty about doing anything for herself and ashamed of having emotional needs seen or met by others. Over the course of treatment, however, she gradually was able to let herself "have" our relationship and allow me to respond to her. With my encouragement, she also expanded two friendships and reestablished ties with several extended family members in a nearby city. Gradually, she became better at seeking support and sharing her personal concerns in each of these adult relationships. As these important changes occurred, her depression and loneliness abated and she stopped turning to Mary as much for her emotional support.

Third, in the course of working on these two issues, the profound deprivations that Mrs. A. had suffered throughout her own life emerged. She had never known her father and, as noted, her mother was both a schizophrenic and an alcoholic. Mrs. A. grew up being shunted back and forth from various homes with relatives when her mother was not lucid or sober, and on several occasions social work agencies placed her in temporary foster homes. It was heartbreaking to learn that she had been sexually molested, as too often occurs in such temporary placements. For the first time, Mrs. A. risked sharing this trauma and could tolerate exploring the feelings of helplessness, rage, and self-loathing that the abuse engendered.

Following this period in which she began to come to terms with her shame and guilt, a lifelong orientation toward depression and compliance improved. Initially, Mrs. A. wanted to use this awareness of her own victimization and chronic depression to further punish herself and feel even more guilty and helpless about helping Mary. By emphasizing my own genuine admiration for the way she had been able to survive and to give so much more to Mary as a parent than she had received as a child, Mrs. A. was gradually able to begin feeling some compassion for herself and her own poignant dilemma. As Mrs. A. allowed me to respond more directly to her own emotional needs she, in turn, became more responsive to Mary. That is, she became more interested in Mary's concerns about school and peers, more responsive to Mary's initiative, and better able to tolerate Mary's negative feelings when Mary was frustrated or angry with her. As noted above, when Mrs. A. became stronger in these ways, we began to use conjoint sessions with Mary to try and translate her personal changes into changes in their current interaction as well.

During these conjoint sessions, I repeatedly focused Mary and Mrs. A. on talking directly to each other about their relationship, rather than about Mr. A., friends, or other topics. For example, I repeatedly gave them cues, such as "What's going on between you two right now?" "What isn't working for you two in your relationship this week?" or "How does this conflict with your dad that you are talking about affect your relationship with your mom?"

As they spoke more directly with each other, I would observe aloud the parentification issues as I heard them occurring. For example, "You two sound like sisters right now. Do you sound like this at home a lot?" or "Mary, you sound like a worried mother. What's going to happen if you stop taking care of your mother like that?"

By highlighting their current interaction in this way, it became even clearer than before that Mary was indeed worried about her mother and had been taking care of her like a parent. More important, it also became clear to everyone that Mrs. A. no longer needed Mary to fulfill this role. On several occasions, Mrs. A. joined me or initiated on her own: (a) acknowledging that Mary had been taking care of her as a parent; (b) appreciating how loving this concern was while still recognizing how burdensome this was to Mary; (c) validating the reality that Mrs. A. had been depressed a lot, rather than continuing to deny how sad she had often seemed; and (d) suggesting the possibility that Mrs. A. was stronger now and no longer needed Mary to take care of her in these ways.

By responding in these new ways in the sessions, Mrs. A. was behaviorally demonstrating to Mary that she was stronger now and no longer needed Mary to be taking care of her in the way she had before. Mary soon tested this new strength, of course, by criticizing something her mother had done. Rather than argue defensively, or shrug and look hurt, Mrs. A. simply said, "Okay, let's talk about it," and proceeded to allow Mary to be angry at her. When they finished their discussion, I punctuated the obvious by saying, "Your mother is stronger now than she used to be . . . I don't think you have to be the parent here anymore."

Significant changes occurred as Mary saw that her mother no longer needed her to take care of her as she had in the past. In particular, Mary's teacher reported that she was doing well in her schoolwork again, succeeding as a member of her school volleyball team, and seemed more active and involved than she had been. It was time to terminate. After discussing several other issues that bear on the treatment process thus far, we will focus on the termination and review the important issues that emerged in this closing phase of treatment.

BALANCING GOALS

With some divorcing parents, balancing divergent goals between mothers, fathers, teachers, and others can be a central therapeutic issue. For several reasons, however, this was not a primary concern with Mary. By enlisting *both* parent's involvement in their daughter's treatment and inviting each of them to share their concerns and suggestions, therapy did not become another arena for reenacting ongoing parental conflicts. And, by proceeding progressively in the three-step treatment plan presented here, therapeutic goals evolved out of the immediately preceding work with joint participation from child, parents and therapist. Let's review this graduated aspect of treatment planning more explicitly.

Mrs. A. initiated treatment for Mary to cope with the crisis of marital rupture. It was important that I accepted at face value the mother's mandate to help her daughter with divorce-related concerns. Only as progress was made on these divorce-related concerns did it become possible to expand the treatment focus to include the broader familial context that was shaping Mary's longer-term developmental problems. If I would have tried to alter or expand Mrs. A.'s original request for treatment, such as soliciting her individual involvement in treatment in the beginning or by requesting conjoint marital sessions, I don't think Mary would have been allowed to enter treatment. Therapists usually need to provide practical help with the parent's view of the presenting problem before they can expand or reframe treatment goals.

By accepting and working within the mother's initial worldview, however, I was able to expand the scope of the problem one step further in phase two of treatment. This occurred as I asked each parent to meet with me for a limited time concerning what they could do to help with Mary's postdivorce adjustment. Most parents will accept one more step if it is presented as an extension of their original goal and initial view of the problem. In this case, even these highly embattled parents made significant improvement in shielding Mary from their intense parental conflict. In contrast, however, several issues that I wished to address were not workable for these parents and I had to relinquish some of my own goals (e.g., both parents' loyalty conflicts and father's authoritarian parenting style) or risk losing the gains we had made.

Similarly, the transition to phase three of treatment entailed new goals and further redefinition of Mary's problem. I was successful in enlisting Mrs. A.'s participation in addressing the parentification conflicts only after we had succeeded in making some progress on the previous, more immediate, goals in phases one and two. Unlike Mrs. A., however, Mr. A. was not able to shift his rigid, externalizing focus from Mary and the parental relationship to address his own problematic parenting style. Cultural and personal factors both played a role here in Mr. A.'s concerns about looking at his own parenting skills and possibly his own upbringing. Strong gender proscriptions against men having emotional problems, needing help or appearing "weak," and cultural differences between us all played a part.

Mary was helped by the initial divorce-education sessions in phase 1, which also met her goals for treatment. This success, in turn, facilitated phase two occurring and the meaningful reduction of exposure to interparental conflict that resulted. Finally, far reaching changes occurred during phase three as Mary came to see her mother as more resilient and capable of managing her own adult life without her assistance. As Mary was progressively relieved of this parentification burden during our conjoint sessions, this became a shared treatment goal for her as it was for her mother and me.

Therapeutic Process

RELATIONAL REENACTMENTS

In phase one of treatment, research findings on children and divorce helped to provide useful guidelines for responding to Mary's divorce-related concerns. In phases two and three, family systems concepts and awareness of structural family relations elucidated the central conflict of parentification. Although these orienting constructs were helpful, the most important aspect of treatment for me was finding corrective responses to the relational reenactments that presented themselves throughout treatment. These three brief examples illustrate how aspects of each client's conflicts were brought into the therapeutic relationship, played out with me along the process dimension, and resolved to some extent in the interaction that transpired between us.

Mother. Mrs. A.'s conflicted feelings about seeking treatment were evident in the initial telephone contact. It was shame laden for her to ask for help for anything from anyone, and these difficulties entering treatment were exacerbated because of our gender and cultural differences. Her life experience led her to expect that often she must comply with White, male authority figures, while naturally wanting to rebel. So, within the first minute of our telephone conversation, the lifelong, painful feelings associated with an oppressive marriage, an exploited childhood, and much cultural discrimination were evoked by her simple human need to ask for help.

Although I was not clear about the specifics until later, I was aware at the time that this was a pivotal moment in treatment. Something about asking for help was clearly reviving unwanted expectations, and it was essential that our process did not reenact a prototypic and problematic relational scenario for her. Therefore, I drew on general impressions I had been gathering to formulate tentative or working hypotheses about what may be occurring for her. For example, what if I responded in some way that suggested that I did in fact need to be the authority? I surmised from her voice and tone, and what she chose to disclose about her marriage, that if I was invested in leading, teaching, or directing and expecting her to dutifully follow, a familiar but deadly relational pattern would reoccur for her, and she would "know" that there was no hope for help or change in this relationship. On the other hand, it would also be problematic for her if I felt intimidated by her cool and challenging tone and withdrew or distanced myself. If so, I would not be able to hear her pain, respond to her real need for help, or be able to actively engage with her and find some common ground for beginning a relationship. This disengagement, as it later became clear, would have recapitulated the lack of response to her genuine emotional needs, which had characterized both her childhood and her marriage. Instead, by finding ways to respond to her that gave her more control in our relationship and assurance that she did not have to comply with me (e.g., "Why don't you meet with me one time only and, after that, you will be able to decide for yourself whether I can be of help"), Mrs. A. experienced a new and more satisfying response to her old relational expectations. One trial learning does not resolve a lifetime of experience, of course, but it did allow treatment to begin for her daughter.

Daughter. In the section on Initial Session, I gave one example of how humor provided a corrective relational experience and allowed Mary and me to begin a collaborative working alliance. Similarly, in the conjoint sessions with mother and daughter, parentification conflicts and other issues were expressed in their current interaction and resolved in the new ways they were able to respond to each other. To illustrate, both Mrs. A. and Mary expected me to take sides against the other—reenacting the father's role in the family and the intense loyalty conflicts that had been operating. If I would have become overidentified with Mary's dilemma and blamed or scapegoated her mother, Mrs. A. could not have become the executive ego or parent in the family, which she eventually was able to do. Or, if I repeatedly sided with Mrs. A., I could not have heard and affirmed Mary's legitimate concerns. Instead, by trying to understand rather than blame, by welcoming differences in perception rather than demanding one reality or "truth," and by allowing both sides to be expressed and heard, we were establishing a level of fairness in their relationship that neither had experienced before. This process enacted by my neutral but concerned role may seem minor, but it created safety where it had not existed before, and permitted mother and daughter to begin talking directly for the first time about the important issues and conflicts between them.

Father.   Finally, significant relational reenactments transpired in the single session with father as well. Mr. A. began our initial contact in an insulting and provocative manner. If I would have acted on my initial impulse to bark back at him in some way (e.g., try to argue, defend, or disprove), our process would have reenacted the combative scenario he had sustained with his wife for many years. Wishing to avoid this, and imagining that perhaps he felt demeaned by seeing a therapist or resented the expectation that another man or Caucasian was going to try to tell him the "right" way to raise his child, I took a light touch with his provocations. By accepting his distaste for therapy and therapists, and focusing instead on his good intentions and sincere wish to help his daughter, we were able to make significant progress in shielding Mary from ongoing parental battles. We would not have achieved this important outcome if he had succeeded in eliciting the same anger, competition, or intimidation in our relationship that he did in others. In this way, I find that many theoretical frameworks are useful but that clients change most readily when we have enacted solutions to their conflicts along the process dimension or in the way we interact together. In contrast, I find that clients do not progress when we have unwittingly replayed their same problematic relational scenarios. Although I have appreciated this basic, orienting concept for many years, I am repeatedly struck by how routinely and centrally the client's core relational patterns are evoked in the process or way we interact together.

IMPEDIMENTS TO TREATMENT

Resistance.   The illuminating psychologist, Helen Block Lewis, often noted that the term *resistance* is frequently a misnomor for shame and guilt. It was initially demeaning for both parents to participate in treatment, and this shame may have been exacerbated for both parents because I am Caucasian and male. Significant conflicts also arose for Mary if she let herself have a relationship with me and allowed me to help her. For example, she anticipated that I was likely to subjugate her as her father did because I was also a male authority figure, she was afraid of betraying her mother by establishing an alliance with another man, and she was violating the family taboo against talking about problems with Whites or others outside the family. These are complex, reality based problems for Mary or any child, and treatment will not progress very far until they are addressed.

I tried to help Mary with these concerns by discussing them directly with her and by expressing how it made sense to me that it was sometimes difficult for her to come to see me. I also gave her repeated opportunities to talk about the good news and the bad news in our relationship (e.g., "What's the best and the worst thing about coming to see me?"). Over time, I also tried to differentiate myself from her conflicts with both parents, for example, being friendlier and more communicative than her father and being more authoritative and mindful of not acting in ways that she could readily perceive as tired, needy, depressed, or confused like her mother. As we talked about these concerns, and she experienced me as different than her parents in these specific ways, it gave her the freedom to explore and better come to terms with the conflicts she had with each parent.

Anxiety/Defense.   When children repeatedly get stuck on the same problem, separate and distinct conflicts they are having with each parent often dovetail or over-lap to create an immobilizing double bind. For example, Mary's core conflict revolved around having her own mind (vis à vis her dominating father), responding to her own needs and interests (vis à vis her needy mother), and proceeding with her own developmental tasks of identity formation. In different but interlocking ways, she struggled with these same conflicts with both parents. Mary's father was highly authoritarian. He was threatening and punitive if Mary freely spoke her own mind, disagreed with him, or acted independently without first seeking his permission. To complicate matters, she had different problems with these same issues vis à vis her mother. That is, Mary could not focus internally and attend to her own feelings, needs, and interests. Instead, she was living outside of herself—vigilantly attuned and highly responsive to the ups and downs in her mother's emotional life. Although this may seem benignly empathic, sensitive, or caring at first, it was not. Mary could not initiate any action on her own behalf without first worrying about the consequences for her mother or do anything for herself without feeling guilty about meeting her own needs rather than her mother's. Thus, Mary was adaptive and competent in the environment—as a result of being afraid to make mistakes with her father and needing to be mature and in control with her mother. However, this outward appearance of competence belied the insecurity, guilt, and worry that prevailed internally. As long as Mary was being good and compliant via her father, and responsible, helpful, and loyal via her mother, she was safe—but at the expense of her own symptomatic development. For example, if Mary was in a situation that called on her to initiate, express her own wishes, or assert on her own behalf, she became anxious and immobilized. Although some of this was culturally "sanctioned," it was not sanctioned to the extent of Mary's symptoms.

Over the course of treatment, I was able to help Mary recognize and label this bind that was constricting her. By elucidating the twin towers of her conflict, and being sympathetic to the very real family interactions that engendered it, she was able to act a little freer with others outside of her family. More significant gains occurred when this issue was made overt and resolved with her mother, as Mrs. A. was able to give Mary permission to stop taking care of her and begin attending to her own schoolwork and friends instead. We were not able to attain parallel changes on this issue with her father, unfortunately, but Mary did make gains in differentiating when she had to comply with others and when she could say no and do more of what she wanted.

In both of these instances, however, cultural factors overlaid these familial conflicts and neither of these changes with mother or father could have occurred without working within Mary's worldview. In this instance, for example, sensitivity to the cultural context meant helping Mary realize that developing her own mind was *not* the same as being disrespectful to her father and that responding to her own needs was not being insensitive to her mother. Mary could progress in treatment only as we were able to articulate and define this new middle ground that preserved cultural prescriptions for respecting and helping parents while balancing this with greater permission for her right to her own life.

Termination and Therapist's Summary Thoughts

Ideally, a successful termination is effected when perceptions of successful change converge from the child, parents, the therapist, and significant others, such as teachers. In this case, each of these figures independently noted that meaningful changes had occurred for Mary. As I observed the clear and direct way in which Mrs. A. and Mary now communicated in our conjoint sessions, I believed that their role reversal had been substantially reduced and replaced with a parent-child relationship for the first time. I began thinking about termination as this new, more appropriate adult-child interaction became consistent in our sessions. About the same time, Mary's teacher reported to Mrs. A. that Mary was doing well at school with friends and seemed happier. After discussing this good news with Mary, I suggested that perhaps our work was finishing up and that she may not need to see me much longer, and Mary agreed.

During the last few months of treatment, Mrs. A. had been renewing contact with her brother who lived in another part of the state and with a foster family that had been supportive of her years ago. I had been encouraging Mrs. A. to explore the possibilities in these family ties and renew them if possible. Whereas many Native American family systems are extended networks with several households sharing childrearing responsibilities and providing role models, Mrs. A. was cut off from these supports. Thus, an important treatment goal was to help her restore these connections and establish affirming relationships within her own family and culture. When a job opportunity became available in this community, Mrs. A. decided to move closer to these support systems. Mary could still see her father regularly, but they would have more family supports than they had ever had and Mrs. A. would not feel so alone. I supported this decision and suggested we meet two more times in order to say good-bye to each other.

Mary moved easily toward termination. She was sad about ending but also felt ready to stop. I strongly supported her stronger, independent feeling, but also reassured her that she could call or come see me if she wanted when she was in town seeing her father.

In contrast, the prospect of ending treatment was far more ambivalent for Mrs. A. In her words, my support had allowed her to be a real parent to Mary for the first time, and she was afraid of losing the effective new parenting stance she had attained once we stopped. Her feelings certainly made sense, but I saw her as being stronger and more effectively in charge now. Although she needed further therapy to continue the recovery work she had started, I thought she had successfully integrated her new, more authoritative parenting skills, had found better ways to get her own adult needs met, and was not likely to fall back on the problematic role reversal with Mary. I shared my more positive assessment of her strength, which she accepted as affirming and not as denying of her needs.

In addition, our ending brought up the intense separation anxieties she had suffered as a child. We worked with the abandonment fears that our ending evoked, and meaningfully linked them to the profound separations she had repeatedly experienced as a child. Rather than turning to Mary for comfort with these separation anxieties, I invited her to call or come see me as needed—especially until she got going with her new therapist in their new town.

This reassurance allowed her to feel more secure again, and she became sad about our ending. As I had done with Mary, we talked together about our relationship, what we had shared and struggled with together, and how we would miss each other. I talked with both of them about how they had enriched my life and that I felt honored to have known them so closely. Treatment stopped soon afterwards and they moved to another city where they made a successful transition.

In closing, I was very moved by this mother and daughter and was sad but glad to see them go. In particular, I admired Mrs. A.'s courage—she was truly a survivor and had been able to give much more to her child than she had received in her own childhood. As I drove home from our last session, I felt inspired by how much some people can do who have been given so little in life. It was a privilege to have touched their lives.

REFERENCES

Alpert-Gillis, L. J., Pedro-Carroll, J. L., & Cowen, E. L. (1989). The Children of Divorce Intervention Program: Development, implementation, and evaluation of a program for young urban children. *Journal of Consulting and Clinical Psychology, 57,* 583–589.

Camara, K. A., & Resnick, G. (1988). Interparental conflict and cooperation: Factors moderating children's post-divorce adjustment. In E. M. Hetherington & J. Aratesh (Eds.), *Impact of divorce, singleparenting, and stepparenting on children* (pp. 169–195). Hillsdale, NJ: Erlbaum.

DiCosta, D., & Nelson, G. (1988). Family and social network factors after divorce in Catholic Italian women and Catholic Anglophone women. In C. Everett (Ed.), *Minority and ethnic issues in the divorce process* (pp. 111–127). New York: Haworth Press.

Duncan, G. J., & Hoffman, S. D. (1985). Economic consequences of marital instability. In M. David & T. Smeeding (Eds.) *Horizontal equity, uncertainty, and economic well-being* (pp. 427–470). Chicago: University of Chicago Press.

Emery, R. E. (1988). *Marriage, divorce and children's adjustment.* Newbury Park, CA: Sage.

Everett, F., Proctor, N., & Cartmell, B. (1983). Providing psychological services to American Indian children and families. *Professional Psychology, 14,* 588–603.

Fine, M., McKenry, P., & Chung, H. (1992). Cultural differences in parental response to divorce. *Journal of Divorce and Remarriage, 17*(3–4), 121–133.

Grych, J., & Fincham, F. (1992). Interventions for children of divorce: Toward greater integration of research and action. *Psychological Bulletin, 111*(3), 434–454.

Guidubaldi, J., Perry, C., & Nastasi, B. K. (1987). Assessment and intervention for children of divorce: Implications of the NASP-KSU nationwide survey. In J. Vincent (Ed.), *Advances in family intervention, assessment, and theory* (Vol. 4, pp. 33–69). Greenwich, CT: JAI Press.

Hetherington, E. M. (1991). The role of individual differences and family relationships in children's coping with divorce and remarriage. In P. Cowan & E. M. Hetherington (Eds.), *Advances in family research: Vol. 2. Family transitions.* Hillsdale, NJ: Erlbaum.

Hetherington, E. M., Cox, M., & Cox, R. (1982). Effects of divorce on parents and children. In M. Lamb (Ed.), *Nontraditional families* (pp. 233–288). Hillsdale, NJ: Erlbaum.

Hetherington, E. M., Cox, M., & Cox, R. (1985). Long-term effects of divorce and remarriage on the adjustment of children. *Journal of American Academy of Psychiatry, 24,* 513–830.

Isaacs, M., & Leon, G. (1988). Race, marital dissolution and visitation: An examination of adaptive family strategies. In C. Everett (Ed.), *Minority and ethnic issues in the divorce process* (pp. 17–31). New York: Haworth Press.

Maccoby, E. E., & Martin, J. A. (1983). Socialization in the context of the family: Parent-child interaction. In E. M. Hetherington (Ed.), *Handbook of child psychology* (Vol. 4, pp. 1–101). New York: Wiley.

Minuchin, S. (1974). *Families and family therapy.* Cambridge: Harvard University Press.

Neff, J., Gilbert, K., & Hoppe, S. (1991). Divorce likelihood among Anglos and Mexican Americans. In C. Everett (Ed.), *Marital instability and divorce outcomes* (pp. 75–97). New York: Haworth Press.

Rutter, M. (1987). Psychosocial resilience and protective mechanisms. *American Journal of Orthopsychiatry, 57,* 316–331.

Santrock, J. W., & Warshak, R. A. (1986). Development of father custody relationships and legal/clinical considerations in father-custody families. In M. E. Lamb (Ed.), *The father's role: Applied perspectives* (pp. 135–166). New York: Wiley.

Teyber, E. C. (1992). *Helping children cope with divorce.* New York: Lexington.

Tharp, R. G., (1991). Cultural diversity and treatment of children. *Journal of Consulting and Clinical Psychology, 59,* 799–817.

United States Department of Health and Human Services. (1990). *Monthly Vital Statistics Report* (No. 13). Washington, DC: Author.

Wagner, R. (1988). Changes in the friend network during the first year of single parenthood for Mexican American and Anglo women. In C. Everett (Ed.), *Minority and ethnic issues in the divorce process* (pp. 89–105). New York: Haworth Press.

Wallerstein, J. S. Corbin, S. B., & Lewis, J. (1988). Children of divorce: A 10-year study. In E. M. Hetherington & J. Aratesh (Eds.), *Impact of divorce, singleparenting and stepparenting on children* (pp. 197–214). Hillsdale, NJ: Erlbaum.

Wallerstein, J. S., & Kelly, J. B. (1980). *Surviving the breakup: How children and parents cope with divorce.* New York: Basic Books.

SUGGESTIONS FOR FURTHER READING

Alpert-Gillis, L. J., Pedro-Carroll, J. S., & Cowan, E. L. (1989). The Children of Divorce Intervention Program: Development, implementation, and evaluation of a program for young urban children. *Journal of Consulting and Clinical Psychology, 57,* 583–589. An excellent school-based, group intervention program for children of divorce.

American Indians and Alaska native families: Emigrants in their own homeland. In M. McGoldrick, J. Pearce, & J. Giordano (Eds.), *Ethnicity and family therapy* (pp. 55–83). New York: Guilford. Useful guidelines for counseling Native Americans.

Gardner, R. (1986). *The boys and girls book about divorce.* New York: Creative Therapeutics. A helpful book for therapists to recommend to young children who are going through a parental divorce.

Teyber, E. (1992). Helping children cope with divorce. New York: Lexington. Helps parents explain the divorce to children, establish custody/visitation arrangements that will benefit children, shield children from parental conflict, and parent more effectively in single-parent and stepfamilies.

Teyber, E. (1996). *Interpersonal process in psychotherapy: A guide for clinical training* (3rd ed.). Pacific Grove, CA: Brooks-Cole. For learning more about the process dimension in counseling relationships.

Chapter 6

BORDERLINE PERSONALITY DISORDER

CASE ILLUSTRATION OF JONATHAN: A 17-YEAR-OLD AFRICAN AMERICAN

Barbara N. Graf, Ph.D.

THE DISORDER

The *Diagnostic and Statistical Manual of Mental Disorders* (DSM-IV; American Psychiatric Association, 1994; hereafter, DSM-IV), describes Borderline Personality Disorder (BPD) as a "pervasive pattern of instability of interpersonal relationships, self-image, and affect." The instability of self-image can be manifested by uncertainty about self-image, sexual orientation, career goals, friends, and/or values. The instability of interpersonal relationships takes the form of intense, unstable relationships marked by periods of extreme overidealization and devaluation. Mood shifts range from depression to irritability to anxiety. Intense anger is a major feature of BPD and can take the form of frequent displays of temper, constant anger, or physical fights. Another major feature of BPD is a chronic feeling of emptiness or boredom. There is great difficulty tolerating being alone and attempts are made to avoid real or imagined abandonment. Impulsivity and self-damaging behavior can be found in the areas of spending, sex, substance abuse, shoplifting, reckless driving, or binge eating. There can be recurrent suicidal threats or self-mutilating behavior.

Although there are now criteria specifying observable symptoms of borderline personality disorder (DSM-IV), the identification of this disorder is fairly recent. It has also been difficult to differentiate borderlines from other personality disorders—especially narcissistic and histrionic personality disorders. Even though the DSM-IV (like the DSM-III), provides specific criteria, Clarkin, Widiger, Frances, Hurt, and Gilmore (1983), found that 60% of the borderline patients in their study also met the criteria for other personality disorders, and Beck and Freeman (1990) note that "no simple borderline profile has been identified," either through the use of traditional assessment tests or empirical studies. In particular, there are often elements of narcissism in borderline functioning. Unlike narcissistic individuals who have some capacity for self-reflection, however, the borderline patient's lack of a cohesive, overall sense of self inhibits his or her capacity for self-exploration. This cardinal feature will help clinicians accurately differentiate the borderline personality disorder.

Despite the many discussions in the literature about this complex disorder, there continues to be much disagreement among clinicians as to the origins of the borderline disorder, how to treat it, and—despite the criteria referenced above—when to apply the diagnosis. Let's look more closely at the history of this fascinating disorder that has generated so much interest and controversy in recent years.

History of the Diagnosis

The historical development of the diagnosis of BPD began in the 1940s from four different clinical observations. In the first, a type of patient was identified who had the appearance of healthy functioning while revealing evidence of primitive thinking on unstructured psychological tests (Rorschach, 1942). A second observation was that some patients who were referred to psychoanalysts and presumed to be neurotic revealed "primitive regressive transferences" (Hoch & Polatin, 1949). For example, these patients would demonstrate intense affect, make very strong dependency demands on the therapist, and become increasingly enraged at the therapist. A third observation came from staff working in psychiatric hospitals who observed a regression in some patients to primitive and highly destructive behaviors (e.g., self-mutilating, suicide attempts) within the supportive confines of hospitals, which had proven helpful to other patients (Gunderson, 1984). The fourth observation came from reports of intense countertransference reactions from therapists—generally reported as feelings of helplessness and/or rage toward the client (Grinker, Werble, & Drye, 1968).

As a result of these early clinical observations, major independent studies by Kernberg, Masterson, and Adler and Buie were undertaken in the 1960s and 1970s, which have greatly influenced current understanding and treatment of borderline personality disorders.

Kernberg worked within a traditional psychoanalytic framework that emphasized biological contributions to borderline functioning, Masterson's developmental approach draws on Mahler's contributions from object relations theory, and Adler and Buie were working within Kohut's theory of self-psychology. More recently, Beck's cognitive approach has also made useful contributions for treating borderlines (1976; 1979).

Kernberg's writing did much to focus current attention on the borderline disorder (1968, 1976; Kernberg, Selzer, & Koenigsburg, et al., 1989). In particular, he focused extensively on the borderline patient's reliance on splitting defenses (e.g., the assignment of either all-good or all-bad attributes to people, with no ability to integrate good and bad or find a middle ground). This will be demonstrated later in the chapter by Jon's tendency to idolize new acquaintances, followed by his total rejection of them when they demonstrated more human or flawed responses. Kernberg believes that splitting is an attempt to defend against the excessive aggression the patient feels as a result of the early childhood frustration or possibly—in his drive-model theory—due to organic or biological causes. The failure to integrate both positive and negative experiences, however, results in the extreme, intense feelings toward others that are a hallmark of the borderline.

In treatment, Kernberg utilized classic psychoanalytic interventions, with emphasis on the necessity of interpreting the patient's negative transference and confronting the patient's splitting defenses.

In contrast to Kernberg's psychoanalytic/biological viewpoint, Masterson drew on Mahler's developmental observations and object relations theory to suggest a more relational or interpersonal genesis of BPD.

Mahler's influence on the understanding of the borderline syndrome came from her observations of mother-child interactions (Mahler, 1968, 1971; Mahler, Pine, & Bergman, 1970, 1975). Mahler described the first 36 months of the infant's life as a period of separation-individuation and she developed a specific, observable timetable with four subphases.

Of particular importance to the development of BPD is the subphase rapprochement. This period, between the 18th and 30th month, involves a complex process whereby the infant experiences rapidly cycling needs to risk venturing out into the world while continuously returning to "home base" for reassurance. This period usually includes the child's tantrums, power struggles, and mood swings.

This struggle between autonomy and dependency is difficult for the parent and the child alike. It is a commonly observable sight: a child climbing in and out of his/her parent's lap; at one moment, rejecting the parent and pushing off and, the next moment, clamoring to return to the lap and be taken care of. It can be a frustrating time for parents. (For some parents, the child's rejection can be too painful; for others, the unyielding dependency demands feel intolerable; and for still others, it is the unending oscillation between the two competing movements that can be so maddening.) As we will see in the following case study of Jonathan, this back-and-forth pattern often continues to be a behavioral feature in borderline adolescents.

Some parents deal with this period by refusing to let go: "You're just going to want to get right back up anyway, so STAY STILL!" Here children's independence is thwarted and they risk enraging the parent if they leave. If this relational pattern continues, this child grows up to have difficulty initiating activity, demonstrates problems with decision making, and tends toward passivity. In contrast, other parents refuse to allow the child to return once he or she ventures off: "You think you're so big for your britches, you can just take care of yourself!" If this relational pattern continues, this child grows up to have problems with his or her self-image, feelings of rejection, isolation, and emptiness. In "normal" and healthy development, the child receives encouragement for his or her initiative and exploration away from secure love yet is still calmly received back for "refueling" when the anxiety and separation increases. In this way, the healthy child, unlike the future borderline, can be both separate and related at the same time. We will see later that this developmental model provides valuable guidelines for how therapists need to respond to their borderline adolescents.

Risks of engulfment or abandonment result for a child when the parent cannot accept the child's alternating needs for individuation and for contact. The child's need for autonomy moves him or her away from the parent until the feelings of isolation are no longer tolerable. The return to the parent reduces the feelings of isolation but at the cost of the self. When the engulfment becomes impossible to tolerate, the child moves away again. This ping-ponging between these two uncomfortable states, the fear of abandonment and the anxiety of enmeshment, creates great difficulty for the child when the parent cannot provide an adequate *holding environment* for both developmental needs. The frustration builds and the feelings of rage and guilt become intertwined, with no clear sense of self. There is no middle ground and no ability to tolerate frustration or ambivalence. Masterson and many other clinicians view the difficulty in negotiating this period of development to be the underlying cause of the borderline syndrome.

Following Mahler, Masterson (1972, 1976; Masterson & Rinsley, 1975) emphasized that the patient's frustration and rage were not based on drives or fantasies but were grounded in the realities of the parent's actual unavailability during the rapprochement substage. In the development of the borderline personality, Masterson saw two distinct ego states emerging. One self-image consists of the good child who is rewarded for passive dependency and the other self-image consists of the bad child or bad self who is criticized and rejected for expressing his or her curiosity, initiative, and other normal or expectable movements toward autonomy. In psychotherapy, Masterson described the first "testing" phase as the borderline client's attempts to test the therapist's effectiveness in setting limits and reliability in being consistently available before risking an attachment.

Masterson writes effectively in teaching clinicians how to confront acting-out behavior in borderline adolescents, interpret resistance, and work through feelings of abandonment. He believes in actively encouraging a patient's move toward individuation—which was not received developmentally—while affirming his or her need for understanding and support. As we have already seen, this essential balance creates a "corrective" or reparative parenting experience for the patient who is struggling with Mahler's rapprochement conflicts.

Working from Kohut's (1971, 1977) model of self-psychology, Adler and Buie (1979) focus on the experience of isolation as the core feature of the borderline personality disorder. They, like Masterson, believe that the patient's needs are reality based and that the resulting frustrations and rages that borderlines characteristically exhibit are a result of a legitimate need for a *self-object relationship.* This complex term describes the general processes of a child's development of sense of "self" or identity through the secure attachment to a significant other or parent. By internalizing (gaining an internal mental representation of the attachment figure) the parent's feelings for and relationship to the child, the child develops a sense of self-esteem and is subsequently able to self-soothe by carrying a cognitive schema of the parent and the parent's loving feelings for the child inside him or her. This allows the child to draw upon this internalized parent or "object" in order to gain nourishment and support in the absence of actual physical contact with the parent. Adler and Buie (1979) believe that the borderline's lack of a strong "self-object" relationship results in feelings of isolation and, subsequently, increasing feelings of frustration and rage. This occurs when the young child does not possess (a) a stable, internal sense of the parent as loving and available or (b) a corresponding sense of self as love-worthy and emotionally connected.

Buie and Adler (1972, 1982) believe that this fundamental experience of isolation (commonly experienced by the client and communicated to the therapist as feelings of emptiness) is defended against by projecting it out onto a world that then appears empty. The unavailability of a holding environment, secure base, or soothing presence in the patient's life results in panic, desperation, and a lack of ability to maintain positive images and memories. It is this holding and soothing presence that Adler and Buie believe the borderline client has missed developmentally and what the therapist must provide in the early stages of therapy. Thus, Kernberg emphasized biological drives, and Masterson emphasized frustration of dependency needs, firm limits, and active encouragement toward individuation. In contrast, Adler and Buie do not believe in interpretations or confrontations. Rather, they encourage therapists to try to respond to the unmet attachment or dependency needs of the borderline client and to provide a stable, consistent, and caring therapeutic relationship.

Cognitive-behavioral conceptualizations of borderline personality disorder are now being utilized more often in treatment (Freeman, Pretzer, Fleming, & Simon, 1990; Beck & Freeman, 1990). As noted above, early studies on BPD and the majority of the current literature on BPD originate from an object-relations or psychoanalytic approach. However, Beck and Freeman (1990) have effectively translated many of these concepts into cognitive-behavioral terminology. For example, Beck believes borderline individuals experience many errors in thinking, or *cognitive distortions,* that often contribute to their illness. One distortion of particular frequency and importance to borderline functioning is called *dichotomous thinking.* This is described as the "tendency to evaluate experiences in terms of mutually exclusive categories" (e.g., good or bad, success or failure, trustworthy or deceitful). This dichotomous thinking (or splitting) will be demonstrated later by Jon's shifts from one extreme to the other in his evaluation of his friends. More so than is usually the case in cognitive therapy, Beck emphasizes that it is the collaborative therapeutic relationship (Beck & Freeman, 1990) that is the most necessary element in changing this dichotomous thinking and successfully treating the borderline patient. Let's turn now from these broad conceptual strokes to the always challenging but potentially rewarding work of treating borderline clients.

CASE ILLUSTRATION

Presenting Problem

Jonathan initially contacted my office after hearing about me from his good friend, Steve, a former client of mine. Both Jon and Steve were part of a very close-knit group of high schoolers at a private, all-male, Catholic high school. As gay young men, they had gravitated toward each other mostly due to their sexual orientation. Within the group they found support, acceptance, and a rescue from their previous feelings of isolation. They confided in each other and occasionally dated each other.

Jonathan phoned me to set up an appointment and told me he heard that I was a safe and understanding person to talk about "things."

I had some hesitation about this referral, as I had already seen two other students referred from this high school group. I was aware that there were difficulties within the group in setting boundaries and defining relationships. Yet, these difficulties made sense to me. These young men were in an environment that valued traditional, stereotypical views of what a man was supposed to be. With one exception, these fellows either received critical judgement from their families or anticipated it thoroughly enough to hide their sexuality. Two of these young men had previously been forced to see a therapist called a change therapist whose practice was based on the belief that their sexual orientation was a "disorder" that therapy could "change," resulting in their becoming heterosexual. Upon finding each other, these young men became friends, lovers, families, and therapists to each other.

I told Jon that my relationships with his friends and the interrelatedness of these relationships might make it more difficult for us, yet I would be happy to see him and join with him in building our own, unique relationship and working through any difficulties. However, I said, it might be easier for Jon to see another therapist and not have to begin with this conflict but that I would leave that decision up to him. He was very clear that he wanted to see me and we made an appointment to meet.

This overlap in the relationships I had with Jonathan and his friends came to the surface in different ways. At times, I was concerned that I was pack leader of a club they belonged to. One of the students told me that he and the other students named me Babs among themselves and that they enjoyed exchanging appointment information: "Oh, you're Babs on Tuesday? I'm Babs on Friday." "You're Babs at four? I'm Babs at two." This overlap was also a factor at a critical point in our later work together.

CLIENT DESCRIPTION

Jonathan bounded into our first session with a high level of energy and much to say. He was dressed fairly Ivy League, with added touches in shoes or wild watch that demonstrated his creative style. Jon was a 17-year-old African American high school senior of medium build. He was bright and articulate yet felt very distant and would not look at me. Early in our first session, he shared his desire to be an actor and I often found myself feeling like an audience. Jon told stories. He talked rapidly and animatedly, gesturing often and occasionally standing up and moving around my office. He had a large smile on his face that often appeared strained. Although understandably nervous at his first therapy session, Jon seemed to be working excessively hard throughout our time together.

This type of storytelling is more common in the beginning of treatment, when there is much information to share. The client's need to be heard and understood is often frustrated by their perception that all information and details must be given in order for me to really see and hear the client. This frustration can sometimes seem like a race against the clock, with the client imparting a great deal of information, yet leaving the session feeling empty. I will often comment on the difficulty in describing one's life to another, how time consuming it must feel and, at times, frustrating.

I believe this process is an important one. Although I sometimes share the client's frustration, I know from experience that when we can give ourselves time to get to know each other, it allows us to slow the session down enough to talk about the feelings underneath the stories. In this arena, we can begin to know each other and make the connection that prevents the client from leaving the session feeling alone.

With Jon, however, all attempts on my part to share feelings or elicit reactions were swiftly rejected. There seemed to be no opportunities for contact or connection.

SOCIAL CONTEXT

Jonathan was the second child of June and Barry. June and Barry had married in their early twenties and soon found their styles and aspirations to be very different. Barry had a small electrical repair shop and June was a secretary. Both had finished high school but June hoped to go on to college. She was able to set very long-term goals, delay gratification, and work hard toward the promise of a return in the future. Barry had no desire to continue his education and liked to have fun. He enjoyed gambling and drinking, which June did not. These pastimes, while not yet causing problems in other areas of his life, began to cause great difficulty between Barry and June, and their fights began to escalate. An additional and major problem was Barry's continued searching for ways to get rich quickly. There were repeated attempts at deals and investments and schemes that became a constant source of conflict for the couple. This increased as they had their first child, Robert, and then, three years later, their last child, Jonathan.

Jon remembers frequent fights about money when growing up. His mother began to work more and more overtime and began taking night classes toward her college degree. Her push for upward mobility made her physically and emotionally unavailable to Jon and he lacked a secure base. His father spent more and more time away from the house as well. Jon came home after school to an empty house but lived in a tight-knit, largely African American community where relatives lived nearby. He remembers feeling lonely yet safe and supported. The greatest difficulty for Jon at that time was the feeling of pressure from his mother. He describes his brother as having been irresponsible and unmotivated and, according to Jon, his family seemed to easily accept that. Excuses were made for his brother and expectations were lowered. For Jon, however, expectations were increased. Obviously bright, Jon became his mother's number-one project. She focused on his school work and the quality of his work around the house. He felt she was never satisfied but quick to criticize and demand more. Jon's perception was that his mother's support came only when he met her expectations or "performed" to her satisfaction. He was unable to express his true needs or feelings.

When Jon was eleven years old, his parents divorced. Jon and his brother moved with their mother to a predominately White community in the suburbs. Jon's memories of this time are most often about his mother's anger and his own feelings of loss and isolation at losing his community. He does not remember feeling loss about his father. He felt deeply out of place in this neighborhood and these feelings increased as he became aware that the sexual feelings he had been having for a long time were not the ones echoed by his peers nor mentioned in the books he read or in the movies he saw.

While public school was fine for his brother, Jon was placed in an all-male, college preparatory, private high school run by the Catholic church. Jon was one of the few students of color. Once again, Jon was faced with high expectations in an environment that felt critical and threatening.

Initially, both Jon and his brother would visit their father in their old neighborhood. Jon repeatedly felt left out. Jonathan reports that his father and brother had always been close but, even without his brother present, he felt that he made his father uncomfortable and that they had great difficulty talking to each other. To this day, Jon does not know whether this was due to Jon's emerging sexuality or his placement in the family as the "one with a future." After a while, Jon visited much less often. This reduction in visitation was never mentioned by Jon's father.

Interestingly enough, Jon's father eventually did get rich quickly—the result of a law suit against the city in which they lived, after being injured in an auto accident with a police car on a high-speed chase. With this money, Barry bought real estate and made investments that allowed him a very comfortable living.

After Barry's change in financial status, Jon's brother began spending more and more time with his father until, upon completion of high school, he moved in with his father full-time. Jon stayed behind with his mother, although he did not feel that he was actually with her. He reported going days at a time without seeing her, only to have her storm into his room to wake him screaming about dishes he had left in the sink or laundry that had not been done. Jon feels their relationship for the past 6 years has been one of absences broken up by screaming fights.

Initial Session

Jon had mentioned "things" he wanted to talk to me about. Initially, I had difficulty learning what those "things" were. Jon began by wanting to talk about his career goals.

CLIENT: God! This is *great* being here. I have a lot of ideas I want to run by someone and get some feedback.

THERAPIST: I'm glad you're here, too. You mentioned on the phone that there were some things you wanted to talk to me about.

CLIENT: Oh, yeah, lots of things. I want to get going on my career; I'm an actor. I haven't really done anything yet but I know exactly how I want things to be. I know I can make it and be really successful. I'm gonna start going out on calls and trying out for things. Going into acting will be a field I can really relate to—more creativity, wilder people, I won't be the only gay or the only Black. It'll be great.

THERAPIST: How is it now? Do you feel like the only gay or the only Black now?

CLIENT: Well, I have my gay friends so that helps, but the school is really straight and in my family or my old neighborhood, I don't know anybody who's gay. And there are no Blacks in my new neighborhood and only a couple at my school. And being a gay, Black man—that's really impossible! I don't know anyone like me.

THERAPIST: Yes. That must be very difficult. How is that for you?

CLIENT: Oh, I'm used to it. That's why if I get into the acting thing, I think it will be much better.

THERAPIST: Tell me more about what it means for you to be gay and Black?

CLIENT: Oh, I told you. It's just extra pressure. When I'm acting I can really be special. I have this idea for a casting call I'm going on. They're looking for a Steve Urkel type, and I saw a pair of glasses at the store that will be just perfect. Here's what I'm going to do.

With that, Jon hiked his pants high up on his chest and began to demonstrate his audition. I found myself looking for a place to land: some opening from Jon where I could enter and start to form a relationship with him. Occasionally, there would be openings, as in his comments about being Black or being gay, but my approaches were quickly pushed aside. I realized that I would need to proceed very slowly with Jon and allow him to set the pace. My plan was to continue to speak to the underlying feelings he was alluding to and attempt a connection with him but to listen carefully to his do-not-enter message and respect his limits. I found myself thinking about how closed off he was and wondering what had forced him to be so protective of himself.

In the first few sessions, this pattern continued. Jon gave me more and more pieces of information as time went on yet still seemed unable to increase his ability to share feelings.

CLIENT: I can't wait to graduate next month and get out of that school.

THERAPIST: Its been hard for you there.

CLIENT: Oh, it's okay, it's almost over. But I think college will be cool. They won't tell you what to do all the time and try to control you.

THERAPIST: You've mentioned how much you hate being told what to do, especially with your mom.

CLIENT: Yeah! She really tries to control me. Look at this bracelet, she hates this thing. She threw a fit yesterday when she saw it and wouldn't talk to me until I took it off. What a bitch.

THERAPIST: Does she battle with you about your appearance often or was this different.

CLIENT: Well, she gets upset at anything different, like these shoes or this watch. You know, I'm sure she knows I'm gay but she never asks anything, never makes any comment. And then she'll get all bent out of shape about something like this bracelet and I think it's 'cause she thinks it's a gay thing.

THERAPIST: You said you're sure she knows you're gay. What makes you think that?

CLIENT: Well, there's my friends. We're always together, no girls anywhere. And some of them dress pretty wild. And she *never* asks me about girls or dates, she just knows better. But she asks my brother about his love life.

THERAPIST: So, there are ways you can tell that she knows, but she never says anything. Have you thought about or wanted to say something to her?

CLIENT: Not too often. A couple times I thought about it, but I just know it will go badly.

THERAPIST: That sounds like the worst of both worlds: You can't talk to her about it or get her help or support, yet it's out enough for you to get attacked about it—and in disguised arenas at that.

CLIENT: Yeah, it stinks.

THERAPIST: Can you tell me more about how it stinks for you, how you know it will go badly between the two of you?

CLIENT: Well, she's just a bitch. What can I say? She's always after me and I don't think she even likes me. She'd be really embarrassed if the family knew I was gay. I mean, she thinks she's doing me a favor if she lets me live in her lousy house.

As our sessions continued, Jon was able to share information of events that were more difficult for him. There was an increased acknowledgement of affect, yet he still tended to swat away any attempt to talk further about these feelings. He used phrases like "What can I say?" "I'm used to it," and "I'm okay" to convey a message to stay away. As this pattern emerged, I was able to make process comments on how difficult these feelings appeared to be for him. For example:

THERAPIST: You know, Jon, you say, "I'm okay" while the look on your face changes and you shake your head. What's happening?

CLIENT: Well, I just hate this, my mom I mean. She's always been this way and it's never going to change. And I've had to learn to just put up with it. It makes me mad and I don't want to think about it.

THERAPIST: So, when you say "I'm okay," that's your way of telling me you're angry and uncomfortable—and want to talk about something else?

CLIENT: Yeah, I guess it is.

In this way, we could acknowledge his need to share information about his life and feel listened to yet recognize his anxiety when we named and explored the feelings he was having. This allowed us to join together and share his difficulty with affect while still respecting the boundary he was setting to limit further exploration.

Case Conceptualization

Jon's difficulty with relationships became the most obvious and the initial area for exploration. Jon did not know how to be with me or with anyone. Jon's situation, being one of the few African Americans in his school and neighborhood and being gay, meant he had no role models and truly had little idea of "how to be" with others. His race and sexual orientation probably increased his sense of isolation and rejection. This problem, connecting, let me know that his difficulties, while deeply aggravated by his present environment, went back to an early time of learning how to form attachments. In both self-psychology (Kohut, 1977), and in object relations theory (Mahler, 1968), children are deeply dependent on their parents for love, attachment, and attention. This results in the formation of a healthy ego for the child. For Jon, this lack of a healthy ego resulted in feelings of isolation coupled with an inability to get outside himself. The anxiety and social uncertainty Jon experienced took all his attention and energy, making it difficult to quiet his inner turmoil enough to understand another's experience. Since it is within the context of relationships that we gain a sense of self, Jon's impairment in relationships caused him problems socially and problems with his self-image.

Jon's difficulty with boundaries alerted me to the likelihood that his boundaries had been invaded and that people were not safe for him. His need to push against the boundaries of others was likely to result in those others either being overrun or being angry. For example, Jon would often show up at his friends' houses late at night without being invited and, at other times, not show up when he was expected. In this way, when Jon's friends felt taken advantage of or became angry or rejected him, Jon recreated his own conflict and reinforced his isolation.

Although Jon fought for this distance, I understood, both from readings and from practice, how acutely painful this isolation was. Yet, Jon's choices with his mother were either to be cast off or to be controlled and criticized. As Masterson emphasized, the two distinct ego states available were the "good child" who was passive and dependent, or the "bad self" who was rejected and criticized. Jon's brother, Robert, had become controlled. This allowed him to stay connected to both his mother and his father. Understandably, Robert later joined the service, where he could be controlled as an adult.

Jon was hungry for attention yet believed that attention came with the risk of criticism (as his mother had criticized him), engulfment (as his mother had attempted to engulf him), or rejection (as his father—and ultimately his mother—had rejected him). Schave and Schave (1989) describe the adolescent's continued need for parents to "function as mirroring and idealizing self-objects; in essence to be there and to be affectively attuned to them." Jon's anger at his parents' inability to perform this function could not be expressed unless he risked further abandonment and the depression that accompanied it. At times, he controlled this anger by splitting it off and projecting it onto others. His ability to elicit this anger was strong. People often became angry at him. As an African American, he experienced a very real risk of criticism, anger, and rejection that aggravated his view of the world as an empty and threatening place. In this way the world doubly reinforced his views, and it was necessary to hide his anger in an environment that was threatened by it.

As an African American gay man, Jon's feelings of isolation were not solely a result of his childhood. The world was not a welcoming place for him. Either his race or his sexual orientation alone were enough to put Jon at risk of attack, even death. In combination, Jon's world was doubly threatening. Additionally, Jon's presence as an African American gay male at a private Catholic school exacerbated his sense of being different and left him most often with the feeling that he did not belong, was not welcomed, and not wanted. As Martin (1971) so clearly states it, "There is a pain brought on by not being like everyone else when it is important that you be like others."

In adolescence, the issues surrounding separation and individuation again become the primary developmental task. Jon's lack of attachment made it all the more difficult. In school and at home, Jon was left to make his own decisions. As he moved into arenas where there was less structure, Jon began to deteriorate. At college, for example, Jon began to cut classes and stopped doing his homework, and his grades began to plunge. This inability to tolerate ambiguity and lack of structure is common in borderline functioning.

The move to college also moved Jon out of the environment that was familiar to him: vacillating between compliance and rebellion. I believe this return to a period of attempted autonomy motivated Jonathan to seek counseling.

Orienting Constructs

In order to gain a picture of Jon or any client, I often use a movie metaphor. I will tell the interns I am supervising to see the client in front of them as the end of the movie. The beginning of the movie is when this person was born, a brand-new baby coming into the world. Your job, as a clinician, is to see the movie, that is, to enter the world of this client and see a picture of what the years and experiences of their life have been like. If you are truly able to do this, the behaviors and symptoms of your client will not only become understandable but will begin to emerge as the best—and sometimes only—choices this person had.

My initial pictures of Jon were of a child who had little opportunity for attention or positive parenting. His mother's rejection of him following her failed attempts to control him and his father's lack of attachment to him left Jon feeling isolated. Gunderson and Zanarini (1989) found that "borderline patients described their relationships with their mothers as conflicted or uninvolved and their relationships with their fathers as uninvolved."

The failure of Jon's mother to successfully navigate the separateness/relatedness period of development (rapprochement) and the continuation of these problematic relational patterns throughout his childhood left Jon with a choice between engulfment and isolation. Jon's brother had complied with his mother's demands and achieved a favored son role in the family. Father's attachment to Jon's brother increased Jon's sense of rejection and left him feeling like there truly was something wrong with him. Although the possibility of intimacy left Jon equally threatened by the potential loss of self, Jon's fundamental experience was one of abandonment.

His parents' later divorce exacerbated these feelings of abandonment. The family's moves, changes in schools, and loss of community all severely compounded his isolation.

Jon's experience of being a gay, African American male, coupled with the moves, changes in school, and loss of community left Jon with no sense of belonging. He had belonged to his extended family and the close-knit neighborhood he had lived in, but then came the move. By leaving this community and placing Jon in a mostly Caucasian school, his family offered no support for Jon's cultural heritage. By providing no adult males of color, Jon had no role model to help his sense of cultural identity.

He might have felt a sense of belonging in his high school, but not as a person of color with an alternative lifestyle. He felt isolated in gay groups, as there were few African Americans. He did not feel he could join with other African Americans without being heterosexual. I wondered if his initial desire to seek treatment with me and to share appointment days and times with his friends at school was another way of attempting to belong, this time by joining the "Babs" club.

Treatment Plans and Intervention Strategy

INITIAL TREATMENT PLAN

My primary initial goal with Jon was to work to establish a collaborative relationship. This was both the most fundamental and most difficult goal of our work together. Jonathan's injuries were in his relationships: originally in his parents' lack of attention and nourishment, lack of structure or limits, and lack of predictability and later recreated in his inability to relate to people. Jon was unable to let people in and unable to leave his own position or egocentrism in order to understand others.

In the beginning of treatment, the goal to establish a relationship meant taking the relationship deeper than the "performance" Jon was currently giving. By performance, I mean Jon's tendency to tell stories without pause for interaction between us nor affective reactions from him. Although Jon was getting the attention he lacked from me, I felt that this experience would ultimately not fill his deeper need to connect with someone. As long as I was an audience for Jon, we were not in real, mutual contact with each other. Additionally, I believe that any healing or growth in therapy takes place within the context of genuine and reciprocal emotional contact; therefore, establishing this in our relationship was a priority.

Establishing our relationship along these lines is an ongoing process throughout the course of treatment, and, ideally, deals with different aspects of the client's conflicts, as the relationship grows and the bond becomes deeper. In the beginning, my goal was to make the session safe enough for Jon to risk becoming more vulnerable and encouraging that vulnerability—while also recognizing his fears and respecting his need to proceed slowly. This was best accomplished by the use of process statements. Instead of pushing for feelings that Jon was not ready to share, as in the previous example of his use of the phrase, "It's okay," we could talk *about* this difficulty and, in later sessions, what made it so difficult to open up. In this way, we were not at cross purposes, but truly collaborating about his difficulties.

Our second short-term goal was to address Jon's difficulty in attending sessions on a regular and timely basis. Again, the use of process comments were helpful in changing Jon's belief that my comments or inquiries about his attendance were attacks or judgments against him. This will be demonstrated more fully later in this section.

An intermediate goal for treatment was to address the deeper conflicts in Jon's relationships based on his personality style. These conflicts took the form of his alternating between idealization and devaluation (new friends quickly went from being "perfect" to being "jerks" who let him down), his mood swings, his poor impulse control (unsafe sex, alcohol use), and his feelings of isolation and engulfment. My goal was to give Jon the holding environment that would allow him to experience a connection without losing himself and to experience independence without retaliation.

I hoped that by being a stable, consistent, and caring presence in his life he could begin to care about himself. I hoped that I could present to Jon a new role model who was neither all-good nor all-bad and be perceived realistically. Most importantly, I wanted him to see that I could survive his rages and not punish or abandon him.

My plan for carrying out these goals was to be caring, supportive, attentive, and patient. I intended to clearly define the rules and boundaries for treatment and consistently address them in order to create a safe, *predictable* environment for Jon. I looked for themes in the topics he addressed and pointed them out to allow him to feel understood and listened to. For example, Jon's relationships in the past consisted of threats to his individuality and threats of abandonment. Jon's unmet needs resulted in a great hunger that he took into his current relationships. This hunger overwhelmed his friends and, when Jon's demands were not met, left Jon feeling betrayed and enraged. These themes allowed us to approach intense material within a framework that Jon could tolerate.

My long-term goals were to reduce Jon's risk-taking behaviors. While his experimentation with drugs and alcohol was not causing difficulties at this time, he was establishing patterns that could cause problems in the future. A great deal of his social life took place in bars, and Jon had a low tolerance for hurt, anger, or frustration. Drugs and especially alcohol gave Jon a short-term escape from these feelings.

I felt this goal was best carried out by facilitating Jon's expression of affect in our work together, resulting in a reduced need to "medicate" these feelings away. We also shared educational information about the effects and interactions of these drugs. Jon was better able to discuss this in an environment where he did not feel judged or attacked.

Another example of risk-taking behavior was in the area of his sexuality. Jon's understandable joy over accepting his sexuality and finding a support group of other like-minded peers initiated a period of much sexual activity. This coming out, combined with an age-appropriate exploration of sexuality and an adolescent fearlessness of consequences, equaled a very high risk for AIDS.

Again, educational information was helpful as there was much misinformation among Jon and his friends. Unfortunately, my attempt to gain credibility with Jon per my belief in his mortality was less successful. He consistently refused to believe that he or his friends could ever become infected. Although I knew that this was again age-appropriate and was the same dynamic that enabled adolescents to behave recklessly in cars or to volunteer for dangerous military assignments, I found myself returning to this topic again and again without success.

REVISED TREATMENT PLAN

As Jon shared more of his history and daily life, I began to realize how devoid of connections his life was. He would gather with his friends but would never say anything of substance to them. They knew little about his life or family. He would go days at a time without even seeing or hearing from his mother and had virtually no relationship with his brother or father. I became increasingly aware of how unusual and difficult it was for Jon to spend time with me and why we were progressing at what I thought to be a slow pace. I realized that, for Jon, it was not slow at all.

This historical lack of connectedness would become most evident when Jon would have difficulty with attendance, begin to tell stories again, or push for special treatment by asking for extra time at the end of sessions or to see me on weekends. These demands were not met but were discussed in the framework of previously identified themes, for example, Jon's unreasonable demands on his friends and the resulting feelings of betrayal and rage. In this way, Jon also tested the consistencies of my boundaries and received the structure and limits he never had at home.

Jon and I were able to identify these patterns and speak to what had caused them to reemerge. More importantly, by becoming aware of the extent of Jon's isolation, I was able to slow down internally and allow the process to unwind.

A second revised goal came as Jon graduated from high school and enrolled in college. At the university, there was no insistence that he attend classes. There were no consequences for not doing the assignments except to fail the course. Without the structure of high school, Jon began to fail.

Jon and I began to focus on his perception of others as people who forced him to "perform." This allowed Jon to take the role of either the victim who complied (and therefore deserved special attention) or the rebel who refused (and became isolated). In college, Jon had no one to take the role of "perpetrator."

Most importantly, we began to focus on this issue in the context of our relationship. We began to explore how his requests for extra time or special treatment and his difficulty with attendance were a part of this same pattern.

BALANCING GOALS

Jon's initial need to tell stories had to be respected. I could make comments about this need or inquire about his feelings, but it was necessary to accept his rejection of my interventions. This was the only way Jon knew how to relate. By respecting this and, at the same time, continuing to make occasional process statements (e.g. "You know, Jon, you've told me a lot of interesting details about the fight you and your friend had last weekend, but I'm still wondering how you felt about all of that. Those feelings seem more difficult for you to talk about."), Jon was not forced into complying with my way of relating but instead provided with a model of another way he could relate.

The issue of attendance was more complicated. Here I believed it was necessary not to compromise. Where our goals could be balanced was in the area of how we addressed this issue. Jon was not attacked or controlled, judged or rejected. Instead, I would ask about his difficulty with attendance and comment on his ambivalence and his struggle (e.g., "Seems like it was hard for you to get here or be here today. I'm wondering if we could put our heads together and try to understand that better"). I tried to communicate that I believed this issue to be very important. The importance of this issue was *not* an indicator of something he was doing wrong but an indicator of the anxiety and pain he might be experiencing.

My goal of reducing his sexual at-risk behaviors remained my goal alone and, therefore, was not realized. This was, at times, frustrating and alarming for me. I heard many instances and details of Jon's exposure to the AIDS virus. I attempted to educate him whenever possible; I also, at times, attempted to firmly confront his behavior and address my deep concerns surrounding his actions. These interventions were consistently batted away by Jon. Vitkus (1993) speaks of the additional therapeutic challenges with borderline patients beyond the complex initial establishment of a relationship. He defines three additional problems: (a) that change "tends to be slow and gradual, and therapeutic plateaus are frequent," (b) that these patients are "unable to project their thoughts into the future . . ." and therefore are unaware of future consequences, and (c) that these patients generally have "few inner resources in terms of ego-strength and impulse control . . ."

Therapeutic Process

RELATIONAL REENACTMENTS

As Jonathan and I moved into the middle stage of treatment, I felt we were becoming closer and that his anxiety was rising as a result. This kind of closer or more intimate relationship was putting Jonathan into uncharted waters, and, historically, relationships brought either the risk of abandonment or the threat of being consumed. It became very helpful at this point that Jonathan and I had been able to identify these themes in past relationships and become aware of vehicles that Jonathan had used in the past to reduce these threats—and thereby reduce his anxiety.

Jonathan began to have difficulty either attending sessions or being on time for them. He would also request additional sessions on days when I was not at the clinic. As these difficulties came up, we would talk about them. For example:

CLIENT: Well, I'm late! But wait until you hear what happened to me. I knew you'd be mad, but I couldn't help it.

THERAPIST: You thought I'd be mad?

CLIENT: Well, maybe not mad, but I *knew* you'd make something out of it. I *knew* you'd want to talk about it. Don't you?

THERAPIST: Well, if you're asking if I think it's important, I do. We've been struggling for some time now about how difficult it is for you to be here. But it sounds like you were worried you'd get in trouble with me, and that seems very different than you and I together trying to work out more manageable ways for you to be here.

CLIENT: (tearfully) I *want* to be here. You have no idea how much I busted my ass to get here.

These encounters were difficult for me as well. On a conscious level, Jonathan was working very hard to get to our sessions. It was at this point in the conflict that Jonathan would exhibit the greatest degree of vulnerability I had experienced with him—and the only times when the pain or tears even made it up to his eyes for me to see. For me, the difficulty was in knowing that Jonathan would only hear my comments and questions as criticisms and not as my awareness that he was in conflict, which I intended.

However, I had learned in the past months that if I did not address these issues, Jonathan would escalate his behavior until I did attend to them. I believed this was because, on an unconscious level, Jonathan was attempting to move me into the only kind of relationship he knew how to have. That is, he would bump up against my boundaries or limits in the hope that I would become angry and reject him. He expected the anger and rejection and heard it even when it wasn't there. He was also very good at creating these feelings in others, and there were times I began to feel angry, too. Luckily, this became a great built-in early warning system alerting me that we were recreating an old relationship of Jonathan's.

On the occasions when I did not address (or did not recognize) one of Jonathan's attempts to push against a limit, Jonathan was not hurt and enraged but distant and disdaining. I believed this was because he could not respect me if he could move me around. And if he could manipulate me, I was no longer safe. Internally, Jonathan felt out of control and I could be of no help to him if I was out of control, too.

In Jonathan's mind, either he was controlling me or I was controlling him. Historically, this *relational template* or *internal working model* is what he had experienced. I was attempting to form a different kind of relationship where I would be in charge of what *I* did and continue to set those limits, in spite of the fact that Jonathan interpreted this as my controlling or criticizing him. This was an important aspect of the corrective experience I was trying to provide for him in treatment.

THERAPIST: You know, I don't underestimate at all how much you want to be here and how hard you work to make that happen. And here you are! I really do see that, Jonathan. But I also believe that it is very difficult for you to be here and that it might help if we put our heads together and tried to understand that. Maybe we could start with how you felt driving over here today.

CLIENT: Well, I *do* want to be here, but sometimes it's really hard. I was thinking today that I don't really have anybody that I can talk to about stuff. I mean, my friends are okay, but there's all this sexual tension all the time. Friends that used to be lovers, lovers that become friends. A couple of my friends will start to see each other romantically and everything changes. The lines get all screwed up. It's easier sometimes just to party and not think about all this stuff.

As we resolved the conflict about being late for therapy, we could proceed to the real issue: relationships and boundaries. Being late for therapy was no longer a testing ground.

Instead, as time went on, new testing grounds appeared. We next dealt with the issue of cancellations (similarly, by focusing on the importance of the issue and the conflict or pain that was being communicated, rather than blaming or attempting to control him). When that was resolved, we moved to Jonathan's asking for additional sessions on days I was not available (again, these demands were not met but instead explored). I continued to feel this barrier between us that prevented Jonathan from sharing his pain with me, yet I believed he was out of ways to push the boundaries surrounding our sessions. However, Jonathan was much more creative than I, and we had one more major conflict to resolve. This proved to be the turning point in our work together.

I was scheduled to see Jonathan at 3:00 P.M. that day. At 1:00 P.M., I walked down the hall to the clinic waiting room to get Steve, a former patient of mine who had recently returned to therapy. Steve was a good friend of Jonathan's and had originally given Jonathan my name and recommended that he see me. As I opened the door to greet Steve, I was surprised to see Jonathan sitting there instead. He jumped up, walked through the door I was holding, and began to walk to my office. I followed behind him thinking that I might have misread my appointment book and that I would check it when we got to my office. However, Jonathan made sure I did not miss the significance of this by turning his head around as we walked down the hall and saying,

CLIENT: This is Steve's appointment time. I asked him to switch with me.

THERAPIST: Yes. I was surprised and thinking I might have misread my schedule.

CLIENT: It's okay though, isn't it?

We were still walking down the hall at this point and I felt uncomfortable with Jonathan's switching the appointments, but I wasn't sure why. His actions hadn't broken any rule. However, over the years, I had learned to both trust my instincts as well as give myself permission to "not know" right away why something wasn't okay. Jonathan's big grin confirmed the feeling I had that this event was significant.

THERAPIST: Actually, it doesn't feel okay, and I'm not sure why. But come on down to my office and let's talk about it.

As we reached my office and sat down, Jonathan began to tell me that he couldn't have made the 3:00 P.M. appointment and how hard he'd worked to solve this problem. He said he knew he *couldn't* cancel or not show and he *knew* I'd be mad, so he had come up with this wonderful solution that I couldn't possibly mind, and here he was.

For me, I became aware of why this wasn't okay, but felt initially bound by my concern over both Jonathan's reaction to this as well as my concern for Steve, who had become enmeshed in this as well. If I held Jonathan to his 3:00 P.M. appointment time, he could come back in two hours; but Steve's appointment time was right now and he would miss his session. I proceeded, knowing it was not my task to rescue Steve from this situation nor to hold back the correct response out of concern for Jonathan's reaction.

THERAPIST: Jonathan, I understand now why this is not okay. First of all, this is *my* schedule and I'm in charge of it. If changes are made, they need to be made through me. It would have been alright for you and Steve to switch appointments if either of you had called me and involved me in the plans. Secondly, this isn't an isolated event. For a long time now, we've talked about how hard it is for you to make your appointments. We've also talked about your pushing limits and people not being there for you. I know this is very difficult, but I *am* here for you and look forward to seeing you later today at 3:00 P.M.

CLIENT: I *knew* it!! You're not gonna see me! I can't *believe* you'd get so nit-picky about this. I tried *so hard* to do the right thing. Nothing I do pleases you! I *can't* come at 3:00 o'clock. I *told* you, I just can't make it. If you want to see me, you see me *now*.

Jonathan continued for a few minutes more. He expressed outrage that I wouldn't see him, felt betrayed by me, and demonstrated more emotion than

I had ever witnessed from him. A couple tears rolled down his cheek as he talked. I listened intently as he talked. When he was finished, I said,

THERAPIST: Jonathan, I can see how hurtful this is for you and how angry you feel. I also know that your whole life you've felt like your mother would pick at you and that there was nothing you could do to please her. I don't feel that way about you and I don't want to join all the people you carry on your shoulders that you have to try and please. However, your appointment time is in two hours and I'll look forward to seeing you then.

CLIENT: I told you, I can't come later.

THERAPIST: Then I'll hope to see you next week at 3:00 P.M.

CLIENT: No way!

As Jonathan slammed the door behind him, my first thoughts were to the degree of pain and rage he was feeling. I felt very sad for him. My next thoughts were doubts about the position I had taken and I went over the alternatives in my head. This was very helpful in reaffirming my assessment, for no other alternative would have been in Jonathan's best interests. Had I not been able to tolerate his feelings of hurt and anger—and adjusted my response to minimize those feelings—I would have sent the message that therapy was not a safe place to have those feelings. My largest concern was his perception of abandonment from me and I wondered if he would come the following week.

I thought about Jonathan during the week as our appointment time approached and I knew that, one way or the other, this would be a turning point. Intellectually, I felt that if he was not able to continue, it was still better to have kept the integrity of our work intact, and maybe that would allow him to return in the future when he was ready. However, on a more personal level, I worried about Jonathan being back out in the world without the slimmest of connections to anyone.

At 3:00 P.M. the following week, Jonathan was sitting in the waiting room. He quietly walked past me down the hall to my office. As I closed the door and sat down, Jonathan reached out his hand to me and, as I held it, he began to sob. He cried for a long, long time.

When he was able to talk, Jonathan began to speak of his loneliness, of always feeling like there was something ugly inside of him and that it was "too much" for anyone else to bear. This feeling of being "too much" surfaced vis à vis his mother, who tried to control him. As her demands became endless, Jonathan attempted to set limits with her and fight for some of his rights. When mother met with his resistance, she would step back, become very distant and tell Jonathan to "just do whatever you want then. I don't care." Jonathan believed this emotional abandonment came because he was too much for her.

With his friends, Jonathan believed he "wanted too much" and that these desires were ugly on his part and needed to be hidden. At times, he expressed, he would get so tired of feeling "wrong" inside that he would want to tell everyone to go to hell.

Jonathan felt his demands might at times be too much or unrealistic, but this time he didn't feel ugly or "too much" and, he said, "somehow, I don't feel so alone." As Masterson (1976) notes, when the therapist sets limits and confronts the client, the client can no longer act out his or her affect. When the therapist creates a safe environment by setting these limits, the painful affect often emerges and the client experiences a meaningful, historical connection that often becomes a turning point in treatment.

IMPEDIMENTS TO TREATMENT

Our largest impediment to treatment was the almost intolerable levels of anxiety that Jonathan felt at increases in intimacy. As we would become closer, Jon would act out this anxiety by pushing away from me, pushing against limits, and breaking rules. He would express rage toward me or attempt to elicit it. As we successfully managed this anxiety, we would have a break-through, such as I've just described. But immediately following a breakthrough, we would move into a period of distance. I understood this to be Jon's need to know that, in the same way he had found out he could get closer, he now needed to know he could *not* get close, as well. These impediments were resolved by commenting on this distance or anxiety yet accepting that it would remain.

Another impediment to treatment was Jon's difficulty in integrating good and bad. Many times, his sessions were dominated by alternating themes of the new, perfect person he had met and the old, worthless friend who had betrayed him. His view of me and of himself alternated in this way as well. Over time, Jon had to recognize that I was a human being with flaws and failings who still honored and cared for him. My caring for him, while not reinforcing his self-view as "special," allowed him to begin considering a middle ground for himself as well.

A major impediment was Jon's lack of a support system or *any* individual who was there for him beyond surface friendships. This greatly limited the amount of anxiety and disruption he could tolerate and, I believe, limited the amount of work we could do. Much of the earlier work referenced above (Gunderson, 1984) involving confrontations and interpretations with borderline patients was done in an in-patient setting where, if they regressed and became destructive, the patients could be safely protected and contained.

Termination and Therapist's Summary Thoughts

Two events led to Jonathan's termination. As it became clear that college was not something he was ready to pursue at this time, Jonathan began to consider a move out of the area. Although I did not believe that our work together had reached a natural conclusion, I felt it very important to not undermine Jon's attempts to become autonomous from me. Jon's childhood attempts at autonomy had been met with parental attempts to control him, followed by threats of abandonment if he did not comply. His religious training and high school education had taken place in an environment that reinforced this view: their rules were clearly defined and not to be debated; participation was total or not at all. Consequently, I believed it was important to let Jon know that, while I thought we might learn more together in the future, I understood his desire to move on now. I reflected on how terribly he had been held back his entire life from pursuing his independence. I assured him that I would remain interested in his whereabouts and available to see him at any time in the future.

This had been discussed for a couple months when the second event occurred. I was offered a position at a new agency that I was very interested in taking. Additionally, I would be able to see my present clients at this new location. Jon felt this would be a time to terminate. Whether the change stirred up difficult feelings and threats of abandonment or this change offered the opportunity to leave as desired, I was not sure at the time. But terminate, he did.

Later, Jon would, many times, come for therapy of a moderate length. Every few years, he returns to the area and sees me for a few months. The issues remain the same, the relationship painstakingly grows, and the terminations always feel abrupt and premature to me.

I have now come to believe that these terminations involve three issues: (a) that Jonathan's coping strategies for avoiding his abandonment despair continued to exert more power than his ability to tolerate this pain; (b) that what appears painstakingly slow to me involves great risk and almost terrifying closeness to Jon, which would not be tolerated were he not given "permission" to terminate; and (c) that, with a symmetry that makes the art of psychotherapy a continual wonder to me, we are recreating his rapprochement phase and cycling through periods of autonomy followed by periods of reunion.

Therapy often involves people reworking issues over time in order to gain a sense of mastery or integration. It was certainly challenging to work with Jon toward such integration but far more rewarding to be able to share in such a rich and valuable relationship.

REFERENCES

Adler, G., & Buie, D. H. (1979). The psychotherapeutic approach to aloneness in borderline patients. In J. LeBoit & A. Capponi (Eds.), *Advances in psychotherapy of the borderline patient* (pp. 433–448). New York: Jason Aronson.

American Psychiatric Association. (1994). *Diagnostic and statistical manual of mental disorders* (4th ed.). Washington, DC: Author.

Beck, A. T. (1976). *Cognitive therapy and the emotional disorders.* New York: International Universities Press.

Beck, A. T., & Freeman, A. (1990). *Cognitive therapy of personality disorders.* New York: Guilford.

Beck, A. T., Rush, J., Shaw, B., & Emery, G. (1979). *Cognitive therapy of depression.* New York: Guilford.

Buie, D. H., & Adler, G. (1972). The uses of confrontation with borderline patients. *International Journal of Psychoanalytic Psychotherapy, 1,* 90–108.

Buie, D. H., & Adler, G. (1982). The definitive treatment of the borderline patient. *International Journal of Psychoanalytic Psychotherapy, 9,* 51–87.

Clarkin, J. F., Widiger, T. A., Frances, A., Hurt, S. W., & Gilmore, M. (1983). Prototypic typology and the borderline personality disorder. *Journal of Abnormal Psychology, 93,* 263–275.

Freeman, A., Pretzer, J., Fleming, B., & Simon, K. (1990). *Clinical applications of cognitive therapy.* New York: Plenum.

Grinker, R., Werble, B., & Drye, R. (1968). *The borderline syndrome: A behavioral study of ego-functions.* New York: Basic Books.

Gunderson, J. G. (1984). *Borderline personality disorders.* Washington, DC: American Psychiatric Press.

Gunderson, J. G., & Zanarini, M. C. (1989). Pathogenesis of borderline personality. In A. Tasman, R. E. Hales, & A. J. Francis (Eds.), *Review of psychiatry.* Washington, DC: American Psychiatric Press.

Hoch, P., & Polatin, P. (1949). Pseudoneurotic forms of schizophrenia. *Psychiatric Quarterly, 23,* 248–276.

Kernberg, O. (1968). The treatment of patients with borderline personality organization. *International Journal of Psycho-Analysis, 49,* 600–619.

Kernberg, O. (1976). *Object relations theory and clinical psychoanalysis.* New York: Jason Aronson.

Kernberg, O., Selzer, M., Koenigsburg, H., et al. (1989). *Psychodynamic psychotherapy of borderline patients.* New York: Basic Books.

Kohut, H. (1971). *The analysis of the self.* New York: International Universities Press.

Kohut, H. (1977). *The restoration of the self.* New York: International Universities Press.

Mahler, M. (1968). *On human symbiosis and the vicissitudes of individuation.* New York: International Universities Press.

Mahler, M. (1971). A study of the separation-individuation process and its possible application to borderline phenomena in the psychoanalytic situation. *The Psychoanalytic Study of the Child, 26,* 403–424.

Mahler, M., Pine, F., & Bergman, A. (1970). The mother's reaction to her toddler's drive for individuation. In E. J. Anthony & T. Bernedeck (Eds.), *Parenthood: Its psychology and psychopathology* (pp. 257–274). Boston: Little, Brown.

Mahler, M., Pine, F., & Bergman, A. (1975). *The psychological birth of the human infant: Symbiosis and individuation.* New York: Basic Books.

Martin, E. (1971). Reflections on the early adolescent in school. In J. Kagen & R. Coles (Eds.), *Twelve to sixteen: Early adolescence.* New York: Wiley.

Masterson, J. (1972). *Treatment of the borderline adolescent: A developmental approach.* New York: Wiley.

Masterson, J. (1976). *Psychotherapy of the borderline adult: A developmental approach*. New York: Brunner/Mazel.

Masterson, J., & Rinsley, D. (1975). The borderline syndrome: The role of the mother in the genesis and psychic structure of the borderline personality. *International Journal of Psycho-Analysis, 56,* 163–177.

Rorschach, H. (1942). *Psychodiagnostics* (5th ed.). Bern, Germany: Hans Huber.

Schave, D., & Schave, B. (1989). *Early adolescence and the search of self: A developmental perspective*. New York: Praeger.

Vitkus, J. (1993). *Casebook in abnormal psychology* (2nd ed.). New York: McGraw-Hill.

SUGGESTIONS FOR FURTHER READING

Fraiberg, S. (1959). *The magic years*. New York: Scribner. Writing from a psychoanalytic perspective, Selma Fraiberg carefully and compassionately takes you into the mind of a child.

Napier, A., & Whitaker, C. (1978). *The family crucible*. New York: Harper and Row. Demonstration of family systems through the use of a case study bringing family dynamics to life.

Teyber, E. (1996). *Interpersonal process in psychotherapy: A guide for clinical training* (3rd ed.). Pacific Grove: Brooks-Cole. Provides a very accessible model of how to incorporate psychodynamic theory and systems theory within the framework of individual treatment and clearly articulates the richness of the therapeutic relationship.

Chapter 7

ATTENTION-DEFICIT/ HYPERACTIVITY DISORDER

CASE ILLUSTRATION OF TIMMY: AN 8-YEAR-OLD BIRACIAL CHILD

Faith H. McClure, Ph.D.
Edward Teyber, Ph.D.

THE DISORDER

Attention-Deficit/Hyperactivity Disorder (ADHD) is a persistent pattern of inattention and/or hyperactivity-impulsivity that is more frequent and severe than the age-appropriate behavior. However, the characterization beyond this general statement, the etiology, and the prevalence have all been in great dispute in the field.

There has been a great debate regarding whether ADHD is a single disorder or multiple disorders. This disagreement is reflected in the diverse descriptive and diagnostic terms that have been used for ADHD. In the past, terms such as *post-encephalitic disorder, minimal brain disorder or dysfunction,* and *hyperkinesis* were used (see Baren, 1994). In particular, the term *hyperactive* has been used in the field, which suggests activity levels as the primary diagnostic feature.

Over the years, the *Diagnostic and Statistical Manual of Mental Disorders* has also wavered in its identification of the disorder. In contrast to the term *hyperactive,* it has noted the significant role of *attention* as a central feature and legitimized the diagnosis for those children who present with the attention deficits without hyperactivity. In DSM-III (American Psychiatric Association, 1980), the disorder was divided into Attention Deficit Disorder with hyperactivity (ADD-H), Attention Deficit Disorder without hyperactivity (ADD-w/o H), and a Residual type. The next version of the manual, DSM-III-R (American Psychiatric Association, 1987) had two categories, Attention Deficit Hyperactivity Disorder and Undifferentiated Attention Deficit Disorder (without hyperactivity). The most recent version, DSM-IV (American Psychiatric Association, 1994), currently lists criteria for three subtypes of ADHD: a predominantly Inattentive Type, a predominantly Hyperactive-Impulsive Type, and the most commonly occurring Combined Type, which we will examine later in the case study of Timmy. The DSM-IV requires that criteria for either one or both of the two basic dimensions of *Inattention* and/or *Hyperactivity-Impulsivity* be present for the past six months, that some of these symptoms be apparent before age 7, and that they cause impairment in two or more settings. Some in the field view these criteria as too stringent. They note, for example, that girls exhibit the Inattentive type more often, a type that may not be observed until age 6 or 7 and that causes difficulty primarily in school settings. Thus, age and pervasive (two or more settings) versus situational (e.g., school or home) requirements for the diagnosis remain issues for future DSM's to address.

The current diagnosis thus focuses on three defining characteristics: inattention, impulsivity, and hyperactivity.

Children who present with primarily the Inattentive Type may have difficulty *focusing* (e.g., listening, organizing, and executing tasks) or may be unable to *sustain* their attention (e.g., staying on task, avoiding distractions, completing their work). These children are therefore often unable to concentrate on the specific task at hand long enough to master basic problem-solving skills or complete complex problems. They have difficulty persisting with tasks until completion, often appear as if their mind is elsewhere, seem to not be listening to instructions, and work in a careless or messy fashion. All too often, the problematic sequence of failure experiences that follows from this can shape their entire life course. Subsequently, academic failure and loss of initiative and a personal sense of efficacy become the pattern. Depression and/or oppositional behavior, as well as antagonistic family relationships often develop. In adolescence, avenues to self-efficacy and meaningful personal relationships give way to increasing frustration, alienation, conduct disorders, and substance abuse, which in turn often lead to a marginalized, nonachieving adulthood (see American Psychiatric Association, 1994; Biederman, 1991; Biederman, Faraone, Mick, Lehman, & Keenan 1991; Wenar, 1994; Wilens, Biederman, Spencer, & Francis, 1994).

Impulsivity is a feature of the Hyperactive-Impulsive Type. Impulsive children act without thinking and cannot inhibit their own behavior or self monitor. They blurt out rapid and irrelevant answers, cannot wait their turn, grab toys and objects from others, talk excessively, interrupt frequently, and are careless in their work and play. Peer relations suffer as much as academic performance, since other children reject or actively avoid their disruptive play. These impulsive children also tend to suffer more accidents and physical injuries from engaging in highly stimulating or reckless behavior without considering the potential consequences of their actions.

In most instances, hyperactivity and impulsivity will occur together. Hyperactive children are described as "driven" or "always on the go." They are more active both while awake and asleep. In school, teachers often complain that they fidget, squirm and cannot remain in their seat, and that they are frequently off-task. At home, parents report that they dart in and out of the house, wear out the furniture from climbing on it, and have difficulty playing quietly or participating in sedentary activities such as being read a story. In adolescence and often into adulthood, the exaggerated gross motor behavior of younger school-age children usually gives way to inner feelings of jitteriness or restlessness.

Thus, children with ADHD experience repeated school failures that result from their inability to focus attention and process the information necessary to generate strategies for solving problems. These experiences lower the children's self-esteem, crush their sense of efficacy, and profoundly undermine their motivation to succeed. Expecting failure, these children lose initiative and think of themselves as "dumb"—often becoming secondarily depressed. Others come to resent instructions to stay on task or become so frustrated because they cannot succeed at anything that they refuse to comply and begin an oppositional trajectory. DSM-IV notes low frustration tolerance, oppositionalism, dysphoria, rejection by peers, and low self-esteem as associated features of ADHD.

All three of the core dimensions of inattention, impulsivity, and hyperactivity will vary across settings, making diagnosis more difficult. For example, ADHD symptoms generally increase in familiar, structured, and task-oriented settings like the classroom and decrease in informal, open settings such as the playground. Symptoms also are more likely to occur in groups than in one-to-one situations and to worsen in situations that are uninteresting or demand sustained attention. Thus, teachers are especially helpful in assessing this disorder, as clinicians may not witness the problematic behavior in a novel, one-on-one testing situation. Additionally, some ADHD children seem to be just *situationally* hyperactive whereas others are more *pervasively* hyperactive. Situationally hyperactive children have a much better prognosis than pervasively hyperactive children, who are more disruptive, function at a lower level at home and school, and are more likely to continue to have problems over time (Rutter & Garmezy, 1983).

Complicating diagnosis and treatment, most ADHD children will not have just this single diagnosis. Thirty to 50% of ADHD children are also *conduct disordered,* for example (Wenar, 1994). Further, approximately 15-20% of children with ADHD have a specific learning disability (Fletcher, Shaywitz, & Shaywitz, 1994). The literature also supports the comorbidity of ADHD with an array of other disorders including mood disorders, anxiety disorders, oppositional defiant disorders, borderline personality disorder, and disorders such as mental retardation and Tourette's syndrome (Biederman et al., 1991; Wenar, 1994).

Although ADHD has its onset in early childhood, it frequently persists into adolescence and adulthood, increasing risk for substance abuse, antisocial behavior, and other forms of psychopathology (Biederman, 1991; Biederman, Newcorn, & Sprich, 1991; Wilens, et al., 1994). Thus, although the "classic" symptoms of inattention, impulsivity, and hyperactivity attenuate somewhat in late adolescence and adulthood, often they leave a profoundly impaired sense of efficacy, a sense of self as incompetent, and poor coping strategies for achieving personal or occupational success in adulthood. Treatment, while often including stimulant medication, is then complicated by these sequelae. For example, physicians are hesitant to prescribe stimulants for adults with ADHD who have comorbid substance abuse. Further, the fact that many adults with ADHD also present with depression often results in use of antidepressants, especially the Selective Serotonin Uptake Inhibitors (SSRIs), which seem to facilitate attention and organization for these individuals. The prevalence rate of ADHD in adulthood has been estimated to range from .3% (Shaffer, 1994) to 2% (Biederman, et al., 1995). Biederman et al. (1995) suggest that 10–60% of childhood ADHD cases persist into adulthood.

ADHD is the problem child of child psychopathology. The etiology of ADHD, just like its core characteristics, has also been in dispute. Although ADHD is more common in first-degree biological relatives and is widely assumed to have an organic basis, there currently is no empirical evidence for any one etiological source. Some researchers suggest that genetic factors play a significant role. Familial aggregation of the disorder has been documented in twin studies, adoption studies, and studies of children at risk by virtue of having a parent who had been previously diagnosed with the disorder (see Biederman, et al., 1995). But, as we will see later, differentiating genetic from environmental contributions is not always easy.

Hypotheses concerning under-overarousal of central nervous system processing or neurotransmitter imbalances remain inconclusive, while hypotheses such as minimal brain dysfunction wither from lack of empirical validation (Wenar, 1994). Other theories, such as dietary causes (e.g., food coloring, additives, sugar), (Wender, 1986), allergies, television, and video games have not received empirical support.

Although some researchers and clinicians have suggested family stress, abuse, and/or disorganization as possible causes of ADHD, the direction of effect is often hard to determine, since having a child with ADHD can disrupt the family's functioning and increase the family's stress levels. Further, to the extent that ADHD is inherited, parents of children with ADHD may themselves have difficulty providing the structure, organization, and flexibility their children need due to their own ADHD symptoms.

One prospective study (Jacobvitz & Sroufe, 1987) suggests that early child-caregiver relationships may indeed play a significant role in the development of ADHD. These researchers followed children from infancy and assessed maternal behavior at 6 months, 2 years, and 3½ years to evaluate which behaviors predicted hyperactivity in kindergarten at age 5 or 6. The results suggested that children with ADHD may have difficulty modulating their own arousal levels stemming from parental insensitivity to the child's own capacity for self-regulation. That is, they found that caregiver's "interventions and initiations" (which they termed "intrusiveness") seemed to disrupt or interfere with the child's internalization of appropriate or adequate self-regulation, the end result being a child with an inability to self-direct or self-regulate.

It thus appears that children's risk for developing the disorder may occur at both the biological and environmental level.

Given the difficulty defining and diagnosing ADHD, it is no wonder that prevalence rates have also been in great dispute. In addition to methodological differences between studies, such as the age of the children evaluated, whether the general population or a clinic population is being assessed, the specific instruments or rating scales and cut-off scores used, conceptual issues such as whether situational (e.g., home or school) and pervasive (i.e., evident in several settings) ADHD symptoms represent the same basic core condition, have yet to be resolved.

Studies that assess situational hyperactivity report rates as high as 30% (see Baren, 1994; McArdle, O'Brien, & Kolvin, 1995). According to DSM-IV (1994), the true incidence rates are 3–5%, while physicians who treat children with this disorder estimate rates of 6–8% (Baren, 1994). Attention Deficit/Hyperactivity Disorder is far more likely to occur in boys than girls, with reported ratios ranging from 4:1 to 9:1 (DSM-IV). Usually diagnosed after age 5 in a school setting, ADHD is responsible for nearly 40% of referrals to child health care professionals (Barkley, 1990).

Life is hard for an ADHD child. The consequences of an inability to sustain attention and inhibit impulses are far reaching. As we will see in the case study of Timmy, the child cannot complete a task, have a success experience, and gain some mastery to disconfirm the pathogenic belief that he or she is "dumb." Having a predictable daily routine, an organized household, and firm but affectionate discipline will provide important buffers for the developmentally vulnerable ADHD child. In contrast, lack of extended family supports, poor child-rearing skills, family instability and marital discord, or feelings of helplessness engendered by poverty, will place this child at much greater risk. Let's look more closely at how the familial and cultural context shape the impact of ADHD.

Just as the ADHD child is faced with his own significant adjustive demands, his parent(s) will also have to cope with their own fatigue, anger and guilt over having a "different" child. In most families with an ADHD child, chronic conflict and antagonism come to characterize family relationships. Parental resentment toward the ADHD child is exacerbated because the child's symptoms vary in different situations, so parents often conclude that the child's problematic behavior is just "willful." By the time the clinician sees the child around age 7 or so, painful family patterns often have become entrenched. For example, parents have felt rejected by their child since infancy because they couldn't soothe their crying baby. In addition they have felt inadequate as parents since the child's toddlerhood, when reasonable attempts at normal discipline went completely unheeded. Several times a day, parents have gone through emotional cycles of feeling overwhelmed by the child's frantic behavior, getting angry and losing their tempers, and withdrawing in guilt. As the child gets older, there is mounting pressure from teachers who are overwhelmed in the classroom to control their child and from grandparents who are critical of the parents and embarrassed to be with the child in public. This increasing control, when the child ought to be more self-directed, illustrates Jacobvitz and Sroufe's (1987) suggestion that parental intrusiveness may undermine the child's ability to self-regulate.

It is heartbreaking for parents to see the pain on their child's face as he repeatedly fails at school, is again rejected by peers, and gradually begins to give up on trying anymore. Family conflicts also escalate as siblings are jealous of the time and attention given to the ADHD child and resent his name calling, grabbing and breaking toys, and temper. Parents tire of refereeing constant fights between the children and often begin to blame each other for the constant tension and discord: "You're too lenient." "You're too harsh." "You never do anything to help." Understandably, single parents are overwhelmed and couples cannot maintain a parental coalition.

Many parents of ADHD children do cope effectively, of course, but added social stressors such as poverty, social isolation or discrimination make school failure, low self-esteem and acting out more likely. These issues are especially salient for minority children, who are often scapegoated because of their race and in some settings are expected to be "inferior." Thus, a minority child who also has ADHD symptoms is even more likely to be singled out, reprimanded frequently, and rejected by teachers and peers. Racial discrimination can thus intensify the rejection and social isolation that is so common for ADHD children. Initiative is even more stifled, reducing the child's opportunities to experience success, feel competent, and develop a positive self-identity.

What can be done to help ADHD children? Stimulant medication (Ritalin, Dexedrine, Cylert) is the predominant pharmacological treatment for ADHD (Schachar & Tannock, 1993; Pelham, 1993). Children are typically given a morning and noon dose and may be given a half dose in the evening. However, because insomnia and appetite loss are frequent side effects, physicians are often concerned about evening doses; they also try to find the lowest possible effective dose and frequently recommend "drug holidays" (e.g., during the summer school break) when children can be taken off the medication(s).

In addition to stimulant medication, tricyclic antidepressants (especially imipramine) are also used (Busch, 1993). The antidepressants seem to be especially useful for children who are emotionally intense or reactive and have significant symptoms of depression and anxiety. Use of medications seems effective in ameliorating the problems with inattention and task orientation that are so problematic for children with ADHD (Wenar, 1994). It helps them become less impulsive, more planful, and better able to sustain attention. Children often report feeling calmer, seem less buffeted around by the reaction of the moment, and are better able to monitor and self-regulate their own behavior with this greater containment. As a result, teachers rate medicated children as more task-oriented, less disruptive, and more appropriate. Medication is not a cure-all, however. That is, although effective use of medication can set the stage for better learning, researchers find that it alone does not result in improved academic performance. The pervasive effects of years of criticism, academic failure, and peer rejection will not be solved with a pill. Also, many are concerned that stimulants in particular are overprescribed simply to make acting-out children from disorganized or high-conflict homes with inadequate discipline more compliant with teachers and parents. Finally, concerns about the side effects of stimulant medications, such as nervousness, insomnia, anorexia, and suppression of growth, have been raised (see Ouellette, 1991).

Treatment of children with ADHD requires a multimodal treatment process that includes behavioral, and cognitive-behavioral interventions in addition to medications (Whalen & Henker, 1991). In these approaches, parents typically receive training in behavior contingency management and child rearing practices. They also participate in support groups with other parents of children with ADHD. These educational interventions are geared to help caregivers provide firm and unambiguous discipline, predictable daily routines, and a structured homelife. Parents are also often encouraged to learn more about the impact of social competence and positive peer relationships on their children; they are also encouraged to become strategic organizers in their children's lives, assist the children in developing self-monitoring and self-regulation strategies, and become advocates for their children (Cousins & Weiss, 1993). Both parents and children seem to benefit from parent-training programs, with parents often reporting reduced parenting stress and increased parenting self-esteem while the children show improvement in the severity of their ADHD symptoms (Anastopoulos, Shelton, DuPaul, & Guevremont, 1993).

Cognitive-behavioral self-regulation approaches are also common (Whalen & Henker, 1991). The goal in these approaches is to help children assert some level of control/constraint on their behavior by teaching them self-monitoring and self-regulation procedures. These procedures, which typically involve "talking" one's self through problem-solving tasks, will be illustrated in the case study that follows.

Children also benefit greatly from social skills training. Learning to follow rules, take turns, and cultivate hobbies or sports activities are all focused on helping these children develop gratifying peer relationships and experience increased self-efficacy.

Working with school personnel and obtaining academic tutoring are often central to an effective treatment approach. This is especially important since academic failure and poor school adjustment, including frequent reprimands and even rejection from teachers, have such profound effects on the development of the child's self-concept and identity.

Thus, the *team* concept, in which school personnel (e.g., classroom teacher, special resource teacher, and/or school psychologist), physician, therapist, and parent(s) communicate and work together, is mandatory for effective outcomes in children with this multifaceted disorder. In particular, therapeutic work with children diagnosed with ADHD must focus on the goal of helping them have success experiences so they can regain some initiative and have improved expectations of mastery. Let's examine these treatment guidelines in the case study of Timmy.

CASE ILLUSTRATION

Presenting Problem

Timmy, an 8-year-old biracial child, was brought to therapy by his mother on the insistence of his school. Timmy was in the third grade and his classroom teacher had been calling his mother almost daily about the problems he was exhibiting. She asked that he be evaluated for Attention-Deficit/Hyperactivity Disorder. School personnel had been requesting that his mother have him evaluated since the first grade but this had not been done in large part because his mother felt embarrassed, felt like a failure, and hoped Timmy would outgrow his negative behaviors. Timmy's problems, which included being intrusive and disruptive in class and with peers, poor attention span, and poor frustration tolerance, had escalated in the past month. A parent-teacher conference was held during which the urgent need for a psychiatric evaluation was communicated to his mother.

Although Timmy's third grade teacher had begun the school year with firm rules that she insisted Timmy adhere to, she now reported feeling overwhelmed by his behavior and allowed him to spend a great deal of the day on the class computer (playing games) since this was one of the few times she could teach without him interrupting. She knew that this was not in his best interest and had requested, in addition to evaluation for medication, consideration of an alternative classroom placement.

According to Timmy's teacher, he seemed unable to sustain attention long enough to complete class assignments and would often shift from one uncompleted project to another. When he did complete assignments, there were many mistakes. He was easily frustrated and would sometimes have temper outbursts which seemed related to this low frustration tolerance. He was often out of his seat, frequently wandered around the class aimlessly, was resistant to direction, and habitually talked out of turn. Timmy also got in trouble for provoking and irritating the other kids (he would, for example, take their work or pencils). The children complained about his disruptiveness and intrusiveness and he was becoming increasingly isolated both in the classroom and on the playground.

Timmy's mother reported that he had always been an active child and that she too felt overwhelmed by what she experienced as his demands. His room was always messy, he did no chores, and he rarely followed directions. She reported that as a single parent she worked long hours so that much of the time Timmy was home with his 14-year-old sister. She acknowledged often finding herself trying to impose strict rules and then just withdrawing and giving up.

Thus, Timmy's experiences both at home and at school vacillated between rigid controls and detachment, even rejection. No one was in sync with him, encouraging him to self-monitor. Thus, over time, Timmy was robbed of the developmentally appropriate process of learning increased self-regulation. The inconsistency in how he was treated (i.e., control and detachment) was all the more confusing for Timmy as a biracial child who also had to negotiate multiple racial and cultural heritages.

Based on the teacher's report, his mother's report, and my observations (which will be described in the next section), Timmy met the DSM-IV (1994) criteria for Attention-Deficit/Hyperactivity Disorder, Combined Type. His symptoms included both inattention and hyperactivity-impulsivity in a variety of settings.

In addition to my evaluation, Timmy was seen by the psychiatrist at the mental health agency I worked for and was placed on the stimulant, Ritalin. At the same time he was tested by the public school psychologist, who found his IQ to be normal but his math achievement scores to be below his grade level.

CLIENT DESCRIPTION

Timmy was a thin, wiry 8-year-old, with dark curly hair and large brown eyes. He and both his parents were biracial (he had African American and Caucasian grandparents). He came to the initial intake session with me accompanied by his mother and 14-year-old sister, Patty. Timmy seemed restless in the waiting room and appeared to examine fleetingly virtually every book and toy in that room. His mother made several ineffectual attempts to contain him (by asking him to sit down) but it was not until his sister took him by the hand that he responded and sat down. Whenever I have an ADHD child referred to me, I like to observe waiting room behavior to see if the symptoms or problems that were described during the phone intake are exhibited there.

The intake occurred in three parts. I first met with the whole family (Patty was included since his mother indicated that she was home with Timmy most of the time). I then met individually with Timmy and individually with his mother. The initial family segment and parent-only segment were to assess the problem and get a sense of the developmental context. In particular, I wanted to get a sense of what the specific problems and/or behaviors were that made them seek therapy, how long and in what settings they were most evident, and ascertain how they had coped thus far. Family disciplinary practices and daily routines were also evaluated. These and the other conceptual factors I was trying to assess are detailed more fully in Chapter 1 (see Conceptual Aspects).

The child-only segment was to observe Timmy in free play. I was particularly interested in evaluating how he would respond to minimal structure. I also wanted to find out what his understanding of the therapy process was—why he was here and what he expected to happen in therapy. In addition, I wanted to learn about his friends ("Do you have any friends?" "Do you have a best friend?" "What is his/her name?" "What do you and (friend) like to do together?"), about his hobbies ("What's your favorite thing to do?" "What do you usually do after school?" "Do you have a favorite television program/book/toy?"), and family life ("What kinds of things do you like to do with your mom and sister?" "Do you guys usually eat dinner together?" "Do you ever play or read books or go places with your mother or sister?"). It has been my experience that even very young children are able to communicate their interests, if not verbally, by the toys they choose to play with. Furthermore, because ADHD children are often experienced as overwhelming by teachers, parents, and peers, who focus exclusively on the problems they present, I wanted to convey early to Timmy that I wanted to know about him and his interests, not just about the problem behaviors. This process, of focusing on him as a person with thoughts, feelings, and expectations, was my attempt to engage with him and let him know that I would in fact be *listening* to him and would not spend all my time trying to control him or reprimand him.

SOCIAL CONTEXT

Timmy was the youngest of two children. His parents had been divorced since he was two (although they had been separated shortly after his birth) and he had very little contact with his father, who lived in another state. His father usually called on special holidays and Timmy saw him approximately once a year. His sister, Patty, was doing well in school. His mother worked as a beautician and was often gone through the afternoon and early evening. The family was rather isolated, with none of their family members living close by. Their primary support came from their church.

Mrs. J. had grown up in another state. She married right out of high school to a man ten years her senior. They moved soon after Patty's birth when her husband had a job transfer. When Patty started preschool, Mrs. J. went to beautician school and has worked at the same place since completing her training.

The problems in her marriage escalated soon after Timmy was born. When her husband was offered a job promotion that meant transferring to another state, he took it and Mrs. J. stayed behind with the children. Although Mr. J. and Patty had developed a warm relationship, he barely knew Timmy. Timmy, therefore, had few adult male relationships.

Since her divorce, Mrs. J. had dated several men, all of whom turned out to be emotionally abusive. Mrs. J. was passive and they were controlling. The relationships were all temporary and unstable and none of the men ever served as positive role models for her children. Mrs. J. also indicated that she had been increasingly depressed in recent months after being sexually assaulted by a former boyfriend.

Mrs. J. decided not to move back to her home state after she and her husband separated. She was embarrassed about the breakup, especially since her parents had disapproved of the relationship in the first place. In addition, her parents held strict religious values and she knew that they disapproved of divorce. She was also quite depressed about the breakup and moving with two young children was a task she did not feel she could manage in her emotional state.

The family lived in an apartment complex but did not know many of the other tenants. As previously mentioned, the church was the primary stabilizing factor in their lives. The minister had in the past provided counseling to the family and was possibly the only stable male figure in Timmy's life.

Mrs. J. reported that Timmy had always been a "difficult" child but, as we will see, it was hard to parcel out all of the multiple contributing factors to his presenting problems. For example, his parents had separated and divorced soon after his birth, his mother was depressed, and his home environment was poorly structured with no consistent daily routines. Although Timmy's school had suggested therapy in the past several years, his mother had persistently avoided the recommendation because she was embarrassed, and her coping style was to withdraw from unpleasant encounters. After the last school conference, she talked to her minister, who assured her that it might be in Timmy's best interest to seek treatment.

Initial Session

During my first office meeting with Timmy, he was accompanied by his mother and sister. I saw them all together initially to clarify the reason(s) for coming in and to get a brief developmental history.

During the intake, Timmy had difficulty remaining in his chair and his eyes darted around the room. He sat on the edge of the chair and his feet and arms seemed to be in frequent motion. During our time alone, I asked him to draw a house, a tree, a person, and draw his family doing something together. He executed these tasks very quickly, without much care, and seemed ready to move on to other activities. (In my office, one side has a small cabinet and a few colorful stacking crates where I keep my toys and art supplies. I also have a sandbox and miniature toys for use in the sandbox. There is also a child's size table and two chairs.) After the drawing activity, choosing my words carefully, I told Timmy, "You can decide what you would like to play with now." I also stated that he could choose if he wanted to play alone or wanted me to join him. He darted off quickly and played briefly with most of the toys in the room, rarely stopping to put things away. He did not ask that I join him and in fact seemed scarcely aware that I was present. His activity was unfocused. I noticed that before he completed examination of one item, he dropped it to pick up another. During this time I sat on the floor (to be at his level), observing. Soon the room was strewn with toys and I surmised that this behavior, on a daily basis, must be overwhelming for a parent to deal with.

Because I like to observe what children will do without structure, I have just a few rules. My rules are simple: it is not acceptable to hit me or throw objects at me, and toys are not to be deliberately broken. For most children (including ADHD children) I also have the rule that, while the child may play with whatever toy they wish, they cannot have more than ten items out at once, which means that at some point they must put something away before they select another toy. During the initial session I did not stop Timmy to put toys away since I wanted to get an assessment of his typical behavior. However, we discussed this at the end of the session, and I indicated that we would follow the rule in the future and that he and I could work together on this follow-through.

As I mentioned, I also asked Timmy about his school, friends, and hobbies.

I went to Timmy's school soon after the intake and sat in the back of the class to observe. His impulsiveness (e.g., blurting out answers), inattention (e.g., focusing on his desk only briefly and then looking around the room), and hyperactivity (e.g., restless movement, tipping his chair backwards, getting out of his seat) were all evident. Part way through my observation hour the teacher moved him to the computer. His restlessness was still apparent there (e.g., he would tip his chair backwards and get on and off it), but this all occurred in a corner of the room so that disturbance of the entire class was minimized.

Case Conceptualization

The impact of biological factors and prenatal events on Timmy's presenting problems is unclear. Regarding her pregnancy, Mrs. J. reported that it had been difficult. She was ill a great deal in the first trimester with nausea and fatigue and then gained about 50 pounds in the last two trimesters. She reported feeling depressed through most of the pregnancy, in large part because she knew that her marriage was troubled.

When Timmy was born, Mrs. J. reported that she found him to be a difficult baby. He had an erratic sleep schedule, which exacerbated her depression, and he was colicky. Because he was fussy and often inconsolable, Mrs. J. felt as if she was failing as a mother from the very beginning. Although his developmental milestones all seemed within normal limits (e.g., walking at about 12 months), his activity level and oppositional behavior (such as refusing to put toys away) made parenting him a chore. In addition, he frequently had accidents, which included falling, pulling things off counters, climbing on furniture, and so forth.

Mrs. J. thus experienced Timmy as demanding and oppositional. Her feelings of failure as a mother were greatly compounded by the breakup of her marriage, when Timmy was a few months old, where she had also felt a failure as a wife. She had little emotional support and worked long hours. Her parenting style vacillated between trying to impose strict structure with Timmy (e.g., limiting where he could go in the house) and giving up (e.g., letting him jump on the furniture) but feeling very angry at him and feeling as if there was not much use in trying. She did at times yell at him, "I just can't manage you. Go to your room and stay there" "Timmy, I don't want to spank you so don't come near me until I've calmed down. Why can't you listen and do as I ask?" "Sometimes it's hard to be around you Timmy, you just drive me crazy." Patty, it seems, was very helpful and would often play with Timmy and keep him occupied.

It thus seemed that Timmy's intense and active temperament interacted with his mother's depleted emotional state to exacerbate whatever biological risk he may have had for ADHD. Her feelings of failure and lack of energy for constructive engagement made it difficult for her to provide consistent limits, nurturing emotional contact, and predictable daily routines. Her interaction with Timmy was primarily negative, and involved either yelling and reprimanding him, or withdrawing from him, often telling him that she just could not manage him and could not stand to be around him because he drove her crazy.

As a preschooler, Timmy also had difficulties in several child care settings where the staff found him oppositional and difficult to manage. He experienced frequent reprimands for his behavior. By the time he began kindergarten in public school, his low frustration tolerance, isolation from other kids who found him unwilling (or unable) to be cooperative and follow the rules, and his inattentiveness were all evident.

These problems continued in the first two grades, where his teachers managed a modicum of control by seating him in the front close to them. Despite this, there were frequent calls from the teachers to his mother and several requests for medication evaluation, since they were convinced he was a child with ADHD. Mrs. J. experienced these encounters with school personnel as further criticisms of her parenting and as more demands on her, which she felt unable to meet, and coped by minimizing her contact with them. She did discuss his problems with the minister at her church and on his advice she took him once to a pediatrician who put him on Ritalin. However, the medication was not taken consistently and there was minimal change in his behavior.

By the time Timmy was in the third grade and the referral to me was made, both his mother and third grade teacher had given up on discipline. Furthermore, Timmy was socially isolated. His world was in many ways unstructured (e.g., no consistent meal times, no consistent bath times) and rejecting (e.g., his mother saying she could not stand to be around him, his peers saying they did not like to play with him and excluding him from their activities). The only consistent relationship he had was with his sister Patty. Timmy was not engaged in school—he rarely got his work done and when he did it was often incorrect. He frequently felt frustrated and seemed unable to express this except by screaming and being oppositional. Disengagement by his mother, peers, and now his teacher, who in giving up on him placed on him few demands or expectations, intensified his experience of the world as unstructured and rejecting. In having his teacher give up on him, Timmy was also robbed of the opportunity to succeed at school and develop a sense of competence.

Thus, Timmy was a young child who had difficulty attending, who seemed unable to control his impulsivity, and who was experiencing frequent negative responses from others. Timmy's status as a biracial youth with little emotional or social support in his neighborhood or school probably exacerbated his sense of isolation and made developing a positive self-concept even more difficult. That is, the rejection he experienced, in part because of his disruptive behavior, was probably intensified by his biracial identity. As a biracial child, he had the additional task of negotiating and integrating several cultural identities, making issues of belonging and social acceptance more salient. Timmy may also have felt scapegoated because he looked different from most of his classmates. Further, the lowered expectations reported by his teacher, who allowed him to play on the computer during class, probably exacerbated his sense of being "inferior." The impact of this was especially troublesome given the sociopolitical climate that often degrades or discriminates against individuals based on race. Except for the church, Timmy's family was also socially isolated. Even in that setting, Mrs. J. rarely responded to invitations to people's homes because she was concerned that Timmy would act out, they would see how "disobedient" he was, and would probably blame it on her parenting. Mrs. J. was understandably sensitive to social rejection and criticism and was concerned about portraying her family in the best possible light.

Orienting Constructs

In my work both with children and adults, I am interested in knowing about their previous relationships with significant others and the "templates" or internal working models of relationships they bring with them to the therapy setting. I try to understand how these templates, such as sense of self (e.g., good, helpless, worthwhile), expectations of others (e.g., demanding, rejecting, critical), primary affects (e.g., sad, ashamed) and repetitive patterns that transpire (e.g., being left, excluded, disappointing others), contributed to the genesis and current maintenance of the presenting problems. When working with young children (especially those under 13), I find it useful to assess the templates of both the child and the primary caretaker and try to understand how they fit or dovetail.

From Mrs. J., I learned that she had grown up in a very strict home where disobedience was not tolerated and was swiftly punished by spankings. Her survival stance was to withdraw and reduce her exposure to her parents' wrath. When she met her ex-husband, she was attracted to his self-confidence and was anxious to leave her parents' sphere of influence. Her parents expressed their disappointment that she did not go to college and become "someone," and she carried with her the sense that she had failed them as a daughter. The failure of her marriage, and later her difficulties parenting Timmy, further entrenched this view of herself as a failure. Her expectations of others, including school personnel, people at her church, and me, was that we would be critical of her and highlight her flaws. Her typical response to these expectations was to withdraw. For example, she seldom returned calls from Timmy's teacher, socialized very little with people at her church, and in the early stages of Timmy's therapy, wanted to send him to the sessions with Patty until I firmly but warmly and supportively emphasized the importance of her presence and participation. As we will see, it was only after repeated attempts to reach her in an empathic, noncritical, nonjudgmental way that she became engaged in therapy and began to utilize all the resources available to her (including group) and follow through with treatment plans. For Mrs. J., it was helpful that I understood how difficult it was for her as a biracial woman and parent to deal with the criticisms she heard of Timmy, which she sometimes felt were leveled not only because of his behavior but also aggravated by his racial identity. I believe that, in the early stages of therapy, my racial identity as an African American female made it easier for her to raise these concerns about race. She expressed great relief when I normalized her feelings of being overwhelmed by noting that this was a common experience for parents of ADHD children. I was also able to let her know that her concerns about the impact of Timmy's racial identity on what she perceived as the school's frequent calls and intolerance of him were understandable. Mrs. J. felt intimidated by the "school authorities" and felt incapable of advocating for her son in that setting. She was visibly relieved when I indicated that I would be happy to attend meetings at the school with her and that we could deal with the school *together*. My goal was to provide a model for relating to school personnel, which included inquiring about the services available there and assertively requesting that Timmy receive those services appropriate to his needs.

Although Timmy may have been born temperamentally an intense, active, and distractible child with low frustration tolerance, he was born at a time when his parents were separating. I surmised that his temperamental style interacted with his mother's emotional state, with the result that responses to his needs were slow in coming, did not come at all, or came at the expense of his initiative and competence (i.e., that responses were rigid and controlling). This, I believe, led to his sense of the world as a place he could not trust to meet his needs, as a place that was unstable and unpredictable. Thus, Timmy, as a biracial child of parents who would soon be divorced, had to deal with issues of belonging and loyalty and try to develop a positive self-identity. However, as a child with moderate ADHD symptoms, who already had difficulty integrating thoughts, feelings, and behaviors, the odds for succeeding and developing a sense of initiative, efficacy, and positive identity were stacked against him.

I hypothesized further that Timmy's difficulty modulating his behavior, combined with the lack of structure and inconsistent limit setting in his home and the lack of a nurturing relationship or secure attachment, reinforced his sense of the world as unstable (inconsistent) and unmanageable. This probably exacerbated his low tolerance for frustration and did not promote in him a sense of proficiency at following directives or instructions. Timmy's lack of competence in following directions and his sense that he could not do things "right" probably contributed to his diminished level of industry or diligence. My guess was that Timmy expected others (including me) to find him unmanageable. Further, that I, like others in his life, would be inconsistent in limit setting (and probably exhibit an all or none controlling style) and ultimately would reject him in anger and disgust and disengage from him. My task, I felt, was to remain actively engaged, to set firm and consistent limits, and to help him find ways to begin providing structure for himself. I hoped to provide for Timmy a *secure base,* that is, a relationship characterized by warmth, caring, consistent engagement, and predictable responses, from which he could "launch," develop a sense of initiative, engage in appropriate social and academic behavior, and ultimately increase his sense of efficacy and positive self-identity. I wanted to let Timmy experience a relationship in which, no matter how demanding and overwhelming he was, the structure, rules, and limits would be enforced, with warmth and caring. These issues will be expanded upon further in the treatment section.

Encouraging the development of initiative and sense of self-efficacy in an environment that is predictable and safe is especially important for young children. I believe that success in later life hinges on being able to make good choices and on feeling competent. Thus, when working with young children, I try to foster and support their choices of activities and celebrate with them the completion of projects and other accomplishments as a way of fueling their sense of efficacy. In my work with Timmy, I tried to create a *psychological holding space* by closely tracking his activities and being warm, supportive, and responsive. I let him know that I was present and willing to join in whatever activities he chose (i.e., actively engaged) but that I also respected his boundaries and would not intrude (supporting his autonomy). I made statements such as, "If you want to play alone that would be fine and if you want me to join you that would be fine too, just let me know." I would then remain close by, usually sitting, kneeling, or crouching on the floor, so that I was easily accessible.

There is a delicate balance in "tracking" the child and conveying presence, availability, and responsiveness without imposing the same agenda or demands that he or she would find at home and at school. Children who come from intrusive, enmeshed families *and* those who come from uninvolved, rigid families will find this stance reassuring: they can then convey to you, the therapist, the experience *they* wish to have for healing to occur. The idea here is to create a safe, welcoming place where the child can maintain his or her boundaries, control the pace of engagement, and be free to choose. Structure based on this sort of therapeutic availability provides a corrective developmental experience for the child and allows him or her to venture out and try new activities, fostering the development of initiative. In turn, the collaborative relationship developed between therapist and child by this secure base almost inevitably makes the child more receptive to suggestions regarding behavioral changes in the child's relationship with family, teachers, and peers. Willing to consider and try out these new behavioral alternatives, the child then begins to experience success with others, which leads to an increased sense of self-efficacy.

This "dance," or engaging sensitivity to the child's needs, is especially relevant for minority children. Helping them develop initiative and explore *alternative pathways to success* is critical since they frequently face racial discrimination and lowered expectations, which can block the traditional routes to success.

Treatment Plans and Intervention Strategy

INITIAL TREATMENT PLAN

Interventions focused on (a) Timmy, (b) the family, and (c) the school. I felt that, with regard to the school environment, I needed to educate Mrs. J. about the many additional services available to Timmy there (such as formal evaluation by a school psychologist, alternative classroom placement, tutoring or being seen by a resource specialist), of which she was unaware. I felt that by informing her of the services available and working with her and the school to find the most appropriate classroom placement for Timmy, I would empower her to be an advocate for her son.

In the family, I felt it important to educate them about ADHD and help them structure the daily routines and physical home environment in a way that would optimize Timmy's functioning. I believed that this would include being empathic with the mother (and in this case, sibling, who had many primary caretaker responsibilities) regarding the strain inherent in having a child with ADHD, teach them the principles of behavior management, and assist them in implementing these new parenting practices.

In my work with Timmy, my goals were to establish a cooperative relationship and help increase his attention span, self-regulation skills, and social skills. Most importantly, I wanted Timmy to develop a positive self-identity and see himself as competent and capable of success. As we will see later, I tried to do this by being emotionally attuned to him on a moment by moment basis, entering into his process and sharing his experience when he permitted, and using this contained contact to model new strategies for succeeding in school and with peers.

As I worked with Timmy and his family, I remained acutely aware of how cultural factors, especially racial identity, might impact their experiences. Gibbs (1989) notes that biracial children and adolescents frequently experience differential treatment from relatives, social rejection in peer relationships, and ambivalent responses from schools. At the same time, they are dealing with issues such as who am I? and where do I fit? It thus became important that I validate the additional challenges stemming from racial identity, help Timmy and his family negotiate more effectively in the system (e.g., get appropriate school services), and help Timmy recognize his potential for success as we worked to increase his sense of competence and esteem.

The therapy goals for Timmy were to:

1. Establish a cooperative relationship;
2. Increase his attention span;
3. Encourage and assist in the development of self-regulation skills;
4. Assist in the development of appropriate social skills and supportive social networks;
5. Help Timmy develop a positive sense of self (including a healthy bicultural identity) and increase his sense of competence and self-efficacy.

The therapy goals for the family were to:

1. Educate the family about ADHD and the interventions necessary to improve the quality of life for all family members;
2. Help the family develop a structured and consistent routine for Timmy;
3. Set up a behavioral intervention program that reinforced compliance with family rules and expectations, while giving Timmy increasing ownership of the program's goals;
4. Be a resource for his mother and sister and provide for them information (including support groups, parent-education groups, and individual therapy) to improve their quality of life;
5. Encourage positive interactions between family members.

The therapy goals for the school setting were to:

1. Help find the appropriate classroom for Timmy;
2. Be a resource to his teacher(s).

The school and family were both open to and welcomed my involvement. I obtained written permission from Mrs. J. that allowed me to interact freely with the school on all matters regarding Timmy.

Individual.   In the therapy setting itself, I tried to ascertain Timmy's interests and allowed him to choose whatever activities he might like. In the early phase, Timmy's unfocused and active style was most apparent. If left to his own devices, Timmy might have emptied all the toys on the floor and recreated, in the therapy room, the chaos and lack of integration that characterized his life. He played with cars, trucks, animals, action figures, transformers, and so forth, usually for brief periods. He often talked to himself and to me as he moved around the room. We had the rule about putting things away after use, and if Timmy wanted to play with toys from different storage units, he was allowed to choose but could not have more than ten items or the contents of one storage unit on the floor at once. I emphasized the fact that he could choose what he wanted to play with but if we had the maximum number of items on the floor and he wanted something else, he had to choose something to put away. I was usually positioned at his level on the floor, readily accessible. When Timmy approached me or offered me a toy, I took it and joined him in play. We talked about the pirates about to attack the ship and the captain of the ship coming up with a plan to save his crew. We brainstormed solutions to the trials and tribulations faced by these brave sailors. In the context of play, we made up adventures, with solutions to the various difficulties our characters faced. Although Timmy was not a child who easily tolerated being read to, storytelling and play acting in the context of play became one way we could be together and describe interpersonal relationships and the various ways people can negotiate them. In the context of these stories and play we also talked about people who looked different from each other, people who had different likes and dislikes, and people who were good at doing some things but not good at doing others as a way for Timmy to begin appreciating his qualities and his uniqueness.

Occasionally, Timmy came in angry after a difficult day at school and tested the limits. Once, for example, he emptied several containers of toys on the floor. I calmly asked him, "Would you like to pick those up by yourself or would you like me to help?" He yelled, "I'm not going to pick them up." I gently took his arm and one container, sat with him on the floor, and began handing him the toys that belonged in that container. We stared at each other for a few moments, then he began to put the toys in. He seemed to be fighting back tears and I said, "Thanks for putting them back Timmy. You seem sad. Are you?" Timmy's response, between the tears, was "I can't do anything right. I hate school, I hate math, this is the worst day of my life." In a soothing voice I let Timmy know that it sounded like he had had a hard day. I also let him know that we could find a way to help him with his math if he wanted that. (He got a math tutor after this incident). I asked him to tell me about his day and what happened. I believe that my staying calm and engaged with Timmy through this process was healing. Timmy's low frustration tolerance and acting out were apparent here. In most relationships, this would have begun a negative escalating cycle. Timmy was clearly aware of the difference in response and toward the end of the session asked me:

TIMMY: Don't you get mad?
THERAPIST: What makes you ask that?
TIMMY: You didn't yell at me when I threw those toys down.
THERAPIST: I do get mad but find it's better to talk about it. Do you think you can tell me when you're mad or sad instead of throwing the toys like you did?
TIMMY: Okay.
THERAPIST: Besides, what I really wanted was for you to put the toys away. I thought that if we worked on it together it would be much better than my yelling. And it worked, and you did a great job putting them away.

One of the important things in my interaction with Timmy as I tried to develop a cooperative relationship was to be present and responsive but not intrusive. I wanted him to feel free to choose to play alone when he wished and to play with me as he wished. I wanted to minimize demands beyond some of the basic limits and rules we had established. I usually followed his lead but conveyed my availability by being at his level, and I often would have in hand a toy that matched his (car, pirate, etc.) so he could interact with my toy if he wanted me to join. Occasionally, I would verbalize our process: "Oops, this truck is really bumping that van." "Michelangelo (a ninja turtle) is really swinging his arm." "That man is getting buried under all the cars and trucks." "Looks like Tyrannosaurus is attacking Brontosaurus." Timmy would sometimes join me and talk about what was happening with the characters or toys. At other times he would say nothing and we would continue playing, sometimes quietly, sometimes commenting on other things happening in our play.

Among the important goals in our work together were to increase his attention span and encourage him to develop problem-solving skills and self-regulating skills. Often, I would color or make something with Play-Doh or build with Legos, side by side with him. I would sometimes make a "mistake" in my coloring or building and softly talk myself through a correction, in large part to model this problem-solving behavior (e.g., "Oh dear, I painted that yellow instead of red. I wonder what would happen if I put this really dark red over it. I need to slow down and do only one part at a time so I won't make too many mistakes." or, "I can't find the right piece for this building. I'm getting frustrated. I better breathe and take a break before I get really mad.").

Timmy often wanted to take things from the office home with him. In responding to this, I had to be careful to not to have him feel I was angry or rejecting but at the same time convey that he would not get his way. I would gently tell him, "These belong in this play room and will be here for you to play with next week. There are a few things you can take home, but you have to work on them before you take them home."

I wanted Timmy to increase his attention span and develop interests that he could share with others. I had paint-by-number posters, coloring books, Play-Doh, stickers, blank cards that could be decorated, and various other art supplies, as well as Legos and other building sets, which I had hoped he would get involved with. I encouraged these types of activities by bringing in supplies consistent with his interests, like pirates and dragons, in large part because completion demanded increased attention, decreased impulsivity, and provided opportunities for problem solving when errors were made and feelings of frustration were evoked. We then together began to do various projects (making books about dragons, pirates, or sailors, coloring posters, building with Legos and so forth). I tried to model problem-solving behavior by softly verbalizing aloud my thinking processes as I worked on my own project at Timmy's side while he worked on his. I would do this by saying something like, "You know I'd really like to get this painting finished today, but it's pretty big. If I do it quickly, it won't look good, the way I want it to. I'd better go slowly, and do it properly. Maybe I'll just need to take lots of breaks. It's better to do it carefully, even though it's really hard to wait until I can finish." His impulsivity was especially evident in the early stages, and he would get frustrated and want to quit. His common phrase was "I can't do it" or "I won't be able to do it right," suggesting he had developed a sense of himself as incompetent and incapable. I would gently suggest we "breathe deeply and take a break" and return to the project later. "Breathe deeply and take a break" became our coping slogan. This became our equivalent of the "stop, look, listen, think" sequence often used to slow down ADHD children and encourage a more thoughtful and less impulsive approach to tasks. I would also point out to Timmy how much of the project was already done, trying to bolster each accomplishment as it occurred ("Wow, that's a great dragon you made with the Play-Doh. Would you like to put him on this plastic plate to dry? You've done a great job and can take him home). Soon Timmy was monitoring his own behavior and was using virtually the same words and thought processes I had modeled in coping with mistakes and other frustrations.

Timmy's interest in pirates and dragons inspired me to bring in a Lego set that had pirates and dragons. I suggested we work on it together over several weeks and indicated that he could take it home when completed. He was very excited but his ability to attend was quite challenged by this project. On the one hand he wanted to take it home that very same day, but his ability to sustain attention was rather deficient. We talked about the feelings of frustration and practiced "breathe and take a break" many times in the following weeks. To his great delight, we did complete the project and took several polaroid pictures of it. He was extremely proud when he took it home and he took his pictures to school to share with his teacher and friends. Throughout the project, I encouraged him and commended him for each completed segment. At the end I noted how, despite feeling frustrated at times, he had stuck with it and now had *successfully* completed a major project. Not only was Timmy's sense of efficacy enhanced, he found a new avenue for communicating with peers—dragons, pirates, and Legos became shared interests between Timmy and some of his peers.

Following this big success, Timmy asked if his sister could join us some-times in the play room. Timmy and I had developed a close and cooperative relationship, and I believed that he wanted to share this pleasant experience with her (He said, "I think Patty would have fun with us. Can she come sometimes?"). I think he also wanted her to model the cooperative, non-intrusive style we had developed (as noted by his statement, "Maybe she and I can play like this at home sometimes too").

Patty joined us in session once a month. She was surprised to see Timmy put toys away with little or no prompting. This of course, had not developed overnight. In fact, in the early stages of therapy I was afraid I might sound like a nag because I frequently found myself reminding Timmy of "the rule" to put things away. Sometimes, I would have to gently touch him on the shoulder and say, "The rule is that you can only have ten toys out at a time. Put something away." As time went on he became adept at following the playroom rules. It seemed he had internalized my verbalizations to the point that a partial prompt was sufficient to evoke a sequence of thoughts for Timmy, which helped him develop his self-regulation skills. I believe that the structure, provided in a matter-of-fact and collaborative way, gave him the corrective experience he longed for. With the structure, rules, a pre-dictable environment, and a warm, consistent relationship, Timmy could feel safe and contained in a way he had not experienced before. He could now try new things without fear that errors would be met with reprimand. He would also not be rejected for "not doing things the right way." In this setting and relationship, he was safe to explore and develop further his sense of initiative.

The issue of doing things "the right way" was one Timmy and I returned to repeatedly in our play and discussions. As a child with ADHD, he had often been reprimanded for not doing things "right." As a biracial child, he also had to contend with how to "fit": Who was he? Which values should he adopt? What was the "right" way to be? I wanted to help Timmy understand that, although there were some basic rules that people were expected to fol-low (e.g., not hurting others), there was no *one* right way to behave at all times. We began to talk about and demonstrate different ways to play games, to solve problems, to make friends, and so forth. We also talked about our similarities and differences. In this process I tried to convey to Timmy how special he was—he had relatives in different parts of the country, he had rel-atives who had different skin colors, and so forth. Having spent my early life in Africa, Timmy and I were able to talk about that and about my relatives who were African, European, and American. In this process I was trying to help Timmy appreciate diversity and celebrate his own multiple heritage.

After Patty began to join us, Timmy agreed that reorganizing his room at home would be a good idea. We talked about how the changes would make both clean up and finding his favorite toys easier. It was my belief that given Timmy's history of difficulties with self-regulation, helping him develop organization and structure in as many areas of his life as possible was useful. At the same time, Timmy needed to have some *ownership* of the changes and decision-making processes rather than having these all imposed by external sources. I believe that this is one of the main reasons interventions with ADHD children often fail to generalize or sustain.

Further, although rigid external controls are unhealthy for most children, they are especially destructive for children whose sociofamilial history includes slavery and systemic discrimination. These children, even more than most, must be given the opportunity to self-regulate and negotiate through life in a flexible and thoughtful way. They are more likely than children belonging to the majority culture to need to explore multiple routes to success.

We got boxes to organize the toys in his bedroom. Patty and Timmy decorated them and actually had fun doing that. Once the boxes were completed, Patty helped Timmy arrange the toys and the room (for example, putting vehicles in one box, animals or dinosaurs in another, action figures or cartoon characters in another, robots in another, and so forth). Although Timmy still was prone to leaving things lie on the floor, the organization relieved the chaos tremendously. One of the by-products of this project and of Patty's monthly sessions with us was that she and Timmy were learning to cooperate and were enjoying each other a lot more. By my example, Patty learned that she could encourage Timmy to do things by using reasoning and collaborative effort, rather than by taking on an authoritarian parental role. Timmy, in turn, became more willing to help Patty with household chores and was more responsive to her requests.

Family.   My intervention with Timmy's family involved helping them understand ADHD and its impact on the family. I like the concepts that Barkley has (Barkley, 1985; Anastopoulos and Barkley, 1988), which are that children with ADHD have a biologically based temperamental style that predisposes them to inattentiveness, impulsivity, and excessive activity levels. Further, that these children are deficient in their capacity for *rule-governed* behavior, that is, it is difficult for these kids to self-regulate and to slow down enough to follow rules. In beginning with an explanation of this sort, the enormous degree of self-blame and guilt that parents have regarding their child's problem behaviors is somewhat diminished. With this explanation, parents are then more receptive to discussions regarding how this child's style can interact with parental characteristics or life experiences (e.g., feeling overwhelmed or emotionally stressed) and family structure (e.g., if chaotic or inconsistent) to exacerbate symptoms. Parents are also able to have more empathy for their children (that is, that the children are not deliberately out to make their parents' lives a misery). In addition, parents of children who could benefit from medication become less resistant and are generally more willing to consider it.

I like to offer families with children who have ADHD a brief (ten week) multifamily educational/therapy group (consisting of three to six families). I find that being in a group helps these families feel that they are not alone or different. The combined input regarding problem behaviors and potential solutions is infinitely richer in a group setting as well. These groups, which incorporate some of the ideas espoused by Barkley and his colleagues (see Anastopoulos and Barkley, 1989), typically involve discussing the character-istics of ADHD (impulsivity, inattention, and hyperactivity) and associated features (such as oppositional behavior, aggressiveness, academic under-achievement, social skills deficits, and so forth). The families are then asked to expand on these and to describe how this has impacted their particular families. During this process, the reciprocal impact of family processes (in-cluding family conflicts and other stressors, excessive control, lack of con-sistent routines, and so forth) are discussed. Then, principles of behavior management (how childrens' behaviors can be modified by attending to an-tecedent events, consequences, and by dispensing rewards and penalties in immediate and consistent ways) are covered. Daily routines are then exam-ined and they are encouraged to develop a more consistent and predictable home routine. I typically help parents with daily routines by handing out a chart that has each weekday listed. Each day is then broken down into com-ponents (mornings, afternoons, evenings, or further into hours as needed). The "must do" tasks for each section of the day are identified and there is a space to indicate completion of the task. Various levels of rewards (requiring different numbers of completed tasks) are then identified. An important note is that children are not expected to have 100% compliance in order to earn rewards, since this is likely to result in frequent failure.

Parents are also taught that their children's problems with attentiveness make it imperative that they issue commands that are direct, specific, brief, and face to face. Further, I emphasize that their children's understanding of the instructions they give will often need to be assessed by asking the chil-dren to restate the directive. In addition, consequences for not following through must be specified in advance (written down in contract form when possible) and follow through on consequences must be consistent.

Use of time out is taught. Together we discuss identifying where the time-out place will be located (e.g., in the study, in the laundry area), how long children will be there (usually, ½ to 1 minute for each year of age), and how compliance problems will be dealt with (for example, a time out chair may need to be placed in the corner of the room and the parent may need to stand behind the chair to make sure the child stays there). The critical nature of helping the children identify behavior they can engage in as an alternative to some of their disruptive behavior (such as jumping on a trampoline instead of on the furniture, playing outdoors rather than running through the house, or establishing one zone of the house as their space with an agreement that at a particular time each day he or she will pick things up) is also discussed. Attention to and reinforcement for positive and appropriate behaviors (some of which we identify together in the group) is emphasized.

Parents are also encouraged to find 10-15 minutes each day for "special time" with their ADHD child. If parents are resistant to doing this daily, I ask them to identify two times in the next week when they will do this. I then request that parents, during this special time, let the child choose the activity and simply follow the child's lead. They are encouraged to be as positive as possible and can simply comment on the process (e.g., "That red truck sure travels fast." "Looks like the animals are all getting together." "Barbie's having a tea party."). They are to try to ignore negative behavior (don't worry about cleaning up, for example, until the *end* of the special time) and verbally reinforce all the positive things they notice (e.g., "You did a great job of putting those cars away."). Parents sometimes need help knowing how to interact in a playful way with their children and I often use this as an opportunity to advocate that parents learn about their children's interests, and I invite them to join me with their child occasionally so I can model playing together. In Timmy's case, his mother joined us a few times and she progressed from being stiff and awkward at the beginning of the initial session (e.g., she sat on a chair at the small child's table in my office, uncertain what to do) to actually having a good time with him (after we brought a boat with sailors and pirates to the table and included her in our play activities and talked).

Finally, the group spends much of the remaining group sessions going over current and potential problem behaviors and together we devise plans for handling these.

Mrs. J. was extremely hesitant to join the multifamily group and, initially, the issues outlined above were discussed individually with her. I made every effort in the first few sessions to empathize with her and acknowledge the stress inherent in raising a child with ADHD. I also aligned with that part of her that truly wanted to be a good parent and instilled hope that things *could* improve. I emphasized that we would work *together* on whatever issues arose regarding Timmy. I believe that my caring, noncritical, responsive style engendered hope in her, decreased her sense of isolation, and contributed greatly to her commitment to therapy and follow through on the plans we developed. Further, as her sense of competence in dealing with Timmy increased, she decided to join the next multifamily group, which provided additional support and healing for her and her family.

When I began working with Timmy's family individually and we first discussed ADHD, I told Mrs. J. that all parents with children who have this disorder have difficulty until they learn some important skills that can help with management. My aim was to relieve some of her guilt and feelings of shame concerning her son. She had, up until this point, accepted personally all of the blame for Timmy's problems and therefore felt like a failure when others pointed out how he misbehaved. I attempted to have her see that his problems had multiple causes, none of which were intentionally caused by her. I aspired to create the hope that, with joint effort, we could find ways to manage Timmy's behaviors.

After discussing the importance of a structured, predictable environment and behavior management principles, a typical day for Timmy was outlined. We identified the issues that caused conflict (e.g., getting himself dressed in the morning, cleaning his room). I also asked his family to identify those things that he did do that were appropriate (e.g., putting his plate in the sink after meals). We set up a chart of tasks for each day (at meal times, homework times, bath times, and so forth) that was put on the refrigerator door, and Timmy was instructed to put on it a smiley face sticker (a box of which was supplied) whenever he successfully completed a task. A certain number of these earned him a reward (a list of desirable rewards was obtained from Timmy). It was important to involve Timmy in the process and give him responsibility for key aspects of the plan as part of the goal of increasing empowerment and self-efficacy. At the end of each month, the goals were reassessed in order to acknowledge accomplishments and make changes that would inspire growth. Although Timmy complained initially about all the expectations ("I can't do that"), he actually responded well to the new system and took some pride in showing me the first week's chart and the fact that he had earned a fair number of smiley face stickers.

As Mrs. J. experienced success in parenting Timmy, her affect improved. When she later joined the ADHD multifamily group, she already had some expertise in the concepts being discussed and this increased her sense of efficacy. She became a somewhat active group member and the group became an important source of support both emotionally and socially.

As mentioned earlier, Timmy was evaluated by the agency's psychiatrist and was prescribed Ritalin. Compliance with the medication regime was emphasized and this was added to Timmy's task chart. He took the noon dose at school, administered by the school nurse. The psychiatrist also discussed possible side effects (potential weight loss, insomnia, growth retardation, and so forth) and recommended that Timmy be off Ritalin during school holidays. The medication seemed to be effective in helping Timmy to calm down and improved his ability to focus at school.

School.   After meeting with Timmy's mother, current teacher, school psychologist, and school principal, the decision was made to place Timmy in a classroom with a lower student-to-teacher ratio. The school psychologist and I then met with Timmy's new teacher to discuss our assessments of Timmy and make recommendations regarding his educational program. Finally, a meeting was held with school personnel (teacher, school psychologist) and his mother to finalize his educational program.

Timmy's new teacher was very competent at implementing behavioral management techniques and her classroom was very well structured. The students had special cards at their desks, which she "starred" throughout the day as reinforcement for good behavior (ADHD children tend to require short-term reinforcement schedules). A fully starred card yielded a special treat. Interpersonal skills (fighting, taking other people's things, learning to share, being kind to others) were addressed frequently throughout the day, often in the context of verbally reinforcing someone for sharing or being kind. She also broke Timmy's work load down into smaller, more manageable components so that, for example, instead of asking him to complete a whole page of math, she asked him to do two or three problems at a time. In this way, he was able to experience frequent completions or "successes," critical to the goal of developing self-efficacy. The teacher also, in the later part of the school year, had students work in pairs on small projects. Her purpose was to foster cooperation and social skills. She also hoped that this cooperation would be useful when the children were moved back to regular classrooms, which was one of the long-term goals for each child.

Timmy also had access to a tutor, who worked with him in a small (two to four) group setting. Timmy was especially weak in his math skills and this tutor helped with how to approach the problems and cope when frustrated. This essentially involved the tutor verbally discussing out loud the thinking process necessary to solve the quantitative tasks. She would verbally describe what needed to be done, anticipate aloud potential feelings of frustration that might be evoked by the task, suggest strategies to untangle these negative emotions (take a deep breath, slow down, do only one part at a time, and so forth) and then walk through solving the problem in a step-wise fashion. Thus, problem solving strategies were modeled for Timmy, providing him with several opportunities each week to practice these skills. I hoped that these self-regulation skills being practiced would transfer to his classroom and other social settings. That is, if Timmy could learn to cope with frustrating situations (in this case math) by talking himself through the problem in a thoughtful rather than impulsive way, he might be able to utilize this same approach in other academic and social settings. In order to succeed in generalizing this new ability, it was essential that this active transfer of skills also be addressed in my individual work with Timmy. Similarly, I would model and verbally reinforce his efforts to thoughtfully solve problems and encourage him to use that approach in social arenas as well.

Timmy's improvement occurred over a period of a year, with joint efforts by his family, school, individual therapy, and medication. His mother and sister improved the structure and daily routine in the home, and his teachers provided him with a predictable learning experience where the limits, expectations, and consequences were clearly established in advance. In therapy, Timmy learned how to operate collaboratively, developed further his problem-solving and self-regulation skills, and had success experiences that enhanced his sense of efficacy ("I can!"). His temper outbursts were shorter and significantly less frequent (he had learned to "talk" to himself and remind himself to "breathe and take a break"). As his behavior improved, his social isolation decreased. He was less intrusive with peers and more able to wait his turn. His participation with his church's youth group increased and he developed a "big brother" relationship with the youth group leader, who became a Big Brother for Timmy.

I saw Timmy once a week for a year. Although he still had occasional temper outbursts when frustrated and was prone to physical restlessness, he was much more contained and manageable and seemed happier. I was able to meet his new fourth-grade teacher and provide information that I felt would assist his transition to that class and be useful over the next academic year.

REVISED TREATMENT PLAN

The treatment plans did not change very much over the year. However, the family's social isolation and their need for increased support became a more prominent focus than initially anticipated. Several factors facilitated this process. One was that, as Timmy's behavior improved, Mrs. J. was more open and responsive to invitations by church friends to visit their homes. She also developed several friendships from the ADHD multifamily therapy group. Toward the latter part of therapy I encouraged her to consider involving Timmy in sports activities. Little League and American Youth Soccer Organization (AYSO) provided additional social outlets for her and structured group activities with other boys for Timmy. Belonging to a team was very important for Timmy, as a biracial child with ADHD symptoms, for whom issues of acceptance and belonging are often so profound. Observing Timmy's pride in his uniforms and his team membership was delightful.

Another issue that arose in the work with Mrs. J. was her depression, which abated somewhat over the year as she felt more efficacious as a parent and became more positively engaged with her children and her new friends. I did, however, provide her with therapy resources. As we headed toward termination (I was leaving the agency), she decided to follow through with the referral I gave her for her own individual therapy.

I was, at the beginning of therapy, very struck by the enormous parenting role Patty had with regard to Timmy, which seemed to come at the expense of her own childhood. In working with Mrs. J., she developed greater self-efficacy and empowerment and resumed her parenting role. This allowed Patty and Timmy to establish a more collaborative and siblinglike relationship, which also became a therapy goal.

The lack of male role models in Timmy's life became more apparent as therapy progressed. I felt that finding a "big brother," preferably from their church, would be a meaningful goal. I encouraged Mrs. J. to talk to her pastor about this possibility. Previously this would not have worked because of Timmy's agitated behavior, which tended to alienate others even if they were patient and well intended. As Timmy's behavior improved, however, it became possible for others to sustain pleasurable contact with him.

Thus, when approached at this time, the youth minister was very responsive and began taking Timmy to sporting events and spending more time
with him.

BALANCING GOALS

One of the aspects of treatment that was difficult to balance was the fact
that Timmy needed structure, order, and direction, but at the same time I
felt it was important that he learn to self-regulate. I wanted to be able to
provide structure without stifling his initiative. Most adults up to this point
in his life had either been overcontrolling or totally disengaged. I felt he
needed something that was different than both of these approaches, even
though my initial countertransference involved the urge to be totally directive with him or totally disengaged, since he was everywhere at once. This
gut reaction, which paralleled that of others, helped me understand easily
how people who encountered him might feel overwhelmed by him. I was,
however, clear about not wanting to repeat this heavy-handed or disengaged
experience and reenact what had been a problematic relational experience
for Timmy.

I feel strongly that people cannot grow until they are able to choose.
Choice fosters initiative, thereby providing more opportunities for mastery
and a sense of responsibility, and for ultimately developing a positive identity. I felt that by introducing choice into his life, I could foster Timmy's
sense of initiative, increase his sense of self-efficacy, and help him take
pride in being responsible, skills that I believed he needed over the long
term. Yet Timmy was a child with ADHD symptoms who also needed structure and limits. My approach was to provide structure and limits but with
warmth, affection, and consistency. Within this structured, warm, contained relationship, options/choices were highlighted and the consequences
of each identified. The security of this relationship freed Timmy to explore
in a more thoughtful way, knowing that mistakes would be seen as learning experiences and accomplishments would be joyfully celebrated. As I
watched Timmy grow and become more thoughtful and appropriately assertive, I was struck by the realization that, as a biracial youth, the lessons of
finding options within limits would be especially meaningful. For minority
youth, the sociopolitical system often places roadblocks and limits, making
exploration of alternative pathways to success imperative. I hoped that
Timmy's lessons as a child with ADHD, exploring and finding alternative
ways of coping and succeeding, would serve him well over time and that he
would continue to actively assess his options and assert himself.

For Timmy, the introduction of choice came gradually. I began by creating and highlighting choice points within various structures (e.g., in setting up his daily routine, I would point out that he had to do his homework,
but he could choose where in the daily routine it fell; once a decision
or choice was made, however, he had to follow through). Highlighting the

options became an important part of our interpersonal process. For example, I would indicate that we could play or work on and finish a project. We talked about prioritizing and what might be gained and/or lost (i.e., given up) by each choice. In our safe, cooperative alliance, exploration, seeing options, choosing, and accepting consequences became salient. The goal was to provide structure and choice and to empower Timmy to use his initiative to self-regulate, which he did.

I also encouraged Timmy's self-evaluative and self-monitoring skills by having him mark his own progress chart at home. Furthermore, in our time together, I hoped that the emphasis on collaboration would help him learn how to cooperate with others, which I felt was central to the development of interpersonal negotiation skills.

Therapeutic Process

RELATIONAL REENACTMENTS

In Timmy's history of relationships, he had never been in sync with anyone. As a biracial child, he had to integrate different racial and cultural heritages. As a child with ADHD symptoms, whose mother was depressed, he had to contend with a minimally involved, overwhelmed, and emotionally depleted parent who had difficulty responding to him and his needs. In school, his teachers had tried to impose structure and often felt that the only way to manage him was to be authoritarian and controlling or give up trying. Thus, in the therapy setting, Timmy tested me to see which category I fell into. Would I be controlling or detached? I hoped that Timmy would not experience me in either of these ways. As I mentioned in the balancing goals section, my goal was to provide structure, in a way that also underscored options, and to be emotionally accessible. I believed that only within a caring relationship would Timmy be able to accept my structure, rules, and limits. I believe it was my sincere caring for Timmy that fostered his participation in his own growth. There was an intimacy in our relationship that Timmy had never experienced before. We would be close together working on paintings, building, and other projects, side by side, or playing with cars, boats, and action figures on the floor. I respected his boundaries and did not intrude but was fully responsive to his invitation to engage with him. He could choose and I made sure to communicate my nonjudgmental acceptance of his decisions. For example, if Timmy moved to another part of the room, I stayed where I was; if and when he chose to return and engage with me, I responded without question.

Timmy and I frequently engaged in parallel interaction, talking together as we worked on our own respective projects. If he chose not to talk with me directly, I would model my own thinking/decision processes in a very soft voice next to him. He could choose to copy this approach if he needed it, but there were no demands that he use *my* way of problem solving. I wanted him to see that another human being respected him and had confidence in the fact that he could make his own good decisions. We could be together emotionally without trying to manipulate each other in any way. I was trying to provide a nurturing relationship for Timmy where he would feel safe and secure and become sufficiently confident to try out behaviors that were new and perhaps frightening to him. I believe that it was this new relationship and this new found security that made the interventions powerful. Without this relationship, all of the behavior modification charts and projects would have been just more meaningless tasks in Timmy's world of isolation. Our relationship over time began to translate into other relationships in Timmy's life. For example, Timmy's sister joined us in session occasionally and here she too learned to be with Timmy in the way that we were together, in this new kind of relationship. His mother also began to spend short periods of time in Timmy's room, just playing with him. Further, about 8 months into treatment, I began to hear from Timmy about shared moments of fun and play with other children.

IMPEDIMENTS TO TREATMENT

Probably the greatest impediment to treatment initially was Mrs. J's depression and her resulting passivity. Timmy needed a more active, engaging, structuring, responsive, eye-to-eye parent. Instead, Timmy was getting an ineffectual and barely responsive parent. As Timmy's negative behavior escalated and got more demanding, Mrs. J. seemed to feel more overwhelmed, and this made her withdraw further: "Oh, no. I can't manage, he's too much for me." was how she reported often feeling. Mrs. J.'s "failure" template, in which she felt that she had failed as a daughter, a wife, and was now failing as a mother, was effected. Timmy and his mother would then engage in a negative escalating cycle, with Timmy becoming more demanding and Mrs. J., more withdrawn and depressed. I entered when this cycle was escalating to a new level.

Mrs. J.'s initial passivity, feelings of ineffectiveness, and experiences of victimization made it difficult for her to implement the interventions. She also had difficulty making clear and direct commands. When she did give instructions, this was done in a way that communicated to Timmy that she didn't really expect him to follow through. Frequently, she would just do the task herself (e.g., pick up the toys, put his clothes in the hamper). The helplessness in her tone of voice was distinct. I responded to her with empathy, support, and encouragement. It was important that she not experience me as a source of further demands, criticism, or failure experiences, since this was the last thing she needed in her already overburdened life. The potential for a problematic reenactment was readily imagined. With this in mind, I framed my interventions in a way that minimized demands (e.g., by setting up the behavior modification programs for Timmy with her in therapy, rather than giving her the tools and asking her to set it up at home). Timmy also had a role in monitoring his own progress, which additionally relieved his mother's burden. I also empathized with her struggles and provided my support in a caring, nonjudgmental way. The combination of Timmy's improved behavior and my noncritical, supportive stance helped her get more involved, and I began to see a greater level of engagement with me and with her children. She did, however, have other personal issues that needed to be addressed beyond her parenting concerns, hence the recommendation for individual therapy.

An additional impediment was Timmy's active, impatient, resistant temperamental style. In the early stages I found myself often reminding him to put toys away or to "breathe and take a break." I was concerned about being too intrusive yet he needed the limits and structure. I tried to do this in a matter-of-fact, supportive way so he did not experience these directives as judgments or rejections. I also was very attuned to appropriate behavior, so I could balance my directives with much praise: "Thanks for telling me that story, you have a great imagination." "You put that away without me even asking. Wow, thanks." "You made that card for me? That's special, I'm going to keep it right here so I can see it every day." It was indeed a relief when Timmy needed fewer and fewer prompts and began to self-regulate more. These successes were always noted and he was praised for this.

Termination and Therapist's Summary Thoughts

I saw Timmy and his family for a year, and therapy was terminated when I left the agency. Prior to my departure, Timmy was transferred to a male therapist and had joined a children's ADHD therapy group. The family was less socially isolated and Timmy was making good adjustment in his new class. Although Timmy had made great progress, I was nevertheless concerned about him and his vulnerability. I felt hopeful, however, that his mother would be a more effective advocate for her son in the school setting in the future, since she had learned a great deal about the school system and the services available there and was less intimidated by school personnel. She was also now seeing her own therapist. I had specifically referred her to a therapist who was very nurturing and had confidence that in that therapeutic relationship her needs could be met. I felt that my relationship with her gave her a sense of empathic connection, a holding environment, where she received validation of her experience and that it was our relationship that helped her to implement the treatment plans we devised. I felt that by finding her a therapist who could provide her with a nurturing experience she could in turn provide that for Timmy. It seemed that Timmy's future pivoted on that possibility.

Although the medication had been helpful for Timmy, it became clear to me once again that the successful treatment of children with Attention-Deficit/Hyperactivity Disorder must also include structure and nurturance in combination.

REFERENCES

American Psychiatric Association. (1980). *Diagnostic and statistical manual of mental disorders* (3rd ed.). Washington, DC: Author.

American Psychiatric Association. (1987). *Diagnostic and statistical manual of mental disorders* (3rd ed. rev.). Washington, DC: Author.

American Psychiatric Association. (1994). *Diagnostic and statistical manual of mental disorders* (4th ed.). Washington, DC: Author.

Anastopoulos, A. D., & Barkley, R. A. (1988). Biological factors in attention deficit-hyperactivity disorder. *Behavior Therapist, 11,* 47-53.

Anastopoulos, A. D., & Barkley, R. A. (1989). A training program for parents of children with attention deficit-hyperactivity disorder. In C. Schaefer & J. Briesmeister (Eds.), *Handbook of parent training: Parents as co-therapists for children's behavior problems* (pp. 83-104). New York: J Wiley.

Anastopoulos, A., Shelton, T., DuPaul, G., & Guevremont, D. (1993). Parent training for attention-deficit hyperactivity disorder: Its impact on parent functioning. *Journal of Abnormal Child Psychology, 21*(4), 581-596.

Baren, M. (1994). ADHD: Do we finally have it right? *Contemporary Pediatrics, 11,* 96-124.

Barkley, R. A. (1985). Attention deficit disorders. In P. H. Bornstein & E. A. Kazdin (Eds.), *Handbook of clinical behavior therapy with children.* Homewood, IL: Dorsey Press.

Barkley, R. (1990). *Attention deficit hyperactivity disorder.* New York: Guilford.

Biederman, J. (1991). Attention deficit hyperactivity disorder (ADHD). *Annals of Clinical Psychiatry, 3*(1), 9-22.

Biederman, J., Faraone, S., Mick, E., Lehman, B. & Keenan, K. (1995). High risk for attention deficit hyperactivity disorder among children of parents with childhood onset of the disorder: A pilot study. *American Journal of Psychiatry, 152,* 431-435.

Biederman, J., Newcorn, J., & Sprich, S. (1991). Comorbidity of attention deficit hyperactivity disorder with conduct, depressive, anxiety, and other disorders. *American Journal of Psychiatry, 148*(5), 564-577.

Busch, B. (1993). Attention deficits: Current concepts, controversies, management, and approaches to classroom instruction. *Annals of Dyslexia, 43,* 5-25.

Cousins, L., & Weiss, G. (1993). Parent training and social skills training for children with attention-deficit hyperactivity disorder: How can they be combined for greater effectiveness? *Canadian Journal of Psychiatry, 38*(6), 449-457.

Fletcher, J., Shaywitz, B., & Shaywitz, S. (1994). Attention as a process and as a disorder. In G. Lyon (Ed.), *Frames of reference for the assessment of learning disabilities.* Baltimore: Paul H. Brooks.

Gibbs, J. (1989). Biracial adolescents. In J. Gibbs, L. Huang, and Associates, *Children of color: Psychological interventions with minority youth.* San Francisco: Jossey-Bass.

Jacobvitz, D., & Sroufe, L. A. (1987). The early caregiver-child relationship and attention-deficit disorder with hyperactivity in kindergarten: A prospective study. *Child Development, 58,* 1488-1495.

McArdle, P., O'Brien, G., & Kolvin, I. (1995). Hyperactivity: Prevalence and relationship with conduct disorder. *Journal of Child Psychology and Psychiatry, 36*(2), 279-303.

Ouellette, E. (1991). Legal issues in the treatment of children with attention deficit hyperactivity disorder. *Journal of Child Neurology, 6*(Suppl.), S68–S75.

Pelham, W. (1993). Pharmacotherapy for children with attention-deficit hyperactivity disorder. *School Psychology Review, 22*(2), 199–227.

Rutter, M., & Garmezy, N. (1983). Developmental psychopathology. In P. H. Mussen & E. M. Hetherington (Eds.), *Handbook of child psychology, Vol. 4, Socialization, personality and social development* (pp. 775–911). New York: Wiley.

Schachar, R., & Tannock, R. (1993). Childhood hyperactivity and psychostimulants: A review of extended treatment studies. *Journal of Child and Adolescent Psychopharmacology, 3*(2), 81–97.

Shaffer, D. (1994). Attention deficit hyperactivity disorder in adults. *American Journal of Psychiatry, 151*(5), 633–638.

Wenar, C. (1994). *Developmental psychopathology* (3rd ed.). New York: McGraw-Hill.

Wender, E. (1986). The food additive-free diet in the treatment of behavior disorders: A review. *Journal of Developmental and Behavioral Pediatrics, 7*(1), 35–42.

Whalen, C., & Henker, B. (1991). Therapies for hyperactive children: Comparisons, combinations, and compromises. *Journal of Consulting and Clinical Psychology, 59*(1), 126–137.

Wilens, T., Biederman, J., Spencer, T., & Frances, R. (1994). Comorbidity of attention-deficit hyperactivity and psychoactive substance use disorders. *Hospital and Community Psychiatry, 45*(5), 421–423.

SUGGESTIONS FOR FURTHER READING

Clark, L. (1989). *The time-out solution.* Contemporary Books. A practical guide to help all parents discipline their children more effectively.

Gibbs, J., Huang, L., and Associates. (1989). *Children of color: Psychological interventions with minority youth.* San Francisco: Jossey-Bass. Useful guidelines for assessing and treating minority children.

Schaefer, C., & Briesmeister, J. (Eds.). (1989). *Handbook of parent training: Parents as co-therapists for children's behavior problems.* New York: Wiley. An effective guide to parent training for parents of ADHD children as well as a range of other presenting child problems.

Whalen, C. K., & Henker, B. (1980). *Hyperactive children: The social ecology of identification and treatment.* New York: Academic Press. An influential clinical text on social factors influencing diagnosis and treatment of ADHD.

Chapter 8

GENDER ORIENTATION

CASE ILLUSTRATION OF TONI: A 19-YEAR-OLD BIRACIAL MAN

Jan Aura, Ph.D.

THE ISSUES

Difficulties don't arise for adolescents because they are gay, lesbian, or bisexual, per se, but do result from the challenges they encounter in integrating a positive identity in a homophobic context. In addition, since sexual orientation is independent of mental disorder (Gonsiorek, 1993), some gay individuals, like some heterosexual individuals, will present with major mental health problems that will intricately interact with their gay, lesbian, or bisexual concerns. There are many good resources for reviewing the therapeutic issues and needs of gay, lesbian, and bisexual adolescents (Gonsiorek, 1993; Mercier & Berger, 1989; Schneider, 1989, 1991; Zera, 1992). In this chapter, I will present issues that are of specific concern to the therapist using a process orientation. In addition, I will try to inform you about my biases, my theoretical conceptualization, and my intervention strategies. I expect, and hope, that you will come to your own conclusions.

Due to extensive sampling problems, it is difficult to predict with any accuracy the number of adolescents who are homosexual. Probably the sample most closely related to the case study presented in this chapter is the incidence of Oberlin College students who self-identified their sexual orientation as heterosexual, gay and lesbian, bisexual, or questioning (Norris, 1992). Thirty-one percent of the Oberlin student body answered a questionnaire about their knowledge and attitudes regarding homosexuality and the victimization of gay students. Seventy-three percent of the women students identified themselves as heterosexual, 5.7% as lesbians, 8.2% as bisexuals, and 12.4% said that they were questioning their sexual orientation. A greater percentage of Oberlin men than women said they were heterosexual

(84.3%), and gay (6.4%), while fewer men indicated they were bisexual (5.2%) or questioning their sexual orientation (4.2%).

Several researchers have noted that there is an increased risk of suicide among homosexual adolescents (Bell & Weinberg, 1978; Roesler & Deisher, 1972; Saghir & Robins, 1973; Remafedi, 1978; Remafedi, Farrow, & Deisher, 1993). The U.S. Department of Health and Human Services task force on youth suicide issued a 1989 report estimating that 30% of completed teen suicides are committed by gay youth each year. They also predicted that gay adolescents are two to three times more likely than their peers to attempt suicide. Remafedi, et al. (1993) found that male homosexual adolescents who attempted suicide adopted a bisexual or homosexual identity at younger ages and had adopted more feminine gender roles than those who did not attempt suicide. Family problems were the most frequently cited reason for attempts. One third of his subjects' first attempts occurred in the same year that they identified their bisexuality or homosexuality, and most other attempts happened soon thereafter. Remafedi also found that homosexual male youth who attempted suicide were more likely than their peers to report sexual abuse, drug abuse, and arrests for misconduct. Additional risk factors for lesbians may include promiscuous heterosexual behavior and pregnancy (Schneider, 1989).

Keep in mind that the younger the adolescent, the more likely they are at risk to experience trauma during the coming out process. Family, peers, and community reactions to sexual orientation are of central importance to adolescents, and younger youth have fewer resources, both practical and emotional, for separation and individuation from their family system, peer school networks, and social/cultural community expectations. Since our culture equates deviation from strict masculine and feminine ideals with homosexuality, those youth who naturally do not conform to gender role expectations, regardless of their sexual orientation, may be externally targeted by anti-gay harassment, discrimination and/or hate crimes. Heterosexuals subjected to antigay harassment will need assistance to understand the social and personal meaning and function of homophobia. For example, condemnation of homosexuality is used to discourage both diversity in sexual behavior as well as diversity in gender identity and sex role adaptation. These heterosexual youth will also need to explore their attitudes about homosexuality and their gender and sex role identity while they recover from the experience of being victimized. Individuals who do not conform to gender role expectations and are homosexual may, as a result of early victimization and "gay-bashing," be forced to recognize a gay, lesbian, or bisexual identity at an earlier age than their peers and before they are psychologically or socially prepared to cope with this realization.

Sociocultural Factors

The cornerstone of overcoming internalized homophobia is to feel connected and a part of humanity while lovingly accepting one's differences and similarities to others. It is difficult for the client to accomplish this within the therapy relationship without the therapist acknowledging a genuine self from which similarities, differences, and connections with the client can be forged. The therapist must reflect acceptance of the client's gay/lesbian self as unique, valid, and of value while acknowledging the broader humanity of the person. If a therapist cannot feel connected in humanity with the client and sees the lesbian/gay client as "other," overidentifies with and sees the client as "the same," or cannot envision the lesbian/gay client as an integral valued part of the larger social community, then homophobia issues will not be resolved within the therapy and referral should be considered (Soboinski, 1990). To more fully understand this conceptualization let us explore models of group identity development.

Adolescence is a time during which a person struggles with issues of identity in a context inclusive of, yet broader than, the family. Who am I in my family, among my peers, in my community, in the world? Each person's self assessment includes identity issues related to gender, race, culture, and socioeconomic class. Several authors have proposed models of identity development or biculturation that outline four or five stages ethnic minority group members go through as they develop self-appreciation and self-actualization (Atkinson, Morten, & Sue, 1989; Bustamante, 1984; Cross, 1978; Solis, 1980). Minority group members in each of these models start by viewing the mainstream majority culture as superior and their primary culture or identity as inferior. They progress through a rejection and intolerance of the majority culture, embracing the minority identity, culture, and people as superior and immersing themselves in their own group's perspective. In the final synthesis/ resolution/integration/autonomy stage the minority group member possesses an inner security, respects and has compassion for both minority and majority individuals, and shows a commitment to social change. These theories have also been expanded to propose similar stages through which majority group members (for example, Euramericans, men, nonhandicapped people, etc.) develop sensitivity to minority group member concerns (Helms, 1984).

By conceptualizing heterosexuals as majority group members and lesbians and gays as minority group members, these models can be used to understand the stages through which heterosexuals and gays and lesbians progress as they resolve their homophobia (Espin, 1987; Lukes & Land, 1990; Walters & Simoni, 1993). Comprehensive models of the stages of coming out or overcoming internalized homophobia incorporate concepts that parallel these biculturation theories. For example, Cass (1979) proposed six stages: identity confusion, identity comparison, tolerance, acceptance, pride, and finally identity synthesis in which a lesbian/gay identity is integrated as one aspect of self. Walters and Simoni (1993) proposed a four stage model of gay male and lesbian group identity attitudes based on one of these biculturation models (Cross's, 1978, model of African American identity development). They described this model as follows:

According to the adapted model, lesbians and gay men in the preencounter stage [Stage I] consider heterosexuality to be "normal" and better and therefore devalue their gayness and idealize all that is heterosexual. In the encounter stage [Stage II], some startling realization or event calls into question their group identity, and they experience anxiety over the struggle to integrate a new cognitive category and to deal with internalized homophobia. In the immersion-emersion stage [Stage III], gay men and lesbians engross themselves in gay and lesbian culture in an attempt to consolidate their group identity while directing their anger outward toward societal homophobia and heterosexism. Achievement of the internalization stage [Stage IV] is characterized by inner security and feelings of self-actualization and self-acceptance as a result of an integrated gay male or lesbian group identity.

Walters and Simoni (1993) found that progression through these four stages is related to an increase in self-esteem. Consistent with the first stages of these models, antigay discrimination in extreme and subtle forms explicitly or implicitly demands the exclusion of gays and lesbians from social institutions (e.g., the church/synagogue, the military, the PTA, the family). The effects of this banishment from belonging are particularly painful for adolescents. Individuals in all but the final stage of these models perceive the world from an "us" versus "others" perspective. From this perspective humanity is split into distinct subgroups by minority and/or majority group membership. These subgroups, in addition to identifying differences, also define acceptability and inclusion (or condemnation and exclusion).

The therapist must be in the last of these stages of dealing with his or her minority and majority group memberships in order to understand, respect, and effectively communicate with the client as he or she progresses through self-identity integration. Otherwise, the therapist will make biased interventions (Task Force on Bias in Psychotherapy with Lesbians and Gay Men, 1990). Experiencing and resolving the rage, defiance, and rejection of majority values, belief systems, and emotional entanglements is vital to healthy identity development of the client and must be tolerated by the therapist. The independence of perspective, which follows from this emotional separation, allows the person to make third order paradigm shifts. Instead of being submerged and thus blinded within a system of beliefs and interactions, with a shift in perspective one can see that there are alternate systems of belief or ways of being that are incompatible to the first system. They then might find themselves submerged within the alternate system of belief. For example, when an adolescent rejects the belief that heterosexuality is superior to homosexuality, there begins understanding of the compulsive nature and pervasiveness of heterosexism (Rich, 1980). As individuation progresses, the individual can make a shift to a perspective that is integrative. They can come to understand their interests and perspective while respecting the interests and perspectives of others. At this point they are ready to relate to people with diverse identities and backgrounds without betraying their own ethnic and gay/lesbian pride.

Gay, lesbian, and bisexual adolescents of color may be progressing through these stages vis à vis their ethnic identity and their homosexual identity at different rates. If they have progressed completely through the stages for either ethnicity or for sexual orientation, it will be much easier for them to make progress on their other minority group membership issues. However, it may be very difficult to progress to the last stage of either ethnic or gay/lesbian identity development without fully experiencing the immersion-emersion stages. For young persons who have not resolved their ethnic identity development, coming out can interfere with this resolution by disrupting the opportunity to effectively immerse themselves in an ethnocentric worldview, if that world view also condemns homosexuality. Alternately, it will be difficult for Black, Asian, Latino or Native American gays and lesbians to immerse themselves within a racist White-identified gay or lesbian community. Although gays and lesbians are as diverse in race, age, and socioeconomic class as the rest of the population, gay culture, identity, and history are most often portrayed as White and male. This can lead gay men and lesbians of color to feel a sense of marginalization and noninclusion within gay/lesbian communities. Bisexuals may feel that there is no identifiable community or group with whom they can identify and be accepted.

The resolution of positive identity formation depends on the ability of a person to feel belonging as an integrated member of various groups (broad social community, ethnic community, lesbian or gay community, friendship network, family, and possibly romantic partnership) while simultaneously maintaining autonomy and a unique sense of self. How a person's struggle to achieve and maintain this integration is strongly affected by their male or female socialization. The therapeutic issues that follow from this conceptualization of overcoming homophobia and attaining identity integration will be discussed in the following case study of a young biracial gay man. For further discussion of some of the process issues faced by lesbians as a result of socialization factors see Vargo (1987) and Krestan and Bepko (1980).

CASE ILLUSTRATION

Presenting Problem

Toni came to the college counseling center in a panic. He couldn't concentrate on the end-of-the-term school work, wasn't sleeping or eating well, and was seriously considering killing himself. He was terrified that he wouldn't be able to cope with the impending graduation and departure of his best friend John, a man with whom Toni was secretly in love.

CLIENT DESCRIPTION

Toni was the eldest son carrying the Spanish surname of his first generation Mexican American father, an accomplished physician. A college junior history major with an emphasis in Latin American studies, Toni was in appearance a short, heavy set, Latino young man with an air of quiet, serious responsibility, except when, spontaneously, a bright, animated, humorous, and unrestrained frolic and defiant mischievousness emerged for a brief moment, only to disappear again as if behind a closed (closeted?) door. What one wasn't likely, at first, to recognize was that Toni's mother was half Central American (El Salvadoran) and half Japanese. Knowing this, gazing into Toni's eyes, you could see the blending of Japanese and Latino features and heritage. He presented in anguish over not being able to meet the expectation of his professors, his family, his intended fiancee, and his friends, while obsessing alternately on thoughts about John and thoughts about suicide.

SOCIAL CONTEXT

Toni was attending a small elite four-year liberal arts college in a large urban area whose mission statement emphasized the valuing of diversity and the need for leaders in a multicultural world community. He was a star student in a strong program emphasizing Latin American studies. Several professors had already volunteered to give Toni recommendations to graduate studies. While he had not kept it a secret, neither had he disclosed nor academically or socially explored his Japanese heritage. He belonged to no campus clubs or organizations (including MECHA), choosing instead to concentrate all his efforts on school work. He had a couple of friends but spent most of his free time at home with his large family. His closest confidante was a young, quiet and shy Latina woman, Teressa, whom family and friends generally assumed would become Toni's fiancee. Teressa attended a large university in the area.

Although Toni had three siblings (two brothers and one sister) and officially lived in a dorm on campus, a separate room in the basement had been given to Toni to use whenever he chose to be at home. He kept his computer in this room and would often retreat from the campus environment to work and to socialize at home. He held a special place in his father's esteem as the oldest son who excelled academically. Toni felt great pressure to live up to his father's expectations of accomplishment and family involvement: a masculine ideal of being the respectable, benevolent patriarchal head of a large family. He had a more personal, emotional side role within the family as a clown (a humorist) with whom family members could have a great time when Toni decided it was time to play. Although his siblings somewhat resented his favored status, Toni was an integral and cared for member of his family.

Toni's nuclear family acted fairly autonomously from extended family relationships. Toni's paternal grandparents and his father's two brothers were conservative working-class Mexican Americans who had disowned Toni's father after he, as a rebellious young premed student, took up motorcycle riding and married a beautiful but headstrong woman of mixed racial background who was not Catholic. The resulting differences in educational background, lifestyle, values, religion, and the angry youthful interactions were never reconciled. This had caused great pain for Toni's father who strongly valued and yearned for familial closeness.

Toni's maternal grandfather had abandoned his wife and three daughters when Toni's mother was still quite young. Shortly after this, he died in an automobile accident that resulted from his drunk driving. His maternal grandmother remained single and supported her children on a waitress' salary, raising them in a Protestant, multicultural, but predominantly Asian community in Hawaii. One of her sisters had married a Cuban American and lived in Florida, while the other married a Euramerican and lived in Seattle. In addition to being at great distances, these families tended to be less functional, struggling with recurrent crises and difficulties. Still, infrequent visits were always interesting for Toni, who more than once noted how the cousins from the three families looked similar in appearance.

Initial Session

Toni was very distraught and nervous at the beginning of his first session. He said he had been feeling suicidal for several months but that a recent conversation had made him acutely upset. He succinctly said that he had told a girlfriend (Teressa) about being in love with someone she had never met. I asked, "How did she respond to your telling her that you are in love with this other person?" He replied, "She was very upset. I guess she wasn't the right person to talk to, but I really need to talk to someone about this." I said, "About being in love with this other person?"

Notice that I carefully responded using gender identification when Toni did so (girlfriend) but consciously, even if it was awkward, avoided reference to gender when Toni did not specify gender (someone). From the initial contact with a new client, it is important to not make assumptions about the gender of romantic partners. For example, if you want to ask about partners you might say "What about relationships? Have you dated, been sexually intimate, or romantically involved with anyone?" Gay clients may test you to see if you operate on a heterosexual assumption. They may be looking for clues about whether or not it is safe to disclose same sex attractions. Purposely using gender neutral terms such as partner and person or avoiding reference to gender until the client gives you this information can help a gay, lesbian, or bisexual client feel safe to disclose. Heterosexual clients will generally quickly correct their omission whereas some gay clients initially go to great lengths to disguise the sex of their partners.

After one furtive look into my eyes, Toni avoided all eye contact while he continued, disclosing his secret attractions to men and his hopeless obsessional love for his friend John, an exchange student leaving in two weeks to return home to his family and girlfriend in France. While he had been attracted to men before, he had always been able to repress his feelings and not acknowledge to anyone but himself his (in his own words) "homosexual tendencies." His choice of terms, nervousness, and reported behavior made it immediately apparent that Toni felt very uncomfortable talking about his sexual and romantic feelings. At moments when he might observe a therapist's reaction to this topic, he avoided eye contact. As a result, it was apparent that he was very concerned about the therapist's value judgments.

When a young client discloses an emerging gay identity or questions his or her sexual orientation with defiance, confidence, or shame, it is important for the therapist to recognize an immediate need to actively convey a nonjudgmental, accepting and nonlabeling response. I am very careful to refer to the client only using terms they themselves have used in self-reference (gay, lesbian, bisexual, etc.). Some terms that in the general culture connote disgust and ridicule, such as queer, faggot, and dyke, are used by activist gays and lesbians as labels of defiant pride. I am comfortable using these terms in this manner if the client initiates this practice. However, if I am uncomfortable with a client's term because it connotes a pejorative value, such as Toni referring disdainfully to his "homosexual tendencies," I will avoid using a label at all. Labels connote identities and it may be a big leap for a client to acknowledge an identity when they are still only disclosing experiences with feelings. It would also be very detrimental for the therapist to impose an identity (heterosexual or homosexual) upon the client. The therapist immediately can begin to reflect a positive value on all sexual orientations by supporting each person's right to self-exploration and self-definition. Still there is a need to respond in a way that is nonjudgmental and encourages further exploration.

Since Toni had used the term *love* in reference to John, I reflected back to Toni, "Your previous feelings for men, but most especially your feelings for John, show you that you have the capability to be sexually attracted to and to romantically love a man." Without any further prompting, Toni began talking about his feelings for women and for Teressa specifically. He talked about caring deeply for her and yet not being sexually attracted nor in love with her. He said he didn't know if he could ever be in love with a woman. I reflected back, "At this point you know that you have the ability to be 'in love' with a man and the ability to love a woman without being sexually attracted to her, but you are not sure if you would ever fall 'in love' with a woman."

This provides a somewhat behavioral assessment of his experience to date while conveying a positive value judgment for sexual/romantic relationships, regardless of gender of the partner, not placing a label or identity on his experience, and leaving the full range of options for choosing a partner open over time, limited only by his own self-definition. People take various lengths of time to come to a definitive assessment of their orientation (nature) and/or preferences (choices) before self-labeling and assuming an identity.

Toni's coping had remained intact as long as his attractions to men could be trivialized and denied. Toni was ready to move beyond this and acknowledged to himself and to the therapist the meaning of his feelings for John. I asked if he had spoken about his feelings for men and women and specifically about his feelings for John with anyone else. He said that only Teressa knew his feelings. Last week, in desperation, he told Teressa that he was sure that he was a homosexual, that he was in love with John, and that he was very upset about John leaving. Teressa responded with intense grief and anger, sharing with Toni her assumption that they would someday be married. Toni said he hadn't expected her to be so upset. Instead of offering him support, Teressa plummeted into her own crisis for which Toni felt responsible. He ended the conversation begging Teressa not to tell his parents anything. It was after this conversation that Toni's suicidal thoughts intensified and he decided to call the counseling center. During the first session we explored the meaning he attached to this conversation (which elements were upsetting and why).

He was not overly concerned about Teressa's moral, religious, or social judgments of homosexuals. He was more directly concerned about losing the relationship with her, leaving him without a close friend, since she expressed a need to not see him for a while. A central theme that emerged was concern about disappointing and alienating significant others by not fulfilling heterosexual role expectations. At one point during this conversation, Toni pointed to a picture in my office of my two children implying that he included me in the universality of people who had fulfilled these expectations. He was making assumptions about me and quite probably projecting attitudes, values, and life experiences onto me. I also regarded this as an indirect question: Who was I, how did I fit into the social structure, and ultimately, what did I expect from him? This implied questioning raised my own considerations about whether or not at this point therapist self-disclosure would be helpful to the client. I always find this an agonizing decision.

I find it, ethically, very difficult to sit with clients discussing their problems and/or experiences related to their gay identity without disclosing that I am a lesbian. However, I think there are times when self-disclosure is not advised. Each individual client relationship needs to be assessed to judge whether therapist self-disclosure will be helpful or not. Without disclosure, the client is likely to assume that the therapist is heterosexual. This makes the consideration of self-disclosure very different for heterosexual, bisexual, and gay therapists. The process issues are crucial in making this decision. For example, a client whose parents have inappropriately disclosed personal aspects of their lives and not respected the client's boundaries may feel very uncomfortable with any personal information about the therapist. Lack of knowledge about the therapist may help contain a manipulative or borderline client from acting out with the therapist. A client who is filled with homophobic self-loathing may, at first, devalue a known gay therapist.

There are, however, important considerations that support therapist self-disclosure. First, a sense of isolation is a difficult problem for individuals when they first recognize same sex attractions. Being able to talk with another gay or lesbian person can immediately help to reduce the experience of being alone. In community settings, such as a college, there may be numerous opportunities for students to be aware of the identity of gay therapists. Therapists may choose to be as open about general aspects of their personal life as their heterosexual colleagues, or they may choose to be open to provide a visible, affirmative, gay or lesbian role model for students. Not correcting the client's heterosexual assumptions can raise issues of trust and honesty when the client is likely at some point to be informed of the therapist's identity. In addition, self-disclosure of *any* sexual orientation by the therapist relates a healthy acknowledgment that each of us is a sexual being, that each of us, as the unique individual we are, belongs to humanity and to the social community, and that sexual/romantic concerns do not need to be hidden. These issues are often of great importance to adolescents. They can be essential for a gay client.

It may be more difficult to establish rapport with a socially withdrawn client who is feeling very dissimilar from the therapist in ethnicity, sexual orientation, and/or sociocultural background, without the therapist overtly acknowledging the reality of these differences. Some characteristics, such as racial identity, may be easier to discern without self-disclosure than others, such as sexual orientation or religious background, which can be hidden. The therapist's verbal acknowledgement of even obvious differences (e.g., gender, race, class) can validate for the client their importance and gives an invitation to talk about how these factors affect the client's experience. This can reduce a sense of isolation or alienation from the therapist and build trust that the therapist sees who they are and recognizes the differences in their experience.

A concern frequently raised as an argument against self-disclosure is that therapist self-disclosure will inhibit or interfere with the emergence of a transference reaction. A central assumption of a process orientation is that the client will reenact central transference and process issues within the therapeutic relationship. (See Chapter 1.) These dynamics will occur regardless of the client's assumptions or knowledge about the therapist (Isay, 1991). Knowledge about the therapist may, however, shape the expression of the transference but not alter the central therapeutic characteristics. For an excellent discussion of ethnocultural factors in transference and countertransference reactions see Comas-Diaz and Jacobsen (1991).

Toni, for example, had already indicated that he was very concerned with meeting other people's expectations. It would make sense that he would want to know as much as he could about me in order to discern what might be my expectations for him. These are transference issues that need to be dealt with within the therapy whether or not there is therapist disclosure. It would be important for the therapist to be on the alert for Toni reenacting his need to live up to other's expectations by trying to meet what he assumed to be either the therapist's heterosexual or gay role expectations.

A second assumption of a process orientation is that the therapist helps facilitate change not primarily by guiding the client to insight but by providing a genuine interaction with the client that is incompatible with the previous maladaptive interaction pattern (a corrective emotional experience). (See Chapter 1.) This is not to be mistaken with assuming that the client's child-hood deficiencies could be made up for by interacting with the therapist, but rather that interactions with the therapist might disrupt previously held patterns and allow the client to break the maladaptive patterns of interaction that block emotional resolution and growth. To accomplish this you must be present and authentic with the client which, most often, will necessitate and be facilitated by limited therapist self-disclosure.

Toni had very little support for a positive gay identity and was isolated from others who also experienced discrimination on the basis of sexual orientation. Limited therapist disclosure can help facilitate a genuine, honest, and alternative response for the client encountering great social pressure to keep romantic/sexual experiences hidden in shame. I felt that it would be helpful for Toni to know that I was a lesbian. If I didn't correct his heterosexual assumption, when he later found out that I was gay, he might feel betrayed. When he accusingly gestured toward the picture of my children assuming that I was heterosexual I asked, "Do you know that I am a lesbian?" He replied no, looked up, made direct eye contact, and became very attentive. I continued, "I ask because I am quite open on campus. For example, I teach a course on lesbian studies so there are opportunities for students to know that I am gay." He asked, again pointing to the picture, "Are those your children?" I responded, "Yes, my partner and I have two children." After a short silence, he noted, "I've always thought that I would have children. Maybe I will still be able to be a father." "You have been thinking that this was one goal you'd have to give up if you acknowledged that you wanted a male partner?" "Yes." He seemed noticeably more relaxed after this exchange.

Therapists who choose to disclose their sexual orientation or leave this up to client assumptions must be careful to reflect the value that all choices/orientations similar or dissimilar to their own are *valid* options and to help clients feel support for whatever identity they adopt for themselves. I often find it helpful to make this therapist value explicit. For example, "I hope you will come to trust that I have no investment in the sex of your partners or of your identity. It is my personal belief that the value of human love and sexuality transcends gender." By this I do not mean to imply that the differences resulting from the gender of one's partner or one's sexual orientation are trivial or insignificant. Also, consistent with my respect for clients' individual perspective and right to self-definition, I allow them to conceptualize whether or not they experience their sexual orientation/identity as a choice, as a social construction, or as an immutable part of their physical inheritance. Perhaps homosexuality is multiply determined, perhaps it is not. I confess, I do not know the answer to this debate. For further discussion of this issue see DeCecco and Elia (1993), Golden (1987), and Kitzinger (1987). There are, however, clinical consequences to the client's conceptualization that need be explored. For example, the clients who are embedded in a fundamental, patriarchal, religious belief system and believe that sexual orientation is a choice, will likely think of their sexual behavior as morally wrong and sinful. A biological model of the cause of homosexuality challenges the basis of the "fundamental" model by proposing that same sex sexual attractions are a natural part of humanity or God's plan. On the other hand, a feminist or humanist perspective assumes the legitimacy of all loving relationships and supports the rights of individuals to prefer or choose same sex relationships, for their merits, over heterosexual relationships, without biological predetermination. The client's beliefs about the origins of their sexual attractions can affect their self-esteem and identity development.

It can also be important not to collude with society's pressure to choose a sexual identity quickly and once and for all. In part, I believe that this pressure to define one's self is a result of straight and gay societies' need to know whether this individual is one of "us" or whether they are one of the "others." I view this as a primary expression of homophobia. Straight and gay peers may place extreme social pressure on adolescents to identify/define themselves, although anecdotally there appears to be increasing support among gay youth for the legitimacy of a range of self-chosen identities, including bisexuality. We may need to explicitly support clients' ambivalence while they work on other issues. For example, a client may first need to resolve family, religious, feminist, or other social issues and come to a positive redefinition of what it means to be gay before self-identifying as a lesbian/gay man. Allowing clients to openly and extensively explore their social and personal concerns about gay issues, as well as their sexuality, without the therapist making assumptions about clients' sexual orientation is important. Of course, occasionally a client's continued ambivalence may become a problem, which can be explored later.

Questions that may facilitate exploration include: What feelings, emotional and/or sexual, have you had for men and/or women? What sexual experiences have you had with men and/or women? When did you first find out about homosexuality? Let's construct a timeline of the major events in your life, including those related to sexuality. (You can also include drug and alcohol use, feelings of being different, etc.) As a child, what fantasies did you have about being a grown up? How do you now imagine what your future might be like as a heterosexual, as a lesbian, as a bisexual?

The first session with Toni ended with an assessment of any alcohol or drug use. Toni drank very little and chose to completely avoid drug use. He felt that there would be no immediate danger of acting on suicidal thoughts before his friend John left. I asked him, in closing, how it felt talking with me. He expressed that he felt very relieved to talk about his feelings, quite comfortable talking with me, and at the same time very apprehensive about what was next: facing the consequences of his acknowledging a gay identity. He wanted to know if he should "come out" to John. I suggested that he take it easy and that we would talk about John at our next meeting.

SUBSEQUENT SESSION

Toni arrived early for his second session. He was feeling in better spirits, in part because his father had paid a surprise visit to his dorm to find out how Toni was doing and to offer support for final exam preparations. Toni immediately wanted to talk to me about "coming out" to John. After his experience with Teressa, I wanted Toni to make a careful assessment about why he wanted to come out to John and about what might be John's possible reactions to his coming out. Given Toni's emotional vulnerability, I was concerned that he (a) make a good judgment about whether this was a good idea at this time, (b) plan what he would say to John and where this conversation would take place, and (c) be prepared for any of John's possible responses. Discussions such as this help the client develop skills and coping strategies to deal with possible discrimination.

As a part of this conversation, we explored the self-negating, hopeless thoughts he had been having (e.g., "I am a disappointment to my family, my professors, and my friends." "While I think most of my family, friends, and professors probably would say that homosexuals and homosexuality was OK, it will never be OK with them that I am a homosexual." "I am a failure." "My future is destroyed." "I am unacceptable." and "I can't live my life as a gay man but I can't live my life as a heterosexual man. In fact, I can't go on living."). We also discussed depression and cognitive-behavioral strategies to address these symptoms, such as exploring the rational/irrational basis of these thoughts, explaining how negative thoughts effect feelings of depression which, in turn, effect our irrational negative thoughts, and clarifying his responsibility to consciously be aware of and to stop or change his thoughts during the day. We discussed the importance of eating well and exercising. I explained to Toni that depression has a strong physiological/biochemical basis that changes gradually. Since Toni had presented very depressed at the first session, we discussed the option of medication. I also mentioned that medication might help relieve some of the obsessive thoughts. He did not want to take medication but said that he would consider this if the symptoms persisted.

During the conversation, it became increasingly clear that Toni had two interpersonal speeds: complete repression, isolation, and inactivity and complete spontaneity, abandon, and recklessness. This behavior was also shown within the therapy session. Toni was quiet and distressed one minute and animated, verbal, and daring a few minutes later. Depending on how extremely the polarities are expressed, these patterns could lead to behaviors that might be dangerous for a gay adolescent. Impulsiveness may lead to such behavior as unwisely coming out to others, engaging in experimental sex, and/or exploring unsafe settings, such as bars and street life that place the adolescent at emotional and physical risk. This shift in behavior can be abrupt and coincides with entering the middle stages of identity development before

personally working through the majority cultures' stereotypes and condemnation of homosexuality. The adolescent is ready to identify with gay
subculture and behavior yet may still have very negative self-esteem. A moderate engagement in personal interaction would involve emotional integration and a capacity to be intimate, for which Toni was not yet ready. I
perceived Toni's willingness to throw his entrenched caution to the wind
and "go for it."

Toni insisted that he not only disclose to John that he was gay but also
that he had romantic feelings for John. He recognized that this was risky.
However, he felt that if he didn't get a response from John about any possibility of returning his feelings, he would continue to obsess about John. Toni
felt that this would be unbearable and that he didn't want to have to write
and then wait weeks for a letter in return. Toni believed that John would be
nonjudgmental, however, he acknowledged that if John did express a hostile,
judgmental, or rejecting response it would be difficult to take. Toni developed a plan about when, where, and what he was going to say. I suggested
that he think about his plan for awhile before acting on it and further suggested that he might want to visit a local gay bookstore to select some reading materials about coming out, or other topics, to be better prepared for his
talk with John. He was very enthusiastic about these plans. I reflected on
this enthusiasm and its contrast to his abstinent denial and inaction for
several years. (This interaction raises interpersonal process as an area
for discussion.)

THERAPIST: You're very animated and showing a great deal of enthusiasm
for visiting the bookstore, for coming out to John, and for finding out
how John will respond to your feelings for him. This is a real contrast
from your years of denying your feelings for men and not acting in any
way on your suspicions of being homosexual. Your shift in behavior is
also a big contrast from just last week, when you were very depressed,
overwhelmed, inactive, and seriously considering killing yourself. You
seem to have two speeds: full stop and full speed ahead.

CLIENT: Yes, that's what it feels like. I'm scared, but I'm not looking back.

THERAPIST: I must admit that I'm a little concerned that your enthusiasm
and spontaneity might also result in a suspension of judgment.

He assured me that he wasn't planning on acting hastily or without caution. I explicitly raised sexuality issues by asking him if he felt informed and
capable of negotiating safe sex if he should choose to be intimate with someone. (This is a topic that should not be avoided with any adolescent.) He felt
that it was difficult to imagine himself in such a situation but that he had no
intention under any circumstances of placing himself at a health risk. I was
very clear in this conversation that I was supporting his choice of continued
sexual abstinence while recognizing that at some point in time he might
make a different choice.

In this case, I think this conversation about negotiating sex was premature. I just wasn't sure how fast he was coming out of the starting gate.

By the end of the second session several issues had been addressed:

1. Short term crisis intervention addressing his suicidal impulses included identifying the immediate hazards causing distress and challenging his coping strategies and establishing a suicide contract.
2. The therapist reflected a positively valued, nonlabeling response to his initial disclosure of same gender sexual attractions.
3. Therapist disclosure of sexual orientation facilitated relationship building, reduced client isolation, and provided a role model of positive self-esteem.
4. The client's depression was addressed through education, limited cognitive-behavioral intervention, and discussion of medication.
5. Reduction of isolation was initiated, and countering homophobia was addressed by referral to a gay bookstore.
6. The therapist and client began problem-solving coping strategies to deal with coming out interactions and with possible experiences of discrimination.
7. Drug and alcohol concerns were assessed.
8. Sexuality and safe sex concerns were raised.
9. A preliminary assessment of central process and family systems issues (relationship interaction patterns that interfered with his coping and growth) was made. For example, Toni appeared to have extreme difficulty initiating separation and individuation when this might involve disappointing others. This component of the therapy will be explored at length.

Case Conceptualization

Adolescents generally struggle with several generic issues: identity, self-esteem, social skills, and individuation within family and community. Resolving these developmental issues is generally fraught with personal pain and angst and exhilaration and triumph. When you add the issue of gay or lesbian sexual orientation to the dilemmas facing the client and the client's family and social networks, you intensify all of the ongoing process issues. For example, parents dealing with their child's individuation with disapproval may, when issues of homosexuality are raised, become outright rejecting, disowning the child.

Several therapeutic issues concerning gay and lesbian adolescents have been identified repeatedly in the literature. Among these are: establishing a positive gay/lesbian identity; eliminating isolation from other gay/lesbian adolescents; addressing issues of homophobia, sexuality, and coming out; integrating multiple cultural/ethnic/community concerns; individuation within the family; and coming to terms with spiritual/religious life. All of this must be accomplished by lesbian and gay adolescents while simultaneously just trying to grow up. Several of these issues were addressed in the initial sessions with Toni.

Central to envisioning effective therapeutic interventions is understanding how the lesbian/gay/bisexual issues interact with the existing process and systems issues facing adolescents within the family, social relationships, identity, community and cultural involvement, and relationship with the therapist. Each of us learns early, within the context of our families and peer relationships, systems or patterns of interaction (the process as opposed to the content of our exchanges with others). We are embedded within a social and cultural matrix of meaning, expectations, and emotional experiences, and it is in this context that we struggle to establish an individual positive sense of self. Without much awareness, a client often brings assumptions about self and others into the therapy relationship expecting that these patterns learned as a child will naturally be replicated in all subsequent relationships.

The homophobic stance of society may replicate and exacerbate certain early relationship issues for the client. For example, the expression of anti-gay discrimination may replicate dysfunctional early parent/child relations, such as the parent seeing the child as "other," assuming the child is bad/evil, lacking an empathetic connection with the child, or requiring the child to deny his or her individual identity, experience, or even reality in order to gain acceptance. When clients' childhood issues with family dysfunction are replicated in adolescence by peer relationships or in their interactions within various social institutions, their coping may become overwhelmed and the process of individuation and emotional growth may be stagnated.

This replication can be very unique and specific for each client. For example, if a client's parent consistently and wrongly assumed that the client's childhood behavior was motivated by an intent to hurt the parent and emotionally berates or condemns the child for this, unresolved challenges to self-esteem will likely remain for the client during adolescence. A young gay man or lesbian with healthy self-esteem will not much care that some people think gays and lesbians are evil and bent on destroying the moral fabric of society. However, if this societal homophobic belief replicates an early childhood interaction pattern, the adolescent may have difficulty emotionally defending against this challenge to their positive sense of self. If they decide to come out to the parent who responds with a repetition or escalation of their classic pattern ("How could you do this to us? Don't you know that you're killing your mother? What kind of a monster are you?"), their coping mechanisms may be temporarily overwhelmed.

As a therapist, you are trying to identify the unique maladaptive systems of interaction, which are replicated over and over again within these primary relationships and then reconstructed or replayed within new adult relationships, including the therapy relationship. Once this connection is understood you can (1) help the client to understand his or her emotional reactions to experiences that replicate these early patterns and (2) observe how these dynamics may affect the therapeutic relationship and conceptualize interventions that interrupt the patterns.

It is the task of the therapist to assess the core process/relationship issues that exist for the client. With Toni, for example, core process issues included primarily focusing upon the expectations, advice, and emotional needs of others while negating, denying, and repressing aspects of himself that did not meet these external definitions or guidelines for being "good." Gonsiorek (1993) refers to a client who described his approach to coping with feelings of inferiority as his "best little boy in the world" syndrome.

This coping strategy led Toni to deny his differences from others (including suppression of homosexual feelings and ignoring his biracial background) and to compartmentalize his life and avoid peer relationships in which he would be expected to address his own personal needs, explore social relationships, and differentiate from familial and academic expectations. It also led him to completely suppress the thoughts, feelings, or behaviors that might betray him, expose his differences to others, or result in rewards (praise, good grades, graduation) which he felt, once he accepted a homosexual identity, he no longer deserved. When Toni had a partial breakthrough in this pattern of suppression, he exploded with activity and action, thus his two speeds: full stop and full steam ahead.

Once core process issues such as these have been identified, the therapist's next task is to ascertain how these issues are being replicated within the various relationship systems of the client (for example, the family, the ethnic community, the gay community, the friendship network, and the school/academic community) and evaluate how the client is having difficulty coping with these replications. This understanding will help guide therapeutic interventions and helps the therapist understand the problematic relationship patterns that will be reenacted with the therapist as well. In the preceding example, the therapist recognized that the parent framed the client's individuation as a personal attack and that the client had difficulty defending against homophobic beliefs that assumed destructive and evil intent on the part of gays. The therapist would be on the lookout for this client behaving as if he expected a similar interaction with the therapist. For example, the client might be acutely sensitive to predicting how the therapist will personally respond to his choices rather than focusing on how his choices will affect himself.

Toni had been unable for a long time to acknowledge and accept his capacity and desire to love men and reconcile this with meeting the expectations of his family, peers, and the academic community he wished to join as a professional. Other aspects of his behavior were also being suppressed in an effort to conform to what he thought were others' expectations. His father, Arturo, had expressed to Toni how painful it had been for him to be rejected by his family, especially by Toni's grandfather. Toni received strong messages from both the Latin and Asian cultures embraced by his parents about the centrality of family. Toni felt that by studying the Latin American experience he could reconnect with his Mexican heritage. His father envisioned a large family of descendants and a close knit, intergenerational family. Toni already felt within broader social communities a hidden marginality due to his mixed racial heritage. He had worked hard to be eligible for graduate studies and feared homophobic discrimination from any future academic colleagues. He felt trapped. A gay identity did not figure into the life he had jointly envisioned with his father. He did not wish to cause his father any further pain, nor did he want to personally experience the pain of separation from family that his father had had to endure.

Orienting Constructs

This formulation was guided by a family systems perspective that acknowledges intergenerational issues and the heroic, often futile, attempts children will make trying to resolve issues that belong to the parents. As children, we are faced not only with our own challenges for personal survival and emotional growth but we are intimately connected to our parents, are emotionally aware of their pain and joy, and with blind devotion and love, wish to do anything to help resolve their intrapsychic and interpersonal dilemmas. The wish to resolve intergenerational pain can persist long after the deaths of the grandparents and parents. These primary desires are related to our attachment strivings and need to ensure our own, and future generations', survival. Certainly, focusing on helping an abusive parent heal old wounds may be a direct attempt to reduce the abuse; however, children often behave in selfless and self-negating ways in an attempt to resolve or reduce parental angst. This self-sacrificial behavior may be very futile; however, admitting that they are not in control of making a difference (which only the parent can do) would result in such hopelessness and grief that children rarely give up. It is helpful for clients to recognize the nobility and the limitations of their efforts and grieve for the losses in their own and in their parent's past.

Toni belonged to a loving family and he wished above all else to retain a favored position within its confines. Yet cultural proscriptions against homosexuality indicated that he had no rightful place within the family structure. He consistently spoke about his fears of disappointing others and was particularly interested in getting me, as an authority figure, to express my advice and expectations. It would be important for me to provide problem-solving guidance to Toni appropriate to his coming-out issues, informing him of local resources and addressing issues of internalized homophobia and external discrimination. While this guidance would be important as Toni established a broader cognitive and relational support system, he would eventually have to confront within the therapy his fear of disappointing others, including the therapist, as he established his own individual identity and integrated his diverse cultural allegiances.

Toni needed to step outside of the system of his family interactions and see the dilemma from a *third order* vantage point in order to realize that being the obedient son did not affect his father's resolution of his own rebellious past, nor was it contributing to Toni's happiness. Establishing this perspective encounters tremendous resistances. It is safer, and more likely to lead to success, for the client first to break these patterns within the therapy relationship. Because these interaction patterns have been reinforced within childhood relationships and replicated with others over many years, it may take repeated interruptions of the pattern within the therapeutic relationship to break the emotional and behavioral hold of the system on the client. It is within the personal interactions between therapist and client during sessions that these patterns can be challenged most directly and effectively.

Treatment Plans and Intervention Strategy

INITIAL TREATMENT PLAN

The treatment plan was conceptualized into three phases, which would roughly follow a sequential implementation. However, each phase, in practice, was initiated during the first sessions and progression on the three phases overlapped. Primary emphasis from phase one to phase two and then phase three followed the sequential plan. I have identified these three phases as phase one: crisis intervention, phase two: gay related themes, and phase three: central process issues.

Phase One: Crisis Intervention. The first phase/priority of the treatment plan was to (a) respond to the immediate crisis that was precipitating a dangerous increase in suicidal ideation, (b) establish rapport and initiate a therapeutic relationship based on integrity, and (c) treat the symptoms of depression through education, cognitive-behavioral interventions, and discussion of medication.

Phase Two: Gay Related Themes. The second phase of treatment was to address several gay related themes and issues as they are raised by the client. These themes include:

1. *Establish a positive gay/lesbian identity.* As mentioned earlier, assisting the client in establishing a positive identity initially involves responding to the client's first disclosures of same gender sexual attractions with a positively valued, nonlabeling reflection of their experience. A client may take months or years exploring the personal meaning of various labels or identities and their own experiences before feeling comfortable with adopting a positive gay, lesbian or bisexual identity.

2. *Reduce isolation.* Informing the client of resources available to them starts the process of reducing their isolation as a gay/lesbian/bisexual person. For example, bookstores offer nonfiction and fiction reading material, women's and gay theme music, and local gay newspapers listing local events, clubs, and organizations. Toni spent several hours during his first solo trip to a gay bookstore browsing through the books and covertly watching everyone who entered the store. He was amazed and delighted at the diversity of the patrons, whom he assumed were mostly gay. Fortunately, the college had an active, culturally diverse gay, lesbian, and bisexual student organization. Over the following months, Toni became a very active member of this campus group. It is very unfortunate that many areas do not have youth groups, necessitating adolescents and young adults to restrict their contacts with the gay community to bars and clubs.

3. *Explore coming out.* Who do you tell you are gay? Who do you decide not to tell? How do you disclose? How does this affect self-esteem, reduction of isolation, increased risk of discrimination and/or emotional disappointment and the establishment of social support and identity? These concerns will most likely involve close friends, the gay community, and family relationships. Toni felt a pressing need to come out to selected others, to no longer hide his gay identity.

Toni's experience coming out to his friend John was very positive. Toni chose the car ride back to campus after spending the day with John at Disneyland to raise the topic. He said that he was noticeably nervous disclosing to John and was thankful that the car ride afforded them the opportunity to talk without having to make much eye contact. John drove the car. I was greatly relieved to hear that John came through as a great friend. He expressed his nonjudgmental acceptance of Toni's homosexuality, told Toni that he was a bit taken aback by Toni's disclosure of romantic feelings for him but that he was glad that Toni had had the courage to express them to him. He spoke of his caring for Toni and how important their friendship was to him but also explained clearly that he had no romantic or sexual feelings for Toni and that he never would. He was looking forward to reuniting with his girlfriend. He suggested that they write and invited Toni to visit him and his girlfriend in Europe in the future. Toni drove him to the airport and they said good-bye the next day. Toni continued for some time to imagine that John's invitation for a visit held out a possibility for a future romantic relationship; however, these fantasies diminished as Toni came out to others and became more involved with gay activities and established gay friends.

4. *Raise health concerns: sexuality, drugs, and alcohol.* The existence of AIDS has changed the experience of adolescents. Hopefully, local schools have provided important information and advice regarding sexual behavior. However, I have found some adolescents who have very little knowledge about sexually transmitted diseases (STDs) or HIV and assume that they are

not at risk or that taking birth control pills solves all of their potential problems. It is important to assess these issues with each client. Be careful not to
make assumptions about sexual activity. Adolescents, regardless of sexual
orientation, may be sexually active with multiple partners, engage in prosti-
tution, or have experienced sexual abuse (e.g., rape, incest). Adolescents
need to know that it is specific behaviors involving the exchange of semen,
blood, vaginal secretions, or breast milk and not nonspecific "having sex"
that places them at risk for HIV infection. It is therefore important to ask or
directly assess specific sexual behaviors and experiences. Since you are an
adult authority, your adolescent clients are not likely to tell you about their
sexual activity without being asked directly. For example, I saw a gay male
client who had been involved as a young teenager in extensive anonymous
and abusive sexual contact with older males. He was often accompanied in
three-party sexual encounters by his best friend and classmate, who later
killed himself in their junior year in high school. These patterns of sexual
contact were intermittent yet recurring during his college years. Yet, this
client reported to me that he had not disclosed any of this sexual activity to
his previous two therapists because they had not asked. I have also heard
adolescents say that they are not having sex with their partner, without vol-
unteering any qualification of this statement, only later to understand that
they meant they were not engaging in vaginal intercourse, although they
were being very sexually active with physical and oral contact. Be specific.
Try not to make any assumptions.

I like to start out with general questions and become more specific. For
example, your questions might include: Have you been sexually active? With
whom have you been sexually active? What sexual activities have you participated in with your partner? With others? How did you communicate
about what would or would not happen? Have you engaged in sexual activities that you later regretted? Have you used a condom when having vaginal
or anal intercourse? When having oral sex? Have you used a dental dam or
Saran Wrap when having oral sex with a/another woman? Is this use consistent? Do you feel that your sexual activities have been mutually agreed upon
and not coercive? Have you ever pressured someone into sexual contact to
which they were not actively consenting? Have you ever been pressured into
sexual contact against your will or choice? How does your knowledge of HIV
affect your feelings about yourself, about your sexuality, and about your relationships? Do you have any questions about STDs or HIV transmission or
about birth control? How comfortable do you feel talking about sex with a
partner? How do you feel talking with me about sexual matters?

Often this topic can naturally follow talking about a current relationship or when taking a relationship history. If the subject does not arise naturally, at some point early in therapy I will initiate this topic by saying that
there are several topics that I routinely ask questions about, including suicide, eating disorders, drug and alcohol use, and sexuality. A nonassertive
adolescent with low self-esteem needs intervention in developing skills to

make responsible choices and negotiate safer sex practices. In addition, sexual behaviors, and thus risk for HIV and STD infection, are strongly affected by drug and alcohol use.

Some research indicates that gay men and lesbians are at higher risk for alcohol abuse. For a review of this research and a discussion of treatment issues see McKirnan and Peterson (1989), Nicoloff and Stiglitz (1987) and Ratner (1993). I like to raise and discuss this issue with using and nonusing clients to provide some education on warning signs and the need for caution. Therapy and emotional growth will not progress for clients who are actively abusing drugs and/or alcohol. I consider the decision to work on personal issues in therapy, with the hope and expectation that once these are resolved the client will cease their substance abuse, to be a major therapeutic error. The focus of counseling with such clients needs to be on alcohol and drug education, assessment of substance use/abuse, confronting denial, and referring to drug and alcohol treatment. Once sobriety is established, personal issues can be productively addressed in therapy.

Effective treatment for lesbian/gay/bisexual clients abusing alcohol or drugs must take gay related issues and treatment interventions into consideration. There are often trends and patterns of use that are influenced by gay communities. For example, I have recently seen among gay adolescent clients and their friends an increase in the use of "crystal," or methamphetamine, a highly refined and especially dangerous version of speed (Genre, 1994). Therapists need to be aware of resources in their area for gay alcohol and drug treatment. For example, Alcoholics Together (gay/lesbian Alcoholics Anonymous), hold meetings in all major metropolitan areas and many smaller communities.

5. *Address cultural concerns.* Gays and lesbians will encounter racism within the gay community and homophobia within various ethnic communities. Young gay men and lesbians of color are more likely to encounter conservative "old world" values within their ethnic communities (Tremble, Schneider, & Appathurai, 1989). These might include an emphasis on strong family relationships, conformity to traditional gender roles, a reliance on religion to define values, and an obligation to give birth to children. These and other cultural values must be taken into consideration when addressing the client's concerns. The therapist does this by gaining an understanding of the familial and cultural context as perceived by the client. Then as the client explores coping strategies, the therapist keeps the final stages of identity development in mind as a goal and helps the client to not remain stuck in fundamental either/or, good/bad, accept everything or reject everything thinking.

A lesbian/gay man of color will need to develop coping/survival skills to be used in their relationships with the dominant White heterosexual community, their ethnic community, and the gay community. For example, clients need to recognize forms of racial and antigay discrimination and ways to behaviorally and psychologically respond in a variety of contexts. Adolescents may want to talk at length about certain relationships or incidents that present challenges to their coping. When Toni attended a Latin American Studies conference one week and a Gay Student's Alliance conference the next week, he spent several sessions sorting out his reactions, talking about the subtle nuances of differences in the behavior he observed and in his interactions with others, and evaluating the various ways he felt belonging, exclusion, comfort, and discomfort in each setting.

Conflicts in allegiances can arise. Adolescents may participate in ethnic peer networks (MECHA, BSA, or Asian Pacific Alliance student organizations) and remain in the closet, or they may participate in gay peer networks and relate to few other peers who share their ethnic background. Will they spend time at family gatherings hiding their sexual orientation or face conflicts when family role obligations are not met? It can be a difficult, but important, struggle to achieve an integrated, positively valued identity. Multiple, interacting forms of overt and covert discrimination will be encountered by individuals who belong to more than one oppressed group. Let's see how some of these issues were taken into consideration with Toni.

Given his biracial heritage, these issues were very complex for Toni. He avoided all group peer socializing prior to acknowledging his homosexuality. He had a few individual friends, spent most of his time studying, and never joined any clubs nor attended any parties. We discussed how this left him with a skill deficit. Avoidance of peer social interaction and experimentation and/or denial of gay/lesbian identity delays resolution of many of the intrapsychic issues of adolescence that reemerge once the person comes out (Malyon, 1982). While Toni immersed himself in the academic study of Latin cultures, he discouraged any social connections with other Hispanic students. Toni had used his academic studies as an effective forum for resolving some biculturation issues and had established a very positive internalized Hispanic pride. He didn't expect, nor did he experience, any exclusion from Hispanic peers as a result of his biracial background, although his Japanese heritage was either unrecognized or largely ignored and regarded as irrelevant. Toni avoided contact with Asian peers, anticipating exclusion from group membership based on his identifiable Mexican and Central American heritage. He expected direct discrimination and exclusion from both ethnic peer groups based on his sexual orientation. As a result, he felt most comfortable starting to overcome his shyness and social awkwardness by joining the campus bisexual, gay, and lesbian organization and becoming an active member. Fortunately the membership of this group was fairly ethnically diverse. It can be very important for adolescents to meet gay/lesbian peers and positive role models who share their cultural/ethnic identity. Large cities usually have formal organizations and informal meeting places (bars & clubs) where gays and lesbians of color can meet each other. However, access to these resources may be limited for people under 21 years of age.

Therapists, in this case a Caucasian lesbian, must be very aware of their own embedment in the social systems and how this affects the therapy process. It was important that Toni not reexperience with the therapist the splitting up of his racial and gay identities. If this pattern were to be replicated, those aspects of Toni's identity similar to the therapist (homosexuality) would be recognized and accepted, while other aspects of his identity dissimilar to the therapist (biracial Hispanic and Asian heritage and identity as a man) would be ignored or rejected. To avoid this pattern the therapist must explore and value all aspects of the client's identity and experience. It will be helpful for the therapist to acknowledge differences in ethnicity and sexual orientation from the client and explicitly explore how this affects the therapeutic relationship.

6. *Reassess family relationships.* The question of whether or not to come out to family members inevitably gets raised. Each gay/lesbian person must personally reassess each of his or her relationships with other family members and establish a level of comfort with their individual identity and with their family roles. Toni's struggle with these issues were central to the third phase of therapy and will be discussed in greater detail below.

7. *Integrate spiritual/religious beliefs.* This may be a central issue for some clients who face painful dilemmas caused by institutionalized religion's antigay doctrine (Clark, Brown, & Hochstein, 1990) and of relatively minor concern for others. During childhood and adolescence, some people experience a strong and intimate spiritual connection. Children who associate this experience with religious beliefs that include condemnation of homosexuals (or at least of homosexual behavior) can be severely challenged when they recognize their capacity for romantically loving a person of their own gender. The rejection from the church is compounded, for those who maintain a belief in the church's doctrine, by a betrayal in their previously loving relationship with God. Gay and lesbian adolescents can resolve these issues in a number of ways. They may maintain their general religious beliefs but modify them to include a loving and accepting God. The Christian Metropolitan Community Church (MCC), the Catholic group Dignity, and gay Jewish temples have meetings in most large cities. In addition to these primarily gay congregations, numerous churches have welcomed gay members. The gay or lesbian adolescent may substantially change religious beliefs yet maintain a strong spiritual connection, for example, by adopting the Wiccan belief in goddesses and gods. Or they may be strongly alienated from any spiritual or religious experience. Toni did not consider religious or spiritual concerns to be a current problem or priority.

8. *Confront internalized homophobia and external discrimination.* This central theme will take several years of sifting through various levels of issues and is addressed when dealing with all of the other issues listed above. A more thorough discussion of this issue was included in the Introduction.

Central Process Issues.   The third phase or element of the treatment plan was to address the *process impediments* to Toni's resolving the conflicting issues he faced coming to terms within his emerging gay identity. For me, process impediments refer to the maladaptive patterns that impede the adolescent client's natural progression toward emotional maturity. For example, Toni had felt stymied, unable to proceed with his individuation within his family and with his personal integration of his sexuality. In many respects, this was a normal individuation process that was stuck in a compliance stage. Toni did not feel that he could risk differentiation, separation, or confrontation and could not envision any integrated resolution. He felt the stakes, complete rejection, were just too high to be faced.

Since Toni previously had tried to win significant others' approval by fulfilling what he thought were their expectations while denying his own needs, I suspected that he might replicate this behavior with me. I suspected that Toni's relying on my advice and approval might be helpful to him while he needed support in dealing with some of the gay issues raised in phase two of the treatment plan. When I suggested he select some gay themes books, fiction or nonfiction, he bought numerous books with a credit card, took incomplete in his classes, and read volumes. When I suggested that it would be helpful to interact with other gay students, he joined the lesbian/gay and bisexual student organization and became an active, responsible, organizing member. But at some point the conflicting expectations from various aspects and relationships in his life would need to be acknowledged, and an individual integration would need to occur. Toni would most likely need to confront me about some real or imagined conflict/difference between us and risk possible rejection in order to more fully individuate. Hopefully, I would be able to genuinely respond to this challenge and stay connected and affirming to Toni's self assertions, which had not occurred in many other formative relationships.

REVISED TREATMENT PLAN

Toni proved to be very adept at avoiding confrontation of conflicting social obligations by compartmentalizing and fragmenting different parts of his life and relationships. As he became more involved with gay organizations, his grades plummeted, he couldn't finish his work or complete applications to graduate school. He spent most of his time on gay-related activities.

In helping Toni come to terms with the conflicting allegiances and divergent expectations in his life, we discussed areas of convergence and conflict. As mentioned earlier, he attended a Latin American Studies conference one weekend and a gay student conference the next, and we discussed the issues this raised for him. We discussed the place his Japanese heritage had in his identity. We discussed his experiences of racial discrimination in the gay community. Toni quickly built a basis of ideological and social support as a gay man. Yet he continued to be deeply conflicted about his academic work and about resolving issues with his family.

BALANCING GOALS

Toni cognitively immersed himself and learned a great deal about gay issues in the year and a half we worked together; however, he did not become involved in any romantic relationships. In part, this was a result of his difficulties grieving the romantic fantasy attachment to John, overcoming peer social skill deficits, and resolving conflicts with family role expectations. In addition, Toni, like many gay men, found it important to firmly establish an individual identity as a gay man before developing the capacity to emotionally interact with a romantic partner. (During this process, Toni chose not to experiment with less committed, primarily sexual interactions with other men.) Women, on the other hand, are more likely to struggle with their lesbian identity issues within the context of relationships (de Monteflores & Schultz, 1978).

No matter what topic Toni needed to address in therapy, his two speeds, complete stop (abject denial of an issue or avoiding the exploration of an issue he considered unresolvable) and full speed ahead (driven to act prematurely on an issue before thoughtful consideration), affected his process. Helping Toni become aware of how this coping style was replicated in our relationship was an underlying theme. We discussed the advantages (avoidance of anxiety and disappointment, delaying dealing with issues he is not emotionally ready to handle, maintaining personal privacy and autonomy, and avoiding negative consequences, etc.) and disadvantages (unmet personal needs, lack of adequate preparation and problem solving, emotional isolation, etc.) of this behavior. We also struggled together to establish the trust and interpersonal engagement necessary to discuss unresolved issues without having to jump to premature closure in order to avoid the discomfort of ambiguity and exploration.

Therapeutic Process

RELATIONAL REENACTMENTS

Toni desperately wanted to come out to his parents, but he had decided that his family would not accept his homosexuality, so he chose not to come out to them. He continued to spend much of each weekend and several nights a week at home. Hiding his activities, books, friends, and so forth from his family was creating much tension and anxiety for Toni. He worried that he was becoming more distant and dissatisfied with his family interactions. He spoke repeatedly of these conflicts and yet felt that he could not decide on any plan to help resolve the problems. During one session he was particularly agitated and frustrated.

CLIENT: We've been talking about my family for some time and I still don't know exactly what you expect me to do. You probably think that since they can't accept me, I should distance myself from them and create my own "gay family."

THERAPIST: You're assuming that I expect you to resolve your family issues in a particular way.

CLIENT: Yes! You think the solution is just to accept the situation and move on, but I can't.

THERAPIST: You're making assumptions about what I think and what I expect you to do.

CLIENT: (raises voice) Well then what do you think?

THERAPIST: I don't know what you should do.

CLIENT: (angrily) Don't give me this nonanswer. What do you think?

THERAPIST: Well, I think you have suggested a very WASP solution to your dilemma. You have to find a solution that is unique to your family and to who you are as a member of your family.

CLIENT: (defiant) As a gay man I don't belong to my family.

THERAPIST: Maybe this makes you more of a member of your family than you were before. You are the son of a man who risked and suffered the loss of family ties to love whom he chose—not whom the family accepted. Yes, your father is a man with many traditional values. However, as a young man he challenged ideas he disagreed with, identified as a motorcycle rebel, and left the Catholic church to marry a Protestant. You're the son of a woman of mixed racial heritage, who understands discrimination and the experience of being bicultural, living in different communities, neither of which completely accept her. Sound familiar? It's not only that you can be different and still be a part of the whole, the family, but that your difference makes you part of the family, a part of the family heritage of difference. Your rebellion involves you in their tradition of rebelliousness. You were making assumptions about what I thought. You might consider carefully what assumptions you might be making about your family. I know it's not what they expect, but *you are* the son of your mother and father.

CLIENT: (neither accepting or rejecting these concepts) I'm going to have to think about this.

A couple of things happened in this exchange: Toni confronted the therapist for the first time. I abandoned my reflective stance to respond genuinely to his concerns. My initial response to his confrontation implied that he could be different from me, a lesbian with a WASP background, and explore options that honored the cultural values that emphasized the centrality and importance of family membership. His defiant response challenged the premise that he could differentiate from others and maintain a sense of belonging. The content of my further response placed a positive value on rebelliousness and specifically identified him as a rebel. This was consistent with the process of what had just occurred (his challenging me). I met his challenge with one of my own: to reconsider his place in his family. This was a direct invitation to continue to explore the option of confronting others and differentiating from them while maintaining a connected relationship with them. There was also the implication that he could also maintain a positive connection with me and others (the gay community) while re-belling/differentiating in his own unique way. Toni successfully completed this interaction by neither agreeing nor disagreeing with me and claiming the right to think about this on his own and come to his own conclusion. This was warmly accepted by the therapist.

Toni canceled the next session, and by the next time we met (two weeks after this conversation) he had come out individually to each of his family members! He was brimming with stories to tell. They had had several argu-ments where he challenged his parents. (Unexpectedly, his mother had been more confrontational, while his father had been more accepting.) Toni began to calm down seeing that his issues were not ignored. Although far from being resolved, the family kept talking about topics he had raised and he continued to be included in family activities, such as plans for the up-coming family camping vacation.

IMPEDIMENTS TO TREATMENT

Toni was balancing his need to make up for lost time, submerging himself in social and emotional growth, with staying focused on school work, graduat-ing, and applying to graduate school. Encouraging a client to delve into deeply conflictual emotional concerns can limit their ability to function ex-ternally in a challenging academic environment. However, failing to address deep emotional concerns can result in self-defeating and counterproductive behavior, which also impedes academic or work accomplishment. Once Toni acknowledged to himself his romantic/sexual attractions to men, he began to have major difficulties with procrastination in school. His grades faltered, he stopped interacting with professors, failed to apply to graduate school, and painfully struggled to complete the work needed to graduate. The amount of stress he experienced because of academic expectations and competing emo-tional conflicts was enormous. Toni needed to positively integrate his ethnic and gay identities and establish solid self-esteem in order to feel that he had a right to excel, receive commendation and rewards, and either pursue gradu-ate work in ethnic studies as a gay man or reassess his career goals. Adding to Toni's ambivalence about completing school requirements was the fact that graduation meant termination from therapy and me at the college counseling center, leaving the college social setting which Toni was just beginning to explore, and temporarily moving back in with his family.

Termination and Therapist's Summary Thoughts

Toni's termination was premature and externally determined by his gradua-tion from college. The last phase of therapy involved active support to over-come the emotional and practical barriers to completing his course work. The last sessions were filled with mixed emotions: a joyous celebration of his accomplishments and a sadness about saying good-bye. A review of his progress helped him feel pride in his personal emotional growth and highlighted future goals, which included resolving the conflicts between career goals and identity issues, establishing new family roles as a gay family member, and exploring romantic relationships with men. I gave him several referrals to therapists in the community, including a recommended referral to a gay Hispanic psychologist. We discussed the changes in our relationship from the beginning of therapy, when he was shocked and pleased to find out that he had a lesbian therapist, to our current relationship in which each of us is a clearly delineated individual who feels genuine care for the other. He brought me a gift of poetry he had written and left after receiving a heartfelt congratulatory graduation hug.

I have tried to illustrate how underlying process variables mediate between adolescents' gay, lesbian, or bisexual identity development and their integration within their families, their ethnic/cultural communities, the gay or lesbian community, their school environment, the broader social community, and the relationship with the therapist. Adolescents are simultaneously struggling to achieve gender, ethnic, and sexual orientation identity development. The influences of multiple identity development are not simply additive, rather they are intricately interactive. In many respects, Toni's experiences with antigay discrimination were mild compared to the experiences of many adolescents, yet his taking the proscriptions of others to heart caused him such pain that he seriously considered killing himself. Fortunately, the resources he ultimately found available to him from his family, friends, and college community helped him through the crisis period accompanying his coming out. Your support for the diverse individual identities of gay, lesbian, and bisexual adolescents and your vision that they deserve a valued, integral, yet differentiated place within the various social/relational systems they encounter can make a tremendous difference to their personal development.

REFERENCES

Atkinson, D. R., Morten, G., & Sue, D. W. (1989). *Counseling American minorities: A cross-cultural perspective.* Dubuque, IA: William C. Brown.

Bell, A., & Weinberg, M. (1978). *Homosexualities: A study of diversity among men and women.* New York: Simon and Schuster.

Bustamante, A. L. (1984). Spiral of cultural identity development. *Calmecac* (pp. 46–52).

Cass, V. (1979). Homosexual identity formation: A theoretical model. *Journal of Homosexuality, 4,* 219–235.

Clark, J. M., Brown, J. C., & Hochstein, L. M. (1989, Winter). Institutional religion and gay/lesbian oppression. *Marriage and Family Review, 14*(3–4), 265–285.

Comas-Diaz, L., & Jacobsen, F. M. (1991). Ethnocultural transference and countertransference in the therapeutic dyad. *American Journal of Orthopsychiatry, 61,* 393–402.

Cross, W. E. (1978). The Thomas and Cross models of psychological nigrescence: A literature review. *Journal of Black Psychology, 4,* 13-31.

DeCecco, J. P., & Elia, J. P. (1993). A critique and synthesis of biological essentialism and social constructionist views of sexuality and gender. *Journal of Homosexuality, 24,* 1-26.

de Monteflores, C., & Schultz, S. (1978). Coming out: Similarities and differences for lesbians and gay men. *Journal of Social Issues, 34,* 59-72.

Espin, O. M. (1987). Issues of identity in the psychology of Latina lesbians. In Boston Lesbian Psychologies Collective (Ed.), *Lesbian psychologies: Explorations and challenges* (pp. 35-55). Chicago: University of Illinois Press.

Golden, C. (1987). Diversity and variability in women's sexual identities. In Boston Lesbian Psychologies Collective (Ed.), *Lesbian psychologies: Explorations and challenges* (pp. 18-34). Chicago: University of Illinois Press.

Gonsiorek, J. (1993). Mental health issues of gay and lesbian adolescents. In L. Garnets & D. Kimmel (Eds.), *Psychological perspectives on lesbian and gay male experiences* (pp. 469-485). New York: Columbia University Press.

Helms, J. E. (1984). Towards a theoretical explanation of the effects of race on counseling: A black and white model. *The Counseling Psychologist, 12,* 153-164.

Isay, R. A. (1991). The homosexual analyst: Clinical considerations. *Psychoanalytic Study of the Child, 46,* 199-216.

Kitzinger, C. (1987). *The social construction of lesbianism.* London: Sage Publications.

Krestan, J., & Bepko, C. (1980). The problem of fusion in the lesbian relationship. *Family Process, 19,* 277-289.

Lukes, C. A., & Land, H. (1990). Biculturality and homosexuality. *Social Work, 35,* 155-161.

Malyon, A. (1982). Psychotherapeutic implications of internalized homophobia in gay men. In J. Gonsiored (Ed.), *Homosexuality and psychotherapy: A practitioners handbook of affirmative models* (pp. 59-70). New York: Haworth Press.

McKirnan, D. J., & Peterson, P. L. (1989). Alcohol and drug use among homosexual men and women: Epidemiology and population characteristics. *Addictive Behaviors, 14,* 545-553.

Mercier, L. R., & Berger, R. M. (1989). Social service needs of lesbian and gay adolescents: Telling it their way. *Journal of Homosexuality, 17,* 75-95.

Morales, E. S. (1989, Winter). Ethnic minority families and minority gays and lesbians. *Marriage and Family Review, 14*(3-4), 217-240.

Nicoloff, L. K., & Stiglitz, E. A. (1987). Lesbian alcoholism: Etiology, treatment, and recovery. In Boston Lesbian Psychologies Collective (Ed.), *Lesbian psychologies: Explorations and challenges* (pp. 283-293). Chicago: University of Illinois Press.

Norris, W. P. (1992). Liberal attitudes and homophobic acts: The paradoxes of homosexual experience in a liberal institution. *Journal of Homosexuality, 22,* 81-120.

Ratner, E. F. (1993). Treatment issues for chemically dependent lesbians and gay men. In L. Garnets & D. Kimmel (Eds.). *Psychological perspectives on lesbian and gay male experiences* (pp. 567-578). New York: Columbia University Press.

Remafedi, G. (1978). Adolescent homosexuality: Psychosocial and medical implications. *Pediatrics, 79,* 331–337.

Remafedi, G., Farrow, J. A., & Deisher, R. W. (1993). Risk factors for attempted suicide in gay and bisexual youth. In L. Garnets & D. Kimmel (Eds.), *Psychological perspectives on lesbian and gay male experiences* (pp. 486–499). New York: Columbia University Press.

Rich, A. (1980). Compulsory heterosexuality and lesbian existence. *Signs, 5,* 631–660.

Roesler, T., & Deisher, R. W. (1972). Youthful male homosexuality. *Journal of the American Medical Association, 219,* 1018–1023.

Sadonick, D. (1994). Kneeling at the crystal cathedral. *Genre, 1,* 40–90.

Saghir, M. T., & Robins, E. (1973). *Male and female homosexuality: A comprehensive investigation.* Baltimore: Williams and Wilkins.

Schneider, M. (1989). Sappho was a right-on adolescent: Growing up lesbian. *Journal of Homosexuality, 17,* 111–130.

Schneider, M. (1991). Developing services for lesbian and gay adolescents. *Canadian Journal of Community Mental Health, 10,* 133–151.

Sobocinski, M. R. (1990). Ethical principles in the counseling of gay and lesbian adolescents: Issues of autonomy, competence, and confidentiality. *Professional Psychology: Research and Practice, 21,* 240–247.

Solis, A. (1980). Races of the Chicano spirit. *Calmecac, 1,* 19–27.

Task Force on Bias in Psychotherapy with Lesbians and Gay Men. (1990). *Bias in psychotherapy with lesbians and gay men* (Final Report). Committee on Lesbian and Gay Concerns, American Psychological Association.

Tremble, B., Schneider, M., & Appathurai, C. (1989). Growing up gay or lesbian in a multicultural context. *Journal of Homosexuality, 17,* 253–267.

Vargo, S. (1987). The effects of women's socialization on lesbian couples. In Boston Lesbian Psychologies Collective (Ed.), *Lesbian psychologies: Explorations and challenges* (pp. 161–174). Chicago: University of Illinois Press.

Walters, K. L., & Simoni, J. M. (1993). Lesbian and gay male group identity attitudes and self-esteem: Implications for counseling. *Journal of Counseling Psychology, 40,* 94–99.

Zera, D. (1992). Coming of age in a heterosexist world: The development of gay and lesbian adolescents. *Adolescence, 27,* 849–854.

SUGGESTIONS FOR FURTHER READING

The list of references to this chapter provides excellent reading for further exploration. However, for those who want to familiarize themselves with the diversity of gay and lesbian experience, culture, and sentiment, I recommend fiction. A good place to start is the short story anthology series:

Nestle, J. L., & Holoch, N. (Eds.). (1990). *Women on women.* New York: The Penguin Group.

Nestle, J., & Holoch, N. (1993). *Women on women II.* New York: The Penguin Group.

Stambolian, G. (Ed.). (1986). *Men on men.* New York: The Penguin Group.

Stambolian, G. (Ed.). (1988). *Men on men, II.* New York: The Penguin Group.

Stambolian, G. (Ed.). (1990). *Men on men, III.* New York: The Penguin Group.
Stambolian, G. (Ed.). (1992). *Men on men, IV.* New York: The Penguin Group.

Or, alternatively, browse in a women's bookstore, a gay bookstore, or a bookstore with good women's and gay selections and pick out literature that seems interesting to you. While you are there pick up the newsletters/magazines for the local gay and lesbian communities.

Chapter 9

SEPARATION ANXIETY DISORDER

CASE ILLUSTRATION OF HENRY: A 10-YEAR-OLD LATINO CHILD

Anthony Zamudio, Ph.D
Nancy L. Wolfe, M.S.

THE DISORDER

In the course of human development, what an infant learns about the nature of its environment is initially defined by its relationships with primary caretakers. The primary caregiver's sensitive reading and prompt response to the infant's needs is crucial in the development of a secure attachment and instrumental in the portrayal of the world as a place in which the child's needs can be met. The attachment figures provide the child with a *secure base,* communicating to the child that they are reliably available to help the child feel secure while exploring and mastering his or her environment. If the mother (or primary caretaker) models power and confidence in *her* negotiation of the world and communicates her belief that the child, too, is capable of such mastery, the child can come to share that perspective. Given this worldview and given confidence about the continuing availability of the caregiver, the child will feel safe to explore this exciting new environment.

In normal development, however, the infant's great joy in developing a secure bond with the caregiver also goes hand in hand with anguish over fear of losing her. As very young children develop into toddlers, they begin to master this separation anxiety in several ways. Through increasing cognitive and affective abilities, the young child becomes better able to hold the image of the caregiver in his or her mind and to experience her loving feelings toward the child during her absence. The ability to crawl, walk, and

talk also seems to counteract the child's sense of helplessness at her departure and to foster the child's initiative and expanding interests in others and
the world at large. When normal development goes awry, however, some
older children *regress* to this panic over separation and develop Separation
Anxiety Disorder (SAD) at some phase between the preschool-school and
adolescent years. Rather than approaching the world with curiosity and confidence, these children remain dependent and cannot separate from caretakers. Thus, the core characteristic that defines SAD is excessive anxiety
about separation from parents and other attachment figures. When there are
no demands to separate, the child is not symptomatic; similarly, when the attachment figure returns, the child's distress is relieved. Let's look more
closely at the symptoms that SAD children present.

When their attachment figures are about to leave, younger children with
Separation Anxiety Disorder may shadow or cling to their parents and cry,
plead, or have temper tantrums in order to make them stay. Reactions to impending separations can be so intense that children may wish they were
dead, threaten suicide, vomit, or have panic attacks (young children's inability to explain their symptoms clearly makes diagnosis of a panic disorder
difficult). Children with SAD also have nightmares, exaggerated fears of
animals and monsters in the dark, and often refuse to sleep alone. Somatic
complaints may include headaches, nausea, and stomach aches for younger
children, while older children may have cardiovascular symptoms, such as
palpitations, dizziness, and faintness. Older children with SAD organize
their lives around avoiding potential separation experiences. Often they cannot go to camp or spend the night away with a friend without feeling distressed, homesick, or yearning for reunion. Some may not even be able to go
on simple errands by themselves. Of particular importance, as many as
three-fourths of SAD children may refuse to attend school in order to be near
the attachment figure. Although there may be some concern about harm to
themselves when separated from caregivers, the essential concern for SAD
children is the worry that some accident, illness, or harm will befall the
caregiver while they are away.

In order to make a diagnosis of SAD, *DSM-IV* (1994) indicates that anxiety over separation must be beyond developmental or expectational norms
(which will vary greatly across cultures), last for four weeks or more, begin
before age 18, and impair or disturb important areas of the child's functioning (e.g., ability to attend school). SAD is a common disturbance; prevalence
estimates are about 4% in children and adolescents. It is one of the few disorders with equal incidence for boys and girls in clinical studies, although
more frequently in females in epidemiological studies. Average age of onset
is nine years, although it can occur anytime between preschool-school and
adolescence. Anxiety about potential separation and avoidance of situations
involving separations (e.g., going away to college or the military) may wax
and wane at different points in development, but the disorder may persist
for many years.

SAD is routinely comorbid with other disorders, especially depression. When social withdrawal results in depression, an additional diagnosis of Dysthymic Disorder or Major Depression may be justified. Child therapists also need to differentiate SAD from other similar or overlapping disorders, especially School Phobia. Some children refuse to go to school because they are afraid of aversive experiences at school, such as being ridiculed by peers or failing academically. Although SAD and School Phobia often overlap, fear of something in the school setting or associated with the school is the defining symptom for school phobic children. In contrast, children with SAD are afraid of separating from the mother or attachment figure, usually because of the fear that some harm will befall her in the child's absence. Epidemiologic studies suggest that children diagnosed with SAD also tend to be younger, female, from lower SES families, and to have more symptoms and Axis 1 disorders than school phobic children, whose overall functioning is much better (Last, Francis, Hersen, Kazdin, & Strauss, 1987a).

SAD also must be differentiated from Panic Disorder. In SAD, the anxiety symptoms concern separation from home and attachment figures (which may escalate to panic levels), whereas in Panic Disorder, the symptoms result from concerns about being incapacitated by the possibility of having an unexpected panic attack. At times, SAD in younger children will precede the development of Panic Disorder with Agoraphobia following puberty (APA, 1994). Adults diagnosed with Panic Disorder and Agoraphobia generally have an earlier onset if they had met the criteria for SAD in childhood (Gruppo Italiano Disturbi d'Ansia, 1989). Additionally, Agoraphobia spectrum avoidance has more sudden onset and severe symptomology when the subject had a history of SAD or School Phobia (Perugi et al., 1988). SAD may precede other psychosomatic disorders as well (Sperling, 1982). Finally, it is important to emphasize that even though SAD children often are demanding and manipulative, they are not malingering. SAD children are genuinely afraid of separation and their anxiety is alleviated only when the attachment figure returns.

Researchers do not yet fully understand the etiology of SAD. There may be a genetic component, as it is more common in first degree relatives and in children of mothers with affective disorders (especially depression) and Panic Disorder with Agoraphobia. One study revealed that 83% of mothers with children diagnosed with SAD or Overanxious Disorder had a history of anxiety disorders themselves. Additionally, 57% of the mothers presented with anxiety disorders while their children were seen for similar problems (Last, Hersen, Kazdin, Francis, & Grubb, 1987b). Another study revealed that mothers of children with SAD were found to be four times more likely to have an affective disorder (mostly Major Depression) than mothers of children with School Phobia (Last et al., 1987a). The study also revealed that compared to school phobic children, children diagnosed with SAD were more likely to meet another DSM diagnosis and be more severely disturbed than school phobic children. Wenar (1994) also suggests that vulnerability to developing SAD may be increased by an insecure attachment, by separation traumas that were uncontrolled and unpredictable, and by a temperamental vulnerability to anxiety in infancy. Whatever the interplay of predisposing factors, SAD usually develops in response to a specific life stressor such as the death of a parent, relative, or pet, an illness of a parent or child, moving to a new neighborhood or school, or immigration. As we see in the case illustration to follow, 10-year-old Henry developed SAD in response to his family moving across country coinciding with a surgery being scheduled for his mother.

Children with SAD tend to come from families that are described as close and caring. Different family interaction patterns can occur (some SAD children are compliant, conscientious, and eager to please), but the most common interaction pattern researchers have identified is a *hostile-dependent* relationship between mother and child. Children with this disorder are often described as demanding, angry, and in need of constant attention—dominating an indulgent mother who gives in and reinforces the child's demandingness (Herbert, 1974). We will see this close intertwining of anger and dependence in the subsequent case study of Henry.

Gardner (1992) describes mothers of SAD children as "overprotective"—not allowing the child to individuate. Like Henry's mother, they often view the world as dangerous and can only feel secure themselves by staying close to the child. As a result, they are often vigilant about the child's whereabouts and constantly check up on him or her. Important treatment complications occur when therapists must differentiate these types of parental insecurities from the reality based threats of crime, neighborhood gangs, and school violence, as occurs in the case study to follow. Indeed, given the high levels of uncontrollable and unpredictable traumas for inner-city children, distinguishing between a mother's realistic concern from overprotectiveness may be difficult. Further, the disruptive nature of these traumas make children's attachment issues and fears regarding separation reasonable. Thus, therapists working with children who live in dangerous neighborhoods have the additional task of addressing the impact of that environment on both the children and parents' behavior and affect. Mothers of SAD children also tend to shelter the child from facing interpersonal problems with peers and others because they perceive their children as too weak or vulnerable. Unfortunately, this "benevolent" act further undermines the child's initiative and sense of efficacy, making him or her fearful to venture out. The result may be further dependence and demandingness, both of which may validate the mother's perception of her child as vulnerable and needy of her protection, fueling further this unhealthy parent-child cycle of overprotection and dependence.

In addition, Gardner emphasizes that there is no meaningful marital coalition in this prototypic family scenario. Father also fails to provide a corrective parental influence on the child, as he accepts the mother's authority passively, is dependent on her as well, or is simply uninvolved in childrearing.

In many families with SAD children, father and child are seen as being in competition with each other for the mother's interest and attention. Much familial conflict results from this competition and lack of marital coalition, as mother and child remain enmeshed in their primary alliance with each other. These issues will be further elucidated in the case illustration to follow.

Sociocultural Factors

Sociocultural factors contribute to and complicate the treatment of Separation Anxiety Disorder. These factors are varied and many, ranging from economic influences to the lack of education. Language, religious, and attitudinal differences about institutions and childrearing practices can be factors as well. Henry, the client in this case, is a 10-year-old Hispanic boy, who lives in the inner city of a major metropolis on the west coast of the United States. The client was born in the United States, his mother was born in Guatemala, and his father was born in Mexico. As we will see, these and other sociocultural factors are significant in the development and maintenance of Henry's presenting problem. Before beginning the case study, we will examine several specific cultural factors that may influence the development of SAD in Hispanic children.

The nature of the world, as children perceive it, is influenced by the nature of their relationship with the primary caretaker and indirectly by the manner in which the primary caretaker views the world. Caretakers' worldviews are colored not only by the relationship they had with their own caregivers but by sociocultural variables as well. Economic factors can influence the probability of real threats in the environment, therefore contributing to a view of the world as a potentially threatening place. This view may be communicated to the child. Further, when dealing with a population from a low socioeconomic level, the incidence of real crime and possible harm is often greater. By being forced to live in the inner city because of low wages and limited sources of transportation, these individuals frequently experience violence as a part of their everyday existence. In addition, gang activities, shootings, drug dealings, robberies, car jackings, molestations, and kidnapings are on the rise in the inner cities of the United States, making fear of becoming a crime victim increasingly a real concern, which can realistically affect the behavior and attitudes of those living amidst such turmoil. These reality-based fears about the possibility of harm make it more difficult for a parent to encourage age-appropriate individuation in a child. Similarly, a therapist's desire to encourage a parent to support the child's separation can be stifled by the therapist's own anxiety which is evoked by witnessing and hearing of such violence. Thus, an important treatment complication occurs with this population because the therapist would like the client to behave more assertively and independently, but the therapist, too, may be realistically apprehensive about potential dangers in the community. As we will see in the case study to follow, the therapeutic task is to assess and address the degree of actual danger which may interact with and/or exacerbate the psychological dimensions noted earlier.

Families moving to the U.S. also have to deal with the stress of immigration itself. Many who come from Central America have lived in areas where Post Traumatic Stress Disorder is more prevalent, whether or not they themselves were directly exposed to war and its consequences (Cervantes, Salgado de Snyder, & Padilla, 1989). These families have often been torn apart with hopes of being reunited at a later date. The multiple separations many of them experience can negatively affect the separation/individuation process for children who have a parent with this background, which may be exacerbated by their apprehension about the American lifestyle (Padilla, Cervantes, Maldonado, & Garcia, 1988). Cervantes et al. (1989) report that those families who have immigrated for political reasons, and who have been exposed to war and dealt with leaving family members behind, can suffer from a significant degree of depression and anxiety. Central American countries, such as Guatemala or El Salvador, have a political history of civil war in which atrocities against the poor and powerless were committed by brutal governments. When a primary caretaker comes from this region, it is often difficult to trust government organizations such as hospitals, schools, or social service agencies. It can take much education and many corrective experiences before this population may be able to trust and utilize government agencies beneficially. Leslie and Leitch (1989) speculate that, in spite of the high level of services available to immigrants, low utilization may also exist out of the fear of being identified as undocumented. This fear of deportation is further increased by a recent California state law (Proposition 187) that not only denies access to medical, educational, and social services to immigrants but also dictates that the foregoing agencies have to notify the authorities when contact is made by undocumented individuals. Unless situations reach *crises levels,* Central Americans will not seek out social and mental health services. Informal social support is often used rather than formal social services and, as a result, their interaction with the larger community is diminished and they may become insulated (Leslie, 1992).

Beyond the realistic potential for harm in the client's environment, language barriers can cause social isolation and the underutilization of mental health services (Acosta, 1984). In recent immigrant populations, failure to acquire the language of the dominant culture may lead to a sense of helplessness and powerlessness and may promote misunderstanding. Everything a person understands about the new culture must be interpreted or inferred and, in this process, accurate or undistorted communication may not occur. The dependence of parents on interpreters, such as their bilingual children is one common solution. In my clinical work, I have noticed that bilingual children find themselves in situations where their role as translators is useful to the family and helps them in their self-esteem in that they feel needed and appreciated. On the other hand, in cases where dysfunctional family relations exist, the bilingual child's role as interpreter can become overburdening for the child and contribute to a grandiose sense of importance, such as the child feeling responsible for his or her family receiving benefits after translating at a social service office.

Parents from lower socioeconomic groups often have less education and poorer reading and writing skills than their children, causing further reliance on their children (Acosta, 1984). In families where parent(s) possess high self-esteem and healthy interdependency between family members exists (Cervantes & Arroyo, 1994), the role of translator can provide children with an opportunity to develop positive social and language skills that increase their self-confidence. If, on the other hand, parent(s) lack self-esteem and are overly dependent on their children for emotional security, then the parent's dependence can make it difficult not only for the parent to let the child individuate but also puts an unnatural burden on the child to care for the parent. This dependent relationship can further create a sense of shame and lack of confidence within the parent and a false sense of omnipotence within the child. The image of the caregiver as a steady and dependable support for the child is also upset by this role reversal, making it difficult for both parent and child to let go of each other. Thus, an important and special feature of treatment with SAD populations, where a bilingual child is the family's interpreter, is addressing parental deficits in language, reading, and writing skills in order to increase the parent's self-esteem and sense of independence, while freeing the child of this caretaking burden.

Other economic and cultural factors can make the separation-individuation process more difficult for this population. In the home countries of this population, families are typically large and extended. It is not unusual that there are many children with a wide range of ages and that other family members, such as grandparents, godparents, aunts, uncles, and cousins, live together or in close proximity. Often, the family needs are given great importance over the needs of the individual (Alvirez & Bean, 1976; Grebler, Moore, & Guzman, 1970), with the family orientation often extending to other family members (Grebler et al., 1970). When this family system functions normally, it is unusual for a child to become overly dependent on one person because a child usually has numerous loving caregivers. Extended families can, in addition, provide for emotional and financial support (Grebler et al., 1970), and assistance with the immigration process (Padilla et al., 1988). Thus, within a functional family system, a child has the opportunity to develop several primary relationships with godparents, aunts, uncles, and siblings that can help them with individuation and socialization processes (Garcia-Coll & Meyer, 1993). If the family experiences separation through death or immigration, however, familial support in child rearing is often lost and a problematic dependency among the remaining family members may result, eliminating the help the extended family can provide in dealing with anxiety and distress (Acosta, 1984). The lack of family support is clearly evident in the case of Mrs. H., whose resources in dealing with the anxiety and distress resulting from immigration and other stressors is limited.

The arrangement of living spaces is also sometimes changed by the immigration process. Many recently immigrated families with limited resources live in single room dwellings where parents and children sleep in the same room, rather than in separate bedrooms as is the custom in American families. Separation from the caregiver (exemplified by having a separate bedroom) establishes the value for autonomy, which, in the United States, comes earlier in life. Evaluating the sociocultural context of infant development (Garcia-Coll & Meyer, 1993) is very important given that children from different ethnic groups place a stronger emphasis on interdependence and cooperation (Kagan, 1977). Thus, the implications of having separate bedrooms may differ for different ethnic populations. In addition to having separate individual spaces, there are differences in the ages at which children are encouraged to become independent. In mainstream America, children may be encouraged to become more independent once they enter school, around age 5, whereas in many Hispanic cultures, independence is not encouraged until later years. In my clinical experience, however, immigrant children sharing living spaces are still able to develop autonomy, separateness, and independence.

It is possible that some of the traditions found in Hispanic cultures may also exacerbate the development of Separation Anxiety Disorder. Having children is perceived by parents in some cultures as valuable, perhaps more so than in other segments of mainstream American society. Bearing and raising children can actually enhance the status of the Hispanic family. Also, the first born male child may carry special status due to family inheritance and leadership traditions. Thus, in many homes, Hispanic children might have less structure imposed by parents and are often perceived as the center of family life. These factors could make the parents of a child with Separation Anxiety Disorder feel less comfortable with imposing the firm limits and consistent consequences that are necessary to alleviate the symptoms of this disorder. In trying to follow the standard treatment guidelines (for example, sending the child back to school even though he or she does not want to go), parents may feel as if they are betraying cultural values. Thus, the conflict arising from what appears to be an appropriate treatment goal clashing against a cultural value would need to be assessed and addressed.

In diagnosing SAD, it is critical that the therapist distinguish between behavior that is normative and adaptive from behaviors that are maladaptive and inhibit the growth and development of the individual. However, as Cervantes and Arroyo (1994) indicate, before diagnosing separation anxiety, it is important to take into account family values of interdependence, neighborhood norms, and forced multiple separations. In other words, some cultural groups place a high value on strong interdependence among family members as opposed to values of independence. Mexican American youth represent a group in which interdependency may often be encouraged.

Kagan's (1977) literature review, for example, documented that Mexican American children are more concerned than other children with cooperative motives rather than competitive motives. This form of socialization has great value and can help a group overcome hardships and maximize their resources. This is especially relevant for Hispanic families who may be faced with the stress of unemployment, financial difficulties, language barriers, and adapting to a lifestyle of the United States. Further evidence for the beneficial effects of social support is provided by Padilla et al. (1988), who found that social support networks for Mexican and Central American immigrants have been very helpful coping resources in dealing with the above stressors. Family and friends were identified as the single most important factor in assisting the immigrants' transition into the United States. In the present case study of Henry, however, the lack of extended familial and community support fostered the developmentally inappropriate dependence between the mother and the child, which in turn created further familial problems by precluding an emotional relationship with the father.

Finally, treatment of the entire family system is also made difficult by the fact that employment opportunities are rare in the inner city and, if there is hope for continuing employment, long hours, few days off, and an inflexible work schedule are to be expected. Because of these factors, conjoint sessions with working parents, which would be helpful in the development of a therapeutic alliance and realignment of family roles, are difficult to arrange because they may threaten greatly needed family income and jeopardize job security. The impact of such factors will be addressed in the following case example.

CASE ILLUSTRATION

Presenting Problem

Henry was brought to an inner-city family health clinic by his mother. For the previous two months he had been reporting stomach pain, headaches, difficulties sleeping alone at night, reluctance to attend school, and resistance to leaving home without his mother. Prior to the clinic visit, Henry had received a physical examination from his pediatrician, who was unable to find an organic basis for his somatic complaints. His mother requested a second opinion from our health clinic. The family physician at our clinic also found no physical problems and requested a psychological evaluation by me, the clinic's psychologist and a bilingual Hispanic man.

Henry's mother indicated that Henry had a history of difficulties with separation beginning in preschool. Throughout preschool, his mother reported that Henry would cling to her, be tearful if she left his sight, and complain of stomachaches. After his first three months of kindergarten, the family moved to the east coast of the United States when Henry's father received a better job opportunity. Henry's symptoms of anxiety increased at his new school, where his attendance was sporadic and academic performance correspondingly poor. For these reasons, his teacher recommended he repeat kindergarten. Henry was then referred to a psychologist and he seemed to respond well, with some decrease in symptoms and improved academic performance. Unfortunately, the treatment terminated prematurely when the family was unexpectedly forced to move back to the inner city on the West Coast after Henry's father experienced work-related problems at his East Coast job.

Upon arrival on the West Coast, Henry was placed in the third grade instead of the second because of his age. Three months after moving, he exhibited symptoms of Separation Anxiety Disorder again. In addition to separation fears, the family's moves and Henry's excessive school absences had disrupted Henry's ability to develop peer relationships. Similarly, his mother's opportunities for establishing social support through community activities were also disrupted by these moves.

Henry's mother (Mrs. H.) also reported that she had been suffering from severe stomach pains that were the result of gall stones. Her physician had recommended hospitalization to remove the stones, but she postponed scheduling the surgery after Henry began showing symptoms of SAD once again. At a time when she was worried about her health, Henry provided companionship and comfort while her husband was consumed by work responsibilities, and she welcomed Henry's attention and dependency.

CLIENT DESCRIPTION

Henry was in the third grade when he first came to the clinic. He was a tall thin boy, with pale skin tone, in contrast to his mother's olive complexion. At his first meeting with the therapist, he was neatly dressed in a T-shirt, jeans, and a popular style of tennis shoes that appeared to be recently purchased. During the initial interview he sat close to his mother, did not make eye contact with me, and spoke in a low monotone voice. His affect was restricted, he answered with head nods and other nonverbal gestures, and he often looked toward his mother, who would respond for him. While Henry spoke both English and Spanish, his mother spoke only Spanish. On occasion, Henry would speak English with me. When this occurred, Henry's mother would sit with a lost look on her face, clearly not comprehending what Henry was saying. Because Henry was born in the United States, he qualified for Medi-Cal coverage, which paid for physical and mental health visits.

SOCIAL CONTEXT

Henry lived in a one bedroom apartment with his natural mother and father. The apartment was located in the heart of the inner city, in a neighborhood that was primarily Latino, with the majority of the population being recently

immigrated Mexican and Central American refugees. Gangs and drug deal-
ers were a major problem in the neighborhood, and community resources
were limited. Henry attended a local public school not far from his home.
The class was overcrowded, and resources for after school programs and
recreational sports were limited.

Because of the mutually dependent mother-child relationship in most
cases of SAD, it is important to include information about the mother of the
child. Mrs. H. was 46 years old and slightly overweight. She was very polite
and respectful toward me. Her attire suggested that she was from a lower socioeconomic group. She wore a simple T-shirt, shoes that were very worn,
and faded shorts. Her dress, in contrast to Henry's, was noticeably more tat-
tered and frayed. She was unadorned, with no makeup, and her graying hair
was pulled straight back. Nonetheless, she carried herself with pride, and
her greatest source of pride appeared to be her son.

Henry's mother, Mrs. H., was born in Guatemala, the second of five children. For unknown reasons, she was given at the age of 1 year, nine months
to a paternal aunt who admired her during a family visit. After several
months of living with her aunt, her grandparents believed that she was not
receiving adequate care, so they took her to live in their home. Consequently, Mrs. H. felt very close to her grandparents and considered that they
were more her parents than her biological parents. Mrs. H. was still confused and resentful over the willingness of her mother and father to give her
up. As an adult she confronted her parents about their reasoning for giving
her away, but this confrontation was not productive and did not provide her
with any useful information to help her resolve her feelings of rejection and
abandonment.

Mrs. H. lived in Guatemala until the age of 33, where she completed a
sixth-grade education. At the age of 17, she became sexually active without
the use of contraception but never became seriously involved in a relationship or pregnant until she approached her 30s. At that time, she became involved with a man who was unwilling to commit to her. She was afraid of
"being alone" for the rest of her life and began trying to conceive a child by
calculating the most likely times of conception and planning her relations
with her partner accordingly. Considering Mrs. H.'s history of profoundly insecure relationships, it is possible that she viewed the possibility of a relationship with a child as something permanent, a bond that she might finally
control. Mrs. H. suspected that she might be pregnant; but, as the relationship grew apart and she realized that her partner would never be willing to
make a long-term commitment, she decided to move to the United States
with members of her extended family.

Upon arriving in the United States, Mrs. H. began working in a factory
to support herself. She reported that after living in the United States for 5
months, she discovered that she was indeed pregnant. She stressed that she
immediately sought prenatal care from a county clinic and was pleased
about being pregnant. Mrs. H. wrote the father of the child but received no
response. She decided to continue with the pregnancy, believing that she

could do a satisfactory job of raising a child on her own as a single parent. Tragically, the female infant was delivered stillborn, due to a malformation in the brain. Unfortunately, Mrs. H. was not given an opportunity to see the infant postdelivery. Consequently, Mrs. H. suspected foul play or a major error by the hospital, in particular suspecting that her and the infant's identification bracelets may not have matched correctly. Believing that the infant had not really died but was somehow switched or taken may have been an attempt both to defend against her own deep feelings of abandonment and inexplicable loss, as well as her own feelings of shame and humiliation over delivering a stillborn child.

Several months after the stillbirth of Mrs. H.'s daughter, Mrs. H. met Mr. H., Henry's father. He was 29 years old and had recently immigrated from Mexico to the United States. They married about a year and a half later, and Henry was born about 6 months later when Mrs. H. was 36 years old. Mrs. H. described Henry's father as a "hardworking" and "good man," and she reported that she felt "safe" with him. Mr. H. was employed in the fast food restaurant business. He and his wife had met on the West Coast, then they moved to the East Coast, where they lived for a little over 2 years when he accepted a job in fast food management. Mr. H. decided to leave his position when he found out that his boss was involved with dangerous individuals, and he became concerned for the safety of his family and himself. This experience also served to reinforce the family's perception of the world as a dangerous place. At intake, Mr. H. was working long, hard hours, without benefits, as a cook in a fast food business. Henry's father was not able to attend therapy sessions often because any hours missed from the low-paying work would result in financial hardship for the family.

Mrs. H.'s only complaint about her husband was the way he treated Henry. She was concerned about how strict he was and the manner in which he would intimidate Henry into complying with his requests. Mrs. H. said that Henry and his father had a competitive relationship in which they were rivals for her attention. Mrs. H. reported that Henry often slept in his parents' bedroom, even though they had a designated place for him to sleep on the sofa in their living room. His mother admitted that she felt sad for him because "he looked so lonely sleeping all by himself," so she routinely had him sleep with her. Mr. H. felt overcrowded and slighted by his wife's decision to put Henry between them, so he slept on a second mattress in their bedroom. Because of Mrs. H.'s own deprivation and insecure attachment in childhood, the concept of being alone seemed to have taken on special significance for her. She was unable to sustain a primary marital coalition with her husband and she was unable to set or follow through with firm limits for Henry. Henry often complained that his mother gave his father more attention than he received and that he was entitled to an equal share. Mr. H. responded by ineffectually explaining to Henry that someday he would grow up and find a wife as good as his mother. By this, Mr. H. was hoping to reduce Henry's insistence on demanding a disproportionate amount of his mother's attention. In response, Henry would become upset and continue to demand all of his mother's attention. This adoration and competition for Mrs. H.'s attention seemed to be highly reinforcing for her. Her relationship with her husband and son did provide a much needed contrast to her childhood experiences of rejection and abandonment and to her relationship with the father of her stillborn child. As a result, she had difficulty in setting limits that were necessary to ease the conflict. If she stopped this competition for her attention, she would be giving up the much needed, constant reassurance that she had never received in her life.

Initial Session

In the first session, Henry was quiet and spoke very little. I wanted to establish an alliance with both Henry and his mother, so I saw the both of them together for about 15 minutes:

THERAPIST: Hello Henry. It's nice meeting you.

HENRY: (Henry nods but avoids direct eye contact.)

THERAPIST: Maybe you can tell me what has been bothering you.

HENRY: (long pause, his mother looking at me and wanting to speak but restraining herself given that I'm giving Henry direct eye contact) My stomach has been hurting me a lot.

THERAPIST: Do you know what has been making you feel that way? (wanting to assess insight or ability to reflect upon himself)

HENRY: (abruptly) I don't know, it just hurts me.

THERAPIST: Gee, that must feel uncomfortable. How long has this been going on?

HENRY: I don't know.

MOTHER: (cannot restrain herself any longer and then interjects) Excuse me doctor, but this has been occurring for a few months now.*

THERAPIST: (At this point, I decided not to be too directive and to ask questions more open endedly to observe mother-son dynamics.) Oh, so what happened a few months ago?

MOTHER: (She continues speaking. As mother speaks, Henry looks directly at her and nods occasionally.) There are some boys in his school that have been bothering him, hitting him. One of them is bigger and, despite telling his teacher, nothing seems to be done.

THERAPIST: I wonder what rough things they are doing (I ask open endedly again to see if Henry can jump into the conversation in any way and give his experience).

MOTHER: (Looking at Henry) Tell the Doctor what they do to you. (She makes it easy for him. He doesn't have to struggle to think or talk in

---

*All of mother's and father's dialogue is in Spanish. Henry's dialogue is in both English and Spanish. My dialogue is in both English and Spanish.

their relationship. She directs him when to speak, and if he pauses or has trouble finding words for his experience, she steps in to express her opinions.)

HENRY: (Speaking in a frustrated and annoyed tone.) When we were on the playground the other day, one of them came up to me and kicked me and hit me on the back. And the teacher didn't do anything when I told her . . . (pause).

MOTHER: (Mother interjects) These boys, doctor, I'm worried because these are bad children who seem to be dangerous.

In the very first few minutes of my session I was faced with trying to distinguish between parental overprotection and realistic concerns, given the violent nature of Henry's community. On the one hand, the information (and the manner in which it is presented) may be a reflection of an overprotective mother who has not allowed Henry to become comfortable with his aggression and to protect and defend himself as do other boys his age. On the other hand, as Cervantes and Arroyo (1994) indicate, neighborhood norms can often involve violence and gang activity, causing anxiety in these situations. I decided to be safe, since I was unfamiliar with Henry's specific school, although I was aware that his neighborhood had a reputation of gang violence, and validate his concern so I could establish an alliance with him and his mother. I felt that if I was playing into any manipulation of either mother or son, there would be plenty of opportunities in our future sessions to address it, rather than risk misinterpreting a reality issue.

THERAPIST: Gee, sounds like the teacher's not listening makes you angry. Mrs. H., how does that make you feel toward the school?

MOTHER: Well, Doctor, I'm very worried about something happening to him, and the fact that the teachers aren't putting a stop to these kinds of things does not seem right. I'm not an educated woman (I have many Hispanic clients who are very humble when they present an opinion against a professional's), but I think something should be done to these students.

HENRY: (nods his head in agreement)

MOTHER: I worry how safe he will be at school.

As mentioned earlier, separation anxiety involves aspects of the mother-child relationship. I decided to meet with the mother alone to establish an alliance with her and not threaten the dependent relationship with Henry. Meeting with her alone would also help further clarify the extent of Henry's separation problem. Thus, Henry was directed to a waiting room next to the therapy office, with the door closed.

MOTHER: Doctor, this problem of his stomachaches and not wanting to go to school is something that began in preschool (Her tone sounded as if she could speak more freely.) He had been doing better after working with a psychologist when we lived on the East Coast. Teachers from

Head Start to kindergarten were very good at understanding him and helping me with him. I was very grateful for that . . .

Mother spoke nonstop, to the point that it was difficult for me to interject questions. I sensed some desperation and experienced a neediness about her that made me want to pull away from her. At the same time, however, I was compelled to help her because I felt compassion for her predicament. I decided that gathering background information would be the best use of the remaining time.

After several minutes into the interview, there was a knock at my door. Smiling, mother said, "I'll bet that's Henry." Opening the door, it was Henry.

HENRY: How much longer are you going to take? (He looked disapproving rather than anxious. He also seemed to want his mother to invite him back in.)
THERAPIST: I know it's difficult to wait outside.
HENRY: 'Cause your taking a long time. . . . (He sounded whiny. He must have been quite angry at me for intruding upon his special relationship.)
THERAPIST: You sound really upset at us for making you wait outside . . . (pause) . . . I can understand you feeling this way . . . I need your help (trying to make him feel a part of our relationship). I want to talk alone more with your mother about some very important information. After she's done, I want to talk with you again, and I will let you know what things she and I review.

When separated from their mother, these children often develop elaborate fantasies about what is being talked about, and answering their questions can help reduce their anxiety.

HENRY: (nods his head in agreement.)
MOTHER: (proudly) I knew he was going to have a hard time with waiting, and I expected him to knock at the door.
THERAPIST: You did?
MOTHER: He likes being with me a lot and wants a lot of my attention.
THERAPIST: How does that make you feel?
MOTHER: I like it that he needs me . . . but aren't all children like that with mothers who love them?

During the time remaining, Mother provided some background history and complained about Henry's opposition over homework assignments. I saw her complaining as a good sign that she could separate somewhat from him. On the other hand, she wasn't able to do this with him in the room. In fact, she asked *me* to instruct Henry to complete his homework assignments and to comply with her requests. She also asked me not to share with Henry the source of this information concerning his noncompliance.

I was immediately concerned about the possible development of *alliances* and felt strongly the need to set boundaries and clarify my role. It also seemed important that I find a way to model being engaged yet maintaining my separateness. My concern, however, was that she not experience me as critical, judgmental, or rejecting.

THERAPIST: What I would like to do is be able to find a way to instruct Henry so he will pay more attention to what *you* say. I also think it is best that we not keep secrets from Henry, or else he won't trust us and the three of us will have difficulty working together. How do you feel about the three of us working together to get Henry to complete his work and for you, as his mother, to have a reasonable authority role with him? After I talk to Henry there may be some things he would like different at home too and we will talk about them later and see if they are reasonable things to work on.

MOTHER: (genuinely) Okay, Doctor. Whatever you think is best.

I brought Henry back into the room and told him (with his mother present) that she had told me about his stomachaches and the difficulty he sometimes has getting his homework and other things done and that we had agreed to work together to improve the situation. I then stated that I wanted to spend time alone with Henry to hear things from his point of view. Mrs. H. seemed surprised at this. I thought it important at this point to address Henry directly. I stated to him that I wanted to spend time alone with him and that we could play with toys and talk together for a while. (In this process I was attempting to delineate one clear boundary. That is, that Henry and I would also have a relationship that was separate from the one I had with his mother.) I then turned to Mrs. H. and thanked her for the information she had given and said that Henry and I would be done in 20 minutes, at which time the three of us would briefly review the session and make plans for future meetings.

An issue that often arises when working with children is the extent to which their counseling time gets shared with parents. My policy when working with children 10 and older is to ask that what occurs during the individual segment be confidential (between child and therapist) with the proviso (stated clearly in the child's presence) that we would tell the parent if the child were engaging in dangerous behavior (e.g., using IV drugs) or were suicidal. Otherwise, the specifics of the session would not be divulged unless the child and I agreed to this in advance. Mrs. H. seemed distressed by this but agreed after I explained the importance of giving Henry the opportunity to express all he thought and felt without fear that it would be told to his mother and potentially displease her. Mrs. H. then reluctantly left the room. Although I utilize these guidelines with most clients, they were particularly relevant given the boundary issues between Henry and his mother, otherwise the same problematic dynamics that occurred in the family would be reenacted in treatment.

After Mrs. H. left, I was aware that Henry didn't seem interested or show curiosity about me and the items (toys, pictures, colors) in my office as other children do, who often either get out of their seats to touch the toys or at the very least look at them from far away. He still seemed more focused on his mother. I warmly invited him to explore the room and explained to him that the purpose of therapy was to talk openly and see if we could together find a way to help him feel safer and enjoy school and his family. By speaking directly to Henry, I hoped to communicate that the therapy environment was one of trust, safety, respect, and openness and that he, as an individual, was a central part of this process. Henry spent most of our time sitting in the same chair but did convey his interest in trains (his family had traveled this way from the East Coast). He also said that he might like to be a pilot when he grows up. His interest in various modes of transportation was fascinating given his presenting problem: fear of separation.

At the end of this intake, I asked Henry and his mother if they would like to be in treatment with me and stated that there were other resources I could provide if they did not feel comfortable with me. The mother said that she wanted to pursue treatment with me because she felt a great sense of respect, courtesy, and understanding from me. I thanked her and told her I would do my best. (With Hispanic patients I often find that at the end of sessions there is often a humble back and forth interchange between us.)

Case Conceptualization

Henry's complaints of stomach pains and separation difficulties can be understood by examining his parents' background, his relationship with his parental figures, his school, and his culture.

Henry's mother had difficulty tolerating separation from Henry due to her own early separation experiences. In her early background, her first attachment was tenuous and prematurely disrupted when, without warning, she was removed from the home where she lived with her parents and older sibling. The reason for her removal was never communicated to Mrs. H., and contributed to her sense of the world as an insecure, uncontrollable, and unpredictable place. She was left with feelings of doubt about her own desirability and self-worth. Such abandonment and rejection experiences seemed to have generated insecurities, influencing her inability to establish a committed relationship throughout her teens and early adulthood. My experience with her in the initial session, which suggested that she was very needy, wanted frequent affirmation, yet also wanted to control the pace and direction of our time together, gave me insight into how others might have experienced her—as demanding and controlling.

Mrs. H.'s desire to conceive a child out of wedlock may be perceived as an attempt to feel whole and desirable. Perhaps in a relationship with a child, she would finally have someone to love and someone who would love her completely in return. This child would depend on her and never leave her as others had before. After many years of not using birth control, she finally conceived this child and began to foster hopes that this pregnancy might help her to overcome her sense of herself as defective and undesirable. Through this pregnancy, she might have finally been able to experience herself as worthy, capable of creativity, and capable of preventing "unexpected disruptions." Moving to the United States also may have offered her the hope of building a new, more secure and fulfilling life. However, all of her hopes for a new start, a new sense of self, and new attachment to a new country were shattered by the stillbirth of her daughter and the difficult social and economic conditions she faced in her new country.

The marriage to Henry's father and Henry's conception again inspired a sense of hope and trust in the future. However, her pattern of self doubt continued as evidenced in her perplexity concerning why Henry's father might be attracted to her, especially considering the fact that she was older than him. However, this age difference had a "positive" side in that it was more probable that her husband would become dependent upon her, satisfying her desire for someone who would need her, cherish her, and never leave her. Further, although this new marriage and pregnancy inspired optimism, it could also have reevoked the trauma of losing the first child. Although fears of fetal demise are common for many women, they are all too real for a woman who has had a previous experience with fetal death, malformation, or trauma. Memories of the death of her own childhood through separation, the real death of her first daughter, and the death of the relationship with the first baby's father may have been reevoked. Fears that she must somehow be defective given her repeated rejections and losses were also understandably evoked. She was, to some extent, delightfully betrayed when her negative expectations were not realized, and Henry was born alive and healthy. Mrs. H. could now hope for a brighter, more emotionally secure future with a husband and son who would love her and not leave her.

After Henry's birth, Mrs. H. became suspicious about not seeing her daughter's body after the delivery. She noted that when Henry was born, his identification bracelet number and her own were identical, while she recalled that the numbers on her daughter's bracelet and hers were different. She requested medical records of her daughter's birth from the hospital, but was unsuccessful in acquiring them. Mrs. H. wondered if there could have been malice or error involved in this matter. She considered that her daughter could have been switched with the deceased child by a staff member or that it might have been a case of mistaken identity. She had felt for many years that her daughter was still alive and she wrote to various officials requesting their help. She reported that she had been told constantly that there was nothing they could do. Though it is possible that such a mix-up could occur, it was more likely that these suspicions served to defend Mrs. H. from dealing with her own feelings of loss and grief for the child, feelings that were intolerably exacerbated by her own extensive history of loss. This unresolved issue had tremendous impact on Mrs. H.'s relationship with Henry. On the one hand, she was distressed and preoccupied with her own concerns but, at the same time, intrusive and demanding of his full attention and devotion. Burdened with the knowledge of his mother's great pain regarding the loss of her daughter, Henry found it difficult to separate from her and become an autonomous being with interests and activities that did not include his mother.

Further, Mrs. H.'s preoccupation hindered her ability to relate to *Henry's* needs and allow his separation. Her suspicions regarding her first child's birth supported her concept of the world as a hostile environment. Given this, how could she ever feel confident in allowing her child to explore the world on his own? Thus, in addition to not wanting to "leave" his mom because of the pain it clearly caused her, Henry was also beginning to internalize his mother's view of the world as a hostile, unsafe place. He began to accept her verbal and nonverbal messages that he could not manage his way in the world without her and that, emotionally, she could not manage without him.

Because Henry was born into a relationship where he was always competing for his mother's attention, he became anxiously attached to her. He never knew when she would be emotionally available to him or when he would be shut out by the sadness and losses of her past. Due to the obsessive preoccupations about her stillborn daughter and the unremitting grief surrounding the unrequited love for the father of the first infant, she was often unable to be emotionally present for Henry. Similarly, Henry's father also experienced Mrs. H.'s preoccupation and emotional absence. In reality, neither Henry nor his father could compete successfully with Mrs. H.'s memories, sorrows, or preoccupation. They could, however, compete with each other for the time she was emotionally available, and this is what they did, vying for control of the small part of her that was intermittently available to them.

Unfortunately for Henry, he did not have a father who was physically and emotionally present to provide a correcting buffer to counter his mother's inconsistent and insensitive parenting. Henry's father worked a great deal and, when he was home, he was often fatigued. Mr. H. expected Henry to be unquestioningly compliant. He also harbored some anger at Henry's "intrusion" in the marital dyad, particularly since Henry usually slept with his mother while he slept in another bed. Clearly, family roles and intergenerational boundaries were not appropriately defined, and Henry and his father often behaved like siblings fighting for the mother's attention. Mother had difficulty setting firm boundaries with Henry but also undermined father when *he* did. Further, the marital coalition lacked strength, with mother taking sides with Henry in criticizing the father's "harsh" manner. While the mother believed that the father was too dominating, the father felt that the mother was too permissive. Thus, the family's primary alliance was between mother and Henry, and it lacked a viable parental subsystem.

This precarious balance suggested the importance of working with the whole family to define more appropriate roles and realign the structure of familial relationships.

Henry's perception of school was a negative one. He wanted to avoid school and stay home partly because of his anxious attachment to his mother and partly because he did not want to respond to the structure and demands imposed by the school setting. He attempted to rationalize this avoidance by externalizing blame onto the school, the teachers, the students, and the system of rules. That Henry had difficulty with initiative, peer relations, and completion of his school tasks is not surprising. Historically, Henry's attempts at autonomy and initiative were sabotaged by his mother's messages, such as that this would represent a loss to her and bring her more pain and that he was weak and needed her because the world was a dangerous place. Any anger Henry might have felt regarding this sabotage could not be expressed directly or assertively to his mother. Further, not taking responsibility for school behavior was safe, since his mother collaborated with him and joined him in blaming others for family problems.

Henry, as a child of parents from two different countries, living in yet a third country, was faced with significant cultural and identity conflicts. His mother's birthplace, language, and physical features were Central American and his father's were Mexican American. These differences, and the animosity that existed within his community between Mexican and Central American families caused him tension and anxiety. Further, within his isolated inner-city home, Henry lacked healthy role models for relating to others and the world. In his school, he looked physically different from many of his classmates and teachers, adding further to his sense of isolation and disconnectedness. Henry's insecure and anxious attachment in his home was further exacerbated by other cultural factors: his family's unstable economic status; the dangerous, volatile neighborhood in which he lived; and the fact that the larger society often devalued people from his ethnic background, simply on the basis of their physical characteristics. Thus Henry was faced with integrating the cultures of his mother and father as well as the culture of the community in which he lived (Garcia-Coll & Meyer, 1993).

Orienting Constructs

Mrs. H.'s history of disrupted attachments made it difficult for her to provide Henry with a secure base from which to launch and become an autonomous, curious, active, joyful child. She sought from Henry the utter devotion she lacked as a child. Any attempts by him to have interests that excluded her were experienced as rejections, further wounding her fragile sense of self. Although she wanted Henry's full attention and devotion, she was unable to give him adequate attention or responsiveness. She was often preoccupied with thoughts of her dead daughter and with questions regarding her parents' reasons for giving her away as a child to relatives who didn't care for her (as evidenced by her grandparents having to remove her from that home). These factors made Henry's attachments to his mother tenuous at best: separating from her wounded her, but she was never fully his when he approached her.

Beyond the issue of disrupted attachments was the issue of real and imagined danger in the environment. The unstable nature of their living situation, including lack of economic security and social support and ongoing violence in their neighborhood, contributed to their sense of the world as a dangerous place. That Henry and his mother viewed the world and people as unkind, uncaring, and often actively malevolent is thus not surprising. Indeed, there were very few experiences in their lives that fostered a sense of trust and expectations of benevolence. This experience and perception of the world as dangerous and of people as likely to be malevolent contributed further to Henry's fear of venturing out and exploring his world. Staying close to his home and his family was the safest alternative. This alternative was not very satisfying to Henry but he lacked the language, emotional support, and psychological sophistication to articulate his feelings and needs. At some level, Henry was angry at his mother for her neediness and demands for his full attention and devotion because it robbed him of his individuality. This anger was further fueled by her incomplete attention and devotion to him. Henry was thus in a no-win situation: his only "safe base" was inconsistently available to him, but he was not allowed to seek security elsewhere because other rewarding relationships would wound her and threaten what he did have with her. Henry's "resolution" was thus expressed in the form of somatic symptoms and fear of separation from his mother.

Treatment Plans and Intervention Strategy

TREATMENT GUIDELINES

Medications play a minor role in the treatment of SAD. There has been some empirical support for the use of the tricyclic antidepressant Imipramine (Gadow, 1991) but efficacy studies have been confounded by problems of comorbidity. It is painful indeed to see preadolescent children become sick to their stomachs or perspire over the impending threat of leaving for school in the morning, and it is equally sad to see parents tyrannized by dependent but demanding children. Fortunately, SAD is readily responsive to treatment.

For Henry and most children with SAD, the first therapeutic guideline is to have the child return to school as soon as possible with attention to the family situation (graduated steps for achieving this will be detailed for Henry and his mother). Family dynamics around the separation are immediately highlighted by this press for more independent functioning, as therapists usually find that the parent gives in and accepts the child's excuses for avoiding school or other separations. Therapists treating SAD must anticipate this parental "sabotage" throughout the course of treatment. Patiently and supportively, therapists must remind parents that when they give in to the child, they are contributing to the pathology. To enable the parent to stop indulging the child and begin setting firmer limits instead, the therapist must become the interim *secure base* for the parent. That is, by providing an empathic *holding environment,* the therapist can help the parent contain and manage more appropriately his or her own separation anxieties aroused by the child's departure. Within the relational context of the parent feeling understood and emotionally "held" by the therapist's attuned responsiveness, the therapist can: (1) help the parent adopt a more firm and authoritative stance with the child, stopping the role reversal and becoming the adult in charge; (2) help the parent better manage his or her own emotions internally, rather than through her child, by becoming better able to identify, experience, and talk about the parent's own unmet dependency needs and separation anxieties with the therapist; and (3) disrupt the problematic cross-general alliance between parent and child by finding new ways to involve the other parent (or other family members) in the child's life (e.g., father-child outings) and work to improve communication in the marriage so that the spouse (or significant others) can begin to hear and respond to the parent's emotional needs.

Additional treatment guidelines involve the school. Therapists working with SAD need to establish cooperative working relationships with school personnel. For example, it may be useful to place the child in a special classroom with a small class size. Much symptomatic improvement can result from increased interaction with the teacher and with other students. It is especially useful when the teacher can encourage a special buddy or otherwise facilitate a close friendship for the child. Therapists can also use the school setting to gradually wean children away from the parent by having the parent accompany the child to the classroom for short amounts of time at the beginning of school and gradually but systematically decrease the parental presence. If the child cannot attend school at all, he or she must spend time at home away from positive reinforcements of the home environment, such as TV, toys, and computer games, to prevent the secondary gains from being symptomatic. The cardinal issue, however, is that the SAD child will only begin to leave the parent more successfully when coaching from the therapist allows the parent to say to the child in a firm and unambiguous voice (i.e., without weeping or looking forlorn): "I will be fine while you are gone, and I want you to go to school now."

INITIAL TREATMENT PLAN

Short-Term Goals

1. Provide a holding environment for mother so she could unambiguously encourage Henry's return to school.
2. Help mother gain insight into how she may inadvertently be contributing to Henry's separation fears.

3. Assess and differentiate real from imagined danger in the school, and facilitate Henry's return to school.

Intermediate Goals

1. Provide Henry with a safe therapeutic environment where he can play out/express himself, including his insecure and anxious attachment to his mother and his fear of the world as malevolent.
2. Help Henry identify his needs, interests, and abilities, and support all attempts at autonomy and initiative.
3. Strengthen the marital dyad and encourage his mother to seek nurturance and support from her spouse, rather than from Henry.

Long-Term Goals

1. Help the family identify interests and support systems in the community.
2. Increase positive contact between Henry and his father.
3. Support appropriate family roles (parental, child, spouse).

Short-Term Goals.   Mrs. H.'s history of frequently disrupted attachments made it clear that she needed therapy in order for her to allow Henry to individuate. Since our center lacked another Spanish-speaking therapist, I decided to divide each session into time alone with Henry, time alone with his mother, and time with both together. I planned to eventually include the dad so that we could have the whole family working together.

In my sessions with Mrs. H., I tried to convey to her that I would do my best to be consistently available to her. I also stated my hope that as we explored her history, we would be able to understand better how her previous experiences contributed to her own and her family's current functioning. I hoped that the security provided by our relationship and insight on her part into the genesis of her own (and Henry's) anxious attachments would make it possible for her to unambiguously encourage autonomy and initiative in Henry.

The initial "mother only" segments of the sessions were thus spent building the relationship, which included listening, being empathic, and validating the disruptive nature of her losses. Mrs. H. was able to share with me how fearful she often was when Henry was away from her—fearful that something might happen to him. We were able to work with this issue and connect it, for example, to the loss of her daughter and the reality of her unstable neighborhood where children were sometimes killed. We then brainstormed ways to increase her sense of security regarding the real dangers in the neighborhood and also differentiated Henry and his life situation from that involving her deceased daughter. I encouraged Mrs. H. to pay close attention to how she expressed (verbally, emotionally, behaviorally) these fears to Henry. I highlighted the long-term benefits of independent functioning for Henry and encouraged her to share her fears with me instead of acting them out with Henry.

In the "child only" segments, I encouraged Henry to find toys and play. I hoped that in this process Henry would begin to identify his own interests. I also hoped that this arena would provide Henry with a safe place to play and master his fears. Mindful of not reenacting his mother's control and intrusiveness, I was careful not to be overinvolved or intrusive, so I kept my comments to a minimum. Henry often seemed conflicted about the extent to which he wanted to include me in his play. He would sometimes deliberately turn his back to me or exclude me in some other overt way. However, he almost always came back to me and handed me the toys at the end of our session. Typically, my response was to say warmly, "I'm glad you came in today, let's put these away together." Again, thinking about how our process could reenact his conflicts, I wanted to communicate full *acceptance* of how he chose to structure his time (i.e., to make unambiguously clear that I was not angry or wounded by the exclusion). Putting the toys away together was important as well because I wanted Henry to realize that he also had responsibility for completion of tasks, including this one.

In the initial "family segments," we focused on getting Henry back to school. We discussed Henry's fears about the school setting itself and his complaints that several boys were bothering him. It turned out that they were not gang members and that there had been no reports of violence on the campus. Henry was able to acknowledge that he could ignore them and spend his recess away from where they were. It seemed, from his description, that they enjoyed teasing him because he was easily upset but that they would likely be discouraged if he firmly said, "I don't like you teasing me," without crying, which we role played and rehearsed. I accompanied Henry's mother to a school conference, where it was decided that Henry would be placed in a smaller class. I was able to model for Mrs. H. how to communicate with the authorities and get appropriate assistance. I also asked the school about what programs were available to Henry (tutoring, free lunch, and so forth) and encouraged Mrs. H. to use these as she saw appropriate. One program, which was recommended, was the Student Study Team (sometimes called the Child Study Team). The Student Study Team is composed of the parent and school personnel (the referring classroom teacher, another classroom teacher who is an ongoing member of the team, the bilingual resource teacher, the resource specialist, the Chapter I learning/reading specialist, the school nurse, and the principal). The team meets on a regular basis, either weekly or bimonthly, to discuss a student who is not experiencing school success. Tests, student work samples, and anecdotal information are analyzed and discussed. Suggestions are made to develop an individual learning program for the child. The mutually agreed upon suggestions of the team are recorded, including a schedule of the follow-up meetings, to monitor progress toward the goals for helping the student become more successful in school. Each member of the team signs the Student Learning Program, and they receive a copy of the form, so each can complete his or her part of the agreement.

Some examples of interventions that might be proposed by the Student Study Team include having the classroom teacher develop, monitor, and reward Henry for improved school attendance, using a Student Behavior Contract signed by the student, the teacher, the parent, and the principal. The resource specialist would arrange for the student to take a battery of tests to determine grade level proficiency of basic skills, appropriateness of current grade placement in relationship to Henry's skill mastery, age, and social interaction with his peers. They would also need to determine if Henry could benefit from special services for remediation of basic skills, which might include tutorial services, reading or math lab services, or special education. The school principal might enlist the volunteer services of a high school or college student, teacher's aide, or parent volunteer, to tutor Henry after school several days a week to remediate math skills, reading and language acquisition, and/or writing skills. The Chapter I reading specialist (or bilingual resource teacher) could provide Mrs. H. with a copy of the school's multicultural activities listed in the School Improvement Plan. They would invite Mrs. H. to attend these activities to increase her understanding of cultural diversity. The Student Study Team would discuss the most appropriate classroom assignment for the student, matching Henry with the teacher who would probably be the most compatible both academically and emotionally.

In the classroom, the teacher could use numerous classroom instructional strategies designed specifically to increase success opportunities for the student on a daily basis. Some of these strategies include modifying time allowed to complete an assignment to meet the student's needs and abilities. The teacher could do a *time-on-task* assessment of the student's classroom behavior to identify ways to help the student increase task completion. Cooperative learning experiences would be provided as much as possible to improve peer relations while increasing task completion. The teacher could modify the number of problems required for student practice to increase the student's attention span. By using small group instruction, the teacher can reinforce learning and increase interest in the subject and in his skills. By providing more hands-on activities, the student can experience more fun in learning. In using a multifaceted approach, the teacher would be more likely to meet the student's preferred learning style. It is also helpful if the teacher can meet with the student to gain information about his preferred subjects and interests, to help in lesson planning, and to jointly find ways to assist the student in successful task completion. The classroom teacher, with the assistance of the learning specialist and/or principal, might develop a Student Progress Sheet where the student can record his grades, tasks completed in the classroom, and homework. This report would be monitored weekly by the classroom teacher and shared at subsequent Student Study Team meetings.

Mrs. H., Henry, and I then met with his new teacher and we devised a return to school plan. During the first week, Mrs. H. would accompany Henry to his classroom but stay in the back until recess. At this point, the teacher would walk Henry out to recess and be his *transitional* object. I asked the teacher if there were any children in the class who might be able to respond supportively to Henry and include him in their activities. I noted Henry's interest in trains and airplanes and the teacher was able to identify another student in the class with similar interests. Thus, during this first week, the teacher engaged both Henry and the other student (Robert) in conversations about trains during recess. Although Henry continued to be distressed about his mom's absence following recess, he did stay at school all week. He continued to complain about stomachaches in the morning, but he was less resistant to getting ready for school.

During the second week Mrs. H. stayed only for the first 45-60 minutes and, at the teacher's signal, left. The teacher would signal Mrs. H. to leave at a time when she was able to be close to Henry's desk so she could again be the transitional object. The teacher would then walk Henry out at recess (preferably with Robert also) and tell Henry where she could be found if he needed her. During the third week, Mrs. H. would take Henry to school but leave as he entered the classroom with the teacher.

An important part of this intervention was to coach Mrs. H. on how to deal with Henry each morning. She was instructed to respond to his functional needs (getting dressed, getting breakfast, and so forth) and clearly state "I want you to go to school today." She was to ignore his complaints and at the end of each day when she picked him up, tell him how proud she was that he was going to school. Knowing how difficult it was for her to deny Henry anything (in this case refusing to let him stay home), I told her that I would check in with her at a certain time for 5 minutes during the first three weeks. During those calls I would say something like: "I can understand that you are questioning if you are doing the right thing and are worried that Henry might become angry at you. As you and I have talked before, Henry will be much better off in the long run if he has an education and can manage on his own. Going to school will help him later when he is ready to find a job. You are being a good mother even though it feels hard right now." Mrs. H.'s involvement in this return to school plan seemed to help her gain a sense of empowerment. I later learned that Mrs. H. developed a good working relationship with the teacher and would frequently talk to her about Henry's progress. This was also facilitated by the school's efforts: they placed Henry with a teacher who spoke Spanish, invited Mr. and Mrs. H. to observe the classroom whenever they wished, and conducted testing to evaluate more formally Henry's educational needs.

Mrs. H.'s issues with boundaries became apparent in her frequent distress calls to me, which were often peppered with "I'm really sorry to bother you doctor." I was faced with the need to balance the issues of limits and boundaries with availability and support. My compromise was to acknowledge my inability to continue responding to the calls but indicate that I could see them twice a week instead. This turned out to be an excellent solution since it seemed to provide Mrs. H. with a greater sense of security and continuity from session to session. I surmised that knowing she would see me in a few days made it more possible for her to contain her anxiety with Henry, and she could let it out with me in session.

Mrs. H.'s improved relationship with bureaucracies (including the agency and the school) made her less suspicious and distrustful of her environment. Her decreased anxiety about the "malevolence" of others was conveyed to Henry by her attitude: she was able to send him to school and let him know she believed the school could provide adequately for him. This change came, of course, later in the therapy process.

Intermediate Goals.   As therapy progressed and the intensity of Mrs. H.'s feelings about her deceased daughter, her parents' giving her away as a child, Henry's safety and so forth subsided somewhat, we began to focus on her marriage. I invited Mr. H. to the sessions and we were able to arrange times so that he could come occasionally. The mother only segments during these times became devoted to "couple" issues with increased focus on sharing, both as a couple and as parents. Mr. H. was very responsive and felt that Henry had usurped his role in his wife's affections and he wanted greater intimacy and privacy. He also felt that his wife was unable to discipline Henry but undermined him when he did. We discussed these issues and tried to develop a strategy on how discipline would be handled.

In my individual sessions with Henry, we began to talk more to each other. I often asked him about his interests, whether he had made any friends at school and about wishes/dreams he had (for example, "If you could wish for any three things, what would they be?"). I paid close attention to his nonverbal language and at times would verbalize what I thought he was communicating (for example, I might ask, "Would you rather play alone right now?"). During one memorable session, Henry was lying on the floor and playing with two action figurines. Suddenly, one of the figurines said (Henry doing the talking for each figure, in Spanish) "I don't want to play with you anymore." The other figure then doubled over and said, "When you say that you hurt me so much. Don't you know that you are my best friend?" At this point, Henry stopped and seemed frozen. His eyes filled with tears. I moved closer to him and said, "People can do different things and have different interests and still care about each other."

During the family segment that followed, Mrs. H. stated that Henry had been rude to her earlier in the week and had yelled that he hated the television program she was watching and wanted to do something else. She reported that she got so upset by his tone that she went to the bathroom and threw up. She then told him how his rudeness made her sick. Henry had, for the rest of the week, been subdued at home, but she wished he would always behave himself. This event illustrated so powerfully the conflict Henry was faced with: (a) expressing his differences with his mother would make her sick, and (b) he needed to contain himself and follow her lead if he wanted her to be healthy. My intervention was to have Mrs. H. acknowledge that

Henry was *not* responsible for her physical illness and that he did not have the power to control her health. I also noted that Henry's interests did not have to match his mom's for him to love her. I tried to elucidate for Mrs. H. the powerful (but negative) impact this event could have on Henry—that it could make him afraid to express himself, to develop his own interests, and to become an independent, assertive human being. I acknowledged that Henry may need to learn how to express himself in an assertive and non-aggressive manner. We spent the rest of the session focusing on this issue of being separate (having separate interests, needs, etc.) but still being connected. I tried to help each identify likes and dislikes and worked to highlight how the differences here made them no less caring about each other. Henry was encouraged to develop his own set of interests, *some* of which might be similar to mom's, some to dad's, and some to none of them.

I monitored Henry's school progress during the first month of his return to school by making a weekly call to his teacher. After the first month, Henry was attending regularly, although he now showed some dependence on the teacher and was only slowly developing age-appropriate relationships.

Long-Term Goals.   As therapy progressed, I continued to work with Mrs. H. to help her understand that for Henry to function more effectively, she needed to express to him her belief that he was capable of doing things for himself and by himself and that she could function in the world without him. To accomplish this, the mother needed to believe this herself. She needed to establish relationships in which she could share the details of her physical problems and her fears about them without threatening the security of Henry's world. This could be accomplished by sharing these concerns with her husband (which might strengthen the marital alliance) and by developing a support network with other adults. The possibilities included strengthening relationships with members of her extended family, making friends with neighbors, joining support groups, or getting more involved in the church. I hoped that by giving Mrs. H. some individual time in session, she could begin to explore her own issues, relieving some of her depression and anxiety. Mrs. H.'s increasing comfort and sense of effectiveness and security within her environment could then set the stage for Henry to feel more comfortable about exploring his own world. He could then be more comfortable in establishing new relationships that did not include his mother, without feeling guilt. Mrs. H. had become the center of Henry's world and vice versa. Henry needed to hear that his mother could fend for herself without him and that she supported his exploration of the world that did not include her.

In addition, I sought to help Mrs. H. feel more confident in herself and comfortable in her requests of Henry and others, including her spouse and the school. I wanted her to feel empowered enough to make honest requests and to expect that others might comply with those requests. She had difficulty communicating clearly and giving direct instructions about what she wanted. Speaking firmly with conviction would help give Henry a model of assertive communication and would likely be rewarded by increased compliance. I had concerns that if the mother was not effective in communicating her own needs, she might express her anger in a passive-aggressive way. Thus, an additional aim of therapy for the mother was to help her become more assertive, to express herself more clearly, and to identify and develop her own interests, with the hope that this would help her feel more powerful and able to cope in her world.

Mrs. H. decided to take English classes through adult education. Her success here prompted her to seek assessment of vocational interests with the goal of obtaining some training, so she could develop marketable skills and eventually contribute to the family's income. She was enlivened by this process and even became an active member of the PTA at Henry's school.

In our individual sessions Henry and I began to address more overtly the bind he had been in: if he developed as a separate, autonomous being, he would hurt his mother and ultimately fail anyway, since he was weak and the world was dangerous. We did this as we built model airplanes or played with train sets.

I was hopeful that in therapy Henry would, in addition to identifying dreams for the future and interests he could engage in in the present, show increased initiative and assertiveness. I asked him if he would be interested and willing to play a modified soccer game in the office. For several weeks we would push the furniture to the side and establish the game rules. As we played, I would verbally cheer Henry on as he tried to get the soccer ball away from me. I would then draw connections between our play and the outside world: when Henry very much wanted something (like he did when he was trying to take the ball away from me), he needed to "challenge" and go for it assertively. Similarly, when he had something that he wanted to hold onto, saying no and keeping it away and to himself (just like he fended me off from taking the soccer ball) was not hurting anybody. We also talked about how this was a necessary part of learning how to get along with and grow up to be as strong as other boys in his class, which Henry wanted to do.

Henry was in the process of changing from a passive and angry child to one who was more assertive and confident. He told me that on one occasion a kid had pushed in front of him in the class line and Henry told him not to and took his place back from this kid. Henry also asked his father if he would play soccer with him and they began doing this several times a week. I enjoyed hearing how Henry wanted to repeatedly engage his father in the same challenge-the-ball exercise that we had been practicing in my office. Henry seemed to relish being able to be so assertive and challenging with his father in this physical way and delighted in seeing his father's determination to protect the ball. Some of the neighborhood kids also began to join Henry and his dad, and Henry had been invited to one of those kids' birthday party. To further these important gains, Henry's parents were encouraged to involve

Henry in a city soccer team where Henry could be involved with and succeed with other boys his age.

Mr. H. continued to attend the sessions as his time permitted. I discouraged Mrs. H. from letting Henry sleep with her and encouraged her to make an alternative sleeping space for Henry that was as pleasant as possible. For example, I encouraged her to let him have a " train" night-light; if possible, buy him a quilt with airplanes or trains on it and so forth. Mr. H. was very much in favor of this and even worked an extra shift to purchase these items.

Mrs. H.'s fear of Henry's anger and possible rejection if she was firm with him was directly addressed. This process was reframed to make her see how, at times, painful or difficult processes are very necessary for good outcomes. I used the example, for her to get her gallstone problem healed she would need to go through treatment—which would likely be painful or difficult—but that the treatment was necessary for her to get fully healed.

Thus, appropriate family roles became focused on more as time progressed. Mr. and Mrs. H. were coached on parenting issues (implementing a time out program, withdrawing certain reinforcements when Henry acted out, rewarding him for appropriate behavior, giving him clear and unambiguous directions about what was expected of him, and so forth). Mr. and Mrs. H. were also encouraged to discuss their differences about parenting in private and not allow Henry to manipulate them using these differences, as had occurred in the past.

Termination was addressed when Mr. H. found a job with medical benefits in an adjoining city. The family realized that they still needed to be in therapy although their overall functioning was significantly improved. We thus agreed to schedule once per month sessions until they connected to a Spanish-speaking therapist in the new city. I was able to support them psychologically as they made the move, and Henry's teacher and school psychologist were very helpful in facilitating his transition to the new school. Although Henry complained of stomachaches the first week at his new school, these complaints had all but disappeared by the time I saw them a month later. Probably the most important factor in adjustment was his mother's improved mental health and her unambiguous statement that she wanted him to go to school and believed that the family and school could together resolve any issues that might arise.

REVISED TREATMENT PLAN

Although working with the whole family had been helpful, I felt that Mrs. H. needed more individual therapy than our sessions provided, since a large focus of that was related to Henry. When the family relocated toward the end of therapy, I was able to find a female therapist for Mrs. H. and a male therapist for Henry. I saw the family once after they moved, primarily to get closure and verify that the transition was relatively smooth. I had two phone contacts with Mrs. H.'s and Henry's new therapists. Mrs. H. seemed to be using her individual therapy well and was processing further the loss of her daughter. She continued to work on learning English and planned to follow through with her vocational interests.

Henry became very involved with a soccer team and his success as a strong player on the team was helpful in developing several friendships. He complained about the impact of therapy on his parents: he was often not pleased about the firmer, more consistent family rules and the stronger coalition between his parents, but his feelings about this became less important as he engaged in more age-appropriate relationships.

BALANCING GOALS

The reality of Henry's world was that it was potentially violent and dangerous. I had to evaluate the contribution of realistic fears to his symptoms but be careful in addressing these and finding ways to increase his actual safety (e.g., being accompanied to school by a parent, not playing in parks known to be frequented by gangs, and so forth), so I did not inadvertently contribute to his perception of the whole world as dangerous and thereby increase his separation fears. I was careful when discussing realistic dangers in his environment to emphasize that this did not represent the whole world.

Although encouraging assertive self-expression in Henry was a reasonable goal, I had to be careful that this goal did not violate culturally sanctioned humility, especially in regard to interacting with elders. I always emphasized that one could be both assertive and polite and gave examples of how that might be expressed (e.g., "May I have the chance to choose a TV program today?" versus pouting but not expressing an opinion or angrily demanding to choose a program). Henry's style had been to pout when things were not going his way, and this passive-aggressive style frequently worked with his mother, who would then give in, exasperated. I pointed out how much unpleasantness this raised for both of them and that learning assertive negotiating skills would serve them both well.

Another major balancing issue concerned Mrs. H.; her history of disrupted relationships made it important that I be consistently present for her. However, her difficulty with maintaining boundaries made it important that I model being separate and boundaried but still connected. Her frequent calls in the early stage of therapy made this issue critical; my solution was to be available to her more frequently (twice a week) but limit contacts between sessions (thereby maintaining that boundary).

Seeing Mrs. H., Henry, and the whole family was at times strenuous. I had to be extremely careful about sharing information from individual segments in the family segments (although I did obtain Mrs. H.'s permission to bring up things from her past if they were relevant and useful in the family segments). In addition to managing the issues between the family members, I had to be an alert time manager. This was especially difficult with Mrs. H. in the beginning, whose need to be heard was at times overwhelming.

Therapeutic Process

RELATIONAL REENACTMENTS

Mrs. H.'s tremendous need to be heard and responded to was evident in the way she captured my attention by her dramatic stories. It was often difficult to end the therapy segments with her in order to meet with Henry or the whole family. That I felt compelled to respond to her and at the same time overwhelmed by her gave me a sense of how Henry must experience her and the burden and guilt he probably felt daily. I often found myself verbalizing what I perceived to be Mom's needs: "It sounds like you have so much pain and at times feel desperate to be heard." She seemed to find this reassuring and it seemed to assure her that the emotions below the words were being heard and responded to.

Mrs. H.'s difficulty with setting limits was evident in her requests to me to tell Henry to do his homework and other requests that I assume the authority/parental role with Henry. I suspected, however, that if I had responded to these requests I would have been viewed as the father was—harsh and stern. This would also have provided Mrs. H. and Henry with another "enemy," further strengthening their unhealthy alliance. Thus, I consistently emphasized my view that she was Henry's parent and that teaching and supporting her in setting limits was the best long-term solution. I was then available to help her process the impact of Henry's anger at her. I was also able to highlight for her how her appropriate limit-setting was contributing to Henry's social and academic progress (he was completing tasks more and learning interpersonal negotiating skills). Henry did not like his mother having private meetings with me and would often pout and knock on the door, especially in the early part of therapy. Mrs. H.'s response was to smile and say she knew Henry would not be able to be away from her. She seemed to reinforce this behavior by almost lovingly telling him he needed to wait outside and suggesting that I wanted this. I asked Mrs. H. if she wanted Henry to be with us during these sessions—which she denied—and I tried gently to show her how confusing her message could be to Henry. Helping her realize the ambiguous quality of her messages and their potential impact was useful. We then agreed to give to give Henry a timer and told him not to knock until the timer went off. I surmised that Henry's behavior was similar at home and robbed his parents of privacy. I was also aware of being irritated at Henry and feeling as though we were competing for Mrs. H.'s attention. I realized that this was indeed how Henry and his father related to each other and felt that helping the family define roles more clearly and the couple's need for privacy was critical. Thus, in the family sessions I encouraged Henry's parents to block out time when they could be alone. I then acknowledged overtly to Henry that he might have negative feelings toward me for making this suggestion and invited him to share these with me. During one individual session, after Henry's parents had implemented my suggestion, Henry had difficulty containing his anger at me and yelled, "I hate you, I don't want to come here anymore," and used several foul words. I let him know that it was okay to be angry at me and to tell me that but use of foul language was not OK. I then continued to be engaged with him, asking him if he wanted me to join him in the game he was playing or not. I believe that my ability to set limits (regarding the foul language) but remain engaged was a critical turning point. After this, Henry began to act out much of his anger in his play (cars crashing, action figures fighting, and so forth). Over time this play became more controlled (the cars would, speeding toward each other, say, "watch out," and not crash; the figures would help each other build their armies and discuss strategy for beating the other side). By this time Henry was including me in his play more consistently and I had the opportunity to suggest alternative strategies for "winning."

Henry's initial therapy behavior, passive disinterest in therapy, was a result of his undeveloped sense of initiative. Permission and encouragement to explore, to include and exclude me as he chose, and to express his feelings (including negative ones) were significant in fostering initiative in him.

Henry's sense of himself as being a victim (i.e., that teachers were unfair and demanding, that father was harsh and stern), which was often supported by his mother, was replayed with me when he accused me of picking on him and making his parents be mean to him. I acknowledged that he might be angry with me but assured him that I harbored no malice toward him. I emphasized that, in fact, I wanted to work with him so he would experience more success and joy at home and at school. Henry was able to grasp this message only as time progressed, and gradually he and I began enjoying each other and playing together with more spontaneity and sharing.

IMPEDIMENTS TO TREATMENT

The reality of violence in Henry's community and possibly his school made me cautious about the extent to which I encouraged Henry's independence and exploration of his world. I often had to distinguish between Henry's realistic and unrealistic or excessive fears and complaints about school. It is not unusual for children to feel singled out and mistreated by teachers, and distinguishing between what was actually occurring and what was imagined was not always easy. The teachers' openness to classroom cooperation and meetings was very useful in this process.

The greatest impediment to Henry's progress was Mrs. H.'s unresolved attachment issues that made it difficult for her to allow Henry to individuate. Mrs. H. needed extensive individual therapy, but the language barrier and limited financial resources made it difficult for us to find an individual therapist for her early on. However, I did find my individual time with her useful in understanding Henry and his presenting problems.

Termination and Therapist's Summary Thoughts

I saw Henry and his family for a year, sometimes seeing them twice a week. We terminated after his family moved to a new city, although I did have one final session with them after they moved. Mrs. H. had an individual therapist and I suggested that she might benefit from being in a support group for parents who had had a child die, such as Compassionate Friends. Although Henry was also connected to a therapist in this new city, the school psychologist suggested he become involved in a school-based counseling program that included group therapy. The opportunity for increased contact with peers seemed like an excellent one. Henry was also involved in a soccer team and his father tried to attend soccer whenever he could. Mr. H. and Henry now had an improved relationship and Mr. H. often coached Henry in soccer at home.

Henry and his parents liked the teacher at his new school, and Henry was especially fond of the cafeteria food. Although Henry's report card confirmed his improvement, he continued to have some academic deficits and would continue to receive special academic assistance.

Mr. and Mrs. H. continued to need help with responding as a parental team but were showing some improvement. Although Mrs. H. sometimes felt guilty when setting firm limits with Henry, she was able to tolerate this better and had a therapist with whom to process the issue. Their marriage was much improved and they were spending more time together.

Clearly, Henry's functioning at school, home, and socially had improved. Although he was still occasionally passive-aggressive and resistant to limits, this had lessened significantly.

In some ways I was sad to see them leave at this point just as the major changes in Henry's life (academic improvement, increased social activities) and in Mrs. H.'s life (greater insight into the genesis of her anxious attachments, vocational goal-setting, and improved social relationships) were occurring. I was pleased that they would continue with therapy elsewhere and felt honored by the trust they had shown by staying in therapy and sharing details of their lives with me.

REFERENCES

Acosta, F. (1984). Psychotherapy with Mexican-Americans: Clinical & empirical gains. In J. Martinez & R. Mendoza (Eds.), *Chicano psychology* (2nd ed. pp. 163–188). New York: Academic Press.

Alvirez, D., & Bean, R. (1976). The Mexican-American family. In C. Mindel & R. Habenstein (Eds.), *Ethnic families in America: Patterns & variations* (pp. 271–291). New York: Elsevier Scientific Publishing.

American Psychiatric Association. (1994). *Diagnostic and statistical manual of mental disorders* (4th ed.). Washington, DC: Authors.

Cervantes, R. C., & Arroyo, W. (1994). *DSM-IV:* Implications for Hispanic children and adolescents. *Hispanic Journal of Behavioral Sciences, 16,* 8-27.

Cervantes, R. C., Salgado de Snyder, V. N., & Padilla, A. M. (1989). Posttraumatic stress in immigrants from Central America and Mexico. *Hospital and Community Psychiatry, 40*(6), 615-619.

Gadow, K. D. (1991). Clinical issues in child and adolescent psychopharmacology. *Journal of Consulting and Clinical Psychology, 59*(6), 842-852.

Garcia-Coll, C., & Meyer, E. (1993). The sociocultural context of infant development. In C. Zeanatt (Ed.), *Handbook of infant mental health* (pp. 56-69). New York: Guilford Press.

Gardner, R. (1992). Children with separation anxiety disorder. In J. O'Brien, D. Pilowski, & O. Lewis (Eds.), *Psychotherapies with children and adolescents: Adapting the psychodynamic process* (pp. 3-25). Washington, DC: American Psychiatric Press.

Grebler, L., Moore, J., & Guzman, R. (1970). *The Mexican-American people: The second largest minority.* New York: Free Press.

Gruppo Italiano Disturbi d'Ansia (1989). Familial analysis of panic disorder and agoraphobia. *Journal of Affective Disorders, 17,* 1-8.

Herbert, M. (1974). *Emotional problems of development in children.* New York: Academic Press.

Kagan, S. (1977). Social motives and behaviors of Mexican-American and Anglo-American children. In J. L. Martinez Jr. (Ed.), *Chicano psychology* (pp. 45-86). New York: Academic Press.

Last, C. G., Francis, G., Hersen, M., Kazdin, A. E., & Strauss, C. C. (1987a). Separation anxiety and school phobia: A comparison using *DSM-III* criteria. *American Journal of Psychiatry, 144*(5), 653-657.

Last, C. G., Hersen, M., Kazdin, A. E., Francis, G., & Grubb, H. J. (1987b). Psychiatric illness in mothers of anxious children. *American Journal of Psychiatry, 144*(12), 1580-1583.

Leslie, L. A. (1992). The role of informal support networks in the adjustment of Central American immigrant families. *Journal of Community Psychology,* 243-256.

Leslie, L. A., & Leitch, M. L. (1989). A demographic profile of recent Central American immigrants: Clinical and service implications. *Hispanic Journal of Behavioral Sciences, 11,* 315-329.

Padilla, A. M., Cervantes, R. C., Maldonado, M., & Garcia, R. E. (1988). Coping responses to psychosocial stressors among Mexican and Central American immigrants. *Journal of Community Psychology,* 418-427.

Perugi, G., Delitito, J., Soriani, A., Musetti, L., Petracca, A., Nisita, C., Maremmani, I., & Cassano, G. B. (1988). Relationship between panic disorder and separation anxiety with school phobia. *Comprehensive Psychiatry, 29,* 98-107.

Sperling, M. (1982). *The major neuroses and behavior disorder in children* (pp. 1-41, 127-172). New York: Aronson.

Wenar, C. (1994). *Developmental psychopathology from infancy to adolescence* (3rd ed.). New York: McGraw-Hill.

Winnicott, D. W. (1965). *The family and individual development* (pp. 3-20). New York: Tavistock/Routledge.

Winnicott, D. W. (1986). *Home is where we start from: Essays by a psychoanalyst.* New York: Norton.

SUGGESTIONS FOR FURTHER READING

Cross, T. L., Bazron, B. J., Dennis, K. W., & Isaacs, M. R. (March, 1989). *Towards a culturally competent system of care: Volume 1. A monograph on effective services for minority children who are severely emotionally disturbed.* CASSP Technical Assistance Center: Georgetown University Child Development Center.

Isaacs, M. R., & Benjamin, M. P. (December,1991). *Towards a culturally competent system of care: Volume 2. Programs which utilize culturally competent principles.* CASSP Technical Assistance Center: Georgetown University Child Development Center.

These monographs are designed to help states and communities plan, design, and implement culturally competent systems of care. Volume 1 defines and identifies specific principles and practical ideas for improving services for African American, Asian American, Latino/Hispanic, and Native American children/families. Volume 2 highlights 11 programs that exemplify specific components of the culturally competent system of care principles. The Royball Family Mental Health Services clinic illustrates effective methods of outreach, such as an on-site, school-based mental health program. The program also utilizes paraprofessional community workers as a means of integrating mental health therapy within the cultural values and beliefs of the Royball clients.

Lopez, S. R., Blacher, J. B., & Shapiro, J. (in press). The interplay of culture and disability in Latino families. In I. Tan Mink, M. L. de Leon Siantz, & P. Berman. (in press). *Ethnically diverse families and childhood disability: Theory, research, and service delivery.* Baltimore: Paul H. Brookes. This chapter helps illustrate the complexity and usefulness of culture in working with Latino families. Clinical material illustrates how cultural dynamics of patient care can often influence compliance issues. The chapter also illustrates the heterogeneity of Latino culture.

Lopez, S. R., Grover, K. P., Holland, D., Johnson, M. J., Kain, C. D., Kanel, K., Mellins, C. A., & Rhyne, M. C. (1989). Development of culturally sensitive psychotherapists. *Professional Psychology, Research, and Practice, 20,* 369–376. The article presents a developmental model of how student-therapists begin integrating a cultural perspective in their clinical case conceptualization. The article is recommended for supervisors helping their supervisees overcome the internal struggles of developing cultural awareness.

Sperling, M. (1982). *The major neuroses and behavior disorders in children* (pp. 1–41, 127–172). New York: Aronson. This is an excellent textbook on understanding various childhood disorders, such as phobias, enuresis, sleep disturbances, and psychosis from a psychoanalytic perspective. The mother-child relationship is an important part of Dr. Sperling's conceptualization of the childhood disorders. Case studies help clarify complex psychoanalytic concepts. This textbook is recommended for all beginning therapists unfamiliar with the application of psychoanalytic concepts.

Chapter 10

RAPE TRAUMA SYNDROME

CASE ILLUSTRATION OF ELIZABETH: AN 18-YEAR-OLD ASIAN AMERICAN

Sandy Tseuneyoshi, Ph.D.

THE ISSUES

The Prevalence of Date Rape

Rape is a grimly prevalent but widely underreported crime. Using data from the National Victim Center and the Crime Victims Research and Treatment Center, Martin (1992) reported that one out of every eight women in this country has been raped, with a total of approximately 683,000 rapes a year. Among individuals raped each year, 84% do not report the rape to the police and 69% fear that others will blame them for somehow causing the rape (Martin, 1992).

This underreporting by victims is also evident in the difference between the number of rapes reported to the police and those reported to community crisis hotlines. For example, in one northwest city, reported rapes totaled 55 for 1992 and 53 for 1993 (Department of Public Safety, 1994), while that city's sexual assault services responded to calls from 3,600 victims during that same time period (Sexual Assault Support Services, 1993). The incidence of rape is also underestimated because a significant number are not considered rape and are therefore not counted (Bart & O'Brien, 1985; Martin, 1992). Rape is especially likely to be discounted or "legitimized" if the victim has had personal involvement with the perpetrator. In dating situations, for example, the victim is likely to be blamed for the rape if she fails to protest early rather than late during "foreplay" (Shotland & Goodstein, 1983).

Although perpetrators of sexual assaults include strangers, casual acquaintances, or someone whom the victims has dated, the risk of a woman being raped by someone she knows is four times greater than the risk of being raped by a stranger (Warshaw, 1988). In a study funded by the National Institute for Mental Health, Warshaw (1988) reported that 25% of the 3,187 women surveyed were victims of rape or attempted rape. Eighty-four percent of those raped knew the rapist, in many cases as classmates or on a first date. In this survey, 57% of the rapes occurred on dates.

Unfortunately, the sexual assault of teen-age girls by classmates, boyfriends, casual friends, and co-workers is commonplace but hidden. In the survey just described, 38% of the rape victims reported that they were 14–17 years old at the time of the assault (Warshaw, 1988). A similar finding was noted by Ageton (1979), who found that almost all of the female teen victims interviewed for that study knew the perpetrator: 56% had been raped by a date, 30% had been raped by a friend, and 11% had been raped by a boyfriend. Since the prime dating age for females is between 16 and 24, and the risk of rape is four times higher for this group than for any other population group, developing effective clinical interventions for teens and young adults is especially important.

As earlier noted, despite the high prevalence of acquaintance rape, it is significantly underreported (Warshaw, 1988). Less than ⅕ of the rape or attempted rape victims in the survey just described reported their rapes to the police and only 27% of women who had been raped identified themselves as rape victims (Warshaw, 1988). Similarly, 78% of the female teen victims in the Ageton study reported that they did not tell their parents about the rape and only 6% reported the assault to the police (Ageton, 1979).

Cultural context plays an important role in determining whether date rape will be reported. Sexual assaults are often underreported because cultural values and beliefs inhibit or discourage women from certain cultural backgrounds from sharing details about rape experiences (Holaday, Leach, & Davidson, 1994). For example, it may take even longer for an Asian American female to seek services because of the shame that she may experience for herself, her family, and her community. As we will see in this chapter, even if she seeks psychological services, the cultural sensitivity and skill of the mental health professional will greatly influence whether she receives the help she needs or terminates therapy after one or two sessions.

Rape Trauma Syndrome

Counselors must be aware that if rape victims do seek help, they may not identify the sexual assault as the presenting problem. Commonly, rape victims will simply present with symptoms of anxiety and/or depression without describing or identifying the precipitating sexual assault. Therapists therefore need to become sensitized to a cluster or pattern of symptoms fitting what is commonly referred to as *rape trauma syndrome*.

Rape trauma syndrome is not a diagnostic category found in the *Diagnostic and Statistical Manual of Mental Disorders,* Fourth Edition (DSM-IV; American Psychiatric Association, 1994; hereafter, DSM-IV). The nosological categories of the *DSM-IV* are based on current symptomatology rather than precipitating events. Utilizing the *DSM* nosology, counselors are likely to observe in sexual assault survivors certain aspects of Post Traumatic Stress Disorder (including sleep disturbances, distressing recollections, emotional numbing, increased arousal), or symptoms reflecting Adjustment Disorder (e.g., diminished occupational, academic, and/or social functioning accompanied by emotional reactions such as anxiety and depression). Rape trauma syndrome, however, identified by Burgess and Holmstrom (1974), focuses on the behavioral, somatic, and psychological reactions presented by victims of forcible and forcibly attempted rape. These responses to rape often occur in three distinct stages: the *acute stage,* the *outward adjustment stage,* and the *renormalization stage.* These stages do not always follow a linear progression and may include regressions as well as premature resolutions, which will be defined below.

In the period immediately following the assault, referred to as the *acute stage,* survivors typically go through a phase of disorganization where they present with symptoms of acute distress that resemble a state of emotional shock (Tyra, 1993). Often, cognitive impairment is manifested in diminished alertness; dulled sensory, affective, and memory functioning; disorganized thought content and/or bewilderment are apparent. Affectively, the victim tends to be characterized by numbness, paralyzing anxiety, hysteria and confusion, or calmness and collectedness. Feelings expressed include fear, humiliation, embarrassment, anger, guilt, revenge, fear of physical violence and death, and self-blame.

In the second stage referred to as the *outward adjustment stage,* the survivor attempts to convince herself and others (often prematurely) that she has resolved the crisis and has returned to a normal lifestyle. Emotionally and interpersonally, however, the rape may have devastating negative impact. The survivor's normal routine may range from minimal or no involvement in occupational or educational activities to overcompensation (i.e., extreme involvement in school or work). Socially, survivors tend to withdraw from contact with relatives and friends. This distancing from people is typically engendered by a host of issues that include a damaged sense of personal security or personal safety, distrust of existing relationships, hesitance to enter new relationships, disturbance in sexual relationships, and fears and phobias specific to the circumstances of the rape.

In the third stage, referred to as the *renormalization stage,* a sense of recovery begins to solidify. Shame or self-blame subsides as the survivor appropriately directs anger toward the perpetrator. As a fundamental sense of trust is restored and fears are resolved, the survivor is no longer plagued by obsessive memories of the attack nor by the concomitant nightmares. The concept of renormalization does not imply that the survivor's life goes on as if the rape had never occurred. For most, significant scars remain.

Cultural Influences in Date Rape

During my 5 years in college counseling centers, only one of nine Asian American rape survivors attempted to report the assault to the police, even though all displayed symptoms of rape trauma syndrome. As supported by the previously cited literature, therapy revealed that the survivor's involvement with the perpetrator tended to "legitimize" the relationship and helped to "prove" the "badness" of the individual, both to herself and to others.

Although cultural factors shape how each client experiences or moves through the rape trauma syndrome stages, there has been little specific research concerning cultural differences in the presentation of rape trauma syndrome. It becomes necessary, therefore, for clinicians to extrapolate from their familiarity with the literature on cultural values. This chapter is limited to Asian American females. The cultural values discussed here also represent the more traditional Asian values, and, therefore, the observations that follow may also be appropriate for Asian international females.

Although Asian Americans who have been sexually assaulted have to deal with issues similar to Euramerican survivors, the manner in which they present and deal with the assault may differ. Cultural values, such as not bringing shame to one's family, not discussing personal or family issues outside of the home, and not talking about sex, may keep the female or family from reporting the sexual assault, seeking help, or fully sharing the trauma with therapists.

Asian American victims often must deal with additional stressors that result from their minority status, their bicultural experience, and the acculturation/assimilation process. These include experiences with prejudice, stereotypes, and racism, experiences that further magnify the disempowering impact of the rape experience.

The race/ethnicity of the perpetrator may add further complexity to these issues. For example, cultural stereotypes surrounding sexuality in the Western world have given rise to male fantasies of ultimate eroticism, sexual prowess, and total submission, and these subjugation fantasies are often targeted toward Asian American females. These factors greatly exacerbate the Asian American victims' recovery process because they serve as additional sources of anxiety, frustration, and conflict.

Within the counseling relationship itself, cultural differences must be attended to, since they can keep Asian American victims from getting the help they need, especially during the initial phase of treatment. For example, it is important for therapists to know that many Asian Americans differ in their communication styles, that is, they tend to be less direct, use fewer verbalizations, show less emotion, and are comfortable with silence. Being aware of this will reduce the likelihood that professionals seeing Asian American clients will misperceive, misdiagnose, or misjudge behaviors such as these. In particular, silence is awkward for some therapists, and they may attempt to manage their own anxiety ineffectively by working hard to fill the silences with words.

Therapists must also be able to process, directly and openly, transference issues regarding racial differences, especially if the therapist is not Asian. A culturally sensitive therapist can do this, for example, by asking the client about potential differences in culture that may exist between the client and therapist, by acknowledging that these differences can have an impact on their relationship, and by inviting the client to talk about any misunderstandings that may arise and educate the therapist about cultural differences that emerge in their work together. Though the client may initially deny that there are any meaningful cultural differences that could be problems, this sincere invitation opens the door for future exploration and gives the client "permission" to raise these issues in the future. If the obvious cultural differences are not made overt, however, it may make it more difficult for the client to reveal these concerns or other unrelated issues or conflicts during the course of treatment.

Generic Considerations in Treating Asian American Clients

Asian Americans represent one of the fastest growing and most diverse American populations of color. They are from backgrounds representing more than twenty different countries and are comprised of at least 29 different subgroups (Yoshioka, Tashima, Ichew, & Murase, 1981). As a result, their immigration patterns, native languages, command of English, degree of assimilation and/or acculturation, family intactness, cultural values, and political and religious beliefs and practices vary (Wong, 1985). In addition, a majority of the Asian population in the United States, with the exception of Japanese Americans, are foreign born (McLoed, 1986). Despite this diversity, which means that differences in social, emotional, and economic status exist among Asian Americans, they are often viewed as a "model" minority with tremendous educational and economic attainment (see Sue & Sue, 1990). They have also been reported to function well in society with few criminal, psychiatric, or divorce rates. These factors, in addition to their high rates of intermarriage with Whites, has led society to erroneously believe that Asian Americans are less prone to the negative impact of prejudice and racism (Sue & Sue, 1990). However, historically and currently, Asians have experienced tremendous prejudice and racism (see United States Commission on Civil Rights, 1992). Examples include denial of citizenship rights (e.g., The Chinese Exclusion Act of 1882, which was repealed only in 1943), concentration camp placement during WWII, and harassment and physical assaults (examples including labels such as "gook" and "the Yellow Peril"; and the 1989 Stockton, California, school attack, during which five Cambodian and Vietnamese children were killed by a man who felt that Asians were responsible for the loss of American jobs). Further, close inspection of Asian enclaves such as the Chinatowns and Japantowns in San Francisco and New York illuminates the fact that many Asians experience poverty, juvenile delinquency, and a myriad of physical and mental health problems. Sue and

Sue (1990) suggest that the discrepancy between "official" and "real" rates of social, economic, and psychological difficulties in the Asian population are probably due in part to cultural factors, including the way in which symptoms are expressed (e.g., somatic or internalizing rather than externalizing ways), family preferences for handling problems themselves rather than seeking outside assistance, and the shame and disgrace associated with having others know about one's social and economic problems.

This brief summary thus highlights the fact that Asians in America are a diverse group with varied social and economic backgrounds, family experiences, and cultural values. Therapists must therefore be careful in how information about Asians is applied to individual clients, since each person's experience will likely be unique. Having said this, it is however helpful for therapists to be aware that some commonalities exist, such as a tendency toward emotional restraint, deference to authority, specified family roles, including a hierarchical family structure, and an emphasis on the family and extended family as important units (Tsui & Schultz, 1983). In addition, among Asians, psychological distress is more likely to be expressed in somatic symptoms, and seeking psychotherapy is typically not a common cultural value (Sue & Sue, 1990).

Therapists working with Asian clients would thus benefit from learning as much as possible about each client's historical and sociopolitical experience and keep each cultural context in mind as they try to establish their credibility as effective helpers. Sue and Zane (1987) write compellingly about the importance of having therapy goals and processes consonant with client cultural values.

Other important cultural value differences between Asian Americans and the mainstream culture exist. One example would be differences regarding "successful" attainment of developmental tasks. That is, most Asian Americans do not encourage the development of autonomy as extremely as Euramericans. For Asian Americans, there is a strong focus on family that emphasizes attachments to the extended family and close ties to the mother. From birth, the fostering of dependency and interdependency is valued in childrearing. Consequently, there is a strong sense of duty or obligation to one's parents. The conscious expression of conflicts between Asian American parents and their children should not be expected since questioning authority, for example, is typically not permitted. In particular, it is generally not acceptable to express anger, resentment, or frustration toward a parent or toward authority figures.

In addition, the Asian American culture tends to discourage the development of intimate relationships with the opposite sex. Typically, Asian American parents discourage their children from dating, and encourage the suppression of sexuality with the goal being to maintain their children's focus on educational achievement. In addition, Asian American culture places a premium on placing other's feelings over one's own, on not verbalizing one's feelings and thoughts, and on being humble and modest.

The emphasis on role, status, and hierarchy in the Asian American cul-ture has great implications for therapists working with this population. One consequence of this, for example, would be to diminish Asian American stu-dents' ability to effectively interact or advocate for themselves with parents, school or university advisors, faculty, staff, and counselors. As we will see in the case study below, all of these cultural factors play a significant role in treating Asian American victims of date rape.

CASE ILLUSTRATION

Presenting Problem

In the Fall quarter of her sophomore year, Elizabeth, an 18-year-old Chinese American college student was sexually assaulted by a male classmate. She had read in a college bulletin and heard from professors that one should make friends by studying with others. In one of her first attempts to estab-lish a friendship with a male peer, Elizabeth met with the following trau-matic event.

With a midterm exam approaching, Elizabeth asked her classmate, Rod, if he would be interested in studying together at the library. Just prior to the library's closing, Rod informed Elizabeth that he had copies of audiotapes with information that was needed for the exam. He suggested that they go to his apartment to listen to the tapes and continue their work.

When they arrived at Rod's apartment, Elizabeth suggested that they use the tape deck in the living room. Rod responded that doing so would disturb his roommate and insisted that they use his bedroom. As soon as he closed the door of the bedroom, Rod jumped on Elizabeth and covered her mouth with his hand. In spite of her attempt to fight him off (she bit him), Rod stuffed her mouth with a cloth and proceeded to rape her. Rod is 6 feet tall; Elizabeth is less than 5 feet.

During the weeks that followed, Elizabeth avoided Rod. After several weeks, Rod confronted her in the lecture hall, asking why she had been avoiding him. Elizabeth responded that the avoidance was caused by what Rod had done to her. Rod denied that he had done anything, invoking the cultural stereotype that although Asian women protest, they are, actually, ready sexual partners. He asserted that Asian American females are willing to do whatever they can to please a man. In addition, Rod told Elizabeth that she knew what she was getting into when she went to his apartment.

A few weeks later, Elizabeth called the city police department and at-tempted to report the rape. They informed her that it was now too late to prosecute and failed to provide her with any referrals such as sexual assault support services or counseling.

During the winter term, Elizabeth found that she was pregnant. She beat her stomach until she was black and blue. She had an abortion without informing her family of the rape or pregnancy. She confided in a friend about the pregnancy, and because she had no money, her friend referred her to an individual in another city who did abortions. For the next several months, Elizabeth was unable to concentrate, felt no motivation to do her schoolwork, and accordingly, her grades fell dramatically.

At the end of the spring term, Elizabeth sought the services of the university's counseling center, distressed because she had been charged with larceny by the department store she had worked for. According to Elizabeth, she did not have any credit cards when she was hired. In order to charge items at this department store, she paid into a credit account. After contributing several hundred dollars to this account, she believed that she could withdraw her money from it whenever she chose to. She attempted to withdraw some money through the business office. They, however, referred her to the personnel office, which told her they could not do it and referred her back to the business office.

Elizabeth was very angry because she felt she had been lied to and denied what was due her. Subsequently, Elizabeth began acquiring articles and charging it to her account—using the credit she had built up. After making purchases equivalent to the credit due her, Elizabeth continued to charge on others' accounts. Prior to this, Elizabeth had never stolen anything. In addition, she did not open the packages after she brought them home but threw them in her closet.

After several weeks of this behavior, security officers confronted Elizabeth. She was disturbed because the security officer wrote in his report that she stole the merchandise simply because she "desired to have nice things," which she felt was not true. Following the formal charge with a crime, Elizabeth was extremely concerned that her name would appear in the paper. She felt sure that family and friends would soon find out. She considered killing herself, since the shame of others knowing felt overwhelming to her.

When Elizabeth came to the counseling center at the end of the spring quarter, she had not discussed the details of the assault or the subsequent problems with anyone. She was referred to me by a male staff member at the counseling center because I am a Japanese American female with a long-standing interest in working with Asian (American and foreign-born) students. During her intake session with the other staff member, Elizabeth stated that a variety of events had occurred but was unable (or unwilling) to give details—especially regarding the rape. The intake worker and I agreed that Elizabeth met the criteria for Major Depression. She reported feeling depressed and had much self-blame and feelings of guilt. In addition, she reported eating and sleeping disturbances, and was suicidal. Elizabeth was also very anxious and had symptoms suggestive of Post Traumatic Stress Disorder, including numbness, nightmares about the rape, social isolation, and hypervigilance.

CLIENT DESCRIPTION

Elizabeth, a short Chinese American student whose hair appeared un-combed, presented in the initial session as distressed. She had a somewhat lost, distant gaze, and looked like a sad, deprived, starved waif whom one could imagine on a poster for a Third World country.

Elizabeth was very soft spoken and, at times, I could count to thirty between her responses. Her upper torso was very petite, whereas her lower torso seemed heavier and more solid. I felt as if her upper body represented her deprivation and her lower body carried the strength and solidness that she had needed to survive.

SOCIAL CONTEXT

Shortly before the assault, Elizabeth had turned 18 years old. She was the older of two girls born to a couple who had emigrated from Hong Kong to the United States. Her father committed suicide when she was about 3 years old. After the suicide, Elizabeth, her mother, and sister moved into the home of her maternal grandparents and their three offspring. Early on, Elizabeth had been told that her father died of a heart attack. Later, when she was 16 years old, Elizabeth was told that her father had killed himself. She was told only that the suicide had been due to the difficulties of adjusting to life in the U.S.

Elizabeth's mother dated frequently, and Elizabeth and her sister were told to never address her as "mother" but to use her first name: Mary. When Elizabeth was 9 years old, Mary wed a Euramerican but did not tell her new husband that she had two daughters! Elizabeth and her sister continued to live with their grandparents while their mother had moved to a separate residence with her new husband.

Mary had a child by her second husband. Sometimes Elizabeth and her younger sister visited Mary and her new family. They were still prohibited from calling her "mother." Elizabeth experienced great difficulty when she saw her half-sister being treated with acceptance and indulged by Mary. In contrast to Elizabeth and Alice (her full-sister), Laura (her half-sister) had a fully decorated room and a closet full of clothes.

Elizabeth described her relationship with Mary as being "cool"; Mary had never been emotionally supportive of Elizabeth. Rather, she issued directives about what Elizabeth should or shouldn't do. Elizabeth also described Mary as only wanting to interact superficially. For example, she would discuss soap operas and movie stars but never ask about how Elizabeth and Alice were coping at their grandparents' home or at school.

Elizabeth's grandfather and grandmother, with whom she lived and was primarily raised by, "hated each other." They fought constantly, often yelling, "I hate you, I'm going to kill you." They also threw appliances, such as the microwave and TV, often breaking them and tossing them out the back door. Tragically, these warring grandparents blamed Elizabeth for most of their problems, even if she wasn't at home when the problem that she was blamed for occurred.

Grandfather, who spoke English, was described as "mean, domineering, and aggressive." He rarely spoke to Elizabeth. Elizabeth felt that her grandfather often told lies about her to her grandmother. Grandmother, who spoke only Chinese, would frequently make nasty statements about Elizabeth. Grandmother's name calling and verbal abuse escalated when Elizabeth was in high school, with the verbal assaults often going on until 3 A.M. Elizabeth would ask her aunt what her grandmother was saying and her aunt would translate, "You are bad . . . you killed your father." Although Elizabeth's uncles and aunt were more benevolent, they worked and attended college and provided little emotional support or protection for Elizabeth and her sister.

Elizabeth's grandparents constantly threatened that when her Social Security check stopped coming at age 18, she would no longer have a place to stay. Both Elizabeth and her sister received checks from Social Security because of their father's death, which were turned over to their grandparents.

Elizabeth and her sister shared a twin bed. Elizabeth stored all her possessions in a cardboard box. Until the end of her junior year in high school, Elizabeth engaged in no extracurricular activities. She had never slept over at a friend's home, was not allowed to have friends over to visit, and had never ridden a bicycle or gone bowling.

Elizabeth attended a public elementary school and did well in school. She lived in a neighborhood with predominantly Euramerican neighbors and attended schools where she and her sister were among the few Asians in attendance. She was often teased at school for being Asian and for dressing differently. Elizabeth remembers that as a child and preteen, she had only two pairs of trousers that she wore continuously. Later, in high school, she tried to fix up old clothes that friends gave to her. At age 14, she began babysitting and working in restaurants to obtain money for clothing and other necessities.

At the end of her junior year of high school, Elizabeth began developing friendships. Prior to this, Elizabeth described herself as having no social skills. One especially supportive friendship that contributed greatly to her development was with a Korean American female whom Elizabeth described as being "Americanized." Elizabeth began to stay over and go on outings with her friend's family. This friend noted to Elizabeth that Elizabeth had broken out of her shell during that year.

During her senior year of high school, Elizabeth began yelling back at her grandmother when her grandmother was verbally abusive and when she tried to forbid Elizabeth from going out of the house. During most of that year, Elizabeth stayed with friends for 3 to 4 day stretches. Although her grandmother accused her of sexual impropriety, Elizabeth had never been involved in any sexual relationships.

For her first term in college, Elizabeth received all Bs. During the following two quarters, her grades began to go down. This correlated with her grandparents' escalating attempts to kick her out of the house because she was turning 18 and her Social Security checks were about to cease. During this time, her grandparents threw her cardboard box of possessions out into the driveway, breaking her most cherished radio, an item she had saved a long time to purchase. Elizabeth felt greatly violated and talked about how this box of possessions had been her "whole world." In fact, one of her daily rituals had been to check her box and see if all her items were intact and still there.

After her grandparents insisted that she leave, Elizabeth's mother took her to her home. The mother (Mary), refused Elizabeth's request to sleep in their home office, but offered her a place in their unfinished garage. Elizabeth declined the offer and stayed with friends during the spring of her freshman year, after which she moved to an apartment with another female friend.

Preimmigration and immigration history reveals that, as a young child, Elizabeth's grandmother saw her own mother killed by Japanese soldiers. The grandparents immigrated to the United States when Mary was 9 but left Mary with an aunt. Mary joined her parents in the United States when she was about 15 years old. By that time, Elizabeth's uncles and aunt had been born.

Mary was invited to Hong Kong to meet an eligible male friend of the family. After reluctantly going to meet him, she was forced to marry him because his family said that they had spent a "fortune" to bring her to Hong Kong. Mary's family also pressured her to marry him to avoid the shame and disgrace that would result if Mary refused and the intended husband's family criticized this refusal.

Initial Session

Elizabeth appeared very distressed at the beginning of our initial session, but her crying was quiet, gentle, and restrained. I could feel the weight of her sadness, pain, and anger for the losses that she had experienced since childhood and the trauma she had endured in the present. I wished to reach out and touch her with a magic wand that would change her life, like the fairy godmother did in Cinderella. I often had the image of holding Elizabeth and rocking her gently—especially when she told me of the hardships that she had endured with so little support.

I believe that, at the start of psychotherapy, it is very important to describe to clients—especially new ones—what therapy is all about. Asian American clients, in particular, tend to have minimal experiences with therapy and think therapy is only for "crazy" people. It is thus important that they have the purpose and process of therapy explained to them. It is important to address these issues in a direct manner. Using humor and culturally familiar terms, I often explain to clients the differences between being "crazy crazy" (psychotic) and "crazy" (neurotic). Usually, I ask them if they are hearing voices coming out of the air or are seeing things. Clients who are not psychotic usually giggle or look at me in amazement.

In view of Elizabeth's presenting problem and history, I shared with her my backpack metaphor, which is a simple but concrete way of describing what therapy involves. I explained that the process of therapy included exploring:

1. What historical rocks/boulders/mountains of feelings were in her backpack, causing her to feel depressed—looking for rock piles of different issues and taking them out one by one and allowing the thoughts, memories, and especially the feelings to be expressed;
2. Dealing more directly with present rocks/issues in her life;
3. Learning how not to put more rocks on her back and how to cope in different and healthier ways (i.e., assertion, communication, negotiation skills); and
4. Examining sources that had helped hold her up (e.g., friends), pushed her down (e.g., mother, grandparents), needed to be developed (e.g., laughing, having fun, relaxing, and getting emotional support from others) or needed to be discarded (e.g., negative self-talk).

Where to begin therapy was a major question. Obviously, there had been many recent stressors and traumatic events, and each of these were exacerbated by her difficult family history. At the end of the first session, I stated that she had certainly been through a lot and recounted what the major issues were that she presented: the rape, abortion, failing academic status, theft charges, and the upcoming trial. Adding to these mounting situational stressors were her painful family history and the most recent familial crisis of being kicked out of her grandparents' home. I was also aware that cultural factors might also be having an impact on each of these events and how they were being coped with. I told Elizabeth that at some point we would get to each one of these issues if she wished.

I viewed Elizabeth as being in crisis because of the rape and felt that she needed issue-oriented crisis counseling. The upcoming trial and the presenting problem of theft that finally brought her in had to be a priority, given the extent of her shame and fear of exposure. I also felt compelled by her poignant developmental history and complex cultural issues but knew that it was essential for her to take the lead in setting our agenda:

THERAPIST: I feel pulled to spend time focusing on your past, as well as the rape, and discussing alternative plans for how you can deal with the theft charges. In time we can focus on each of these, and anything else you would like to talk about. What would you like to focus on first?

She opted to talk about her fears regarding the upcoming trial. Elizabeth stated that charging merchandise to other accounts was wrong, recognizing that this was something that had never crossed her mind prior to the rape. She could not believe that she had done it. I offered to talk with her public defender about the impact of the rape and what I felt was going on with her psychologically prior to and during the theft.

THERAPIST: Elizabeth, it seems as though during the past nine months the rape, the abortion, and being kicked out of your home were all traumatic losses . . . and it was as though not being given your money by the department store was, as they say, the straw that broke the camel's back. These events were like large boulders being thrown on your back. Now, you already had in your backpack the mountains of feelings you suffered from losing your mother and your father in childhood, and the hurt and anger from living with your grandparents. In combination with the rape and theft charge, I can see how it has all been just too much pain for you to bear, especially when you have had to handle it without support from anyone.

Her pained expression told me emphatically that she believed that I understood her. For the first time, the tension in her face softened and I knew that this empathic link allowed our relationship to begin.

Regarding the rape, I conveyed to Elizabeth that she would have control over what details she wanted to share and when she wanted to share them. She then proceeded to tell me the details of the events leading up to the assault. Sadly, Elizabeth blamed herself that the rape happened and thought that she had not fought hard enough. In light of the self-blame, it was imperative that I validate that she had been raped against her will and that it was not her fault. I acknowledged her courage and emphasized the fact that she did the best that she could under the circumstances. I also affirmed that it was ludicrous for the rapist, Rod, to claim that she wanted sex—highlighting the reality that a willing sexual partner does not struggle with and bite her lover's hand! Elizabeth said that this validation was "good to hear" and she felt a sense of relief from the guilt. I told her that many victims of sexual assault feel guilt and/or shame and blame themselves. I again assured her that she had done the best she could, and I told her directly that Rod was the one with the problem. Victims of assault need to hear directly and unambiguously where the responsibility for the problem resides. Although it may seem obvious to the counselor that it doesn't bear repeated emphasis, the client is traumatized, not thinking clearly, and her guilt necessitates clear, direct and repeated clarifications. Before we ended, I explained to Elizabeth the following:

THERAPIST: There may be times during our work together when you may feel that I don't understand you, hurt your feelings, or when you may have feelings such as anger or hurt at something I say or do. If that should happen, I really want you to let me know about this, even though I know this would be hard for you to do, given your culture and family. From your history, I know that you have not had much practice at this. But I hope you will try. If you don't tell me these things directly, you probably will begin to hold your feelings in. Then it would become very hard for you to trust me or work with me. It would probably get in the way of our relationship like it does with your family. Perhaps we could do it another way by talking and working it out together. I hope you will practice with me. Also, if along the way you have any questions, I hope that you will ask me, even if it is hard to do.

I believe a statement of this sort is important in that it explicitly gives permission, encouragement and hope for a different kind of relationship, i.e., one that does not parallel or recapitulate the problems of the past. This is especially important with Asian American clients because many will find it difficult to disagree with or question an "authority" figure such as a counselor.

Case Conceptualization

Elizabeth is a late adolescent who experienced significant losses and deprivation throughout her childhood and adolescence. She had little nurturance or support from her narcissistic mother, or any other adult figures, and lived in fear of her combative and rejecting grandparents. Elizabeth was also teased and rejected by other children because she was Asian and poor, and she was lonely and isolated until her mid-high-school years. Feeling responsible for her younger sister's well-being and needing to mother her, Elizabeth had minimal opportunities to explore and experience all that there is for children and adolescents to do.

I believed that the recent expulsion from her grandmother's home, the rape, and the abortion represented further rejection and abuse of her, and that these factors triggered her credit card rebellion. After the department store gave her the runaround about the money that Elizabeth believed was rightfully hers, she rebelled against this felt injustice and "took" the money that she felt was due her. I believe that this process of "taking" (though wrong), unconsciously represented her taking back some of the love that she had been entitled to from her past but which had been unfairly withheld from her.

Compared to other Asian immigrant families, Elizabeth's family was atypical in terms of their nonsupport of her educational achievement and goals. The family is usually most central to Asian American families, yet her mother gave up her two daughters for a husband, and her grandparents forced Elizabeth out when her Social Security check stopped coming.

In spite of the atypical cultural background, it is important for one to consider the difficulties that immigrant families face in the quest to survive and adjust to a life in America. Elizabeth's father spoke little English, married and immigrated to America hoping to find the American dream. Shortly after the birth of his second child, he jumped off a bridge. The dream had gone tragically sour.

Mary had only recently been reunited with her parents and was soon forced by them to marry and separate from them again. Perhaps, needing to find security and acceptance in a new land, she married a Euramerican male at the expense of losing her children. I have observed similar feelings of abandonment and difficulties with intimacy among other Asian American clients from immigrant families, who had been left behind, had preceded their parents to this country, or had been separated after immigration. The differences in outcome seem to have depended on the degree of benevolence of the relative with whom the client stayed, the length of the separation, and the ages at which the separation and reunion occurred. It is interesting to track intergenerational patterns wherein Elizabeth's grandmother lost her mother early in her life. Mary was separated at about 9 years of age from her mother, and Elizabeth, in turn, lost her mother when she was 9 years old. Attachment bonds and primary relationships were fragile and broken in all three generations.

Elizabeth was in the conforming stage of racial/cultural identity development, a stage characterized by self-depreciation and rejection of one's own cultural identity (Sue & Sue, 1990). She said that she hated being Chinese and did not want to learn Chinese because she heard her grandmother say hateful things about her in Chinese. The racial taunts she heard as a child also had a negative impact on her identity, and the trauma of the rape was also similarly overlaid with cultural stereotypes—all of which propelled Elizabeth away from achieving any positive cultural or racial identity.

Orienting Constructs

In general, I view life from an Eastern orientation, operating according to negatively and positively charged forces—yin and yang. This perspective helps me to understand my clients with regard to characteristics that predominate and those that are in the background waiting to be developed. The goal is to attain balance and possess the flexibility to move back and forth. The therapeutic work is to focus on the client's imbalance and to help support and nurture the side that needs to emerge and develop.

I use a lot of visual metaphors in my work to create images or pictures that help me and my clients to *see* their issues more clearly. Clients often embellish my images or take off with metaphors of their own. For example, I sometimes use the metaphor of plants to think and talk with clients about their problems. I ask myself and the clients what kind of gardeners they had to help them grow and thrive. Did they have the basic water and shelter? Did they have support, sunshine, and fertilizer? Were they pruned too much or given too much fertilizer? What does the client's tree look like now? If different parts of the tree represent developmental areas, such as personal, interpersonal, and academic/career, what branches are blossoming with flowers and leaves? Which sides have buds yet to bloom? In what areas has growth been stunted?

I also ask myself, if this client started off in life with an empty backpack on her back—standing straight up to the world, emotionally responsive and open to experiences, what happened to make her feel the way she does now? What kind of rocks (feelings) did Elizabeth throw in her backpack because she faced rejection? What are these feelings? Are they rocks of sadness, anger, confusion? What piles of rocks have accumulated into mountains? How heavy are the rocks? How has she protected herself from further pain (defenses)? Has she built walls to protect herself, and how high and thick are the walls? What support has she had to hold up the backpack? Is she able to acknowledge her feelings and assert her thoughts and feelings to others? How much practice does she have doing this? What impact does this backpack of rocks have on her present relationships? Such visual metaphors and colloquial expressions often sound unsophisticated, but for certain clients they greatly facilitate a true working alliance.

In Elizabeth's case, her primary gardeners had abandoned her, physically and emotionally. The substitute grandparent gardeners gave minimal water and shelter, no fertilizer, and no sunshine. They attacked and pruned her. Elizabeth resonated and came to life emotionally as I used this visual language with her.

Elizabeth had a very heavy backpack that had chronically depressed her. She had thrown rocks and boulders filled with all her sadness, anger, and pain into her back pack and they had piled up into mountains. There were mountains of losses and mountains of having been persecuted, rejected, and scapegoated. The walls built by these mountains kept Elizabeth from getting close to others emotionally. She was unaware that she stored these feelings and was no longer able to acknowledge that she even had feelings. Elizabeth had no support to help her with her load; nevertheless, she used the strength that she had developed to help hold up her sister's load. Elizabeth had difficulties standing up straight, literally, and the recent events made it almost impossible for her to even hold her head up.

The result was that Elizabeth had a shame-based sense of self, no sense of importance or validity for her own feelings, and no expectations of understanding or acceptance from others. Despite all of this, she still possessed an inner-strength that enabled her to survive. I observed that the validation, support and encouragement I offered to Elizabeth, and especially my willingness to advocate on her behalf with police and professors, were received with disbelief. There was an initial questioning that I would actually want to do something for her and, then, deep expressions of appreciation. I also observed that it was difficult for Elizabeth to express her feelings to me—to actually break down and cry freely remained a threat to her.

Treatment Plans and Intervention Strategy

INITIAL TREATMENT PLAN

Short-Term Goals

1. My first goal was to address the theft charges and upcoming trial and sentencing. We needed to do this because Elizabeth's increasing anxiety about this impending stressor was extremely high. I thought Elizabeth's coping resources would be exhausted and the risk for suicide increased.

2. Another goal was to stabilize her rape trauma and abortion-related symptoms. I wanted to do this by exploring her sense of hopelessness, shame, violation, and so forth. I also planned to focus on the cultural stereotypes that were a part of the rape, because Elizabeth was very disturbed by the rapist relating this to her. In addition, it was important that Elizabeth develop new coping techniques for dealing with her feelings instead of repressing them.

3. My third goal was to provide Elizabeth with support regarding her academics: offering her assistance concerning her classes, and helping her seek help from the Dean of Students with her academic standing. Her academic attainment was very important to her, and her inability to concentrate, her decreased motivation, and her declining grade point average (GPA) that resulted were constant reminders of the sexual assault that also contributed to her low self-esteem and depression.

4. My last short-term goal was to help Elizabeth problem-solve with regard to the issues arising from the rape and abortion. The goal here was empowerment and would probably include taking action against perpetrator (e.g., report the rape and the perpetrator's use of cultural stereotypes in justifying his behavior to the Affirmative Action office and the Dean of Students). For rape survivors, reporting sexual assaults can be significant in helping them appropriately place the responsibility and blame on the rapist, where it belongs, and no longer on themselves. However, I broached this issue carefully because I know that there are often cultural prohibitions against sharing information of this sort, and I wanted Elizabeth to feel empowered to act when she felt ready to.

Intermediate Goals

1. My first intermediate goal was to help Elizabeth identify her feelings, needs, thoughts, and limits in relationships. She then needed to learn how to express them by developing assertiveness and negotiation skills.

2. Given her history of emotional abuse, Elizabeth had an inordinate amount of negative self-talk, and a goal was to decrease the negative self-talk, increase positive self-talk, and teach her techniques for dealing with the negative self-talk (e.g., thought stopping).

Long-Term Goals

1. My first goal was to explore the impact of childhood and family issues on Elizabeth's sense of self and on her present relationships. I believed that Elizabeth had minimal understanding of how much her past history was influencing her pre- and postsexual assault.

2. I thought that one of the most important goals was to explore the impact of cultural values, minority status, prejudice, and racism on Elizabeth's racial/cultural identity. This was necessary because I believed that Elizabeth's rape was in part an act of bigotry that had powerful violating and defiling aspects. The rape not only recapitulated her social and familial experiences with bias and disaffection wherein those in authority derogated her but also fueled a sense of shame.

Underlying all of the specific goals was the necessity of developing a corrective therapeutic relationship in which safety, trust, and hope were established. Developmentally, Elizabeth had had very little afforded her with respect to material goods, nurturing experiences of love, support, caring, or having someone to depend on.

With an Asian American client like Elizabeth, the feelings that you convey nonverbally that show you care will be more important than the words you say. Again, behaviors are more important than words. Many Asian American clients grew up never having seen their parents cry, or they have never cried in front of anyone else. They have never expressed their needs and wants nor have they ever expressed negativity or expressed what they did not like. A significant number of Asian American clients whom I have worked with consider this to be "complaining." They need to be invited and given permission, that is, told that it is alright to cry or to "complain."

Short-Term Goals. The issues defined under the short-term goals were the most anxiety-provoking for Elizabeth. After having experienced a series of stressors, the theft charges had thrust her into crisis and propelled her to seek help.

Elizabeth was severely depressed and anxious. The possibility that her family or friends would find out about the charges terrified her to the point that she regarded suicide a viable solution, which was especially troublesome since this coping approach had been modeled by her father. I therefore suggested a referral to the student health center for a medication evaluation. Elizabeth did not want medication, however, because she was afraid of becoming addicted. It was important for me to validate her feelings about suicide and medications and also about the impact of culture and family on the way she was thinking and feeling. At the same time, it was critical to have her explore alternative cognitive and behavioral strategies for dealing with the overwhelming feelings she was experiencing.

Elizabeth expressed an inordinate amount of negative self-talk and self-blame about various stressful events and how she had dealt with these problems. I believed that her inordinate amount of negative self-talk had it's roots in her history of abuse and the Asian worldview. Among Asians, lack of resolve and determination are often considered to be evidence of human failure. Research findings suggest that Asians tend to attribute their distresses to personal weaknesses, rather than to others (Ichikawa, 1989). Asians also tend to believe that mental health is maintained by avoidance of morbid thoughts and the exercise of will power (Sue, 1976; Sue & Morishima, 1982) Thus, the causes of failure as well as the causes of emotional stress are internally ascribed.

In contrast to failure attributions, causes of success are more externally ascribed by the Japanese, Chinese, and Chinese Americans, compared to Euramericans (Chandler, Shama, Wolf, & Planchard, 1981; Hsieh, Shybut, & Lotsof, 1967). Hsieh et al. (1967) explain this difference by noting that the individual-centered American culture places a high premium on self-reliance, individualism, and status achievement through personal efforts. In contrast, the situation-centered Chinese culture places high value on the group, tradition, social role expectations, and harmony with the universe. Clearly, Elizabeth operated according to the Asian worldview, and it was important that I acknowledge this and take it into consideration during the course of therapy.

In order to be culturally competent, therapists working with people of color cannot limit themselves to the conventional role of working only in the fifty minute hour. According to Atkinson, Thompson, and Grant (1993), the therapist may have to assume alternative roles that include adviser, advocate, facilitator to indigenous support and healing systems, consultant, and agent of social change. For example, a therapist in the role of cultural mediator would help to point out and interpret perspectives of Asian American culture to individuals outside the Asian American culture and also help to point out and interpret perspectives of Euramerican culture to the Asian American client. The therapist's role would depend on the client's level of acculturation, the locus of the problem's etiology, and the goals of helping.

Recognizing the power imbalance that Elizabeth experienced with the majority culture and the personal depreciation and emotional deprivation she experienced in her family, I felt that it was critical for her to have the experience of someone reaching out to her. She needed me to go beyond the limits of the usual therapeutic relationship and extend active help and support in dealing with the judicial system. Her family's immigrant status and her level of acculturation seemed to require that she have an advocate in this very important area, where she had little knowledge and felt disempowered. Therefore, I called Elizabeth's public defender and explained the events that led up to her being charged with theft. He asked that I write a letter that described and explained her history, the rape, and the abortion, and her psychological state at the time of the thefts. This was to be presented in court.

I told her that if she wanted me to go to court with her on the day of the trial, I would. She looked very relieved and nodded emphatically. I attended the trial with her and walked with her to the probation office. Elizabeth's focus changed from suicide as an option to how she would deal with each issue that arose, including the sentencing, which might include jail time and a work detail. Much to her relief, by some good fortune, her name never appeared in the newspaper section of court proceedings.

I have come to believe that when one works with individuals who have been sexually assaulted, one must be knowledgeable about the internal and external grievance procedures and the effectiveness and fairness of these systems. Without this understanding, one might urge clients to go alone to report the rape. Telling their stories to persons who are insensitive and unresponsive may further traumatize the victims. Given the cultural values and differences in communication styles of victims of color, it is even more critical that therapists go with victims whenever possible to provide emotional support, to help clarify questions asked of the survivor, or to help explain to the investigator details that are necessary for thorough reporting. Therapists may be the only persons whom the survivors have trusted enough to tell the details.

As a result of the rape, abortion, and subsequent distress and depression, Elizabeth's motivation and concentration had decreased considerably. At times, she was unable even to get out of bed. Her GPA for the quarter following the attack was 0.7. She despaired that no one would want to help her, since the police did not help her when she telephoned them. The police apparently did not even give her any referrals to sexual assault or other support services when she originally reported the rape. Given her history of deprivation and lack of support, I felt it necessary to extend myself to her. I offered to contact professors or to arrange for her to meet with the Dean of Students who would, if necessary, be able to help her retroactively withdraw from classes. She did not want me to contact the dean, but asked me to contact professors for her. I contacted her professors, who responded positively. Elizabeth wanted to attempt to finish the quarter, and we were able to find a way for her to do that.

Intermediate Goals.   Understandably, Elizabeth had been holding in her feelings regarding the rape and abortion. Early on, I had shared with her the backpack metaphor and explained that, in time, it would be good if she could get rid of some of the feelings that were depressing her. I also shared with her the common and varied feelings that sexual assault survivors experience. Elizabeth indicated that when she found out she was pregnant it was clear to her that she would have an abortion, since she viewed the pregnancy as an extension of the rape. As we talked about Elizabeth's experiences with abuse and violation, her range of feelings emerged. Often, we would sit together in silence as Elizabeth struggled to find ways to share her experiences and begin to metaphorically empty her backpack.

It is especially important when working with Asian American clients to pay attention to nonverbal cues, since they tend to place less credence on direct verbal confrontations and emotional expressiveness. I usually watch the eyes; in a split second one might see a flash of feeling signaling that something is going on. As I watched Elizabeth's nonverbal cues, I was able to tell when it was acceptable to go deeper into feelings or that some impact had been made. Conversely, it is critical that therapists be mindful of their own nonverbal expressions, as Elizabeth and other Asian American clients often attend more to our actions than our words.

In response to my affirmation of her experience, Elizabeth increasingly allowed herself to express her anger at the male who raped her, and she began to decrease the self-blame and negative self-talk that had permeated her responses in the initial phase of treatment. She was, however, still very fearful of seeing him. He apparently had transferred to a school in the South after Elizabeth told him she was going to report him. At the end of winter term, right before finals, Elizabeth ran into Rod's roommate. The roommate assumed that she had had a positive relationship with Rod and informed her that Rod would be coming into town. Elizabeth was in a state of panic for the next week and, on her way to a final exam, she was sure she saw him walking with his roommate. Elizabeth "fell apart." She was unable to take the exam, as she was flooded with fear and memories of the rape.

As we processed this crisis, I suggested that relationships could be different for her now than they had been in the past. We began to explore and define what she might need and/or not need from others when feelings emerge. The concept that her thoughts, needs, and feelings were valid and acceptable and that she deserved to have things given to her emotionally was foreign to her. This new way of thinking and caring I conveyed to her was necessary for Elizabeth to begin thinking about other possibilities for relationships.

THERAPIST: Your family expressed feelings to each other and to you in a certain way, some because of culture, some because of the family you grew up in. Even though you grew up with this, you can learn a different way now. You can choose and learn a way that is going to be the best for you. What, in fantasy, do you think someone could do for another if someone were crying? I know you've watched movies on TV. What have you seen people do when someone is hurt? and what would you like that for yourself?

I had Elizabeth begin to write up a list of what she needed in relationships. I told her it was very important that she write down concrete details. For example, I need support was not enough. She needed to write down, I need someone to give me a hug, ask me questions, such as ask how I feel, or validate my feelings.

I taught Elizabeth a method of asserting her feelings, thoughts, and needs using the DESC method (Bower & Bower, 1976). DESC is an acronym for *D*escribe the situation or behavior, *E*xpress her feelings and thoughts, *S*pecify her needs and changes in the behavior she desires, and give *C*onsequences—positive and negative to her and the other individual. Elizabeth was able to use this method when she talked to her mother about her feelings regarding her mother's emotional unresponsiveness. Since many Asian clients often feel that any direct expression is aggressive, differences between assertiveness and aggressiveness had to be clarified. In particular, the fact that assertiveness involved expressing needs and feelings while still being respectful to the other was emphasized.

I explained to Elizabeth that she needed a lot of practice. I find that many clients think that their inability to get their needs responded to indicates that they are in some way defective. It is important, therefore, that they understand that they did not have good models of positive communication from which to learn positive and effective communication skills. With Asian American clients, the impact of Asian values (i.e., specified family roles and the hierarchical family structure) on communication also needs to be discussed, and they need help finding ways to express their feelings within this cultural context. In my experience, helping clients find ways to express their needs *respectfully* is often the key.

In addition, Elizabeth needed to weed out those individuals in her life who were not supportive of her and not willing to try to listen and change behaviors that were harmful to her. As I worked with Elizabeth (and that I find true of many Asian American clients), I had to be careful to not emphasize the Euramerican values that focus on independence from family but help her grow and have her needs responded to in ways that were compatible with family interdependence, which is a part of Asian culture.

Elizabeth's family was different from other Asian American families. We talked about Elizabeth trying to find out whether her mother was willing to hear her and to make changes in the way she related to her. It turned out that in Elizabeth's case, she had to get most of her needs met and feelings affirmed from individuals other than her family, since they continued to be unsupportive of her.

THERAPIST: You can't make someone change. However, you're not asking the other person for something unreasonable like a Mercedes Benz that they may be unable to afford. If the other person can't or won't respond to you, then perhaps you need to find others who can. If someone says that you are forcing or making them to change, then you could say no—that it is up to them if they want to try or not. If the other person doesn't want to change, then you have to look at what the consequences are for you, and make your decisions based on what you need. Nobody is perfect but the other person's willingness to try and make changes is what is important.

One of the most important reasons that Elizabeth needed to learn how to assert herself was that her Asian American communication values ran counter to what is valued in the majority Euramerican culture. I realized that Elizabeth would need to be able to assert herself to be successful, to advocate for herself (e.g., with professors or employers), and to deal with the probability of sexual or racial harassment or discrimination in the future. Elizabeth, like many Asian American clients, needed to understand the importance of dealing flexibly with others and how cultural factors impacted appropriate use of these skills. I encouraged Elizabeth to learn to selectively use different skills to her advantage and noted that learning assertiveness and communication skills, which are valued by the majority culture, in no way devalued her Asian values. I wanted her to appreciate the fact that rather than being disadvantaged, students of color are more advantaged because they can have bi- or tricultural communication competence and be able to negotiate and function effectively in multiple cultural contexts.

Long-Term Goals.   The listing of short-, intermediate-, and long-term goals within this section does not imply that these goals were compartmentalized and addressed serially. In particular, the long-term goals cited in this section were addressed throughout treatment, not only at the end. From the beginning, issues regarding family experiences and how these were impacting current thoughts, feelings, events, or relationships were identified and addressed. For example, with regard to her family history, I shared with Elizabeth the metaphor about her being a plant. She chose to be a rose. We explored how her rose bush was abandoned, trampled on, and neglected by her gardeners. At the earliest sessions I presented Elizabeth this:

THERAPIST: I don't know if your parents/grandparents were good or bad people, but in my assessment they did not *behave* like good parents. Good parents not only provide a roof over your head, clothe, and feed you but also provide you with emotional support. From what I know about you, it seems that you rarely received love or support from them.

Elizabeth had wondered if something was wrong with her that her father killed himself, that her mother would not claim her as her daughter, and that her grandparents would kick her out of the house once her financial contribution to the family ended. Elizabeth needed to hear that she was not to blame and to have her pathogenic belief that she was not lovable repeatedly disconfirmed by the experience of being cared about, which I tried to provide. I told her that her caretakers had failed in their responsibilities to parent her in a positive and healthy manner, not that they were sick or bad people who intended to hurt her.

Elizabeth dropped out of an ethnic studies class after the sexual assault. However, she retook this class in the spring quarter of the following school year. I happened to be a guest lecturer one day in her class on Asians in America: Prejudice and Racism. I had shown part of the movie *Who Killed*

Vincent Chin? a documentary about the first civil rights trial involving an Asian American. I was very emotional during the delivery, crying and angry at times, especially because I was an Asian American activist in Michigan when Vincent Chin was killed and when his case was brought to trial.

Following this, Elizabeth had much to talk about in the next session. I asked her how it was for her to see me in her class and she said that it had been very positive. Elizabeth said that she too cried through the presentation. She had not known about the case and she had a lot of anger and disbelief regarding the information I had shared.

We focused then on her experiences growing up in a West Coast community, about her family's immigration to and adjustment in America, about the racial issues involved in her mother marrying a Euramerican male and abandoning her children, about what her experiences have been as an Asian American and as a person of color, and about the emergence of similar issues in her sexual assault. After this class, Elizabeth decided that she wanted to pursue a teaching credential, hoping to teach ethnic history/studies. She especially wanted to teach students of color so that they would grow up having a better sense of themselves and their culture. Elizabeth, it seemed, was beginning to develop a more positive cultural identity.

REVISED TREATMENT PLAN

As treatment progressed, I became increasingly interested in teaching Elizabeth how to manage stress more effectively through relaxation. I usually give my abuse clients relaxation skills training. However, I did not initially include achievement of the relaxation as a treatment goal because of Elizabeth's extreme distress during the initial phase of therapy. I was concerned, however, because she continued to have difficulty falling asleep and also spent many waking hours worrying and thinking about her problems. Early on, she had rejected a referral for medication that might have helped alleviate many of these symptoms. I believed that Elizabeth needed to learn exercises that would help her achieve the relaxation state as a way to cope with this difficult period. I also felt that these skills would increase her resilience in dealing with future stressors.

First, I discussed with Elizabeth the impact of stress on one's body through the autonomic nervous system, the importance of relaxation to bring her body back to a balanced state, how to attain the relaxation state, and how to incorporate relaxation exercises into her life. I explained to her that she needed to shut her brain off for a while. I noted that this method was inexpensive and not in any way harmful to her body. Most importantly, she could have control over this process.

I like to try out different types of relaxation techniques, since the effectiveness of each approach varies by individual. During our sessions I put Elizabeth through different relaxation exercises, such as the use of imagery, meditation, and self-hypnosis. I also taped the relaxation exercises so that my voice would be a continuing source of comfort to her at home. Elizabeth responded to these exercises with an increased sense of calm. My experience is that many Asian Americans tend to somaticize their problems, and using imagery that focuses on relaxing internal organs, muscles, and nerves, is especially useful with this population. On the self-hypnosis tape I presented affirmations and goals for positive changes in her life, such as increased relaxation, increased self-confidence, increased ability to concentrate and retain information read, increased identification and assertion of personal needs/feelings/limits, and increased ability to choose and work on developing more supportive relationships.

Elizabeth used the tape religiously and stated that it helped her fall asleep at night. She also reported that she once felt panicked when she thought that her roommate had recorded over the relaxation tape. The tape represented a concrete way for me to provide a constant holding environment and secure connection for Elizabeth, which was especially important given her history of insecure attachments.

I also felt that Elizabeth had suffered so much injustice and capriciousness in her life, and had paid so dearly for the rape, that the rapist should experience consequences. I hoped that this process would empower Elizabeth and help her recognize that although she had experienced much victimization in the past, she could now take some action. I hoped that she would report the rape to such campus officials as the Student Conduct Coordinator. Elizabeth, however, did not feel that she could do this. She noted that her rapist had left campus and believed that nothing could be done. In addition, I knew that she was still blaming herself and that publicly talking to others about the rape would add to her feelings of shame. Although I had my own thoughts about what should be done with the rapist, I realized that "forcing" her to report would only dynamically replay the demand/compliance routine that she had experienced in much of her life and I very much wanted this decision to be her own. That is, it would have been counterproductive for me to act on my own feelings and pressure her to do it my way, potentially reevoking in our relationship the same concerns that the rapist or her caretakers had evoked originally by taking control. Recognizing that my goals might differ from hers, I wondered how our process felt to her.

THERAPIST: How do you feel about me urging you to report the rape to the Student Conduct Coordinator? . . . Does this feel similar in any way to when your mother or grandmother tells you to do something? . . . I wonder if you ever feel any of the same angry feelings toward me that you do with them?

She denied feeling the same way with me, saying that she felt different with me because I cared about what happened to her. I invited her to tell me if ever she felt pushed by me to act in a way she was not comfortable with.

I relinquished my goal of pursuing consequences for her rapist after suggesting once that she could write a letter to the Dean of Students at his present university if she wished. However, I did suggest to Elizabeth that she might want to think of ways that he could "pay," even if this was limited to fantasizing. Elizabeth said that she had been thinking of this and thought of writing his name on all the women's bathroom walls saying that he was a rapist. Together we elaborated on this fantasy, giving her an opportunity for ventilation through fantasy as a means of cognitively beginning to shift the blame and shame on to the perpetrator rather than keeping it on herself.

BALANCING GOALS

I believe that I was able to contribute to balancing both Elizabeth's goals and the university's goals. Elizabeth came to therapy because an imbalance in her personal life was having an impact on her ability to be successful in her academic program. Her family history and her family's expectations of her, although she did not live with them, were a thorn in her side. Through the course of therapy, heavier emphasis was placed on her personal life, realizing that she could not perform to the best of her ability academically until she addressed those issues. Eventually, Elizabeth was able to heal, grow, and blossom in the personal and academic areas of her life.

One issue I had to try to balance was Elizabeth's needs for personal growth and assertiveness, which were necessary for survival, and how her cultural values might impact this. I tried to deal with this by helping her understand that she could *respectfully* assert herself and have her needs met without seeming self-centered or culturally inappropriate.

I also had to walk a fine line between my belief that reporting Rod would empower Elizabeth and her reticence to file this report. I chose to deal with this by suggesting that she report and giving her information about reporting avenues but not forcing her and honoring her choice to not report.

Therapeutic Process

RELATIONAL REENACTMENTS

Initially, Elizabeth arrived 15 to 20 minutes late for her 9:00 A.M. sessions and always apologized for being late. I understood the severity of her depression and could see that she was having difficulty even getting out of bed and taking care of herself. I also understood the ambivalence she had about coming in. She had sought help at the counseling center when she felt desperate, as she had been "crying all the time," although these tears were never shared with another. I don't believe she trusted or believed that someone would really want to support and help her. To have someone listen to her would be monumental, given her history. Further, up until this point, she had never shared with anyone in or outside her family the details of the sexual assault, the theft or criminal proceedings, and so forth. Her reluctance to share was partially based on Asian cultural values, which discourage the disclosing of problems outside the family. Not bringing shame and dishonor to the family is more critical than bringing honor to the family.

Many times, when one discovers "resistance" such as this, that is, when a client repeatedly arrives late for sessions, some beginning therapists may think they need to confront that resistance. For example, therapists ineffectively address clients' resistances by saying, "You have been late and you are being resistant," or, "Your being late must mean that you are defending against forming a relationship with me." On the other hand, therapists can ignore the important message the client is giving them by being late and choose not to raise the issue of lateness. Fortunately, there are other more effective ways to work with resistance, rather than blaming the client or ignoring it. Instead, one can address resistance more effectively without even having to use the words *resistance* or *defense*. Being Asian American helps me, I believe, say things to clients that they don't want to hear, without making them feel criticized or blamed. Culturally, I was taught to do what would not hurt someone's feelings, and this guides how I respond to manifestations of client resistance. Personally, I do not hesitate in being direct, and as a colleague once told me, I have the ability to cut to the issue with the clarity of a samurai sword, but do it with the gentleness of a cherry blossom falling on your face.

To illustrate, I chose to address the issue of Elizabeth's lateness by acknowledging how difficult it must be for her to get out of bed, given her depression. I wanted to normalize her experience and provide an understanding response. At the same time, we focused on how hard it must have been for her to keep inside all that had happened to her. I also acknowledged that she had so little practice expressing her feelings, needs, and thoughts. I told her that, given all of that, trusting and believing that I wanted to help would take time. The only thing about her being late was that it gave us less time to talk and work together.

Elizabeth related that it was easier to talk to me because I was Asian and female than to the Euramerican male intake worker; she had felt such a distance from him as he took notes throughout the intake. Elizabeth felt she couldn't talk to him about the details of the rape. She reported that the reason he referred her to me was that she kept telling him, "you don't understand, you couldn't understand." The comments that I made about being Asian and the impact of Asian family values helped her feel more understood. As her depressive symptoms decreased, her trust of me increased, and her punctuality also increased.

How might a non-Asian therapist similarly establish credibility and rapport with an Asian American client like Elizabeth? My primary suggestion is that obvious cultural differences (such as race, gender and so forth) be addressed directly by asking the client how he or she feels about working with a therapist who is different, and by asking the client's personal, familial, and cultural perspective on various issues. This process will help therapists articulate problems from the client's cultural perspective and be able to address issues in a culturally sensitive manner. Doing this will signal to clients the therapist's sensitivity to cultural influences and increase rapport and credibility.

During the treatment process, issues from Elizabeth's past relationships emerged, regarding her expression of deep feelings. The seeds of hope that I felt I started to plant and fertilize were that, although Elizabeth did not choose her gardeners/parents, she certainly could choose her present gardeners/friends, partners. The responsibility for changing her life and relationships to positive experiences lay with her. We focused on how the best resolution she could have was to go on and live a productive and satisfying life. The first goal in this process was to identify what her feelings were and what she needed when she expressed herself to others.

How I explore this issue depends on the kinds of experiences the client has had in having his or her feelings responded to. With Asian clients, I acknowledge family and cultural norms of giving/receiving support.

THERAPIST: I know that in most Asian families (that includes Japanese, Chinese, Korean, Vietnamese, etc.) people don't share feelings, nor receive support for these feelings. I had one Asian student say, "All my parents care about is my head and stomach." We are taught to hold our feelings in, have a blank face, accept the situation, and move on. Is this how it was for you?

Time was spent in exploring and staying with her pain, sadness, anger about her experiences with her grandmother, uncles, aunt, mother, and father. In Elizabeth's case, she had had no experiences with expressing sad and painful feelings or getting emotional support. Initially, she wanted to know what could be accomplished by crying with another. I answered her question directly using the backpack metaphor. I took time to explain to Elizabeth that she had lived many years, during which she had accumulated rocks, and that these rocks are filled with feelings that never have been expressed. I suggested that, if she began to unload (share) the rocks, boulders, and mountains of feelings, she would feel lighter. I warned Elizabeth that she might, in fact, feel worse in the beginning. However, I likened it to carrying heavy shopping bags around. When we finally sit down, we do not immediately feel great; rather, we may moan and groan, feeling the aches and pain, and then we feel better.

I then wanted to address with her why I thought she was having difficulties expressing her feelings to me, given her history. As stated earlier, my being Asian made it easier for her to relate to me, and she expected me to understand because I was a therapist. I thought that my being Asian, however, also made her hesitate to express feelings because she expected me to respond like her mother or grandparents.

I could really feel the conflict she was experiencing, as I recalled how difficult it was for me to directly express my negative feelings in front of someone else, even to my therapist, given *my* Asian background. I told her that I had to work hard at expressing my feelings. Relating my history and struggles to her had a positive impact, and she was able to begin to open up. It was especially important to tell her that I knew it wouldn't be easy at first but that she needed practice and that it would get easier each time she did it. Again, I suggested that she could practice with me.

Termination and Therapist's Summary Thoughts

Elizabeth and I had worked together on a weekly basis for about 20 sessions through the summer and up to the beginning of the winter term, when I went on leave for two months. When I returned from leave, I saw her on a drop-in basis until the end of the school year. The anxiety and depressive symptoms that she had initially presented had abated. She had moved from the outward adjustment stage to the renormalization stage of rape trauma syndrome. For example, she was reaching out and establishing closer relationships with females. Elizabeth was also reestablishing a high school friendship with a male friend that began to blossom into a romantic relationship. She was beginning to have "first" experiences such as learning to ride a bicycle, going bowling, going out of town to the coast, and going to a Shakespearean festival.

Elizabeth had also been able to use her assertiveness skills to confront her mother about the way her mother communicated with her and to express to her mother what she needed from her. Her mother responded in a positive way the first time she tried this new mode of communication. Unfortunately, however, her mother was not able to continue to respond in this supportive manner. We talked about how her mother was also bound by her culture and her family history and that this also kept her from being able to respond to Elizabeth differently. Having tested these waters with her mother to see what she could have there, Elizabeth refocused her hopes and efforts on the current friendships she was choosing and developing. Elizabeth felt that things were better for her and I too felt that her life had stabilized and that she was beginning to blossom.

Developmental and relationship crises push students to seek help during these times. Different issues emerge at choice points during a student's tenure at the university, and termination with an individual therapist may mean they will reconnect with the same or a different therapist at a later date. It is essential to convey to clients that there will be occasions in the future when they may benefit from seeing a therapist again and frame this as a strength they have in recognizing when they need the support. Therapists also often come to be seen as an extension of the client's family, especially for clients of color, and they may in the ensuing years maintain occasional contact.

Elizabeth brought up termination before I went on leave because she was concerned that I was busy and had many students to see. My impending departure rekindled feelings that her needs were not important. To address this we focused on her feelings that I, too, was leaving her.

THERAPIST: Elizabeth, I wonder how you feel, knowing that you believe I am too busy to see you and that I will be leaving. You have experienced many losses in your family in which individuals have left you or have not been there for you. We have talked about your sad and angry feelings toward them, and I am wondering what you are feeling toward me right now.

Elizabeth reiterated that my being female and Asian was very helpful to her, as I could understand, explain, and confirm for her experiences, thoughts, and feelings regarding the rape and issues of culture. She expressed to me deep gratitude for the help I had given her all along the way. I knew that it would still be difficult for her to express a negative feeling about me directly to me, so I persisted:

THERAPIST: I am happy that I was able to be here for you. I know you feel grateful, but I also think it's really normal in a relationship to have two different feelings toward someone at the same time. Has there ever been a time that I have disappointed you or said or did something that hurt your feelings? If there is, I'd like to know. You've talked about things that you would have liked to tell your family but felt that you couldn't. Again, you might not be able or want to do these things with them. However, you might use me to practice.

Elizabeth said that she was sad but insisted that there was nothing she was angry about with me. As we explored why, she clarified that experiences with me were very different from those with her family because I listened to her and respected her. She also stated that she knew she had me to talk to if she needed to come back. I told her that I could not guarantee that I would be at the counseling center forever, but that I would be available for her in whatever way I could, as long as I worked there. I also let her know that she could have a similar positive experience with another therapist. In addition, I expressed that there still were issues about family history that she might want to deal with in time. Elizabeth still had a long way to go in terms of getting rid of the rocks in her backpack, and there was still an overwhelming amount of pain that had not emerged or been dealt with.

When I said this to Elizabeth, I truly felt very warm, loving, and caring feelings for her. She thanked me and I said that she was welcome. I told her that she knew where my office was, and to drop in or call me if she needed to talk. I also gave her "homework"—to have fun and play. Earlier, I suggested to her that she watch a lot of movies—comedies, describing to her the research indicating that laughter benefits mental health. I told her she needed to laugh a lot to make up for lost time!

Elizabeth did drop in to see me periodically after I returned from my leave, as issues in her present relationships evoked her pain, much of this exacerbated by her family history. Before the assault, her GPA for the quarter was 2.7. After the assault it was 0.7. Now, three years later, it was 3.7 for the current quarter. Elizabeth switched from a business to a sociology major, as she continued to want to teach ethnic studies. She was very excited about her goals and about wanting to have an impact on the positive cultural development and sense of self of students of color.

Elizabeth also stopped in to see me one day after she picked up her transcript. She was very happy to see that her grades had improved since she had decided on a sociology major and career. She was especially pleased that she had earned an A for her ethnic studies class. Seeing her transcript for the first time, however, rekindled a host of painful feelings about her childhood, being kicked out of her grandparents home, the rape, the abortion, and the criminal charges. The grades reminded her of these events, and she now felt safe enough with me to cry with me as she talked. Later, Elizabeth expressed appreciation that she had me and also had a new boyfriend with whom she could talk.

Elizabeth and I continued to meet periodically when she wanted to discuss personal and/or academic problems. In one of our last meetings, Elizabeth expressed her interest in participating in a study abroad program in Asia (I had referred her previously to the Study Abroad Program at the International Students office).

ELIZABETH: I am really excited! I want to learn Chinese. I feel bad about not knowing how to speak more Chinese than utterances like, "I'm going to kill you," which my grandmother said to me. Did I ever tell you that 2 years ago my father's parents wrote my sister and me, wanting to know how we were? They sent pictures and we sent some back. I'd like to meet them. Maybe they will be more positive and kinder, the type of grandparents I never had.

I reflected enthusiastically that this interest in her cultural background was in such contrast to her perspective when she first came in to see me. The exploration of sexual stereotyping surrounding the rape and the ethnic studies class seemed to have helped her to evaluate and change her feelings about being Asian and Chinese. I wondered aloud whether her having a relationship with me, an Asian American female, also contributed to that change.

ELIZABETH: Sometimes, I wish you were my mom.

She began to cry and I reached out and held her hand. I gave her a hug. She continued to stay with her feelings as we sat together in silence. We then talked about object relations theory in a way that she could understand.

THERAPIST: Someday soon, for example, you will leave for Hong Kong or to graduate school and you will not see me. We will say good-bye. However, I will always be with you on another level. I will be in some part of your heart and you will know that I am with you. You will carry me with you wherever you go.

Elizabeth then asked me if I thought she would be a good mother. I told her that I thought that she already had experiences mothering her sister. I related that she would be a good mother especially if she has a positive relationship with her partner in which she continued to get the kind of emotional support she needs. If not, she may end up feeling angry and resentful towards her child. This was in direct contrast to her earlier presentation, during which she expressed negative feelings about being in a romantic relationship or having children.

This was one of our final sessions together before the school year ended. Although Elizabeth still had much to work through, given her history of betrayal and abuse, I believe that her dialogue illustrates genuine movement, growth, and resilience. I felt strongly that she had a much brighter future ahead of her and was grateful for the way in which she had enriched my life and experiences as a therapist.

References

Ageton, S. (1979). *Sexual assault among adolescents: A national study (final report)*. Rockville, MD: National Institute of Mental Health.

American Psychiatric Association. (1994). *Diagnostic and statistical manual of mental disorders* (4th ed.). Washington, DC: Author.

Atkinson, D. R., Thompson, C. E., & Grant, S. K. (1993). A three dimensional model for counseling racial/ethnic minorities. *The Counseling Psychologist, 21,* 257–277.

Bart, P. B., & O'Brien, P. H. (1985). *Stopping rape: Successful survival strategies.* Elmsford: Pergamon Press.

Bower, S. A., & Bower, G. H. (1976). *Asserting yourself.* Menlo Park: Addison-Wesley.

Burgess, A. W., & Holmstrom, L. L. (1974). Against rape. *The American Journal of Psychiatry, 131,* 981–986.

Chandler, T. A., Shama, D. D., Wolf, F. M., & Planchard, S. K. (1981). Multiattributional causality: a five cross-national study. *Journal of Cross-Cultural Psychology, 12,* 207–221.

Department of Public Safety. (1994). *Analysis of crime and police activity, City of Eugene, Oregon.* Eugene, OR: Author.

Holaday, M., Leach, M., & Davidson, M. (1994). Multicultural counseling and intrapersonal value conflict: A case study. *Counseling and Values, 38*(2), 136–142.

Hsieh, T., Shybut, J., & Lotsof, E. (1967). Internal versus external control and ethnic group membership: A cross cultural comparison. *Journal of Consulting Psychology, 33,* 122–124.

Ichikawa, F. V. (1989). Japanese children's self-concepts and beliefs about academic achievement. *Dissertation Abstracts International, 49*(7-B).

Martin, L. C. (1992). *A life without fear.* Nashville: Rutledge Hill Press.

McLoed, B. (1986). The Oriental Express. *Psychology Today, 20,* 565–570.

Prince, J. S., Miller, T. K., & Winston, R. B. (1977). *Student developmental task inventory guidelines.* Athens, Georgia: Student Development Associates.

Sexual Assault Support Services. (1993). *Annual report 1991–1993.* Eugene, Oregon: Author.

Shotland, R. L., & Goodstein, L. (1983). Just because she doesn't want to doesn't mean it's rape: An experimentally based causal model of the perception of rape in a dating situation. *Social Psychology Quarterly, 46*(3), 220–232.

Sue, D. W., & Sue, D. (1990). *Counseling the culturally different: Theory and Practice* (3rd ed.). New York: Wiley.

Sue, S. (1976). Conceptions of mental illness among Asian- and Caucasian-American students. *Psychological Reports, 38,* 583–592.

Sue, S., & Morishima, J. K. (1982). *The mental health of Asian Americans.* San Francisco: Jossey-Bass.

Sue, S., & Zane, N. (1987). The role of culture and cultural techniques in psychotherapy: A critique and reformulation. *American Psychologist, 42,* 37–45.

Tsui, P., & Schultz, G. L. (1985). Failure to report: When psychotherapeutic engagement fails in the treatment of Asian clients. *American Journal of Orthopsychiatry, 55,* 561–569.

Tyra, P. (1993). Older women: Victims of rape. *Journal of Gerontological Nursing, 19*(5), 7–12.

United States Commission on Civil Rights. (1992). *Civil rights issues facing Asian Americans in the 1990s.* Washington, DC: U.S. Government Printing Office.

Warshaw, R. (1988). *I never called it rape: The Ms. Report on recognizing, fighting, and surviving the date and acquaintance rape.* New York: Harper & Row.

Wong, H. Z. (1985). Training for mental health service providers to Southeast Asian refugees: Models, strategies, and curricula. In T. C. Owen (Ed.), *Southeast Asian mental health treatment, prevention, services, training, and research* (pp. 345–390). Washington, DC: National Institute of Mental Health.

Yoshioka, R. B., Tashima, N., Ichew, M., & Murase, K. (1981). *Mental health services for Pacific/Asian Americans.* San Francisco: Pacific American Mental Health Project.

SUGGESTIONS FOR FURTHER READING

Counseling of People of Color

Atkinson, D. R., Thompson, C. E., & Grant, S. K. (1993). A three dimensional model for counseling racial/ethnic minorities. *The Counseling Psychologist, 21,* 257–277. Validates the way that I have worked with students of color and helps therapists use nontraditional methods to work more effectively with peoples of color.

Pedersen, P. (1988). *A handbook for developing multicultural awareness.* Virginia: American Association for Counseling and Development.

Sue, D. W., & Sue, D. (1990). *Counseling the culturally different:* Theory and Practice (3rd. ed.). New York: Wiley.

Both are excellent in providing information about and suggestions on how to work with people of various cultures.

The Culture of Color

Takaki, R. (1989). *Strangers from a different shore: A history of Asian Americans.* New York: Penguin Books. If one is going to treat Asian Americans or other peoples of color, one must know of their history and experiences in America. A history, not from a Eurocentric point of view, has rarely been included in the curricula. This one is an excellent start.

Psychological Issues in Chinese-American Children

Sue, D., Sue, D. W., & Sue, D. M. (1983). Psychological development of Chinese-American children. In G. J. Powell (Ed.), & J. Yamamoto, A. Romero, & A. Morales (Assoc. Eds.), *The psychosocial development of minority group children.* New York: Brunner/Mazel.

Sue, S., & Chin, R. (1983). The mental health of Chinese-American children: Stressors and resources. In G. J. Powell, J. Yamamoto, A. Romero, & A. Morales (Eds.), *The psychosocial development of minority group children.* New York: Brunner/Mazel.

Relational Aspects of Psychotherapy

Kell, B. L., & Mueller, W. (1966). *Impact and change.* Englewood Cliffs, NJ: Prentice-Hall.

Teyber, E. (1996). *Interpersonal process in psychotherapy* (3rd ed.). Pacific Grove, CA: Brooks-Cole.

The relational aspects of psychotherapy and the importance of the interpersonal process in therapy. Both are excellent.

Chapter 11

Group Therapy With Seriously Emotionally Disturbed Children

Case Illustration of Sam: A 9-Year-Old African American Child

Cassandra N. Nichols, M.S.

The Disorder

Sam was a 9-year-old African American fourth-grader in a private education-treatment facility for children and adolescents. His case file indicated that he had been given multiple diagnoses since his kindergarten year, including Attention Deficit/Hyperactivity Disorder, Oppositional Defiant Disorder, a learning disability, and early signs of psychosis. Based on these problems and his poor school performance and adjustment, Sam was designated as a Severely Emotionally Disturbed (SED) child (Morgan, 1989). It was this education-based designation that warranted his placement at the facility where I worked as his therapist and case manager.

One of my early recollections of Sam was a morning when I was called by the school principal, who had found him attempting to peel off the skin on his arm. In this early incident, Sam's needs, his feelings toward significant others, the impact of race on his life was evident. Sam had decided that because I was "such a nice and pretty lady who don't never get mad when I do such bad things" and because I had "no kids to take care of me when men come around," he was going to "be my son". The only impediment in his mind to this scenario was a racial one: I was White and he was Black.

Sam, like other children, was reenacting his major conflicts with significant persons in his life with me. And he was doing this, not in a symbolic or indirect transference mode, but in a more overt way. This process, which I have come to observe repeatedly in children in treatment facilities, goes beyond merely *wishing* that an important authority figure in their life were the nurturing and loving parent they never had and frequently involves telling a teacher, social worker, or therapist directly that they want him or her to become their parent. In this, as in other therapy settings, this reenactment of relationships with primary attachment figures ideally allows the therapist to use the therapeutic relationship as a vehicle for change. By examining the discrepancy between what the child believes is an ideal parent (i.e., an emotionally responsive therapist who can provide safe boundaries and secure limits) and the child's experience of his or her own parents, the therapist is able to work to heal problems within the family.

For troubled ethnic minority children, however, this transference can take on an additional dimension. Specifically, for children of color working with a Caucasian therapist, this transference may include his or her awareness of racial or prejudicial treatment of ethnic minorities by some members of the dominant culture. These children may come to believe that in order to be loved or be taken care of by the therapist they need to become more "White." For other children, however, the opposite may occur and they may mistrust the therapist and reject any attempts to establish a relationship. Therapists must then be sensitive to the overlay of race on the relationship and specifically ask the child how he or she feels about working with a therapist of another race. The therapist must also inquire about what the child's experiences have been with individuals of the therapist's racial group. In doing so, therapists can address more directly the child's feelings or concerns and provide the child with a new, positive, and appropriate experience. In this process, issues of identity can be addressed, and therapists can help the children take pride in their differences and uniqueness.

Sam's early statements also suggested that he saw his role in his family setting as that of "protector." This alerted me to the possibility that the issue of protection of self and significant others was central for Sam, and, like race, was going to be a central theme in our work together.

This chapter describes Sam's treatment in group therapy for latency-aged acting-out boys. The group consisted of boys from various ethnic and cultural backgrounds. My challenge was to establish my credibility as a Caucasian female therapist and provide healing, corrective experiences for them.

I will first discuss the clinical features of group therapy with children. Because an integral part of my therapy with Sam was embedded within a multicultural context, I will also briefly present an overview of some of the relevant sociocultural factors to consider when working with African American children. Finally, I will discuss Sam's case in terms of its relevant developmental history and presenting problems, case conceptualization, treatment plans, and intervention strategy, including therapeutic process and termination issues.

Group Therapy (Clinical Features)

For the past five decades, group therapy has gained acceptance as one of the most corrective psychological modalities for children (Schiffer, 1984). The group approach is seen as particularly effective for latency-aged children because they are developmentally in a phase when socialization and peer relationships become a prominent feature of their lives. Peer relationships exert an enormous influence on their prosocial or problematic behavior. As such, peer relationships act as a *major psychosocial pathway* toward the development of the child's identity and self-concept (Schaefer, Johnson, and Wherry, 1982). Because children's personalities are so strongly developed within social contexts, group therapy can serve as the arena for the examination and modification of both social and personal problems.

Thus, group therapy may well be the preferred mode of treatment for many children. This may be especially true for children who come from multicultural settings. First, many minority cultures have traditionally depended upon a variety of group activities to bring families, clans, and tribal groups together for cultural, religious, and social activities. As a result, the development of ethnic minority children is often embedded in an interdependent or cooperative orientation (Ho, 1992). Group therapy, therefore, may represent an extension of this relational orientation frequently observed in ethnic minorities. Second, groups consisting of individuals from diverse ethnic backgrounds may permit members to value differences, learn alternative communication styles, and practice a variety of problem-solving and coping strategies (McKinley, 1991). These factors may have additional significance for children who live or go to school in ethnically diverse environments where learning how to cohabitate cooperatively becomes increasingly important. Group therapy may be a safe arena for examining and appreciating the similarities and differences of each ethnic group and may help children begin to "find their place in the world" with others. However, despite the benefits of group therapy, a child's appropriateness for this interpersonal encounter has to be assessed and pivots in part on his or her attachment history.

In order to benefit from group therapy, a child must have formed in his or her early history a significant attachment with a primary caretaker. Attachment is a necessary precondition for group therapy because of the particular social nature of this treatment modality. More specifically, group therapy is an effective therapeutic approach because it serves as an interpersonal context in which children can experiment with and practice new relational behaviors (Yalom, 1985). However, children will not be appropriate for group therapy if they are unmotivated or unable to establish relationships, since some basic level of reciprocity is necessary for this process to be effective. It is also helpful if by the time the child reaches latency, he or she has had a history of forming an attachment to some type of social group (e.g., sports team, Scouts, or other organized club). In sum, group therapy is appropriate and effective for children who are able to trust others and participate in a reciprocal helping relationship.

Due to the extended nature of many ethnic minority families, children of color are often able to bond with other family members if their biological parents are not readily available. The extended kinship patterns and flexibility in caretaking roles within minority families makes it possible for a variety of figures in the child's life to perform the nurturing and caretaking functions in the absence of the child's natural parents. Thus, in the context of this heritage of collective development, ethnic minority children are very likely to have a prior sense of belonging to some group or affiliative network of people.

Overview of Sociocultural Factors

In order to have an understanding of the social and psychological implications of working with an ethnically heterogeneous therapy group, therapists must have some knowledge of and familiarity with the cultural values and expectations of the children and their families. Although therapists must consider the ethnic and cultural backgrounds of each of the children in a group being formed, I will focus only on Sam's African American sociocultural concerns.

FAMILY STRUCTURE

The family structure for many ethnic minority individuals is established within a deep relational and cultural context (Sue & Sue, 1990). For most African American families, this structure is based upon strong kinship ties that may extend beyond the immediate family to include extended family and members of the community. Involvement in church and a strong commitment to religious and spiritual values are frequently characteristic of this kinship foundation. Role flexibility within the family enables members to share a degree of versatility in traditionally expressive (e.g., childrearing) and instrumental (e.g., "bread winner") tasks (See Gibbs, Huang, et al., 1989). As a component to this flexibility in family roles, older children may be expected to take on the responsibility of caring for younger children or to contribute economically to the family. This may be especially true if the family is, like many ethnic minority families in the United States, economically disadvantaged or impoverished. Thus, European norms of developing an independent or highly autonomous sense of self, separate from one's community, may not be a culturally consonant goal for African American children.

According to the U.S. Census Bureau (1987) nearly half (42.7%) of all African American children under 18 years old lived in families below the poverty line. A large majority of these families were characterized by poor financial conditions, residential segregation, and high unemployment rates. These factors place excessive demands on parents who may have to devote much energy toward their economic survival, diminishing their ability (in time or energy) to be with their children. For single-parent or teenage-parent families, these demands become extreme. Although other family members may be able to serve as helpers or buffers, this is less true of those who have had to relocate frequently and those who are isolated or estranged from their families or community.

African American families have the dual responsibility of socializing their children to operate within their culture and its values as well as within the broader culture, which has often been prejudicial and discriminatory. While the task of establishing a positive identity is challenging for all children, it is more so for African American children, who have to operate within their own *and* the predominantly White culture. This difficulty is compounded for troubled families by lack of appropriate role models.

It is important for therapists to realize that the sociopolitical experiences of African Americans, which includes racial discrimination and the history of slavery, impacts the willingness of many to use mental health services. Those who do seek therapy often go only if in crisis and prefer African American therapists (Sue & Sue, 1990). Furthermore, many drop out prematurely (Sue & Sue, 1977). The reasons for this are myriad and may include lack of credibility on the part of some therapists who fail to take into account the client's sociocultural background when conducting assessments and developing interventions (Sue & Zane, 1987).

THERAPIST

In order for Caucasian therapists to work with ethnic minority children, it is necessary that they have the flexibility or openness to respect and enter into differing worldviews. For Caucasian therapists, as well as therapists of all racial groups, it is critical that they explore and closely examine their own worldviews and the factors that have contributed to these views. Only then can they decenter and enter the child's subjective worldview. This process will also facilitate therapist's development of a *non-defensive* therapy stance, which invites children to express their similarities and differences, as well as agreements and disagreements, more openly. In this way, therapists will be able to encourage children to operate using more flexible coping strategies and will help them develop openness to differing viewpoints. Clearly, there is no distinct set of therapeutic "techniques" that can be applied to children of different ethnic groups. It is necessary for therapists to be able to incorporate into their own value system alternative definitions and interpretations of family constitution, identity, and normative behavior. In working with African American children for example, therapists would need to take into account the influence of kinship and family. It would also be important for the therapist to understand the impact of racism, poverty, and acculturation on the family, its structure and functioning, and on the child's emotional well-being.

CASE ILLUSTRATION

Presenting Problem

Sam began to receive therapy services shortly after he was designated by his school's psychologist as Severely Emotionally Disturbed (SED) (Hagborg & Konigsberg, 1991; Morgan, 1989; Trupin, Forsyth-Stephens, & Low, 1991). The SED label is not a psychological diagnosis but is a loosely defined "umbrella" diagnosis used mostly by school administrators to cover a variety of psychological problems impacting the child's educational adjustment. These problems are believed to be *emotional* in nature and may include such psychological diagnoses as Attention Deficit/Hyperactivity Disorder, Conduct Disorder, Oppositional Defiant Disorder, mood disorders, elimination disorders, academic skills disorders, any of the pervasive developmental disorders, as well as development delays. Common for all children diagnosed as SED is a history of aggression or physical acting out at school.

Sam, in addition to having been diagnosed at different times with Attention Deficit/Hyperactivity Disorder, Oppositional Defiant disorder, a learning disability, and early signs of psychosis, had been a victim of physical and emotional abuse and lived in a neighborhood where gang activity and drug abuse were rampant.

Children diagnosed as SED by a school psychologist are usually first placed in a special classroom within their public school district for children with similar problems. If the child is unable to improve in such a classroom, the school district will then refer him or her to a specialized and highly-structured treatment facility for education and therapy services. Most programs for SED children (such as our facility) have small classroom sizes (six to eight children per classroom) that almost always operate according to a behavior modification model. The personal therapy model, however, is at the discretion of the therapist.

With Sam and the other children, I used an interpersonal process model of treatment (Strupp & Binder, 1988; Kiesler & Van Denburg, 1993) that incorporated sensitivity to ethnic and cultural socialization norms. From this perspective, a child's behavior can be best understood by attending to the basic relational patterns he or she repeatedly establishes with others. Presenting problems or symptoms represent the interpersonal strategies children have adopted to cope with the pain engendered by certain problematic relational scenarios that they recreated over and over with important care-givers. In treatment, the therapist tries to help the child recognize the mal-adaptive relational pattern that the child is beginning to create with the therapist and other children, and then try to help the child enact new and more satisfying solutions that do not follow the old scripts or interpersonal patterns. The process of providing a "corrective emotional experience" or real life experience of change will be discussed further throughout the un-folding of this chapter (Alexander, 1963).

Although placed within a fourth grade classroom, Sam's grades and achievement scores indicated he was far below the fourth-grade level in most academic areas. This did not appear to be due to a deficit in intellec-tual capacity but rather, to the lack of time Sam had actually spent in the classroom over the past 4 years. He began kindergarten, like most children, at age 5, but half way through the school year he began to exhibit aggressive behavior (i.e., fighting with other children, breaking classroom toys) and appeared easily distracted in comparison to his classmates (e.g., Sam often became bored during class and would daydream or pick on the other chil-dren). He was promoted to the first grade; but, according to school records, he was often tardy or missed several days of school at a time. Continued fighting in the classroom resulted in numerous suspensions for his aggres-sive behavior. By the second grade, he was attending only a half-day of school due to his problematic behavior. Teachers continued to promote him (rather than holding him back for his subsequent academic problems) be-cause no teacher wanted him to repeat the year in his or her classroom. Due to his oppositional and often aggressive behavior, teachers were frustrated and sometimes frightened of Sam. By the third grade he was placed in a classroom for SED children in the same district. His clinical presentation was similar to that observed in children diagnosed with Conduct Disorder. However, due to the significant impact of his psychological problems on his academic performance and school adjustment, coupled with a probable learning disorder, Sam was designated as SED, which allowed him to receive special academic and psychological services paid for by his school district. Once in the SED class, Sam did not last long. His aggressive behavior contin-ued and he began to physically threaten a teacher's aide. His new teacher was unable to control his behavior, so Sam was referred to our facility. When Sam started school at his new placement, he was angry, withdrawn, and assaultive toward another student on his first day.

CLIENT DESCRIPTION

Sam was an average-sized, handsome, 9-year-old African American child with a dark, warm complexion. His hair was cut in a style popular for young males—shaved short and close to the scalp with a flat top and a small braided and beaded ponytail in back. He wore a small gold hoop earring in his left ear and a large gold chain around his neck with a BMW medallion.

Like many urban boys in the early 1990s, Sam wore baggy denim pants many sizes too big and cinched at the waist with a belt, a large T-shirt nearly down to his knees, and expensive high-top sneakers.

When brought to my office for the first time, he swaggered in, immediately sat down, and initially refused to talk to me. Rather than attempting to engage him, I told Sam I was willing to hang out with him whenever he was ready and, if he chose, he could help me decorate the bulletin board in my office. After about 5 minutes of sitting with an immobile granite-like expression on his face, Sam got up and silently handed me pieces of construction paper while I stapled. Before our session was over, Sam pointed out that I was not much taller than he (I am a little over five feet tall). He smiled, and his entire face lit up. I surmised that my physical size and nonchalant style reduced any sense of judgment or threat from me he may have anticipated. Sam's previous experiences with "authority" figures probably taught him to be wary, and had I forced him to engage with me, he would likely have responded with a more angry and hostile stance. My plan for establishing new relational patterns or corrective emotional experiences was to develop a relationship with Sam that minimized hierarchy and authority but communicated instead respect and cooperation.

Sam's understanding of why he was placed in our facility was simply that he was a "bad child." He saw himself as "not good" like the other children and was happiest when he was attending school on a half-day schedule. That way, he was able to play most of the day without adult involvement or constraints. He let me know immediately that his plan was to "get into lots of trouble" at the facility, so the school "would have to place me back on half-day." Although the principal told him from the outset that half-days were not an option at our school, Sam was out to prove him wrong.

SOCIAL CONTEXT

Sam's parents, Morris and Chantae, were 16 years old when Sam was born. At that time, both parents dropped out of high school, without returning to earn a diploma or GED. His parents never married and remained together only sporadically in the subsequent years. Chantae's own mother was also 16 years old when she gave birth to her daughter, and Chantae had little contact with her biological father. Chantae was raised by her maternal grandparents, Raymond and Annie, after her mother moved to Tennessee with her new husband (not Chantae's father) when Chantae was 6 years old. Raymond and Annie had three other children living at home (two daughters and one son), who were 10 to 15 years older than Chantae. Raymond died when Chantae was 10 years old. Chantae continued to live with her grandmother until Sam was 5 years old. Then she and Sam moved in with Chantae's boyfriend, Luke. Chantae had an unpredictable relationship with Luke—sometimes going with him and at other times returning to Morris, Sam's biological father. For the next two years, Chantae and Sam moved back and forth between Luke's house, her grandmother's house, and Morris's parents, depending upon the status of Chantae's relationships. During that time, Chantae often left Sam for days or even weeks with her grandparents or with Morris and his parents.

Chantae never worked and supported herself and Sam with Welfare and Aid to Dependent Children. During her late teenage years, she got involved in illicit drug use, and by the time Sam had started school at our facility, Chantae was rumored to be on crack cocaine. Morris worked mostly odd construction jobs and had a police record since his adolescence for petty theft, carrying a weapon, and noncompliance in school. He was arrested for armed robbery two years prior to Sam's enrollment at our facility for holding up a convenience store. Sam was found asleep in the back seat of his father's car in front of the convenience store at the time. Morris was placed in the local state penitentiary and was due to be paroled sometime in the next year.

Over the past year, Chantae began leaving Sam with Annie for longer periods of time and was often gone for months at a stretch. She had a child, fathered by Luke, named Yazmine who was 11 months old when Sam started school. School records with attached Child Protective Services (CPS) reports indicated that his mother had been accused of physically abusing Sam on numerous occasions. For instance, records indicated that he came to school on a number of occasions with untreated welts and cuts. Records did not indicate any sexual abuse. As a result of the abuse and Chantae's inconsistent living situation, Annie was given primary parental custody over him (although Chantae was still able to live or visit unsupervised in the home). A social worker was assigned to Sam and visited the home once a month.

Although Sam reported a close relationship with his great-grandmother, he also felt very protective toward his mother and baby sister. He often worried about his mother's health and welfare and believed that once his father was released from prison, the two would get married so "we could all be a family". Although Annie loved her great-grandson, she was in her mid-60s and, over the past two years, had more difficulty controlling Sam's behavior. She, therefore, did not discipline him much. Sam was never assaultive towards her or any of his aunts who lived at home, but, on occasion, would run away for hours at a time when angry. His family reported that Sam was not involved with any neighborhood gangs or drug use, but they were worried that he may soon become associated with "the wrong kind of people". His uncle Markus had been a stable male figure in Sam's life up until Sam was 6 years old. Then, Markus joined the army, however, and had contact with his nephew only a couple times a year after that.

Sam had not been successful academically in school, but this appeared to be due to his family turmoil rather than due to an intellectual incapacity. Within the first week at our facility, Sam began to demonstrate a certain amount of street smarts. For example, his new teacher reported that while accompanying Sam to recess on the first day, another teacher was in the hallway counting the children's lunch money. Without stopping or changing his

walking stride, Sam was able to glance once at the teacher's hands and report how much money she was holding in one and five dollar bills. On the
next day, he was caught breaking into the classroom computer's security
lock in order to play Nintendo while he was supposed to be practicing his
multiplication tables on the computer.

He was also well-coordinated and enjoyed sports, especially basketball.
Even though he was initially determined to get expelled from the facility,
underneath it all Sam had a bright and sociable nature. As a result, the staff
felt positive about his appropriateness for our program and his potential for
future success.

Initial Session

INDIVIDUAL THERAPY

Before placing Sam in group therapy, I saw him for four individual therapy
sessions. When working with children, especially in a treatment facility, utilizing both individual and group therapy simultaneously can allow the therapist to work with the same issues on a personal one-to-one basis as well as in
a social arena. Usually, one form of therapy serves as the primary mode
while the other is secondary. In Sam's case, I wanted to use group therapy as
the primary treatment, with our individual sessions as a way to process relevant issues from the group. First, though, I needed to establish a working alliance with him.

Sue and Zane (1987) discuss the importance for the therapist to demonstrate a degree of credibility when working with ethnic minority children.
This achieved credibility refers to the child's perception of the therapist as
an effective and trustworthy person who wishes a positive and successful
therapeutic outcome for him or her. For ethnic minority clients, this type of
credibility can best be accomplished by the therapist's interpersonal skills
and the extent to which he or she can convey to the child nonjudgmental
acceptance. Given the frequent negative encounters minority children who
end up in therapy typically have had with authority figures prior to therapy,
they are appropriately skeptical of the therapist's ability and desire to be
helpful. A therapist who acts in a strict authoritarian fashion may not be
able to formulate a working alliance because this relational style will only
dynamically replay the experiences the child has had leading up to treatment. At the same time, they need structure and a clear sense of expectations within a warm and caring relationship. In other words, the treatment
goals and techniques are secondary to the quality of the therapeutic relationship. Beyond the words spoken, the therapist's tone of voice and body
language must convey respect and interest.

Although many children may be unaware of the role of the therapist,
Sam (due to his experiences with the school and social work system) had
some type of idea of what a therapist does. To him a therapist was a person

who "meddles in your family stuff" but at the same time "could be fun." During our individual sessions together, it appeared that my initial credibility was going to be based upon whether or not the "fun" was worth the "meddling."

In my office I have only a few rules: no taking or breaking my toys and the sand needs to stay in the sandbox. Although the treatment facility followed a strict behavior modification program, therapy was not contingent upon the children's behavior. Therapy, therefore, was something separate from their treatment plan in school and, as a result, most children enjoyed the refuge of the therapy hour. Furthermore, my simple rules made sense to the children, and I had relatively few behavioral problems.

Occasionally, however, the children engaged in testing, which usually had a physically threatening quality to it. With Sam, this occurred at the end of our second session together. Sam and I had spent the session playing basketball with my small indoor hoop and sponge-like basketball. I typically remove my shoes and jewelry when I play. When I went to find my watch at the end of our time, it was not where I had placed it. Sam glared at me, fists clenched. "You think I took it" he yelled, "You're just like the rest of them." I responded with "Actually Sam, I was hoping you would help me look for it, it may have fallen." Sam glared at me for what seemed like an eternity. The tension in the room had suddenly escalated and it seemed as though Sam was ready to pounce. His breathing had become more rapid and his jaw quivered slightly. I began to look under a chair when Sam put his hand in his trouser pocket at threw the watch at me, "Take your stinking thing," he said. I had not accused Sam of taking it and was surprised that, having taken it, he was willing to relinquish it so quickly. Although his fury was on the surface, he also seemed close to tears. I believed Sam was testing me to see if I would become angry and assume the authoritarian, punitive, and rejecting stance he had so often endured. It made sense to me that he, like other children in his circumstances, was trying to figure out this relationship and how we would interact.

THERAPIST: Thanks for giving it back to me Sam.

CLIENT: And? (continuing to glare and clench his fists).

THERAPIST: I don't like having my things taken without permission, but I hope you and I can work it out.

CLIENT: That's it?

THERAPIST: What do you mean, Sam?

CLIENT: You're not going to take me to the principal or something?

THERAPIST: No Sam. I think this one we can work out together. There is one more thing. I did not like it when you threw it at me. But I do appreciate having it back. If there is something in this office that you would like to have, let's talk about it first, okay?

CLIENT: (Sam unclenched his fist and seemed much calmer) Well don't you be so stupid and leave things like that around. Others might not give them back so easily.

In this episode, I was aware of how easily our interaction could have escalated into a power struggle. I wanted to convey to Sam that there were limits (stealing was not OK; throwing things at me was unacceptable) but do this in a way that was not rejecting or punitive. I also hoped that I could begin giving Sam a different language for communicating his wants (i.e., he could ask) and begin modeling for him how to convey feelings without acting them out (in this instance, by telling him that I didn't like the watch being thrown at me, yet did this calmly without anger).

Sam and I began to establish a collaborative relationship. Together we made up elaborate basketball rules as we played in the office—rules necessary for getting around the desk, taking equal turns, and the number of points allotted for certain types of baskets. As we played together I tried to demonstrate to Sam that I valued his input on how we spent our time together and that I was willing to invest my energy to learn what he enjoyed. This process went a very long way in helping us establish a caring, reciprocal working relationship. During this time, Sam was beginning to settle into school, had taken a leadership role in the classroom (which at times had a negative quality, including provoking fights between groups of children), and had discovered that the facility was one place he could not "get kicked out of." Sam appeared to look forward to our time together, and I knew our relationship was off to a good start when, as I was returning Sam to his classroom he stopped, turned to me and said, "You play pretty good basketball for a short White woman!"

Sam and I had one other encounter that involved threat during the early phase of therapy. On a morning before one of our individual sessions, Sam had a verbal altercation with another child and, as a result, was sent to time-out. By the time he came to my office he was sullen and withdrawn. He was uncommunicative and angry during most of the session, so I allowed him to play mostly by himself in my office as a way to provide him with the space he needed to calm down. On the way out of our session he ran into Ron, the child he had argued with that morning. In front of my office door (with me unintentionally caught standing between the two) the two boys began to glare at one another, clenching their fists. The tension was intense and the probability of a physical altercation was high. I knew I needed some way to defuse the tension and give them each an out. Speaking in a gentle, but firm voice:

THERAPIST: The two of you had a difficult morning together. . . .

SAM: Yeah. (moving closer to Ron, seeming ready to attack) And I spent a half an hour in time-out because of this asshole. He's not going to get away with it. (Sam was now pushing against me since I was standing between him and Ron.)

RON: Man, you are *nothing*. (He too seemed ready to attack.) I have no problem making something out of this with you!

THERAPIST: Yes, you could fight and someone will get hurt. Sam, I'd like it if you would take off on that side of the hall (nodding to my left) and

Ron, I'd like it if you would take off on that side of the hall (nodding to the right).

SAM: I'm not running from him!

THERAPIST: No, that not what I'm saying. I'm asking both of you to leave at the same time to find a place—any place away from each other—and cool down. I don't care where it is—just somewhere quiet on the school grounds. You two can fight and *both* get into trouble and be losers, *or,* you can go your separate ways and *both* be winners.

I slowly backed away from the boys. Sam and Ron continued to glare at one another, but they slowly backed away also. They walked away in the opposite direction from one another down the hallway, although they continued to peer back at each other. Sam found a place under the stairway where he sat for a half an hour before he returned to class on his own. I made it a point to praise each child individually before they went home that day for making the appropriate choice not to fight under such tempting circumstances. I was also silently relieved that I did not get into a power struggle that I surely would have lost.

These two examples are intended to portray some of the realities of working with children like Sam. They are often angry and hostile but there is generally an element of self-preservation in that stance. Sam's life experiences had taught him to be vigilant. Furthermore, he didn't know whom he could trust. In his home and neighborhood, a tough guy exterior was a realistic survival stance. His experiences with authority figures in school and other settings had also been disempowering, further validating his need for a self-protective posture. He had, for example, experienced criticism and denigration and was labeled a troubled child with "serious emotional disturbances." The reality was that underneath this hostile and sullen stance was a young child trying to cope with deep emotional wounds, lacking the language needed to manage his deep pain. I knew that I needed to find a way to respond to his pain but, more importantly, to promote his sense of *efficacy* in new and more adaptive ways.

GROUP

The group was composed of five 8- and 9-year-old boys, each of whom I had seen approximately four times in prior individual sessions. All of the boys had common presenting problems involving acting-out behavior and noncompliance in school. According to the *DSM-IV* (American Psychiatric Association, 1994), these children would have received diagnoses such as Conduct Disorder, Oppositional Defiant Disorder, Dysthymia, Post-Traumatic Stress Disorder, or Attention Deficit/Hyperactivity Disorder, in addition to a learning disorder. Because these psychological diagnoses had so profoundly affected their academic performance and school adjustment, they were given the education system-based designation of SED, which then justified their need for special academic and psychological services to be paid for by their school districts.

Although group memberships usually consists of six to eight members, given the aggressive behavior of these children, I decided on a smaller, more manageable group. This way, structure and limit setting was easier to establish. All of the children had exhibited periods of time (ranging from a few days to two weeks) in which they were not aggressive towards others in class. This indicated to me that they had at least enough ego strength and self-control to inhibit their acting-out behavior for a reasonable length of time to participate in the group.

Rather than including only a homogeneous ethnic membership, the group was composed of children from different ethnic groups. This allowed the children to work on their own personal issues in a positive interracial social context that was reflective of the ethnic minority make-up of the facility and most of their neighborhoods. The group was composed of two African American boys (Sam and Donnie), two Hispanic boys (Jose and Manuel, both of Mexican descent), and one Caucasian boy (Paul) who lived in a mixed Hispanic and Caucasian neighborhood. Although both of the Hispanic children spoke Spanish, they were born in the United States and spoke fluent English. The challenge at the beginning of group therapy was to make overt any racial tension between the children while developing rules about how this tension was going to be handled by myself and the group participants in future sessions.

FIRST GROUP CONTACT

I knew before our group met that these children often played cooperatively together during recess and in classroom activities. When anger erupted, however, the children would often use racial slurs against one another. In order to develop a comfortable and cohesive environment in which the children could begin seeing the influence of the group as positive and desirable, we were going to have to discuss any possible racial tension from the onset. During our initial group session, Sam gave us the opportunity to begin this discussion. He appeared angry because he believed that I was no longer going to see him in individual sessions. Although we had discussed our schedule beforehand, that is, that he, like the other children, was going to be seen in individual as well as group sessions, Sam believed that my time was going to be taken away from him. Shortly after the children assembled in my office, Jose picked up the basketball that Sam and I had frequently used.

SAM: Hey! You can't play with that!

JOSE: Who says? (passing the ball to Paul)

SAM: I say, and I'm bigger than you!

JOSE: It doesn't belong to *you*, it belongs to Ms. Cassie—being bigger doesn't matter.

SAM: Listen you dumb wetback, when *I'm* here the basketball is mine 'cause I'm a better player, so put it back!

At hearing "dumb wetback," Jose and Manuel looked at one another and clenched their fists. In order to diffuse the tension and potential fight, I began to set immediate limits.

THERAPIST: (making eye contact with each of them and speaking in a firm but soothing voice) Sam, Jose, Manuel, Donnie, and Paul, I need you to sit down right where you are.

Sam, take a deep breath. What just happened?

SAM: (arms folded and looking away) Jose was using *our* basketball, the one we use for our games. I think you should keep it for me and not allow anyone else to play with it.

THERAPIST: I understand that you like to play basketball, and I enjoy the special time that we spend together. I wonder if you are worried that perhaps if Jose or someone else is in my office with us for this group, maybe you or I will not be able to spend any more time together?

SAM: (Still silent but turns his face briefly toward me.)

THERAPIST: There are some things that we need to talk about, but first, let's plan out our schedules for when I will be seeing each of you alone—just like we all talked about before. I'll get out our appointment cards, and with each of you, we will come up with a time that we will meet—just you and I together.

The boys' heated discussion was significant for all of them, but especially for Sam. He wanted reassurance that our time together was special and that we were going to continue our relationship on a one-to-one basis. Realizing that Sam wanted to save face with the other boys and because our relationship was rather new (as was my relationship with all of the boys), I did not want to delve deeper into this issue with him right then. Rather, I wanted him to feel heard by me and I wanted to assuage his concern. In order to maintain an atmosphere of collaboration with the children, I keep appointment cards in my desk, and together we come up with a time that works best for therapy appointments. Most children seem to appreciate the grown-up nature of keeping an appointment card and are able to tape them to their classroom desk to remind them of their therapy time. I went around the room, kneeled down, and faced each child to make our appointment. In this way, each boy had the opportunity to feel special and see that no other child was given more individual time than the others. Sam and Jose both appeared appeased.

Next, I wanted to address the racial name calling and need for group therapy rules.

THERAPIST: (getting out a large sheet of butcher paper and tacking it to the wall) Now that that has been settled, let's talk about some rules. I need all of you to help in coming up with some important rules for our group so no one feels left out or feels like others have done something to make him angry. Sometimes when we are mad at other people we call them names. What are some names that we might call people when we are angry? If you think a name is too bad to say out loud, you can spell it out for us. I'll write it on this paper.

PAUL: Um, Jerk, waste-case, dweeb . . . .

SAM: Ugly, bagger, retard, fool . . . .

JOSE: Stupid, goob, asshole . . . .

The boys continued coming up with all of the derogatory names they could think of, first with slang terms, then mild profanity and Spanish curse words (which all the children knew). By the end, the boys were having fun together coming up with their own funny combinations such a "snot-breath" and "nose-hair-head." Now, racial slurs needed to be addressed.

THERAPIST: What great imaginations you all have! Sometimes though, when a person *really* wants to get someone mad or in order to *really* hurt their feelings, he might call them a bad word that has to do with their race or color or religion. We're going to make the same word list, but this time we're going to do it a little bit differently. Jose and Manual, I want you two to come up with a list of hurtful words that someone might call you because you are Mexican American. Donnie and Sam, a list of hurtful words someone might call you because you are African American. And Paul, a list of bad words directed at you because you are White. No group can help out the other group.

At first the children were hesitant about this exercise, but once we got started, we were able to fill up the other side of the paper with many possible racial slurs and their combinations. Since all the boys had attended racially mixed schools, none of these words were new or surprising to them. What made it a different experience for them was that this time these words were discussed out in the open and in a nonangry, noncontemptuous, and nonthreatening way. In order to address this sensitive but important matter, I wanted to diffuse the heated quality of the subject.

THERAPIST: Sam, if someone called a White boy one of these words (pointing to my list of White slurs), how do you think he might feel?

SAM: Well, he might feel angry or dissed (disrespected).

THERAPIST: Yes, you're right. That is how he might feel. Manual, how do you think a Hispanic might feel if someone called him some of these words? (pointing)

MANUAL: He could feel hurt inside, maybe like he is different from other people or maybe that he has to do something, so no one will think he is a wuss (sissy).

Around the room I went, asking each boy to address the racial slurs of a child from a different ethnic minority group. No child had to address his own feelings about his own ethnic group or risk placing themselves on the line. The issue was addressed and together in a collaborative fashion we decided that our first rule was "No capping" (name calling). We took the paper off the wall, rolled it up, tied a ribbon around it, and placed it in my closet in case we ever needed to turn to it for future reference.

WORKING ALLIANCE

The relationship between therapist and client is a central feature of therapy. The effectiveness of the therapists interventions pivot on the quality of this relationship and the process enacted between therapist and client. It is necessary, in this relationship, for the therapist to be genuinely able to discover something of personal worth in the client and have the best of intentions for him or her. On the client's part, he or she must be motivated to change and trust that the therapist is willing and equally motivated to help in this change process. For ethnic minority children, the ability to form a working alliance may not simply be effected by the capacity to form interpersonal relationships; it may also be effected by the child's concept of the racial differences between them and by the therapist's ability to handle these differences. That is, a level collaboration may be influenced by the child's concept of the therapist's achieved *credibility* (i.e., effectiveness and trustworthiness) and ability to provide help in spite of any racial differences (Sue & Zane, 1987). Although I had no difficulty in genuinely *liking* Sam and seeing psychological strengths in him, I initially struggled with my own feelings of inadequacy around the issues of credibility and ability to help.

During the first few individual and group sessions with Sam, the beginning of a working alliance had been established. I had attempted to be nonjudgmental, and nonpunitive (e.g., when Sam took my watch), yet clear and firm in my rules and expectations (e.g., letting him know that taking without permission was not OK). I felt that Sam was beginning to recognize that this relationship would be different from other relationships. However, I began to struggle at times with my ability to handle our racial, cultural, and economic differences. Although intellectually I was able to separate myself from these social concerns, emotionally I felt overwhelmed at times with what appeared to be a vicious cycle for Sam of poverty and discrimination. My lower-middle-class upbringing was not easy, but, perhaps because of my status as a Caucasian or "majority" member of society, I was raised to believe in *hope*—or the expectation that as bad as life can be, circumstances can always get better, if you worked hard enough. I knew that I needed to explore whether Sam, given his life circumstance and negative experiences with the social and school system, had hope that good things could be part of his future, or that he had the efficacy to effect change or have an impact on his world.

Additionally, my culture ingrained within me the idea of upward mobility. My parents worked hard so I could economically surpass them, and, thereafter, it was expected that I would work hard to provide my own children with the opportunities I never received. I realized, however, that the economic and social odds against Sam were embedded in a sociopolitical context that made getting out of the inner-city neighborhood and upward mobility that much more challenging. I found myself wanting to protect Sam from his environment and what I saw as a menacing future. Interestingly, *Sam shared the same protective concern for me.* That is, he had his own desire to protect me from what he believed was my own inability to take care of myself. Based on my knowledge of Sam's history, I knew he felt he needed to protect the other women in his life (i.e., mother, great-grandmother, baby sister, aunts). I began to wonder if this role of protector was one of the arenas in which Sam felt some sense of importance and experienced a modicum of control. It thus became important to understand the genesis of this and its current function. I didn't want Sam to be in this parentified role with me and thereby reenact his developmental problems in therapy. At the same time, however, I wanted to change this thoughtfully without rejecting an important part of his identity or injuring his self-esteem or taking away one of the few tools he had for fashioning an attachment or, more poignantly, perhaps protecting himself from further physical abuse from his mother.

The following dialogue demonstrates how Sam's desire to protect me was played out. During one of the first few group sessions together, a few of the boys began to test the limits of the group. They spoke in low voices in the corner of my office, intentionally loud enough, though, for me to hear.

DONNIE: I don't want to be here or even in school today. Will someone run with me? Maybe to the arcade or something?

MANUEL: I'd run, but I've got a home visit this weekend, and I don't want a demotion in points. Maybe next week.

JUAN: I'll run. If we do it soon from this office, the hall monitors won't be able to get us right away, and we could be there for awhile and move on. This gringa can't stop us.

PAUL: I'll get food from her desk. Sam, you coming?

SAM: That's stupid! What if she *does* try to stop you? I'm not going to hurt the lady and you're not neither. She's been real nice. In fact, if you touch her, I'll be *on* you.

DONNIE: You're just saying that because you *like* her. You're the one who's stupid—there's three of us and you. What you gonna do about that?

SAM: I told you—I will be *on* you quicker than you think!

THERAPIST: I'm not hard of hearing. I can hear all of you just fine. Manuel and Sam, you are both making a good choice not to run. Donnie, Juan, and Paul if you want to run—okay. I'm not going to stop you—there's the door. But first, I'd like you each to think about your choices. Donnie, you go up a level tomorrow and running will jeopardize that. Juan and Paul, you both have basketball tryouts after school. If you choose to run you will be off the team.

JUAN: I'm not—I'll run another day. I want to play ball after school. They're giving out uniforms. Paul?

PAUL: Maybe I'll stay, then. Donnie, we'll go another day.

DONNIE: (out loud now and speaking directly at me) I'm running anyway. Those are all stupid reasons to not run, and you're stupid for thinking that moving up a level will keep me here!

SAM: (approaching Donnie) You're dissing her. You *can't* do that, and I won't let you.

THERAPIST: Sam, I appreciate your concern but I can take care of myself. Move away from Donnie. You have been doing fine up until now—you don't want to get into a fight and have to go into time out. What I do need you to do right now is to move away from Donnie, let him leave if that is his choice, and go about your own business. The same goes for everyone else. You know your choices—make them now and let's get on with our group.

A potentially assaultive situation in group is always a spur-of-the-moment circumstance. All the boys except for Donnie wound up staying in group. Donnie left to save face, and after sitting in the hallway for 5 minutes, he returned to group. Sam spent about the same amount of time saving his own face by sitting in the corner of the room and tapping the wall with his foot. Both boys needed to cool down, and, as they did, I continued to resume our group activity for the day. Sam and Donnie eventually calmed down, quietly returned to the group when they were ready, and began to interact somewhat together. I waited until our next group meeting together before I addressed what had happened in our earlier meeting.

In addition to adding a new rule to the group about having the boys leave for a cool down period rather than act out, I wanted to explore the issue of Sam's apparent need to take care of me. I wondered if this was an expression of Sam's transference (i.e., of the protectiveness he felt toward his mother and other female relatives). I also wondered if this was perhaps one of the coping strategies he used at home to stave off abuse or punishment. I was also concerned that perhaps Sam's protectiveness toward me was actually in response to some expression on my part of needing protection. I felt it was important to pursue this issue further as I examined my own concerns regarding protectiveness.

To reinforce group cohesiveness, I began our next session with a group drawing activity. I had all the boys share a large sheet of butcher paper, asked them to come up with a scene from school, and then I instructed them to draw the scene together with each of them cooperating in some activity. They chose to draw together an afternoon ice-cream party.

THERAPIST: I really enjoy having you all cooperate together today with your drawing. I especially like the scene you're drawing with all of you having fun together at the party. Can you each tell me what you are doing in the picture?

JUAN: I'm getting ready to play kick-ball. I get to be team captain and Paul's on my team.

PAUL: (laughing) Yeah—and when we win, we get a trophy!

MANUAL: We could all be on the same team—just us from the group and we'll play against some other kids.

DONNIE: Sam and me will play—I'll draw me practicing with you (pointing at Sam). What do you think?

SAM: Okay—but I'll draw Ms. Cassie in the picture. The staff is boring and she will probably have more fun watching us.

THERAPIST: Sam, you seem to think that it is pretty important that I am taken care of at this party. Can you tell me more?

SAM: Well, I don't know. We're having more fun than the staff and maybe you don't want to be alone.

JUAN: She's a grown-up. Grown-ups like to be with other grown-ups, not kids.

THERAPIST: Sometimes grown-ups like to be with other kids and sometimes they like to be with other grown-ups and still other times they like to be alone. What do some of you others think?

PAUL: My mom is alone a lot since my dad left. She says she's busy all day and being alone is *good* for her.

THERAPIST: Do you ever worry about her?

PAUL: Sometimes. I used to feel that maybe she was lonely and that I should stay with her more when she was home and stuff, but she says she's okay and that she needs to worry about *me* and not the other way around. I think she's okay.

SAM: My mom is by herself without nobody a lot. Sometimes she gets sick or gets in trouble with the police or with bad people. She can't help it. Grandma says its because she and my aunts never learned to take care of themselves. With my dad gone, she just gets in trouble more. My dad and grandma say I'm now the man of the house, so I have to look out for her.

With this session, Sam's protectiveness toward me began to make sense. Sam saw his mother and aunts as helpless. This belief was reinforced by his grandmother and by his father who reminded Sam, during prison visitation days, "You're the man of the house. Look after your mother and her sisters—they need to be taken care of". In the neighborhood where Sam lived, being taken care of often meant protection from physical harm. Sam was often commended by his great-grandmother, father, and other family members for protecting his "helpless" mother. In short, Sam's own worth was attached to his ability to safeguard the women in his family. Although I certainly had my own reasons for wanting to protect Sam, his protective behavior toward me had to do with his own beliefs about how he viewed his own self-worth and how he saw his mother and other "alone" women such as myself. These two sessions helped me to understand a number of relational themes for Sam: how he saw his worth in the world, how he saw himself in relation to his mother, and how he behaved toward people (at least women) he cared for. I realized that a principal goal of our work together must be for Sam to learn that he could relate to me differently than to the other women he was close to and that he could experience my responding to him, rather than my needing him to take care of me. I also wanted him to know that I would not be punitive, abandoning, or in any way abusive based on his protectiveness toward me. Indeed, I would remain consistently engaged regardless of his behavior. I also felt that it was going to be important to help Sam find other ways of receiving positive attention from his family, perhaps through successful academic and sports activities. On my part, I realized that I needed to remember just how resilient Sam was. In spite of the setbacks of his life circumstances, he was experiencing increased success in this setting. My task was also to help him access more fully whatever resources were available to him in his family and community.

Case Conceptualization

Sam's behavioral problems came to the attention of school personnel once he began school, but the basis for his difficulties had started years before. Sam was raised in an impoverished household and neighborhood marked by gang and drug activity. It appeared that few rules or behavioral constraints were placed upon him, and, by the time he started school, Sam was an unruly, angry, and acting-out child. Additionally, Sam was frequently physically abused by his mother. Like many abused children, Sam learned to read his environment well. In order to predict when abuse was going to occur, he learned how to decipher and interpret the actions and feelings of others around him. This made him a highly vigilant child: sensitive to the needs of others sometimes yet "sneaky" and somewhat deceitful at other times. That is, Sam related to others in an approach-avoidance manner: he was likable and enjoyable to be around, but sometimes he would lash out and hurt others, using what he knew about an individual's vulnerabilities against him or her. In this way, Sam successfully kept others at arm's length.

I hypothesized that part of Sam's vigilance and protective behavior toward me had a great deal to do with his own family's parentification of him. Having given birth at age 16, Sam's mother was unable to take care of her own emotional needs, let alone the physical and psychological needs of her young son. Sam was inappropriately placed in the position of *parent* when, at a very early age, he began to meet his mother's need for "protection" from others. While parentified children such as Sam may feel special and grown-up for being their family's "little man," they miss out on the opportunity to be children themselves. Given this parentification, compounded by the vigilance learned from an abusive environment, children (such as Sam) can only be "adult" for so long before their own helplessness and rage erupts into anger and acting-out behavior. Indeed, given his age and limited sociofamilial resources, much of Sam's early acting-out behavior could be seen as a cry for help being expressed in ways consonant with his developmental level. Given Sam's range of behaviors—withdrawal, coopera-tion, and rage—which seemed to shift without warning, it was no wonder that he had a host of different diagnoses from various professionals through-out his young life.

In addition to his family problems, Sam lived in an impoverished and vi-olent inner-city neighborhood. He had witnessed from an early age both petty and violent crimes. I hypothesized that his acting-out behavior was due not only to the turbulence and inconsistency at home but also to the same type of violence that was occurring in his neighborhood on an even larger scale. I hypothesized that Sam's tough guy exterior may have been an externalization of anxiety (possibly PTSD) and/or depression, borne out of his inconsistent and frequently violent sociofamilial circumstances. I hy-pothesized further that Sam's ability to convey his feelings and needs was greatly limited, in large part by his developmental level and inadequate par-enting. I thus saw his symptoms, which included hypervigilance, with-drawal, sullenness, anger, assaultiveness, but also cooperation and caring, as reflections of his courageous and creative attempts to cope.

In spite of these psychological problems, Sam had a great deal of per-sonal strength. He was a highly likable and intelligent child with a wonder-ful sense of humor. Other children and adults were often drawn to him. He also showed potential leadership qualities (for example, he could rally the other children into earning behavior points for special events).

Although Sam continued to have difficulty controlling his anger, he demonstrated that he could learn from past experience and that he could take on another person's perspective. For example, Sam no longer assaulted someone when he was angry but sometimes walked away or verbally jousted. In addition, he could also see that I set limits with him and did not allow him to fight with others in the group because I cared about him, not because I thought he was a "bad kid" who needed to be put down. This in-creasing ability to control his anger, and more accurately read my intentions regarding him, were important points, because without such consciousness or capacity for empathic understanding, he could have exhibited strong so-ciopathic characteristics. In fact, the capacity he had to trust and engage me, coupled with the absence of stronger pathology, indicated to me that there were some strengths in his homelife (perhaps from his great-grand-mother) that were worth pursuing for family therapy.

Orienting Constructs

Sam's sense of self was borne out of his individual, familial, and cultural ex-periences. Sam was born to a teenage mother who had difficulty providing him with a sense of security and safety. His mother was frequently absent and was, when present, physically abusive. In addition, the family had limited fi-nancial resources and lived in a neighborhood where threat of physical harm was a daily reality. Furthermore, Sam was referred to as the man in his family, which he believed meant protecting the women in his life. The impossibility of this task, given his developmental level and available resources must have engendered an immense sense of helplessness and inadequacy in him. All of these factors, in combination, contributed to the rage he sometimes expressed.

For Sam, being a child meant being vulnerable and at risk for abuse. Being hypervigilant produced a sense of being in control. Sam took this stance one step further and was frequently on the offensive, a stance which made him feel safer and less vulnerable to attack. This then became his template for coping with the world. In addition, Sam's experiences of failure and reprimand in a variety of educational settings validated further his need for this hypervigilant attacking stance.

Sam received affirmation in his family primarily when he took the role of "protector." To be affirmed, he needed to take care of others. This, however, was an impossible task. His pathway to efficacy was a hopeless one. Sam was desperately in need of finding new pathways to developing a sense of efficacy and receiving positive affirmation.

Given Sam's history, it made sense that he would be vigilant and testing of my trustworthiness, on the one hand, and anxious to be my protector, on the other. My ability to set limits without being abusive or authoritarian, to respond to his acting-out without leaving or abandoning him, to welcome his expression of needs and feelings (especially those beneath the "attacking" stance) without asking him to respond to mine, and to help him identify the multiple possible pathways to a greater sense of efficacy (i.e., rewarding relationships, sports, academics, and so forth) were crucial.

Sue and Sue (1990) aptly discuss how African American values have been heavily shaped by social class variables, such as racism and discrimination, which may affect an African American client's ability to trust a Caucasian therapist. It appeared that in Sam's case, distrust of me was further due to the abuse and neglect he had received from his mother. Children who have been abused or neglected will often demonstrate a pattern of hypervigilance and pseudoadult behavior (Wenar, 1994). Underneath this highly responsible veneer, however, normal development is thwarted and children develop faulty communication, difficulty in bonding with others, and retarded initiative. These children may repeatedly demonstrate a pattern of approach-avoidance behavior in therapy, in which the child may initially come close to the therapist but will also attempt to sabotage this relationship by either direct or covert means. It is important to note that this type of behavior is a reflection of the child's internal state: "If I allow myself to feel close to the therapist, she may eventually leave or hurt me." This internal state is further reflective of a core issue of worthiness: "If I were somehow different [i.e., a smarter, better looking, or a perfect child] I would never have been physically hurt or abandoned in the first place." For many seriously mistreated children, the child's message to him- or herself as a result of this abusive treatment may be simply, "I am a mistake. I never should have been born."

This approach-avoidance behavior and emerging internal conflict was demonstrated about 4 months into group therapy. Even though the children in the group had all been labeled at some point in their life as "delinquent," it was rare for them to steal toys or materials from my office. My office had become a refuge for most of the children and, as such, had developed into a "space" that they had come to value and appreciate. Given this context, when Sam pilfered a small mechanical action figure one day, it became a therapeutic issue. Not only had he stolen the item but he had informed the other group members about the purloined toy during recess after one of our sessions. The children were agitated, not impressed, by this behavior. I believe that they felt violated when something they respected had been taken. Additionally, the children had come to like Sam—even seen him as a leader. To have him take something of "theirs" was a transgression against their relationship. The following group discussion illustrates how this approach-avoidance conflict as it was played out in group. Following this, Sam and I addressed this critical point individually as well.

DONNIE: Um, what do you think should happen if someone steals something from the group? Like a toy or something.
THERAPIST: Well, do you have something in mind? What do you think?
DONNIE: I think that if someone *takes* something that he should be punished—he should lose points and should have to leave the group.
THERAPIST: That sounds pretty harsh, Donnie. You sound kind of mad.
DONNIE: Well, yeah. I mean we all share in here, and if people *take* things, then we'll have nothing left.
THERAPIST: What do others think or feel—about what should happen if someone steals something from the group?
JUAN: I think it depends. If its something big like a radio, you should call the police. If its a toy, then the person should just be kicked out.
MANUAL: Yeah, he should be kicked out because nobody can trust him again.
PAUL: Maybe he should be just temporarily kicked out—maybe for just a couple of times. I mean *something* has to happen to him.
THERAPIST: Can any of you think of a reason that someone may take something from the group that doesn't belong to them?
PAUL: Because maybe they don't have nothing at home. Or maybe because they wanted to just do a dare.
MANUAL: (looking over at Sam) That's a stupid dare! Nobody will like someone who steals something that we can't use anymore!
THERAPIST: (quietly) Sam, I've noticed that you haven't said anything. What's up?
SAM: (pulling the item out of his pocket and throwing it across the room) Nothing's up! You are all a bunch of narcs! It was just a small dumb toy, and I was going to put it back!

THERAPIST: Sam, thank you for returning the toy. I understand that you are upset right now. You can leave for some quiet time if you'd like or you can stay—its up to you.

Sam chose to remain in the group but moved to a corner of the room to get some distance from the other members. I wanted to address how the other boys were feeling about their own anger and mistrust towards Sam, but at the same time I wanted to address Sam's process over getting "caught" and his resulting feelings of anger and perhaps shame. Most important, Sam was testing me publicly to assess whether I could impose limits and still remain caring and emotionally connected to him. He had not received this fundamental response in other relationships. Furthermore, if I passed this test, Sam would not have to stay focused on the surface feelings of anger. Instead, he could move beyond the reactive feelings of anger to the original feelings of hurt and shame that his life experience had repeatedly engendered. The effectiveness of my response (i.e., limit setting with respect and care) let him know behaviorally that this was a safe place to begin dealing with the more vulnerable feelings.

Mueller and Kell (1966) describe the affective constellations of anger-sadness-shame that often emerge when central conflicts begin to be unearthed during the course of therapy (e.g., reactive anger, sadness or hurt, and shame or anxiety over feeling sad or hurt). Sam was readily in touch with the anger he felt as a result of his abuse and neglect. What was becoming increasingly clear to me was that his anger was a mask or response to deeper feelings of hurt and vulnerability. Sam was, not surprisingly, angry because his mother was unable or unwilling to take care of Sam's natural child-like state of dependence and vulnerability. I suspected that underneath the sadness and longing, however, were even deeper feelings of shame over unmet attachment needs, that is, to be loved, cherished, and protected by his mother and family. For a child like Sam to actually experience such vulnerability and not have them embraced by a primary caretaker is too painful for a developing and unsupported self to tolerate. Consequently, anger becomes a much easier emotion to express and serves as a way to protect one's self. The following dialogue illustrates how Sam was permitted to express some sadness over the rejection by his friends when he was caught stealing.

THERAPIST: So, have any of you done something that you later regretted? Maybe something that, when you did it, was not so smart, that you didn't really think through—that when you think about it now you kinda say to yourself, Ugh, why did I *do* that?

JUAN: One time after I got my room painted, I put stickers on the wall that wouldn't come off. Now, I have these dumb stickers in some places and peeled paint in other places.

THERAPIST: What did your family do when they found out?

JUAN: My dad was mad! He hollered and hollered for a while.

PAUL: Once when I was supposed to be minding my sister, I went across the street to play with my friend and she followed me. She almost got hit by a car!

THERAPIST: What happened then?

PAUL: My mom got angry and put me on restriction for a week!

THERAPIST: How did you feel?

PAUL: Bad, man. I mean my sister is a pain and all, but I don't want her dead or nothing.

THERAPIST: What do any of you think Paul's mom should have done when she found out that his sister almost got hit by a car and it was *his* fault for not watching her?

MANUEL: I think being put on restriction is good.

THERAPIST: Then what?

MANUEL: That's it. I mean its not like he didn't already feel bad.

THERAPIST: So you're saying that sometimes we do things that we regret and make us feel bad inside?

MANUEL: Yup.

THERAPIST: Do you think that maybe that's how Sam feels? that maybe he didn't think first about stealing the toy and now he feels bad?

JUAN: Maybe.

THERAPIST: Do you think that maybe it's okay to do something you regret but that sometimes we just make mistakes? Maybe friends would understand that?

PAUL: Yeah, I guess. We all do dumb things. Like you said—that's okay.

At this point Sam shyly and unobtrusively became more engaged in the group and recommenced his play. Later, during our individual session together he confided that making mistakes was *not* "okay" in his family and that often his mother would stay angry at him for days when he did something "dumb." She would also yell and sometimes hit him. He also intimated his belief that that was why she left him so much—because he did "dumb" things. After finding that he could do dumb things with me, like stealing, and still receive firm limits and care, Sam felt safe enough to risk experiencing and revealing his sadness. I offered him the corrective experience that he had not received often enough: I did not threaten to leave, I did not diminish his feelings, and I let him know that regardless of his "bad" behaviors I was still with him and for him.

SAM: (crying) Maybe if I were good—you know, like kids on TV—my mom wouldn't get so angry . . . or leave.

THERAPIST: Because somehow its *your* fault that your mom gets mad at you . . . ?

SAM: (nods his head)

THERAPIST: And only if you were *perfect* like actors on TV your mom might be like those moms on TV and everything would be okay.

SAM: (cries and nods his head)

THERAPIST: Even though, Sam—and this is important so I'd like you to listen carefully—there is *no such thing* as a perfect child or grown-up. Actors pretend—they're not real. Just like your friends here said, they make all kinds of mistakes—*that* is real.

SAM: But if I could be good . . . I mean sometimes I am for a long time. But then I mess up . . .

THERAPIST: Yes, like today you "messed up." And that's it. You messed up, just like Juan has done, and Paul, and Manuel, and everyone else. And I still like you, and I'm not going anywhere . . . and I look forward to having you come back.

Treatment Plans and Intervention Strategy

INITIAL TREATMENT PLAN

My initial treatment plan included the establishment of a working alliance and the development of group cohesiveness. My hope was that by establishing a positive therapeutic relationship between me, Sam, and the group that was dependable, trustworthy, and supportive, the foundation would be set for further, more in-depth work. These initial goals included addressing issues related to race and establishing rules for appropriate behavior in the group, such as, no physical or verbal assault or ridicule allowed.

Once these initial goals were met, I hoped to use the group as a place where Sam could begin to learn more socially appropriate behaviors and the rewards that come from healthy, affirming interpersonal relationships. For instance, Sam demonstrated at times a charming and humorous personality. I hoped he could learn to use this side of himself to take on a more positive leadership role, rather than use it as a vehicle for instigating others and receiving negative attention from his teacher. In addition, I wanted Sam to learn better impulse control and problem-solving skills. These included recognizing potentially volatile situations and triggers for his anger and making more appropriate responses, such as walking away. The group was an especially appropriate vehicle for dealing with these issues, since the young men could together generate solutions to problems and practice with each other more appropriate responses. I thus hoped that the group and I might provide for Sam this consistent, safe, *holding* environment, where he could begin to acknowledge, express, and have his some of his normal, age-appropriate, socialization and developmental needs met.

Let me try to highlight further what I mean by using the group and our therapeutic relationship to provide a *containing* environment. Because Sam's family did not provide much empathic support for the normal and predictable feelings that resulted from his developmental experiences, Sam was unable to manage emotions such as sadness, shame, anxiety, or even happiness. This was compounded by the physical abuse he had experienced from his mother and was further fueled by the series of humiliations he had experienced in educational and other settings. His low socioeconomic status and race are also not valued by the majority culture, further contributing to his feeling that the world was unsafe, threatening, and demeaning. In order for Sam to begin to heal, it was going to be necessary for him to identify and experience his range of feelings and learn to express them and his needs in more flexible ways. This time, however, it could occur in a relational context characterized by empathy, care, and concern, where his feelings could be managed and "held." This meant that when Sam's feelings of need or depreciation emerged in treatment, I could affirm, welcome, and respond compassionately to them, rather than be overwhelmed and/or threatened by them, as had occurred with rejecting others in his past.

Finally, the last phase of therapy included Sam's ability to internalize me and our relationship as a way to begin *transitioning* into developing a sense of himself as a worthy and lovable individual—separate from others around him yet still connected to the people and family members he cherished. More specifically, I hoped that Sam would be able to use our relationship and connection together as a source of strength to draw upon during times of need. In a sense, I hoped to become for Sam a sort of *transitional object.*

Sam was increasingly able to use our relationship as a tool for security and strength. This was most evident when he began to struggle with making appropriate behavioral choices that involved acting out or running away. During the middle to later phases of our work together, he spent a period of time seemingly regressing back to old aggressive and withdrawn behaviors that he had previously given up. Looking back at some of these experiences, I believe he was testing the environment and me before he made some crucial progress in therapy. It was as if he was mulling over whether or not risking feeling was worth some of the pain that accompanies change.

Sam was making tremendous progress in therapy but the depth of his woundedness was made evident about 8 months into therapy. In this particular instance, Sam had gotten extremely angry at one of the other members for what he believed was cheating during a game in group. A similar circumstance 8 months before would probably have led Sam to either hit the other child or to run away from school. In this instance, Sam did not assault the child, but stood up, clenched his fists, teetered on his feet for what felt like an interminable amount of time, and then ran out of my office and headed for the back fence that separated the school from the adjoining neighborhood. According to our facility policy, leaving the school property without permission was grounds for police and parental involvement. Children who "ran" also lost all behavioral points and special privileges. Sam climbed the fence and, rather than jumping down on the other side and running further, he stopped and perched himself. In essence, Sam was "on the fence" both literally and figuratively. If he ran further, he may have spent some time in detention. The situation that tipped off his anger, however, was too overwhelming for him to handle in a more appropriate manner. Sam sat on the fence to cool down and think things through.

The fact that Sam could respond so intensely to what seemed like a relatively minor incident alerted me to the possibility that his feeling like he was in an unfair no-win situation was a hopelessly familiar and painful scenario. Sam was in a no-win situation in this incident; he was in a no-win situation with his mother; and, as a black male trying to succeed in his inner-city environment and in this sociopolitical context, he was again in a no-win situation. Thus, this incident evoked the same feelings he had experienced in his early life (i.e., rage and helplessness). Sam was, however, beginning to respond differently to these profound affects, which in the past had resulted in assaultive behavior on his part.

I could see Sam outside my window and had asked the facility staff to keep an eye on him but to leave him alone. After about an hour, it began to rain and, by this time, Sam had missed lunch. I walked outside to a table where Sam could see me and I left his jacket, umbrella, and lunch, and I went back to my office. As soon as I left, Sam climbed down, took his things, and returned to the fence. A couple hours later I walked into my office from a meeting, and Sam was sitting under a table drawing a picture.

THERAPIST: I'm glad you're back. Do you want to talk?

SAM: (shakes his head no)

THERAPIST: That's fine. The school bus will be here in about an hour and a half to take you home. I've got paperwork and a few errands to run until then. You can stay there until you have to go home and I'll just leave you alone. I'll leave it up to you to let me know if you need anything. One last thing: You made two good choices today—you did not hit Donnie and you did not run. I'm proud of you.

True to my word I went about my business and left Sam alone. I went to a meeting and when I returned, Sam had gone home. On my desk he left a painstakingly drawn picture of our group together. I was in the middle with the boys standing around me. I could see that Sam saw the group as a type of community or family and that he was internalizing me as a more benevolent template or inner voice.

REVISED TREATMENT PLAN

The basic treatment goals were not revised much, but in addition to group and individual sessions, I did pursue family therapy for Sam's great-grandmother and aunts. There appeared to be potential for change within the family, and they were quite open to receiving help in learning how to handle Sam more effectively. With the help of Sam's social worker, I also found a community anger-control program for him. The anger-control program, held at a local church, was designed to keep children such as Sam out of gangs. Through this program, Sam was able to develop relationships with other children under positive circumstances, and he was able to develop alternative ways of managing his anger.

There were two issues that I was aware of when I initiated therapy with Sam's family. First, Sam's great-grandmother and aunts appeared somewhat isolated from any aid or support within their community. Second, I did not know how amenable they would be to having a female Caucasian therapist. With these two considerations I decided to run a larger family therapy group with Sam's family and two other families who had children from their same neighborhood. Additionally, I had a male, African American co-therapist to counterbalance any issues that may have arisen due to my gender and ethnicity. Included in the treatment plan were psychoeducational approaches to parenting, such as addressing issues of discipline (i.e., consistent enforcement of firm rules and limits with logical (non-abusive) consequences, reinforcement of appropriate behavior, and so forth) and exploration of ways to increase the amount of community support for each family. In addition to having these families begin supporting one another, other community resources, such as recreational groups and church-based youth groups, were identified.

BALANCING GOALS

Throughout our treatment together, the challenge was to balance the goal of establishing and maintaining a strong and supportive relationship while helping Sam to see that he did not have to do anything to take care of me or be anyone other than himself to receive care and nurturance from me. Sam believed that in order to receive the support he deserved as a child, he had to be my protector. Sam had learned from his childhood experiences that taking care of others was one way to receive positive attention. He was willing to go to any length, including peeling off his skin, to receive my love and affirmation. My task was to convey that I could care about him even though I may not always approve of his behaviors. For example, I needed to let him know that I didn't like it when he took things from my office without permission but that I still liked him and wanted to continue working with him.

My other challenge was to see beyond Sam's external "angry" presentation and not overreact with the same intimidation and/or counterattack this had usually elicited from others. I did this by recognizing that the extent to which Sam seemed threatening to me reflected the depth of his woundedness. By responding in a consistent, even, nonreactive way, I was able to provide for Sam the safe environment from which he could then access the other more threatening feelings that his anger protected. Sam soon learned that the affects of hurt, shame, and hopelessness were understandable and acceptable to me. This containment then made it possible to begin developing alternative ways of expressing his needs and setting limits with others. For example, we began role playing what to say and do when angry, identified cool-down activities he could engage in when angry (such as drawing or sports), and considered the consequences of his anger in each situation.

Therapeutic Process

RELATIONAL REENACTMENTS

One especially powerful reenactment occurred in the example discussed earlier when Sam stole a toy from my office. For good reasons, Sam watched my response to this test very carefully. His mother would have used this type of behavior to confirm that he was "bad" and justify why she left him, and the system would have used this to place him in juvenile hall. In contrast, my response to set firm limits but remain emotionally available and caring differentiated me from his mother and the system. Clearly, I had to set limits to help Sam know that there would be predictable consequences to his behavior. He had not felt the safety of secure boundaries in the past, and he needed it now. In addition, both the group and I were able to show compassion for Sam while still disapproving of his behavior. Sam had not received this essential developmental experience from his family or the system, and it was a new and corrective experience that proved to be a watershed in treatment.

In this experience, Sam also was able to deal with me directly on issues of color for the first time (i.e., Sam: "You only get mad at me because I'm Black! You wouldn't do anything if I were White like Paul!"). It also revealed his ambivalence toward me in that I represented what he wanted in a parent but what he hated in the system (i.e., Sam: "Man, I can't make you out. I like you sometimes, but you'll change just like the other White teachers do."). This ambivalence was also expressed by Sam toward his mother, whom he loved dearly but who consistently failed him by her abuse and abandonment. I understood that a huge component of what Sam hated was the arbitrariness or unfairness that he perceived in both his mother and in the sociopolitical system. For Sam, such unfairness evoked both the helplessness and rage that led him to so many of his troubles. This issue was illustrated, for example, in the episode when Sam ran and sat on the fence when he thought that another child had cheated at a game.

IMPEDIMENTS TO TREATMENT

Initially, I wondered if my gender and race might impact the development of a strong alliance. Sam and I were, however, able to form a strong bond. The biggest impediment that did occur on my part had to do with my own feelings of protectiveness toward Sam. Although Sam was protective towards me for reasons that involved his family history, my feelings towards him included my own process of questioning our racial, cultural, and economic differences.

Through the process of pursuing this issue with colleagues, I explored the literature on some of the barriers that may occur between a Caucasian therapist and an African American client (e.g., Jones & Seagull, 1977;

Pinderhughes, 1973). Consistent in the literature is the necessity of examining one's own values when working with ethnic minorities. Greene (1985) suggests four areas that may emerge during the therapy process as impediments. These areas include racism or prejudice, "color blindness," paternalism, and the unquestioning acceptance of African American power. The first area is clear: this involves the therapist's feelings of unconscious or conscious superiority over the client as a result of race. Color blindness involves ignoring issues pertaining to the individual's race, with the belief that no social or cultural differences actually exist between races. From a paternalistic standpoint, the therapist interprets all of the client's problems as a result of race or prejudice, thus ignoring any other alternatives or contributors. Finally, the idea of unquestioning acceptance of Black power involves the therapist's attitude that because racism exists, any thoughts, feelings, or behaviors on the part of the client—regardless of the pathology—is justified. I considered each of these areas carefully, but none seemed to adequately address my process. My dual feelings of protectiveness and being overwhelmed about Sam's life did not seem to be due to issues involving prejudice, ignorance, or even exaggeration over racial matters. Turning back into the interpersonal process literature, I was reacquainted with the issue of *survivor guilt* that led me to understand my feelings toward Sam.

According to Niederland (1981), survivor guilt is a fundamental human conflict that involves a biologically-based concern for and sensitivity to the pain of significant others that makes it difficult for an individual to be comfortable or successful if these others are not. Although this idea of survivor guilt originally concerned the experiences of Holocaust survivors in relation to those loved ones that had perished, Modell (1971) believes that this issue is one of universal significance and may include a wide variety of situations. Even though the idea of survivor guilt had not been directly connected to the social inequalities that exist between Caucasians and ethnic minorities, I began to examine if this was at least partially the reason for my initially protective feelings toward Sam and feeling overwhelmed about his prognosis given his family background and the social, environmental, and political odds against him. I wondered if I was experiencing guilt over the probability that I would never experience what he has experienced.

By formulating my issue in this manner, I was able to keep this special form of guilt from operating in our relationship, for example, by being less firm with Sam than he needed me to be. Had I allowed this "protectiveness" to lead to indulging Sam's provocativeness and testing without setting the firm limits that he needed, I would have been responding in a way that sounds similar to Green's notion of paternalism. A paternalistic stance implies dependence that the therapist might encourage by focusing solely on the client's vulnerability issues instead of supporting the client's active strivings toward efficacy as well. I did not wish Sam to be dependent upon me; just the opposite. I wished for him to develop a sense of personal power that would make him less dependent on others. Initially, his situation seemed simply overwhelming to me and I felt *guilty* over not knowing immediately what to do for this child. Discussing my concerns with colleagues and delving into the literature helped me make sense of this.

Sam and I had also had similar transference issues with one another that involved feelings of protectiveness. Exploring our mutual conflicts regarding protection made it possible for Sam and me to not repeat the destructive patterns he had experienced in other relationships, where he had received the confusing message, "I can take care of you," but at the same time, "You overwhelm me. I am not capable of taking care of you." Exploring with a helpful supervisor the roots of these issues in my own background and in our current relationship permitted me to treat Sam effectively and provide the corrective relational/emotional experiences he needed in order to change. We did this together by repeatedly making overt how he tried to take care of me at times and my reassuring him that I knew he cared about me but that he did not need to take care of me in order for me to care about him. The other primary way we did this was by exploring together the impact it had on me and others when he was threatening and challenging.

Termination and Therapist's Summary Thoughts

Therapy ended almost 2 years later when Sam successfully returned to public school. The timing of our termination was planned ahead of time and occurred slowly over a period of 6 months. During that 6-month period Sam was gradually mainstreamed back into public school. We were able to address together the anxiety-arousing issues that emerged over the separation. I contacted the teacher at his new school and was able to involve her in this transition process. Two of the boys from our group were also transferring to Sam's school, so they had the advantage of sharing this process together.

Sam's angry outbursts had all but ceased at this point, and he had learned to draw upon a large repertoire of problem-solving skills when he did feel anger or sadness. For instance, Sam liked to sketch and color. In group, I often had the children make pictures about their feelings or thoughts. Sam began to keep a journal of his drawings and, as time progressed, his pictures were accompanied by personal writings and creative stories. His journal became an important method for expressing his emotions. Additionally, he was athletic and enjoyed being outdoors. When feelings of anger overwhelmed him, Sam learned to utilize physical activity as a way of letting off steam. Finally, Sam's social skills had improved tremendously. He developed the ability to form positive relationships with a number of the facility staff and knew how to tell them when something was bothering him.

The shame he once experienced over having unmet needs of love and care had diminished greatly. He was now involved in a group through his church, which supported their youth to be proud of their African American heritage. Additionally, Sam's family continued in family therapy and became more adept at setting firm limits and enforcing these in consistent and appropriate ways (e.g., restricting him when he had broken a curfew). Sam grew especially close to one of his aunts who had been living with him and his great-grandmother. Sam's mother continued to float in and out of his life, which was often disruptive for him. It became especially important for the family to include her in the parenting classes and to insist that she too follow the disciplinary practices they were now using. Fortunately, Sam now had family and community support to counteract some of the potentially hurtful repercussions that stemmed from his mother's inconsistent presence and emotional unavailability. Sam smiled more, began to excel in school, and demonstrated more positive leadership skills, such as being voted in as class vice president.

Sam had indeed grown in our 2 years together and had the potential for continued success. He was now more aware of his "triggers" and had a greater repertoire of responses. I was also thrilled to see that Sam had learned to acknowledge his own achievements and felt more positive about himself. I was aware, however, that as an African American male, he would likely have to cope with a great deal of arbitrary unfairness of the sort that had ignited his acting-out behavior. He also continued to live in a neighborhood that was menacing and that did not support expression of his tender side. Further, his mother continued to be inconsistently available. However, Sam did have a caring great-grandmother and a supportive aunt who planned to continue therapy for Sam and themselves after he left our facility. Sam's family was also now more involved in their church and in youth groups where support and socialization needs could be met. I hoped also that Sam's increased sense of efficacy and wider behavioral repertoire would serve him well in the many challenges he is likely to face.

REFERENCES

Alexander, F. (1963). The dynamics of psychotherapy in light of learning theory. *American Journal of Psychiatry, 20,* 440–448.

American Psychiatric Association (1994). *Diagnostic and Statistical Manual of Mental Disorders,* (4th ed.). Washington, DC: Author.

Gibbs, J., Huang, L., et al. (1989). *Children of color: Psychological interventions with minority youth.* San Francisco, CA: Jossey-Bass.

Greene, B. A. (1985). Considerations in the treatment of Black patients by white therapists. *Psychotherapy, 22,* 389–393.

Hagborg, W., & Konigsberg, B. (1991). Multiple perspectives of therapeutic change and the severely emotionally disturbed adolescent. *Psychotherapy, 28,* 292–297.

Ho, M. H. (1992). *Minority children and adolescents in therapy.* Newbury Park, CA: Sage.

Jones, A., & Seagull, A. A. (1977). Dimensions of the relationship between the Black client and the White therapist. *American Psychologist, 32,* 850–855.

Kell, B., & Mueller, W. B. (1966). *Impact and change.* Englewood Cliffs, NJ: Prentice-Hall.

Kiesler, D. & Van Denburg, T. (1993). Therapeutic impact disclosure: The last taboo in psychoanalytic theory and practice. *Clinical Psychology and Psychotherapy, 1*(1), 3–13.

Kunjufu, J. (1985). *Countering the conspiracy to destroy Black boys* (Vol. 1). Chicago: African American Images.

McKinley, V. (1991). Group therapy as a treatment modality of special value for Hispanic patients. *Social Work with Groups, 13,* 255–266.

Modell, A. H. (1971). The origin of certain forms of preoedipal guilt and the implications for a psychoanalytic theory of affects. *International Journal of Psychoanalysis, 52,* 337–346.

Morgan, S. (1989). Clarifying the federal definition of severely emotionally disturbed. *Journal of Instructional Psychology, 16,* 173–179.

Niederland, W. G. (1981). The survivor guilt syndrome: Further observations and dimensions. *Journal of American Psychoanalytic Association, 29,* 413–426.

Pinderhughes, C. A. (1973). Racism and psychotherapy. In C. Willie, B. Kramer, & B. Brown (Eds.), *Racism and mental health.* Pittsburg: University of Pittsburg Press.

Schaefer, C. E., Johnson, L., & Wherry, J. N. (1982). *Group therapies for children and youth.* San Francisco, CA: Jossey-Bass.

Schiffer, M. (1984). *Children's group therapy.* New York: Free Press.

Strupp, H., & Binder, J. (1988). *Time limited dynamic therapy.* New York: Basic Books.

Sue, D. W., & Sue, D. (1990). *Counseling the culturally different: Theory and practice* (2nd ed.). New York: Wiley.

Sue, S. (1977). Community and mental health services to minority groups: Some optimism, some pessimism. *American Psychologist, 32,* 616–624.

Sue, S., & Zane, N. (1987). The role of culture and cultural techniques in psychotherapy: A reformation. *American Psychologist, 42,* 37–45.

Sullivan, H. S. (1953). *The interpersonal theory of psychiatry.* New York: Norton.

Trupin, E., Forsyth-Stephens, A., & Low, B. (1991). Service needs of severely disturbed children. *American Journal of Public Health, 81,* 975–980.

U.S. Bureau of the Census. (1987). *Statistical abstracts of the United States.* Washington, DC: U.S. Government Printing Office.

Wenar, C. (1994). *Psychopathology from infancy through adolescence* (3rd ed.). New York: Random House.

Yalom, I. D. (1985). *The theory and practice of group psychotherapy.* (3rd ed.). New York: Basic Books.

SUGGESTIONS FOR FURTHER READING

Axelson, J. (1985). *Counseling development in a multicultural society.* Belmont, CA: Brooks-Cole. This provides a good *general overview* on multicultural issues in counseling. While this text does not address the needs of children, it does provide a well-conceptualized description of the roles culture, social structures, and worldviews play in the therapy relationship. It also provides a sociodevelopmental explanation of human growth from the viewpoints of various ethnic minority groups (e.g., African American). It also challenges readers to assess how *they* relate to various groups of people in society, thereby effectively addressing the role counselors themselves play in the psychotherapy relationship.

Ho, M. (1992). *Minority children and adolescents in therapy.* Newbury Park, CA: Sage. This book includes the historical context of various ethnic groups and provides practical techniques for group, family, and individual psychotherapy. Understanding the historical context of groups (e.g., African Americans) helps counselors appreciate the sociocultural legacy of each group. They can then use this understanding in their conceptualizations of client dynamics and behavior.

Vargas, L. & Koss-Chiono, J. (Eds). (1992). *Working with culture: Psychotherapeutic interventions with ethnic minority children and adolescents.* San Fransisco, CA: Jossey-Bass. This text is excellent for describing social problems and issues that may be of specific concern for ethnic minority children and adolescents. For instance, the chapters on African Americans address concerns such as self-esteem and identity in adolescents from middle-class families, therapeutic issues for children in foster care, and racial socialization. Together with the Ho and Axelson's texts, *Working with Culture* provides a well-rounded picture of pertinent issues for many African American children.

Chapter 12

CONDUCT DISORDER

CASE ILLUSTRATION OF BRIAN: A 10-YEAR-OLD AFRICAN AMERICAN CHILD

David Chavez, Ph.D.
Nancy L. Wolfe, M.S.

THE DISORDER

Most therapists are likely to treat Conduct Disorder, since one third to one half of all child and adolescent referrals involve conduct problems, aggressiveness, and antisocial behavior (Wenar, 1994). According to DSM-IV (American Psychiatric Association, 1994), prevalence estimates suggest that this disorder may occur in 6–16% of the population of males under the age of 18 and 2–9% of females in that same age range. A diagnosis of Conduct Disorder, as established by the DSM-IV, requires "a repetitive and persistent pattern of behavior in which either the basic rights of others or major age appropriate societal norms or rules are violated" (1994, p. 85). According to DSM-IV, three behaviors from any of these four main groupings of behavior must have been present in the last 12 months, with at least one present within the last 6 months, for a person to receive a Conduct Disorder diagnosis:

Aggression to People and Animals

1. Often bullies, threatens, or intimidates others.
2. Often initiates physical fights.
3. Has used a weapon that can cause serious physical harm to others (e.g., a bat, brick, broken bottle, knife, gun).
4. Has been physically cruel to people.
5. Has been physically cruel to animals.

6. Has stolen while confronting a victim (e.g., mugging, purse snatching, extortion, armed robbery).
7. Has forced someone into sexual activity.

Destruction of Property

8. Has deliberately engaged in fire setting with the intention of causing serious damage.
9. Has deliberately destroyed others' property (other than by fire setting).

Deceitfulness or Theft

10. Has broken into someone else's house, building, or car.
11. Often lies to obtain goods or favors or to avoid obligations (i.e., "cons" others).
12. Has stolen items of nontrivial value without confrontation of a victim (e.g., shoplifting, but without breaking and entering; forgery).

Serious Violation of Rules

13. Often stays out at night despite parental prohibitions, beginning before age 13.
14. Has run away from home overnight at least twice while living in parental or parental surrogate home (or once without returning for a lengthy period).
15. Is often truant from school, beginning before age 13.

Additionally, the disturbance in behavior must cause significant impairment in social, academic, or occupational functioning. Individuals who are 18 years of age or older and who do not meet the criteria for Antisocial Personality Disorder can still be diagnosed with Conduct Disorder.

The DSM-IV makes a distinction between Childhood-Onset Type, in which at least one criterion characteristic of Conduct Disorder is met before age 10, and Adolescent-Onset Type, in which none of the criteria is met before age 10. In a majority of individuals, there is a reduction of symptoms by adulthood. Early onset however, as in the case of Brian, can be predictive of poorer prognosis and increased risk of adult Antisocial Personality Disorder or Substance-Related Disorders.

According to Wenar (1994), there are two sub-groups of Conduct Disorders. The first is the *undersocialized* or *solitary aggressive* type, which is defined by fighting, disobedience, temper tantrums, uncooperativeness, impertinence, and restlessness. These individuals are typically aggressive, impulsive, fail to learn from experience, and lack feelings of guilt or anxiety. This subtype is considered to be the most severe type, with poorer prognosis including greater likelihood of Antisocial Personality Disorder and Substance Abuse Disorder. Brian was a child who fell into this category. Therefore, early intervention was extremely important in order to avoid the possibility of such an extremely negative outcome later in his life.

Children and teens who exhibit another cluster of behaviors have been termed *socialized* or *group aggressive* type or *delinquents*. Typical behaviors for this group include having conduct disordered companions, being truant from school and home, being loyal to delinquent friends, stealing with others, lying, and setting fires. This group has been socialized with a deviant set of values and typically comes from lower socioeconomic level homes. It is especially important when working with children and adolescents from different cultural groups to assess the extent to which behaviors exhibited by these individuals are due in part to environmental factors, since it is not uncommon in some places for individuals to be threatened with physical harm if they refuse to join a gang and engage in activities of this sort. Understanding the environmental context can have significant implications for intervention.

These subgroups (undersocialized/aggressive and socialized/group aggressive) are not included as subcategories of Conduct Disorder in DSM-IV, but still aid in helping clinicians make distinctions that might be useful in understanding the development of problem behaviors and differential treatment outcomes.

Wenar (1994) notes that in normal development, socialization and the development of self-control are facilitated when secure attachment and basic trust are formed between the child and the primary caretakers. These caregiving relationships, based on affection and nurturance, become the most important part of the child's developing world. Keeping these secure ties intact is of primary importance for normal development. When the parent-child relationship develops normally, the child internalizes the parent's rules and loving feelings for the child, and the capacity for empathy and sympathy become possible. This reassuring and responsive relationship allows the child to form a link between parental directives and the feelings of affection that bond the relationship between the child and the primary caregivers. As this occurs, the child moves away from his or her egocentric perspective and becomes more willing to forgo his own impulses and incorporate or take on the perspective of the parent. It is in the context of this stable, consistent, and trustworthy relationship that children can learn what is expected of them, how to attain goals, and to develop strategies for delaying immediate gratification. In order for this to be possible, the child's memory must become sophisticated enough to remember the socialization messages that the parents give, which occur progressively through the toddler and preschool years. Thinking must also develop so that the child is able to move from literal interpretation of messages to the more abstract, allowing generalization from one situation to the next.

In the child with Conduct Disorder, this socialization process goes awry. It has been theorized that for the "conduct disordered child," the primary attachment bond, necessary in the socialization process, is insecure or in some way becomes disrupted. Longitudinal data following children from early to middle childhood supports this hypothesis (Erickson, Sroufe, & Egeland, 1985; Renken, Egeland, Marvinney, Mangelsdorf, & Sroufe, 1989).

This may be caused by the mother or primary caregiver's inability to parent effectively or it may be the result of a bidirectional interaction between a temperamentally difficult child and an overwhelmed parent. Active, willful, intense boys with a short attention span are more difficult to raise and can be more vulnerable to the stressors of family conflict and disorganization. Waters, Posada, Crowell, and Keng-ling (1993) suggest that even if we cannot trace disruptive behavior problems etiologically to attachment problems, the behavior problems themselves will inevitably disrupt the *secure base* relationship. Regarding temperament, Campbell (1991) also found that certain "difficult to raise" kindergarten children who were aggressive, noncompliant, hyperactive, and inattentive were at risk for continued problems. Thus, a negative escalating cycle may develop, with the child's behavioral problems persisting, which may then increase stress on the family and the marital coalition and cause conflict in the mother-child relationship. Campbell hypothesizes that stressed mothers become more restrictive and negative in reaction to impulsive and difficult children. Often the mother's more stern reaction is ineffective and only serves to make the child less compliant.

In addition, excessive environmental stressors (i.e., poverty, unemployment, illness, etc.) and maternal psychological disturbances (i.e., depression) can weaken the parent-child relationship and put the child at greater risk for behavior disturbances. In a study by Egeland, Kalloske, Gottesman, and Erikson (1990), maternal depression was positively correlated with an increase in the child's disruptive behavior. Additionally, they found that if stimulation, predictability, and organization in the home was low and stressors, such as financial difficulty or illness was high, behavior problems were more likely to occur. While conduct disorders may be diagnosed for children of all social and racial groups, it is especially important in designing treatment plans for minority children that the cultural context is examined and that interventions are devised that will be consonant with their specific cultural values. For example, it is important for therapists to be aware of how different cultures express affection and bonding. Further, in some settings, gang members and other individuals whose values differ from those of the mainstream culture may be the primary attachment figures who impact the client's values and behavior. Thus, if the primary attachment relationship is disrupted or is contributing to dysfunction, it is important to provide the child the opportunity to establish a bond with someone who will be sensitive to and accepting of differences in self-expression and relating and who will model behavior that will enhance the client's functioning.

Sociocultural Factors

The skilled clinician is a person who takes all factors of the client's world into consideration when making a diagnostic assessment and planning treatment. Even though there may exist some commonalities among clients from certain cultural groups, each client's worldview will be sculpted by a unique combination of influences. The case illustration that follows describes Brian, an African American child. Understanding the cultural factors that may impact the clinical presentation and treatment of African American children will therefore be briefly discussed in this section.

It is critical to remember that not all African American families are the same and that there is significant variation based on family background, economic and social standing, value systems, and the degree of acculturation to mainstream American norms (Allen & Majidi-Ahi, 1989). There are however, some commonalities that are worth exploring when working with African American children that may enable clinicians to be most effective.

We know that African American clients are more likely to drop out of therapy than White clients at a rate of 52.1% compared to 29.8% (Sue, 1977). This high drop-out rate may be attributed to many possible causes. One of these, according to Allen and Majidi-Ahi (1989), is the pervasive suspiciousness that many African American Americans have toward White therapists and White institutions. This attitude seems natural given the history of African Americans in America, plagued by slavery, deprivation, and discrimination. Racism is something that African Americans contend with on a daily basis, and their caution about White institutions can be seen as self-protective and adaptive.

Furthermore, the psychology field itself has been known to demonstrate a bias against African Americans by seeing cultural differences as "cultural deviance." Often, clinical diagnoses are further biased by the influence of social class and the fact that African Americans are still overrepresented in lower income levels in the United States. For example, Hollingshead and Redlich (1958) found that class influenced the severity of a clinical diagnosis, with the most severe diagnoses being given to lower-class clients. They also observed that mental illness was rarer for the affluent, compared to the lower classes. These findings suggest not only probable discrepancies in ability to make unbiased diagnoses cross culturally but suggest that diagnoses and interventions are effected by racial oppression and poverty.

Differences in family structure and socialized gender roles could also lead to misdiagnosis of "abnormality" by therapists who are unaware of cultural variations. Women in the African American community have traditionally worked in order to supplement the low wages of their male partners. This has led to the development of more flexibility between the roles of males and females and the reliance on extended family for added support (Hill, 1972). Women are often socialized in a way that encourages assertiveness, while men are encouraged to show emotion and be nurturing (Lewis, 1975). Both of these trends were witnessed in Brian's adoptive mother and father in treatment. The mother was strong and forceful, while the father demonstrated a great deal of gentleness and nurturance. They also demonstrated their ability to utilize these "alternative" gender roles as therapy demanded in order to help Brian. Lewis (1975) also found that African

American families were more likely to share responsibilities and decisions concerning child care. In a study comparing African American and White families in the Midwestern United States (Gillum, Gomez-Marin, & Prineas, 1984), African American families were found to be less likely to express conflict openly, were more achievement oriented, were more likely to have a moral-religious outlook, and were more organized and controlled than White families. These also happened to be some of the differences that Mrs. B., Brian's mother, explained about her family's worldview as we worked together to design treatments that would fit them personally.

Other factors that influence the clinician's experience with African American clients have to do with communication differences. According to Allen and Majidi-Ahi (1989), it is not common for lower-income African Americans to nod or say "uh-huh" when they have heard something. They suggest that, without this information, a therapist might consider an African American child who sits quietly while being given direction sullen or uncommunicative, when in reality this is a culturally normal manner of relating. Because of this lack of verbal feedback, the therapist may need to rely more on non-verbal information with these clients. These authors also note that it is normative for African Americans to engage in conversation while engaged in another activity and that it is not considered necessary to maintain eye contact in the context of the activity. Because of these differences in communication, it is common for misinterpretations and miscommunications to occur if the therapist is unaware of the range of normative responses for any culturally differing group.

Allen and Majidi-Ahi (1989) note further differences that influence the success of treatment for the African American client. For example, many African American clients place more value on interpersonal warmth rather than the technical competence of the clinician. This makes it important that therapists establish rapport and a collaborative alliance with the clients in order to keep them engaged in the therapeutic process. Moreover, since African American clients often belong to a network of extended family members, therapeutic interventions can often be more productive when members of that network are included in therapy and attempts are made to improve the family system as a whole. Furthermore, providing social, spiritual, economic, vocational, recreational, personal, and psychological assistance, rather than individual psychotherapy or pharmacotherapy only, is likely to yield better outcomes. Knowledge of community referrals, along with creativity and sensitivity to individual needs, is therefore critical in helping clients from many non-mainstream cultures.

Thus, it is important that therapy begin with the assessment of the client's unique worldview. One way that counselors-in-training can do this is by asking clients about the ideas, values, and goals that they view as most important to them in their lives. Armed with this information about the client's world, the therapist can help the client brainstorm options for problem solutions that fit the client's personal value system. The therapist can work with the client to clarify the problems and the direction of therapy best suited for that person in that context. The client then has the option of choosing the solutions that best fit their lives from a custom designed menu of possible solutions collaboratively discovered by the client and the therapist together.

CASE ILLUSTRATION

Presenting Problem

Brian, a 10-year-old African American child who was brought into therapy by his adoptive mother. The relationship between Brian and his parents was conceived one Sunday morning in church. On that morning, Pastor A. had focused on the sad reality that too many African American children were living their entire lives in the foster care system because they were less likely to be adopted than White children. He noted further that many of the African American children who had been adopted were adopted by White families since there were too few African American families who were willing to take them. He was concerned about the difficulty these children would have developing a proper racial identity in transracial adoptions, and there was consensus among the congregation that same-race adoptions were a better option, if possible. Pastor A.'s predominantly African American congregation was touched by his plea for more African American families to adopt these unwanted children. In the weeks that followed, some members of the church actually began to organize a formal church project that aimed to give some of these unadoptable children permanent homes with members of their congregation.

Mrs. B. and her husband, who had both always been strongly affiliated with the church, were emotionally touched by his adoption message and sought to follow Pastor A.'s plea to rescue children in need of a home. In their desire to meet their Christian ideals, they started adoption proceedings. The adoption process was time consuming and complicated, but Mr. and Mrs. B. were tenacious. After a little more than a year, they were given custody of Brian, age 10, and his natural sister Alisha, age 8. Brian and Alisha were welcomed into a family consisting of Mr. and Mrs. B. and their biological son, Nathan, age 11. The couple were hopeful that they could provide these children with the loving home they had always missed.

The family didn't know much about the background of the children, except that their natural parents had a history of drug and alcohol abuse. The children had been placed in foster care when Alisha was an infant and Brian was about 2 years old. Neither child remembered their biological mother or father and had lived in a series of foster homes since their removal from their natural parents. Not much was known about the conditions in the previous foster care placements, other than the fact that one set of foster parents with whom Brian and Alisha had lived were currently being prosecuted for sexual molestation of several of their other foster children. There was a strong suspicion that Brian and Alisha might also have been victims of this foster family's sexual abuse.

Brian was brought into therapy because he was acting-out seriously since being placed with his newly adoptive family. The primary concern was that Brian had molested his sister shortly after the children moved in. To Mrs. B.'s knowledge, this had occurred three or four times. However, Brian also behaved in a sexually inappropriate way with Nathan. Mrs. B. reported that she had caught Brian "doing things" to Nathan but was so offended and embarrassed by the behavior that she was unable to go into detail about the acts. She also stated that Brian was physically confrontational with Nathan much of the time. In addition, Brian was discovered stealing tapes and other possessions from Nathan's bedroom. He even tried to sell Nathan's bike to another kid down the street. According to Mrs. B., Nathan was a quiet and passive boy and didn't know how to handle Brian's aggressive acts, and she was seriously alarmed with Brian's behavior and the extent to which it was making her biological son's life miserable.

Mrs. B. also complained that Brian was never compliant with her requests. He was also noncompliant at school and engaged in fights on the playground. She noted further that sometimes Brian would be out in the yard just talking to himself and that she was worried that he was "just plain nuts."

Brian had also become identified as the "problem" in the neighborhood. For example, he had been throwing rocks at neighbors' windows and at passing cars. He defecated in the flower bed; then, when neighborhood children came by, he picked up his own feces and chased them around with it.

At the time Mrs. B. first came in, she wanted to explore with me the hypothesis that Brian might truly be psychotic, in the hope that she might be able to undo the adoption arrangement. I explained that since the agreement was already final, returning Brian on the basis of him being somehow "defective" was not a likely possibility. We ended up discussing this hope several more times in therapy before we moved into exploring ways to facilitate Brian's adjustment. I could understand how Mr. and Mrs. B.'s idealized idea about adoption had been truly shattered. By the time Brian was brought into therapy Mrs. B. was indeed very disillusioned. This was not the child that she had dreamed and hoped for, and I could empathize with her feelings of regret regarding their decision to adopt him, which I conveyed to her. My empathy and nonjudgmental stance were critical in developing a relationship with her. Once she realized that she could not "return" Brian, her tenacity and creative problem-solving skills became strengths that contributed to Brian's eventual adjustment.

CLIENT DESCRIPTION

Brian was a good-looking child of average height and weight. He always came neatly groomed and well dressed. He appeared to be racially mixed, with both African American and Euramerican features, but, since we had very little information about his heritage, it was difficult to assess what his genetic combination might have been. Brian presented as a quiet sullen child who maintained an initial aloofness that made sense, given the tremendous rejection and lack of stability that had characterized his early life. Although polite, he rarely initiated discourse or play in the early stages of therapy.

SOCIAL CONTEXT

The family lived in a predominately White neighborhood. They maintained ties to the African American community through their church, which was outside their area of residence. This same-race contact was extremely important for the family, since they felt that cultural values and practices between their own race and the mainstream majority culture were quite different. The mother verbalized how these differences were especially apparent in the parenting practices of African American families compared to families of other races. For instance, Mrs. B. made it clear that she believed it was normal for African American mothers to spank their children. I knew from research and experience that, for some groups, corporal punishment was normative. Speaking in a manner that did not challenge her cultural beliefs, I listened to her stance on spanking but expressed the hope that we could identify a range of interventions that might prove effective for Brian. I also mentioned that spanking in anger could become out of control and dangerous and, although it signaled which behavior to stop, it did not teach alternative behavior. These became areas for further exploration later in therapy.

At this initial meeting, I needed to let Mrs. B. know, in a way that would not alienate her, that by law, I would have to report to Children's Protective Services if I thought Brian was being physically abused. I knew I would be in a difficult position if I were faced with having to report. If indeed the mother were found to be abusive, Brian would once again be without a family. Given Mrs. B.'s fantasy about returning Brian, this felt like an extremely dangerous issue, and I was concerned that she might consider this one tactic to rid herself of Brian. I emphasized that if it came to this, CPS was likely to remove all three children. I hoped that Mrs. B. would not consider this option because I believed that the best hope for Brian would be to keep him in therapy and help the family learn more effective parenting skills. I hoped for those reasons that I would not have to report to CPS, but I also knew that I would report if I found out that Brian was currently being hurt. Fortunately, although Mrs. B. believed in firm and sometimes stern discipline, she was not abusive.

Initial Session

During the initial session, I saw both Brian and his mother separately. I interviewed his mother first in order to get an idea about Brian's background and problems from her perspective. Mrs. B. was a tall, large-framed woman who was slightly overweight. She worked as a teacher's aide in the public schools and always came to sessions neatly groomed in attire that would have been appropriate for her occupation.

Mrs. B. made it clear to me that she and her family felt strongly linked to their cultural identity as African Americans. Because of this, she indicated that she was very skeptical about whether I, a Latino male, might be able to help her and Brian in therapy. She wondered whether I could understand her way of parenting and her cultural values, which she assumed were different from mine. It has been my experience with clients of color that many assume that regardless of race, therapists are members of an institutionally racist occupation and may have difficulty honoring their cultural values. In Mrs. B.'s case, she stated clearly that she was skeptical of mental health institutions' ability to find viable solutions for her or other African American clients. She described her previous experience with a White female therapist, who insisted that the family try interventions that were incompatible with their value system, such as having family meetings to decide the rules that would exist in the house. These discussions sensitized me to Mrs. B.'s need to be heard, have her viewpoints acknowledged, and have therapy develop in a highly collaborative manner. Clearly, we would need a solid, trusting relationship, and interventions would need to be presented as suggestions with all demand or authoritarian qualities greatly reduced.

In our initial meeting, I assured Mrs. B. that even though I am not African American, my goal would be to explore the family's personal values and help them find solutions or options that would fit them personally. I also assured her that it was not my purpose to impose my personal value system upon her and her family. I told her that I was aware that some of my colleagues had very specific cookbook values about child rearing, but I realized that often these approved formulas do not fit African American or Latino families. My response must have been reassuring enough because she responded in a positive manner and was engaged enough to proceed with therapy, which would last for the next 11 months.

The early stages of therapy were difficult in that Mrs. B. wanted quick solutions but was hesitant to implement the behavior modification plans that started by changing one behavior at a time. She would state, "I don't think you understand, this may work well for White families, but it won't work for us." I maintained a supportive stance and would then explain, "I have respect for what you're telling me, but in order to help you, we have to find some common ground. These are interventions that have worked for individuals from many backgrounds." I would then address each behavior and intervention, query if and how it violated any personal or cultural value, and then proceed with the intervention after asking her if she would be willing to try it for a specified period of time. I assured her that she did not have to become White to accept these interventions, and we could modify those aspects that she found offensive so that the changes would fit for her as an individual and as an African American.

In my individual time with Brian, I found him quiet and sullen, but relatively cooperative. When I asked him why his mother had brought him to therapy, he told me that he did not act "good" at home because his mom made him mad. Brian was unable to articulate exactly what she was doing to create this anger in him. I asked him about the rules in his new home and he reported that he didn't know exactly what the rules were and this was confusing for him. In the weeks to come we would work toward clarifying those expectations in combined sessions with Brian and his mother.

As the session progressed, Brian continued to be quiet and sullen. He seemed suspicious or distrustful of this new experience he was being thrust into. I tried to make him feel at ease as I told him how the therapy would work. I told Brian that we would be talking together, and playing together, and I would see if I could help him and his family get along better. I showed him around the playroom, allowing him to see the selection of toys available. As we went through each section of the room, from one toy to another, he would examine each item, quietly manipulate it, then put it back in it's place. We made a tour of the room, and I told Brian that if he wanted, we could start playing today. In a somewhat sullen voice, he replied that he would wait until next time. I got a sense that he felt intimidated by this new place. I imagined that I was intimidating too. I am a big man, had a large beard, and given his probable molestation, it was possible that adult males might induce considerable fear in him. I knew it would be important to be quiet and gentle in therapy with Brian, letting him make the choices about how fast to go in this new arena. I felt that this was especially important given his lack of choices and history of being disempowered as a result of frequent foster placement changes and probable sexual molestation.

Even though Brian most clearly met the DSM-IV criteria for Conduct Disorder by his sexual perpetration, physical aggression and cruelty, and petty thievery, I also suspected that depression and anxiety might be underlying issues, perhaps fueling his acting-out behavior. I also did not rule out the possible contribution or interaction of Post Traumatic Stress Disorder, considering its common occurrence in sexual abuse survivors. However, I believed that to a large extent Brian's caution and fear also stemmed from his horrific experiences with the social welfare system's bureaucracy and his history of rejection and abuse by adults. I was an adult and I worked for what he might have perceived as one of the institutions that had failed to protect him and care for him. It would be my job in therapy to prove that I was not another exploitative person and that I could offer him caring and support following his victimization, something different from his previous experiences.

Case Conceptualization

While there were a multitude of issues that needed addressing in this case, three main points served as organizing principles in the formulation of intervention with Brian: (a) issues of rejection and abandonment in Brian's life, (b) the issue of sexual abuse, both its perpetration by Brian as well as his probable victimization, (c) the need to intervene with his adoptive parents to increase both their levels of nurturance and their effectiveness.

ADDRESSING FEELINGS OF REJECTION AND ABANDONMENT

Brian had lived a life in which each day reminded him that he was somehow unlovable, inferior, and worthy of rejection. From his point of view, he had been rejected by his natural parents, since they were unable to care for him. Internally, he might have wondered why he had been born into a world with parents who were so unfit and cared so little for him that he was taken from them. Feelings of rejection and abandonment were intensified by being tossed from one uncaring, emotionally disconnected foster family to another. And finally, upon adoption, it seemed that even here he would not gain the approval of his adoptive mother, no matter what he did. Brian's racial identity may have exacerbated his experience of being unworthy since members of the majority culture sometimes devalue people from his racial background.

It all seemed so unfair and out of his control. He had been helpless from the beginning, powerless to make any decision that really mattered in his life. The only thing that was clear for Brian was the fact that he had never been nurtured and loved, that people treated him as inferior, and that he had endured one rejection after another as he bounced from one foster home to the next. These experiences contributed to his perception of himself as defective. I hypothesized that Brian's acting-out gave him a sense of control and power by providing a "justification" for the rejection he had experienced and the abandonment he anticipated from the new family. His acting out was thus a defense against his powerlessness in the face of frequent abandonments and possible sexual victimization. This defense represented an attempt to impact the outcome of the adoption, which he expected to end in rejection and removal from the home.

Brian had come to view the world as an unpredictable place, and all decisions important in impacting the pain in his life were out of his control. So Brian seized power in the small ways that he could. He was stuck with a dominating adoptive mother, so Brian controlled by ignoring her and failing to comply with her demands. He attempted to take power in the relationships in which he was able to dominate, molesting his sister Alisha and abusing his more passive adoptive brother, Nathan.

Brian identified with the aggressors in his life and his destructive acting-out was a manifestation of this identification. I suspected that Brian's history of disrupted attachments robbed him of feelings for his victims. Further, since so many of the events in his life occurred without regard to his needs— and he did not have the power to remove himself from his life of pain—he "seized" power by inflicting pain upon those less powerful than himself. Thus, the issues of rejection and abandonment were interconnected with the second issue of sexual abuse.

ABUSE IN BRIAN'S LIFE

Because of the drug and alcohol abuse history of his natural parents, it is doubtful that a secure attachment had been formed between Brian and his mother, even though he reportedly lived with her for 2 years. Regardless of the quality of that relationship however, whatever attachment had been formed was disrupted when the children were pulled from the mother's custody and put into foster care. The foster care homes that followed were numerous and, even if the children started to become attached to a foster family, that was destroyed by the frequent custody changes. Not only were these relationships brief and disrupted but if Brian had been molested as suspected, he would also come to know the nature of his relationships with adults as frightful, hurtful, and dangerous. Through his life experiences, which appeared to also include molestation, this young child had come to know the world as a dangerous and unpredictable place. He had come to be distrustful of adults and guarded about getting emotionally attached to anyone, since it would only end in the sorrow of separation or abuse. He learned that he could not trust or rely on anyone in the world but himself. He learned that even to rely on himself alone was a dangerous position, given the fact that he had power to change very little in his world of pain. This lead him to control and inflict pain on others as a way of dealing with his own pain.

Finkelhor and Brown (1985) write compellingly about the impact of sexual abuse and note that it can result in traumatic sexualization, a sense of betrayal, feelings of powerlessness, and stigmatization. Brian's history, including his probable sexual victimization, had left him feeling ineffective and powerless. He had no consistent advocates and had experienced betrayal first by his biological family and later by the system that was supposed to care for him but had placed him in homes where he had been victimized. Finally, if Brian had indeed been sexually abused, his concept of sexual activity would have been shaped by this experience. Brian, for instance, may have come to see sexual contact as one way to be in control of others and to get them to respond to him.

INCREASING PARENTS' EFFECTIVENESS AND NURTURANCE

Brian's adoptive parents consisted of a controlling mother and an adoptive father who took on few parenting responsibilities. Brian thus lacked any warm or affectionate attachment to an authority or parental figure, something necessary for internalizing and following through on rules and expectations. He responded to his adoptive mother's attempts to control him by being noncompliant and by acting out in ways that would distress her (e.g., attacking Nathan or Alisha, or defecating outdoors). In this way he was not completely under her control nor was he completely powerless. Her expectations of complete obedience and his disempowering life experiences were fuel for his acting-out. Brian's adoptive father's minimal parenting in the early stages of therapy may have represented *emotional absence* that had also characterized many of his foster care experiences. Thus, Brian in his new home was faced with two parents whom he may have seen as either unresponsive (father) or controlling (mother). Further, as is often the case with children with Conduct Disorder, the parents appeared to lack an effective strategy for disciplining Brian and for providing for his emotional needs. Often these two issues go hand in hand, and I believed that providing concrete guidance would facilitate their ability to parent him more effectively (e.g., by setting and enforcing reasonable rules) as well as help them emotionally connect with their new son. In turn, I was convinced that helping Brian's adoptive parents learn to empathize with Brian's plight would lead them to develop empathy as well as develop and enforce appropriate limits, which I believed would greatly reduce his acting-out. Warmth and consistent limits that were clearly identified were, I believed, the key here.

Orienting Constructs

Brian had been referred to our clinic because of the strong suspicion of sexual abuse from his previous foster placement and his acting-out behavior. Sexual abuse was suspected not only because of the impending prosecution of the foster family for sexual abuse of other children placed in their home but also because of Brian's molestation of his sister and his other sexual acting-out behavior. Such behavior commonly occurs in children who have been molested themselves. This premise helped to organize my conceptualization of Brian's problems and was instrumental in establishing the goal of eventually helping Brian to process the emotional impact that such abuse had on his life. I hoped that eventually he could begin to articulate how that experience had impacted his own life emotionally and how his own sexual perpetration might impact the life of his victims. I hoped that by developing empathy for himself as a victim, and for his own victims, he would be safe from further perpetration in his life. I also hoped to help Brian find more appropriate ways to express his pain and gain empowerment (i.e., a sense of control and competence) in his life. These issues will be further elaborated in the treatment section.

The other construct that served to focus my treatment of this client is attachment theory and *internal working models.* I related to Brian as a boy who had never had a secure emotional bond with an attachment figure. His own internal concept of himself in relationship to others had been formed by his history of repeated trauma and left him with three problematic "templates" for interpersonal relations. Specifically (a) because Brian lacked a loving relationship in his life, he did not expect or feel he deserved one; (b) because he was abandoned throughout his life, he expected to be rejected and experienced himself as not love worthy; thus, he feared risking emotional commitment in his new home; and (c) because he had been exploited and sexually abused, he was distrustful of others and experienced himself as powerless and shameful. These painful developmental experiences shaped Brian's current, symptomatic reactions to his new family in which he tried to gain empowerment by shaming others. His sexual molestation of Alisha, attempted molestation of Nathan, and public defecation can be seen in this light. Although his behavior made sense given his history, his hostile and provocative behavior was maladaptive and further alienated him from members of his new adoptive family. In treatment, Brian needed to be given opportunities to test new ways of relating that did not fit the three old templates. The challenge was to help him grasp how previous conceptualizations about the nature of the world and relationships accurately fit the past but may not fit the present. I hoped that if my relationship with Brian could be characterized by warmth, caring, and active engagement, where he was not able to elicit anger and rejection in me even if my rules were violated, it would help to redefine what human relationships could provide. I could then in the context of this new kind of relationship help Brian internalize rules and ways of behaving that would enhance his quality of life, especially his relationship with his family. Thus, by not allowing him to reconstruct our relationship along the same old familiar and problematic lines, I hoped to utilize our relationship to provide him a new and better solution. In turn, I also aimed to give his family the tools they needed to provide Brian a more corrective experience at home, one that involved developing caring relationships where rules were enforced in an atmosphere of warmth and fairness. My hope was that if Brian and his adoptive family began to value each other, the parents would be willing to invest in the effort that effective parenting demands, and he would internalize their rules, which would lead to more rewarding family relationships.

Treatment Plans and Intervention Strategy

My treatment plan was organized across the three conceptualization issues I addressed earlier: (a) Brian's issues of abandonment and rejection, (b) Brian's sexual molestation, and (c) Brian's adoptive parents' parenting skills.

Short-Term Treatment Goals

1. Begin to establish a corrective emotional relationship with Brian that addresses issues of abandonment and rejection.
2. Openly address molestation issues, including Brian's molestation of his sister and the possibility of Brian's own sexual molestation.
3. Take steps to stop Brian's molestation of Alisha, and begin to work through feelings related to his own victimization.
4. Develop a trusting working relationship with the mother and deescalate the level of conflict between Brian and his mother at home.

Intermediate Treatment Goals

1. Continue to foster trust in my relationship with Brian. Help Brian to clarify what he is willing to do to obtain greater acceptance by his new family: What behaviors are expected? and What are the consequences and rewards?
2. Educate the parents about the normal development of 10-year-olds and common side effects of molestation, foster placement, and adoption.
3. Teach the parents more effective parenting skills and how they might be applied in the home.
4. Explore ways to enhance Brian's social skills. Encourage and support appropriate interaction with neighbors, school mates, and church members. Find ways to foster cooperation, self respect, and self-esteem.

Long-Term Treatment Goals

1. Through my relationship with Brian, provide a corrective emotional experience that permits him to work through issues of rejection and abandonment. Help Brian to integrate empathy, self control, and social skills into all areas of his life.
2. Uncover and work through molestation issues, especially feelings of powerlessness and shame. Help Brian identify and develop interests that would enhance his sense of competence.
3. Develop consistent and appropriate parenting practices in the family. Encourage Brian's father to share parenting responsibilities and take a more active role in Brian's emotional development.

INITIAL TREATMENT PLAN

As I began treatment with Brian, I considered Brian's molestation of Alisha and his own possible molestation to be central to his current problems, and I felt that these issues needed to take priority in treatment. It was important to help Brian find a way to stop the molestation of his sister because I was worried about her and because Brian might be removed from this home, as he had been removed from numerous foster homes in the past. Psychologically, this would have reenacted Brian's experience of being abandoned and fueled his sense of powerlessness, to which he may have reacted by increased acting out in an attempt to defend against his feelings of powerlessness. In addition, the probability of being adopted permanently again would be slim, and Brian would probably be further exposed to victimization. Finally, if he were removed from this home, he would lose the only stable relationship in his life, that which he had with his sister Alisha. I hoped to help make the molestation stop so that Brian would not lose the best chance he had been given in life thus far. I was also concerned about Alisha and the way in which she was being victimized. It was clear that this had to be addressed immediately.

Since Brian was a child perpetrator and was receiving treatment while still a child, I felt optimistic about his potential for a successful outcome. I felt great compassion for this young child who had endured so much pain that he would, in turn, inflict pain upon others.

In the beginning of treatment, Brian was reticent about playing with the toys in the playroom. I felt that this reticence was in part a manifestation of Brian's hesitance to engage with me (after all, this might represent another relationship he would soon lose). It may also have represented one way in which Brian could exert control over yet another situation where his wishes had not been ascertained and he was being forced to comply. Our first sessions, therefore, were spent talking to each other as I tried to convey my interest in him. I wanted to get a sense of who he was and what his world was like, so I asked him many questions that he answered in a sullen voice with intact but brief answers.

THERAPIST: How do you feel, talking to me?
BRIAN: (Shrugs)
THERAPIST: Do you feel like you were forced to come?
BRIAN: (Shrugs again)
THERAPIST: I know that sometimes adults force children to do things they don't want to do. Sometimes they do it because they care and want to be helpful, but sometimes they do it to be mean and hurtful. I think your mother brought you here because she would like it if you all got along better. I think she wants to be helpful. I know I want to be helpful.
BRIAN: (begins to look at therapist, suggesting that he hears this.)
THERAPIST: I can't help your family without your help Brian. Perhaps you and I can have fun together here and also find ways to have fun with your family without anybody being hurt or made to feel bad.

Brian's barely perceptible nod suggested that he heard me but his reluctance to engage quickly made sense given his history.

Given my grave concern about Brian's molestation of his sister, I felt the need to address this early.

THERAPIST: Brian, do you know what I mean when I use the term *molest?*
BRIAN: Yeah, you mean when you touch and play with someone's private parts.

THERAPIST: Your mother tells me that you molested your sister Alisha. Did that really happen Brian?

BRIAN: Yes.

THERAPIST: How did you feel about doing that to her?

BRIAN: (sits without making eye contact and does not answer)

THERAPIST: Were you glad about what you did to her?

BRIAN: No! (The reply is forceful and angry.)

THERAPIST: Were you sad about what you did to her?

BRIAN: No. (The reply is unemotional and stoic in nature.)

THERAPIST: Were you sorry that you did that to her?

BRIAN: (hesitantly looks away from my direction as he responds) Yeah.

THERAPIST: How many times did it happen Brian?

BRIAN: (tone is again sullen and angry) I don't know!

THERAPIST: Do you think it will happen again?

BRIAN: I don't think so.

THERAPIST: I'm glad to hear that, Brian. Brian, did anything like that ever happen to you?

BRIAN: No!

THERAPIST: Brian, this is an uncomfortable topic to discuss. Are you feeling uncomfortable?

BRIAN: No!

THERAPIST: You appear angry to me. Are you angry?

BRIAN: NO!

THERAPIST: What's that strong "no" about?

BRIAN: I don't know!

THERAPIST: I think that there are a couple of possible reasons. First of all, if something like that did happen to you, you may be angry at the person who did it. You may also be angry at me for bringing it up. Does that sound right to you?

At this point, Brian softened and shrugged his shoulders. After probing a bit more, with Brian again tensing up, I sensed that this was as close as I was going to get, and I decided to back off. Even though we appeared to reach a dead end with regard to this topic, once Brian entered therapy, molestation of his sister would never be reported again. I believe that by making my knowledge about the molestation of his sister explicit, coupled with interventions to provide more appropriate ways of relating to individuals (which will be discussed in more detail later), Brian was able to end the molestation. I did on several occasions tell Brian how proud I was of his decision to not molest Alisha anymore. We also discussed together ways to express feelings that did not hurt others. Although I asked Brian again if anything similar to his sister's molestation had ever happened to him, his response was a blank. He then looked away from me and he quickly said that nothing like that had ever happened to him. I subsequently steered him toward the anatomically correct dolls, wondering if his play with them would provide a hint of his own victimization. He showed me how he had touched his sister and used his finger to penetrate her but once again denied that he had ever experienced such a violation himself. There were blocks in the therapy playroom with phallic or orifice symbols on them. These blocks will often be a source of interest for children who have endured molestation, but Brian avoided them and continued to deny that he himself had been a victim. When I saw Brian's resistance, I told him I could understand that if he had been hurt himself, it must be scary, embarrassing, and uncomfortable to talk about it. I wanted to assure Brian that if something like that really did happen to him, I'd be sad and concerned for him. I also let him know that some children who are hurt in that way feel angry and hurt and sometimes try to hurt others in the same way they were hurt. I said their feelings were understandable but that they usually learned it was better to talk about it to an adult they trust and to try and find other ways to feel good about themselves. I closed by letting him know that if it's not safe and not a good time in our relationship to discuss something like this, he's the one to make that decision. I was aware that trust would need to develop between us before Brian felt comfortable enough to disclose what would have been a humiliating, degrading, and disempowering experience had he been molested. This was not something an already disempowered child would divulge to yet another "untrustworthy" adult. I would need to prove to Brian that I was an adult of a different sort, and I needed to find ways to let Brian know that not all relationships in life would be ones in which he would be the inferior, the powerless, and the loser.

I did let Brian know that if he had ever been molested and wanted to talk about it, I would be available and responsive but would not *force* him to talk about it. I was aware that forcing him to talk about it would only dynamically replay the force-compliance routine that characterizes victimization and I wanted to emphasize that in our relationship Brian had the power to choose when to discuss this issue.

Normally I do not request that the parent attend every session, but in this family's case, I thought it would be important because Brian was so unclear about expectations at home. It has been my experience in working with conduct disordered children that family interventions are often the most powerful, and I typically try to include *at least* one parent in the treatment process. Mrs. B. would join us for 30 minutes of our 1½ hour session. This time would be spent clarifying rules and expectations and collaborating in the development of behavior modification plans. I hoped this would clarify ways in which Brian might become successful within the home and I also hoped to teach the mother some parenting skills in the process. I wanted to use this time to help both Brian and his mother develop empathy for each other; and I tried to voice each one's point of view in ways that would make it palatable to the other.

Mrs. B. was very disturbed by Brian's lack of compliance with her requests in the home. I knew that if Brian could improve in this area, both he and his new mother would be much happier. It would also represent a small success in therapy on which we could build. I began by discussing with Mrs. B. what behaviors she would like to see change. Her initial responses had an angry, demanding quality yet were rather nonspecific and global, such as "I want him to be a good responsible child." In reality, Brian had no idea what being a "good, responsible child" entailed behaviorally; therefore, defining the mother's behavioral expectations became our mission during the conjoint part of our sessions.

As therapy progressed, we talked about attending to cues in Brian's behavior, learning to distinguish when he was headed for misbehavior, and how to intervene early and prevent the behavior from escalating. For example, when Brian began to tease Nathan, to intervene before he became aggressive and separate them. We also talked about using time-outs, in which Mrs. B. (or Nathan or other family member) and Brian could be apart from each other when they were angry, then return and settle the dispute after they had both calmed down. I talked to Mrs. B. about identifying a time-out place (like a chair facing a corner) and giving Brian a timer set with 5 minutes, with instructions not to leave until the timer went off. If necessary, Mrs. B. might need to stand behind the chair with no verbal interaction except to put her hand on Brian's shoulder if he tried to stand up. Once Brian realized her seriousness about this, there would eventually be less need for her to stand close by during time-outs. I thus attempted to implement behavior modification plans that would teach Mrs. B. more planning ways to control Brian's behavior.

We started out by defining some behaviors that Brian could work on developing. When I asked Mrs. B. if she could be more specific about what she would like Brian to do, her first reply was that she wanted him to listen to everything that she said. I explained that this was too broad, and it would be difficult to figure out whether Brian were really listening or not. We discussed how it would be easier if we chose a behavior that could be witnessed and measured. Mrs. B. made it clear that one of the things that she expected Brian to do each day was to make his bed and clean up his room, which he regularly failed to do. I explained that our new plan would work best if we started out working with just one behavior, and later on we might be able to add more. So, Brian agreed that he would try making his bed everyday. I explained that for a new behavior, it's asking too much that Brian be perfect the first week, so we agreed that he could miss making his bed one day out of the week and still get a reward. I asked Brian what kind of a prize would be worth working for. There was a special comic book that Brian loved. He had always seen it in the convenience store but had never had any money to buy it. Mrs. B. promised to buy it for him if he complied with their agreement. We drew up a contract that had a definition of the target behavior (i.e., making his bed), the expected frequency (number of times the behavior is required per week, in this case, 6 out of 7 times), and anticipated reward if the contract was fulfilled (the comic book). Brian and his Mom both signed the contract. In addition I gave them a Star Chart on which Brian could plot his daily achievement by placing shiny metallic stars on the days of the week in which he had performed his target behavior. An excited look came over Brian's face as we discussed his reward, as if he had already earned the treasure.

The following week, Mrs. B. and Brian returned. Brian looked intimidated and depressed. I had informed both of them that the initial period of our conjoint time would be spent checking up on progress and readjusting for the next week's work. During this portion of the session, Mrs. B. immediately complained that Brian had "failed," and said she "knew he could never do what he was told." When I asked how many times he had made his bed, the mother replied that he had made it 6 out of the 7 days, but it had taken much prodding to get him to do it. Because of that, she didn't feel that he should have the magazine. I tried to explain to Mrs. B., in a sensitive manner, that it was important that the rules not be changed after the session. If we wanted Brian to be better at home, it was important that he get what he had earned, otherwise the plan would not work. I also empathized with her feelings of frustration at having to remind him but highlighted the fact that he had indeed successfully met the goals set. This example represents the difficulty sometimes faced with designing behavioral interventions. I have since learned the importance of asking families what they think the problems might be that would arise with the plan we have designed, and together we brainstorm solutions to the potential loopholes. In this instance, I suggested that for the following week, we could add to the contract making the bed before breakfast in the morning and that she needn't remind him. He either did his chore by that time, or he did not. We talked about how all changes to the contract would need to be agreed upon by all of us. Mrs. B. seemed to understand the system better, and she then agreed to give him the magazine after all as acknowledgement of his meeting the contract as originally written. I believed that this became the point in therapy when Brian started to realize that I wanted things to be more fair for him in his relationship with his mother. He saw that I might be his advocate and not his enemy, as other adults had been in his history. Confirmation of this fact for Brian, however, was still weeks away. This incident also signaled Mrs. B.'s willingness to listen to reason, and I made overt this assessment as a positive quality to both Brian and Mrs. B. This was the beginning of helping them identify those aspects of their relationship that were positive and worth building upon.

The weeks that followed continued to be difficult. Mrs. B. continued to have difficulty with consistent follow through. For example, the following week, Brian didn't get his reward, even though he had met the agreement stipulated in his contract, because he acted-out at school. We again stressed the importance of rewarding appropriate behavior while trying to modify inappropriate behavior. The week after that, Mrs. B. judged some other behavior, instead of the target behavior, in deciding that Brian lacked behavioral control that week. It became clear to me that Mrs. B. had high expectations and difficulty acknowledging the successes. In fact, it seemed as though she was actively sabotaging the system and setting Brian up to fail—further fueling his sense of powerlessness, which in turn led him to respond by acting-out more. She complained about the behavior modification process and groaned about our focusing on this little stuff, "when he's such a big problem." I assured her that I understood how overwhelmed she must feel and tried to help her understand why the inconsistency and seemingly arbitrary changes in our contracts could only be counterproductive given Brian's history. For the first few weeks, it was difficult for me to control my counter-transference. I felt angry at her and wondered if she was encouraging me to reject her, just as she appeared to be rejecting Brian. I also hypothesized that her behavior may have something to do with her own templates and made a note to spend some time with her discussing her own family history so I could respond to her in a more empathetic fashion. I realized that to some extent she was set in her ways and resistant. I felt, however, that keeping a calm, patient, understanding, and nonjudgmental stance with her was critical in keeping her involved with Brian's treatment. I knew that I needed to model for her an ability to remain engaged and responsive, despite her criticism and expressed dissatisfaction. I believed that this stance in our relationship was essential in order to enable her to adopt a similar one in her relationship with Brian.

Thus, during the following month of therapy, I met for a short time with Mrs. B. alone. During this time I wanted her to get a sense that I understood how difficult this adoption experience had been for her and her family; and indeed, I believed that this had been the case. She and her husband had hoped to help the children, and, in the process, their lives had been unraveled.

I also spent some time getting a sense about who Mrs. B. was before all of this had happened in her life. She was the oldest child from a large family. She had been raised in the inner city when it was a less violent place. Her father had been absent from the household and her mother worked long hours to support the children. The money from a single income, in a family with many children, didn't stretch far enough and the family was fairly economically deprived. Since Mrs. B. was the oldest child in the family, she became the designated parent when the mother was gone. It was a huge responsibility for her as a young girl and forced her to grow up before her time. Mrs. B. seemed older and more worn than her age, and I felt badly that she, like Brian, had a tough life full of unfairness. I also felt badly that what she had hoped would be a turn of good will toward these parentless children, had turned into what she considered a huge, unanticipated burden. I thus learned to relate to Mrs. B. out of empathy for her. I saw that her intentions were good, indicated by her consistency in attending therapy sessions and her devotion in trying to help Brian in the face of her frustration. Beneath her gruff exterior, she was a kind woman. It was to her kind interior, and her own sense of deprivation, that I hoped to appeal in order to help her understand the painful reality of Brian's life. I hoped that if she could understand his perspective, she might be able to love him more and be more forgiving of him.

To accomplish this, I needed to make an empathic bid to Mrs. B. I responded to the feelings behind her sabotaging attempts toward the behavior modification plans. I responded by saying, "I can see how much he really wants your affirmation and that it's so hard for you to give it right now. I know you've had so much struggle in your own life and that you didn't get the kind of nurturance he is asking for and needs." This needed to be a tactful bid, so that it wouldn't be heard as punitive, angry, or manipulative. This was a delicate situation. I wanted Mrs. B. to feel a compassionate connection with me, as if I had an arm of understanding around her, while saying, "This poor little guy." I hoped to provide a *secure base,* or safe empathic place for the mother during our time together. I wanted this relationship of caring for her to say: He's probably looking for a place he can come to, and I understand that he does it in ways that are hard for you to deal with; But what he's really doing, underneath, is wanting more of you.

It was my job to help the mother see that beneath this acting-out, there was a hurting little child. One way to do this was by acknowledging the child inside the mother and responding to mother's little kid. In some ways, my job was to model how one can understand that negativity and criticism mask pain and frustration. I also wanted to be the cognitive interpreter for Brian's mother of his behavior on a deeper level. Brian's real message was, "I want to be loved and cared about by you." I could then translate to the mother, "He really likes you, wants your love, you're important." This was a way of being affirming to the mother in a situation that on the surface seemed anything but affirming. It was also important that, when Brian had done well, I acknowledge his mother's contribution to that success. By doing this, I could model how to show affirmation or approval of the child in his legitimate success.

In about the fourth session, the adoptive father presented to therapy with Brian and his adoptive mother. Mr. B. was a police officer and had taken some time off of work because of a job-related injury. He came to the therapy session dressed informally in a sweat shirt and casual pants. He was a huge man, about 6 feet 5 inches, heavily built, and a little overweight.

When Mr. B. came to therapy, I hoped to promote the idea that he and Mrs. B. could function as a team. I found that Mr. B. was more capable of being emotionally available than Mrs. B. was at this time, and I encouraged her to invite Mr. B.'s participation in working with Brian at home. Mr. B., I learned, had grown up in the suburbs in a family that was working class. There were fewer children in his family of origin compared to Mrs. B.'s, so consequently they were more financially stable. Mr. B.'s father had also been absent, and without a father role model, Mr. B. had never learned from his own family how to be part of an active husband and wife parenting team. He consequently spent lots of time at work and seemed psychologically absent to the family. I encouraged that he play a more active role in the family by assisting his wife in monitoring Brian and following through on behavior modification plans. This could also relieve Mrs. B. of some of the parenting burden, which she had seemed to take on by herself, just as she had parented her siblings alone in her family of origin.

Even though the father was an impressively large and physically powerful man, he was kind and gentle. Though he towered over his wife, she was definitely the one in charge. I thought of Mr. B. as "the lieutenant," taking orders from his wife, "the general." It was interesting to see them interact. Every time he would respond, she would appear to invalidate or contradict his response. I came to recognize that this represented her way of interacting and was perhaps a manifestation of her need to maintain control and have her perspective validated. This made sense per her history of having been given responsibility for her siblings, with little validation for how well she had managed. However, even though Mrs. B. seemed to override her husband's opinion about most things, she had respect for his superior understanding of technical issues. This included his understanding of the dynamics involved in the behavior modification contracts. He really understood the purpose of the behavioral interventions and how to implement them. He was very task oriented and would translate to Mrs. B. exactly what she needed to do in order for the behavior modification plans to work. Though I myself had done this in the past few weeks, with limited success, Mr. B. was able to not only put what Mrs. B. needed to do into words that she better understood but he was able to keep the program in check during the week. It was very instructive for me to observe him and the way in which he was able to get his message across. This reinforced for me the importance of seeing as many members of a family as possible when working with conduct disordered children and identifying each member's strengths and trying to utilize those strengths. Mr. B. came for the next 6 weeks while he was still off work. He was optimistic compared to her pessimistic outlook, and Brian made great gains during that period of time. He was doing well in attaining behavioral goals and received the rewards that he had earned. Everyone acknowledged his improvement, except Mrs. B. (in part because Brian had been cast into the "bad boy" role), whose own life experiences, including much adversity, made her suspicious of success, and she questioned if it would last. I acknowledged her concerns but tried to instill optimism by noting how much progress we had made despite Brian's horrendous early history.

During this same period of time, Brian and I were continuing to strengthen our relationship. During the first few weeks, Brian was sullen and noncompliant. He did not want to play, which I viewed as his attempt to exert control over the situation. I tried to align with his need for control by emphasizing that *he* could choose what games to play with. Brian then tested me by deliberately breaking several toys. I let him know that this behavior was not acceptable but continued to be warm and engaged with him.

In this process, I began to disconfirm Brian's view that people would eventually reject him and that all he had to do to speed this process was act-out. In setting limits, I conveyed to Brian my view that he was worth the effort. This experience seemed to help strengthen our relationship.

Over time, I realized that both Brian and I were marking time, dreading the conjoint portion of therapy with Mrs. B. At this point, I shared my insight with Brian and asked him if he felt similarly. He agreed and shared that he was really quite frightened of his new mother. I attempted to join with him by talking about how powerful and at times demanding she was. I told him that I thought he had a tough role to play because it seemed so difficult to make her happy. In addition, I wondered aloud that if she was always going to be unhappy and feel that he was a "bad boy," that he may often feel he might as well misbehave so that at least he would feel he deserved her anger. This appeared to be a powerful thing to say to him. He stared in wonder, as if he couldn't believe his ears and was afraid to speak for fear of breaking the spell. I also shared that while this was a difficult person to deal with, I thought that, deep down, she cared about him and that the task he and I had was to draw that out of her. I also reassured him that our relationship would be different. I did have rules that had to be obeyed, but they were, I thought, reasonable, consistent, and few. While there would be consequences to not obeying the rules, I would always care about him.

This exchange appeared to change the nature of our sessions. He began to play with toys in the playroom. His favorite activity was playing war. He would go to the sand table and create elaborate scenes with the male army figures. In the first several weeks, the theme was always the same. The "little guys" would be pitted against the "big guys." It was as if Brian could not imagine that the battle could ever be fair. It would be a tremendous battle in which Brian would provide the sounds of the explosions, the humming of the tanks, and the screams of the dying soldiers. The outcome, however, was always the same, and the little guys would always lose. He was fixed in this pattern, and I could see in his metaphor of battle that this was the theme of Brian's life. He too was a little guy, with a history of his own failed battles, and without the hope of ever having enough power to win. Throughout this early stage, my role was that of an observer who relayed what I was seeing both metaphorically and literally.

One day, remarking yet again how much I enjoy playing war, he finally invited me to play. Brian set me the task of representing the big soldiers, and he took the army comprised of smaller soldiers. Over time, the battle scenes generated detailed conversations between Brian and me about battle strategies. I introduced to him the idea that the small characters didn't always have to lose, that they could be more clever, cunning, and planning. They could also be more agile, run faster, and hide better because they were less bulky. We talked about how some really smart military men would be in a position so high that they could get what they wanted purely by negotiation skills, saving many lives. We started to look at, and talk about, all of the ways a small guy could develop himself in order to be successful in our mock battle scenes. I hoped to offer options to Brian as he vicariously replayed over and over again his own position of powerlessness in his life: his past sexual abuse, his history of repeated abandonments, and his current rejection from his new adoptive mother.

I suggested in one session that we mix up the sizes of the soldiers in our armies, with each side having big soldiers and smaller soldiers. He was bewildered by this at first, but he was willing to give it a try. Brian began to love playing with the mixed-size armies and he enjoyed the creative strategies that we planned. We talked about how each type of soldier had his own assets and how the little guys could sometimes be the best if they were smart. Our soldiers began to develop relationships with each other and when one guy got hurt in battle, other fellow soldiers would drag him into a fox hole, call for the medic, and the men would try to care for him in the meantime and hope that he survived. We imagined together what it might be like emotionally to be hurt in battle. I said I really wouldn't want to lose that man, not only because he was a good soldier but because he was also a great buddy. I wanted Brian to understand that all of the men were important, not only as battle objects but as members of the team and as friends to each other. The battle scenes became an important way to build trust in our relationship and to cognitively develop alternative strategies that could translate into Brian's real life. We discussed for example, instead of throwing feces at neighbors to get their attention, using other more socially appropriate behaviors. Over time, Brian was able to generate numerous alternatives, such as inviting kids over to play with his wrestling men, asking them if he could join a game in progress, and pitching in to help a neighbor complete a chore.

Brian's original noncompliance and petty thievery had largely disappeared. However, on one occasion, Brian tried to slip his favorite army character into his pocket. We had established early in therapy the rules of the playroom. They were very simple. Brian could use any toy in the room. However, the toys couldn't be intentionally broken or used to hurt others, they had to stay in the therapy room, and they had to be put away before the end of the session. On this particular occasion, about 2½ half months into our sessions, Mrs. B. had been particularly difficult. Brian, according to Mom, was slipping; and she asserted that what I was doing was not working. She found that she needed to come down harder and harder on Brian. Although I disagreed with her assessment based on my observations and the reports from Brian and Mr. B., I dealt with Mrs. B. relatively passively by asking her to be patient. Following the session, Brian told me he forgot something in the playroom, and we returned to it. At this time, Brian proceeded to pilfer the soldier that had always been considered the leader, the most clever of them all. As he picked up his jacket, I saw Brian put the little plastic soldier into his pocket. I told Brian that he would have to leave the soldier in the playroom because that was the rule, but I could understand why he might like to take him, so he could continue to have fun with him at home. I said I understood why this soldier was special—he was loved and admired by others, not criticized and rejected as can sometimes happen to soldiers. I wanted Brian to know that I could understand his motivations and the world from his point of view. I also wanted him to understand that it was possible to be with an adult who could impose structure consistently and benevolently, while, at the same time, staying attached in the relationship. It was important for Brian to know that, rather than being judged only by his breach of the rules, I regarded his acts as being separate from the core of who he was, the core that I saw as lovable and valuable in an enduring way. I wanted to focus on the consequence of the behavior, rather than how his testing behavior effected my value for him as a person. I hoped that my voice conveyed a matter-of-fact tone. I wanted Brian to know that my feelings for him would not change, even while he tested my consistency and availability with his behavior. Brian needed to know that no matter how he tested me, I could stay emotionally connected to him. I watched Brian pull the army guy out of his back pocket and put him back in his place. We finished the session as usual that day, and I told him that I would be looking forward to our next session together. I believed that I had successfully passed his test. I could set firm limits for Brian and, at the same time, be accepting of him as a person. This, I felt, created safety for Brian and allowed us to develop a relationship characterized by trust. Although I believe that a crucial component of this particular behavior was Brian's taking a representation of me—a soldier—to help him battle his mother, I knew that I needed to respond to the inappropriateness of stealing. I considered that I would perhaps have to give Brian something concrete (perhaps another soldier) as a representation and reminder that battles could be resolved in a variety of ways. I wondered if Brian felt that I had let him down in the conjoint session, and, now, not only was he alone once again but he would have to deal with a larger-than-life mother over the next week. In retrospect, a more effective intervention at the time of the stealing incident would have been to note Brian's "abduction" of the soldier and ask him what made him take him. This would have provided useful information as to whether Brian could yet address his needs directly, and in the event that he could not, would have provided me an opportunity to discuss the possibility that he experienced the interaction with his mom as an abandonment on my part.

Indeed, in the following session, Mrs. B. was less amenable to suggestions, and I found myself working doubly hard. I decided to acknowledge her strengths and validated her efforts as a parent by asking her how she thought we should proceed. This seemed to surprise her, and she acknowledged that some of the things we had done had worked. She was then much more amenable to continuing the interventions, and I thereafter credited her role and declared how her following through made a major difference in Brian's success.

Developing empathy for others was a major goal of therapy. Brian needed to understand that he was not the only person who was small and picked on, that others who went through painful experiences had feelings similar to his own. I wanted him to increase his repertoire of appropriate responses when these feelings arose. I began doing this by the way that we talked about the army characters and their feelings and subjective experiences with war; then I loaned Brian books to read and take home.

The books were a series I had collected that used fantasy characters to demonstrate how it felt to be hurt by bigger, bully characters. The books also explored various creative alternative solutions to obtain more power in situations where one feels powerless. If we had read the stories together in session, the activity would have seemed below his level because the books were designed for children a little younger than Brian, but the reading level was just right for Brian's abilities. So the books became part of his homework assignment. I said, "These books may seem a little easy for you, but the message of the characters is the important part. See if you can understand the lesson that the book teaches and we'll talk about it next week." One of the books, for example, was the story of a small dinosaur who was constantly being physically hurt and humiliated by a huge mean dinosaur [from the book *Tyrone the Horrible* by Hans Wilhelm, New York: Scholastic Inc.]. They lived in the same neighborhood and the big bully dinosaur would steal the smaller dinosaur's lunch. He would tease him, punch him, embarrass him, and hurt him physically. The smaller dinosaur had a difficult time getting to sleep at night because he kept thinking about ways he might be able to avoid the bully. The small dinosaur, Boland, thought with his friends about ways in which he could react that might change the situation. He tried every option he could think of. He offered the mean dinosaur ice cream, he tried to ignore him, and he tried to fight back, but all of these options ended in disaster. Finally, the small guy walked by the bully with a sandwich, which was quickly stolen by the big dinosaur. This time, however, the little dinosaur had been clever. He had filled the sandwich with flaming hot peppers that burned his mouth, and the bully never bothered him again. Brian liked these stories because they were like our battle scenes in which the little guys could find ways to prevail through their own creativity and cleverness. We continued to discuss how it felt to be in the losing position and explored various options to become empowered. Brian and I were able to use these books and our play with the army men to explore times when Brian himself had felt powerless and how he might respond in the future when faced with disempowering experiences.

Other than the reading homework, what Brian chose to do in our weekly sessions was usually the same. The only deviation from the battle scenes with the soldiers was Brian bringing in wrestling figures from his collection at home, but the theme was the same. It would always be life-like human figures fighting each other. There was a lack of creativity to the play. Brian was unsophisticated and undefended in the way he compulsively repeated the conflicts that had been his life experiences. The play during my time with Brian in therapy would never move from confrontational scenes, but he showed growth in his ability to articulate the conflict between the soldiers, and the characters gradually became capable of showing emotions and capabilities beyond their potential for aggression. Brian's growth could be witnessed by his transition from the "splitting" that was observed in the early battle scenes, in which soldiers were either large or small, good or bad, powerful or powerless, or winners versus losers. Later battles were filled with people on both sides who were more real and three dimensional in character. This transition was an indication of growth for Brian. As an observer and participant, I verbalized my observations about how the soldiers had grown and were not all good/bad, powerful/powerless or winners/losers but sometimes won and sometimes lost, sometimes did bad things that didn't make *them* bad or unlovable. Occasionally, we would bring these issues closer to home and talk about whether Brian had ever thought he was bad just because he had *done* something bad and so forth.

Based on this growth, I returned to the issue of possible molestation. Broaching the subject tentatively, I told Brian that when he felt the time was right, perhaps he could answer some questions I had about the possibility of his being forced to engage in sexual behavior against his will. I made it clear that the choice was up to Brian, and at this time he chose to not discuss this issue. However, he agreed to let me know if some time felt right in the future. Unfortunately, I left the agency before Brian was able to address this issue directly and, in transferring him to a new therapist, made note of the importance of this in later therapy. I felt that as Brian began to feel more powerful and gained greater understanding of the fact that something bad happening to him did not make him a bad person, he would be more open to addressing this painful experience.

Brian's parents gradually learned better ways to cope with his difficult behavior. They learned new skills and gained at least some understanding of what it had been like to live in Brian's world of repeated rejections and abuses. The parents learned slowly how to plan Brian's day better in order to avoid problems, for example, getting him up earlier, and having a schedule of activities for before and after school. This list of activities with their deadlines was posted on Brian's bulletin board as well as in the kitchen. The behavior modification plans that involved extinguishing undesirable behaviors (e.g., Brian could use foul language no more than once/day to get a star, which was gradually reduced to no more than 5 times/week and later to 3 times and finally to no times/week) and developing more desirable ones (e.g., making his bed by 7:45 A.M. each morning) became more successful as Mr. B., who was more consistent in implementation of the program, increased his participation. The interest that Mr. B. had in Brian meant a lot to Brian, since Mr. B. seemed to be more willing to become interpersonally connected to Brian and affirming of him than had Mrs. B. I encouraged the parents to get Brian involved in some group sports and church activities in order to develop cooperation skills and more age-appropriate social skills. Brian and Nathan both joined Little League, got involved in soccer and in their church's youth group. In these arenas, they began to share more positive experiences, which was enhanced by Mr. B.'s participation and engagement with them.

REVISED TREATMENT PLAN

In the initial session, the mother had stated that Brian would purposely disobey her. I had inferred this to mean that he might be passive-aggressive, but as I gathered information from Brian, I began to wonder if cognitive deficits might be causing some of his confusion. Upon further inquiry, I realized that Brian had large lapses of memory and could not even recollect things that should have been important to him. I asked him to keep track of the number of times his mother had to ask him to go to bed each night, and this was difficult for him to do. He often couldn't remember the homework assignments. I began to inquire further, and it turned out that he couldn't even remember what had happened in past therapy sessions. Furthermore, he couldn't remember fun things he had done in the recent past. This memory dysfunction is a characteristic very common in children with Conduct Disorder, and it is suggested by some neuropsychologists to be a major contributor to the transgressions (see Kazdin, 1987 for review); I realized that I had to teach Brian some strategies that could help him improve his memory.

I began this work by helping Brian to remember through elaborate rehearsal. We would repeat the rules of the playroom many times during the session, until Brian himself was able to repeat the rules by heart. Additionally we would make lists that helped remind Brian of important things. This included putting a list of the playroom rules on a chart that we posted on the back of the playroom door. We would also make lists together for the coming week that were designed to help Brian remember homework or other things (e.g., making his bed or taking the trash out) that he planned to do during the week. Part of our weekly session involved questioning Brian to assess what was important for him that week. I would then write what he wanted to accomplish in that week on a piece of paper that included each day of the week divided into morning, afternoon, and evening; he would post this in his room when he got home. We talked about how important it was to check the paper at least three times each day at home (before school, after school, before bed), and I always asked him how much he was able to do from his list during the next therapy session. I often modeled the use of lists in therapy, as we checked off our clean-up list at the end of each session.

We thought up rhymes and funny stories associated with things that Brian needed to remember. I told Brian to remember the saying, They'll think I'm being *bad,* if I don't make my *bed.* While this rhyme had its utility, it was also important to emphasize that Brian *was not* bad if he did not make his bed. On the contrary, because he was essentially a good boy, he was motivated to keep his parents from *thinking* this. Another rhyme we used was I must check my *list* or something will be *missed.* We repeated the words together, exaggerating the rhythm and the rhyme. The rhymes appeared to be helpful in remembering his daily tasks, and we would repeat them as we discussed his homework progress for the last week. We would also chant the rhyme before he left, when we discussed the goals for the week ahead. Brian seemed to like this silliness that we shared together, and it served its purpose by enhancing Brian's ability to remember his daily assignments. It also taught him a skill he could apply in the future. These strategies were also conveyed to the parents and they learned to incorporate them into their parenting with Brian. Mr. B., a funny and creative man, seemed to enjoy making up rhymes and songs for all the children. Mrs. B. shook her head and smiled as she described how her husband was "getting into" reminding the kids of their chores with a little song or poem. I was very pleased that what had been a negative task for Mrs. B. (reminding Brian and the others of their chores) had become an amusing family event.

BALANCING GOALS

One of the most difficult aspects of balancing goals in this case was my feeling of urgency to address the molestation and perpetration issues with Brian—before a trusting therapeutic relationship had fully developed. I quickly came to like Brian. His quietness reminded me of myself as a child, and I felt a deep sadness for the pain that Brian had suffered in his short and intensely difficult life. I felt deep concern that if Brian continued to molest his sister, his new family would have a reason to have him removed from the home. After his tumultuous life history, with multiple separations, this would have been probably the worst yet, since it would require that he be separated from his sister—the only lasting relationship in his life. I believe I pushed too hard, trying to get him to talk about his own possible sexual abuse, and in retrospect wonder if I should have pushed less. I also believe however, that there was a beneficial effect in discussing Brian's perpetration right from the beginning. It made it clear that I knew what had happened (removing the air of secrecy that so often shrouds molestation), we had an opportunity to discuss the possibility of it happening again, and I was able to open the door to future discussions as our relationship strengthened. Since the family was fully aware of Brian's potential, we also discussed ways in which they could better supervise the children to prevent Brian from further sexual acting-out. I believe that the reason Brian was never caught molesting his sister again was the full disclosure within the family and the therapy setting, and not because he had become more cunning in his perpetration.

The other difficulty was managing Mrs. B. She was challenging for me because she evoked lots of negative countertransference. I found her to be rigid, resistant, and complaining. I used my experience of her to imagine what Brian's experience of her might be, and this helped me to develop even more empathy for the little boy. Even though she was difficult, I knew I needed to establish a working relationship with her to be able to keep Brian in therapy. If I alienated her, she would pull him from the treatment as she had done with their first therapist. So, I had to find ways to bridge this gap I felt between Mrs. B. and myself. I responded to the feelings behind her frustration, I learned about her own history so I could understand her behavior, and I learned from Mr. B. the language and style she seemed to respond to. Over time, I was able to successfully join with the mother, and this change in our relationship moved her. I also knew that she deserved a great deal of credit for bringing Brian to therapy, which I conveyed to her.

When Mr. B. came to therapy, I promoted the idea that Mr. and Mrs. B. function as a team. I encouraged him to play a more active role in the family by assisting his wife in monitoring Brian and following through on behavior modification plans. Further, since he was an athletic man interested in sports, I suggested that he help Brian and Nathan join sporting activities. When Mr. and Mrs. B. worked together on the program they saw that it worked. This reinforced and encouraged the father's participation without alienating the mother. Further, given Mrs. B's history of parenting her siblings with very little assistance, this process of shared parenting was very therapeutic for her. I recommended that she and her husband might benefit by further dividing parenting tasks. So, part of the intervention was to find out what each parent's strengths were and what each could do better or best, and they were encouraged to operate in that sphere. It happened that Mom could do the caretaking in functional areas (i.e., getting the kids to school), while Dad could take care of emotional nurturing, which included playing and talking to them more.

Therapeutic Process

RELATIONAL REENACTMENTS

What I expected Brian to recreate with me in therapy was his role as the kid not worthy of being loved. I thought that acting-out would be a major problem in the treatment setting. This did indeed occur to some extent in the initial part of therapy. Compared to many children with Conduct Disorder, however, it was relatively minimal and all but disappeared when he learned to trust our relationship and became connected to me. I had a sense that Brian had been the loser with adults so many times that he had conceded to being "powerless" with them unless he acted-out. Brian was surprised by the respect I gave him as we played army, side by side. Our process together was enacting a solution to his conflicts as we talked about our strategies together as *equals,* rather than I being the directing adult and he being the submissive child. He couldn't believe that I would consider him capable of making good decisions, and, because of that, he was initially cautious with me. It took him some time to become less skeptical about my credibility, but as Brian began to feel more powerful, and he saw that I was consistent and sincere, he gradually began to trust me.

I also believed that Brian was quite depressed at the onset of treatment. As time progressed, he saw that he would not be a victim in our relationship, which helped him move beyond his ritual of the little men losing to the big men. He was free to try new plans and think about new ways of conceptualizing the battle field. These changes may have seemed small in the context of Brian's life, but, for him, these were great leaps. The rigidity in his play reflected the repetitive theme of his life, that of powerlessness and victimization; and his attempt to defend against these was evident in his acting out, especially in his victimization of others. Within our relationship, and with his new family, there was now the possibility for more positive outcomes. In many ways this was threatening for Brian, because there had been predictability and a security that came from his knowing that he would always lose. In many ways this consistent pain and turmoil had become a primary attachment for him; it was the only thing he could really count on throughout his life. Like all children who have suffered such life experiences, he would feel insecure and threatened as the prospect of a better life became possible since this was foreign and unfamiliar to him. This expectation that all relationships with him would eventually fail induced Brian's caution and suspicion about his new family life and our relationship. Over time, however, consistent warmth and respect lead to increased trust on his part in our relationship. In time this generalized somewhat to the relationship between Brian and his adoptive parents as they also began to interact more positively and share pleasurable activities.

IMPEDIMENTS TO TREATMENT

The biggest impediment to change was Mrs. B. Even though she seemed committed to helping Brian, she continued to be stubborn in her adherence to her own rules, which changed often. She was inconsistent in following through on the behavior modification plans we developed and often expected things to deteriorate. It was difficult for her to make clear specific requests of the children and even harder for her to be objective about rating their behavior (especially positive behavior) and delivering fair and consistent consequences. No matter how much I tried to educate her about the power of positive reinforcement, she seemed to cling to the adverse control she had grown up with. She scolded, nagged, and degraded Brian until he complied, and when he finally did, it was not good enough. Even though Brian had made significant gains from therapy, Mrs. B. still had a difficult time admitting his progress. Her expectations for future failure made it hard for her to accept and enjoy current successes. Mr. B., on the other hand, could see that Brian had improved in small ways, and his acknowledgment of Brian's changes enabled Brian to feel more valued in the home and more confident in himself. I tried to maintain periodic phone contact with Mr. B., since he was unable to attend therapy regularly, to keep him involved in Brian's therapy work and to keep Brian's door to approval open in the home.

I also recommended a parenting group run by the church where Mrs. B. could have feedback from other parents whose cultural values matched hers but who had been able to effectively utilize positive reinforcement. This group also provided emotional and social support for her.

Termination and Therapist's Summary Thoughts

Therapy had lasted 11 months with Brian and his family when I accepted another professional position and would be leaving the clinic. I felt concerned about the impact that this premature ending might have on Brian. I feared that once again Brian would feel that he was being involuntarily forced away from a relationship that he had begun to trust. In his life of abrupt and artificial endings, I feared that the close of our relationship would also be traumatizing. I disclosed the termination date as soon as I decided to take the new position. This allowed us about a month before termination to talk about the ending. I began to summarize with Brian where we had come from, how much progress he had made, and where he would go next. We had made major gains in his home life. There had been no more reports of molesting his sister, and the sexual acting out behavior with Nathan had stopped. He and Nathan still punched each other and fought, but it occurred less frequently now, and they also had some positive activities in common (soccer, baseball, church youth group). Brian was more compliant with his mother, even though she still had difficulty acknowledging his improvement. The biggest gain at home, however, was the increased participation of Mr. B. in helping Mrs. B. manage Brian's behavior and his increased involvement in fun activities with all the children. Brian had learned to respect Mr. B. He was a "big guy" who was gentle, attentive, dependable, and consistent. This was a twist that was new to Brian. I felt that I had also shown Brian that, at least sometimes, big guys could be respectful, sincerely caring, and fair.

I felt that in our short time together, Brian began to feel like a more valuable person. Many people in his world were working together to improve his life. He learned some alternative ways of conceptualizing problems and more adaptive ways to behave; and he no longer experienced himself as a powerless victim who could gain control only by victimizing others. Although his mother was still skeptical about Brian's therapeutic gains, I sensed she was open to continued work if she hooked up with the right therapist. Interestingly, she asked that the next therapist also be a man of color. While I did not think Brian could only work with a therapist of color, I did refer the family to a therapist that I personally knew to be culturally sensitive and, because he was a man of color, he was also likely to keep Mrs. B. involved with therapy. I also knew that this therapist would be sensitive and caring enough to be able to provide Brian with the holding environment he needed in order to continue building trust and developing in a positive direction.

I wanted to see Brian increase his social skills and therefore referred him to group therapy with other boys. I also thought that other activities involving social skills would be helpful. Mr. B., on my recommendation, signed the boys up for sports, and Brian and Nathan were set to play on a team for the next baseball season and were going to soccer practices. I also encouraged church activities that could help Brian to develop further the skills that would help him get along better with others and to build a network of nurturing relationships.

About two weeks from the actual termination date, I wanted Brian to address directly the end of therapy with me. I said to Brian, "I think you know what it's like to leave. You've had to leave a lot of places. Do you think it will be difficult?" Brian replied in a quiet voice, "Yes." "Do you think it will be sad?" He nodded affirmatively this time. His eyes welled with tears, but he could not articulate his sadness. I told him that our relationship had meant a lot to me, and that I would miss him. He could not speak, but the tears began to stream onto his cheeks, and I saw proof of this bond that had grown between us.

It was difficult for me to terminate with Brian because I had come to feel a real connection with him and to understand his pain. I was concerned that, if the family did not make the right connection in therapy, Brian would be stranded without the support the family needed to achieve Brian's long-term therapy goals. I felt better as it became clear that the family would indeed go to the therapist I had recommended. I also felt good about the improved relationships within the family. Even though there was still much work to be done, Brian had made significant progress. I could feel sure that I had given Brian something that would never be taken away or separated from him, that is, the experience of being with someone who really cared about him and the hope that his life could be different. These were gifts that would last a lifetime.

REFERENCES

Allen, L., & Majidi-Ahi, S. (1989). African American Children. In J. Taylor Gibbs & L. Nahme Huang (Eds.), *Children of color: Psychological interventions with minority youth* (pp. 148–178). New York: McGraw-Hill.

American Psychiatric Association. (1994). *Diagnostic and statistical manual of mental disorders* (4th ed.). Washington, DC: Author.

Campbell, S. B. (1991). Longitudinal studies of active and aggressive preschoolers: Individual differences in early behavior and in outcome. In D. Cicchetti & S. L. Toth (Eds.), *Rochester Symposium on Developmental Psychopathology: Vol. 2. Internalizing and externalizing expression of dysfunction* (pp. 57–90). Hillsdale, NJ: Erlbaum.

Egeland, B., Kalloske, M., Gottesman, N., & Erikson, M. E. (1990). Preschool behavior problems: Stability and factors accounting for change. *Journal of Child Psychology and Psychiatry, 31,* 891–909.

Erickson, M. F., Sroufe, L. A., & Egeland, B. (1985). The relationship between quality of attachment and behavior problems in preschool in a high risk sample.

In I. Bretherton & E. Waters (Eds.), Growing points in attachment theory and research. *Monographs of the Society for Research in Child Development, 50* (Serial No. 209, Nos. 1-2), 147–186.

Finkelhor, D., & Brown, A. (1985). The traumatic impact of child sexual abuse: A conceptualization. *Journal of Orthopsychiatry, 55*(4), 530–541.

Gibbs, J. T. (1989). African American Adolescents. In J. Taylor Gibbs & L. Nahme Huang (Eds.), *Children of color: Psychological interventions with minority youth* (pp. 148–178). New York: McGraw-Hill.

Gillum, R., Gomez-Marin, O., & Prineas, R. (1984). Racial differences in personality, behavior, and family environment in Minneapolis school children. *Journal of the National Medical Association, 76,* 1097–1105.

Hill, R. B. (1972). *The strengths of Black families.* New York: Emerson Hall.

Hollingshead, A., & Redlich, F. (1958). *Social class and mental illness.* New York: Wiley.

Kazdin, A. (1987). *Conduct disorders in childhood and adolescence.* Newbury Park, CA: Sage.

Lewis, D. (1975). The Black family: Socialization and sex roles. *Phylon, 36,* 221–237.

Renken, B., Egeland, B., Marvinney, D., Mangelsdorf, S., & Sroufe, L. A., (1989). Early childhood antecedents of aggression and passive-withdrawal in early elementary school. *Journal of Personality, 57,* 257–281.

Sue, S. (1977). Community mental health services to minority groups: Some optimism, some pessimism. *American Psychologist, 32,* 616–624.

Waters, E., Posada, G., Crowell, J., & Keng-ling, L. (1993). Is attachment theory ready to contribute to our understanding of disruptive behavior problems? [Special issue] *Development and Psychopathology, 5*(1–2), 215–224.

Wenar, C. (1994). *Developmental psychopathology from infancy to adolescence* (3rd ed.). New York: McGraw-Hill.

SUGGESTIONS FOR FURTHER READING

Gibbs, J. T., Nahme Huang, L., et al. (1989). *Children of color: Psychological interventions with minority youth.* San Francisco: Jossey-Bass. Provides excellent information about cultural differences and culturally sensitive treatment planning.

Sue, D. W., & Sue, D. (1990). *Counseling the culturally different.* New York: Wiley. Provides a summary of the research in the field of cross-cultural counseling and infers how this material can be applied.

Wenar, C. (1994). *Developmental psychopathology from infancy to adolescence* (3rd ed.). New York: McGraw-Hill. Provides a summary of research on child and adolescent psychopathology. Reviews etiology and treatment approaches. The chapter on Conduct Disorders and inadequate self-control is of particular interest.

Chapter 13

SPIRITUAL VALUES CLARIFICATION

CASE ILLUSTRATION OF LINDA:
A 16-YEAR-OLD DEPRESSED DAUGHTER
OF MISSIONARY PARENTS

John Powell, Ph.D.

THE ISSUES

She rose slowly from her chair as I entered the waiting room, neither resisting nor imitating the self-extending manner of her parents. Her movements were slow and her countenance sad. Her thin frame was covered by a print dress and her straight hair tied with a ribbon. When my eyes turned to her she offered a reluctant handshake. In a moment of silence she spoke in a barely audible voice, "I'm the one my dad called about." She seemed to smile ever so slightly during this split-second, then lowered her eyes. They remained downcast as we walked toward my office.

Such was my introduction to Linda, a 16-year-old Caucasian daughter of missionary parents who had returned to the States for the specific purpose of obtaining treatment for her. They had become increasingly concerned as reports from her overseas boarding school indicated first subtle, then more substantial changes in her mood and behavior. After relevant consultation with school and mission personnel in East Africa, the decision was made for the family to take an early furlough. Medical testing in both Africa and the States had ruled out tropical diseases or other physical maladies accounting for her symptoms. Both she and her parents, though resisting it at first, now seemed ready to think of depression and/or other psychological problems as strong possibilities.

I subsequently saw Linda in an outpatient private practice setting over a period of eighteen months.

Depression

Depression is a complex yet all-too-common phenomenon. The *Diagnostic and Statistical Manual of Mental Disorders* (American Psychiatric Association, 1994) details the symptoms of mood disorders (which includes Major Depressive Episode) and depressive disorders, indicating a range of reported prevalence for Major Depressive Disorder. Linda's symptoms would have best fit this category had it existed in its present form at that time. The DSM-IV reports "The lifetime risk for Major Depressive Disorder in community samples has varied from 10% to 25% for women and 5% to 12% for men." (p. 341). It (both single and recurrent) is reported to be twice as common in adolescent and adult females as in adolescent and adult males.

In being considered as having a Major Depressive Disorder, Single Episode, Linda not only satisfied the criteria for Major Depressive Episode (as required for this diagnosis) but medical tests and her behavior had ruled out other likely possibilities of inclusion in other categories. Significant criteria included seven of the nine listed: (1) a depressed mood most of the day, nearly every day; (2) markedly diminished interest or pleasure in all, or almost all, activities most of the day, nearly every day; (3) significant weight loss when not dieting or weight gain (a change of more than 5% of body weight in a month) (5) psychomotor agitation or retardation nearly every day; (6) fatigue or loss of energy nearly every day; (7) feelings of worthlessness or excessive or inappropriate guilt nearly every day; (8) diminished ability to think or concentrate, or indecisiveness, nearly every day (DSM-IV, p. 327, in abbreviated form).

Both the symptoms and underlying causes of depression are complex. They vary by age and other variables, though the central factors are depressed mood and loss of interest and pleasure. Added to these are often subjective feelings of sadness or hopelessness, loss of appetite or overeating with subsequent weight loss or gain, sleep disturbance, low energy and/or fatigue, diminished capacity to think or concentrate, feelings of worthlessness and/or guilt, and thoughts of death, dying and/or nonexistence. There is often impairment in social and occupational functioning, sometimes seriously so. Panic attacks and agoraphobia may accompany symptoms of depression, and anxiety can also be manifest. For adolescents and children, a common symptom may be negativism and/or agitation and, in some cases, antisocial behavior. Agitation and irritability along with anxiety and phobias, are most common in children; negativism and antisocial attitudes more common in adolescent depression. Irritability is also quite often present as a symptom in adolescents.

For Linda, prominent features were depressed mood, loss of interest and pleasure, a sad countenance, fatigue, some mild to moderate irritability, and a degree of anxiety that sometimes seemed close to panic. Further, the depression was clearly affecting her education and schooling. The origins of these features were not understood by her at first, and it became an early task for us to hear about them together, begin relating them to her history and experiences, and try to discover their connections and origins. As we began to talk, it was important also to assess her experiences and listen for additional aspects of her depression as well.

In adolescents, depression may be tied to feelings of rejection and/or disapproval, oppositional behaviors, sulkiness, grouchiness, aggression, withdrawal and/or retreat, school difficulties, decrease in personal grooming and hypersensitivity to rejection or noninclusion. Worthlessness, guilt, and low self-esteem are frequently present, but many times not clearly defined internally or made manifest as in adults. The yet developing ego structure of adolescents makes it more difficult to get at the source dynamics for depression, and many of the above-noted symptoms and/or behaviors—even the generalizing affect of depression itself—may be thought of as covers for other more basic but ill-defined emotions that may underlie the depression.

Issues such as acceptance of self and acceptability to others, decision making ability, peer and romantic relationships, separation from parents, changing views of the family, future orientation and planning, and changes in sibling and extended family relationships are often associated with adolescent depression. Disruptions of relationships, usually with a heavy component of disappointment, are common. Many times, loss, fear of loss, and transitions or change are precipitants—not infrequently "stored" from earlier experiences.

Anger can often be a major component. Many adolescents, angry about rejection, mistreatment, lack of nurture, or other real or imagined deficits in caring, may direct their anger inward when there seems no clear way of expressing it otherwise. The shifts from agitation or negativism to sadness and meloncholy can sometimes be understood as attempts to deal with anger, albeit at a deeply unconscious level. The internal experience of anger but lack of its expression can be further compounded by fear of rejection or misunderstanding if it is expressed. The extent of this disowned anger in depression, as well as high comorbidity with anxiety, is sometimes not fully appreciated by therapists. In Linda's situation, as will be seen later, these features were important to understanding her.

Depression is not without its physiological components, both as a result and a cause. Adolescents experiencing depression almost inevitably experience physiological symptoms (e.g., appetite change, sleep disturbances, fatigue) as a result of inner struggles and conflicts. In more severe situations, vegetative signs are present. The development of depression from purely physiological causes may be more difficult to determine. The DSM-IV rules out the primary diagnosis of major depressive episode or Major Depression if organic factors have initiated and maintained the disturbance. It is always important, of course, to consider such possibilities in arriving at a diagnostic understanding of the psychological symptoms.

In the case of someone like Linda, most of whose life has been spent in the tropics under less than ideal public health conditions, it is particularly important to be aware of the possibility of other than psychosocial causes. For example, dinghy fever, a tropical disease especially well known to expatriates who live in rural, tropical climates, is known to produce symptoms looking suspiciously like depression.

Sociocultural Factors

As I sought to understand Linda and her distress, it was crucial to begin learning of her background and relationships as a prelude to her therapy. The sociocultural aspects of her life and specific development of depression call for a perspective going beyond "adolescent depression." Linda can be understood partly from the situation she is in as a *Third-Culture Kid*, or TCK, a term coined by Ruth Useem as a result of seminal studies begun some thirty-odd years ago (Useem & Downie, 1976; Useem, 1993). Children who spend a majority of their developmental years in a culture other than that of their parents were found to have discernible differences when compared to their North American-reared counterparts. Additional studies tend to confirm this (MK-CORE, 1993).

TCKs, as defined by Useem, include four groups of children: Those whose families are in (a) the international business community, (b) the diplomatic corps, (c) overseas military operations, and (d) missionaries. Of the four groups, the families most involved in and deeply integrated into the host culture are missionaries. Traditionally, the children of such parents have come to be known as MKs (for Missionary Kids) as well as TCKs. Because of their parents' work, it is not unusual for many to attend boarding school for a portion of and, in some cases, most of their precollege educational careers.

While this is becoming less common, some children begin boarding as early as 7 years of age. Many, however, may live most of their late childhood and adolescent years in a boarding home at a mission or international boarding school. There are, of course, periodic visits from and with parents, vacations in their parents' home, and regular visits up to a year's duration (usually on a 2½- to 4-year cycle) to their parents' home culture (e.g., North America). Efforts are usually made for significant parental involvement and/or communication with the school, though actual practices vary widely among schools, mission organizations and geographic areas.

It is not unusual for children growing up in such situations to spend substantial time in their early developmental years immersed in the host culture as well as in the expatriate or mission culture within their country of service. Thus, there is a sense of alienation from their parents' home culture and something of an identification with the host culture; yet, they can never fully join the host culture as a full-fledged member. They must often make extra efforts to "reenter" the home culture of their parents. Such a situation has implications for identity formation, separation and autonomy, and usually suggests a trajectory of development with unique features. As it were, these children and adolescents essentially develop a culture of their own; thus the term, *Third-Culture Kid.* A variety of research attempts have been made to better understand this (e.g., see Austin, 1983).

Many MKs whose parents are from North America but live overseas are fluent in at least one language other than English. They may also have passable language skills in a less standard language (such as a tribal tongue or regional trade language) as well, depending on parents' work and location. When they are young, they often develop a high degree of comfort with children from the host culture, a pattern which characteristically carries over into comfort and enjoyment of ethnic diversity in adulthood.

As MKs move into later adolescence and young adulthood, they tend to be most comfortable with others who have had extensive cross-cultural experiences and to be knowledgeable about the world beyond their years. Integration into standard North American adolescent culture is seldom easy. Even during times of furlough, American games such as Trivial Pursuit and discussions of the latest musical groups or clothing fads are anathema to them. The lack of world awareness and interest seen in their North American peers do, for some, fuel a sense of themselves as "odd" and "unacceptable."

The weight of evidence regarding such MK adolescents returning to North America for college suggests they are knowledgeable and educated beyond their years. They attend and are successful in college to a very high degree (see articles in Tetzel & Mortenson, 1986; Echerd and Arathoon, 1989). One recent large scale study found that 96% attend college, 73% attain at least an undergraduate degree, and 68% do so with a grade point average of 3.0 or better on a 4-point scale (MK-CORE, 1993).

Compared to adolescents raised in North America, however, they may lag somewhat in psychosocial development and experience a lack of self-confidence as they return to the culture of their parents (at least by some standards—see Mortenson, 1987, above). They often, in many respects, have more skills relating to adults than with a range of same-age peers, especially their monocultural peers.

Their lives have been marked by many transitions, and most have become adept at change. This is sometimes problematic for MKs, however, and the shock and disjuncture often experienced upon reentry to American culture can bring forward unresolved issues of grief and loss from previous unresolved transitions. Add to this the usual developmental issues and struggles of this age group, especially those of identity and separation, and one can readily see some possibilities for depression. However, it is not usually these issues alone that result in the development of depression among MKs.

While the great majority successfully negotiate such transitions, there are some casualties. For example, the anticipation of a permanent move and the expectation of the disbanding of a group of high school classmates who will be widely scattered upon graduation usually requires some attention for successful negotiation. The lack of interpersonal support during this period can be a factor in depression, and is sometimes experienced or interpreted by the person as some type of internal deficit. Once the class scatters, there is seldom a "hometown" to which one can return. Their identity, then, seems to become one more of affiliation and relationship rather than one which is grounded in a highly specific location, even though identification with the country in which they grew up may remain strong.

While identity is yet forming, some of the external anchors of belonging that hold it in place while the ego grasps for a more secure internal position are threatened by these changes and transitions. Even the imagination of this loss is for some a precipitant of depression; for others, the experience of unmourned losses creates depression.

Herrmann (1977), using Ericksonian developmental theory as a grounding, has shown the struggles and effects of identity formation for MKs of college age. She demonstrates identity as a task of unique aspects for MKs. For those who continue to struggle with identity and who lack these internal and external supports, depression is likely. Yet, even with identity as a central issue the overall outcomes are remarkably successful. A more recent large scale study of adult MKs spanning a range of years reveals a rather high degree of existential well-being among this group (Andrews, 1993).

Family relationships and connections with others central to the MK's development are important factors in understanding depression. As Schubert and Powell (1989) point out, solid and trusting relationships are very important for the successful negotiation of these myriad transitions and as a deterrent to depression. The overseas missionary community actually contains several levels of culture and subculture. These include such things as the ethos of the particular mission organization, the broader overseas missionary enterprise, the specific work situation (hospital, school, church planting, etc.) in which the MK and his or her family live and work, and the sometimes delicate subcultures composed of national citizens and missionaries working together in church and ministry matters. Blending such transitions is an important part of development as a MK (Powell, 1989).

It is important also to understand Linda in terms of her own Christian beliefs and values. The context of her parents' Christian faith, the purpose for which they earlier made a career commitment to live and work overseas, and the environment of service and activity created by the living out of these beliefs, are crucial to who she is. Many of her values, self-perceptions and understanding of life had been and were continuing to be shaped by these beliefs and by the individual commitment made by her to become a Christian at an earlier age. These areas of her life were also influenced by others, such as the interpretation of Christian principles and beliefs made by those surrounding her, and the consistency (or inconsistency) with which these were translated from spoken or written word to behavior. The latter had an important influence on her sense of self and on her own beliefs and interpretations.

Her experiences as a teenager who had developed depression include understanding not only her and her family but the broad context of Christianity in which she lived; more specifically, missionary and boarding school life, growing up in a culture that could never become fully her own, the requirements of juggling and sorting at least two clearly defined cultures (home and host) as well as many subcultures, and the usual developmental issues of being adolescent all had their effect. I will try to show how the context of her parents' "home" churches, their extended families, and their activities during this current furlough also exerted their influence.

CASE ILLUSTRATION

Presenting Problem

Linda's changes in mood and behavior began soon after she arrived for her junior year (11th grade) at school the preceding August. By late January, they had magnified and precipitated her family's premature return to the States. She had become a fearful, melancholic and withdrawn young woman—at times childlike in some verbalizations and overly mature in others. These characteristics stood in sharp contrast to the usual active, outgoing, and inquisitive girl described by her parents as typical up to a year earlier. She had been a teen who had become increasingly popular among her school friends and had looked forward to her junior year in boarding school. While usually earning As and B+s, her grades had slipped, her energy seemed drained, and she had seemingly lost interest in school and almost all pleasurable activities.

Her parents, friends and school/mission officials were aware of and concerned about these changes. Since physical causes seem to have been ruled out, many thought that Christmas break at her parents' work location would help. She seemed to feel more secure and a bit happier there and showed some improvement. Both parents, however, described her as seeming different and had continued to express concern. She seemed reluctant to share with them anything she was thinking about or feeling, and could only describe her fear and pain, unable to attach it to specific objects or events. She frequently apologized for not doing better.

As we sat in those moments of the first session and I heard of this contrast, I found it hard to imagine that her parents were talking of the person sitting so dejectedly across from me. I felt internally conflicted; there was the unspoken expectation by her parents that I would provide the help that might restore her to this earlier self, yet her own despondency caused me to temporarily question whether I could provide what might be needed. This seemed to stimulate a quasi-conscious exploration of both my own faith and the skills and understanding I would need to help her.

Linda had indeed shown some slight improvement during Christmas break and returned to school seeming partially cheerful. She had left the village with a hope that things would be better, partly because of her own prayers as well as those of her parents. Her father, especially, had spent many hours attempting to encourage her and sharing his work activities with her during the weeks of break. She said she knew her parents loved her and wanted her to be better. She didn't want to disappoint them.

Her return to school, however, was traumatic. She felt she had already caused too much concern on the part of her friends and others at school; this became more acute as she realized she wasn't making it. She felt she was taking space in the boarding home that "someone else deserved more than I." She was late for breakfast the first morning, hardly ate, and was fearful as she walked to classes. She stated that she "knew" that the houseparents were upset with her. She had become so upset by noon that one of them came to the classroom building to take her back to the house. She cried for awhile and then felt better. With a lot of attention and encouragement, she succeeded in staying at school two weeks. She then became more serious, devoid of any cheer or humor, felt extremely tired and began losing weight. Then began the steps which eventually brought her to my office.

She at first seemed relieved to be coming to the U.S., but then began realizing the enormity of not seeing her friends again for some time—maybe never, if she didn't get better. She now felt guilt for taking her parents away from their work. Further, she wondered how this would be explained to those in her parents' home church, and to concerned relatives. Even after her parents left the first session and we were alone, she could add little more about her concerns than had already been noted. Her symptoms had become more pronounced after subsiding during the initial stages of reentry to the States. She was not attending school here, was frightened to leave her house and had begun spending long periods alone in her room. She became either sullen, irritable, or anxious at any attempt to get her to consider school or social activities.

Linda seemed caught between three worlds: that of her own painful and unexpressed feelings underlying the depressive symptoms, the world of creeping realization that she had less a sense of belonging here than she had in the boarding school, and the strong but subtle expectations she held for pleasing her parents and living up to these internalized standards. She seemed eager for help, but helpless in knowing how to receive it.

CLIENT DESCRIPTION

Linda was an attractive, thin-featured 16 year old (nearly 17) with straight, rather long, blondish hair. She referred to herself at one point as a dishwater blonde. She carried herself somewhat straightforwardly in spite of her downcast eyes and the sluggish movements that sometimes dominated. Behind her sad countenance, there seemed a connection with me through an occasional glance from her dark brown eyes, perhaps seeking to convey something, and sometimes almost pleading. These glances were seldom longer than a second, usually followed by withdrawal and aversion. In spite of her obvious pain and the silent pauses, she seemed to attend to my comments or questions and at some level be considering them. It was as if she was watching very closely and attempting to read my expectations. At other moments she seemed to be testing me as though she were hopeful. Yet, the feeling of her discouragement and distress was pervasive and expressed itself in passivity.

In the initial phases of that interview, she did seem free to make occasional comments even with her parents present. I observed that these seldom revealed feelings or perspectives, however, but mainly factual details. Her parents seemed gentle and caring in their descriptions of her, and were generally nonintrusive. I had learned something of their journey to this point from the phone conversation with her father, and Linda supplied additional details of her school experience. Her parents detailed further aspects of her medical tests and their decision to bring her for psychotherapy. Linda agreed that she wanted help but didn't know what to do or expect. She and her parents each seemed close to desperation but tried to present themselves as hopeful.

Linda described her present houseparents and some of her friends but could only say, "This year in school was different—it wasn't the same as before," even when asked to describe these differences. Feeling that she might have more to say and desiring to see how she would relate to me alone, I asked her parents to leave for the latter half of the initial interview. The most significant event, in addition to further background information, was a flash of anger when I asked more broadly about the houseparents she had had in her previous years. She seemed particularly distressed when mentioning one in particular.

As noted earlier, Linda's symptom picture met the criteria for Major Depressive Disorder, Single Episode. However, features of Agoraphobia and the possibility of Panic Disorder were clearly worthy of pursuit. I was concerned at that time, however, that I may have been too quick to form a diagnostic opinion and needed to be cautious in subsequent sessions to look for additional material. Other than previous experience with MKs, which provided a kind of intuitive context, little was at first evident as to the dynamics in her symptom development nor the specific precipitant(s) for their onset. Her early separation from parents, frequent changes of boarding school personnel, general aspects of the dangers faced by the overseas missionary community, and the seeming attachment to Africans during her early years were compelling features to follow up on. But the significant clinical picture was one of depression.

SOCIAL CONTEXT

Linda was born in a mission hospital in East Africa, as was her sister ahead of her. The second and last of Ed and Esther's two children, she is 9 years her sister's junior. Each had attended the same boarding school. With their age difference, Linda had not spent substantial time with her sister Sally, except during vacations at home in the village and during furloughs in the States. However, she reported that Sally had been significant to her in the 2 years of overlap at school, and she seemed to have a deep, though not intimate, affection for her.

According to Linda's parents, their two daughters were strikingly different. Sally was described as caring but brash, who "tells things as they are" but who seemed to have a tender underside. She excelled in athletics during high school and completed a degree in physical therapy, holding a position in an urban hospital known for its treatment of a diverse ethnic population. She and Linda had continued a more or less regular correspondence through the years.

Esther acknowledged some mild episodes of depression during their adjustment to Africa and in the months of language study. She also admitted to some mild episodes following the birth of Sally, her first child, though had received no psychotherapy or medication for it. She had not experienced this with Linda. There was no other indication of depression in the immediate family.

Linda's parents described her as "the sensitive one." She seemed always to identify with the underdog, would shed tears easily when seeing or hearing of someone being mistreated, and seemed to feel things deeply. She often seemed unable to express what she was feeling, however, especially if she considered it a negative feeling such as anger.

Ed and Esther had been educated at a Christian liberal arts college in the midwest. They had become Christians early in life and independently made commitments to serve in overseas missions during a spiritual emphasis week at the college. Not long after, they became interested in one another.

Each parent came from a midwestern family. Ed had grown up on a farm, Esther in a county seat town in the same state some 100 miles away. Ed was the youngest of three brothers and four sisters; Esther was the middle of five children, two older brothers, two younger sisters. Their parental families were intact and most members of their extended families continued to be active in community and church affairs, primarily in small or rural midwestern communities. They tended to be farmers, small business owners, or teachers. One of Esther's sisters and her husband had taught for a 3 year period at a missionary boarding school in South America. Esther felt especially close to this sister and had shared with her the details of Linda's situation. Ed and Esther, however, had not been free in sharing this information with other family members, nor had they shared much with their Stateside church constituency. There seemed to be a quality of avoidance or denial, perhaps shame, in describing to others the reasons for their early return. Linda felt this and was also aware of their attempt to publicly cover their anxiety about her with smiles and platitudes.

While no other family members in the generation of Linda's parents served as career missionaries, there appeared to be general support by family members. There was usually enthusiastic interest in pictures and stories about their work in East Africa, and on two occasions over the years they had received visits from relatives.

Both Ed and Esther had developed friendships with members of minority groups (of which there were not many where they grew up) during their high school years. Each felt these friendships had been instrumental in their decision to work in Africa. During furlough visits they often made a point to see the families of these friends. Linda pointed out later that, even though they attempted to cover it, some members of her mother's extended family were prejudiced and occasionally made derogatory comments about Africans. She felt her maternal grandmother had been especially so. These feelings were sometimes couched in silent disapproval or veiled comments about visits to minority friends. Linda recalled enjoying these visits, especially to one particular African American family, when they were on furlough. Esther indicated that on one occasion, when Linda was quite small, she had become visibly upset when one of her uncles made disparaging comments about Africans.

Linda's parents seemed to share a deep commitment to one another and to their children. They were respectful in their communication and seemed to have a good awareness of boundaries. However, two features in their family life emerged with clarity early in our contacts: (a) Anger or disapproval was seldom acknowledged directly and therefore not processed; and (b) interpersonal conflicts were downplayed or denied. Esther seemed more willing than Ed to express negative affect (and probably experienced more of it than he); Ed tended to paint a smiling face on nearly any situation.

These characteristics had not gone unnoticed by Linda. During therapy she offered insightful observations about her sister and revealed some insights about what had probably been a period of rebellion for Sally. Further, the wishes of the parents for Linda and her sister were very strong but tended to be expressed more by subtle disapproval or overly strong approval, rather than through direct communication at both ends of that continuum. I sensed this to be true in their expectations of me as well.

Through church affiliation and personal religious conviction, the majority of their extended family members was familiar with Christian missions and believed in their importance. Most, however, had stayed pretty close to home after completing schooling or service in the military. This seemed to provide some stability for Linda during furlough times. Visits to the States sometimes caused her to wonder why she couldn't live and attend school all in one place, like most of her cousins.

The extended family cultures were largely middle class and of conservative/evangelical religious background. Their behavior and verbalizations were grounded in the basic values of small town friendliness, respect, and helpfulness to others, fortified by their Christian beliefs. Linda's parents seemed to take some pride, especially her mother, in the fact that the families were seen as solid citizens and respected members in their communities. Those same values had obviously been operational in Ed and Esther's 27 years of life and work in Africa.

There was no reported history of mental illness in the family of either parent, although one of Esther's aunts had evidently been mentally retarded. In gathering family history, Esther indicated that this had been a shame to the family and seldom had been referred to directly as she was growing up. An uncle of Ed's had his farm repossessed during the Great Depression and Ed seemed to feel a sense of shame in this. A family value seemed to be: Always be good and look good, and even if things aren't good, try to appear as though they are. This value, among others, played an important role in understanding Linda and her treatment.

Initial Session

Linda's mild manner and depressed mood made it difficult at first to know where best to try to join with her. Her voice was at times barely audible and her pace of response slow. Yet, in the first few minutes of our meeting, I had seen the hint of a smile and what seemed some glances of anger, suggesting a bit more life and availability of affect than her demeanor indicated. In our first 30 minutes with her parents in the room, she had been given easy opportunity to speak, and they waited patiently for her sometimes delayed responses. Linda seemed somehow to take on her mother's anxiety about the situation and at times make it her own. At others, she seemed repelled by her parents' concern, but mainly in subtle ways, seeming confused or dejected.

In these initial moments, I felt for a few seconds that her parents were quietly examining me and my suitability for working with their daughter. Due, perhaps, to my consultation work with overseas mission organizations, they had been referred by mutual acquaintances, and I felt some pressure to provide the best help possible. In a few minutes, however, I felt less scrutinized by either them or Linda and realized that my reaction was probably due more to my own anxiousness about providing the help I thought was expected as much as it was their subjecting me to some sort of test. I realized that such feelings are not unusual for therapists and are eloquently described by Teyber (1996). However, as I caught myself responding more to this subtle concern than to Linda herself, I was able to acknowledge it internally and begin to experience freedom in attempting to join with her. As I refocused my attention, I noticed that Linda seemed somehow a bit stronger and, though anxious, seemed to be developing a comfortableness with me. This clearly seemed to be a response to my own sense of having overcome some inward anxiousness and having become more present to her. My experience was consistent with that described by Aponte and Winter (1987) in terms of increased self-knowledge and its use in the therapeutic relationship.

After her parents left the room, Linda moved her chair ever so slightly so as to face me more directly. After a short silence she asked if I had ever been to Africa. The dialogue went something like this:

CLIENT: Have you ever been to Africa?
THERAPIST: Yes, I have.
CLIENT: Did you like it?
THERAPIST: I thought it was different and beautiful.
CLIENT: (after a pause) I miss being there. (long pause followed by the quivering of her lower lip and eventual tears) I wish I were there.
THERAPIST: Is it better there than here?
CLIENT: Not always. (long pause)
THERAPIST: Not always?
CLIENT: No. (long pause) It depends on where you are and who you're with.
THERAPIST: M-m-m-m-m
CLIENT: Right now, I'd like to be with Annie, walking through the village watching the children play.
THERAPIST: That sounds enjoyable. What's it like?
CLIENT: But I'm not there . . . (followed by a flow of tears and deep sobs) . . . and I don't know if I'll ever get back.

It seemed in that short interchange that Linda had trusted me with something important to her—that she missed Africa and was grieving the possibility that she may never return. (Later in the session I learned that she had been noncommunicative about this to her parents, almost as if to protect them in their decision to bring her to the States.) I chose not to follow up on her affect at that moment, but to wait and see what direction she would take. When she regained her composure, she shifted back to my visit in Africa, asking in more detail about it. I felt this was an important part of building our relationship. We shared several observations about places we had each been, and she learned that I had at one time actually been on the campus of her boarding school.

As we continued this discussion, I sensed a slight withdrawal and began having second thoughts about being so disclosing of this information. She then asked, "Do you know some of the teachers and staff at (the boarding school)?" When I told her I didn't, she paused for a time, then seemed to relax. I took the risk of verbally observing this by saying "When I told you I didn't know anyone at (the boarding school), you seemed somehow relieved." She became silent, almost withholding in manner. After some moments, I noted this by saying "You seem very quiet . . . almost like you've drawn back a little." After a few seconds she said "I was afraid you might know Mrs. T." I replied, "No, I don't . . . would that be important to you?" "Yes," she said, "I'm glad you don't know her." Then she was silent.

I broke the silence by shifting to some questions about her symptoms and how they had developed and attempted in my mind to form some hypotheses about her depression. It seemed to have a fairly discernable onset, but it was difficult to get at any specific event, relationship, or series of events to quite understand it. However, I was beginning to see some of her strengths and defense patterns. She was very observant and perceptive of others' feelings, seemed to have a vocabulary for expressing what she saw, and was clearly motivated for help. But she seemed to use information from her acute perception to deflect her own feelings, especially if they were anything but positive, and she seemed to defend against them with a level of denial that provided an interesting contrast to this strength of perception. As our time expired, I shifted to the practical aspects of our working together. With her parents present, arrangements were made for further assessment and meetings.

As I reflected on the session, I was aware of a certain delight in seeing more energy than I would have suspected from the phone conversation with her father. But I was also aware of an inward tension . . . a countertransferential pull toward wanting to quickly reduce her seemingly helpless distress. At the same time I experienced an appreciation for the hint of inward resilience I saw. I later learned that more people had been responding to the side of this tension that seemed to say, Help me, relieve me of this, rather than the side that said, I'm resilient, let's find a way out of this. The inward tension I felt later proved to parallel her own.

In the next two sessions I took the dual stance of getting relevant information while attempting to join more with her as a person, both in pain and in potential. She affirmed her mother's earlier description of herself as having been outgoing, friendly and inquisitive, all of which had changed for her over the past months. I learned that she had done volunteer work with other students in literacy classes for African children who lived near her school, and that she seemed to identify with Africans in some important ways, especially those who had been mistreated or seemed sad or discouraged.

Linda had been popular among her peers, seen as someone who would listen and who was very reliable. Her grades had, until recent months, placed her on the honors list. During the summers she had assisted her mother in providing first aid treatment and assisting with literacy and Bible study classes for villagers who came to the growing mission church and in outreach activities that her parents had begun in earlier years. She seemed to have been on a good track of development. I found myself liking her but becoming frustrated by her present depression and agoraphobia, and at times a bit angry at her occasional oppositional stance. These were seen more, it seemed, when she talked about God or her Christian faith. When I sought to explore this further, she would often respond with an unusual delay or look petulant. This seemed significant.

Linda could at first detail no particular precipitating event for the depression and was spotty in her description of intrapsychic processes associated with her sadness, fear, and withdrawal. Yet, she seemed bright and began giving me glimpses into her anger, strengths, and personal faith. I had on one or two occasions experienced again some fleeting seconds of anxiousness about helping her as I had in our first session. These now seemed tied to some uncertainties regarding hypotheses for understanding her depression. But as I began to see her strengths, a sense of hope emerged that dispelled this uncertainty. Further, she seemed to trust me while still wanting to test me, and I was now finding a good level of comfort.

In these sessions, she sometimes had small bursts of energy when talking of something she enjoyed (such as Africa) but was more often prone to appear sad, have some delay in response, and occasionally make disparaging comments about herself along with hopeless comments about the future (e.g., "I know I'll never get back to Africa." "I don't think I'll be able to finish high school."). Since rejection and/or loss and low self-esteem are often at issue in adolescent depression, I began to listen more closely for openings that might lead to a better understanding of those aspects in her symptoms. In one session the following exchange took place:

THERAPIST: Each time you mention Africa, you seem to brighten up but then become sad.

CLIENT: Oh . . . you don't like me when I'm sad.

This was an interesting clue to the possibility that she was trying to discover what my expectations were and then trying to meet them, although I did not address it directly at the time.

THERAPIST: I don't like it *that* you're sad, because I believe it covers some beautiful parts of yourself.

CLIENT: I'm sorry I'm sad . . . it doesn't make it good to be around me. (Long silence) A lot of people don't like to be around me.

THERAPIST: A lot of people?

CLIENT: Well, most people. (long silence, in which she looked at the floor and began quietly sobbing)

THERAPIST: Some particular people?

CLIENT: (long silence) Maybe. (further silence) Well, one person.

THERAPIST: One person?

CLIENT: Yes, one person. (pause) Mrs. T.

THERAPIST: The person you asked me if I knew?

CLIENT: Yes.

THERAPIST: She doesn't want to be around you because you're sad?

CLIENT: Well, not just sad. She thinks I'm not a good Christian.

THERAPIST: Not a good Christian?

CLIENT: She accused me of being a volunteer at the literacy program just so I could be with Rob, not because I loved the people who come there. Rob is just a good friend who's really good in literacy work. (pause) And I started crying because what she said hurt and it's not true. Then she said she didn't like being around crybabies . . . she wanted her students to be strong people. (pause) Then she just walked off. (long silence and tears)

THERAPIST: And then?

CLIENT: I tried to tell Christine, my roommate, but she seemed too busy. I was afraid to tell Mom and Dad because I knew they would worry. (pause) I was really trying to be a good Christian, but . . . (more tears and finally deep sobs)

THERAPIST: (after a long pause and some recovery on Linda's part) It really hurt to be thought of as not being a good Christian.

CLIENT: I really tried . . . (more tears)

THERAPIST: You really try hard to live out being a Christian . . .

CLIENT: . . . and sometimes nobody seems to notice . . . and I wonder even if God notices . . . (long pause)

At this point, it seemed that Linda began trusting me enough to reveal one of the events that had hurt her and had been hard for her to express to anyone. It touched on some important areas for her. Her Christian faith was keenly important to her. Related to this was also her need to protect her parents, something I later learned she thought was part of being a good Christian. She didn't wish for her parents to worry about her being unhappy at school. As the clue had suggested at the beginning of this interchange, she had become quite good at discerning what her parents' (and others') expectations were and usually tried to conform to them. This was partly recapitulated with me in this session and I was able to take a first step toward understanding and helping to change it. Others would be taken later.

As we got to know one another, she revealed many instances of hurt at school that she did not convey to her parents (or anyone) for fear of not pleasing them, having her feelings rejected, or being left out. By subtly knowing what people expected and trying to meet these expectations, the chances for rejection were decreased. Some of her stories were not unlike those of Van Reken in the book *Letters Never Sent* (Van Reken, 1988). It was also becoming clear that Linda felt alone, perhaps even abandoned by God, in living out her faith. Yet, she needed to protect her parents from knowing of this loneliness, as she saw it, even as an act of this faith. This conflict, yet unacknowledged, was one of the origins of her pain. And perhaps she was beginning to question God as well.

Before this session ended, she had sobbed more and seemed in greater pain. I was tempted to extend the session. To have done so, I now know, would have been to emphasize her weakness. Instead, I told her I felt privileged to have been told some of her deeper feelings and believed she was strong for having spoken so clearly about them. She looked at me somewhat quizzically and then smiled slightly, indicating with nonverbals her readiness to leave.

Reflecting on this session I came again to the notion of being tested, but in a different way. She now seemed to be testing me *not* so much about my capacity to help but whether I had a need for her to not be sad, as per her father. The deeper test seemed to be whether I could tolerate the pain and sadness she had accumulated over a period of time and that was no longer being contained.

Passing tests often becomes an important therapeutic step. Showing her that I could allow her to be sad, unlike her father, would be one way of passing this test, especially in the framework of her attempts to read my expectations and provide what I expected. The delicate emotional footwork involved in passing such tests can then lead to the provision of emotionally corrective experiences. In this case, the task would be to help her express the depth of this sadness and pain without the fear of its being denied or discounted, however subtly, and allowing her to begin touching the fullness of her own reality. A step toward this had been taken.

Case Conceptualization

The appearance of Linda's first symptoms had coincided with her leaving the family's village home at the end of the summer and arriving at boarding school. While this had generally been routine for her (though not without some tears and anxieties each year), this year seemed different. Even over the summer, as she recalled, she had a creeping sense of foreboding about her return. She tried to keep telling herself that her junior year would be the best ever and that when she returned to school everything would be alright.

As she reviewed the latter months of the previous year, she began to realize that there had been several disappointments which she had brushed aside, telling herself they were minor and "not to worry about them." Loss of self-esteem is often a contributor to the development of depression, especially in adolescents, and her "storing" these disappointments had begun having its effect. On a couple of occasions she attempted to mention these disappointments to her parents but felt doing so raised her mother's anxiety, so she kept them to herself. The disappointments generally had to do with people not keeping promises they had made to her and having been overlooked in various school and boarding home activities.

Several clearer hypotheses now presented themselves. With the onset of symptoms being associated with return to boarding school, it seemed reasonable to believe that aspects of separation were at play. I hypothesized that the several disappointments from last year that she had disclosed to me were only a sampling of others that had occurred over a period of time. She had not admitted these fully to herself, nor, given her rather sensitive nature, had she risked creating difficulty or being disliked by mentioning them to anyone. Instead, she attempted to ignore them at one level and, at another, to pray and believe that God would take care of them. When things became worse rather than better, she began to think, first, that she was not "doing things right" and, second, wondering if God was to be trusted with such things.

Linda's outgoingness and enthusiastic spirit had, over time, become predictable parts of her personality. It was these to which most people seemed to respond, not to attempts to express "negative things." Her parents were delighted with these qualities but also seemed bothered, usually in an indirect way, when things were not going well for her. Linda had not felt at liberty to disclose some of her loneliness, disappointments, or fears to her parents but instead tried to respond to them in ways she knew they would like: being cheerful and outgoing. As the younger child, she had heard her parents' comments and concerns about some of Sally's behavior and development; her natural sensitivity helped deepen her wish not to be the object of such comments.

I conjectured that she had at some early point also decided not to cause stress for them as Sally, who was more expressive and assertive, had done. Instead she found ways to prevent disclosing any of her own feelings that might distress them. In this regard, the cheerfulness and outgoingness was a useful defense. It had worked so well, in fact, that she had also learned not to share negative feelings or hurts with others. In many cases, she also tried to keep them from herself. She was no longer being successful. The avoidance of her own affect and her undeveloped capacity to assert her own needs contributed significantly to her depression. This made it hard for her to know just how she did feel, what she really wanted, and what she was really like . . . all coming to the fore during the "identity" stage of development so important to adolescence and described with particular emphasis for missionary children by Taylor (1988).

Given the glimpses of anger in our early contacts, I hypothesized that Linda was experiencing much more anger than she was aware of. Up to now she had not found adequate channels for experiencing or expressing it. Instead, as is often true in the dynamics of depression, she was unconsciously directing it inward. Several features might have accounted for her anger:

1. She was disappointed with herself for not being the "strong" person she believed she should be. This was true regarding both her wish to not cause her parents anguish about her being away at boarding school (as she believed her sister had caused) and in wishing to demonstrate Christ's sufficiency in caring for her as she sought to follow him in her Christian walk. As she began to experience some disappointments and distress the preceding year, she began to feel that she was failing in each of these. She had become angry at her "weakness." I noted this not only as an important psychological dynamic but also a spiritual one.

2. She also began experiencing something more accurately described as resentment. She was finding it increasingly hard to leave her parents' home after such a short visit each summer, even though she enjoyed school, her friends, houseparents, and most teachers. At times, her tears in my presence seemed to be those of anger; at others, they were clearly tears of grief. She missed the closeness of her parents and, in anticipating plans for college that would be developing this year, realized that she would be leaving Africa permanently while her parents stayed. She would then have neither Africa nor her parents and she was frightened. It seemed there were some things yet to do before this larger separation could take place. Her open expression of missing Africa and often reflecting on its beauty and meaning for her was a metaphor for many other things she had missed or was missing.

Given the adaptive stance of cheerfulness and outgoingness she had taken, which was now failing, she saw no avenue for reclaiming what she had missed or claiming others that might yet be available. She experienced little capacity to deal with the anger and resentment within her and felt hopeless and/or powerless to take action to make things better.

Several individual comments from Linda, as well as the observed interactions with her parents, led me to hypothesize that a strong element in the development and maintenance of her depression was the assumed protectiveness of her parents. She did not want to disappoint them, cause them worry or concern, or create for them unnecessary work. She wished to please them by following their example of Christian commitment, although she had not yet reached the maturity to incorporate as her own all that such a commitment might mean.

There seemed to be an emerging tension between these wishes and her own needs. Though she could not yet verbalize it, at some level she wished to express her hurts and disappointments and receive her parents' soothing comfort. This tension seemed especially true with her father: he often sought to comfort her, would listen, and share experiences; yet, he seemed not to want to hear specifically about her pain, meeting such attempts with platitudes or gently changing the subject. Her mother seemed more expressive of her own feelings and needs, but Linda felt these too often took a twist such that Linda then felt responsible for responding to those rather than expressing her own. From this, a certain "giving up" had emerged. Her intrapsychic response was a deep grieving and a depressive hopelessness. She seemed to be quietly mourning the loss of something she deeply desired but yet knew little about within herself.

As our therapy progressed, I learned of two incidents that rounded out an understanding of some of the separation issues about which I had earlier conjectured. Linda had entered boarding school (at age 7, 2nd grade) when her sister Sally, 9 years older, was a junior (11th grade). Linda had especially looked up to her. Sally was excellent in athletics and seemed to take a strong interest in her little sister, often spending extra time with her in the initial weeks. But during first semester Sally broke her leg, which, because of complications, required her to be on crutches most of that school year. She had evidently become discouraged herself, her grades had dropped, and because of inactivity in the usual events, so had her friendships. Linda seemed to accept Sally's changes, but as we later looked back at the impact of Sally's apparent withdrawal and her own disappointments, the fears that kept Linda from fully entering into her own junior year seemed to recapitulate some of Sally's, 9 years earlier.

A second incident involved a break-in occurring at the school during Christmas break of her sophomore year. The bandits had entered several of the dormitories, vandalizing individual rooms as well as other parts of the hall. Personal items belonging to several of the girls had been taken. When Linda returned, she not only found her room a mess but had great difficulty sleeping those first few nights. Throughout the remainder of that year she sometimes awoke in the night thinking she had heard someone in her room. Interestingly, this event had not been mentioned until sometime later in therapy.

Not only had she experienced anxiety about her safety following that event, she found she was missing a locket containing a small photo of her parents that they had given her for Christmas during her first year at school. She felt extremely guilty for having left it at school. This appeared to be, again, something Linda adapted to well at the time, but in recent months she had been having dreams where fears for safety, threats of loss, and guilt had been themes. In some respects, she seemed to be internalizing responsibility for the emotional deprivation it now became clear she was experiencing. In spite of their deep concern for her, her parents seemed at some level unable to connect with Linda's tender sensitivity and needs for comfort and security; this event seemed to have underlined this.

Orienting Constructs

The constructs of separation and loss, grief, unmet needs for comfort, inward directed anger, protection of parents, feelings of failure and worthlessness, and questions about her acceptability to God were important in understanding Linda and providing orientation for our work together. It was also important to acknowledge her demonstrated resiliency, genuine sensitivity to the needs of others, developing capacity for sound relationships as demonstrated by the friendships she had with both adults and peers, and her sense of identity with her family and with aspects of the African culture. Her Christian commitment seemed to be related to each of these and was an important orienting construct in understanding many of the others.

Linda seemed to know, at one level, that her own Christian faith, ironically, contained the knowledge and wisdom to address each of the issues that tied in with her depression. Yet, at the same time, the feelings of failure to have adequately appropriated this faith in overcoming hurt and difficulty seemed to exaggerate her sense of guilt and inadequacy and to fuel the depression.

The somewhat different relationships she had with each of her parents seemed an important issue. Already, an interesting father transference with me was beginning to develop. I was aware of my countertransference in wishing to protect her from further pain as she underwent therapy, even though my intellect told me (1) that she had some underlying strengths that needed to be surfaced and utilized, and (2) that I would need to provide some direct and honest expression of feelings and acceptance that would, in turn, allow and encourage her to express the full range of her own anger, resentment and doubts. Further, it would be important for her to experience anger as something that did not in itself disrupt and break relationships but could produce clarification and closeness if healthily experienced and expressed.

Linda had from outward appearances been healthy and adaptive in her development and had, indeed, developed many strengths. However, because of several seemingly small but not understood or processed experiences through the years, she had built up unresolved issues that had come to a head partly through some resonant events (e.g., Mrs. T's comments about her Christian faith) and partly through a realization that her completion of school and departure from Africa were imminent. The anticipation of this further separation and the uncertainty of what was to come became increasingly painful. She had been quite successful in utilizing the part of her personality that was outgoing and cheerful in making successful adaptations, but it had also become a defense that denied her access to and expression of painful events that might have been easily negotiated or resolved had there been the permission and place to reveal and process them as they occurred. They had now caught up with her.

Further, Linda had experienced a variety of losses through the years that she had not sufficiently grieved. Each of her transitions seemed to have involved one or more losses that she had not acknowledged but had been covered with denial or platitudes. These had resulted in what was now a *compacted grief.* Helping her review and grieve these losses emerged as an important orientation to follow as our work together unfolded.

With respect to her Christian theology, she seemed not to have been predisposed to fully understand the concept of grace nor to allow herself to it in spite of its importance in her Christian faith. Rather, especially in her present circumstances, she felt unworthy of the acceptance and comfort she desperately wanted and felt she should be blamed and perhaps punished. The concepts of grace, forgiveness, and reconciliation, though not mentioned in those words to this point, became important orienting points as well. I followed some of the ideas and steps so poignantly described by Smedes (1984).

Further, it was clear that Linda's denial of her own anger and negative feelings by believing that they should not be expressed to her parents would be important to tackle. An important orienting construct would be to provide in our relationship the experience of surfacing and expressing those feelings and finding that they were accepted, did not destroy our relationship, or cause me to withdraw. Being on the lookout for such opportunities would yield for her important corrective emotional experiences.

Linda's reactions to me within the first hour had, in spite of the pervading depression, indicated some aliveness and conveyed the idea that the presentation of depression was not a full presentation of Linda. After our first session, I found myself entertaining notions of secondary gains from her depressive symptoms. This idea could find support in the fact that she had, over the past several weeks, gained the whole of her parents attention, as well as that of a number of others. Further, it seemed reasonable that in the development of the depression, she had short-cut the enormity of her fears about future separations by causing them to happen all at once, putting them more quickly behind her. Thus, I reasoned, she had both gained the attention (comfort?) she sought from parents and short-circuited her fears all at the same time.

However, in subsequent sessions, this hypothesis withered away. In one session, this interaction assisted in its dissipation:

CLIENT: Dad does seem to be a lot more available to me than he was in Africa.

THERAPIST: How do you mean?

CLIENT: He seems to let me talk anytime I want to, even in middle of the night. I was crying and couldn't sleep last night and he came to my room to see what was wrong. We went into the kitchen and fixed some milk and crackers and we talked for a long time.

THERAPIST: About . . . ?

CLIENT: Just about Africa, some things I had been thinking about.

THERAPIST: Um . . . like . . . ?

CLIENT: About leaving Africa. Some things I used to like to do there. (long pause) Then he told me about some things he used to like to do there, too, that he missed, like going to the river sometimes and seeing if he could spot any hippos. He said he missed some of the Africans he worked with at church.

THERAPIST: How was it to hear those things from him?

CLIENT: I already knew that . . . not about the hippos but that he missed being there and that he missed his friends . . . (she trailed off and began to show some tears) . . . even though he never told me.

THERAPIST: That affects you somehow?

CLIENT: It makes me sad . . . He and Mom have been so good to me, and I've let them down . . . I've made them leave what they love. (more tears) I wish we could have all stayed . . . but here we are . . . because of me.

THERAPIST: What's that like?

CLIENT: I hate myself for it . . . (grimacing and clenching her fists) . . . I really tried to stay there, but I couldn't get better and now I've disappointed everybody. (pause) Why don't Mom and Dad just leave me here and go back?

The idea of secondary gains seemed less likely to me after this exchange because of the continuing guilt, self-recriminations, and worthlessness along with her own remorse over leaving Africa. There was still a strong need to protect her parents, presumably to assure their love and/or her security. Even though we had not discussed it directly at this point in therapy, it was unquestionably there and probably inconsistent with the secondary gains hypothesis. The interchange, however, did reveal further the depth of the conflict between wishing for something from her parents and wanting to protect them at the same time. There seemed to be considerable fear beneath that and the belief that she couldn't do things very well without them.

Treatment Plans and Intervention Strategy

INITIAL TREATMENT PLAN

I find it useful to attempt a projection of therapy into the traditional three-stage model: the beginning stage, middle or working through stage, and the termination stage. While in reality the exact progression between stages is not always discernable, such projections early in therapy are instructive for providing guidelines for the development of intervention strategies.

I saw Linda's situation as rather complex, because it included not only depression but involved cross-cultural, developmental and religious issues that would need to be considered for eventual resolution. For the beginning stage, I believed that four goals were important. It is the middle stage of therapy that is longest, and its success is usually related to meeting these initial goals before plunging into it too rapidly.

The first goal was simply that of establishing an environment and offering a relationship in which Linda would feel comfortable and begin expressing herself. It was especially important for her to express her feelings in as complete a manner as possible if we were to make the necessary progress. It was clear that her sensitivity often resulted in her being much too other-directed, and I was already a bit concerned about the father transference I saw developing as well. She seemed to be orienting to what she believed my needs were and seemed at times to hold back verbalizing feelings that her nonverbals suggested she was experiencing.

At the same time I was not unaware of the countertransferential pull toward making things better for her without her doing the necessary work of self-exploration and risk taking. On two or three occasions I found phrases of reassurance (that things would work out well) forming in my mind, when I yet had no clear understanding of how that would be. I did not wish to respond in such a way as to cause our relationship to recapitulate that which she had established with her father by carefully reading his expectations, denying her negative feelings, and providing what he wanted in order to have *something* with him—even if it didn't fully meet her needs.

Unless Linda's feelings and needs were more fully recognized, expressed, and worked through, it would risk leaving her with the unresolved situation of feeling she must protect me from her feelings and wishing for something she knew she needed but didn't get. To minimize the contamination of my own countertransference and the possibility of responding as her father might, I made it a point to check in with a colleague now and then.

A second goal for this stage was to establish a sense of separateness of myself from her parents, the missions community, and the church as she had known and experienced them. I believed it important that she be able to utilize her own strengths to form a relationship with me and to test these strengths later as we got into the probable uncertainty and distortion that can come with more intimate disclosure. I was already having second thoughts about having disclosed my experiences in Africa and the fact that I had been on the campus of her boarding school. In my attempts to establish a connection with her, I wondered in retrospect if some of my eagerness had not been as much directed toward reassuring her parents of my credentials as of making a connection with Linda. My goal now was, as much as possible, to ensure that she would have the freedom to be herself in a relationship that was clearly separate from others, one existing solely for her benefit. She needed to begin experiencing me as aware of but outside her more familiar circles and subcultures. In this respect, I was reminded of the importance accorded tight boundaries in therapy by such writers as Langs (1985).

The third goal related to the question of identity, that is, to assess and understand it better and to recognize its place in this stage of her development. Though I could make some assumptions, it seemed important to grasp a better understanding of how Linda was identifying herself and what anchorages she had most internalized at this point in her identity formation. In one respect she saw herself as a child of Africa, yet she was also a child of missionary parents, a Christian, a student in boarding school, and a friend and helper to many. These, if understood and integrated well, could clearly become strengths but would need more work before they were fully owned or integrated by her. At the beginning, however, they seemed areas of confusion that needed clarification before we went too far into other areas. It would be important to hear from her how she viewed these important facets of her identity and to affirm the strengths in them as we traversed more dangerous ground.

Finally, the fifth goal was to help her clarify her own goals in therapy so a mutually agreed upon contract could be struck. When we initially approached this, her goals were simply, "To get back in school where I belong, to stop being depressed, and to let Mom and Dad get back to what they want to do." As we worked further on these, she was able to be more definitive. The following interchange, which took place in the context of a discussion about how she tended to identify herself, reveals something of this process in developing mutual goals:

CLIENT: Well, I guess being an MK is okay.
THERAPIST: Okay?
CLIENT: Well, I guess so. I mean, that's what I am and what I've been ever since I was born.
THERAPIST: So what's that like?
CLIENT: Well, it's being a daughter of missionary parents . . . (she smiles) . . . someone who is with other MKs and missionaries a lot, and somebody who usually goes to boarding school. (long pause) And somebody who gets depressed when they shouldn't.

THERAPIST: Oh, gets depressed when she shouldn't? How so?

CLIENT: Well, you're supposed to do things you may not believe in and aren't like you. You have to please people or they'll be unhappy with you. And you always have to smile even if you don't feel like it . . . this is depressing . . .

THERAPIST: Trying to please people can make you depressed even though you're smiling?

CLIENT: Yes. I don't like to smile when I have to. (long silence and change of body posture to one of sullenness and disengagement)

THERAPIST: Did something just happen inside you? . . . with your feelings?

CLIENT: Well, maybe.

THERAPIST: I noticed you changed the way you were sitting and the way you stopped looking my direction when you talked about being depressed and smiling anyway.

CLIENT: Yeah. (long pause) Maybe, maybe something did change . . . well, I guess it did (sitting more alertly now)

THERAPIST: Like . . . ?

CLIENT: Like maybe feeling kinda mad.

THERAPIST: Mad . . . ?

CLIENT: Maybe. (pause, and with more energy) Yeah, mad.

THERAPIST: H-m-m-m

CLIENT: Well, I know there are a lot of reasons I'm depressed. It isn't just being an MK. I don't like myself, other people don't like me, I cause problems for my Mom and Dad, I take your time, I don't seem any better . . . (She breaks into tears. After a pause and some recovery on her part, she looks up at me.)

THERAPIST: Linda, what you've just said seems very real . . . like you didn't have to be someone you're not.

CLIENT: (more engaged now) I'm tired of it . . . tired, tired, tired! . . . How was I different?

THERAPIST: What you've just said seems to have come from deeper inside you . . . and seems to express some pain and discouragement and anger, all things you really feel. It didn't seem like it was just depression. You seemed to be connected with yourself in a deeper way.

CLIENT: (pause) That's what I want, to be connected with myself. I think I used to be, but not anymore.

This interchange resulted in an important emotionally corrective experience. She had found, for the first time in our relationship, that her deeper feelings of hurt, anger, and disappointment could be expressed and not damage our relationship. Rather, it seemed to help her find a sense of connectedness with herself and laid the foundation for actually making our relationship stronger.

Following this we were able to talk more fully about her wish to be better connected and to discuss some elements I saw—such as wanting to please and not disappoint her parents, feeling she was failing as a Christian, and being fearful of separations, sometimes just those of leaving her room or house. Her reference to and experience of anger as we sat together was not lost, and we came back to that in the session summary. We had begun to set some mutually derived goals and discussed in more detail what therapy might include.

Thus, some further goals became:

- To understand how it was so important to not disappoint her parents and what that meant to her;
- To explore why she felt she was failing as a Christian;
- To examine her fears about separation.
- To help her discover and express more of her feelings, especially her "not happy" feelings.

She also mentioned the strong desire to return to the school in which she had enrolled here, but we agreed that other "internal" goals may be more important first. She seemed to understand that working toward these goals would be related to overcoming her depression, though I was careful to not imply a guarantee of that. We also agreed to work on strategies for overcoming some of her withdrawal and/or agoraphobic behaviors. Attendant to that, I began to think of specific strategies she could utilize for taking some steps away from those behaviors. With these mutually derived goals, I also began thinking of intermediate goals along these following lines:

- To help her experience permission to feel her anger, express it, and begin attaching it to relevant events and objects.
- To help her begin making connections between her needs for approval and comfort (e.g., pleasing her parents and others) and her difficulty in expressing her own feelings and needs.
- To explore more fully her own personal understanding of God vis à vis the details of her faith and personal relationship with God, thus helping her express herself somewhat more independently of parents' faith and wishes.
- To assist her in seeing the extent to which she was a "protector" of her parents feelings and concerns and to begin understanding why and how this had developed.

In looking to the longer-range goals of therapy, I believed the following were reasonable and over a period of months could probably be achieved:

- Help her legitimize her feelings, especially those of anger and discouragement and to develop means for asking for what she needed so as to minimize these as disruptive feelings for her.
- Attain a level of separation from her parents and their needs and establish a sense of identity and individuation appropriate to her age level.

- Achieve some increased integration of her faith with other aspects of her experience and identity in a manner that she experienced as her own, rather than the simple incorporation of external values that may or may not be hers.

It would be necessary to consult with her parents and have them in a session from time to time. Her depression, in part, was linked to them and it would be important to incorporate changes that I hoped Linda would undergo into their understanding also. Their strong interest in her recovery was of importance, and with the probability of her remaining with them for most of the ensuing year, it would be crucial to utilize their availability. Further, along the lines articulated by Minuchin and Fishman (1981), it would be important for some family understanding to take place for Linda to experience a more satisfactory outcome.

REVISED TREATMENT PLAN

As therapy unfolded, two major themes developed that resulted in some revision of my earlier treatment plans. The first concerned a new realization of the depth to which Linda had experienced losses she had seldom acknowledged and probably never grieved. The second dealt with a better understanding of the pressures and stresses her parents were feeling due to the apparent lack of understanding on the part of some friends for having left their work in East Africa early. Both were having their differential affects upon Linda. The former resulted in some regression in our work; the latter in revealing more clearly just how responsible Linda felt for making things go OK for her parents.

After some three months in therapy, Linda had reached the point where she was able to get out more on her own and, though the prospect of full-time school attendance was quite fearful for her, arrangements had been made for her to begin driver's education as a step toward returning. At the conclusion of her first lesson, the instructor asked her to move the car from the place they had parked to a slightly different location while he was still present in the car. To this point she had felt good about this first venture back toward a more regular life, and she had expected some affirmation. When she started to move the car, however, she had put the gear in reverse rather than forward, pressed too hard on the accelerator, and struck a car behind her. The physical damage was minimal, but to her yet fragile ego it was severe. While the instructor's words were kind, she sensed a disapproval in him that set off a chain of self-recrimination and guilt.

After we had discussed this in some detail, the following exchange took place:

THERAPIST: How might you understand the severe guilt and put-downs of yourself which followed what happened there?

CLIENT: I don't know, but I know I've felt them before.

THERAPIST: That's interesting . . . anything come to mind?

CLIENT: Well, no . . . well, maybe. Do you remember Mrs. T.?

THERAPIST: Sure.

CLIENT: Well . . . there was more than one Mrs. T.

THERAPIST: More than one?

CLIENT: Well, not really. But now I'm remembering some other teachers and houseparents I had earlier in school who were like Mrs. T.

THERAPIST: In what way?

CLIENT: Oh, kind of mean. Well, real mean. They would act like they liked you but really didn't. And sometimes they would be just outright mean, like Mrs. T. did when she told me I wasn't a good Christian.

THERAPIST: Tell me more about them.

Linda went into some detail describing two other teachers whom she felt were mean, who had without warning attacked her in some vulnerable spot. Later in the session:

THERAPIST: So it seems that a lot of times when you were expecting some-one to compliment you, they would somehow turn on you instead?

CLIENT: Yeah, yes . . . it seemed like I lost some things before I ever had them . . . a lot of things.

The sessions following this exchange focused on the number of transitions Linda had made over the years: numerous trips between her parents' village station and the mission headquarters in a major city, each of which meant several overnights; her transition to boarding school at age 7; her sister's relative inability after her accident to tend to Linda in elementary school; an emergency trip to the States by her father when his mother died, and her grandmother not being here when they came on their next furlough; and many others. In most cases, even though her parents had been warm and comforting, Linda had not felt permission since an early age to express how she really felt about these changes and losses, and had never really grieved. The grieving of these losses, one by one, became an important goal and focus for a number of sessions.

Near the end of these discussions, Linda came in some 10 minutes late (she had never been late before) and seemed more dejected. After some preliminaries this discussion took place:

CLIENT: I almost didn't come today.

THERAPIST: Oh, how come?

CLIENT: I just didn't.

THERAPIST: You know me well enough to know I won't let you get by with that kind of answer! (both of us chuckle mildly)

CLIENT: Yeah, you won't. (pause, with some evidence of humor and then eyes become watery) I didn't want to come because I don't want to say good-bye.

THERAPIST: Say good-bye? What do you mean?

CLIENT: Well, I'll have to stop seeing you sometime, won't I?

THERAPIST: In time.

CLIENT: That's what I realized as we've been talking about all these things I've lost. (pause) Not coming to see you will be just another loss.

THERAPIST: Just another loss?

CLIENT: It might be.

THERAPIST: Perhaps not just another loss . . . because you can make this one different.

CLIENT: Why will this be any different?

THERAPIST: Because I think you're learning some better ways to experience loss . . . some more healthy ways.

CLIENT: Will I know them before we stop meeting?

THERAPIST: That's one of the things you've been working on.

CLIENT: H-m-m-m

THERAPIST: I can tell you what my part in it will be.

CLIENT: What?

THERAPIST: I'll be very honest with you about what I'm thinking and feeling when we say good-bye. And I'll want to hear what you're thinking and feeling, too. We'll plan to take plenty of time to do that. You might call that a good good-bye.

CLIENT: I don't know if I can do that . . . it sounds like just another hurt.

THERAPIST: Yes, good-byes and losses are often painful, but facing and expressing the pain at the time is an important part of getting through it okay.

CLIENT: Well, if you say so. I guess I see a little bit of what you mean. I still need to learn a lot about that. You won't kick me out before I'm ready, will you?

THERAPIST: I don't have any plans like that.

As the session progressed, Linda brought up the question of how God was supposed to help when she felt bad about leaving somebody or losing something and said she felt that a lot of times he didn't. After some discussion, I asked her if she knew the Book of Acts very well. She replied that she had studied it and sometimes read it in her personal devotional time. I asked her if she would read the portion where the apostle Paul says good-bye to his friends and fellow workers from Ephesus (Acts 20:18–38, especially 36–38), where he told them they had become "very dear" to him. I asked her to let me know in our next session what she thought about it. She agreed.

This was the first direct attempt in utilizing biblical passages in helping her understand and cope with some of her issues, even though we had several times discussed elements of Christian faith. I realized there was a risk involved, that of possibly being identified with some persons of her background she saw as duplicious or insincere. Also, I wondered if this would put too much emphasis on our own parting, which I believed would be some months away. However, this seemed a reasonable risk in light of the present focus on her losses. I believed it might assist her to integrate her faith in meeting some of the practical issues.

With respect to the second theme, that of her parents' increasing stress from the perception of friends, I felt it necessary to focus on this directly with them at some point; their handling of it seemed clearly to be affecting Linda. Perhaps helping them become somewhat more real and disclosing to friends would also relate to their becoming more so with Linda.

BALANCING GOALS

There was not a great inconsistency between the goals of Linda's parents and Linda herself. Each seemed committed to the process that would relieve Linda of her symptoms and allow her to return to the happier adolescent she had seemed to be earlier. As time went on, all were able to understand that meeting these goals would require some risks in facing areas that would be painful and with which the parents, especially, might not feel altogether comfortable. It would be important to maintain this somewhat delicate balance common to working with family issues: being especially careful not to blame the parents, on the one hand, nor, on the other, to identify with Linda. It seemed important also to help the parents expand their worldview in such a way that anger would not be seen as disrespectful, bad, or dangerous.

Linda seemed more quickly than her parents to grasp the importance of this as she began risking expressions of her anger, first with me and later with them. It was important to keep them apprised of her needs and development sufficiently to ensure their continued support but to encourage Linda to take the initiative for that as much as possible. Knowing this might create tension within the family if the balance noted above was not sufficiently maintained, the words of Christ recorded in John 8:32 came to mind as a hope for each of them: "You shall know the truth, and the truth shall make you free."

An important aspect of Linda's development, interrupted by her situation, was identity development. This issue was made more complex both from her status as an MK and by the limiting situation she was now in: being in a somewhat alien culture, not attending school, and having fewer opportunities for stimulation that would facilitate this development. An understanding of her development vis à vis her Christian commitment was likewise crucial, and in this respect some of the work by Fowler (1981) on stages of faith was helpful in understanding this.

It would be important also to understand her development in terms of the maladaptive patterns she had developed, that is: turning her anger inward rather than attaching it to its relevant object and expressing it, protecting her parents by reporting only positive feelings and happenings, feeling responsible for things that were not hers to be responsible for, and her view of herself as unworthy or guilty.

In a more specific sense, the general goals of helping her develop a clearer sense of identity also raised important issues regarding her Christian faith. The years between 16 and 22 are crucial ones for the questioning and reinterpretation of religious faith and identity. From my assessment, I believed that Linda's religious faith was much more that of an intrinsic nature than an extrinsic one (Allport, 1968), but it was still developing. I needed to keep some balance between the goals of helping her develop an identity appropriate to her age, helping her integrate her Christian faith in similar ways, and assisting her in coming to terms with feelings she had been unable to express.

The integration of her Christian faith with her obvious strengths, the depth of pain over her ungrieved losses, and the fuller development of her identity would be important goals. Further, she needed assistance with separation/individuation issues. To achieve this, along with better identity development, it would be important to balance her Christian faith, her MK identity, the mission subculture, and the myriad aspects of being a TCK. While I believed her parents found these goals generally acceptable, I also believed that they might have to endure some pain and insightful resolution themselves to eventually reach them. Hearing Linda express negative affect, especially if it was anger at them, their work, her school, or the mission, might be difficult for them.

Therapeutic Process

RELATIONAL REENACTMENTS

Over the 18 months of our work together, Linda's progress was at times steady, at times rocky. Early in our contacts I sought psychiatric consultation with the question of medication for her depression. The resulting conclusion was that utilizing it ran the risk of blunting the affect necessary for her improvement. This proved to be a good decision, for the transference developed quickly and there was some decrease in symptoms fairly early (especially those of withdrawal/agoraphobia). Also, the patterns of her core conflicts surfaced in discernible ways as she began to experience the intensity of her anger and loss-related grief and to examine the blocks to their experience and expression that she felt from her parents and had developed within herself. One core conflict was the need to express these feelings and the fear of rejection or nonacceptance if she did. Another was the need for nurture and comfort and the fear that it would be withheld if she were not happy and nearly perfect. The latter seemed to have been translated even into her relationship with God.

There was no question of the reality of Linda's pain as we delved into specifics under the depression. I sometimes found myself being angry *for* her, especially after some grueling exchanges about her hopelessness, worthlessness, and the losses she hadn't grieved. I knew she had pain and anger she wasn't able to express except in her symptoms. I also continued to guard myself against trying to take that away *for* her, or even to take too much responsibility for helping her express it in our sessions. My counter-transference surfaced from time to time as either wanting to take the re-sponsibility for making it better for her or, like her father, putting a smiling face on it and pretending it wasn't there.

After we had met for several months, her 17th birthday occurred. She was actually able to celebrate it with some recovered cheerfulness. Her older sister had come home for that weekend; another missionary family in which there were adolescents Linda's age attended, and this was a boost for Linda. In the fall, after we had been meeting some 6 or 7 months, she was able to begin school. With some placement exams, she was able to start her senior year, although there was still a question of making up some additional requirements during the year.

As these months had passed, she had slowly begun expressing her feel-ings more clearly, becoming more aware and less frightened of the effect if she admitted them. In one session, as she began getting more in touch with her anger about there being no one there to help her express the pain of loss she felt during a particular transition, an important exchange took place:

CLIENT: I guess I was kind of mad, maybe lonely, too, in not being able to tell anyone. I didn't really know I was mad.
THERAPIST: Do you remember more specifically what you felt?
CLIENT: Well, mainly lonesome. I wished I could talk to my dad.
THERAPIST: What would have happened if you could?
CLIENT: He would comfort me . . . just by being together. I probably wouldn't tell him I was lonesome . . .

At this point she seemed to be deep in thought. When she looked up again her mood had changed from one of quiet but painful reflection to something less acute, almost dull.

CLIENT: I was just thinking of some good times and telling my dad about them. He seemed to like to hear those things, sometimes more than once. (pause) I remember doing a project in science that I really liked. It was about Machu Picchu in Peru, you know, that mysterious city in the Andes where the population seemed to disappear without a reason. No-body seems to know what happened. Suzie—she was my project part-ner—and I really worked hard on this. We wrote to the States for some pictures . . . (pause, catches herself) What were we just talking about?
THERAPIST: You were telling me about your loneliness and anger. You even seemed to be feeling some of it as we talked.
CLIENT: Did I? H-m-m-m
THERAPIST: Something just happened here, I think, that may be important to understand. Could you go back to telling me about your loneliness and anger for a minute?

CLIENT: I don't think so . . . I don't feel it right now.

THERAPIST: Do you remember feeling anything else when you started telling me more about it?

CLIENT: No, not especially . . . well, maybe that I shouldn't be telling you about it.

THERAPIST: Not telling me . . .

CLIENT: You wouldn't want to hear it . . . even though I knew *you* would, because you've been trying to get me to talk more about it. It's kinda hard to talk about.

THERAPIST: With me?

CLIENT: Well, with anyone.

THERAPIST: Anyone?

CLIENT: Well, with Dad, I guess. He wouldn't want to hear about those things.

THERAPIST: What would he want to hear about?

CLIENT: Good things.

THERAPIST: Like you started to tell me after you thought about him, and didn't remember what you had been talking about before?

CLIENT: Yeah . . . Yes . . . Maybe, maybe . . . I think so.

Further discussion helped her discover just how patterned this type of response had become. She had reenacted with me the same pattern she had established with her father. Wishing to talk about something "negative," but, sensing his desire not to hear that, switching to something positive and submerging the other feelings. Following this, she seemed gradually more free to allow the negative feelings to be put into words. During this period there was a discernible lifting of her depression.

A significant amount of time was spent reviewing her past losses and the unresolved hurt and grief she had been carrying. Many pertained to simple oversights she had experienced, more acutely than others, perhaps, because of her greater sensitivity to the importance of relationships and acceptance. Some incidents she remembered were abusive in quality, though she had not to that point construed them as such. Many of her recollections related to the losses she felt but didn't express as she and her family had made various transitions.

On one occasion she had been confined to her room for several days (except for meals and classes) for not having obtained an excuse for missing chapel. She missed it because she had stopped to help one of the African workers on campus who had fallen and injured herself, but this was somehow overlooked or misunderstood. She had stopped to assist, feeling compassion for the woman and believing, as she discussed it later, it was an expression of her Christian faith.

While she was grounded, a former schoolmate who was a close friend came back for a brief visit, and Linda was not allowed to see her. Though she had felt that this was grossly unfair, she had never reported it to her parents.

As we discussed this, her woundedness from the event was poured out in tears, and in time she was able also to acknowledge the rage she had suppressed for so long. Expressing the depth of feeling over this event seemed to widen the channels for a myriad of other events that she recalled and discussed.

On several occasions transactions took place between us that resulted in a corrective developmental recapitulation for her. On such an occasion I came to our session with my left arm in a sling due to a slight injury, experiencing some mild pain. She seemed to take more than usual interest in just how badly I was injured. As I quickly sought to redirect her toward the issues we had been working on, she seemed less involved than in previous sessions. After a couple of unsuccessful attempts to get into much depth with her, this exchange ensued:

CLIENT: Are you sure you're all right?

THERAPIST: Yes, it's happened before and should be fine in a few days . . . but my being hurt seems to draw your attention, with the sling and all.

CLIENT: I'm not used to seeing you that way. It's different.

THERAPIST: Can you tell me how this makes things seem different?

CLIENT: Well, I want you to be healthy. (laughs) Well, I guess, really, it makes it harder . . . to talk . . . to talk to you.

THERAPIST: Talk to me . . . about . . . ?

CLIENT: Oh, I don't know. (pause) Do you want me to get you a drink of water or something?

THERAPIST: Thanks, but no. I'm doing fine. I guess I'm just interested in how it's harder for you to talk to me today.

CLIENT: Oh, I don't know. I guess it's just hard to talk about myself when I know you're hurt or in pain.

THERAPIST: That's interesting . . . how so?

CLIENT: It just seems . . . just seems, I guess . . . that I ought to be taking care of you somehow. (pause, looks up) Well, you know, I know you're taken care of and everything or you wouldn't be here . . . (trails off)

THERAPIST: Yes, my shoulder is being taken care of, but it seems that my injury does have a certain effect on you. Like it draws on you somehow to want to take care of me.

CLIENT: Well, I want to make sure you're okay . . . yeah.

THERAPIST: Does that seem to be a familiar feeling for you?

CLIENT: Well, sometimes you make me think of my folks . . . I don't mean you're old or anything . . . and I don't feel good when they're hurt. I want to take care of them.

THERAPIST: How do you usually do that?

CLIENT: Oh, I just try to figure out what will help and do it . . . like cleaning the house if I'm in the village, or running errands . . . stuff like that.

THERAPIST: So you asked if I'd like to have a glass of water earlier. Things like that?

CLIENT: Yeah, things like that.

THERAPIST: But it seemed like you did another thing, too.

CLIENT: What was that?

THERAPIST: You didn't want to talk to me about your concerns as you had in the last sessions . . . perhaps didn't want to say anything about the hurts we had been talking about recently.

CLIENT: Huh . . . no, I didn't . . . feel like it today.

THERAPIST: I wonder if that's also a familiar thing for you.

CLIENT: (pause, seems deep in thought) Yes, yes . . . I didn't want to tell my folks anything that might hurt them. It was just hard to do. I knew they loved me and were concerned for me and that they worked hard, I didn't want . . . I didn't want them to be hurt because I was hurt . . . or to worry . . .

This exchange eventually led into a productive discussion of her protectiveness toward her parents. She began to realize that she had negated her own needs out of a sense of not wanting to upset or distress them. She learned that she had subtly taken cues from her father's gentle avoidance of painful or unpleasant things and avoided bringing them up. She also learned that she had been reluctant to mention painful things to her mother because she feared her overreaction to them. Her response to each had been to submerge her own feelings and needs, and she began to see how this had contributed to her depression. As we continued to work on her grieving process, she also realized more fully how these accumulated griefs had been significant contributors to her depression as well.

As she became more aware of these things, her interest in understanding how they related to her faith emerged more fully. One such issue was anger. The model of her father—never to express it—and that of her mother—to make an exaggerated response to it—had given her little permission to fully experience and express her own. She wondered if it was even right to do so. Given her knowledge of the Bible, I asked her during the week to read the latter part of the 4th chapter of Ephesians and to look especially at the passage in verse 26 about being angry and not sinning ("Be angry and sin not . . . ," NASB version). I also asked her to look at the passage in the Gospel of John where Christ throws moneychangers out of the temple. The discussions that followed gave her permission to talk *about* anger in a valued context one step removed from her actual experience, and helped her gradually move into her own experience in a full and releasing way.

The earlier excursion into the Book of Acts (where the apostle Paul said good-bye to leaders in the church at Ephesus) had been helpful. It provided permission within the context of her Christian beliefs to express herself in the pain of loss and partings. These glimpses into biblical examples and principles regarding anger also were helpful. Concurrent with these excursions, she kept a diary, something she had done earlier but gave up when the depression became more profound. This seemed to allow her to "test" some of her understandings and feelings before expressing them to me and eventually became an important vehicle for expressing them to others also. Her diary entries became over a period of time less questioning and reflective of unresolved pain and more integrative of her self-understanding, identity, and Christian faith.

In addition to loss and anger, we also incorporated biblical readings and reflections involving God's acceptance and love for her. We discussed at length the meaning of the commandment to honor her mother and father—how she could follow that and still express her own needs and develop a clearer sense of identity. A significant outcome of the latter was her eventual decision to risk experiencing and expressing her anger and other negative feelings even though she feared being misunderstood and not liked for doing so. She had developed the conviction that, in time, doing so would make her more healthy and that, perhaps later, her parents would see that and she would honor them by being more capable of a better and fuller relationship with them. An insightful concept, I thought, for someone 17 years old.

An important focus was also on the concepts of grace and forgiveness. Tournier (1961) has provided seminal work in understanding these broad concepts, and writing was particularly helpful as applied to Linda's situation. Linda could provide a good definition of grace from her Christian education: "the unmerited favor of God." However, her strivings to be always pleasant and happy by avoiding anger and other negative feelings, and to live up to the perfection she believed her Christian faith required, seemed to leave little room for its actual operation.

As she became more aware of and began to own negative feelings, she was surprised that I still accepted her in spite of them. She gradually experienced that God might also accept them. As she realized that she had little control over whether or not I chose to accept her and her feelings, she could acknowledge that she actually had little control over what God chose to accept. As she examined this in light of other Christian beliefs about God, such as his omniscience and love, she began to experience less need for controlling things by denying her feelings and being pleasant and perfect. Perhaps God would meet her needs if she let go of some of her strivings and looked at what was already being provided for her.

Linda had always been quick to forgive, also as a way of being pleasant and avoiding conflict. As we worked together she began to realize she was paying a very high price for this in emotional stress and depression. To do this so automatically meant a further denial of the hurts or other wrongs perpetrated against her. Forgiveness, to be complete, requires that the wronged person weigh fully the effect of the wrong that has been perpetrated, and then decide whether to take on all the consequences of that wrong doing on oneself. In deciding to do so, the perpetrator is left free of the consequences or results. We worked through several examples where she had been hurt or overlooked, examined the consequences of that hurt or wrong doing in detail, and discussed whether she would choose to take on all those as her own. This cast a different light on what she was doing in "forgiving" others and also allowed her to look at how she experienced the forgiveness of Christ as a basic part of her faith. In time she became much more discerning and understanding as she chose to forgive others.

As she continued to make progress, several significant events took place. During Thanksgiving of her senior year, she was able to attend a retreat for MKs in their freshman year of college or in the last two years of high school. She seemed a different person when she returned, exclaiming that there were so many other people there "just like me!." This event greatly enhanced her identity as an MK and TCK, and she began valuing her past experiences in a new way. The speaker had talked about MKs feeling like "ugly ducklings" as they returned to North America and were so frequently misunderstood by peers here. He developed this idea throughout the weekend, using that story to help MKs see that they were really swans, just placed temporarily with ducks. He also talked about the redemptive process that takes place from a Christian view as MKs realize their fuller identities. The richness of their cross-cultural upbringing and even their hurts and loneliness can be redeemed as characteristics that eventually bring them happiness and allow them to develop productive careers. The swan analogy continued to be significant throughout her therapy.

A similar event involved the discovery of a poetic booklet written by a woman who, like Linda, had grown up of missionary parents in Africa. It was entitled simply *I Am Green* (unpublished). The author spoke openly of her own struggles in finding an identity after returning to the States. She experienced the "yellows" of the African sun and her many memories of growing up there as fundamental parts of herself. She also experienced the "blues" of being an American, but often misunderstood as one, especially as she attempted to make a successful transition to life in the States after so long in Africa. Blending these was hard, she wrote. She spoke of loss and pain but also of joy and hope, not wanting to give up either part of herself. As the author found ways of blending these parts of herself, she, like the ugly duckling who discovered he was really a swan, discovered that she was, in her fullness, really "green," as she blended the blue and yellow parts of herself. This discovery allowed the author to experience and embrace her fuller identity. Linda was undergoing a similar process.

These events, and several others, helped Linda to think more about the grace of God. She had felt somehow that she did not deserve nor could have even anticipated these experiences, but they came to her at the right time. She ultimately understood these as "acts of grace" that she could allow herself to accept as further evidence that God did indeed love her, and she had little control over that except in her response. This view, developed over a period of some weeks, allowed her to make a significant change in the way she viewed herself (less guilty, fewer feelings of worthlessness) and helped free her to interact with others much less fearfully. She seemed less anxious and speculated that she probably did not need to work so hard at being perfect to maintain her faith. She had made significant progress, and soon after Christmas and Easter had passed she mentioned our termination.

It came when she told me she had been accepted at the college her parents attended. She mentioned fears about how she would make the transition. This stimulated discussion about both the many other transitions she had made earlier and now understood better and that which was taking place in our work. While the thoughts of college and termination brought temporary fears, they also helped to put in focus the strength of our work and looking beyond it.

At this point my own concerns had shifted from trying to stay on course with goals, managing my countertransference, and responding to the concerns of Linda's parents to interacting rather freely and spontaneously with her. I felt that she would indeed be ready for termination by the time she left for college. Therapy had begun its shift from the middle stage to termination. The tasks were shifting to those of affirming and consolidating gains and helping integrate her insights with possibilities and plans.

IMPEDIMENTS TO TREATMENT

In retrospect, the largest impediment to treatment was Linda's pattern of turning her anger inward in order to protect her parents (and others) from her "negative" feelings. These patterns had developed from real experiences in her family dynamics and were enhanced through misunderstood expectations of her Christian and missionary subculture. Further, living in a foreign culture of which she had become a significant part (which ultimately turned out to be a valuable strength for her) also added to a greater struggle in developing an identity that would incorporate these various aspects of faith and culture.

I came to understand the dynamics of her parents' relationship with one another as an impediment to treatment, as we met occasionally to review progress or look at a particular issue. Her father's difficulty in hearing Linda's pain and "not happy" feelings was related to an attempt on Ed's part to compensate for what he felt were his wife Esther's exaggeration of negative feelings and overanxious responses. While this related foundationally to his own history, his patterned response to Esther's overexaggerations had left him almost devoid of the ability to hear feelings of hurt, anger, or despair or to express them himself. I wanted, as a guideline, for him to experience my acceptance of the pain or fear that he covered with these patterned responses, in the hope that he might be able to realize the same with Linda. While some progress was made with this, I was not altogether successful.

As therapy with Linda progressed and she began finding and expressing her anger in my presence, she found her tentative attempts to do so with her parents initially thwarted. In discussing this in one session, I found myself getting somewhat angry and began to express it.

CLIENT: I wish it were different . . . I tried to talk to Dad about it but it didn't work.

THERAPIST: How didn't it work?

CLIENT: Well, he just didn't seem to want to hear about it. He told me that all these things will work together for good and to try to concentrate on something hopeful. I couldn't concentrate on something hopeful, I just wanted him to understand that I didn't like what had happened (referring to an event of unfairness at school the preceding year).

THERAPIST: That you were mad about it?

CLIENT: Yeah, that I thought it was unfair . . . it hurt and I know it made me mad, too.

THERAPIST: That makes me mad.

CLIENT: What?

THERAPIST: It makes me mad that your dad won't listen to you.

CLIENT: Oh . . .

THERAPIST: And that your mother gets overconcerned once you express something that's not gone well for you.

CLIENT: Oh.

THERAPIST: You want to tell them about it and they either can't listen or get all worked up about it. That makes me mad. It's not what you need.

CLIENT: (after a long pause and a noticeable drawing back) It's okay.

THERAPIST: I don't think it is, Linda.

CLIENT: (looks down . . . several moments of silence)

At this point I began worrying that I may have gone too far in expressing my own feelings and had frightened her with the expression of anger itself, especially anger directed at her parents. After a long silence and some thoughts of possible incompetence on my part:

THERAPIST: Linda, I notice you've pulled your feet in your chair and curled up. Could you tell me what's happened for you?

CLIENT: I'm kinda scared.

THERAPIST: Scared?

CLIENT: I don't like it when anybody gets mad.

THERAPIST: When I'm mad?

CLIENT: (reluctantly) Yes.

THERAPIST: It's hard for you to be angry and hard to be around someone who's angry. I think that's really understandable in light of the experiences you've shared with me. Can you say more about what it's like to be with me right now, knowing that I've just expressed being mad.

CLIENT: Well, it's easier now.

THERAPIST: How?

CLIENT: Well, it just is. . . . We're talking about it.

This paved the way for her understanding that she could continue to be more accepting of her own anger and that could lead to less fear of it in others. As she implied above, she was able to see more fully that experiencing it and talking about it in our relationship did not damage the relationship, as she had previously felt, but actually enhanced it. It also led to a discussion about an individual being angry at someone and that it didn't mean rejection of the person. At the conclusion of the following session, having processed this further, we agreed to have her parents in for a session or two to talk about this.

The first of the two sessions we had with them was difficult in that the pattern she had described was acted out within the session. As Linda attempted to tell about the school incident (an approach we had agreed on) her father responded with some gentle but nonetheless diverting platitudes, and her mother became anxious. When we ended that session, I felt we had moved too soon on this. Linda was probably not quite ready for this intensity with them, and her father had seemed especially uncomfortable, having presumably concluded that I felt he was not attending properly to Linda.

In the next session, however, he had evidently been giving this much thought and probably had discussed it with someone. (I later learned that he had met with his pastor about it.) He began by acknowledging what I had tried to point out, and went into some detail about his own history (excluding comment about his and Esther's relationship, however) and how he disliked anger and unpleasantness. He at first defended his position, but later seemed to soften. That all this had been discussed in Linda's presence was significant for her and a step in overcoming a major impediment.

In time, Linda was able to see how she had adapted to her father's dynamic (and her mother's, too) by not expressing what she needed to express. This pattern had permeated much of her behavior at boarding school and become an impediment to the more integrated development of her affect and, to some extent, her identity. As this impediment was gradually removed—her parents are to be commended for the risks they took in engaging me on this issue—Linda's significant growth in therapy continued.

Other ipediments, such as the pressure perceived by Linda's parents and family to "keep up a good face" and to make a show of strength and progress for the "Christian community" were also gradually addressed. The integration of biblical principles regarding honesty and integrity were given attention particularly in matters of affect. These became important groundings both in work with Linda and those occasional meetings with her parents.

As time approached for our termination, Linda reminded me of our earlier discussion about "good good-byes." We incorporated some important aspects of that discussion into our termination.

Termination and Therapist's Summary Thoughts

Once the gradual shift toward the termination phase began some 4 months prior to ending, Linda's spirits seemed to remain fairly stable and much of her former cheerfulness returned. However, it was balanced with an underside of reality that now took into account a better understanding of how and why she had become depressed. She was experiencing a new appreciation for feelings, even negative ones. In this process she was incorporating important understanding of herself into the ongoing development of her identity.

The decision to terminate was made, in part, by her decision to attend college some 200 miles away. Yet, I believe we would have reached termination at approximately the same time anyway. The fact that she was back on track with her educational plans was perhaps one indication of the success of our work together. We spent several sessions reviewing progress, clarifying elements of her dynamics, and consolidating the gains she had made. Some slight regression and return of mild depression helped us affirm the actual gains she had made and to acknowledge that some areas still needed work. We also discussed her future, what college might be like, how it compared with boarding school, and how she could form new friendships that allowed her to express things she previously had difficulty doing. The friendships she had formed during her last year of high school bore witness to her capacity to do this. Two of her friends would be attending the same college; one would be her roommate.

As I look back on what I have written, I am aware of the impact that Linda had on me as we worked together—which I still carry. The barely audible voice I first encountered had changed into one of greater confidence, though not without occasional tentativeness. The downcast eyes had looked up and, later, ahead. She was clearly grasping the future and seemed much more capable of doing things to make it positive. Her thin frame seemed to show more vitality. She had regained the ten pounds or so she had lost. There was spontaneity that, her parents told me, seemed to be beyond the cheerfulness that they had so valued earlier on. Her clear Christian commitment, now beginning to be lived out in ways more connected to her own reality, seemed to be on a trajectory of better understanding and application. She was no longer depressed.

Nearly all the mutual goals we had set together were met to one degree or another. Others showed progress but were not met to the extent I had hoped. As I look back, I do so in admiration of Linda's hard work, of her parents' openness and support, and with gratitude to God for the goals that were accomplished. Like a parent, perhaps, I must admit to wishing that a bit more had been done and, also, that I might have been there to see it all accomplished. But therapy is not the same as parenting, even though it bears some of the same qualities. Even in the therapist's often required stance as antithetical parent—that is, manifesting qualities in the relationship that are different from and have the emotional impact of helping undo the effects of negative patterns in the real parental relationship—therapy is still not the same as parenting. The therapist may occasionally manifest and experience such qualities, especially of wanting to participate in just a bit more success, but must forever remain clearly separate. It was undoubtedly time for Linda to go.

As we terminated, I shared with Linda how much I valued her and her successes in therapy. We talked of many of our experiences together, laughed at some of the times we had miscommunicated, and affirmed that the relationship had been a good one. I was tempted to offer a follow-up session now and then as she made her adjustment to college and came back for an occasional visit. But I thought better of it. She did not raise it as a desire then, nor has she ever contacted me again for another session. I take this as a silent statement that she was really ready to say good-bye and that this transition was a completely healthy one for her. As a statement of my own faith, I trust that she is using the things she learned in therapy and is living happily and productively.

REFERENCES

Allport, G. W. (1968). *The person in psychology: Selected essays.* Boston: Beacon Press.

Andrews, L. A. (1993). *Existential well-being among adult MKs.* Report to MK-CART/CORE annual meeting, Colorado Springs, CO.

Aponte, H. J., & Winter, J. E. (1987). The person and practice of the therapist: Treatment and training. In M. Baldwin & V. Satir (Eds.), *The use of self in therapy.* New York: Haworth Press.

Austin, C. N. (1983). *Cross-cultural re-entry: An annotated bibliography.* Abilene, TX: Abilene Christian University Press.

American Psychiatric Association. (1994). *Diagnostic and statistical manual of mental disorders* (4th Ed.). Washington, DC: Author.

Echerd, P., & Arathoon, A. (Eds.). (1989). *Understanding and nurturing the missionary family.* (Compendium of the International Conference on Missionary Kids, Quita, Ecuador, January, 1987, Vol. I.) Pasadena, CA: William Carey Library.

Echerd, P., & Arathoon, A. (Eds.). (1989). *Planning for MK nurture.* (Compendium of the International Conference on Missionary Kids, Quito, Ecuador, January, 1987, Vol. II.) Pasadena, CA: William Carey Library.

Fowler, J. W. (1981). *Stages of faith: The psychology of human development and the quest for meaning.* San Francisco: Harper & Row.

Herrmann, C. B. (1977). *Foundational factors of trust and autonomy influencing the identity formation of the multicultural lifestyled MK.* Unpublished doctoral dissertation, Northwestern University, Evanston, IL.

Holy Bible (New American Standard Version, NASB). (1960). LaHabra, CA: The Lockman Foundation.

Langs, R. (1985). *Madness and cure.* Salt Lake City: New Concept (Gardner) Press.

Minuchin, S., & Fishman, H. C. (1981). *Family therapy techniques.* Cambridge, MA: Harvard University Press.

MK-CORE. (1993, April). *Preliminary findings from the AMK Study.* Unpublished report to the constituent group at the annual meeting of MK-CART/CORE, Colorado Springs, CO.

Powell, J. (1989). Personal integration: Blending transition, learning and relationships. In P. Echerd & A. Arathoon (Eds.). *Planning for MK nurture.* Pasadena, CA: William Carey Library.

Schubert, E., & Powell, J. (1989). Depression and suicide. In P. Echerd & A. Arathoon (Eds.), *Understanding and nurturing the missionary family.* Pasadena, CA: William Carey Library.

Smedes, L. B. (1984). *Forgive and forget: Healing the hurts we don't deserve.* San Francisco: Harper & Row.

Taylor, M. H. (1988). Personality development in the children of missionary parents. *The Japan Christian Quarterly, 42*(2), 42–47.

Tetzel, B. A., & Mortenson, P. (Eds.). (1986). *New directions in missions: Implications for MKs.* (Compendium of the International Conference on Missionary Kids, Manila, Philippines, 1984) West Battleboro, VT: ICMK

Teyber, E. (1996). *Interpersonal process in psychotherapy: A guide for clinical training* (3rd ed.). Pacific Grove, CA: Brooks-Cole.

Tournier, P. (1961). *Guilt and grace.* New York: Harper and Row.

Useem, R. H., & Downie, R. D. (1976). Third-culture kids. *Today's Education* (Sept.–Oct., pp. 103–105).

Useem, R. H. (1993). Third culture kids: Focus of major study. *Newslinks: The Newspaper of International Schools Services.* Princeton, NJ: International Schools Services.

Van Reken, R. E. (1988). *Letters never sent.* Chicago: Davic C. Cook Publishing.

SUGGESTIONS FOR FURTHER READING

Baldwin, M., & Satir, V. (Eds.). (1987). *The use of self in therapy.* New York: Haworth Press. This edited volume contains some rich material for understanding and being more sensitive to the use of self in psychotherapy. Most selections in one way or another challenge the therapist to look into his or her own life and dynamics as well as that of the client, and search out ways of better understanding how the relationship may bring about desirable change. The piece by Robert Aponte is particularly helpful in pointing to many of the subtleties so important to the effective use of the person as therapist.

Lynch, J. J. (1977). *The broken heart.* New York: Basic Books. This compassionate volume brings crucial elements of human understanding into the sometimes too "clinical" world of therapy. It helps the therapist keep in mind his or her own vulnerability and provides much insight on how this can be an adjunct rather than a hindrance to effective therapy.

Mueller, W. J., & Kell, B. L. (1972). Coping with conflict: Supervising counselors and psychotherapists. New York: Appleton-Century-Crofts. An excellent source for elucidating the fine nuances necessary to utilizing one's own feelings, perceptions and ideas as facilitative of change. While focusing on supervision, it reveals many aspects of conflict and its experience and expression, too often outside the full awareness of either client or therapist. Its discussion of process, motive, and resolution are unparalleled.

O'Donnell, K., & O'Donnell, M. (1988). *Helping missionaries grow: Readings in mental health and missions.* Pasadena, CA: William Carey Library. This pithy volume covers a number of issues regarding the spiritual and mental health of those Christian missionaries working cross-culturally. A variety of areas are covered. It touches on issues for families and the children of missionaries, and provides a number of insights important to understanding the relationships, conflicts, and stresses experienced by this group.

Tournier, P. (1968). *A place for you.* New York: Harper & Row. This volume, one of a number translated into English from Tournier's rich work, provides a sense of direction and hope for those seeking a "place" (broadly defined). It takes some broad questions of life and, in a Christian context, explores how moving to a sense of identity and place can take place healthily and integratively.

ABOUT THE EDITORS

Faith H. McClure, Ph.D., is an assistant professor of psychology at California State University, San Bernardino. She grew up in South Africa during apartheid. Dr. McClure received a Ph.D. in clinical psychology from UCLA and is licensed in California. Her research interests are in the areas of multicultural issues in mental health, sexual and substance abuse, and resilience.

Edward Teyber, Ph.D., a clinical psychologist, is a professor of psychology and director of the Psychology Clinic at California State University, San Bernardino. He is also the author of *Helping Children Cope with Divorce* and *Interpersonal Process in Psychotherapy.* He has published research articles on the effects of marital and family relations on child adjustment and has contributed articles on parenting and postdivorce family relations to popular-press newspapers and magazines. Dr. Teyber is also interested in supervision and training, and he maintains a part-time private practice.

ABOUT THE CONTRIBUTORS

Jan Aura received her Ph.D. in clinical psychology from UCLA. Currently she is an adjunct professor in the Women's Studies Department of Occidental College and in private practice in Culver City and Pasadena, California. Previously she has worked as a college Ombudsman, the director of a college counseling center, and in a private practice and training setting at the Los Angeles Family Institute. She has four general areas of clinical specialties: Young adult and adult issues (identity, individuation, peer relationships, sexuality, eating disorders, drugs and alcohol); survivors of abuse (childhood and adult sexual assault survivors, P.T.S.D., adult children of alcoholics); couple and family systems (alternative and nontraditional family systems); and employment difficulties. She loves backpacking, gardening, swimming, skiing and watching her two children, Jamie and Jordan, play sports.

Dorli Burge received a Ph.D. in clinical psychology from UCLA and an M.A. in early childhood education from California State University, Northridge. She works as a research associate with Dr. Constance Hammen at the UCLA Psychology Department and as a psychotherapist in private practice. Prior to her training in clinical psychology, she worked for several years as an infant development specialist, focusing on the complexities of parent–child interaction. Her research has studied parent–child interactions of depressed mothers and their children and, more recently, the effect of attachment on adolescent functioning.

David Chavez received a B.A. from Harvard and an M.A. and Ph.D. from University of California, Berkeley. He is currently an assistant professor in the Psychology Department at California State University, San Bernardino and practices part-time in the Inland Empire of California. He has interests in preventive interventions with children, parents, and families, and in cross-cultural research.

Barbara N. Graf received a B.A. from Antioch University, an M.A. in marriage and family counseling from Azusa Pacific University's California Family Study Center, an M.A. and a Ph.D. in clinical psychology from

California School of Professional Psychology. She is the director of Loyola University Law School's on-campus psychological counseling program. In her private practice in Pasadena, California, she works with children, adolescents, and adults.

Cassandra N. Nichols received an M.S. degree in counseling psychology from California State University, San Bernardino, and is a doctoral candidate in counseling psychology at Ball State University. She has worked in the area's public school system; in her private practice she counsels children and their families. Her research and practice interests include group therapy with ethnically diverse children, gender and achievement, and sibling attachment.

John Powell received a Ph.D. in psychology from the University of Missouri, Columbia. He is a professor and psychologist at the Michigan State University Counseling Center, where he provides psychotherapy and clinical training as well as teaching and research supervision. His interests include psychotherapy supervision, cross-cultural adaptation, and the relationship between Christianity and psychology. He also conducts a part-time private practice and frequently provides psychological consultation to overseas mission organizations.

M. Dawn Terrell, Ph.D., a clinical psychologist, is assistant professor of psychology at San Francisco State University and director of the SFSU Psychology Clinic. She has authored or coauthored papers on ethnocultural factors and substance abuse, psychotherapy with multiethnic adolescents, and assessment with culturally diverse populations. In addition to eating disorders and substance abuse, her clinical and research interests include issues associated with ethnic and gender identity development. She maintains a psychotherapy and consultation practice.

Sandy Tsuneyoshi received her Ph.D. in clinical psychology at Michigan State University. She has done internships in California, Hawaii, and Michigan. She was on staff at MECCA (Multi-Ethnic Counseling Center Alliance) and at the Olin Health Center branches of Michigan State University Counseling Center. Presently, she is on staff at the University of Oregon Counseling Center. She has been pro-active in the development and APA accreditation of a predoctoral training program there. Outreach, psychotherapy, and advocacy for American and international students of color are among her special interests.

Nancy L. Wolfe received an M.S. degree in counseling psychology from California State University, San Bernardino. She has worked for Planned Parenthood as a teen intervention counselor and an HIV counselor for the past several years. She has also had experience working with severely emotionally disturbed adolescents and adolescent sexual perpetrators. She is interested in pursuing her research in human psychology and health where they may interact with culture and family.

Anthony Zamudio received a B.A. in Social Ecology from UC Irvine and a Ph.D. in Clinical Psychology from UCLA. He received child and family therapy training at the San Fernando Valley Child Guidance Clinic, where he was actively involved in programs for children and families from low-income Spanish-speaking communities. Currently, he is the Behavioral Science Director of the USC/California Medical Center Family Residency Program, where he teaches and supervises medical residents and psychology interns. He also has a private practice where he works with children and families.